AN INQUIRY INTO T
CAUSES OF THE WEA

ADAM SMITH was born at Kirkcaldy, on the east coast of Scotland, in 1723. He was educated first at the local burgh grammar school and then at Glasgow University, where he studied under Francis Hutcheson, Professor of Moral Philosophy and the father of Scottish philosophy. In 1740 Smith was awarded a Snell Exhibition to Balliol College, Oxford, where he found the standard of teaching disappointingly low but the library resources good. He abandoned his Oxford studies in 1746 and two years later delivered a course of lectures in Edinburgh on 'Rhetoric and Belles Lettres', subsequently adding to it a series on civil law. These lectures did much to establish Smith's early reputation. In 1751 he was appointed Professor of Logic at Glasgow, and in the following year was transferred to Hutcheson's old chair of Moral Philosophy. Smith held this appointment until 1763, during which time he published a work based largely on his lectures, *The Theory of Moral Sentiments* (1759). With David Hume, he founded the Select Society and helped to write, in 1755, the first, abortive, *Edinburgh Review*. In 1764 he resigned his professorship to become tutor to the young Duke of Buccleuch, with whom he travelled extensively in France, meeting some of the leading 'philosophes' of the day. It was in France that Smith began to draft the *Wealth of Nations*, though the bulk of it was written after his return in 1766 to Kirkcaldy. The book was finally published in 1776. In 1777 Smith took up residence in Edinburgh, having been appointed to a post of Commissioner of Customs. He was elected Rector of Glasgow University in 1787. Smith died in Edinburgh on 17 July 1790 and was buried in the Canongate churchyard.

KATHRYN SUTHERLAND is Reader in Bibliography and Textual Criticism and Professorial Fellow of St Anne's College, Oxford. She has published widely on fictional and non-fictional writings of the Scottish Enlightenment and the Romantic periods. She has edited an edition of *Mansfield Park* by Jane Austen and, for Oxford World's Classics, Adam Smith's *An Inquiry into the Nature and Causes of the Wealth of Nations*.

OXFORD WORLD'S CLASSICS

For over 100 years Oxford World's Classics have brought readers closer to the world's great literature. Now with over 700 titles—from the 4,000-year-old myths of Mesopotamia to the twentieth century's greatest novels—the series makes available lesser-known as well as celebrated writing.

The pocket-sized hardbacks of the early years contained introductions by Virginia Woolf, T. S. Eliot, Graham Greene, and other literary figures which enriched the experience of reading. Today the series is recognized for its fine scholarship and reliability in texts that span world literature, drama and poetry, religion, philosophy and politics. Each edition includes perceptive commentary and essential background information to meet the changing needs of readers.

ADAM SMITH

An Inquiry into the Nature and Causes of the Wealth of Nations

A Selected Edition

Edited with an Introduction and Notes by
KATHRYN SUTHERLAND

OXFORD
UNIVERSITY PRESS

OXFORD
UNIVERSITY PRESS

Great Clarendon Street, Oxford OX2 6DP

Oxford University Press is a department of the University of Oxford.
It furthers the University's objective of excellence in research, scholarship,
and education by publishing worldwide in

Oxford New York

Athens Auckland Bangkok Bogotá Buenos Aires Cape Town
Chennai Dar es Salaam Delhi Florence Hong Kong Istanbul Karachi
Kolkata Kuala Lumpur Madrid Melbourne Mexico City Mumbai Nairobi
Paris São Paulo Shanghai Singapore Taipei Tokyo Toronto Warsaw

with associated companies in Berlin Ibadan

Oxford is a registered trade mark of Oxford University Press
in the UK and in certain other countries

Published in the United States
by Oxford University Press Inc., New York

Editorial material © Kathryn Sutherland 1993

The moral rights of the author have been asserted

Database right Oxford University Press (maker)

First published as a World's Classics paperback 1993
Reissued as an Oxford World's Classics paperback 1998

British Library Cataloguing in Publication Data

Data available

Library of Congress Cataloging in Publication Data

Smith, Adam, 1723–1790.
An inquiry into the nature and causes of the wealth of nations /
Adam Smith; edited with an introduction by Kathryn Sutherland.
p. cm.—(Oxford world's classics)
Includes bibliographical references and index.
1. Economics. I. Sutherland, Kathryn. II. Title. III. Series.
HB161.S65 1993 330.15'3—dc20 92–40956

ISBN 0–19–283546–7

9

Printed in Great Britain by
Clays Ltd, St Ives plc

ACKNOWLEDGEMENTS

I am grateful to Professors Andrew Skinner, R. H. Campbell, and William B. Todd, the editors of the Glasgow Edition of *An Inquiry into the Nature and Causes of the Wealth of Nations* (1976), for permission to reproduce their text in this selected edition. I am particularly indebted to Marilyn Deegan, for reading and commenting on my typescript and for advice and criticism on various points; and to Judith Luna, for her encouragement of the project and for great patience during its many delays.

CONTENTS

INTRODUCTION

Who owns the *Wealth of Nations*? Since the early nineteenth century Smith has been the patron saint of *homo economicus*. Victorian liberal economists invoked his work to justify the pursuit of individual self-interest in a free market. The political and economic trends of the more recent past—the drive to privatization, the concentration on the profit motive as the key to market effectiveness and economic co-ordination—in Thatcherite Britain and Reaganite North America (but also in St Petersburg and Moscow), claim descent from Smith. His name is taken by the Adam Smith Institute, a right-wing think-tank whose aim is to devise policy based on market principles; but his interpreters and descendants include Karl Marx. For not only did Smith view merchants and manufacturers with deep suspicion, but he considered the sign of a properly functioning market system to be the maximization of material benefits to society's lowest members. The comprehensiveness of his vision of a self-regulating market appears to confirm him as the founding father of economic conservatism; but against his celebration of capitalism as the surest means of wealth accumulation should be set a pessimism at the dehumanizing potential of industrial society which appears to anticipate Marx's alienation theory. Nor should we too readily conflate Smith's socio-economic prescriptions with conditions in the late twentieth century. His experience as an eighteenth-century citizen was of pre-industrial, small-scale technology. He does not anticipate the high-technology, multinational interests of modern institutions, the dangerous consumption of non-renewable natural resources, or the problems of post-industrial unemployment. Immediately relevant in the ideological climate of the late twentieth century, the *Wealth of Nations* is firmly embedded in a complex of assumptions surrounding the birth of a consumer society in the eighteenth century.

I

> There is nothing which requires more to be illustrated
> by philosophy than trade does . . . A merchant seldom
> thinks but of his own particular trade. To write a good
> book upon it, a man must have extensive views.
>
> (Samuel Johnson)

If the significance of Adam Smith's *Inquiry into the Nature and Causes of the Wealth of Nations* has been too narrowly restricted to no more than the beginnings of technical economics, this is in some measure the consequence of his own famous exposition of the division of labour. As a plea for specialization, it is a theory which appears to justify modern interpreters in editing out of consideration Smith's complicating deliberations on the nature of law, government, and social and individual morality as they affect the operations of a market economy. In the 1970 Penguin edition of the *Wealth of Nations*, for example, Books 1 and 2 form the substance of a work 'solely concerned with Smith's contribution to the principles of economics', and Book 3 is included simply 'in order to make the maximum use of the available space'. In justification, the editor, Andrew Skinner, anticipates his readers' response by arguing that '[i]t would probably be agreed that the first two books contain the central part of Smith's work as a theoretical economist, and the real basis of a profoundly influential system of thought'.[1] With less tactical skill, the same argument is employed to explain the complete absence of Book 5 from the recent Everyman reprint of 1991: Book 5, the reader is assured, adds nothing new. D. D. Raphael concludes his Introduction by observing that: 'Books I–IV do, however, contain the whole of what Smith had to say in carrying out his aim, "An Inquiry into the Nature and Causes of the Wealth of Nations".'[2]

---

[1] *The Wealth of Nations, Books I–III*, ed. Andrew Skinner (Harmondsworth: Penguin, 1970), 7.

[2] *The Wealth of Nations*, ed. D. D. Raphael (London: Random Century Group, 1991), p. xxvii.

What both these editions fail to acknowledge is the importance of that man of 'extensive views' whom Dr Johnson
described in explaining Smith's qualifications for writing on
economics.[3] It is the original embedding of the economic
argument within a wider cultural, intellectual, and historical
enquiry which the present selected edition attempts to reinstate
against the more traditional view of the *Wealth of Nations* as
the 'classic' economics textbook. By including large sections
from all five books, the discursive context of Smith's model
becomes apparent. An enquiry in five books, the *Wealth of
Nations* sites economic activity within the framework of a
wide-ranging discussion of social institutions and human
propensities. The effect of its extended description is to complicate and problematize economic analysis by driving the economic impulse deeper into the recesses of human personality as
the natural basis of our psychological and social existence.

Book 1 is concerned to outline that division of labour which
constitutes the wealth of nations, and to establish a new
division of society into landlords, wage-earners, and capitalists,
who in their various combinations activate and keep in motion
the mechanism of the economic process. As Smith summarizes
his argument so far in the 'Conclusion' to Chapter 11:

The whole annual produce of the land and labour of every country, or
what comes to the same thing, the whole price of that annual produce,
naturally divides itself . . . into three parts; the rent of land, the wages
of labour, and the profits of stock; and constitutes a revenue to three
different orders of people; to those who live by rent, to those who live
by wages, and to those who live by profit. These are the three great,
original and constituent orders of every civilized society, from whose
revenue that of every other order is ultimately derived. (p. 155)

Book 2 is concerned with accumulation, in its economic and
psychological aspects—with productive and unproductive labour, the virtues of parsimony, and the human urge to better
our condition (that is, to amass greater and greater wealth).

---

[3] *Boswell's Life of Johnson*, ed. G. B. Hill, revised L. F. Powell, 6 vols.
(Oxford: Clarendon Press, 1934–50), ii. 430.

Taken together, Books 1 and 2 do, indeed, form an economic treatise—Smith's demonstration of what constitutes the wealth of nations, and in particular the wealth of the modern commercial nation. But without Book 3 their argument would lack the significant historical dimension which eventually reveals how it is that the humblest beneficiary of the division of labour, the 'industrious and frugal peasant' of the opening chapter, excels in his material comforts the African king, 'the absolute master of the lives and liberties of ten thousand naked savages' (p. 20).

For Book 3 is dedicated to historical explanation, to the historical and geographic relation of town to country, and in particular to the emergence of the ur-capitalist protagonist from the medieval contest for dominance between the town guilds and the feudal landowners. Smith's subject, broadly historicized here, is the relation between those legislative and administrative institutions which constitute and protect human society, and that individual liberty from regulation which is the motor of economic development. Is society a community of private interests or of public regulation?

Book 4 ranges widely while purporting to be a critique of two systems of political economy—Mercantilism and Physiocracy (roughly speaking, the commercial and the agricultural systems)—within which all previous writings on the management of a national economy are here classified. Mercantilism, the still feudally minded philosophy of wealth through trade, dominated economic thought and practice between the mid-sixteenth and late seventeenth centuries. It recognized the need to safeguard a potent national economy through high import tariffs and state intervention. 'Physiocracy' is the label attached to the doctrines of a group of eighteenth-century French economists, led by François Quesnay, who argued, in contrast, that mercantile stock is 'sterile', and that agriculture is the only source of wealth because it alone produces a surplus, other manufactures merely reproducing what they consume. Most of Book 4 is concerned to expose the flaws in the Mercantilist system, under whose intricate controls, it is claimed, the British and other European economies have been severely hampered.

Only the last chapter gives an outline of and qualified praise to the agricultural or Physiocratic model, familiar to Smith from his long stay in France in the 1760s. Smith's sustained attack on Mercantilism is contextualized within a topical consideration of domestic and foreign policies—the corn laws at home and the state of Britain's colonies in North America and India—and provides him with the opportunity to cast in an attractive light his own arguments for free competition in trade.

Book 5 is the longest. Representing over a quarter of the length of the *Wealth of Nations*, its concern with the duties of government in a free society goes some way towards adjusting those notions of 'natural liberty' expounded in the more narrowly commercial sections of the work, and in particular in Book 4. Here Smith's subjects are the legitimate forms of government expenditure, the means of raising revenue to support such expense (taxation), and a critical discussion of public debt. Among expenditure devolving to the state, he lists: the remuneration of members of the armed forces; of administrators of justice; and of those who maintain public works and institutions, including, in some cases, educators. Smith's views on the state organization of services are highly topical in the late twentieth century—in the emphasis placed on considerations of efficiency, the role of markets, and the possibilities of some services being self-financing.

Taken together, as they need to be, these five books represent more than a theoretic collectivity or practical handbook of writings on trade, manufacture, money, wealth, and so on; their larger subject, the struggle for individual liberty and general prosperity in history, is shared with other panoramic narratives, both factual and fictional, of the eighteenth-century Enlightenment. Further, certain major subjects and themes give structure and coherence to, or establish contradictory reverberations within, a work which is often merely rambling and repetitively expansive.

The *Wealth of Nations* is an exercise in history; more particularly, it is a work of stadial history (of history 'by stages') in the service of modern commercial society. In common with other philosophical historians of the eighteenth century, Smith accepted the stadial explanation of human development as a way of accounting for cultural-economic differences between societies and the relation of material to psychological agents. According to the theory in its generally deployed form, there are four types of economic organization through which societies will, in the course of nature, progress in fixed order—the hunting, shepherd, farming, and commercial economies—and to each of these stages certain social and political organizations and even certain personality traits will correspond.[4] In its application, particularly in French and Scottish historical debate in the second half of the eighteenth century, the theory renders social difference largely conformable to modes of subsistence, and in some cases, notably in less advanced societies, to climate and topographical factors too, with law and government virtually secondary aspects of the social fabric arising out of these circumstances. Though as a theory of causation the stadial subsistence theory becomes more complex, encompassing at a primary level more variables as society enters its modern phase, always uppermost is the shaping role played by the acquisition of property and the means of production in developing a fully human and social identity, a verdict corroborated by the great weight of Smith's complementary writings on ethics, government, law, and other topics, all of which assume implicitly the emergence of the commercial state.

In giving historical elaboration to the rise, progress, and decline of the empires of Greece and Rome, and the breakdown of the feudal order in Europe during the Middle Ages, Chapters 2 and 3 of Book 3, and Chapter 1 of Book 5 provide systematic consideration of the four socio-economic stages, and suggest the inevitability of modern commercial society. Both sections draw heavily on Smith's earlier work as recorded in his *Lectures on Jurisprudence* (dating from the early 1760s). Their wide sweep of the past is characteristic of the stylized history

---

[4] The stadial theory is well explained in Ronald L. Meek, *Social Science and the Ignoble Savage* (Cambridge: Cambridge University Press, 1976).

writing of other Scottish Enlightenment thinkers, especially David Hume, Adam Ferguson, and Smith's pupil at Glasgow, John Millar. Like them, Smith does not mean to imply that history as mere antiquity has any prescriptive force, but that, as the record of how differing modes of subsistence connect at various stages with the development of social institutions and forms of government, history is both materially instructive and capable of generating laws for understanding all social change:

But what all the violence of the feudal institutions could never have effected, the silent and insensible operation of foreign commerce and manufactures gradually brought about. (p. 264)

Among nations of hunters, as there is scarce any property, or at least none that exceeds the value of two or three days labour; so there is seldom any established magistrate or any regular administration of justice . . . It is in the age of shepherds, in the second period of society, that the inequality of fortune first begins to take place, and introduces among men a degree of authority and subordination which could not possibly exist before . . . Civil government, so far as it is instituted for the security of property, is in reality instituted for the defence of the rich against the poor, or of those who have some property against those who have none at all. (pp. 407–13)

What the reader needs to be alert to is the material base of Smith's own interpretation of history, and in particular the implied definition of human progress which the stadial theory contains. Is the concept merely descriptive or precisely evaluative? Is it an impartial observation of change as sequence, or a celebration of 'modern' society as the acme of human potential? We have for answer a statement from *Lectures on Jurisprudence*:

Thus at last the age of commerce arises. When therefore a country is stored with all the flocks and herds it can support, the land cultivated so as to produce all the grain and other commodities necessary for our subsistence it can be brought to bear . . . such a society has done all in its power towards its ease and convenience.[5]

---

[5] *Lectures on Jurisprudence* (1762–3), i. 32 (p. 16). References to Smith's Works, unless otherwise stated, are to the relevant page/section in the *Glasgow Edition of the Works and Correspondence of Adam Smith* (Oxford: Clarendon Press, 1976–83). See Select Bibliography for full details.

In its profitable assimilation of the flocks and herds of the 'second age' of shepherds and the grain of the 'third age' of farmers, Smith's 'fourth age' appears as the ultimate goal of history's serial unfolding. The propelling materialism of the stadial theory of social change includes a retrospective justification, even a celebration, of late eighteenth-century commercial capitalism. History's progressive unfolding comes dangerously close at this point to assuming the shape of a closed narrative, as Europe, with Britain at its head, enters the final glorious phase, history's happy ending. Out of history is born commerce, and in particular, the commercial empire and complexly diffused consumption patterns of Georgian England. It is difficult not to be wooed, whether conscious or not of the effect of that manipulatory possessive ('necessary for *our* subsistence') which steals into an otherwise impersonal description of '*a* country' (emphases added). Here is Britain, advanced as far as industry will allow, a land of opulence, beyond further progress. Scientific observation shades imperceptibly into the unsubtly oppositional 'us/them' of imperialist rhetoric. It is this colonizing undertow of stadial history which provides the context for Walter Bagehot's famous witticism that Smith set out to show 'how from being a savage, man rose to be a Scotchman'.[6] Further, in providing a materialist history, Smith and the other philosophical historians of the eighteenth century can be seen to identify a politics of cultural transformation which again occupies historians, anthropologists, and literary critics, among others, engaged in cultural studies in the present day.

Much of the exemplifying history of the *Wealth of Nations* is in fact geography, not historical evidence from within British society, but contemporary cross-cultural analogy. The nomadic Tartars and Arabs who people Smith's second age of shepherds are, like the commercial Scots, men of the eighteenth century; a favourite ground for the erecting of comparisons is the 'primitive' social organization, recently recorded, of the North

[6] 'Adam Smith as a Person' (1876), in *Bagehot's Historical Essays*, ed. Norman St John-Stevas (London: Dennis Dobson, 1971), 86.

American Indians. Smith's theorization of commercial capitalism is inscribed upon a vast geo-historical space which effectively represents the hegemonic ambitions of Britain at this
time, as the centre of an international network of trade and
consumption and the locus of 'civilized' values. Yet it is also
important to note the limitations built into this model: the
Wealth of Nations contains an attack upon empire. Like Gibbon, the first volume of whose *Decline and Fall of the Roman
Empire* appeared in the same year as the *Wealth of Nations*,
Smith's concern is with the inherent instability of empire.
Their shared thesis was that large empires were a drain on the
vigour, and undermined the virtue, of their masters. Though
something of a commonplace at the time, in 1776, the year of
their publication, the argument was given some point by the
insurrection of the American colonies and the Declaration of
Independence, as well as by continuing corruption in the
British East India Company.

In Book 4 we are told that there is no economic case for
colonies and so for empire, because the monopolies which
empire establishes, of whatever kind, impoverish the homeland.
Monopoly, the 'sole engine of the mercantile system' and the
leading economic principle of empire, is viewed by Smith as
inimical to that free trade and international competition in
which lies the spur to industry and the wealth of nations. In
challenging Mercantilism, Smith effectively demolishes the
economic case for empire as he does the case for slavery.
Finally, in a powerful concluding paragraph to the whole work,
emphasis is placed on the illusoriness of empire, its insubstan-
tiality, its character as a fantasy of power: the space that it fills
and the resources that it represents, it is argued here, have
existed in the national imagination only. The effect of Smith's
rhetoric on the eve of war is to de-territorialize America, the
ultimate fantasy empire.

The *Wealth of Nations* also embodies a justification of commerce
and the free-market economy in terms of a social ethic of
'natural liberty'. The epithet 'natural' is the most overworked

word in the *Wealth of Nations*, and the most difficult to pin down. 'Nature', Raymond Williams wrote, 'is perhaps the most complex word in the language.'[7] In eighteenth-century usage this was certainly so, and Smith's argument 'from nature' structures the *Wealth of Nations* as a dialogue between the word's various meanings. Williams distinguishes three 'areas of meaning' in terms of which the word develops, and all three are significant to Smith's analytic survey of the wealth of nations. First, 'Nature' is 'the essential quality and character of something' (as indicated in the title *An Inquiry into the Nature and Causes of the Wealth of Nations*); secondly, it is 'the inherent force which directs either the world or human beings or both' (Smith's economy is the result of compelling human psychology—the way we are—and inevitable development—the way things are); thirdly, it is 'the material world itself, taken as including or not including human beings' (for Smith this implies the existence of a set of discoverable laws, or a state of nature, sometimes to be contrasted with an existing, regulated state of society and things).

In the opening chapter Smith observes of the country workman that his habit 'of indolent careless application' is 'naturally, or rather necessarily acquired' (p. 16), and this conjunction or substitution of the epithets 'natural' and 'necessary' occurs in a range of economic contexts: '[t]he liberal reward of labour, therefore, as it is the necessary effect, so it is the natural symptom of increasing national wealth' (p. 73). 'The owner of the stock which employs a great number of labourers, necessarily endeavours, for his own advantage, to make such a proper division and distribution of employment' among his workers, while '[t]he greater their number, the more they naturally divide themselves into different classes and subdivisions of employment' (p. 87–8). 'That order of things which necessity imposes in general . . . is, in every particular country, promoted by the natural inclinations of man' (p. 229). 'But the study of

[7] Raymond Williams, *Keywords: A Vocabulary of Culture and Society* (revised edn., London: Fontana, 1983), 219.

his own advantage naturally, or rather necessarily leads [the individual] to prefer that employment which is most advantageous to the society' (p. 289). The effect of the authority of the conjunction is to impose the arrangements of the free market as both inevitable and in accordance with the uninhibited workings of human nature. In other words, the attribution of 'natural' and 'necessary' to the workings of the economy within a particular model (the free market) suggests that what is described is a normal state of affairs and, importantly, that the description is itself neutral, value-free.

Elsewhere, at Book 1, Chapter 7, there is a discussion of 'natural price' in relation to 'market price' which is crucial in Smith's advocacy of a system in which markets are allowed to work freely without outside interference. According to Smith, the free market, left to itself, will 'naturally' produce that balance of supply and demand on which its successful operation depends; yet at the same time, the natural economic forces at work in the market never actually equate market with natural price. Here 'natural' draws on the connotations of 'natural law', and implies that there is a scientific principle at work in the market. Though market price can at any particular time be at, above, or below natural price, depending on the relation between supply and demand, natural price functions, according to Smith, as a centre of gravity producing an equilibrium in the tension between supply and demand comparable to the equilibrium worked by the force of gravity for moving bodies (p. 56). The idea, like the working of the principle it assumes, is problematic.

Within the large corpus of writings on natural law in the works of seventeenth-century jurists and philosophers, including Grotius and Pufendorf in the Netherlands and Germany, and John Locke in England,[8] 'natural liberty' exists between two

---

[8] Hugo Grotius, *De jure belli ac pacis* (Of the Law of War and Peace) (1625); Samuel von Pufendorf, *De jure naturae et gentium* (Of the Law of Nature and Nations) (1672), and *De officio hominis et civis* (Of the Whole Duty of Man) (1673); John Locke, *Two Treatises of Government* (1690).

possibilities—between the state of nature in which primitive man and woman were believed actually to exist, and a utopian ideal of freedom. The distinction is important, for it explains why Smith's use of the epithet 'natural' constantly pushes against its transparent function of describing how things are in an unhindered free market, and how it goes further, attributing value, in the form of moral approbation, to certain exemplary economic and social models: in other words, it explains how economic *de*scription shades into *pre*scription, despite the fact that the original argument from nature is posited on a reading of human nature as a collection of morally unadopted energies, neither good nor bad. Accordingly, descriptive and analytical epithets give way to evaluative terms throughout Book 3, a historical account of 'the natural progress of things toward improvement', which bristles with 'naturals' and 'necessaries'. At points in the argument here (as at Book 3, Chapter 3, for example), the free market even appears to be directly responsible for social liberty, the dissolution of feudalism and bond-labour being attributed to market pressures from commerce and manufacture.

Elsewhere, in the breathtaking vision of economic and political freedom with which Smith concludes Book 4, 'the obvious and simple system of natural liberty' is also that 'perfect liberty' (p. 354) which is to be set against the interventionist strategies of regulated colonial trade and mercantile investment. Smith's model assumes a society of independent manufacturers and merchants whose conduct is self-policing in the context of free-market relations:

All systems either of preference or of restraint, therefore, being thus completely taken away, the obvious and simple system of natural liberty establishes itself of its own accord. Every man, as long as he does not violate the laws of justice, is left perfectly free to pursue his own interest his own way, and to bring both his industry and capital into competition with those of any other man, or order of men. (p. 391)

Earlier, the 'just liberty' of the common workman to employ his labour as he sees fit is defended against the constricting effects of apprenticeship regulations (p. 120). The 'system of natural liberty' extends, it appears, to all sectors of the economy from the humblest to the most powerful member. The figures of the merchant and the labourer lend support to Smith's project to show how the evolution of a free-market economy is identical with the realization of a comprehensive social ethics of 'natural liberty'. The task of political economy, as Smith sees it in Book 4, is to criticize the contingent and historically derived laws of regulation by reference to this 'system of natural liberty', which guarantees free competition in terms of a complex network of self-interested endeavour and self-imposed checks on behaviour. In *Lectures on Jurisprudence*, reference is made to a 'natural balance of industry' and to the 'natural connection of all trades'.[9] 'Liberty', in this context, means the freedom of social exchanges in the market. But, like the positioned examples of the merchant and the labourer, the free market as a method of organization is merely a discursive formation, a rhetorical strategy which ultimately fails to explain just how such a society comes into being.

The final effect of Smith's rhetoric is to signal a shift in the social role of economic activity itself at this point in the late eighteenth century, a shift which assumes the abolition of a traditional regulatory system at the same time as it describes (but in fact prescribes) a new model of free commercial enterprise. It is this new model which is comprehensively endorsed in terms of a whole range of naturalizing strategies—in terms of human nature; in terms of natural law; inevitably, freely, even innocently of intended outcome; and, paradoxically, in terms of moral approval. The inclusiveness of these strategies ensures the impossibility of imagining any alternative social, political, or economic structure.

Most readers consider the emphasis to fall in the *Wealth of Nations* on its model of the workings of the economy. This

---

[9] *Lectures on Jurisprudence* (1766), 233–4 (p. 498).

model supposes a situation where there are three main forms of economic activity—agriculture, manufacture, and trade—carried on by means of three components of production—land, labour, and capital, or the input of, as Smith defines them, 'the three great, original and constituent orders' into which society falls at the 'commercial stage' (p. 155). These are landlords, workers, and capitalists, who variously combine to keep in motion the mechanism of the economic process and to whom three kinds of return accrue—rent, wages, and profits, all of which may enter into the cost of a commodity but each of which differs from the other two. According to Ronald Meek, it is this new tripartite division of the socio-economic structure, and, in particular, the acknowledgement of the importance of its third component, the capitalist and the capitalist's profits, which distinguishes the *Wealth of Nations* as a paradigmatic text. Writing in 1973, Meek extends from the natural sciences to economics T. S. Kuhn's specialist use of the term 'paradigm' (in his *Structure of Scientific Revolutions* (1962)) in order to explain what he sees as the universal acceptance of Smith's analysis and the 'shift in perception' it can be said to have occasioned. As a result of the *Wealth of Nations*, Meek argues, our figuring of economic structures was decisively changed.[10] Through the combinations of these three orders and three productive components is guaranteed that growth which constitutes the wealth of nations; and it comes about by means of a further combination of psychological and technological factors.

The *Wealth of Nations* opens with the division-of-labour theory as the essential starting-point for economic growth. Smith was not the first social or economic thinker to identify the division of labour as the key to productivity in commercial

---

[10] *Precursors of Adam Smith*, ed. Ronald L. Meek (London: Dent, 1973), p. viii. However unsatisfactory as an explanatory model Kuhn's ideas now appear, their appropriation from the 'hard' sciences signals something important and enduring in the modern history of economics, to do with the status that practitioners have sought for economics, since Smith, as a scientific discipline grounded in testable theories.

society. Anticipations of his argument are to be found in the economic pamphleteers of the 1690s, in the writings of Sir William Petty and John Locke, and in Bernard Mandeville's *Fable of the Bees* (1723). In the early eighteenth-century period- ical the *Spectator*, itself the literary agent of the new consumer society, the aptly named merchant Sir Andrew Freeport ex- plains to an unspecialist, middle-class readership the advantages of a division of labour, using Petty's example of a watch:

It is certain that a single Watch could not be made so cheap in Proportion by one only Man, as a hundred Watches by a hundred; for as there is vast Variety in the Work, no one Person could equally suit himself to all the Parts of it; the Manufacture would be tedious, and at last but clumsily performed: But if an hundred Watches were to be made by a hundred Men, the Cases may be assigned to one, the Dials to another, the Wheels to another, the Springs to another, and every other Part to a proper Artist; as there would be no need of perplexing any one Person with too much Variety, every one would be able to perform his single Part with greater Skill and Expedition; and the hundred Watches would be finished in one fourth Part of the Time of the first one, and every one of them at one-fourth Part of the Cost, though the wages of every Man were equal. The Reduction of the Price of the Manufacture would increase the Demand of it, all the same Hands would be still employed and as well paid. The same Rule will hold in the Cloathing, the Shipping, and all the other Trades whatsoever. And thus an Addition of Hands to our Manufactures will only reduce the Price of them; the Labourer will still have as much Wages, and will consequently be enabled to purchase more Conveni- ences of Life; so that every interest in the Nation would receive a Benefit from an Increase of our working People.[11]

The episode is instructive, showing how already in 1711 what we take to be the basis of Smith's model of more than sixty years later is being popularized as part of a new form of social description. His own famous example of the manufacture of pins had received exemplary status in 1755, when Denis Diderot's

[11] *The Spectator*, ed. Donald F. Bond, 5 vols. (Oxford: Oxford University Press, 1965), No. 232. All subsequent references (by essay number) are included in the text and are to this edition.

Encyclopédie entry described eighteen different stages in its manufacture (see my explanatory note to p. 12 of the text).

But Smith extends the manufacturing model when he writes that '[t]he division of labour . . . so far as it can be introduced, occasions, in every art, a proportionable increase of the productive powers of labour' (p. 13). Consequently, he asserts, philosophy, just like pin-making, will 'in the progress of society' subdivide into distinct branches; and he concludes that as each philosopher 'becomes more expert in his own peculiar branch, more work is done upon the whole, and the quantity of science is considerably increased by it' (p. 18). He even goes so far as to suggest that differences in talents and genius are traceable less to natural endowment than to the effects of labour specialization (p. 23).

Smith argues that when each individual concentrates on one skill or function to the exclusion of others, technical innovations, in the form of new machinery or modifications to old processes, will result (pp. 16–17); but that, in the course of such specialization, workers will inevitably reduce their own self-sufficiency and render themselves dependent on other specialized workers for those wants which independent labour can no longer supply. The consequence is a diversified economy kept healthy by the self-interested motives of all its contributors to co-operate freely in the practice of exchange. An equation might be drawn between the opulence of a society and its economic growth on the one hand, and its complex division of labour and pattern of mutual dependence on the other.

That Smith finds his model effective over the whole range of human activity results from the fact that it is grounded not in wisdom, design, or benevolence, but in a natural human propensity to truck and barter, and in an equally instinctive regard for personal interest. He writes:

man has almost constant occasion for the help of his brethren, and it is in vain for him to expect it from their benevolence only. He will be more likely to prevail if he can interest their self-love in his favour, and show them that it is for their own advantage to do for him what he requires of them. . . .

As it is by treaty, by barter, and by purchase, that we obtain from one another the greater part of those mutual good offices which we stand in need of, so it is this same trucking disposition which originally gives occasion to the division of labour. (pp. 22–3)

Just as the economic growth which constitutes the wealth of nations is accelerated by the specialization and technological advances consequent upon the division of labour; so, to the same extent, commercial prosperity is fuelled by certain psychological factors which ensure that '[e]very man . . . lives by exchanging, or becomes in some measure a merchant' (p. 31).

At the core of the human psyche and of the socio-economic process lies desire. Desire takes various forms. At Book 1, Chapter 11, '[t]he desire of food is limited in every man by the narrow capacity of the human stomach; but the desire of the conveniencies and ornaments of building, dress, equipage, and household furniture, seems to have no limit or certain boundary' (pp. 152–3). These are desires 'which cannot be satisfied, but seem to be altogether endless'. Smith expresses here the tenets (grounded in behavioural psychology) of an expansionist philosophy of commerce which assumes human appetite as the motor of historical change and consumption as the key to prosperity. Such arguments had been voiced as early as the 1690s, in the pamphlets of liberal economists and merchants like Dudley North, Nicholas Barbon, and Henry Martyn (see my explanatory note to p. 153 of the text).

Later, it is the desire to save rather than the desire to consume which is said to ensure economic growth: 'But the principle which prompts to save, is the desire of bettering our condition, a desire which, though generally calm and dispassionate, comes with us from the womb, and never leaves us till we go into the grave' (p. 203). Smith entitles the chapter in which the distinction is made, 'Of the Accumulation of Capital', and its argument works to complicate the doctrine of economic amoralism in terms of which Mandeville famously accounted for an emergent capitalism. Mandeville had objected that virtue is an obstacle to economic activity, which is best promoted by the operations of vice in the service of pleasure and happiness within an expanding luxury market. Together, luxury and vice increase employment, raise the standard of living, and guarantee economic progress.[12] Smith suggests that, among those agents which maximize pleasure and happiness, frugality, even more than luxury, is economically and psychologically decisive; by frugality people better their condition and win social approval. This is not a return to a Mercantilist economics of virtue, but a complication of the new economics of self-interest by a recognition of the legitimacy of a secondary (even accidental) morality in regulating the economy, since public approbation is an aspect of private esteem. It is effects, not motives, which matter.

Smith's argument that 'prudence' and 'parsimony', rather than conspicuous consumption, promote the social approbation which we all covet, is expanded in a section added to the *Theory of Moral Sentiments* in 1790, where he states:

The desire of becoming the proper objects of this respect, of deserving and obtaining this credit and rank among our equals, is, perhaps, the strongest of all our desires, and our anxiety to obtain the advantages of fortune is accordingly much more excited and irritated by this desire, than by that of supplying all the necessities and conveniencies of the body, which are always very easily supplied.[13]

In arguing in the *Wealth of Nations* that frugality is a powerful economic stimulus, Smith distinguishes between the greater quantity of productive labour which savings set in motion and the limited productive power of revenue. Both contribute to the maintenance of a consumer economy; but paradoxically, it is frugality which fuels consumption in the long term, while 'prodigality', it is suggested, will exhaust it (p. 199).

Smith's larger contention is that the complex of desires which drive human behaviour (the basic desire or need for food and shelter; the competitive desire for conspicuous consumption; and the socialized desire for approval) fuel and regulate the

[12] This is the thesis of Bernard Mandeville's, *The Fable of the Bees: Or, Private Vices, Publick Benefits* (1714; expanded 1723).

[13] *The Theory of Moral Sentiments*, VI. i. 3 (p. 213).

economy in all its aspects. Importantly, reason plays no part; nor do the nobler impulses: mutual dependence may be as important a strand in Smith's argument as economic growth, but its basis is self-interest in the context of the psychological compulsion to exchange. As Smith commented earlier in *Lectures on Jurisprudence*:

We may observe that these principles of the human mind which are most beneficial to society are by no means marked by nature as the most honourable. Hunger, thirst, and the passion for sex are the great supports of the human species. Yet almost every expression of these excites contempt. In the same manner, that principle in the mind which prompts to truck, barter, and exchange, tho' it is the great foundation of arts, commerce, and the division of labour, yet it is not marked with any thing amiable.[14]

But who or what constitutes the wealth of nations? Who are Smith's exemplary labourers and producers? Which economic activities best promote the progressive march of society? Smith's larger discussion of the progress of riches hangs on the rise in importance of towns, but also on the industry of the countryside. The wealth of nations is conceived of in terms of vaguely defined regional interests and collectives, of local situations—the words he prefers are 'societies' and 'neighbourhoods' (p. 53)—which are fictionalized as vignettes of the inside of a manufactory, the seasonal labour of the small farm, and always, the dynamic co-operation of a town and its environs. The *Wealth of Nations* is a work in which argumentative drives are often at odds with the themes and models of its more expansive communication; hence, those contradictory shifts of emphasis which make it much more than a 'scientific' treatise; hence, too, those narrative and digressive modes whose procedures build in, by means of allusive devices, ambivalent assessments of the idea of progress in human affairs.

The obvious hero of Smith's tale of wealth accumulation is the capitalist—the merchant, the entrepreneur, or master-manufacturer. He it is whose enterprise maintains colonies in

---

[14] *Lectures on Jurisprudence* (1766), 300–1 (p. 527).

Virginia and Maryland (p. 221) and whose individuated energies epitomize the competitive drive which is the key to the general character of modern commercial society. Not only is it clear that trade and manufactures are more profitable than agriculture (p. 125), but 'in all the modern states of Europe' manufacturing productivity and trade have served to subsidize improvements in the agricultural sector, thus completely inverting the 'natural order of things', whereby capital is directed first to agriculture and only afterwards to manufacture and trade (p. 232). Furthermore, while country landowners tend to be negligent of their estates, 'merchants are commonly ambitious of becoming country gentlemen', and are in consequence great improvers of land (p. 259). But Smith's commercial facilitator bears little relation to Sir Andrew Freeport, the London merchant of the *Spectator* essays. Where Sir Andrew is a man of 'natural Eloquence, good Sense, and Probity of Mind', 'of indefatigable Industry, strong Reason, and great Experience', who is 'pleasanter Company than a general Scholar' (*Spectator* 2, 549), Smith's merchant or master-manufacturer is an amoral figure at best, self-serving, narrowly motivated, and not to be trusted. He belongs to 'an order of men, whose interest is never exactly the same with that of the publick, who have generally an interest to deceive and even to oppress the publick, and who accordingly have, upon many occasions, both deceived and oppressed it' (pp. 157-8).

The assumption which runs through the *Wealth of Nations*, that we are the jobs we do, that personality is a function of work and of socio-economic circumstance, combines with a Lockean interpretation of the human mind in which mental alertness corresponds to the range of sensations received. Where business renders the merchant deceitful, an indolent life-style leaves the country landlord stupid (p. 155). In the case of the factory hand, a complex subdivision of labour can result in an incapacity for extended thought (p. 429). In contrast to all of these, the agricultural worker can display a mental agility and intellectual superiority, the direct consequences of a labour which is undivided, independent, and varied. At the heart of the *Wealth of Nations* lies a contradiction: between two models of production—the one 'natural', the other virtuous; and between two modes of argument—the one scientific, the other moralized. If natural man is a merchant, virtuous man is a farmer.

'Agriculture is of all other arts the most beneficent to society.'[15] While rejecting the economic basis of the French Physiocratic position—that the labour of the farmer uniquely produces more than he requires for subsistence—Smith nevertheless celebrates at several points the superiority of agricultural productivity. This is not a matter of the size of profits—other manufactures regularly exceed agriculture; rather, it relates to a deep-rooted and exemplary notion of virtuous productivity. At times Smith only just avoids the unabashedly moralized economics of Dr Johnson, who proclaimed in 1756 that: 'Agriculture . . . and agriculture alone, can support us without the help of others in certain plenty and genuine dignity.'[16] Behind Smith's praise of the rural life lies a traditional opposition of town and country values, reaching back to Cicero and Horace, and especially to Virgil—to a classical ideal of virtuous work. Virgil's *Georgics* provided a didactic poetics of rural life and agronomic improvement (an instructional treatise on farm management *and* a poem, a work of literature), whose influence is more readily noted in the eighteenth-century vogue for poetic essays celebrating the workings of the rural economy. An idealizing fiction centring on the productive life in the country, the *Georgics* also provides a more open-ended model which can extend to a treatment of industry in the economy as a whole. The subject of John Dyer's poem *The Fleece* (1757) is the British wool industry; other topics for 'Georgic' poetry at this time included cider-making and sugar production—John Philips's early *Cyder* (1708) and James Grainger's *The Sugar-Cane* (1764); in higher style, there is the reflective philo-

---

[15] Ibid. 298 (p. 522).
[16] 'Further Thoughts on Agriculture' (1756), in *Political Writings*, ed. Donald J. Greene, Yale Edition of the Works of Samuel Johnson (New Haven, Conn. and London: Yale University Press, 1958–ꞏ), x (1977), 124.

sophizing, as well as practical advice on country matters, of William Cowper's *The Task* (1785). In the *Wealth of Nations*, Smith's Georgic hero is the 'common ploughman':

Not only the art of the farmer, the general direction of the operations of husbandry, but many inferior branches of country labour require much more skill and experience than the greater part of mechanick trades. The man who works upon brass and iron, works with instruments and upon materials of which the temper is always the same, or very nearly the same. But the man who ploughs the ground with a team of horses or oxen, works with instruments of which the health, strength, and temper are very different upon different occasions. The condition of the materials which he works upon too is as variable as that of the instruments which he works with, and both require to be managed with much judgment and discretion. The common ploughman, though generally regarded as the pattern of stupidity and ignorance, is seldom defective in this judgment and discretion. He is less accustomed, indeed, to social intercourse than the mechanick who lives in a town. His voice and language are more uncouth and more difficult to be understood by those who are not used to them. His understanding, however, being accustomed to consider a greater variety of objects, is generally much superior to that of the other, whose whole attention from morning till night is commonly occupied in performing one or two very simple operations. (pp. 126–7)

The second half of the eighteenth century saw enormous improvements in agricultural technology and management in Scotland. But if the Smithian economy celebrates agricultural productivity, Smith himself was also the champion of a commercial expansion against which, by the end of the century, the agrarian politics of Wordsworth's poetic protests would be levelled. The local, virtuous agrarianism to which the *Wealth of Nations* is entailed seems already in 1776 to be a nostalgic model, a relict of the 'third stage' of social progress. This to some extent reflects the transitional status of Smith's text and the marginalization of the moral critique in economic writings after him.

Smith ends the important first chapter of the *Wealth of Nations*, concerning the economic primacy of a division of labour, by refashioning the details of his argument into a picture of the domestic accommodation of the common workman within commercial society. Economic prosperity is defined in terms of 'the great multiplication of the productions of all the different arts . . . which occasions . . . that universal opulence which extends itself to the lowest ranks of the people' (p. 18). Debated throughout the eighteenth century were the competing moral and economic advantages of the doctrines of beneficial luxury and of lower-class poverty. It is Hume's opinion in 1742 that 'the great advantage of England above any nation at present in the world, or that appears in the records of any story', consists in the extended division of wealth down to the labouring classes.[17] While still assuming a hierarchical division of society into men and masters, the exemplary descriptions by which Smith assembles his economic model signal the mundaneness of production and consumption, as in the case of the humble pin on which the whole sophisticated structure turns.

In the older Mercantilist explanations of wealth which Smith writes to dismantle, it was an article of faith that the subordination of ranks within a closed economy served national security, and that the self-interested pursuit of free trade might unsettle the providentially fixed establishment of rich and poor, of consumer-citizens and subsistence labourers. The labourer-consumers who people Smith's text appear to propose a dangerous levelling of social distinctions. What recent commentators have described as 'the democratization of consumption' and 'the consumer revolution'[18] taking place in the course of the eighteenth century is celebrated in Smith's text as the broad base upon which a wealthy economy stands. The hierarchical model of society, Smith suggests, will be modified during the commercial stage by those multilateral networks which promote the interdependent pursuit of mutual benefits in accordance

---

[17] David Hume, 'Of Commerce', in *Essays Moral, Political, and Literary* (London: Oxford University Press, 1963), 271–2.

[18] Joyce Appleby, 'Ideology and Theory: The Tension between Political and Economic Liberalism in Seventeenth-Century England', *American Historical Review*, 81 (1976), 515; and Neil McKendrick, John Brewer, and J. H. Plumb, *The Birth of a Consumer Society: The Commercialization of Eighteenth-Century England* (London: Hutchinson, 1983), 13.

with which manufactures and commerce thrive. Hence Smith's concern (at Book 1, Chapter 8) with the level at which common labour should be recompensed, and his thesis that in a low-wage economy consumption and, therefore, productivity suffer.

Unlike society at the feudal stage, commercial society is organized on a horizontal axis. It is not the exclusive luxury markets of the few, but the purchasing power of the workman, the growing demand for mass-produced goods, and the urge to imitative buying which constitute the real wealth of nations. The commodities Smith cites are conspicuously humble—the workman's 'coarse linen shirt', 'earthen or pewter plates', 'his bread and his beer'—but in their fashioning, so complex a network of trade and manufacture has been called into operation that it 'exceeds all computation'. It is for this reason that 'the accommodation of an European prince does not always so much exceed that of an industrious and frugal peasant, as the accommodation of the latter exceeds that of many an African king' (pp. 18–20). Comparisons such as this work to complicate the apparent amoralism of Smith's economics of self-interest. His larger argument is for the practical usefulness of consumption to all members of society, however unfettered its workings may be by moral regulation; but the process whereby '[w]hat was formerly a seat of the family of Seymour, is now an inn upon the Bath road' and the 'marriage-bed of James the First of Great Britain' becomes a night's lodging in a Dunfermline alehouse (p. 210) jeopardizes any simple amorality, by appearing to imply the late working of an economic *and* moral retribution/redistribution. The challenge contained in Smith's vision of the economy from below is echoed in Dr Johnson's democratized understanding of society at this time: 'The true state of every nation is the state of common life.'[19] It explains the composition of those who people Smith's wealthy nation—Spitalfield silk-weavers, London journeymen tailors, Scottish cotters and stocking-knitters, Birmingham factory-hands, and everywhere small shopkeepers and farmers.

[19] Samuel Johnson, *A Journey to the Western Islands of Scotland*, ed. J. D. Fleeman (Oxford: Clarendon Press, 1985), 17.

Finally, whose labour does not contribute to the wealth of nations? There are two large categories, the one problematic and the other entirely absent from Smith's model of production. At Book 2, Chapter 3, the subject of unproductive labour is raised. Both productive and unproductive labour, it is asserted, contain value; but the value of productive labour is added to the goods it manufactures, so as to be used later, while the value of unproductive labour, 'how honourable, how useful, or how necessary soever', is fixed in no permanent (that is, vendible) commodity and is consumed at once. Only productive labour, therefore, replenishes circulating capital and so contributes directly to the wealth of nations. Unproductive labourers number among them 'some both of the gravest and most important, and some of the most frivolous professions': actors, musicians, politicians, poets, lawyers, doctors, and even economists (pp. 191–2). Their work, as we might now say, is service-oriented or concerned with the representation of material society at the ideological level. Though Smith insists on the usefulness and necessity of unproductive or performative labour, the very opposition which he sets up exposes that dilemma over the reproduction of value as culture or well-being (as opposed to well-doing) which is at the heart of the late twentieth-century debate over the place of education, the arts, and medicine within the economy.

But if unproductive labour exists in paradoxical relation to the wealth of nations, women's labour is virtually absent from the Smithian economy: his is a narrowly male model of production and consumption. This in itself is instructive, since recent economic and social historians have shown how women's active engagement in labour outside the home—in workshops and factories, in textile industries and down mines—was an important contribution to the proto-industrialization of Britain in the eighteenth century. Smith's famous pin might even be termed a feminized example—pins being commonly made at this time *with* as well as *for* female labour; while it has been suggested that the growing market for mass-produced goods 'took much of its new impetus to consume from the

earnings of women and children'.[20] At Book 1, Chapter 10, we
find Smith's only clear reference to a female worker, when he
notes the contribution to the precarious cottager economy of the
woman's spinning, a grossly underpaid employment (p. 116
and note). His calls in the same chapter for the abolition of
apprenticeship regulations, in the interests of free trade and
healthy competition, were subsequently criticized by female
commentators, among them Priscilla Wakefield, as appearing to
justify the erosion of women's rights to certain forms of employment (midwifery and shop-work), and relegating them to unskilled labour without decent training.[21]

It might be argued that the emphasis which Smith, together
with other eighteenth-century social commentators, places on
the importance of population-growth to commercial improvement in itself suggests women's crucial contribution to the
nation's wealth; but the sense we have of the marginalization
of women's economic activity in Smith's text is better explained
in terms of the kind of scientific description which the *Wealth
of Nations* begins to establish. The eventual consequence
of Smith's method was to be the professionalization of the
discourse of the economist; by rendering the disciplinary model
more exclusive at a theoretic and analytical level, he in fact
refines the social model he purports to describe. Editing out
of account women's labour is one stage towards the eventual
establishment of the serious study of political economy.

Smith died in 1790, fourteen years after the publication of the
Wealth of Nations and six years after Matthew Boulton and
James Watt patented the rotary-motion steam engine. Written

[20] Neil McKendrick, 'Home Demand and Economic Growth: A New View
of the Role of Women and Children in the Industrial Revolution', in *Historical
Perspectives: Studies in English Thought and Society*, ed. Neil McKendrick (London: Europa, 1974), 172.
[21] Priscilla Wakefield, *Reflections on the Present Condition of the Female Sex;
With Suggestions for its Improvement* (London, 1798). For a summary of women's
work experiences in the period, see Jane Rendall, *Women in an Industrializing
Society: England 1750–1880* (Oxford: Basil Blackwell, 1990).

on the eve of the large-scale emergence of industrial technology and urban expansion which steam-power inaugurated, the *Wealth of Nations* anticipates some of its worst disadvantages: not the more modern fear that machinery would displace human labour, but the threat to individual integrity and social harmony. If technological innovation and economic growth hang upon the division of labour, so too do the inspirational and moral poverty of the individual. The multifarious activities of the many, working separately but restrictively to achieve a single, narrow objective, is a recipe for 'mental mutilation' (p. 435). Where the labourer works from early childhood for the largest part of every day at a limited range of simple operations, Smith argues, he 'has no occasion to exert his understanding, or to exercise his invention . . . He naturally loses, therefore, the habit of such exertion, and generally becomes as stupid and ignorant as it is possible for a human creature to become . . . His dexterity at his own particular trade seems, in this manner, to be acquired at the expence of his intellectual, social, and martial virtues' (pp. 429–30). An end-product whose value is no longer remotely equatable with the value of the labour of the individual spells the depersonalization of work, even the reification of the worker, as seems virtually implicit even in Smith's early optimistic image of the hand, dislocated into exaggerated activity by the subdivision of labour: 'The rapidity with which some of the operations of those manufactures are performed, exceeds what the human hand could, by those who have never seen them, be supposed capable of acquiring' (p. 16).

Smith's remedy for the negative aspects of economic growth is that the state should take responsibility, in its own interest, for providing basic compulsory education and encouraging 'publick diversions' of a wholesome kind. Smith is not suggesting that entertainment be state-controlled, but rather that the state should allow 'entire liberty to all those who for their own interest would attempt, without scandal or indecency, to amuse and divert the people'. However, the social and moral price paid for the specialized division of labour is so high that the state is under an obligation to compensate its members through basic education, regardless of any obvious advantages to itself. Only in this way can responsible citizenship be ensured. Smith senses the necessity for providing the new urban labourer, 'sunk in obscurity and darkness' in the great city and a prey to 'low profligacy and vice', with something to replace the mutual support and control previously exercised by the small village community (pp. 440–1).

Like the views of other educationalists and social commentators of the period, Smith's suggestions for encouraging individual responsibility and mutual toleration have much to do with the safeguarding of commercial society. John Millar, his pupil at Glasgow University, contrasts the stupidity and lassitude of the workman in an advanced society with the vigour of his earlier counterpart, arguing that, '[u]nlike the mechanics of a commercial nation . . . the inhabitants of a rude country have separately preserved, and kept in action, all the original powers of man'.[22] One persuasive argument for the reintroduction of a Scottish militia at this time was that it would provide 'mechanical' man with the opportunity to rediscover that 'virtue' (military strength) which marked the character of his forbear, the integrated warrior-producer (see my explanatory note to p. 405 of the text). It is important to note that, for all the economic buoyancy of Smith's commercial vision, the material progress it implies is attended by no corresponding moral advance: the divided commercial personality is the subject of Book 5. Ultimately, Smith's is not an optimistic view.

For Smith, self-interest is a powerful connective force between man's ethical and economic conduct. In a famous passage at Book 4, Chapter 2, he argues that behind its discontinuous individual promptings may even be discerned a more comprehensive control, promoting long-term universal benefit; and this he terms 'an invisible hand' (p. 292). In his earlier *Theory of Moral Sentiments*, he had already argued that an 'invisible hand' distributes, with some approach to equality, the 'neces-

[22] John Millar, *An Historical View of the English Government*, 4 vols. (London, 1803), iv. 151.

saries of life', despite the unequal division of wealth in commercial society.[23] Now he argues that the self-interested individual unintentionally maximizes the wealth of society for all its members. For all its providential weighting, the invisible hand is not the attribute of a celestial designer, directing the world from on high. Smith assumes a society of independent agents whose conduct is self-policing in the context of free-market relations and the laws of nature, which are, as we have seen, one and the same in his view. But in Book 5, the longest book, the picture appears to be adjusted, when Smith propounds the duties of the statesman in a society of natural liberty. Laws and institutions, we learn, evolve in response to society's increasing material complexity and the effect of modes of subsistence on human personality. The suggestion is clear, that men and women are ever more straitened in the interests of material development. While 'progress' dictates the emergence of the commercial stage, moral health lies in the agrarian and earlier stages. The distinction points to a paradox at the heart of commercial society: Smith's society of natural liberty, his self-regulating market, eventually needs a statesman at the helm; and the 'invisible hand' must give way to the guiding hand.

II

> Edinburgh is a hot-bed of genius. —I have had the good
> fortune to be made acquainted with many authors of the
> first distinction; such as the two Humes, Robertson,
> Smith, Wallace, Blair, Ferguson, Wilkie, etc. and I have
> found them all as agreeable in conversation as they are
> instructive and entertaining in their writings.

> (Tobias Smollett)

So writes Matthew Bramble, the picaresque tourist of Smollett's novel *Humphry Clinker* (1771), on his first introduction to Edinburgh society.[24] In the second half of the eighteenth

---

[23] *The Theory of Moral Sentiments*, IV. i. 10 (pp. 184–5).

[24] Smollett, *The Expedition of Humphry Clinker*, ed. Angus Ross (Harmondsworth: Penguin, 1967), 269–70.

century, Scotland, and in particular Edinburgh and Glasgow, provided the focus for Britain's major intellectual activity. This ascendancy can be traced back to the Act of Union of 1707, when Scotland and England alike ceased to exist and were incorporated in a United Kingdom of Great Britain. Politically, the aims of the Union's English architects were to reduce Scottish power and to assimilate Scottish government into a Westminster-centred structure. In the long term this was only too successful; but paradoxically, and perhaps consequently, Scotland's lost parliamentary autonomy, and in particular the dichotomy it established between national identity and economic and cultural progress, can be seen as precipitating a northern intellectual rebirth unmatched in the securer environment of the south.[25] In the age of Dr Johnson the great 'English' thinkers were almost all Scots: in David Hume, Adam Smith, and James Boswell the times produced the greatest philosopher, economist, and biographer writing in English.

In the search for the beginnings of Scottish Enlightenment thinking, the early enthusiastic reception and circulation within the northern universities of the ideas and method of Isaac Newton, 'the Miracle of the present Age' as Addison called him (*Spectator* 543), must be prominent. In particular, the Newton of the *Opticks* (1701; in English 1704) held out an all-embracing theoretical method for rendering knowledge systematic, and brought closer the possibility of a social and moral science of man founded on the inductive laws derived from the evidence of experience as ordered by the penetrating eye of the observer. Hume, in his *Treatise of Human Nature* (the title continues: *being an attempt to introduce the experimental method of reasoning into moral subjects*) (1739–40), adapted Newtonian principles of experiment and observation to the scientific formulation of the mechanisms of behaviour and the field of morality. Importantly, the Scottish thinkers were keenly aware

[25] See the argument offered in Nicholas Phillipson, 'The Scottish Enlightenment', in *The Enlightenment in National Context*, ed. Roy Porter and Mikuláš Teich (Cambridge: Cambridge University Press, 1981), 32.

of the analogical drive within Newton's universalizing methodology; they absorbed the Newtonian model into their programme of intellectual advance through interdisciplinary and wider cultural co-operation. The learned clubs and societies which sprang up throughout Scotland in the course of the eighteenth century witness, among other things, to an associative theory of the advancement of knowledge. In such clubs professors of arts and sciences mixed with Scotland's progressive landed interest and with merchants and members of the professions. Inevitable consequences of such interchanges were the redefinition of the parameters of academic and polite discourse, and the greater accountability which the literati felt their enquiries owed to issues of civil and political moment. The invigorating atmosphere of sympathetic debate suggested one enquiry as the context for another; within such a commodious intellectual design, disciplines were not seen as rigidly separate but rather as co-ordinated systems, actively seeking out definitive information through mutual relations.

Smith was an eminently clubbable man. In 1754, with Hume and the painter Allan Ramsay, he was a founder member of the celebrated Select Society, a formal debating society which, during its ten years of activity, earned the status of a North British Academy and came to include in its membership the full diversity of Scotland's aspirant leadership—aristocratic, military, secular- and clerical-intellectual, and commercial. Influenced by Hume's writings, members pushed further their discussions of ideas of morality and virtue, interpersonal relations, and the origin and organization of a modern commercial state. As Roger L. Emerson notes in his close analysis of its composition, the Society channelled intellectual speculation along predictable lines, its minuted programme of questions for debate revealing an 'economic-political-social' bias which reflects the preoccupations of 'men interested in change, its likely directions, and problematic consequences'.[26]

---

[26] Roger L. Emerson, 'The Social Composition of Enlightened Scotland: The Select Society of Edinburgh, 1754–1764', *Studies on Voltaire and the Eighteenth Century*, ed. Theodore Besterman, 114 (1973), 295.

'All the world are ambitious of a place amongst us', commented Hume to Ramsay;[27] and from his *Enquiry concerning the Principles of Morals* (1751) can be deduced an explanation. 'But why, in the greater society or confederacy of mankind', Hume asks here, 'should not the case be the same as in particular clubs and companies?'[28] The club is an ideal model of, and an initiation into, society at large. Most of those whom we associate with the high noon of the Scottish Enlightenment were in the 1750s members of the Select Society: after Hume and Smith, Hugh Blair, a Church of Scotland minister and soon to be the first professor of Rhetoric and Belles Lettres at Edinburgh University; William Robertson, already leader of the Church Moderates and later an influential historian of Scotland and America, Principal of Edinburgh University and, from 1763, Historiographer Royal for Scotland; Adam Ferguson, Professor of Natural Philosophy and later of Moral Philosophy at Edinburgh and a pioneer sociologist; and Henry Home, Lord Kames, who, uniting legal, philosophical, historical, and literary investigations with the more practical concerns of agricultural improvement, was perhaps the representative Enlightenment man.

Smith's economic theories form one complementary part in an ambitious science of man, comprising enquiries into human nature, social relations, ethics, the nature of progress, the origins of language, the history of institutions, religion, the maintenance of government, and the history of astronomy. In contrast to his emphasis on a division of labour as the prerequisite of a thriving economy, the philosophic model he constructs is distinguished by the reciprocal accessibility of its constituent parts—by their clubbableness. It is a network of mutually verifiable truths, arrived at by a process of empiricism and conjecture. Philosophy, in Smith's definition, is 'the science of connecting principles'; but it is so only as 'that science which

[27] Cited ibid. 298.

[28] David Hume, *An Enquiry concerning the Principles of Morals*, ed. L. A. Selby-Bigge, revised P. H. Nidditch (3rd edn., Oxford: Clarendon Press, 1975), 281.

pretends to lay open the concealed connections that unite the various appearances of nature'.

Systems in many respects resemble machines. A machine is a little system, created to perform, as well as to connect together, in reality, those different movements and effects which the artist has occasion for. A system is an imaginary machine invented to connect together in the fancy those different movements and effects which are already in reality performed.[29]

In the student notes which we have of his *Lectures on Rhetoric* for the Glasgow University session 1762/3, Smith applies the same model to verbal exposition itself, preferring over the unconnected 'Aristotelian' style of debate the 'Newtonian method', in which 'the phaenomena which we reckoned the most unaccountable' are 'all deduced from some principle (commonly a wellknown one) and all united in one chain'.[30]

The diverse arguments of the *Wealth of Nations* can all be deduced from the empirical beginning: 'I have never known much good done by those who affected to trade for the publick good' (p. 292). Moreover, the economic structure which is here propounded is one way of making sense of and connecting the evidence available in discrete form in the real world, but the model itself does not have objective existence in that same world. Smith is careful to point out that 'in all the modern states of Europe' the 'natural order' on which he bases his economic system 'has ... been, in many respects, entirely inverted' (p. 232). As a way of regulating contiguous fragments, system-making is essentially an imaginative exercise, and one that is inexhaustible. Smith recognizes the constant need there will be to adjust the relationship between part and whole, to invent new systems, since the possibilities for combination will be limited only by the limitless, by our powers of *repres-entation*.

In Book 5, in the course of outlining the deleterious effects on the human intellect of the division of labour, Smith distin-

---

[29] *Essays on Philosophical Subjects*, 51 and 66.
[30] *Lectures on Rhetoric and Belles Lettres*, Lecture 24, p. 146.

guishes 'those few' individuals who, set apart from the normal activity of over-specialized production, are free to observe and to 'contemplate' the variety which such multiplied narrowness brings into existence:

In a civilized state . . . though there is little variety in the occupations of the greater part of individuals, there is an almost infinite variety in those of the whole of society. These varied occupations present an almost infinite variety of objects to the contemplation of those few, who, being attached to no particular occupation themselves, have leisure and inclination to examine the occupations of other people. The contemplation of so great a variety of objects necessarily exercises their minds in endless comparisons and combinations, and renders their understandings, in an extraordinary degree, both acute and comprehensive. (p. 431)

This is as good a picture as we could hope for of the economist as hero, the disengaged Newtonian spectator, whose mind is 'necessarily' exercised 'in endless comparisons and combinations'. In his opening chapter Smith imagines a factory in which each different branch of production is 'placed at once *under the view of the spectator*' (p. 11); and he remarks subsequently: '*I have seen* a small manufactory of this kind' (p. 12), '*I have seen* several boys . . .' (p. 15); and at the end of the chapter, '[*o*]*bserve* the accommodation of the most common artificer . . . *examine* . . . all the different parts of his dress . . .' (pp. 18–19) (emphases added). It is the economist who, by an act of imagination and observation, assembles the general truths of life from its unordered particulars, creating a temporary stability and shape from its infinitely discrete fragments.

What Smith describes as the economist's method is essentially a poetic or a fictional process. Earlier in the century, in the *Spectator*, Addison and Steele had created a literary periodical around the observations and conversations of the fictional Spectator Club, a cross-section of 'polite' members who represent the respectable limits of the new consumer society. Its collective authorial persona, 'Mr Spectator', describes himself as one who lives in the world 'rather as a Spectator of Mankind, than as one of the Species; by which means I have made my self a Speculative Statesman, Soldier, Merchant, and Artizan, without ever medling with any Practical Part in Life' (*Spectator* 1). It is this informed awareness combined with special exclusion which guarantees his privileged status as a spectator and which provides his authority with his readers, a mixture of squirearchy and bourgeoisie, of country and town values. It is from the polite culture and heterodox alliances of the Spectator Club that the clubbable environment of Edinburgh intellectual society can be seen to derive.[31] Inherently protean in their view of commercial society, the *Spectator* essays form a stream of impressions linked by association, a succession of incidents and reflections which exemplify the spectrum of values (economic, social, literary, moral) which are negotiable currency in the commercial society. London provides their focus, its changing panorama and the extent of its trade affording the Spectator 'a kind of *Emporium* for the whole Earth' (*Spectator* 69).

For Smith, an integrated universe is the product of analogical thinking. Behind his own limited contribution to language theory (in his 'Considerations concerning the first formation of languages') lies the general eighteenth-century philosophic concern with the origin and development of language, written and spoken, and the question of the relationship that obtains between things and descriptions of things. He speculates in the *Wealth of Nations* on whether 'the propensity to truck, barter, and exchange one thing for another . . . be one of those original principles in human nature, of which no further account can be given; or whether, as seems more probable, it be the necessary consequence of the faculties of reason and speech' (p. 21). As the original commerce between persons or groups in society, the linguistic transaction provides the paradigm for all other social forms and systems, since in language meaning

---

[31] See Nicholas Phillipson, 'Adam Smith as Civic Moralist', in *Wealth and Virtue: The Shaping of Political Economy in the Scottish Enlightenment*, ed. Istvan Hont and Michael Ignatieff (Cambridge: Cambridge University Press, 1983), 179–202; and J. G. A. Pocock, 'Cambridge Paradigms and Scotch Philosophers: A Study of the Relations between the Civic Humanist and the Civil Jurisprudential Interpretation of Eighteenth-Century Social Thought', ibid. 240.

is created by one process being equated with and substituted for another in a more or less complex system of exchange.

This primary intersection of language and trade is apparent in Smith's attempts to describe the market. At Book 3, Chapter 1, the reader is told that 'the town is a continual fair or market, to which the inhabitants of the country resort, in order to exchange their rude for manufactured produce' (p. 230). The market is a place; but it is also an assembly and a network of communications (originally a market-place was a point of convergence of major roads in the centre of a town). For Smith, and after Smith for the modern interpreter, the market illuminates many of the features which characterize advanced societies. As the primary mechanism for the distribution of goods, the market is both a concrete and tangible entity—the point of sale and/or the company who gather to buy and sell—and it is an abstraction, a concept of spending controlled by supply and demand. In the *Wealth of Nations*, the market as place, with all its connotations of an older moral economics of face-to-face dealings, already seems abandoned to the more abstract usage. But whether it is a place which facilitates a process or the process itself, it is, as Peter Stallybrass and Allon White remark, 'an agent of transformation . . . a conjuncture of discourses . . . the point of intersection of different cultures'.[32]

As London is 'a kind of *Emporium* for the whole Earth', and as the merchant is the great assembler and converter, knitting 'Mankind together in a mutual Intercourse of good Offices' (*Spectator* 69), so Smith's text is, finally, an assemblage of different modes of saying, in which the discourses of history, literature, anthropology, and ethical and scientific description compete and are exchanged. Smith began his professional career in Edinburgh in 1748 delivering public lectures on Rhetoric and Belles Lettres; and his work as a stylistician continued after his appointment, first to the Chair of Logic and then to the Chair of Moral Philosophy at Glasgow Univer-

[32] Peter Stallybrass and Allon White, *The Politics and Poetics of Transgression* (London: Methuen, 1986), 36.

sity. An interest in rhetoric pre-dated his study of economics. In the mid-century debates of the Select Society a concern with the refinement of the English Language in Scotland was recognized as inseparable from the encouragement of progressive economic models; so much so that the foundation of modern economics and the disciplined study of English language and literature (both of which the Scottish eighteenth-century intellectual enquiry anticipate) can be seen as mutually implicated. As a 'classic' economics text the *Wealth of Nations* remains entailed to other disciplinary forms with which it shares the shaping and description of commercial society. It is this dialogic convergence, this comprehensiveness, which begins to explain why it has made such a persuasive contribution to subsequent ideological history.

NOTE ON THE TEXT

This selected edition is based on the text of the two-volume Glasgow edition of *An Inquiry into the Nature and Causes of the Wealth of Nations* (1976), edited by R. H. Campbell and A. S. Skinner, the text established by W. B. Todd. This is the definitive modern edition of the text, prepared by examining the first six editions against the important first and third editions. Smith's own notes, indicated here by superscript numerals, are retained at the foot of the page; editorial notes, indicated by asterisks, are placed at the end of the text. As in the Glasgow edition, variations in spelling (ancient/antient, public/publick, shown/shewn, and so on) remain unaltered as witness to the orthographic licence which Smith himself allowed on the several occasions he revised his work.

Although the exigencies of space in the present series dictate that this is a selected edition of the *Wealth of Nations*, I have departed from the usual practice of selectors in attempting to represent the breadth of Smith's analysis and have tried not to sacrifice its wide cultural, intellectual, and historical concerns to a narrower economic reading. Consequently, large sections from Books 4 and 5 are included. Excised material is indicated by dots (. . .) in the text.

The first edition of the *Wealth of Nations* was published in London on 9 March 1776 by the firm of Strahan and Cadell. It appeared in two volumes, at a cost of one pound and sixteen shillings, and was sold out in six months. A second edition appeared in 1778 and a third in 1784. To the third edition Smith made several important additions, in particular to Book 4, Chapters 4 and 5 ('Of Drawbacks' and 'Of Bounties'). He also added a new chapter to Book 4 (Chapter 8), entitled 'Conclusion of the Mercantile System', and a new section to Book 5, Chapter 1. The Scottish historian William Robertson had written to Smith on 8 April 1776, after completing his 'first reading of the *Inquiry*', to suggest the usefulness of an index to the work: 'As your Book must necessarily become a Political or Commercial Code to all Europe, which must be often consulted both by men of Practice and Speculation, I should wish that in the 2d Edition you would give a copious index.'[1] This was supplied for the third edition. The fourth edition is dated 1786, and the fifth and final edition to be published in Smith's lifetime appeared in 1789, the year of the French Revolution. Before Smith's death the work had been translated into German (1776–8), French (1778–9, 1788), and Danish (1779–80).

[1] *The Correspondence of Adam Smith*, ed. E. C. Mossner and I. S. Ross (Oxford: Clarendon Press, 1977), 193.

SELECT BIBLIOGRAPHY

Modern Editions of Smith's Works

All page references to Smith's works in the Introduction and Explanatory Notes to this edition are to the *Glasgow Edition of the Works and Correspondence of Adam Smith* (Oxford: Clarendon Press, 1976–83). Short titles refer to the six incorporated works:

I *The Theory of Moral Sentiments*, ed. D. D. Raphael and A. L. Macfie (1976)

II *An Inquiry into the Nature and Causes of the Wealth of Nations*, ed. R. H. Campbell and A. S. Skinner; textual editor W. B. Todd, 2 vols. (1976)

III *Essays on Philosophical Subjects*, ed. W. P. D. Wightman, J. C. Bryce, and I. S. Ross (1980)

IV *Lectures on Rhetoric and Belles Lettres*, ed. J. C. Bryce (1983)

V *Lectures on Jurisprudence*, ed. R. L. Meek, D. D. Raphael, and P. G. Stein (1978)

VI *The Correspondence of Adam Smith*, ed. E. C. Mossner and I. S. Ross (1977)

Modern Editions of *The Wealth of Nations*

An Inquiry into the Nature and Causes of the Wealth of Nations, ed. Edwin Cannan, 2 vols. (London: Methuen, 1904), based on the fifth edition of 1789 (the last in Smith's lifetime) collated with the first edition of 1776; with introduction, notes, marginal summary, and an enlarged index.

The Wealth of Nations, Books I–III, ed. Andrew Skinner (Harmondsworth: Penguin, 1970; revd. 1974); unannotated, but with a long introduction concentrating on its contribution to 'classical' economics.

An Inquiry into the Nature and Causes of the Wealth of Nations, ed. R. H. Campbell and A. S. Skinner; textual editor W. B. Todd, 2 vols. (Oxford: Clarendon Press, 1976), the definitive Glasgow edition (see above); with a general introduction and commentary, mainly on economic matters.

The Essential Adam Smith, ed. Robert L. Heilbroner and Laurence J. Malone (Oxford: Oxford University Press, 1986); contains selections from all five books of *The Wealth of Nations*, together with selections from *The Theory of Moral Sentiments*, *The History of Astronomy*, and *Lectures on Jurisprudence*; unannotated, but with brief introductions to each section.

The Wealth of Nations (Everyman's Library, 1910; repr. London: Random Century Group, 1991), with a new introduction by D. D. Raphael; Books I–IV only, unannotated.

Biographical Studies

Campbell, R. H. and Skinner, A. S. *Adam Smith* (London: Croom Helm, 1982).

Rae, John *Life of Adam Smith* (London, 1895; repr., with additional material by Jacob Viner, New York, 1965).

Ross, Ian *Life of Adam Smith* (Oxford: Clarendon Press, in preparation).

Stewart, Dugald 'Account of the Life and Writings of Adam Smith, LL.D.' (1794), in Adam Smith, *Essays on Philosophical Subjects*, ed. W. P. D. Wightman, J. C. Bryce, and I. S. Ross (Oxford: Clarendon Press, 1980).

General Studies

Blaug, Mark *Economic Theory in Retrospect* (4th edn., Cambridge: Cambridge University Press, 1985), ch. 2.

Bryson, Gladys *Man and Society: The Scottish Inquiry of the Eighteenth Century* (1945; repr. New York: Augustus M. Kelley, 1968)—a classic, if dated, analysis of the subject.

Hirschman, A. O. *The Passions and the Interests: Political Arguments for Capitalism before its Triumph* (Princeton, NJ: Princeton University Press, 1977).

Hollander, Samuel *The Economics of Adam Smith* (Toronto: University of Toronto Press, 1973).

Hont, Istvan and Ignatieff, Michael (eds.), *Wealth and Virtue: The Shaping of Political Economy in the Scottish Enlightenment* (Cambridge: Cambridge University Press, 1983)—an important contribution from a civic-humanist perspective, setting Smith in his wider intellectual context.

Hutchison, Terence *Before Adam Smith: The Emergence of Political Economy* 1662–1776 (Oxford: Basil Blackwell, 1988).

McCloskey, Donald N. *The Rhetoric of Economics* (Brighton: Harvester, 1986).

Macfie, A. L. _The Individual in Society: Papers on Adam Smith_, University of Glasgow Social and Economic Studies, 11 (London: George Allen and Unwin, 1967).

McKendrick, Neil, Brewer, John, and Plumb, J. H. _The Birth of a Consumer Society: The Commercialization of Eighteenth-Century England_ (London: Hutchinson, 1983).

Meek, Ronald L. (ed.), _Precursors of Adam Smith_ (London: Dent, 1973)—contains extracts from Cantillon, Hutcheson, Hume, Turgot, Mirabeau, Quesnay, Steuart, and Tucker.

Raphael, D. D. _Adam Smith_, Past Masters series (Oxford: Oxford University Press, 1985).

Rendall, Jane _The Origins of the Scottish Enlightenment 1707–76_ (London: Macmillan, 1978)—a useful collection of documents on different aspects of the moral, social, and historical thought of Smith's contemporaries.

—— 'Virtue and Commerce: Women in the Making of Adam Smith's Political Economy', in Ellen Kennedy and Susan Mendus (eds.) _Women in Western Political Philosophy_ (Brighton: Harvester, 1987), 44–77.

Skinner, Andrew S. _A System of Social Science: Papers relating to Adam Smith_ (Oxford: Clarendon Press, 1979).

—— and Wilson, Thomas (eds.), _The Market and the State: Papers in Honour of Adam Smith_ (Oxford: Clarendon Press, 1976)—reviews themes of the _Wealth of Nations_ as they appear in our own time.

Werhane, Patricia H. _Adam Smith and his Legacy for Modern Capitalism_ (Oxford: Oxford University Press, 1991).

Critical Contexts

Barrell, John _An Equal Wide Survey: English Literature in History, 1730–80_ (London: Hutchinson, 1983).

Copley, Stephen 'The "Natural" Economy: A Note on some Rhetorical Strategies in Political Economy—Adam Smith and Malthus', in Francis Barker _et al._ (eds.), _1789: Reading Writing Revolution_ (University of Essex, 1982), 160–9.

—— (ed.), _Literature and the Social Order in Eighteenth-Century England_ (Beckenham: Croom Helm, 1984).

Feingold, Richard _Nature and Society: Later Eighteenth-Century Uses of the Pastoral and Georgic_ (Hassocks: Harvester, 1978).

Heinzelman, Kurt _The Economics of the Imagination_ (Amherst, Mass.: University of Massachusetts Press, 1980).

MacLean, Kenneth *Agrarian Age: A Background for Wordsworth*, Yale Studies in English, 115 (New Haven, Conn.: Yale University Press, 1950).

Raven, James *Judging New Wealth: Popular Publishing and Responses to Commerce in England 1750–1800* (Oxford: Clarendon Press, 1992).

Sekora, John *Luxury: The Concept in Western Thought, Eden to Smollett* (Baltimore, Md.: Johns Hopkins University Press, 1977).

Shell, Marc *The Economy of Literature* (Baltimore, Md.: Johns Hopkins University Press, 1978).

—— *Money, Language, and Thought: Literary and Philosophic Economies from the Medieval to the Modern Era* (Berkeley and Los Angeles, Calif.: University of California Press, 1982).

Sutherland, Kathryn 'Fictional Economies: Adam Smith, Walter Scott, and the Nineteenth-Century Novel', *English Literary History*, 54 (1987), 97–127.

Webb, Igor *From Custom to Capital: The English Novel and the Industrial Revolution* (Ithaca, NY: Cornell University Press, 1981).

Williams, Raymond *The Country and the City* (London: Chatto and Windus, 1973).

A CHRONOLOGY OF ADAM SMITH AND HIS TIMES

Date	Adam Smith	Historical/Cultural Events	Publications
1723	Born in Kirkcaldy, Fife, Scotland.	Adam Ferguson (d. 1816) born.	Mandeville, *Essay on Charity and Search into the Nature of Society* (in *Fable of the Bees*, 2nd edn.)
1724			Defoe, *Tour through . . . Great Britain* (-1726); Lafitau, *Mœurs des sauvages amériquains*.
1727		Accession of George II. Sir Isaac Newton (b. 1642) dies.	Newton, *Principia*, translated into English.
1733		Mandeville (b. 1670) dies. Kay's flying shuttle.	Voltaire, *Letters on the English Nation*. Pope, *Essay on Man* (-1734).
1735		Abraham Darby smelts iron from coke.	
1736		Porteous Riots. Gin Act. James Watt (d. 1819) born.	

Year	Life	Historical and cultural events	Literature
1737	Becomes, at the usual age of 14, a student at Glasgow University and a pupil of the moral philosopher Francis Hutcheson. Glasgow was already an intellectual centre of the Scottish Enlightenment.	Tom Paine (d. 1809) born. Stage Licensing Act.	
1739		War with Spain.	Hume, *Treatise of Human Nature* (–1740).
1740		War of Austrian Succession (–1748). Boswell (d. 1795) born.	Richardson, *Pamela*. Thomson and Mallet, *Alfred* (inc. 'Rule Britannia!').
1740–6	Wins a Snell Exhibition to Balliol College, Oxford, where he spends the next six years, his studies largely self-directed.		
1741			Hume, *Essays, Moral and Political* (–1742).
1745		Landing of Charles Edward Stuart (the Young Pretender); Battle of Prestonpans.	
1746	Back in Scotland.	Battle of Culloden and defeat of Jacobite Rebellion. Disarming of Highlands Act.	

Date	Adam Smith	Historical/Cultural Events	Publications
1747		Heritable Jurisdictions Act. Hutcheson (b. 1694) dies.	Richardson, *Clarissa* (–1748). Hogarth, *Industry and Idleness*.
1748		Treaty of Aix-la-Chapelle. Second Disarming of Highlands Act.	Montesquieu, *De l'esprit des lois*. Hume, *Philosophical Essays concerning Human Understanding*.
1748–51	Through the patronage of the philosopher and jurist Henry Home, later Lord Kames, Smith gives a series of public lectures in Edinburgh on Rhetoric and Belles Lettres, later adding a series on civil law.		
1751	Appointed to the Chair of Logic at Glasgow University.		D'Alembert, Diderot, et al., *Encyclopédie* (–1766). Hume, *Enquiry concerning the Principles of Morals*.
1752	Appointed to the Chair of Moral Philosophy, previously held by his former teacher Hutcheson, at Glasgow. Moral philosophy was a subject which at this time included natural theology, ethics, jurisprudence, and political economy.	Gregorian calendar adopted in Britain.	Hume, *Essays Moral, Political, and Literary* and *Political Discourses*.
1754		Society of Arts founded.	Hume, *History of Great Britain* (–1761).

1755		Hutcheson, *System of Moral Philosophy*. Johnson, *Dictionary*. Rousseau, *Discours sur l'inegalité*.
1756	Seven Years War (–1763).	
1755–6	Provides two contributions to the short-lived *Edinburgh Review*: one a review of Dr Johnson's *Dictionary*; the other an extended letter to the editors on the relevance to Scotland's intellectual advance of the learning and literature of Europe, and of England and France in particular.	
1757	Militia Act. Battle of Plassey. Warrington Academy founded (–1786). Blake (d. 1827) born.	Brown, *Estimate of the Manners and Principles of the Times*. Dyer, *The Fleece*.
1758	Nelson (d. 1805) born.	Hume, *Enquiry concerning Human Understanding*.

Date	Adam Smith	Historical/Cultural Events	Publications
1759	*The Theory of Moral Sentiments*, the first of the two major works published in Smith's lifetime.	British Museum opened. Capture of Quebec. Burns (d. 1796) born.	Robertson, *History of Scotland*. Goldsmith, *Present State of Polite Learning*.
1760		Accession of George III. Capture of Montreal.	Macpherson, *Fragments of Ancient Poetry* ('Ossian').
1761	Smith's 'Considerations Concerning the First Formation of Languages' published in the *Philological Miscellany*.	Bridgewater Canal cut.	Rousseau, *La Nouvelle Héloise*.
1762		Westminster Paving Commission established. Act for Registering Infant Poor.	Kames, *Elements of Criticism*. Hurd, *Letters on Chivalry and Romance*. Rousseau, *Du contrat social*.
1763		Peace of Paris.	Macaulay, *History of England*, vol. i.

1764–6		1764
Journeys to the Continent as tutor to the young Duke of Buccleuch, appointed by his stepfather, Charles Townshend, later Chancellor of the Exchequer. Smith spends time in Toulouse, Geneva, and Paris. In Toulouse he probably begins in earnest the *Wealth of Nations*, a book with its roots in the Glasgow years; in Geneva he meets Voltaire, and in Paris he gains entry to the salons of Madame de Boufflers and Mademoiselle de l'Espinasse, where he meets members of the French 'school' of economists, the so-called Physiocrats, who surrounded François Quesnay, the king's physician.	Black measures latent heat. Harrison's chronometer. Grant of *diwani* (land revenues) to East India Company.	Reid, *Inquiry into the Human Mind*.
	1765	
	Stamp Act. American Mutiny Act. Soho Works, Birmingham, built by Boulton.	Johnson's edition of Shakespeare. Blackstone, *Commentaries on the Laws of England*. Percy, *Reliques of Ancient English Poetry*.

Date	Adam Smith	Historical/Cultural Events	Publications
1766–7	Briefly in London, working with Lord Townshend. During this time Smith is elected to the Royal Society and enlarges his intellectual and literary circle.	Death of James Stuart. Repeal of Stamp Act. American Declaratory Act. Food Riots. Grand Trunk Canal projected. Rousseau in England (–1767).	1766
1767–73	Returns to Kirkcaldy to study and to write. In particular, he is at work on the *Wealth of Nations*. In 1767 the third edition of the *Theory of Moral Sentiments* is published, with 'Considerations Concerning the First Formation of Languages' as an appendix.	Royal Crescent, Bath, begun. Wallis visits Tahiti.	Ferguson, *Essay on Civil Society*. 1767
		Cook's First Voyage (–1771). Royal Academy founded.	*Encyclopedia Britannica* (–1771). Arthur Young's *Tours* commenced. 1768
		Watt's condenser patented.	Robertson, *History of Charles V*. 1769

Year		
1770	Boston Massacre. Falkland Islands crisis. Hargreave's Spinning-Jenny patented. Wordsworth (d. 1850) born.	Burke, *Thoughts on Present Discontents.* Raynal, *Histoire des deux Indes.* Goldsmith, *Deserted Village.*
1771	Arkwright's first spinning-mill. Walter Scott (d. 1832) born. Warren Hastings appointed Governor of Bengal.	Millar, *Observations concerning the Distinction of Ranks.* Mackenzie, *The Man of Feeling.*
1772	Cook's Second Voyage (–1775). Partnership of Boulton and Watt. Coleridge (d. 1834) born.	Foote's *The Nabob* first performed. Ferguson, *Institutes of Moral Philosophy.*

Date	Adam Smith	Historical/Cultural Events	Publications
1773-7	Mainly spent in London, apart from an extended visit to Kirkcaldy. Smith is now formally admitted to the Royal Society and he extends his acquaintance with Edmund Burke, Samuel Johnson, Edward Gibbon, and perhaps Benjamin Franklin.		
1773		Pownall's Corn Law. East India Regulating Act. Boston Tea Party. Adelphi Lottery.	Goldsmith, *She Stoops to Conquer.*
1774		Failure of proposed examination reform at Cambridge University. Copyright law settled by Lords. Priestley discovers oxygen.	Kames, *Sketches of the History of Man.* Warton, *History of English Poetry* (–1789).
1775		War of American Independence, battles of Lexington and Concord. Watt's improved steam-engine. Lunar Society's first formal meeting. Jane Austen (d. 1817) born.	Burke, *Conciliation with the Colonies.* Johnson, *Journey to the Western Islands.* Spence, *Real Rights of Man.*

Year			
1776	Publication of *An Inquiry into the Nature and Causes of the Wealth of Nations*. The first edition is sold out in six months.	American Declaration of Independence. Battle of Long Island. Hume (b. 1711) dies. Cook's Third Voyage (–1779). National Report on poor-relief expenditure.	Bentham, *Fragment on Government*. Gibbon, *Decline and Fall of the Roman Empire* (–1788). Paine, *Common Sense*. Price, *Observations on Civil Liberty*.
1777			Robertson, *History of America*.
1778	Smith is granted an appointment as Commissioner of Customs and Salt Duties in Scotland and sets up home in Edinburgh. Second edition of the *Wealth of Nations*.	War with France. Rousseau (b. 1712) dies. Voltaire (b. 1694) dies.	Burney, *Evelina*.
1779		War with Spain. Crompton's 'mule'. First iron bridge. Machine riots. Cook (b. 1728) dies.	Alexander, *History of Women*. Johnson, *Lives of the Poets* (–1781). Hume, *Dialogues concerning Natural Religion*.

Date	Adam Smith	Historical/Cultural Events	Publications
1781		Cornwallis surrenders at Yorktown. Arkwright's patent overturned. Watt's rotary steam-engine.	
1782		Kames (b. 1696) dies. Battle of the Saints.	Ferguson, *Roman Republic*. Rousseau, *Confessions* (-1789). Laclos, *Les Liaisons dangereuses*.
1783		Peace of Versailles.	Blake, *Poetical Sketches*. Crabbe, *The Village*.
1784	Third edition of the *Wealth of Nations*, considerably expanded and the definitive edition as far as Smith was concerned.	India Act. Johnson (b. 1709) dies.	Young, *Annals of Agriculture* (-1809).
1785		Cartwright's power-loom.	Cowper, *The Task*. Wilkins (trans.). *Bhagvat-Geeta*.
1786	Fourth edition of the *Wealth of Nations*.	Coal gas used for lighting.	Burns, *Poems in the Scottish Dialect*.

Date	Life	Date	Historical events	Literary works
1787–9	Smith appointed Rector of Glasgow University.	1787	Impeachment of Warren Hastings (–1795). United States Constitution signed.	
		1788	Celebration of centenary of Glorious Revolution. Convict settlement at Botany Bay. Byron (d. 1824) born.	
1789	Fifth edition of the *Wealth of Nations*.	1789	Fall of the Bastille. Mutiny on the *Bounty*. Declaration of Rights of Man.	Blake, *Songs of Innocence*.
1790	Smith dies in Edinburgh and is buried in the Canongate churchyard.	1790		Burke, *Reflections on the Revolution in France*. Wollstonecraft, *Vindication of the Rights of Men*.
1794	Dugald Stewart's 'Account of the Life and Writings of Adam Smith' is published in the *Transactions of the Royal Society of Edinburgh*.			

Date	Adam Smith	Historical/Cultural Events	Publications
1795	Publication by his literary executors, Joseph Black and James Hutton, of Smith's *Essays on Philosophical Subjects*, together with Stewart's reprinted 'Account of the Life'. The *Essays*, comprising 'The History of the Ancient Logics and Metaphysics', 'The History of the Ancient Physics', 'The History of Astronomy', 'Of the Affinity between certain English and Italian Verses', 'Of the External Senses', and 'Of the Nature of that Imitation which takes place in what are called the Imitative Arts', represent all that was allowed to survive from the sixteen folio volumes of manuscripts burnt at Smith's own request after his death.		

An Inquiry into the Nature and Causes of the Wealth of Nations

CONTENTS

II   BOOK II
                    Of the Nature, Accumulation, and Employment
                    of Stock

INTRODUCTION AND PLAN
OF THE WORK

THE annual labour of every nation is the fund which originally supplies it with all the necessaries and conveniences of life which it annually consumes, and which consist always, either in the immediate produce of that labour, or in what is purchased with that produce from other nations.

According therefore, as this produce, or what is purchased with it, bears a greater or smaller proportion to the number of those who are to consume it, the nation will be better or worse supplied with all the necessaries and conveniences for which it has occasion.

But this proportion must in every nation be regulated by two different circumstances; first, by the skill, dexterity, and judgment with which its labour is generally applied; and, secondly, by the proportion between the number of those who are employed in useful labour, and that of those who are not so employed. Whatever be the soil, climate, or extent of territory of any particular nation, the abundance or scantiness of its annual supply must, in that particular situation, depend upon those two circumstances.

The abundance or scantiness of this supply too seems to depend more upon the former of those two circumstances than upon the latter. Among the savage nations of hunters and fishers,* every individual who is able to work, is more or less employed in useful labour, and endeavours to provide, as well as he can, the necessaries and conveniencies of life, for himself, or such of his family or tribe as are either too old, or too young, or too infirm to go a hunting and fishing. Such nations, however, are so miserably poor, that, from mere want, they are frequently reduced, or, at least, think themselves reduced, to the necessity sometimes of directly destroying, and sometimes of abandoning their infants, their old people, and those afflicted with lingering diseases, to perish with hunger, or to be devoured by wild beasts. Among civilized and thriving nations, on the contrary, though a great number of people do not labour at all, many of whom consume the produce of ten times, frequently of a hundred times more labour than the greater part of those who work; yet the produce of the whole labour of the society is so great, that all are often abundantly supplied, and a workman, even of the lowest and poorest order, if he is frugal and industrious, may enjoy a greater share of the necessaries and conveniences of life than it is possible for any savage to acquire.

The causes of this improvement, in the productive powers of labour, and the order, according to which its produce is naturally distributed among the different ranks and conditions of men in the society, make the subject of the First Book of this Inquiry.

Whatever be the actual state of the skill, dexterity, and judgment with which labour is applied in any nation, the abundance or scantiness of its annual supply must depend, during the continuance of that state, upon the proportion between the number of those who are annually employed in useful labour, and that of those who are not so employed. The number of useful and productive labourers, it will hereafter appear, is every where in proportion to the quantity of capital stock which is employed in setting them to work, and to the particular way in which it is so employed. The Second Book, therefore, treats of the nature of capital stock, of the manner in which it is gradually accumulated, and of the different quantities of labour which it puts into motion, according to the different ways in which it is employed.

Nations tolerably well advanced as to skill, dexterity, and judgment, in the application of labour, have followed very different plans in the general conduct or direction of it; and those plans have not all been equally favourable to the greatness of its produce. The policy of some nations has given extraordinary encouragement to the industry of the country; that of others to the industry of towns. Scarce any nation has dealt equally and impartially with every sort of industry. Since the downfal of the Roman empire, the policy of Europe has been more favourable to arts, manufactures, and commerce, the industry of towns; than to agriculture, the industry of the country. The circumstances which seem to have introduced and established this policy are explained in the Third Book.

Though those different plans were, perhaps, first introduced by the private interests and prejudices of particular orders of men, without any regard to, or foresight of, their consequences upon the general welfare of the society; yet they have given occasion to very different theories of political œconomy;* of which some magnify the importance of that industry which is carried on in towns, others of that which is carried on in the country. Those theories have had a considerable influence, not only upon the opinions of men of learning, but upon the public conduct of princes and sovereign states. I have endeavoured, in the Fourth Book, to explain, as fully and distinctly as I can, those different theories, and the principal effects which they have produced in different ages and nations.

To explain in what has consisted the revenue of the great body of the people, or what has been the nature of those funds which, in different ages and nations, have supplied their annual consumption, is the object of these Four first Books. The Fifth and last Book treats of the revenue of the sovereign, or commonwealth. In this Book I have endeavoured to show; first, what are the necessary expences of the sovereign, or commonwealth; which of those expences ought to be defrayed by the general contribution of the whole society; and which of them, by that of some particular part only, or of some particular members of it; secondly, what are the different methods in which the whole society may be made to contribute towards defraying the expences incumbent on the whole society, and what are the principal advantages and inconveniencies of each of those methods: and, thirdly and lastly, what are the reasons and causes which have induced almost all modern governments to mortgage some part of this revenue, or to contract debts, and what have been the effects of those debts upon the real wealth, the annual produce of the land and labour of the society.

BOOK I

Of the Causes of Improvement in the
productive Powers of Labour, and of the Order
according to which its Produce is naturally
distributed among the different Ranks of the
People

CHAPTER I

Of the Division of Labour

THE greatest improvement in the productive powers of labour,
and the greater part of the skill, dexterity, and judgment with
which it is any where directed, or applied, seem to have been
the effects of the division of labour.*

The effects of the division of labour, in the general business
of society, will be more easily understood, by considering in
what manner it operates in some particular manufactures. It is
commonly supposed to be carried furthest in some very trifling
ones; not perhaps that it really is carried further in them than
in others of more importance: but in those trifling manufactures which are destined to supply the small wants of but a
small number of people, the whole number of workmen must
necessarily be small; and those employed in every different
branch of the work can often be collected into the same
workhouse, and placed at once under the view of the spectator.
In those great manufactures, on the contrary, which are destined to supply the great wants of the great body of the people,
every different branch of the work employs so great a number
of workmen, that it is impossible to collect them all into the
same workhouse. We can seldom see more, at one time, than

those employed in one single branch. Though in such manufactures, therefore, the work may really be divided into a much greater number of parts, than in those of a more trifling nature, the division is not near so obvious, and has accordingly been much less observed.

To take an example, therefore, from a very trifling manufacture; but one in which the division of labour has been very often taken notice of, the trade of the pin-maker;* a workman not educated to this business (which the division of labour has rendered a distinct trade), nor acquainted with the use of the machinery employed in it (to the invention of which the same division of labour has probably given occasion), could scarce, perhaps, with his utmost industry, make one pin in a day, and certainly could not make twenty. But in the way in which this business is now carried on, not only the whole work is a peculiar trade, but it is divided into a number of branches, of which the greater part are likewise peculiar trades. One man draws out the wire, another straights it, a third cuts it, a fourth points it, a fifth grinds it at the top for receiving the head; to make the head requires two or three distinct operations; to put it on, is a peculiar business, to whiten the pins is another; it is even a trade by itself to put them into the paper; and the important business of making a pin is, in this manner, divided into about eighteen distinct operations,* which, in some manufactories, are all performed by distinct hands, though in others the same man will sometimes perform two or three of them. I have seen a small manufactory of this kind where ten men only were employed, and where some of them consequently performed two or three distinct operations. But though they were very poor, and therefore but indifferently accommodated with the necessary machinery, they could, when they exerted themselves, make among them about twelve pounds of pins in a day. There are in a pound upwards of four thousand pins of a middling size. Those ten persons, therefore, could make among them upwards of forty-eight thousand pins in a day. Each person, therefore, making a tenth part of forty-eight thousand pins, might be considered as making four thousand eight hundred pins in a day. But if they had all wrought separately and independently, and without any of them having been educated to this peculiar business, they certainly could not each of them have made twenty, perhaps not one pin in a day; that is, certainly, not the two hundred and fortieth, perhaps not the four thousand eight hundredth part of what they are at present capable of performing, in consequence of a proper division and combination of their different operations.

In every other art and manufacture, the effects of the division of labour are similar to what they are in this very trifling one; though, in many of them, the labour can neither be so much subdivided, nor reduced to so great a simplicity of operation. The division of labour, however, so far as it can be introduced, occasions, in every art, a proportionable increase of the productive powers of labour. The separation of different trades and employments from one another, seems to have taken place, in consequence of this advantage. This separation too is generally carried furthest in those countries which enjoy the highest degree of industry and improvement; what is the work of one man, in a rude state of society, being generally that of several in an improved one. In every improved society, the farmer is generally nothing but a farmer; the manufacturer, nothing but a manufacturer. The labour too which is necessary to produce any one complete manufacture, is almost always divided among a great number of hands. How many different trades are employed in each branch of the linen and woollen manufactures, from the growers of the flax and the wool, to the bleachers and smoothers of the linen, or to the dyers and dressers of the cloth! The nature of agriculture, indeed, does not admit of so many subdivisions of labour, nor of so complete a separation of one business from another, as manufactures. It is impossible to separate so entirely, the business of the grazier from that of the corn-farmer, as the trade of the carpenter is commonly separated from that of the smith. The spinner is almost always a distinct person from the weaver; but the ploughman, the harrower, the sower of the seed, and the reaper of the corn, are often the same. The occasions for those different sorts of labour returning with the different seasons of the year, it is impossible that one man should be constantly employed in any one of them. This impossibility of making so complete and entire a separation of all the different branches of labour employed in agriculture, is perhaps the reason why the improvement of the productive powers of labour in this art, does not always keep pace with their improvement in manufactures. The most opulent nations, indeed, generally excel all their neighbours in agriculture as well as in manufactures; but they are commonly more distinguished by their superiority in the latter than in the former. Their lands are in general better cultivated, and having more labour and expence bestowed upon them, produce more, in proportion to the extent and natural fertility of the ground. But this superiority of produce is seldom much more than in proportion to the superiority of labour and expence. In agriculture, the labour of the rich country is not always much more productive than that of the poor; or, at least, it is never so much more productive, as it commonly is in manufactures. The corn of the rich country, therefore, will not always, in the same degree of goodness, come cheaper to market than that of the poor. The corn of Poland, in the same degree of goodness, is as cheap as that of France, notwithstanding the superior opulence and improvement of the latter country. The corn of France is, in the corn provinces, fully as good, and in most years nearly about the same price with the corn of England, though, in opulence and improvement, France is perhaps inferior to England. The corn-lands of England, however, are better cultivated than those of France, and the corn-lands of France are said to be much better cultivated than those of Poland. But though the poor country, notwithstanding the inferiority of its cultivation, can, in some measure, rival the rich in the cheapness and goodness of its corn, it can pretend to no such competition in its manufactures; at least if those manufactures suit the soil, climate, and situation of the rich country. The silks of France are better and cheaper than those of England, because the silk manufacture, at least under the present high duties upon the importation of raw silk, does not so well suit the climate of England as that of France. But the hard-ware and the coarse woollens of England are beyond all comparison superior to those of France, and much cheaper too in the same degree of goodness. In Poland there are said to be scarce any manufactures of any kind, a few of those coarser household manufactures excepted, without which no country can well subsist.

This great increase of the quantity of work, which, in consequence of the division of labour, the same number of people are capable of performing, is owing to three different circumstances; first, to the increase of dexterity in every particular workman; secondly, to the saving of the time which is commonly lost in passing from one species of work to another; and lastly, to the invention of a great number of machines which facilitate and abridge labour, and enable one man to do the work of many.

First, the improvement of the dexterity of the workman necessarily increases the quantity of the work he can perform, and the division of labour, by reducing every man's business to some one simple operation, and by making this operation the sole employment of his life, necessarily increases very much the dexterity of the workman. A common smith, who, though accustomed to handle the hammer, has never been used to make nails, if upon some particular occasion he is obliged to attempt it, will scarce, I am assured, be able to make above two or three hundred nails in a day, and those too very bad ones. A smith who has been accustomed to make nails, but whose sole or principal business has not been that of a nailer, can seldom with his utmost diligence make more than eight hundred or a thousand nails in a day. I have seen several boys under twenty years of age who had never exercised any other trade but that of making nails, and who, when they exerted themselves, could make, each of them, upwards of two thousand three hundred nails in a day. The making of a nail,* however, is by no means one of the simplest operations. The same person blows the bellows, stirs or mends the fire as there is occasion, heats the iron, and forges every part of the nail:

In forging the head too he is obliged to change his tools. The different operations into which the making of a pin, or of a metal button,* is subdivided, are all of them much more simple, and the dexterity of the person, of whose life it has been the sole business to perform them, is usually much greater. The rapidity with which some of the operations of those manufactures are performed, exceeds what the human hand could, by those who had never seen them, be supposed capable of acquiring.

Secondly, the advantage which is gained by saving the time commonly lost in passing from one sort of work to another, is much greater than we should at first view be apt to imagine it. It is impossible to pass very quickly from one kind of work to another, that is carried on in a different place, and with quite different tools. A country weaver,* who cultivates a small farm, must lose a good deal of time in passing from his loom to the field, and from the field to his loom. When the two trades can be carried on in the same workhouse, the loss of time is no doubt much less. It is even in this case, however, very considerable. A man commonly saunters a little in turning his hand from one sort of employment to another. When he first begins the new work he is seldom very keen and hearty; his mind, as they say, does not go to it, and for some time he rather trifles than applies to good purpose. The habit of sauntering and of indolent careless application, which is naturally, or rather necessarily acquired by every country workman who is obliged to change his work and his tools every half hour, and to apply his hand in twenty different ways almost every day of his life; renders him almost always slothful and lazy, and incapable of any vigorous application even on the most pressing occasions. Independent, therefore, of his deficiency in point of dexterity, this cause alone must always reduce considerably the quantity of work which he is capable of performing.

Thirdly, and lastly, every body must be sensible how much labour is facilitated and abridged by the application of proper machinery.* It is unnecessary to give any example. I shall only observe, therefore, that the invention of all those machines by which labour is so much facilitated and abridged, seems to have been originally owing to the division of labour. Men are much more likely to discover easier and readier methods of attaining any object, when the whole attention of their minds is directed towards that single object, than when it is dissipated among a great variety of things. But in consequence of the division of labour, the whole of every man's attention comes naturally to be directed towards some one very simple object. It is naturally to be expected, therefore, that some one or other of those who are employed in each particular branch of labour should soon find out easier and readier methods of performing their own particular work, wherever the nature of it admits of such improvement. A great part of the machines made use of in those manufactures in which labour is most subdivided, were originally the inventions of common workmen, who, being each of them employed in some very simple operation, naturally turned their thoughts towards finding out easier and readier methods of performing it. Whoever has been much accustomed to visit such manufactures, must frequently have been shewn very pretty machines, which were the inventions of such workmen, in order to facilitate and quicken their own particular part of the work. In the first fire-engines,* a boy was constantly employed to open and shut alternately the communication between the boiler and the cylinder, according as the piston either ascended or descended. One of those boys, who loved to play with his companions, observed that, by tying a string from the handle of the valve, which opened this communication, to another part of the machine, the valve would open and shut without his assistance, and leave him at liberty to divert himself with his play-fellows. One of the greatest improvements that has been made upon this machine, since it was first invented, was in this manner the discovery of a boy who wanted to save his own labour.

All the improvements in machinery, however, have by no means been the inventions of those who had occasion to use the machines. Many improvements have been made by the ingenuity of the makers of the machines, when to make them became the business of a peculiar trade; and some by that of those who are called philosophers or men of speculation, whose trade it is, not to do any thing, but to observe every thing; and who, upon that account, are often capable of combining together the powers of the most distant and dissimilar objects. In the progress of society, philosophy or speculation becomes, like every other employment, the principal or sole trade and occupation of a particular class of citizens. Like every other employment too, it is subdivided into a great number of different branches, each of which affords occupation to a peculiar tribe or class of philosophers; and this subdivision of employment in philosophy, as well as in every other business, improves dexterity, and saves time. Each individual becomes more expert in his own peculiar branch, more work is done upon the whole, and the quantity of science is considerably increased by it.

It is the great multiplication of the productions of all the different arts, in consequence of the division of labour, which occasions, in a well-governed society, that universal opulence which extends itself to the lowest ranks of the people. Every workman has a great quantity of his own work to dispose of beyond what he himself has occasion for; and every other workman being exactly in the same situation, he is enabled to exchange a great quantity of his own goods for a great quantity, or, what comes to the same thing, for the price of a great quantity of theirs. He supplies them abundantly with what they have occasion for, and they accommodate him as amply with what he has occasion for, and a general plenty diffuses itself through all the different ranks of the society.

Observe the accommodation of the most common artificer or day-labourer in a civilized and thriving country, and you will perceive that the number of people of whose industry a part, though but a small part, has been employed in procuring him this accommodation, exceeds all computation. The woollen coat, for example, which covers the day-labourer, as coarse and rough as it may appear, is the produce of the joint labour of a great multitude of workmen. The shepherd, the sorter of the wool, the wool-comber or carder, the dyer, the scribbler, the spinner, the weaver, the fuller, the dresser, with many others, must all join their different arts in order to complete even this homely production.* How many merchants and carriers, besides, must have been employed in transporting the materials from some of those workmen to others who often live in a very distant part of the country! How much commerce and navigation in particular, how many ship-builders, sailors, sail-makers, rope-makers, must have been employed in order to bring together the different drugs made use of by the dyer, which often come from the remotest corners of the world! What a variety of labour too is necessary in order to produce the tools of the meanest of those workmen! To say nothing of such complicated machines as the ship of the sailor, the mill of the fuller, or even the loom of the weaver, let us consider only what a variety of labour is requisite in order to form that very simple machine, the shears with which the shepherd clips the wool. The miner, the builder of the furnace for smelting the ore, the feller of the timber, the burner of the charcoal to be made use of in the smelting-house, the brick-maker, the brick-layer, the workmen who attend the furnace, the mill-wright, the forger, the smith, must all of them join their different arts in order to produce them. Were we to examine, in the same manner, all the different parts of his dress and household furniture, the coarse linen shirt which he wears next his skin, the shoes which cover his feet, the bed which he lies on, and all the different parts which compose it, the kitchen-grate at which he prepares his victuals, the coals which he makes use of for that purpose, dug from the bowels of the earth, and brought to him perhaps by a long sea and a long land carriage, all the other utensils of his kitchen, all the furniture of his table, the knives and forks, the earthen or pewter plates upon which he serves up and divides his victuals, the different hands employed in preparing his bread and his beer, the glass window* which lets in the heat and the light, and keeps out the wind and the rain, with all the knowledge and art requisite for preparing that beautiful and happy invention, without which these northern parts of the world could scarce have afforded a very comfortable habitation, together with the tools of all the different workmen employed in producing those different conveniencies; if we examine, I say, all these things, and consider what a variety of labour is employed about each of them, we shall be sensible that without the assistance and co-operation of many thousands, the very meanest person in a civilized country could not be provided, even according to, what we very falsely imagine, the easy and simple manner in which he is commonly accommodated. Compared, indeed, with the more extravagant luxury of the great, his accommodation must no doubt appear extremely simple and easy; and yet it may be true, perhaps, that the accommodation of an European prince does not always so much exceed that of an industrious and frugal peasant, as the accommodation of the latter exceeds that of many an African king, the absolute master of the lives and liberties of ten thousand naked savages.*

CHAPTER II

Of the Principle which gives occasion to the Division of Labour

THIS division of labour, from which so many advantages are derived, is not originally the effect of any human wisdom, which foresees and intends that general opulence to which it gives occasion. It is the necessary, though very slow and gradual consequence of a certain propensity in human nature which has in view no such extensive utility; the propensity to truck, barter, and exchange one thing for another.

Whether this propensity be one of those original principles in human nature, of which no further account can be given; or whether, as seems more probable, it be the necessary consequence of the faculties of reason and speech, it belongs not to our present subject to enquire. It is common to all men, and to be found in no other race of animals, which seem to know neither this nor any other species of contracts. Two greyhounds, in running down the same hare, have sometimes the appearance of acting in some sort of concert. Each turns her towards his companion, or endeavours to intercept her when his companion turns her towards himself. This, however, is not the effect of any contract, but of the accidental concurrence of their passions in the same object at that particular time. Nobody ever saw a dog make a fair and deliberate exchange of one bone for another with another dog. Nobody ever saw one animal by its gestures and natural cries signify to another, this is mine, that yours; I am willing to give this for that. When an animal wants to obtain something either of a man or of another animal, it has no other means of persuasion but to gain the favour of those whose service it requires. A puppy fawns upon its dam, and a spaniel endeavours by a thousand attractions to engage the attention of its master who is at dinner, when it wants to be fed by him. Man sometimes uses the same arts with his brethren, and when he has no other means of engaging them to act according to his inclinations, endeavours by every servile and fawning attention to obtain their good will. He has not time, however, to do this upon every occasion. In civilized society he stands at all times in need of the co-operation and assistance of great multitudes, while his whole life is scarce sufficient to gain the friendship of a few persons. In almost every other race of animals each individual, when it is grown up to maturity, is intirely independent, and in its natural state has occasion for the assistance of no other living creature. But man has almost constant occasion for the help of his brethren, and it is in vain for him to expect it from their benevolence only.* He will be more likely to prevail if he can interest their self-love in his favour, and shew them that it is for their own advantage to do for him what he requires of them. Whoever offers to another a bargain of any kind, proposes to do this. Give me that which I want, and you shall have this which you want, is the meaning of every such offer; and it is in this manner that we obtain from one another the far greater part of those good offices which we stand in need of. It is not from the benevolence of the butcher, the brewer, or the baker, that we expect our dinner, but from their regard to their own interest. We address ourselves, not to their humanity but to their self-love, and never talk to them of our own necessities but of their advantages. Nobody but a beggar chuses to depend chiefly upon the benevolence of his fellow-citizens. Even a beggar does not depend upon it entirely. The charity of well-disposed people, indeed, supplies him with the whole fund of his subsistence. But though this principle ultimately provides him with all the necessaries of life which he has occasion for, it neither does nor can provide him with them as he has occasion for them. The greater part of his occasional wants are supplied in the same manner as those of other people, by treaty, by barter, and by purchase. With the money which one man gives him he purchases food. The old cloaths which another bestows upon him he exchanges for other old cloaths which suit him better, or for lodging, or for food, or for money, with which he can buy either food, cloaths, or lodging, as he has occasion.

As it is by treaty, by barter, and by purchase, that we obtain from one another the greater part of those mutual good offices which we stand in need of, so it is this same trucking disposition which originally gives occasion to the division of labour. In a tribe of hunters or shepherds a particular person makes bows and arrows, for example, with more readiness and dexterity than any other. He frequently exchanges them for cattle or for venison with his companions; and he finds at last that he can in this manner get more cattle and venison, than if he himself went to the field to catch them. From a regard to his own interest, therefore, the making of bows and arrows grows to be his chief business, and he becomes a sort of armourer. Another excels in making the frames and covers of their little huts or moveable houses. He is accustomed to be of use in this way to his neighbours, who reward him in the same manner with cattle and with venison, till at last he finds it his interest to dedicate himself entirely to this employment, and to become a sort of house-carpenter. In the same manner a third becomes a smith or a brazier,* a fourth a tanner or dresser of hides or skins, the principal part of the clothing of savages. And thus the certainty of being able to exchange all that surplus part of the produce of his own labour, which is over and above his own consumption, for such parts of the produce of other men's labour as he may have occasion for, encourages every man to apply himself to a particular occupation, and to cultivate and bring to perfection whatever talent or genius he may possess for that particular species of business.

The difference of natural talents in different men is, in reality, much less than we are aware of; and the very different genius which appears to distinguish men of different professions, when grown up to maturity, is not upon many occasions so much the cause, as the effect of the division of labour.* The difference between the most dissimilar characters, between a philosopher and a common street porter, for example, seems to arise not so much from nature, as from habit, custom, and education. When they came into the world, and for the first six or eight years of their existence, they were, perhaps, very much alike, and neither their parents nor play-fellows could perceive any remarkable difference. About that age, or soon after, they come to be employed in very different occupations. The difference of talents comes then to be taken notice of, and widens by degrees, till at last the vanity of the philosopher is willing to acknowledge scarce any resemblance. But without the disposition to truck, barter, and exchange, every man must have procured to himself every necessary and conveniency of life which he wanted. All must have had the same duties to perform, and the same work to do, and there could have been no such difference of employment as could alone give occasion to any great difference of talents.

As it is this disposition which forms that difference of talents, so remarkable among men of different professions, so it is this same disposition which renders that difference useful. Many tribes of animals acknowledged to be all of the same species, derive from nature a much more remarkable distinction of genius, than what, antecedent to custom and education, appears to take place among men. By nature a philosopher is not in genius and disposition half so different from a street porter, as a mastiff is from a greyhound, or a greyhound from a spaniel, or this last from a shepherd's dog. Those different tribes of animals, however, though all of the same species, are of scarce any use to one another. The strength of the mastiff is not, in the least, supported either by the swiftness of the greyhound, or by the sagacity of the spaniel, or by the docility of the shepherd's dog. The effects of those different geniuses and talents, for want of the power or disposition to barter and exchange, cannot be brought into a common stock, and do not in the least contribute to the better accommodation and conveniency of the species. Each animal is still obliged to support and defend itself, separately and independently, and derives no sort of advantage from that variety of talents with which nature has distinguished its fellows. Among men, on the contrary, the most dissimilar geniuses are of use to one another; the different produces of their respective talents, by the general disposition to truck, barter, and exchange, being brought, as it were, into a common stock, where every man may purchase whatever part of the produce of other men's talents he has occasion for.

CHAPTER III

That the Division of Labour is limited by the Extent of the Market

As it is the power of exchanging that gives occasion to the division of labour, so the extent of this division must always be limited by the extent of that power, or, in other words, by the extent of the market.* When the market is very small, no person can have any encouragement to dedicate himself entirely to one employment, for want of the power to exchange all that surplus part of the produce of his own labour, which is over and above his own consumption, for such parts of the produce of other men's labour as he has occasion for.

There are some sorts of industry, even of the lowest kind, which can be carried on no where but in a great town. A porter, for example, can find employment and subsistence in no other place. A village is by much too narrow a sphere for him; even an ordinary market town is scarce large enough to afford him constant occupation. In the lone houses and very small villages which are scattered about in so desert a country as the Highlands of Scotland, every farmer must be butcher, baker and brewer for his own family. In such situations we can scarce expect to find even a smith, a carpenter, or a mason, within less than twenty miles of another of the same trade. The scattered families that live at eight or ten miles distance from the nearest of them, must learn to perform themselves a great number of little pieces of work, for which, in more populous countries, they would call in the assistance of those workmen. Country workmen are almost every where obliged to apply themselves to all the different branches of industry that have so much affinity to one another as to be employed about the same sort of materials. A country carpenter deals in every sort of work that is made of wood: a country smith in every sort of work that is made of iron. The former is not only a carpenter, but a joiner, a cabinet-maker, and even a carver in wood, as well as a wheel-wright, a plough-wright, a cart and waggon maker. The employments of the latter are still more various. It is impossible there should be such a trade as even that of a nailer in the remote and inland parts of the Highlands of Scotland. Such a workman at the rate of a thousand nails a day, and three hundred working days in the year, will make three hundred thousand nails in the year. But in such a situation it would be impossible to dispose of one thousand, that is, of one day's work in the year.

As by means of water-carriage a more extensive market is opened to every sort of industry than what land-carriage alone can afford it, so it is upon the sea-coast, and along the banks of navigable rivers, that industry of every kind naturally begins to subdivide and improve itself, and it is frequently not till a long time after that those improvements extend themselves to the inland parts of the country. A broad-wheeled waggon, attended by two men, and drawn by eight horses, in about six weeks time carries and brings back between London and Edinburgh near four ton weight of goods. In about the same time a ship navigated by six or eight men, and sailing between the ports of London and Leith,* frequently carries and brings back two hundred ton weight of goods. Six or eight men, therefore, by the help of water-carriage, can carry and bring back in the same time the same quantity of goods between London and Edinburgh, as fifty broad-wheeled waggons, attended by a hundred men, and drawn by four hundred horses. Upon two hundred tons of goods, therefore, carried by the cheapest land-carriage from London to Edinburgh, there must be charged the maintenance of a hundred men for three weeks, and both the maintenance, and, what is nearly equal to the maintenance, the wear and tear of four hundred horses as well as of fifty great waggons. Whereas, upon the same quantity of goods carried by water, there is to be charged only the maintenance of six or eight men, and the wear and tear of a ship of two hundred tons burden, together with the value of the superior risk, or the difference of the insurance between land

and water-carriage.* Were there no other communication between those two places, therefore, but by land-carriage, as no
goods could be transported from the one to the other, except
such whose price was very considerable in proportion to their
weight, they could carry on but a small part of that commerce
which at present subsists between them, and consequently
could give but a small part of that encouragement which they
at present mutually afford to each other's industry. There could
be little or no commerce of any kind between the distant parts
of the world. What goods could bear the expence of land-
carriage between London and Calcutta?* Or if there were any
so precious as to be able to support this expence, with what
safety could they be transported through the territories of so
many barbarous nations? Those two cities, however, at present
carry on a very considerable commerce with each other, and
by mutually affording a market, give a good deal of encouragement to each other's industry.

Since such, therefore, are the advantages of water-carriage,
it is natural that the first improvements of art and industry
should be made where this conveniency opens the whole world
for a market to the produce of every sort of labour, and that
they should always be much later in extending themselves into
the inland parts of the country. The inland parts of the country
can for a long time have no other market for the greater part
of their goods, but the country which lies round about them,
and separates them from the sea-coast, and the great navigable
rivers. The extent of their market, therefore, must for a long
time be in proportion to the riches and populousness of that
country, and consequently their improvement must always be
posterior to the improvement of that country. In our North
American colonies the plantations have constantly followed
either the sea-coast or the banks of the navigable rivers, and
have scarce any where extended themselves to any considerable
distance from both.

The nations that, according to the best authenticated history,
appear to have been first civilized, were those that dwelt round
the coast of the Mediterranean sea. That sea, by far the greatest

inlet that is known in the world, having no tides, nor consequently any waves except such as are caused by the wind only,
was, by the smoothness of its surface, as well as by the
multitude of its islands, and the proximity of its neighbouring
shores, extremely favourable to the infant navigation of the
world; when, from their ignorance of the compass, men were
afraid to quit the view of the coast, and from the imperfection
of the art of ship-building, to abandon themselves to the
boisterous waves of the ocean. To pass beyond the pillars of
Hercules, that is, to sail out of the Streights of Gibraltar, was,
in the antient world, long considered as a most wonderful and
dangerous exploit of navigation. It was late before even the
Phenicians and Carthaginians,* the most skilful navigators and
shipbuilders of those old times, attempted it, and they were
for a long time the only nations that did attempt it.

Of all the countries on the coast of the Mediterranean sea,
Egypt seems to have been the first in which either agriculture
or manufactures were cultivated and improved to any considerable degree. Upper Egypt extends itself nowhere above a few
miles from the Nile, and in Lower Egypt that great river breaks
itself into many different canals, which, with the assistance of
a little art, seem to have afforded a communication by water-
carriage, not only between all the great towns, but between all
the considerable villages, and even to many farm-houses in the
country; nearly in the same manner as the Rhine and the Maese
do in Holland at present. The extent and easiness of this inland
navigation was probably one of the principal causes of the early
improvement of Egypt.

The improvements in agriculture and manufactures seem
likewise to have been of very great antiquity in the provinces
of Bengal in the East Indies, and in some of the eastern
provinces of China; though the great extent of this antiquity
is not authenticated by any histories of whose authority we, in
this part of the world, are well assured. In Bengal the Ganges
and several other great rivers form a great number of navigable
canals in the same manner as the Nile does in Egypt. In the
Eastern provinces of China too, several great rivers form, by

their different branches, a multitude of canals, and by communicating with one another afford an inland navigation much more extensive than that either of the Nile or the Ganges, or perhaps than both of them put together. It is remarkable that neither the antient Egyptians, nor the Indians, nor the Chinese, encouraged foreign commerce, but seem all to have derived their great opulence from this inland navigation.

All the inland parts of Africa, and all that part of Asia which lies any considerable way north of the Euxine and Caspian seas, the antient Scythia, the modern Tartary and Siberia, seem in all ages of the world to have been in the same barbarous and uncivilized state in which we find them at present. The sea of Tartary is the frozen ocean which admits of no navigation, and though some of the greatest rivers in the world run through that country, they are at too great a distance from one another to carry commerce and communication through the greater part of it. There are in Africa none of those great inlets, such as the Baltic and Adriatic seas in Europe, the Mediterranean and Euxine seas in both Europe and Asia, and the gulphs of Arabia, Persia, India, Bengal, and Siam, in Asia, to carry maritime commerce into the interior parts of that great continent: and the great rivers of Africa are at too great a distance from one another to give occasion to any considerable inland navigation. The commerce besides which any nation can carry on by means of a river which does not break itself into any great number of branches or canals, and which runs into another territory before it reaches the sea, can never be very considerable; because it is always in the power of the nations who possess that other territory to obstruct the communication between the upper country and the sea. The navigation of the Danube is of very little use to the different states of Bavaria, Austria and Hungary, in comparison of what it would be if any of them possessed the whole of its course till it falls into the Black Sea.

CHAPTER IV

Of the Origin and Use of Money*

WHEN the division of labour has been once thoroughly established, it is but a very small part of a man's wants which the produce of his own labour can supply. He supplies the far greater part of them by exchanging that surplus part of the produce of his own labour, which is over and above his own consumption, for such parts of the produce of other men's labour as he has occasion for. Every man thus lives by exchanging, or becomes in some measure a merchant, and the society itself grows to be what is properly a commercial society.

But when the division of labour first began to take place, this power of exchanging must frequently have been very much clogged and embarrassed in its operations. One man, we shall suppose, has more of a certain commodity than he himself has occasion for, while another has less. The former consequently would be glad to dispose of, and the latter to purchase, a part of this superfluity. But if this latter should chance to have nothing that the former stands in need of, no exchange can be made between them. The butcher has more meat in his shop than he himself can consume, and the brewer and the baker would each of them be willing to purchase a part of it. But they have nothing to offer in exchange, except the different productions of their respective trades, and the butcher is already provided with all the bread and beer which he has immediate occasion for. No exchange can, in this case, be made between them. He cannot be their merchant, nor they his customers; and they are all of them thus mutually less serviceable to one another. In order to avoid the inconveniency of such situations, every prudent man in every period of society, after the first establishment of the division of labour, must naturally have endeavoured to manage his affairs in such a manner, as to have at all times by him, besides the peculiar produce of his own industry, a certain quantity of some one commodity or other, such as he imagined few people would be likely to refuse in exchange for the produce of their industry.

Many different commodities, it is probable, were successively both thought of and employed for this purpose. In the rude ages of society, cattle are said to have been the common instrument of commerce; and, though they must have been a most inconvenient one, yet in old times we find things were frequently valued according to the number of cattle which had been given in exchange for them. The armour of Diomede, says Homer, cost only nine oxen; but that of Glaucus cost an hundred oxen.* Salt is said to be the common instrument of commerce and exchanges in Abyssinia; a species of shells in some parts of the coast of India; dried cod at Newfoundland; tobacco in Virginia; sugar in some of our West India colonies; hides or dressed leather in some other countries; and there is at this day a village in Scotland where it is not uncommon, I am told, for a workman to carry nails instead of money to the baker's shop or the ale-house.*

In all countries, however, men seem at last to have been determined by irresistible reasons to give the preference, for this employment, to metals above every other commodity. Metals can not only be kept with as little loss as any other commodity, scarce any thing being less perishable than they are, but they can likewise, without any loss, be divided into any number of parts, as by fusion those parts can easily be re-united again; a quality which no other equally durable commodities possess, and which more than any other quality renders them fit to be the instruments of commerce and circulation. The man who wanted to buy salt, for example, and had nothing but cattle to give in exchange for it, must have been obliged to buy salt to the value of a whole ox, or a whole sheep at a time. He could seldom buy less than this, because what he was to give for it could seldom be divided without loss; and if he had a mind to buy more, he must, for the same reasons, have been obliged to buy double or triple the quantity, the value, to wit, of two or three oxen, or of two or three sheep. If, on the contrary, instead of sheep or oxen, he had metals to give in exchange for it, he could easily proportion the quantity of the metal to the precise quantity of the commodity which he had immediate occasion for.

Different metals have been made use of by different nations for this purpose. Iron was the common instrument of commerce among the antient Spartans; copper among the antient Romans; and gold and silver among all rich and commercial nations.

Those metals seem originally to have been made use of for this purpose in rude bars, without any stamp or coinage. Thus we are told by Pliny,'* upon the authority of Timaeus, an antient historian, that, till the time of Servius Tullius, the Romans had no coined money, but made use of unstamped bars of copper to purchase whatever they had occasion for. These rude bars, therefore, performed at this time the function of money.

The use of metals in this rude state was attended with two very considerable inconveniencies; first, with the trouble of weighing; and, secondly, with that of assaying* them. In the precious metals, where a small difference in the quantity makes a great difference in the value, even the business of weighing, with proper exactness, requires at least very accurate weights and scales. The weighing of gold in particular is an operation of some nicety. In the coarser metals, indeed, where a small error would be of little consequence, less accuracy would, no doubt, be necessary. Yet we should find it excessively troublesome, if every time a poor man had occasion either to buy or sell a farthing's worth of goods, he was obliged to weigh the farthing. The operation of assaying is still more difficult, still more tedious, and, unless a part of the metal is fairly melted in the crucible, with proper dissolvents, any conclusion that can be drawn from it, is extremely uncertain. Before the

---

' Plin. Hist. Nat. lib. 33. cap. 3. ['King Servius was the first to stamp a design on bronze; previously according to Timaeus, at Rome they used raw metal.' Pliny, *Natural History*, XXXIII. xiii translated by H. Rackham in Loeb Classical Library (1952), ix. 37.] [Campbell and Skinner]

institution of coined money, however, unless they went through this tedious and difficult operation, people must always have been liable to the grossest frauds and impositions, and instead of a pound weight of pure silver, or pure copper, might receive in exchange for their goods, an adulterated composition of the coarsest and cheapest materials, which had, however, in their outward appearance, been made to resemble those metals. To prevent such abuses, to facilitate exchanges, and thereby to encourage all sorts of industry and commerce, it has been found necessary, in all countries that have made any considerable advances towards improvement, to affix a publick stamp upon certain quantities of such particular metals, as were in those countries commonly made use of to purchase goods. Hence the origin of coined money, and of those publick offices called mints; institutions exactly of the same nature with those of the aulnagers and stampmasters* of woollen and linen cloth. All of them are equally meant to ascertain, by means of a publick stamp, the quantity and uniform goodness of those different commodities when brought to market. . . .

It is in this manner that money has become in all civilized nations the universal instrument of commerce, by the intervention of which goods of all kinds are bought and sold, or exchanged for one another.

What are the rules which men naturally observe in exchanging them either for money or for one another, I shall now proceed to examine. These rules determine what may be called the relative or exchangeable value of goods.

The word VALUE, it is to be observed, has two different meanings, and sometimes expresses the utility of some particular object, and sometimes the power of purchasing other goods which the possession of that object conveys. The one may be called 'value in use;' the other, 'value in exchange.' The things which have the greatest value in use have frequently little or no value in exchange; and, on the contrary, those which have the greatest value in exchange have frequently little or no value in use. Nothing is more useful than water:* but it will purchase scarce any thing; scarce any thing can be had in exchange for it. A diamond, on the contrary, has scarce any value in use; but a very great quantity of other goods may frequently be had in exchange for it.

In order to investigate the principles which regulate the exchangeable value of commodities, I shall endeavour to shew,

First, what is the real measure of this exchangeable value; or, wherein consists the real price of all commodities,

Secondly, what are the different parts of which this real price is composed or made up.

And, lastly, what are the different circumstances which sometimes raise some or all of these different parts of price above, and sometimes sink them below their natural or ordinary rate; or, what are the causes which sometimes hinder the market price, that is, the actual price of commodities, from coinciding exactly with what may be called their natural price.

I shall endeavour to explain, as fully and distinctly as I can, those three subjects in the three following chapters, for which I must very earnestly entreat both the patience and attention of the reader: his patience in order to examine a detail which may perhaps in some places appear unnecessarily tedious; and his attention in order to understand what may, perhaps, after the fullest explication which I am capable of giving of it, appear still in some degree obscure. I am always willing to run some hazard of being tedious in order to be sure that I am perspicuous; and after taking the utmost pains that I can to be perspicuous, some obscurity may still appear to remain upon a subject in its own nature extremely abstracted.

CHAPTER V

Of the real and nominal Price of Commodities, or of their Price in Labour, and their Price in Money

EVERY man is rich or poor according to the degree in which he can afford to enjoy the necessaries, conveniencies, and amusements of human life. But after the division of labour has once thoroughly taken place, it is but a very small part of these with which a man's own labour can supply him. The far greater part of them he must derive from the labour of other people, and he must be rich or poor according to the quantity of that labour which he can command, or which he can afford to purchase. The value of any commodity, therefore, to the person who possesses it, and who means not to use or consume it himself, but to exchange it for other commodities, is equal to the quantity of labour which it enables him to purchase or command. Labour, therefore, is the real measure of the exchangeable value of all commodities.*

The real price of every thing, what every thing really costs to the man who wants to acquire it, is the toil and trouble of acquiring it. What every thing is really worth to the man who has acquired it, and who wants to dispose of it or exchange it for something else, is the toil and trouble which it can save to himself, and which it can impose upon other people. What is bought with money or with goods is purchased by labour as much as what we acquire by the toil of our own body. That money or those goods indeed save us this toil. They contain the value of a certain quantity of labour which we exchange for what is supposed at the time to contain the value of an equal quantity. Labour was the first price, the original purchase-money that was paid for all things. It was not by gold or by silver, but by labour, that all the wealth of the world was originally purchased; and its value, to those who possess it and who want to exchange it for some new productions, is precisely equal to the quantity of labour which it can enable them to purchase or command.

Wealth, as Mr. Hobbes says, is power.* But the person who either acquires, or succeeds to a great fortune, does not necessarily acquire or succeed to any political power, either civil or military. His fortune may, perhaps, afford him the means of acquiring both, but the mere possession of that fortune does not necessarily convey to him either. The power which that possession immediately and directly conveys to him, is the power of purchasing; a certain command over all the labour, or over all the produce of labour which is then in the market. His fortune is greater or less, precisely in proportion to the extent of this power; or to the quantity either of other men's labour, or, what is the same thing, of the produce of other men's labour, which it enables him to purchase or command. The exchangeable value of every thing must always be precisely equal to the extent of this power which it conveys to its owner.

But though labour be the real measure of the exchangeable value of all commodities, it is not that by which their value is commonly estimated. It is often difficult to ascertain the proportion between two different quantities of labour. The time spent in two different sorts of work will not always alone determine this proportion. The different degrees of hardship endured, and of ingenuity exercised, must likewise be taken into account. There may be more labour in an hour's hard work than in two hours easy business; or in an hour's application to a trade which it cost ten years labour to learn, than in a month's industry at an ordinary and obvious employment. But it is not easy to find any accurate measure either of hardship or ingenuity. In exchanging indeed the different productions of different sorts of labour for one another, some allowance is commonly made for both. It is adjusted, however, not by any accurate measure, but by the higgling and bargaining of the market, according to that sort of rough equality which, though not exact, is sufficient for carrying on the business of common life.

Every commodity besides, is more frequently exchanged for, and thereby compared with, other commodities than with labour. It is more natural, therefore, to estimate its exchangeable value by the quantity of some other commodity than by that of the labour which it can purchase. The greater part of people too understand better what is meant by a quantity of a particular commodity, than by a quantity of labour. The one is a plain palpable object; the other an abstract notion, which, though it can be made sufficiently intelligible, is not altogether so natural and obvious.

But when barter ceases, and money has become the common instrument of commerce, every particular commodity is more frequently exchanged for money than for any other commodity. The butcher seldom carries his beef or his mutton to the baker, or the brewer, in order to exchange them for bread or for beer, but he carries them to the market, where he exchanges them for money, and afterwards exchanges that money for bread and for beer. The quantity of money which he gets for them regulates too the quantity of bread and beer which he can afterwards purchase. It is more natural and obvious to him, therefore, to estimate their value by the quantity of money, the commodity for which he immediately exchanges them, than by that of bread and beer, the commodities for which he can exchange them only by the intervention of another commodity; and rather to say that his butcher's meat is worth threepence or fourpence a pound, than that it is worth three or four pounds of bread, or three or four quarts of small beer. Hence it comes to pass, that the exchangeable value of every commodity is more frequently estimated by the quantity of money, than by the quantity either of labour or of any other commodity which can be had in exchange for it.

Gold and silver, however, like every other commodity, vary in their value, are sometimes cheaper and sometimes dearer, sometimes of easier and sometimes of more difficult purchase. The quantity of labour which any particular quantity of them can purchase or command, or the quantity of other goods which it will exchange for, depends always upon the fertility or barrenness of the mines which happen to be known about the time when such exchanges are made. The discovery of the abundant mines of America* reduced, in the sixteenth century, the value of gold and silver in Europe to about a third of what it had been before. As it cost less labour to bring those metals from the mine to the market, so when they were brought thither they could purchase or command less labour; and this revolution in their value, though perhaps the greatest, is by no means the only one of which history gives some account. But as a measure of quantity, such as the natural foot, fathom,* or handful, which is continually varying in its own quantity, can never be an accurate measure of the quantity of other things; so a commodity which is itself continually varying in its own value, can never be an accurate measure of the value of other commodities. Equal quantities of labour, at all times and places, may be said to be of equal value to the labourer. In his ordinary state of health, strength and spirits; in the ordinary degree of his skill and dexterity, he must always lay down the same portion of his ease, his liberty, and his happiness. The price which he pays must always be the same, whatever may be the quantity of goods which he receives in return for it. Of these, indeed, it may sometimes purchase a greater and sometimes a smaller quantity; but it is their value which varies, not that of the labour which purchases them. At all times and places that is dear which it is difficult to come at, or which it costs much labour to acquire; and that cheap which is to be had easily, or with very little labour. Labour alone, therefore, never varying in its own value, is alone the ultimate and real standard by which the value of all commodities can at all times and places be estimated and compared. It is their real price; money is their nominal price only.

But though equal quantities of labour are always of equal value to the labourer, yet to the person who employs him they appear sometimes to be of greater and sometimes of smaller value. He purchases them sometimes with a greater and sometimes with a smaller quantity of goods, and to him the price of labour seems to vary like that of all other things. It appears to him dear in the one case, and cheap in the other. In reality, however, it is the goods which are cheap in the one case, and dear in the other.

In this popular sense, therefore, labour, like commodities, may be said to have a real and a nominal price. Its real price may be said to consist in the quantity of the necessaries and conveniencies of life which are given for it; its nominal price, in the quantity of money. The labourer is rich or poor, is well or ill rewarded, in proportion to the real, not to the nominal price of his labour.

The distinction between the real and the nominal price of commodities and labour, is not a matter of mere speculation, but may sometimes be of considerable use in practice. The same real price is always of the same value; but on account of the variations in the value of gold and silver, the same nominal price is sometimes of very different values. When a landed estate, therefore, is sold with a reservation of a perpetual rent, if it is intended that this rent should always be of the same value, it is of importance to the family in whose favour it is reserved, that it should not consist in a particular sum of money.* Its value would in this case be liable to variations of two different kinds; first, to those which arise from the different quantities of gold and silver which are contained at different times in coin of the same denomination; and, secondly, to those which arise from the different values of equal quantities of gold and silver at different times. . . .

Equal quantities of labour will at distant times be purchased more nearly with equal quantities of corn, the subsistence of the labourer, than with equal quantities of gold and silver, or perhaps of any other commodity. Equal quantities of corn, therefore, will, at distant times, be more nearly of the same real value, or enable the possessor to purchase or command more nearly the same quantity of the labour of other people. They will do this, I say, more nearly than equal quantities of almost any other commodity; for even equal quantities of corn will not do it exactly. The subsistence of the labourer, or the real price of labour, as I shall endeavour to show hereafter, is very different upon different occasions; more liberal in a society advancing to opulence than in one that is standing still; and in one that is standing still than in one that is going backwards. Every other commodity, however, will at any particular time purchase a greater or smaller quantity of labour in proportion to the quantity of subsistence which it can purchase at that time. A rent therefore reserved in corn is liable only to the variations in the quantity of labour which a certain quantity of corn can purchase. But a rent reserved in any other commodity is liable, not only to the variations in the quantity of labour which any particular quantity of corn can purchase, but to the variations in the quantity of corn which can be purchased by any particular quantity of that commodity.

Though the real value of a corn rent, it is to be observed however, varies much less from century to century than that of a money rent, it varies much more from year to year. The money price of labour, as I shall endeavour to show hereafter, does not fluctuate from year to year with the money price of corn, but seems to be every where accommodated, not to the temporary or occasional, but to the average or ordinary price of that necessary of life. The average or ordinary price of corn again is regulated, as I shall likewise endeavour to show hereafter, by the value of silver, by the richness or barrenness of the mines which supply the market with that metal, or by the quantity of labour which must be employed, and consequently of corn which must be consumed, in order to bring any particular quantity of silver from the mine to the market. But the value of silver, though it sometimes varies greatly from century to century, seldom varies much from year to year, but frequently continues the same, or very nearly the same, for half a century or a century together. The ordinary or average money price of corn, therefore, may, during so long a period, continue the same or very nearly the same too, and along with it the money price of labour, provided, at least, the society continues, in other respects, in the same or nearly in the same condition. In the mean time the temporary and occasional price of corn may frequently be double, one year, of what it had been the year before, or fluctuate, for example, from five and twenty to fifty shillings the quarter. But when corn is at the latter price, not only the nominal, but the real value of a corn rent will be double of what it is when at the former, or will command double the quantity either of labour or of the greater part of other commodities; the money price of labour, and along with it that of most other things, continuing the same during all these fluctuations.*

Labour, therefore, it appears evidently, is the only universal, as well as the only accurate measure of value, or the only standard by which we can compare the values of different commodities at all times and at all places. We cannot estimate, it is allowed, the real value of different commodities from century to century by the quantities of silver which were given for them. We cannot estimate it from year to year by the quantities of corn. By the quantities of labour we can, with the greatest accuracy, estimate it both from century to century and from year to year. From century to century, corn is a better measure than silver, because, from century to century, equal quantities of corn will command the same quantity of labour more nearly than equal quantities of silver. From year to year, on the contrary, silver is a better measure than corn, because equal quantities of it will more nearly command the same quantity of labour.

But though in establishing perpetual rents, or even in letting very long leases, it may be of use to distinguish between real and nominal price, it is of none in buying and selling, the more common and ordinary transactions of human life.

At the same time and place the real and the nominal price of all commodities are exactly in proportion to one another. The more or less money you get for any commodity, in the London market, for example, the more or less labour it will at that time and place enable you to purchase or command. At the same time and place, therefore, money is the exact measure of the real exchangeable value of all commodities. It is so, however, at the same time and place only.

Though at distant places, there is no regular proportion between the real and the money price of commodities, yet the merchant who carries goods from the one to the other has nothing to consider but their money price, or the difference between the quantity of silver for which he buys them, and that for which he is likely to sell them. Half an ounce of silver at Canton in China may command a greater quantity both of labour and of the necessaries and conveniencies of life, than an ounce at London. A commodity, therefore, which sells for half an ounce of silver at Canton may there be really dearer, of more real importance to the man who possesses it there, than a commodity which sells for an ounce at London is to the man who possesses it at London. If a London merchant, however, can buy at Canton for half an ounce of silver, a commodity which he can afterwards sell at London for an ounce, he gains a hundred per cent. by the bargain, just as much as if an ounce of silver was at London exactly of the same value as at Canton. It is of no importance to him that half an ounce of silver at Canton would have given him the command of more labour and of a greater quantity of the necessaries and conveniencies of life than an ounce can do at London. An ounce at London will always give him the command of double the quantity of all these which half an ounce could have done there, and this is precisely what he wants.

As it is the nominal or money price of goods, therefore, which finally determines the prudence or imprudence of all purchases and sales, and thereby regulates almost the whole business of common life in which price is concerned, we cannot wonder that it should have been so much more attended to than the real price.

In such a work as this, however, it may sometimes be of use to compare the different real values of a particular commodity at different times and places, or the different degrees of power over the labour of other people which it may, upon different occasions, have given to those who possessed it. We must in this case compare, not so much the different quantities of silver for which it was commonly sold, as the different quantities of labour which those different quantities of silver could have purchased. But the current prices of labour at distant times and places can scarce ever be known with any degree of exactness. Those of corn, though they have in few places been regularly recorded, are in general better known and have been more frequently taken notice of by historians and other writers. We must generally, therefore, content ourselves with them, not as being always exactly in the same proportion as the current prices of labour, but as being the nearest approximation which can commonly be had to that proportion. I shall hereafter have occasion to make several comparisons of this kind. . . .

CHAPTER VI

Of the component Parts of the Price of Commodities

IN that early and rude state of society which precedes both the accumulation of stock and the appropriation of land, the proportion between the quantities of labour necessary for acquiring different objects seems to be the only circumstance which can afford any rule for exchanging them for one another. If among a nation of hunters, for example, it usually costs twice the labour to kill a beaver which it does to kill a deer, one beaver should naturally exchange for or be worth two deer. It is natural that what is usually the produce of two days or two hours labour, should be worth double of what is usually the produce of one day's or one hour's labour.

If the one species of labour should be more severe than the other, some allowance will naturally be made for this superior hardship; and the produce of one hour's labour in the one way may frequently exchange for that of two hours labour in the other.

Or if the one species of labour requires an uncommon degree of dexterity and ingenuity, the esteem which men have for such talents, will naturally give a value to their produce, superior to what would be due to the time employed about it. Such talents can seldom be acquired but in consequence of long application, and the superior value of their produce may frequently be no more than a reasonable compensation for the time and labour which must be spent in acquiring them. In the advanced state of society, allowances of this kind, for superior hardship and superior skill, are commonly made in the wages of labour;* and something of the same kind must probably have taken place in its earliest and rudest period.

In this state of things, the whole produce of labour belongs to the labourer; and the quantity of labour commonly employed in acquiring or producing any commodity, is the only circumstance which can regulate the quantity of labour which it ought commonly to purchase, command, or exchange for.

As soon as stock has accumulated in the hands of particular persons, some of them will naturally employ it in setting to work industrious people, whom they will supply with materials and subsistence, in order to make a profit by the sale of their work, or by what their labour adds to the value of the materials. In exchanging the complete manufacture either for money, for labour, or for other goods, over and above what may be sufficient to pay the price of the materials, and the wages of the workmen, something must be given for the profits of the undertaker of the work who hazards his stock in this adventure. The value which the workmen add to the materials, therefore, resolves itself in this case into two parts, of which the one pays their wages, the other the profits of their employer upon the whole stock of materials and wages which he advanced. He could have no interest to employ them, unless he expected from the sale of their work something more than what was sufficient to replace his stock to him; and he could have no interest to employ a great stock rather than a small one, unless his profits were to bear some proportion to the extent of his stock.

The profits of stock, it may perhaps be thought, are only a different name for the wages of a particular sort of labour, the labour of inspection and direction. They are, however, altogether different, are regulated by quite different principles, and bear no proportion to the quantity, the hardship, or the ingenuity of this supposed labour of inspection and direction. They are regulated altogether by the value of the stock employed, and are greater or smaller in proportion to the extent of this stock. Let us suppose, for example, that in some particular place, where the common annual profits of manufacturing stock are ten per cent. there are two different manufactures, in each of which twenty workmen are employed at the rate of fifteen pounds a year each, or at the expence of three hundred a year in each manufactory.* Let us suppose too, that the coarse materials annually wrought up in the one cost only seven hundred pounds, while the finer materials in the other cost seven thousand. The capital annually employed in the one will in this case amount only to one thousand pounds; whereas that employed in the other will amount to seven thousand three hundred pounds. At the rate of ten per cent. therefore, the undertaker of the one will expect an yearly profit of about one hundred pounds only; while that of the other will expect about seven hundred and thirty pounds. But though their profits are so very different, their labour of inspection and direction may be either altogether or very nearly the same. In many great works, almost the whole labour of this kind is committed to some principal clerk. His wages properly express the value of this labour of inspection and direction. Though in settling them some regard is had commonly, not only to his labour and skill, but to the trust which is reposed in him, yet they never bear any regular proportion to the capital of which he oversees the management; and the owner of this capital, though he is thus discharged of almost all labour, still expects that his profits should bear a regular proportion to his capital. In the price of commodities, therefore, the profits of stock constitute a component part altogether different from the wages of labour, and regulated by quite different principles.

In this state of things, the whole produce of labour does not always belong to the labourer. He must in most cases share it with the owner of the stock which employs him. Neither is the quantity of labour commonly employed in acquiring or producing any commodity, the only circumstance which can regulate the quantity which it ought commonly to purchase, command, or exchange for. An additional quantity, it is evident, must be due for the profits of the stock which advanced the wages and furnished the materials of that labour.

As soon as the land of any country has all become private property,* the landlords, like all other men, love to reap where they never sowed, and demand a rent even for its natural produce. The wood of the forest, the grass of the field, and all the natural fruits of the earth, which, when land was in common, cost the labourer only the trouble of gathering them, come, even to him, to have an additional price fixed upon them. He must then pay for the licence to gather them; and must give up to the landlord a portion of what his labour either collects or produces. This portion, or, what comes to the same thing, the price of this portion, constitutes the rent of land, and in the price of the greater part of commodities makes a third component part.

The real value of all the different component parts of price, it must be observed, is measured by the quantity of labour which they can, each of them, purchase or command. Labour measures the value not only of that part of price which resolves itself into labour, but of that which resolves itself into rent, and of that which resolves itself into profit.

In every society the price of every commodity finally resolves itself into some one or other, or all of those three parts; and in every improved society, all the three enter more or less, as component parts, into the price of the far greater part of commodities.

In the price of corn, for example, one part pays the rent of the landlord, another pays the wages or maintenance of the labourers and labouring cattle employed in producing it, and the third pays the profit of the farmer. These three parts seem either immediately or ultimately to make up the whole price of corn. A fourth part, it may perhaps be thought, is necessary for replacing the stock of the farmer, or for compensating the wear and tear of his labouring cattle, and other instruments of husbandry. But it must be considered that the price of any instrument of husbandry, such as a labouring horse, is itself made up of the same three parts; the rent of the land upon which he is reared, the labour of tending and rearing him, and the profits of the farmer who advances both the rent of this land, and the wages of this labour. Though the price of the corn, therefore, may pay the price as well as the maintenance of the horse, the whole price still resolves itself either immediately or ultimately into the same three parts of rent, labour, and profit.

In the price of flour or meal, we must add to the price of the corn, the profits of the miller, and the wages of his servants; in the price of the bread, the profits of the baker, and the wages of his servants; and in the price of both, the labour of transporting the corn from the house of the farmer to that of the miller, and from that of the miller to that of the baker, together with the profits of those who advance the wages of that labour.

The price of flax resolves itself into the same three parts as that of corn. In the price of linen we must add to this price the wages of the flax-dresser, of the spinner, of the weaver, of the bleacher, &c. together with the profits of their respective employers.

As any particular commodity comes to be more manufactured, that part of the price which resolves itself into wages and profit, comes to be greater in proportion to that which resolves itself into rent. In the progress of the manufacture, not only the number of profits increase, but every subsequent profit is greater than the foregoing; because the capital from which it is derived must always be greater. The capital which employs the weavers, for example, must be greater than that which employs the spinners; because it not only replaces that capital with its profits, but pays, besides, the wages of the weavers; and the profits must always bear some proportion to the capital.

In the most improved societies, however, there are always a few commodities of which the price resolves itself into two parts only, the wages of labour, and the profits of stock; and a still smaller number in which it consists altogether in the wages of labour. In the price of sea-fish, for example, one part pays the labour of the fishermen, and the other the profits of the capital employed in the fishery. Rent very seldom makes any part of it, though it does sometimes, as I shall shew hereafter.* It is otherwise, at least through the greater part of Europe, in river fisheries. A salmon fishery pays a rent, and rent, though it cannot well be called the rent of land, makes a part of the price of a salmon as well as wages and profit. In some parts of Scotland a few poor people make a trade of gathering, along the sea-shore, those little variegated stones commonly known by the name of Scotch Pebbles.* The price which is paid to them by the stone-cutter is altogether the wages of their labour; neither rent nor profit make any part of it.

But the whole price of any commodity must still finally resolve itself into some one or other, or all of those three parts; as whatever part of it remains after paying the rent of the land, and the price of the whole labour employed in raising, manu-facturing, and bringing it to market, must necessarily be profit to somebody.

As the price or exchangeable value of every particular com-modity, taken separately, resolves itself into some one or other or all of those three parts; so that of all the commodities which compose the whole annual produce of the labour of every country, taken complexly, must resolve itself into the same three parts, and be parcelled out among different inhabitants of the country, either as the wages of their labour, the profits of their stock, or the rent of their land. The whole of what is annually either collected or produced by the labour of every society, or what comes to the same thing, the whole price of it, is in the manner originally distributed among some of its different members. Wages, profit, and rent, are the three original sources of all revenue as well as of all exchangeable value. All other revenue is ultimately derived from some one or other of these.

Whoever derives his revenue from a fund which is his own, must draw it either from his labour, from his stock, or from his land. The revenue derived from labour is called wages. That derived from stock, by the person who manages or employs it, is called profit. That derived from it by the person who does not employ it himself, but lends it to another, is called the interest or the use of money. It is the compensation which the borrower pays to the lender, for the profit which he has an opportunity of making by the use of the money. Part of that profit naturally belongs to the borrower, who runs the risk and takes the trouble of employing it; and part to the lender, who affords him the opportunity of making this profit.

The interest of money is always a derivative revenue, which, if it is not paid from the profit which is made by the use of the money, must be paid from some other source of revenue, unless perhaps the borrower is a spendthrift, who contracts a second debt in order to pay the interest of the first. The revenue which proceeds altogether from land, is called rent, and belongs to the landlord. The revenue of the farmer is derived partly from his labour, and partly from his stock. To him, land is only the instrument which enables him to earn the wages of this labour, and to make the profits of this stock. All taxes, and all the revenue which is founded upon them, all salaries, pensions, and annuities of every kind, are ultimately derived from some one or other of those three original sources of revenue, and are paid either immediately or mediately* from the wages of labour, the profits of stock, or the rent of land.

When those three different sorts of revenue belong to different persons, they are readily distinguished; but when they belong to the same they are sometimes confounded with one another, at least in common language.*

A gentleman who farms a part of his own estate, after paying the expence of cultivation, should gain both the rent of the landlord and the profit of the farmer. He is apt to denominate, however, his whole gain, profit, and thus confounds rent with profit, at least in common language. The greater part of our North American and West Indian planters are in this situation. They farm, the greater part of them, their own estates, and accordingly we seldom hear of the rent of a plantation, but frequently of its profit.

Common farmers seldom employ any overseer to direct the general operations of the farm. They generally too work a good deal with their own hands, as ploughmen, harrowers,* &c. What remains of the crop after paying the rent, therefore, should not only replace to them their stock employed in cultivation, together with its ordinary profits, but pay them the wages which are due to them, both as labourers and overseers. Whatever remains, however, after paying the rent and keeping up the stock, is called profit. But wages evidently make a part of it. The farmer, by saving these wages, must necessarily gain them. Wages, therefore, are in this case confounded with profit.

An independent manufacturer, who has stock enough both to purchase materials, and to maintain himself till he can carry his work to market, should gain both the wages of a journeyman* who works under a master, and the profit which that master makes by the sale of the journeyman's work. His whole gains, however, are commonly called profit, and wages are, in this case too, confounded with profit.

A gardener who cultivates his own garden with his own hands, unites in his own person the three different characters, of landlord, farmer, and labourer. His produce, therefore, should pay him the rent of the first, the profit of the second, and the wages of the third. The whole, however, is commonly considered as the earnings of his labour. Both rent and profit are, in this case, confounded with wages.

As in a civilized country there are but few commodities of which the exchangeable value arises from labour only, rent and profit contributing largely to that of the far greater part of them, so the annual produce of its labour will always be sufficient to purchase or command a much greater quantity of labour than what was employed in raising, preparing, and bringing that produce to market. If the society was annually to employ all the labour which it can annually purchase, as the quantity of labour would increase greatly every year, so the produce of every succeeding year would be of vastly greater value than that of the foregoing. But there is no country in which the whole annual produce is employed in maintaining the industrious. The idle every where consume a great part of it; and according to the different proportions in which it is annually divided between those two different orders of people, its ordinary or average value must either annually increase, or diminish, or continue the same from one year to another.

CHAPTER VII

Of the natural and market Price of Commodities*

THERE is in every society or neighbourhood an ordinary or
average rate both of wages and profit in every different employment of labour and stock. This rate is naturally regulated,
as I shall show hereafter,* partly by the general circumstances
of the society, their riches or poverty, their advancing, stationary, or declining condition,* and partly by the particular nature
of each employment.

There is likewise in every society or neighbourhood an
ordinary or average rate of rent, which is regulated too, as I
shall show hereafter, partly by the general circumstances of the
society or neighbourhood in which the land is situated, and
partly by the natural or improved fertility of the land.

These ordinary or average rates may be called the natural
rates of wages, profit, and rent, at the time and place in which
they commonly prevail.

When the price of any commodity is neither more nor less
than what is sufficient to pay the rent of the land, the wages
of the labour, and the profits of the stock employed in raising,
preparing, and bringing it to market, according to their natural
rates, the commodity is then sold for what may be called its
natural price.

The commodity is then sold precisely for what it is worth,
or for what it really costs the person who brings it to market;
for though in common language what is called the prime cost
of any commodity does not comprehend the profit of the
person who is to sell it again, yet if he sells it at a price which
does not allow him the ordinary rate of profit in his neighbourhood, he is evidently a loser by the trade; since by
employing his stock in some other way he might have made
that profit. His profit, besides, is his revenue, the proper fund
of his subsistence. As, while he is preparing and bringing the

goods to market, he advances to his workmen their wages, or their subsistence; so he advances to himself, in the same manner, his own subsistence, which is generally suitable to the profit which he may reasonably expect from the sale of his goods. Unless they yield him this profit, therefore, they do not repay him what they may very properly be said to have really cost him.

Though the price, therefore, which leaves him this profit, is not always the lowest at which a dealer may sometimes sell his goods, it is the lowest at which he is likely to sell them for any considerable time; at least where there is perfect liberty, or where he may change his trade as often as he pleases.

The actual price at which any commodity is commonly sold is called its market price. It may either be above, or below, or exactly the same with its natural price.

The market price of every particular commodity is regulated by the proportion between the quantity which is actually brought to market, and the demand of those who are willing to pay the natural price of the commodity, or the whole value of the rent, labour, and profit, which must be paid in order to bring it thither. Such people may be called the effectual demanders, and their demand the effectual demand; since it may be sufficient to effectuate the bringing of the commodity to market. It is different from the absolute demand. A very poor man may be said in some sense to have a demand for a coach and six; he might like to have it; but his demand is not an effectual demand,* as the commodity can never be brought to market in order to satisfy it.

When the quantity of any commodity which is brought to market falls short of the effectual demand, all those who are willing to pay the whole value of the rent, wages, and profit, which must be paid in order to bring it thither, cannot be supplied with the quantity which they want. Rather than want it altogether, some of them will be willing to give more. A competition will immediately begin among them, and the market price will rise more or less above the natural price, according as either the greatness of the deficiency, or the wealth and wanton luxury of the competitors, happen to animate more or less the eagerness of the competition. Among competitors of equal wealth and luxury the same deficiency will generally occasion a more or less eager competition, according as the acquisition of the commodity happens to be of more or less importance to them. Hence the exorbitant price of the necessaries of life during the blockade of a town or in a famine.*

When the quantity brought to market exceeds the effectual demand, it cannot be all sold to those who are willing to pay the whole value of the rent, wages and profit, which must be paid in order to bring it thither. Some part must be sold to those who are willing to pay less, and the low price which they give for it must reduce the price of the whole. The market price will sink more or less below the natural price, according as the greatness of the excess increases more or less the competition of the sellers, or according as it happens to be more or less important to them to get immediately rid of the commodity. The same excess in the importation of perishable, will occasion a much greater competition than in that of durable commodities; in the importation of oranges, for example, than in that of old iron.

When the quantity brought to market is just sufficient to supply the effectual demand and no more, the market price naturally comes to be either exactly, or as nearly as can be judged of, the same with the natural price. The whole quantity upon hand can be disposed of for this price, and cannot be disposed of for more. The competition of the different dealers obliges them all to accept of this price, but does not oblige them to accept of less.

The quantity of every commodity brought to market naturally suits itself to the effectual demand. It is the interest of all those who employ their land, labour, or stock, in bringing any commodity to market, that the quantity never should exceed the effectual demand; and it is the interest of all other people that it never should fall short of that demand.

If at any time it exceeds the effectual demand, some of the component parts of its price must be paid below their natural rate. If it is rent, the interest of the landlords will immediately prompt them to withdraw a part of their land; and if it is wages or profit, the interest of the labourers in the one case, and of their employers in the other, will prompt them to withdraw a part of their labour or stock from this employment. The quantity brought to market will soon be no more than sufficient to supply the effectual demand. All the different parts of its price will rise to their natural rate, and the whole price to its natural price.

If, on the contrary, the quantity brought to market should at any time fall short of the effectual demand, some of the component parts of its price must rise above their natural rate. If it is rent, the interest of all other landlords will naturally prompt them to prepare more land for the raising of this commodity; if it is wages or profit, the interest of all other labourers and dealers will soon prompt them to employ more labour and stock in preparing and bringing it to market. The quantity brought thither will soon be sufficient to supply the effectual demand. All the different parts of its price will soon sink to their natural rate, and the whole price to its·natural price.

The natural price, therefore, is, as it were, the central price, to which the prices of all commodities are continually gravitating. Different accidents may sometimes keep them suspended a good deal above it, and sometimes force them down even somewhat below it. But whatever may be the obstacles which hinder them from settling in this center of repose and continuance, they are constantly tending towards it.

The whole quantity of industry annually employed in order to bring any commodity to market, naturally suits itself in this manner to the effectual demand. It naturally aims at bringing always that precise quantity thither which may be sufficient to supply, and no more than supply, that demand.

But in some employments the same quantity of industry will in different years produce very different quantities of commodities; while in others it will produce always the same, or very nearly the same. The same number of labourers in husbandry will, in different years, produce very different quantities of corn, wine, oil, hops, &c. But the same number of spinners and weavers will every year produce the same or very nearly the same quantity of linen and woollen cloth. It is only the average produce of the one species of industry which can be suited in any respect to the effectual demand; and as its actual produce is frequently much greater and frequently much less than its average produce, the quantity of the commodities brought to market will sometimes exceed a good deal, and sometimes fall short a good deal of the effectual demand. Even though that demand therefore should continue always the same, their market price will be liable to great fluctuations, will sometimes fall a good deal below, and sometimes rise a good deal above their natural price. In the other species of industry, the produce of equal quantities of labour being always the same or very nearly the same, it can be more exactly suited to the effectual demand. While that demand continues the same, therefore, the market price of the commodities is likely to do so too, and to be either altogether, or as nearly as can be judged of, the same with the natural price. That the price of linen and woollen cloth is liable neither to such frequent nor to such great variations as the price of corn, every man's experience will inform him. The price of the one species of commodities varies only with the variations in the demand: That of the other varies, not only with the variations in the demand, but with the much greater and more frequent variations in the quantity of what is brought to market in order to supply that demand.

The occasional and temporary fluctuations in the market price of any commodity fall chiefly upon those parts of its price which resolve themselves into wages and profit. That part which resolves itself into rent is less affected by them. A rent certain in money is not in the least affected by them either in its rate or in its value. A rent which consists either in a certain proportion or in a certain quantity of the rude produce, is no doubt affected in its yearly value by all the occasional and temporary fluctuations in the market price of that rude produce: but it is seldom affected by them in its yearly rate. In settling the terms of the lease, the landlord and farmer endeavour, according to their best judgment, to adjust that rate, not to the temporary and occasional, but to the average and ordinary price of the produce.

Such fluctuations affect both the value and the rate either of wages or of profit, according as the market happens to be either over-stocked or under-stocked with commodities or with labour; with work done, or with work to be done. A publick mourning raises the price of black cloth* (with which the market is almost always under-stocked upon such occasions) and augments the profits of the merchants who possess any considerable quantity of it. It has no effect upon the wages of the weavers. The market is under-stocked with commodities, not with labour; with work done, not with work to be done. It raises the wages of journeymen taylors. The market is here under-stocked with labour. There is an effectual demand for more labour, for more work to be done than can be had. It sinks the price of coloured silks and cloths, and thereby reduces the profits of the merchants who have any considerable quantity of them upon hand. It sinks too the wages of the workmen employed in preparing such commodities, for which all demand is stopped for six months, perhaps for a twelvemonth. The market is here over-stocked both with commodities and with labour.

But though the market price of every particular commodity is in this manner continually gravitating, if one may say so, towards the natural price, yet sometimes particular accidents, sometimes natural causes, and sometimes particular regulations of police,* may, in many commodities, keep up the market price, for a long time together, a good deal above the natural price.

When by an increase in the effectual demand, the market price of some particular commodity happens to rise a good deal above the natural price, those who employ their stocks in supplying that market are generally careful to conceal this change. If it was commonly known, their great profit would tempt so many new rivals to employ their stocks in the same way, that, the effectual demand being fully supplied, the market price would soon be reduced to the natural price, and perhaps for some time even below it. If the market is at a great distance from the residence of those who supply it, they may sometimes be able to keep the secret for several years together, and may so long enjoy their extraordinary profits without any new rivals. Secrets of this kind, however, it must be acknowledged, can seldom be long kept; and the extraordinary profit can last very little longer than they are kept.

Secrets in manufactures are capable of being longer kept than secrets in trade. A dyer who has found the means of producing a particular colour with materials which cost only half the price of those commonly made use of, may, with good management, enjoy the advantage of his discovery as long as he lives, and even leave it as a legacy to his posterity. His extraordinary gains arise from the high price which is paid for his private labour. They properly consist in the high wages of that labour. But as they are repeated upon every part of his stock, and as their whole amount bears, upon that account, a regular proportion to it, they are commonly considered as extraordinary profits of stock.

Such enhancements of the market price are evidently the effects of particular accidents, of which, however, the operation may sometimes last for many years together.

Some natural productions require such a singularity of soil and situation, that all the land in a great country, which is fit for producing them, may not be sufficient to supply the effectual demand. The whole quantity brought to market, therefore, may be disposed of to those who are willing to give more than what is sufficient to pay the rent of the land which produced them, together with the wages of the labour, and the profits of the stock which were employed in preparing and bringing them to market, according to their natural rates. Such commodities may continue for whole centuries together to be sold at this high price; and that part of it which resolves itself into the rent of land is in this case the part which is generally paid above its natural rate. The rent of the land which affords such singular and esteemed productions, like the rent of some vineyards in France of a peculiarly happy soil and situation, bears no regular proportion to the rent of other equally fertile and equally well-cultivated land in its neighbourhood. The wages of the labour and the profits of the stock employed in bringing such commodities to market, on the contrary, are seldom out of their natural proportion to those of the other employments of labour and stock in their neighbourhood.

Such enhancements of the market price are evidently the effect of natural causes which may hinder the effectual demand from ever being fully supplied, and which may continue, therefore, to operate for ever.

A monopoly* granted either to an individual or to a trading company has the same effect as a secret in trade or manufactures. The monopolists, by keeping the market constantly under-stocked, by never fully supplying the effectual demand, sell their commodities much above the natural price, and raise their emoluments, whether they consist in wages or profit, greatly above their natural rate.

The price of monopoly is upon every occasion the highest which can be got. The natural price, or the price of free competition, on the contrary, is the lowest which can be taken, not upon every occasion, indeed, but for any considerable time together. The one is upon every occasion the highest which can be squeezed out of the buyers, or which, it is supposed, they will consent to give: The other is the lowest which the sellers can commonly afford to take, and at the same time continue their business.

The exclusive privileges of corporations, statutes of apprenticeship,* and all those laws which restrain, in particular employments, the competition to a smaller number than might otherwise go into them, have the same tendency, though in a less degree. They are a sort of enlarged monopolies, and may frequently, for ages together and in whole classes of employments, keep up the market price of particular commodities above the natural price, and maintain both the wages of the labour and the profits of the stock employed about them somewhat above their natural rate.

Such enhancements of the market price may last as long as the regulations of police which give occasion to them.

The market price of any particular commodity, though it may continue long above, can seldom continue long below its natural price. Whatever part of it was paid below the natural rate, the persons whose interest it affected would immediately feel the loss, and would immediately withdraw either so much land, or so much labour, or so much stock, from being employed about it, that the quantity brought to market would soon be no more than sufficient to supply the effectual demand. Its market price, therefore, would soon rise to the natural price. This at least would be the case where there was perfect liberty.

The same statutes of apprenticeship and other corporation laws indeed, which, when a manufacture is in prosperity, enable the workman to raise his wages a good deal above their natural rate, sometimes oblige him, when it decays, to let them down a good deal below it. As in the one case they exclude many people from his employment, so in the other they exclude him from many employments. The effect of such regulations, however, is not near so durable in sinking the workman's wages below, as in raising them above their natural rate. Their operation in the one way may endure for many centuries, but in the other it can last no longer than the lives of some of the workmen who were bred to the business in the time of its prosperity. When they are gone, the number of those who are afterwards educated to the trade will naturally suit itself to the effectual demand. The police must be as violent as that of Indostan or antient Egypt (where every man was bound by a principle of religion to follow the occupation of his father, and was supposed to commit the most horrid sacrilege if he changed it for another) which can in any particular employment, and for several generations together, sink either the wages of labour or the profits of stock below their natural rate.

This is all that I think necessary to be observed at present concerning the deviations, whether occasional or permanent, of the market price of commodities from the natural price.

The natural price itself varies with the natural rate of each of its component parts, of wages, profit, and rent; and in every society this rate varies according to their circumstances, according to their riches or poverty, their advancing, stationary, or declining condition. I shall, in the four following chapters, endeavour to explain, as fully and distinctly as I can, the causes of those different variations.

First, I shall endeavour to explain what are the circumstances which naturally determine the rate of wages, and in what manner those circumstances are affected by the riches or poverty, by the advancing, stationary, or declining state of the society.

Secondly, I shall endeavour to show what are the circumstances which naturally determine the rate of profit, and in what manner too those circumstances are affected by the like variations in the state of the society.

Though pecuniary wages and profit are very different in the different employments of labour and stock; yet a certain proportion seems commonly to take place between both the pecuniary wages in all the different employments of labour, and the pecuniary profits in all the different employments of stock. This proportion, it will appear hereafter,* depends partly upon the nature of the different employments, and partly upon the different laws and policy of the society in which they are carried on. But though in many respects dependent upon the laws and policy, this proportion seems to be little affected by the riches or poverty of that society; by its advancing, stationary, or declining condition; but to remain the same or very nearly the same in all those different states. I shall, in the third place, endeavour to explain all the different circumstances which regulate this proportion.

In the fourth and last place, I shall endeavour to show what are the circumstances which regulate the rent of land, and which either raise or lower the real price of all the different substances which it produces.

CHAPTER VIII

Of the Wages of Labour

THE produce of labour constitutes the natural recompence or wages of labour.

In that original state of things, which precedes both the appropriation of land and the accumulation of stock, the whole produce of labour belongs to the labourer. He has neither landlord nor master to share with him.

Had this state continued, the wages of labour would have augmented with all those improvements in its productive powers, to which the division of labour gives occasion. All things would gradually have become cheaper. They would have been produced by a smaller quantity of labour; and as the commodities produced by equal quantities of labour would naturally in this state of things be exchanged for one another, they would have been purchased likewise with the produce of a smaller quantity.

But though all things would have become cheaper in reality, in appearance many things might have become dearer than before, or have been exchanged for a greater quantity of other goods. Let us suppose, for example, that in the greater part of employments the productive powers of labour had been improved to tenfold, or that a day's labour could produce ten times the quantity of work which it had done originally; but that in a particular employment they had been improved only to double, or that a day's labour could produce only twice the quantity of work which it had done before. In exchanging the produce of a day's labour in the greater part of employments, for that of a day's labour in this particular one, ten times the original quantity of work in them would purchase only twice the original quantity in it. Any particular quantity in it, therefore, a pound weight, for example, would appear to be five times dearer than before. In reality, however, it would be twice as cheap. Though it required five times the quantity of other goods to purchase it, it would require only half the quantity of labour either to purchase or to produce it. The acquisition, therefore, would be twice as easy as before.

But this original state of things, in which the labourer enjoyed the whole produce of his own labour, could not last beyond the first introduction of the appropriation of land and the accumulation of stock. It was at an end, therefore, long before the most considerable improvements were made in the productive powers of labour, and it would be to no purpose to trace farther what might have been its effects upon the recompence or wages of labour.

As soon as land becomes private property, the landlord demands a share of almost all the produce which the labourer can either raise, or collect from it. His rent makes the first deduction from the produce of the labour which is employed upon land.

It seldom happens that the person who tills the ground has wherewithal to maintain himself till he reaps the harvest. His maintenance is generally advanced to him from the stock of a master, the farmer who employs him, and who would have no interest to employ him, unless he was to share in the produce of his labour, or unless his stock was to be replaced to him with a profit. This profit makes a second deduction from the produce of the labour which is employed upon land.

The produce of almost all other labour is liable to the like deduction of profit. In all arts and manufactures the greater part of the workmen stand in need of a master to advance them the materials of their work, and their wages and maintenance till it be compleated. He shares in the produce of their labour, or in the value which it adds to the materials upon which it is bestowed; and in this share consists his profit.

It sometimes happens, indeed, that a single independent workman has stock sufficient both to purchase the materials of his work, and to maintain himself till it be compleated. He is both master and workman, and enjoys the whole produce of his own labour, or the whole value which it adds to the materials upon which it is bestowed. It includes what are usually two distinct revenues, belonging to two distinct persons, the profits of stock, and the wages of labour.

Such cases, however, are not very frequent, and in every part of Europe, twenty workmen serve under a master for one that is independent; and the wages of labour are every where understood to be, what they usually are, when the labourer is one person, and the owner of the stock which employs him another.

What are the common wages of labour depends every where upon the contract usually made between those two parties, whose interests are by no means the same. The workmen desire to get as much, the masters to give as little as possible. The former are disposed to combine in order to raise, the latter in order to lower the wages of labour.

It is not, however, difficult to foresee which of the two parties must, upon all ordinary occasions, have the advantage in the dispute, and force the other into a compliance with their terms. The masters, being fewer in number, can combine much more easily; and the law, besides, authorises, or at least does not prohibit their combinations,* while it prohibits those of the workmen. We have no acts of parliament against combining to lower the price of work; but many against combining to raise it. In all such disputes the masters can hold out much longer. A landlord, a farmer, a master manufacturer, or merchant, though they did not employ a single workman, could generally live a year or two upon the stocks which they have already acquired. Many workmen could not subsist a week, few could subsist a month, and scarce any a year without employment. In the long-run the workman may be as necessary to his master as his master is to him; but the necessity is not so immediate.

We rarely hear, it has been said, of the combinations of masters; though frequently of those of workmen. But whoever imagines, upon this account, that masters rarely combine, is as ignorant of the world as of the subject. Masters are always and every where in a sort of tacit, but constant and uniform combination, not to raise the wages of labour above their actual rate. To violate this combination is every where a most un-popular action, and a sort of reproach to a master among his neighbours and equals. We seldom, indeed, hear of this com-bination, because it is the usual, and one may say, the natural state of things which nobody ever hears of. Masters too some-times enter into particular combinations to sink the wages of labour even below this rate. These are always conducted with the utmost silence and secrecy, till the moment of execution, and when the workmen yield, as they sometimes do, without resistance, though severely felt by them, they are never heard of by other people. Such combinations, however, are frequently resisted by a contrary defensive combination of the workmen,* who sometimes too, without any provocation of this kind, combine of their own accord to raise the price of their labour. Their usual pretences are, sometimes the high price of provi-sions; sometimes the great profit which their masters make by their work. But whether their combinations be offensive or defensive, they are always abundantly heard of. In order to bring the point to a speedy decision, they have always recourse to the loudest clamour, and sometimes to the most shocking violence and outrage. They are desperate, and act with the folly and extravagance of desperate men, who must either starve, or frighten their masters into an immediate compliance with their demands. The masters upon these occasions are just as clamor-ous upon the other side, and never cease to call aloud for the assistance of the civil magistrate, and the rigorous execution of those laws which have been enacted with so much severity against the combinations of servants, labourers, and jour-neymen. The workmen, accordingly, very seldom derive any advantage from the violence of those tumultuous combinations, which, partly from the interposition of the civil magistrate, partly from the superior steadiness of the masters, partly from the necessity which the greater part of the workmen are under of submitting for the sake of present subsistence, generally end in nothing, but the punishment or ruin of the ringleaders.

But though in disputes with their workmen, masters must generally have the advantage, there is however a certain rate below which it seems impossible to reduce, for any considerable time, the ordinary wages even of the lowest species of labour.

A man must always live by his work, and his wages must at least be sufficient to maintain him. They must even upon most occasions be somewhat more; otherwise it would be impossible for him to bring up a family, and the race of such workmen could not last beyond the first generation. Mr. Cantillon* seems, upon this account, to suppose that the lowest species of common labourers must every where earn at least double their own maintenance, in order that one with another they may be enabled to bring up two children; the labour of the wife, on account of her necessary attendance on the children, being supposed no more than sufficient to provide for herself. But one-half the children born, it is computed, die before the age of manhood. The poorest labourers, therefore, according to this account, must, one with another, attempt to rear at least four children, in order that two may have an equal chance of living to that age. But the necessary maintenance of four children, it is supposed, may be nearly equal to that of one man. The labour of an able-bodied slave, the same author adds, is computed to be worth double his maintenance; and that of the meanest labourer, he thinks, cannot be worth less than that of an able-bodied slave. Thus far at least seems certain, that, in order to bring up a family, the labour of the husband and wife together must, even in the lowest species of common labour, be able to earn something more than what is precisely necessary for their own maintenance; but in what proportion, whether in that above-mentioned, or in any other, I shall not take upon me to determine.

There are certain circumstances, however, which sometimes give the labourers an advantage, and enable them to raise their wages considerably above this rate; evidently the lowest which is consistent with common humanity.

When in any country the demand for those who live by wages; labourers, journeymen, servants of every kind, is continually increasing; when every year furnishes employment for a greater number than had been employed the year before, the workmen have no occasion to combine in order to raise their wages. The scarcity of hands occasions a competition among masters, who bid against one another, in order to get workmen, and thus voluntarily break through the natural combination of masters not to raise wages.

The demand for those who live by wages, it is evident, cannot increase but in proportion to the increase of the funds which are destined for the payment of wages. These funds are of two kinds; first, the revenue which is over and above what is necessary for the maintenance; and, secondly, the stock which is over and above what is necessary for the employment of their masters.

When the landlord, annuitant,* or monied man, has a greater revenue than what he judges sufficient to maintain his own family, he employs either the whole or a part of the surplus in maintaining one or more menial servants. Increase this surplus, and he will naturally increase the number of those servants.

When an independent workman, such as a weaver or shoemaker, has got more stock than what is sufficient to purchase the materials of his own work, and to maintain himself till he can dispose of it, he naturally employs one or more journeymen with the surplus, in order to make a profit by their work. Increase this surplus, and he will naturally increase the number of his journeymen.

The demand for those who live by wages, therefore, necessarily increases with the increase of the revenue and stock of every country, and cannot possibly increase without it. The increase of revenue and stock is the increase of national wealth. The demand for those who live by wages, therefore, naturally increases with the increase of national wealth, and cannot possibly increase without it.

It is not the actual greatness of national wealth, but its continual increase, which occasions a rise in the wages of labour. It is not, accordingly, in the richest countries, but in the most thriving, or in those which are growing rich the fastest, that the wages of labour are highest. England is certainly, in the present times, a much richer country than any part of North America. The wages of labour, however, are much higher in North America than in any part of England. In the province of New York, common labourers earn[2] three shillings and sixpence currency, equal to two shillings sterling, a day; ship carpenters, ten shillings and sixpence currency, with a pint of rum worth sixpence sterling, equal in all to six shillings and sixpence sterling; house carpenters and bricklayers, eight shillings currency, equal to four shillings and sixpence sterling; journeymen taylors, five shillings currency, equal to about two shillings and ten pence sterling. These prices are all above the London price,* and wages are said to be as high in the other colonies as in New York. The price of provisions is every where in North America much lower than in England. A dearth has never been known there. In the worst seasons, they have always had a sufficiency for themselves, though less for exportation. If the money price of labour, therefore, be higher than it is any where in the mother country, its real price, the real command of the necessaries and conveniencies of life which it conveys to the labourer, must be higher in a still greater proportion.

But though North America is not yet so rich as England, it is much more thriving, and advancing with much greater rapidity to the further acquisition of riches. The most decisive mark of the prosperity of any country is the increase of the number of its inhabitants. In Great Britain, and most other European countries, they are not supposed to double in less than five hundred years. In the British colonies in North America,* it has been found, that they double in twenty or five-and-twenty years. Nor in the present times is this increase principally owing to the continual importation of new inhabitants, but to the great multiplication of the species. Those who live to old age, it is said, frequently see there from fifty to a hundred, and sometimes many more, descendants from their

---

[2] This was written in 1773, before the commencement of the present disturbances.

own body. Labour is there so well rewarded that a numerous family of children, instead of being a burthen is a source of opulence and prosperity to the parents. The labour of each child,* before it can leave their house, is computed to be worth a hundred pounds clear gain to them. A young widow with four or five young children, who, among the middling or inferior ranks of people in Europe, would have so little chance for a second husband, is there frequently courted as a sort of fortune. The value of children is the greatest of all encouragements to marriage. We cannot, therefore, wonder that the people in North America should generally marry very young. Notwithstanding the great increase occasioned by such early marriages, there is a continual complaint of the scarcity of hands in North America. The demand for labourers, the funds destined for maintaining them, increase, it seems, still faster than they can find labourers to employ.

Though the wealth of a country should be very great, yet if it has been long stationary, we must not expect to find the wages of labour very high in it. The funds destined for the payment of wages, the revenue and stock of its inhabitants, may be of the greatest extent, but if they have continued for several centuries of the same, or very nearly of the same extent, the number of labourers employed every year could easily supply, and even more than supply, the number wanted the following year. There could seldom be any scarcity of hands, nor could the masters be obliged to bid against one another in order to get them. The hands, on the contrary, would, in this case, naturally multiply beyond their employment. There would be a constant scarcity of employment, and the labourers would be obliged to bid against one another in order to get it. If in such a country the wages of labour had ever been more than sufficient to maintain the labourer, and to enable him to bring up a family, the competition of the labourers and the interest of the masters would soon reduce them to this lowest rate which is consistent with common humanity. China has been long one of the richest, that is, one of the most fertile, best cultivated, most industrious, and most populous countries in the world. It seems, however, to have been long stationary. Marco Polo, who visited it more than five hundred years ago, describes its cultivation, industry, and populousness, almost in the same terms in which they are described by travellers in the present times.* It had perhaps, even long before his time, acquired that full complement of riches which the nature of its laws and institutions permits it to acquire. The accounts of all travellers, inconsistent in many other respects, agree in the low wages of labour, and in the difficulty which a labourer finds in bringing up a family in China. If by digging the ground a whole day he can get what will purchase a small quantity of rice in the evening, he is contented. The condition of artificers is, if possible, still worse. Instead of waiting indolently in their work-houses, for the calls of their customers, as in Europe, they are continually running about the streets with the tools of their respective trades, offering their service, and as it were begging employment. The poverty of the lower ranks of people in China far surpasses that of the most beggarly nations in Europe. In the neighbourhood of Canton many hundred, it is commonly said, many thousand families have no habitation on the land, but live constantly in little fishing boats upon the rivers and canals. The subsistence which they find there is so scanty that they are eager to fish up the nastiest garbage thrown overboard from any European ship. Any carrion, the carcase of a dead dog or cat, for example, though half putrid and stinking, is as welcome to them as the most wholesome food to the people of other countries. Marriage is encouraged in China, not by the profitableness of children, but by the liberty of destroying them. In all great towns several are every night exposed in the street, or drowned like puppies in the water. The performance of this horrid office is even said to be the avowed business by which some people earn their subsistence.

China, however, though it may perhaps stand still, does not seem to go backwards. Its towns are no-where deserted by their inhabitants. The lands which had once been cultivated are no-where neglected. The same or very nearly the same annual labour must therefore continue to be performed, and the funds destined for maintaining it must not, consequently, be sensibly diminished. The lowest class of labourers, therefore, notwithstanding their scanty subsistence, must some way or another make shift to continue their race so far as to keep up their usual numbers.

But it would be otherwise in a country where the funds destined for the maintenance of labour were sensibly decaying. Every year the demand for servants and labourers would, in all the different classes of employments, be less than it had been the year before. Many who had been bred in the superior classes, not being able to find employment in their own business, would be glad to seek it in the lowest. The lowest class being not only overstocked with its own workmen, but with the overflowings of all the other classes, the competition for employment would be so great in it, as to reduce the wages of labour to the most miserable and scanty subsistence of the labourer. Many would not be able to find employment even upon these hard terms, but would either starve, or be driven to seek a subsistence either by begging, or by the perpetration perhaps of the greatest enormities. Want, famine, and mortality would immediately prevail in that class, and from thence extend themselves to all the superior classes, till the number of inhabitants in the country was reduced to what could easily be maintained by the revenue and stock which remained in it, and which had escaped either the tyranny or calamity which had destroyed the rest. This perhaps is nearly the present state of Bengal, and of some other of the English settlements in the East Indies.* In a fertile country which had before been much depopulated, where subsistence, consequently, should not be very difficult, and where, notwithstanding, three or four hundred thousand people die of hunger in one year, we may be assured that the funds destined for the maintenance of the labouring poor are fast decaying. The difference between the genius of the British constitution which protects and governs North America, and that of the mercantile company which oppresses and domineers in the East Indies, cannot perhaps be better illustrated than by the different state of those countries.

The liberal reward of labour, therefore, as it is the necessary effect, so it is the natural symptom of increasing national wealth. The scanty maintenance of the labouring poor, on the other hand, is the natural symptom that things are at a stand, and their starving condition that they are going fast backwards.

In Great Britain the wages of labour* seem, in the present times, to be evidently more than what is precisely necessary to enable the labourer to bring up a family. In order to satisfy ourselves upon this point it will not be necessary to enter into any tedious or doubtful calculation of what may be the lowest sum upon which it is possible to do this. There are many plain symptoms that the wages of labour are no-where in this country regulated by this lowest rate which is consistent with common humanity.

First, in almost every part of Great Britain there is a distinction, even in the lowest species of labour, between summer and winter wages. Summer wages are always highest. But on account of the extraordinary expence of fewel, the maintenance of a family is most expensive in winter. Wages, therefore, being highest when this expence is lowest, it seems evident that they are not regulated by what is necessary for this expence; but by the quantity and supposed value of the work. A labourer, it may be said indeed, ought to save part of his summer wages in order to defray his winter expence; and that through the whole year they do not exceed what is necessary to maintain his family through the whole year. A slave, however, or one absolutely dependent on us for immediate subsistence, would not be treated in this manner. His daily subsistence would be proportioned to his daily necessities.

Secondly, the wages of labour do not in Great Britain fluctuate with the price of provisions. These vary every-where from year to year, frequently from month to month. But in many places the money price of labour remains uniformly the same sometimes for half a century together. If in these places, therefore, the labouring poor can maintain their families in dear years, they must be at their ease in times of moderate plenty, and in affluence in those of extraordinary cheapness. The high price of provisions during these ten years past has not in many parts of the kingdom been accompanied with any sensible rise in the money price of labour. It has, indeed, in some; owing probably more to the increase of the demand for labour, than to that of the price of provisions.

Thirdly, as the price of provisions varies more from year to year than the wages of labour, so, on the other hand, the wages of labour vary more from place to place than the price of provisions. The prices of bread and butcher's meat are generally the same or very nearly the same through the greater part of the united kingdom. These and most other things which are sold by retail, the way in which the labouring poor buy all things, are generally fully as cheap or cheaper in great towns than in the remoter parts of the country, for reasons which I shall have occasion to explain hereafter.* But the wages of labour in a great town and its neighbourhood are frequently a fourth or a fifth part, twenty or five-and-twenty per cent. higher than at a few miles distance. Eighteen pence a day may be reckoned the common price of labour in London and its neighbourhood. At a few miles distance it falls to fourteen and fifteen pence. Ten pence may be reckoned its price in Edinburgh and its neighbourhood. At a few miles distance it falls to eight pence, the usual price of common labour through the greater part of the low country of Scotland, where it varies a good deal less than in England. Such a difference of prices, which it seems is not always sufficient to transport a man from one parish to another, would necessarily occasion so great a transportation of the most bulky commodities, not only from one parish to another, but from one end of the kingdom, almost from one end of the world to the other, as would soon reduce them more nearly to a level. After all that has been said of the levity and inconstancy of human nature, it appears evidently from experience that a man is of all sorts of luggage the most difficult to be transported. If the labouring poor, therefore, can maintain their families in those parts of the kingdom where the price of labour is lowest, they must be in affluence where it is highest.

Fourthly, the variations in the price of labour not only do not correspond either in place or time with those in the price of provisions, but they are frequently quite opposite.

Grain, the food of the common people, is dearer in Scotland than in England, whence Scotland receives almost every year very large supplies. But English corn must be sold dearer in Scotland, the country to which it is brought, than in England, the country from which it comes; and in proportion to its quality it cannot be sold dearer in Scotland than the Scotch corn that comes to the same market in competition with it. The quality of grain depends chiefly upon the quantity of flour or meal which it yields at the mill, and in this respect English grain is so much superior to the Scotch, that, though often dearer in appearance, or in proportion to the measure of its bulk, it is generally cheaper in reality, or in proportion to its quality, or even to the measure of its weight. The price of labour, on the contrary, is dearer in England than in Scotland. If the labouring poor, therefore, can maintain their families in the one part of the united kingdom, they must be in affluence in the other. Oatmeal* indeed supplies the common people in Scotland with the greatest and the best part of their food, which is in general much inferior to that of their neighbours of the same rank in England. This difference, however, in the mode of their subsistence is not the cause, but the effect of the difference in their wages; though, by a strange misapprehension, I have frequently heard it represented as the cause. It is not because one man keeps a coach while his neighbour walks a-foot, that the one is rich and the other poor; but because the one is rich he keeps a coach, and because the other is poor he walks a-foot.

During the course of the last century, taking one year with another, grain was dearer in both parts of the united kingdom than during that of the present. This is a matter of fact which cannot now admit of any reasonable doubt; and the proof of it is, if possible, still more decisive with regard to Scotland than with regard to England. It is in Scotland supported by the evidence of the publick fiars,* annual valuations made upon oath, according to the actual state of the markets, of all the different sorts of grain in every different county of Scotland. If such direct proof could require any collateral evidence to confirm it, I would observe that this has likewise been the case in France, and probably in most other parts of Europe. With regard to France there is the clearest proof. But though it is certain that in both parts of the united kingdom grain was somewhat dearer in the last century than in the present, it is equally certain that labour was much cheaper. If the labouring poor, therefore, could bring up their families then, they must be much more at their ease now. In the last century, the most usual day-wages of common labour through the greater part of Scotland were sixpence in summer and five-pence in winter. Three shillings a week, the same price very nearly, still continues to be paid in some parts of the Highlands and Western Islands. Through the greater part of the low country the most usual wages of common labour are now eight-pence a day; ten-pence, sometimes a shilling about Edinburgh, in the counties which border upon England, probably on account of that neighbourhood, and in a few other places where there has lately been a considerable rise in the demand for labour, about Glasgow, Carron, Ayrshire, &c.* In England the improvements of agriculture, manufactures and commerce began much earlier than in Scotland. The demand for labour, and consequently its price, must necessarily have increased with those improvements. In the last century, accordingly, as well as in the present, the wages of labour were higher in England than in Scotland. They have risen too considerably since that time, though, on account of the greater variety of wages paid there in different places, it is more difficult to ascertain how much. In 1614, the pay of a foot soldier was the same as in the present times, eight pence a day.* When it was first established it would naturally be regulated by the usual wages of common labourers, the rank of people from which foot soldiers are commonly drawn. Lord Chief Justice Hales, who wrote in the

time of Charles II. computes the necessary expence of a labourer's family, consisting of six persons, the father and mother,
two children able to do something, and two not able, at ten
shillings a week, or twenty-six pounds a year. If they cannot
earn this by their labour, they must make it up, he supposes,
either by begging or stealing.* He appears to have enquired very
carefully into this subject.[3] In 1688, Mr. Gregory King, whose
skill in political arithmetick is so much extolled by Doctor
Davenant,* computed the ordinary income of labourers and
out-servants to be fifteen pounds a year to a family, which he
supposed to consist, one with another, of three and a half
persons. His calculation, therefore, though different in appearance, corresponds very nearly at bottom with that of judge
Hales. Both suppose the weekly expence of such families to be
about twenty pence a head. Both the pecuniary income and
expence of such families have increased considerably since that
time through the greater part of the kingdom; in some places
more, and in some less; though perhaps scarce any where so
much as some exaggerated accounts of the present wages of
labour have lately represented them to the publick. The price of
labour, it must be observed, cannot be ascertained very accur-
ately any where, different prices being often paid at the same
place and for the same sort of labour, not only according to the
different abilities of the workmen, but according to the easiness
or hardness of the masters. Where wages are not regulated by
law, all that we can pretend to determine is what are the most
usual; and experience seems to show that law can never regulate
them properly, though it has often pretended to do so.

The real recompence of labour, the real quantity of the
necessaries and conveniencies of life which it can procure to
the labourer, has, during the course of the present century,
increased perhaps in a still greater proportion than its money
price. Not only grain has become somewhat cheaper, but many

---

[3] See his scheme for the maintenance of the Poor, in Burn's History of the
Poor-laws. [R. Burn, *History of the Poor Laws* (London, 1764), 135–60.] [Camp-
bell and Skinner]

other things from which the industrious poor derive an agreeable and wholesome variety of food, have become a great deal cheaper. Potatoes, for example, do not at present, through the greater part of the kingdom, cost half the price which they used to do thirty or forty years ago. The same thing may be said of turnips, carrots, cabbages; things which were formerly never raised but by the spade, but which are now commonly raised by the plough. All sort of garden stuff too has become cheaper. The greater part of the apples and even of the onions consumed in Great Britain were in the last century imported from Flanders. The great improvements in the coarser manufactures of both linen and woollen cloth furnish the labourers with cheaper and better cloathing; and those in the manufactures of the coarser metals, with cheaper and better instruments of trade, as well as with many agreeable and convenient pieces of houshold furniture. Soap, salt, candles, leather, and fermented liquors have, indeed, become a good deal dearer; chiefly from the taxes which have been laid upon them.* The quantity of these, however, which the labouring poor are under any necessity of consuming, is so very small, that the increase in their price does not compensate the diminution in that of so many other things. The common complaint that luxury extends itself even to the lowest ranks of the people,* and that the labouring poor will not now be contented with the same food, cloathing and lodging which satisfied them in former times, may convince us that it is not the money price of labour only, but its real recompence, which has augmented.

Is this improvement in the circumstances of the lower ranks of the people to be regarded as an advantage or as an inconveniency to the society? The answer seems at first sight abundantly plain. Servants, labourers and workmen of different kinds, make up the far greater part of every great political society. But what improves the circumstances of the greater part can never be regarded as an inconveniency to the whole. No society can surely be flourishing and happy, of which the far greater part of the members are poor and miserable. It is but equity, besides, that they who feed, cloath and lodge the whole body of the people, should have such a share of the produce of their own labour as to be themselves tolerably well fed, cloathed and lodged.

Poverty, though it no doubt discourages, does not always prevent marriage. It seems even to be favourable to generation. A half-starved Highland woman frequently bears more than twenty children, while a pampered fine lady is often incapable of bearing any, and is generally exhausted by two or three. Barrenness, so frequent among women of fashion, is very rare among those of inferior station. Luxury in the fair sex, while it enflames perhaps the passion for enjoyment, seems always to weaken, and frequently to destroy altogether, the powers of generation.*

But poverty, though it does not prevent the generation, is extremely unfavourable to the rearing of children. The tender plant is produced, but in so cold a soil and so severe a climate, soon withers and dies. It is not uncommon, I have been frequently told, in the Highlands of Scotland for a mother who has borne twenty children not to have two alive. Several officers of great experience have assured me, that so far from recruiting their regiment, they have never been able to supply it with drums and fifes from all the soldiers children that were born in it. A greater number of fine children, however, is seldom seen anywhere than about a barrack of soldiers. Very few of them, it seems, arrive at the age of thirteen or fourteen. In some places one half the children born die before they are four years of age; in many places before they are seven; and in almost all places before they are nine or ten. This great mortality, however, will every where be found chiefly among the children of the common people, who cannot afford to tend them with the same care as those of better station. Though their marriages are generally more fruitful than those of people of fashion, a smaller proportion of their children arrive at maturity. In foundling hospitals, and among the children brought up by parish charities, the mortality is still greater than among those of the common people.*

Every species of animals naturally multiplies in proportion to the means of their subsistence, and no species can ever multiply beyond it.* But in civilized society it is only among the inferior ranks of people that the scantiness of subsistence can set limits to the further multiplication of the human species; and it can do so in no other way than by destroying a great part of the children which their fruitful marriages produce.

The liberal reward of labour, by enabling them to provide better for their children, and consequently to bring up a greater number, naturally tends to widen and extend those limits. It deserves to be remarked too, that it necessarily does this as nearly as possible in the proportion which the demand for labour requires. If this demand is continually increasing, the reward of labour must necessarily encourage in such a manner the marriage and multiplication of labourers,* as may enable them to supply that continually increasing demand by a continually increasing population. If the reward should at any time be less than what was requisite for this purpose, the deficiency of hands would soon raise it; and if it should at any time be more, their excessive multiplication would soon lower it to this necessary rate. The market would be so much under-stocked with labour in the one case, and so much over-stocked in the other, as would soon force back its price to that proper rate which the circumstances of the society required. It is in this manner that the demand for men, like that for any other commodity, necessarily regulates the production of men; quickens it when it goes on too slowly, and stops it when it advances too fast. It is this demand which regulates and determines the state of propagation in all the different countries of the world, in North America, in Europe, and in China; which renders it rapidly progressive in the first, slow and gradual in the second, and altogether stationary in the last.

The wear and tear of a slave, it has been said, is at the expence of his master; but that of a free servant is at his own expence. The wear and tear of the latter, however, is, in reality, as much at the expence of his master as that of the former.

The wages paid to journeymen and servants of every kind must be such as may enable them, one with another, to continue the race of journeymen and servants, according as the increasing, diminishing, or stationary demand of the society may happen to require. But though the wear and tear of a free servant be equally at the expence of his master, it generally costs him much less than that of a slave. The fund destined for replacing or repairing, if I may say so, the wear and tear of the slave, is commonly managed by a negligent master or careless overseer. That destined for performing the same office with regard to the free man, is managed by the free man himself. The disorders which generally prevail in the œconomy of the rich, naturally introduce themselves into the management of the former: The strict frugality and parsimonious attention of the poor as naturally establish themselves in that of the latter. Under such different management, the same purpose must require very different degrees of expence to execute it. It appears, accordingly, from the experience of all ages and nations, I believe, that the work done by freemen comes cheaper in the end than that performed by slaves.* It is found to do so even at Boston, New York, and Philadelphia, where the wages of common labour are so very high.

The liberal reward of labour, therefore, as it is the effect of increasing wealth, so it is the cause of increasing population. To complain of it is to lament over the necessary effect and cause of the greatest publick prosperity.

It deserves to be remarked, perhaps, that it is in the progressive state, while the society is advancing to the further acquisition, rather than when it has acquired its full complement of riches, that the condition of the labouring poor, of the great body of the people, seems to be the happiest and the most comfortable. It is hard in the stationary, and miserable in the declining state. The progressive state is in reality the chearful and the hearty state to all the different orders of the society. The stationary is dull; the declining, melancholy.

The liberal reward of labour,* as it encourages the propagation, so it increases the industry of the common people. The

wages of labour are the encouragement of industry, which, like
every other human quality, improves in proportion to the
encouragement it receives. A plentiful subsistence increases the
bodily strength of the labourer, and the comfortable hope of
bettering his condition, and of ending his days perhaps in
ease and plenty, animates him to exert that strength to the
utmost. Where wages are high, accordingly, we shall always
find the workmen more active, diligent, and expeditious, than
where they are low; in England, for example, than in Scotland;
in the neighbourhood of great towns, than in remote country
places. Some workmen, indeed, when they can earn in four
days what will maintain them through the week, will be idle
the other three. This, however, is by no means the case with
the greater part. Workmen, on the contrary, when they are
liberally paid by the piece, are very apt to over-work themselves, and to ruin their health and constitution in a few years.
A carpenter in London, and in some other places, is not
supposed to last in his utmost vigour above eight years. Something of the same kind happens in many other trades, in which
the workmen are paid by the piece; as they generally are in
manufactures, and even in country labour, wherever wages are
higher than ordinary. Almost every class of artificers is subject
to some peculiar infirmity occasioned by excessive application
to their peculiar species of work. Ramuzzini, an eminent Italian
physician, has written a particular book concerning such diseases.* We do not reckon our soldiers the most industrious set
of people among us. Yet when soldiers have been employed in
some particular sorts of work, and liberally paid by the piece,
their officers have frequently been obliged to stipulate with the
undertaker, that they should not be allowed to earn above a
certain sum every day, according to the rate at which they were
paid. Till this stipulation was made, mutual emulation and the
desire of greater gain, frequently prompted them to over-work
themselves, and to hurt their health by excessive labour. Excessive application during four days of the week, is frequently
the real cause of the idleness of the other three, so much and
so loudly complained of. Great labour, either of mind or body,

continued for several days together, is in most men naturally followed by a great desire of relaxation, which, if not restrained by force or by some strong necessity, is almost irresistible. It is the call of nature, which requires to be relieved by some indulgence, sometimes of ease only, but sometimes too of dissipation and diversion. If it is not complied with, the consequences are often dangerous, and sometimes fatal, and such as almost always, sooner or later, bring on the peculiar infirmity of the trade. If masters would always listen to the dictates of reason and humanity, they have frequently occasion rather to moderate, than to animate the application of many of their workmen. It will be found, I believe, in every sort of trade, that the man who works so moderately, as to be able to work constantly, not only preserves his health the longest, but, in the course of the year, executes the greatest quantity of work.

In cheap years, it is pretended, workmen are generally more idle, and in dear ones more industrious than ordinary. A plentiful subsistence, therefore, it has been concluded, relaxes, and a scanty one quickens their industry. That a little more plenty than ordinary may render some workmen idle, cannot well be doubted; but that it should have this effect upon the greater part, or that men in general should work better when they are ill fed than when they are well fed, when they are disheartened than when they are in good spirits, when they are frequently sick than when they are generally in good health, seems not very probable. Years of dearth, it is to be observed, are generally among the common people years of sickness and mortality, which cannot fail to diminish the produce of their industry.

In years of plenty, servants frequently leave their masters, and trust their subsistence to what they can make by their own industry. But the same cheapness of provisions, by increasing the fund which is destined for the maintenance of servants, encourages masters, farmers especially, to employ a greater number. Farmers upon such occasions expect more profit from their corn by maintaining a few more labouring servants, than by selling it at a low price in the market. The demand for servants increases, while the number of those who offer to supply that demand diminishes. The price of labour, therefore, frequently rises in cheap years.

In years of scarcity, the difficulty and uncertainty of subsistence make all such people eager to return to service. But the high price of provisions, by diminishing the funds destined for the maintenance of servants, disposes masters rather to diminish than to increase the number of those they have. In dear years too, poor independent workmen frequently consume the little stocks with which they had used to supply themselves with the materials of their work, and are obliged to become journeymen for subsistence. More people want employment than can easily get it; many are willing to take it upon lower terms than ordinary, and the wages of both servants and journeymen frequently sink in dear years.

Masters of all sorts, therefore, frequently make better bargains with their servants in dear than in cheap years, and find them more humble and dependent in the former than in the latter. They naturally, therefore, commend the former as more favourable to industry. Landlords and farmers, besides, two of the largest classes of masters, have another reason for being pleased with dear years. The rents of the one and the profits of the other depend very much upon the price of provisions. Nothing can be more absurd, however, than to imagine that men in general should work less when they work for themselves, than when they work for other people. A poor independent workman will generally be more industrious than even a journeyman who works by the piece. The one enjoys the whole produce of his own industry; the other shares it with his master. The one, in his separate independent state, is less liable to the temptations of bad company, which in large manufactories so frequently ruin the morals of the other.* The superiority of the independent workman over those servants who are hired by the month or by the year, and whose wages and maintenance are the same whether they do much or do little, is likely to be still greater. Cheap years tend to increase the proportion of independent workmen to journeymen and servants of all kinds, and dear years to diminish it.

A French author of great knowledge and ingenuity, Mr. Messance, receiver of the tailles in the election of St. Etienne, endeavours to show that the poor do more work in cheap than in dear years, by comparing the quantity and value of the goods made upon those different occasions in three different manufactures; one of coarse woollens carried on at Elbeuf; one of linen, and another of silk, both which extend through the whole generality of Rouen.* It appears from his account, which is copied from the registers of the publick offices, that the quantity and value of the goods made in all those three manufactures has generally been greater in cheap than in dear years; and that it has always been greatest in the cheapest, and least in the dearest years. All the three seem to be stationary manufactures, or which, though their produce may vary somewhat from year to year, are upon the whole neither going backwards nor forwards.

The manufacture of linen in Scotland, and that of coarse woollens in the west riding of Yorkshire, are growing manufactures,* of which the produce is generally, though with some variations, increasing both in quantity and value. Upon examining, however, the accounts which have been published of their annual produce, I have not been able to observe that its variations have had any sensible connection with the dearness or cheapness of the seasons. In 1740, a year of great scarcity,* both manufactures, indeed, appear to have declined very considerably. But in 1756, another year of great scarcity, the Scotch manufacture made more than ordinary advances. The Yorkshire manufacture, indeed, declined, and its produce did not rise to what it had been in 1755 till 1766, after the repeal of the American stamp act.* In that and the following year it greatly exceeded what it had ever been before, and it has continued to advance ever since.

The produce of all great manufactures for distant sale must necessarily depend, not so much upon the dearness or cheapness of the seasons in the countries where they are carried on, as upon the circumstances which affect the demand in the countries where they are consumed; upon peace or war, upon the prosperity or declension of other rival manufactures, and upon the good or bad humour of their principal customers. A great part of the extraordinary work, besides, which is probably done in cheap years, never enters the publick registers of manufactures. The men servants who leave their masters become independent labourers. The women return to their parents, and commonly spin in order to make cloaths for themselves and their families. Even the independent workmen do not always work for publick sale, but are employed by some of their neighbours in manufactures for family use. The produce of their labour, therefore, frequently makes no figure in those publick registers of which the records are sometimes published with so much parade, and from which our merchants and manufacturers would often vainly pretend to announce the prosperity or declension of the greatest empires.

Though the variations in the price of labour, not only do not always correspond with those in the price of provisions, but are frequently quite opposite, we must not, upon this account, imagine that the price of provisions has no influence upon that of labour. The money price of labour is necessarily regulated by two circumstances; the demand for labour, and the price of the necessaries and conveniencies of life. The demand for labour, according as it happens to be increasing, stationary, or declining, or to require an increasing, stationary, or declining population, determines the quantity of the necessaries and conveniencies of life which must be given to the labourer; and the money price of labour is determined by what is requisite for purchasing this quantity. Though the money price of labour, therefore, is sometimes high where the price of provisions is low, it would be still higher, the demand continuing the same, if the price of provisions was high.

It is because the demand for labour increases in years of sudden and extraordinary plenty, and diminishes in those of sudden and extraordinary scarcity, that the money price of labour sometimes rises in the one, and sinks in the other.

In a year of sudden and extraordinary plenty, there are funds in the hands of many of the employers of industry, sufficient to maintain and employ a greater number of industrious people than had been employed the year before; and this extraordinary number cannot always be had. Those masters, therefore, who want more workmen, bid against one another, in order to get them, which sometimes raises both the real and the money price of their labour.

The contrary of this happens in a year of sudden and extraordinary scarcity. The funds destined for employing industry are less than they had been the year before. A considerable number of people are thrown out of employment, who bid against one another, in order to get it, which sometimes lowers both the real and the money price of labour. In 1740, a year of extraordinary scarcity, many people were willing to work for bare subsistence. In the succeeding years of plenty, it was more difficult to get labourers and servants.

The scarcity of a dear year, by diminishing the demand for labour, tends to lower its price, as the high price of provisions tends to raise it. The plenty of a cheap year, on the contrary, by increasing the demand, tends to raise the price of labour, as the cheapness of provisions tends to lower it. In the ordinary variations of the price of provisions, those two opposite causes seem to counterbalance one another; which is probably in part the reason why the wages of labour are every-where so much more steady and permanent than the price of provisions.

The increase in the wages of labour necessarily increases the price of many commodities, by increasing that part of it which resolves itself into wages, and so far tends to diminish their consumption both at home and abroad. The same cause, however, which raises the wages of labour, the increase of stock, tends to increase its productive powers, and to make a smaller quantity of labour produce a greater quantity of work. The owner of the stock which employs a great number of labourers, necessarily endeavours, for his own advantage, to make such a proper division and distribution of employment, that they may be enabled to produce the greatest quantity of work possible.

For the same reason, he endeavours to supply them with the best machinery which either he or they can think of. What takes place among the labourers in a particular workhouse, takes place, for the same reason, among those of a great society. The greater their number, the more they naturally divide themselves into different classes and subdivisions of employment. More heads are occupied in inventing the most proper machinery for executing the work of each, and it is, therefore, more likely to be invented. There are many commodities, therefore, which, in consequence of these improvements, come to be produced by so much less labour than before, that the increase of its price is more than compensated by the diminution of its quantity.

CHAPTER IX

Of the Profits of Stock

THE rise and fall in the profits of stock depend upon the same causes with the rise and fall in the wages of labour, the increasing or declining state of the wealth of the society; but those causes affect the one and the other very differently.

The increase of stock, which raises wages, tends to lower profit. When the stocks of many rich merchants are turned into the same trade, their mutual competition naturally tends to lower its profit; and when there is a like increase of stock in all the different trades carried on in the same society, the same competition must produce the same effect in them all.

It is not easy, it has already been observed, to ascertain what are the average wages of labour even in a particular place, and at a particular time. We can, even in this case, seldom determine more than what are the most usual wages. But even this can seldom be done with regard to the profits of stock. Profit is so very fluctuating, that the person who carries on a particular trade cannot always tell you himself what is the average of his annual profit. It is affected, not only by every variation of price in the commodities which he deals in, but by the good or bad fortune both of his rivals and of his customers, and by a thousand other accidents to which goods when carried either by sea or by land, or even when stored in a warehouse, are liable. It varies, therefore, not only from year to year, but from day to day, and almost from hour to hour. To ascertain what is the average profit of all the different trades carried on in a great kingdom, must be much more difficult; and to judge of what it may have been formerly, or in remote periods of time, with any degree of precision, must be altogether impossible.

But though it may be impossible to determine, with any degree of precision, what are or were the average profits of stock, either in the present, or in antient times, some notion may be formed of them from the interest of money. It may be laid down as a maxim, that wherever a great deal can be made by the use of money, a great deal will commonly be given for the use of it; and that wherever little can be made by it, less will commonly be given for it. According, therefore, as the usual market rate of interest varies in any country, we may be assured that the ordinary profits of stock must vary with it, must sink as it sinks, and rise as it rises. The progress of interest, therefore, may lead us to form some notion of the progress of profit. . . .

In our North American and West Indian colonies, not only the wages of labour, but the interest of money, and consequently the profits of stock, are higher than in England. In the different colonies both the legal and the market rate of interest run from six to eight per cent. High wages of labour and high profits of stock, however, are things, perhaps, which scarce ever go together, except in the peculiar circumstances of new colonies. A new colony must always for some time be more under-stocked in proportion to the extent of its territory, and more under-peopled in proportion to the extent of its stock, than the greater part of other countries. They have more land than they have stock to cultivate. What they have, therefore, is applied to the cultivation only of what is most fertile and most favourably situated, the lands near the sea shore, and along the banks of navigable rivers. Such land too is frequently purchased at a price below the value even of its natural produce. Stock employed in the purchase and improvement of such lands must yield a very large profit, and consequently afford to pay a very large interest. Its rapid accumulation in so profitable an employment enables the planter to increase the number of his hands faster than he can find them in a new settlement. Those whom he can find, therefore, are very liberally rewarded. As the colony increases, the profits of stock gradually diminish. When the most fertile and best situated lands have been all occupied, less profit can be made by the cultivation of what is inferior both in soil and situation, and less interest can be afforded for the stock which is so employed.

In the greater part of our colonies, accordingly, both the legal and the market rate of interest have been considerably reduced during the course of the present century. As riches, improvement, and population have increased, interest has declined. The wages of labour do not sink with the profits of stock. The demand for labour increases with the increase of stock whatever be its profits; and after these are diminished, stock may not only continue to increase, but to increase much faster than before. It is with industrious nations who are advancing in the acquisition of riches, as with industrious individuals. A great stock, though with small profits, generally increases faster than a small stock with great profits. Money, says the proverb, makes money. When you have got a little, it is often easy to get more. The great difficulty is to get that little. The connection between the increase of stock and that of industry, or of the demand for useful labour, has partly been explained already, but will be explained more fully hereafter* in treating of the accumulation of stock. . . .

In a country which had acquired that full complement of riches which the nature of its soil and climate, and its situation with respect to other countries allowed it to acquire; which could, therefore, advance no further, and which was not going backwards, both the wages of labour and the profits of stock would probably be very low. In a country fully peopled in proportion to what either its territory could maintain or its stock employ, the competition for employment would necessarily be so great as to reduce the wages of labour to what was barely sufficient to keep up the number of labourers, and, the country being already fully peopled, that number could never be augmented. In a country fully stocked in proportion to all the business it had to transact, as great a quantity of stock would be employed in every particular branch as the nature and extent of the trade would admit. The competition, therefore, would everywhere be as great, and consequently the ordinary profit as low as possible.

But perhaps no country has ever yet arrived at this degree of opulence. China seems to have been long stationary,* and had probably long ago acquired that full complement of riches which is consistent with the nature of its laws and institutions. But this complement may be much inferior to what, with other laws and institutions, the nature of its soil, climate, and situation might admit of. A country which neglects or despises foreign commerce, and which admits the vessels of foreign nations into one or two of its ports only, cannot transact the same quantity of business which it might do with different laws and institutions. In a country too, where, though the rich or the owners of large capitals enjoy a good deal of security, the poor or the owners of small capitals enjoy scarce any, but are liable, under the pretence of justice, to be pillaged and plundered at any time by the inferior mandarines,* the quantity of stock employed in all the different branches of business transacted within it, can never be equal to what the nature and extent of that business might admit. In every different branch, the oppression of the poor must establish the monopoly of the rich, who, by engrossing the whole trade to themselves, will be able to make very large profits. Twelve per cent. accordingly is said to be the common interest of money in China, and the ordinary profits of stock must be sufficient to afford this large interest.

A defect in the law may sometimes raise the rate of interest considerably above what the condition of the country, as to wealth or poverty, would require. When the law does not enforce the performance of contracts, it puts all borrowers nearly upon the same footing with bankrupts or people of doubtful credit in better regulated countries. The uncertainty of recovering his money makes the lender exact the same usurious interest which is usually required from bankrupts. Among the barbarous nations who over-run the western provinces of the Roman empire, the performance of contracts was left for many ages to the faith of the contracting parties. The courts of justice of their kings seldom intermeddled in it. The high rate of interest which took place in those antient times may perhaps be partly accounted for from this cause.

When the law prohibits interest altogether, it does not prevent it. Many people must borrow, and nobody will lend without such a consideration for the use of their money as is suitable, not only to what can be made by the use of it, but to the difficulty and danger of evading the law. The high rate of interest among all Mahometan nations is accounted for by Mr. Montesquieu, not from their poverty, but partly from this, and partly from the difficulty of recovering the money.

The lowest ordinary rate of profit must always be something more than what is sufficient to compensate the occasional losses to which every employment of stock is exposed. It is this surplus only which is neat or clear profit. What is called gross profit comprehends frequently, not only this surplus, but what is retained for compensating such extraordinary losses. The interest which the borrower can afford to pay is in proportion to the clear profit only.

The lowest ordinary rate of interest must, in the same manner, be something more than sufficient to compensate the occasional losses to which lending, even with tolerable prudence, is exposed. Were it not more, charity or friendship could be the only motives for lending.

In a country which had acquired its full complement of riches, where in every particular branch of business there was the greatest quantity of stock that could be employed in it, as the ordinary rate of clear profit would be very small, so that usual market rate of interest which could be afforded out of it, would be so low as to render it impossible for any but the very wealthiest people to live upon the interest of their money. All people of small or middling fortunes would be obliged to superintend themselves the employment of their own stocks. It would be necessary that almost every man should be a man of business, or engage in some sort of trade. The province of Holland* seems to be approaching near to this state. It is there unfashionable not to be a man of business. Necessity makes it usual for almost every man to be so, and custom every where regulates fashion. As it is ridiculous not to dress, so is it, in some measure, not to be employed, like other people. As a man of a civil profession seems aukward in a camp or a garrison, and is even in some danger of being despised there, so does an idle man among men of business. . . .

In reality high profits tend much more to raise the price of work than high wages. If in the linen manufacture, for example, the wages of the different working people; the flax-dressers, the spinners, the weavers, &c. should, all of them, be advanced two pence a day: it would be necessary to heighten the price of a piece of linen only by a number of two pences equal to the number of people that had been employed about it, multiplied by the number of days during which they had been so employed. That part of the price of the commodity which resolved itself into wages would, through all the different stages of the manufacture, rise only in arithmetical proportion to this rise of wages. But if the profits of all the different employers of those working people should be raised five per cent. that part of the price of the commodity which resolved itself into profit, would, through all the different stages of the manufacture, rise in geometrical proportion to this rise of profit. The employer of the flax-dressers would in selling his flax require an additional five per cent. upon the whole value of the materials and wages which he advanced to his workmen. The employer of the spinners would require an additional five per cent. both upon the advanced price of the flax and upon the wages of the spinners. And the employer of the weavers would require a like five per cent. both upon the advanced price of the linen yarn and upon the wages of the weavers. In raising the price of commodities the rise of wages operates in the same manner as simple interest does in the accumulation of debt. The rise of profit operates like compound interest.* Our merchants and master-manufacturers complain much of the bad effects of high wages in raising the price, and thereby lessening the sale of their goods both at home and abroad. They say nothing concerning the bad effects of high profits. They are silent with regard to the pernicious effects of their own gains. They complain only of those of other people.

CHAPTER X

Of Wages and Profit in the different Employments of Labour and Stock

THE whole of the advantages and disadvantages of the different employments of labour and stock must, in the same neighbourhood, be either perfectly equal or continually tending to equality. If in the same neighbourhood, there was any employment evidently either more or less advantageous than the rest, so many people would crowd into it in the one case, and so many would desert it in the other, that its advantages would soon return to the level of other employments. This at least would be the case in a society where things were left to follow their natural course, where there was perfect liberty, and where every man was perfectly free both to chuse what occupation he thought proper, and to change it as often as he thought proper. Every man's interest would prompt him to seek the advantageous, and to shun the disadvantageous employment.

Pecuniary wages and profit, indeed, are every-where in Europe extremely different according to the different employments of labour and stock. But this difference arises partly from certain circumstances in the employments themselves, which, either really, or at least in the imaginations of men, make up for a small pecuniary gain in some, and counter-balance a great one in others; and partly from the policy of Europe, which no-where leaves things at perfect liberty.

The particular consideration of those circumstances and of that policy will divide this chapter into two parts.

PART I

Inequalities arising from the Nature of the Employments themselves

The five following are the principal circumstances which, so far as I have been able to observe, make up for a small pecuniary gain in some employments, and counter-balance a great one in others: first, the agreeableness or disagreeableness of the employments themselves; secondly, the easiness and cheapness, or the difficulty and expence of learning them; thirdly, the constancy or inconstancy of employment in them; fourthly, the small or great trust which must be reposed in those who exercise them; and, fifthly, the probability or improbability of success in them.

First, The wages of labour vary with the ease or hardship, the cleanliness or dirtiness, the honourableness or dishonourableness of the employment. Thus in most places, take the year round, a journeyman taylor* earns less than a journeyman weaver. His work is much easier. A journeyman weaver earns less than a journeyman smith. His work is not always easier, but it is much cleanlier. A journeyman blacksmith, though an artificer, seldom earns so much in twelve hours as a collier, who is only a labourer, does in eight. His work is not quite so dirty, is less dangerous, and is carried on in day-light, and above ground. Honour makes a great part of the reward of all honourable professions. In point of pecuniary gain, all things considered, they are generally under-recompensed, as I shall endeavour to show by and by. Disgrace has the contrary effect. The trade of a butcher is a brutal and an odious business; but it is in most places more profitable than the greater part of common trades. The most detestable of all employments, that of public executioner, is in proportion to the quantity of work done, better paid than any common trade whatever.

Hunting and fishing, the most important employments of mankind in the rude state of society, become in its advanced state their most agreeable amusements, and they pursue for pleasure what they once followed from necessity. In the advanced state of society, therefore, they are all very poor people who follow as a trade, what other people pursue as a pastime.* Fishermen have been so since the time of Theocritus.⁴ A poacher is every-where a very poor man in Great Britain.* In countries where the rigour of the law suffers no poachers, the licensed hunter is not in a much better condition. The natural taste for those employments makes more people follow them than can live comfortably by them, and the produce of their labour, in proportion to its quantity, comes always too cheap to market to afford any thing but the most scanty subsistence to the labourers.

Disagreeableness and disgrace affect the profits of stock in the same manner as the wages of labour. The keeper of an inn or tavern, who is never master of his own house, and who is exposed to the brutality of every drunkard, exercises neither a very agreeable nor a very creditable business. But there is scarce any common trade in which a small stock yields so great a profit.

Secondly, the wages of labour vary with the easiness and cheapness, or the difficulty and expence of learning the business.

When any expensive machine is erected, the extraordinary work to be performed by it before it is worn out, it must be expected, will replace the capital laid out upon it, with at least the ordinary profits. A man educated at the expence of much labour and time to any of those employments which require extraordinary dexterity and skill, may be compared to one of those expensive machines. The work which he learns to perform, it must be expected, over and above the usual wages of common labour, will replace to him the whole expence of his education, with at least the ordinary profits of an equally valuable capital. It must do this too in a reasonable time, regard being had to the very uncertain duration of human life, in the same manner as to the more certain duration of the machine.

⁴ See Idyllium xxi. [Idyll xxi, 'The Fishermen', begins, 'It is Poverty . . . that alone can rouse the crafts', translated by R. C. Trevelyan, *The Idylls of Theocritus* (Cambridge, 1947), 66–8.] [Campbell and Skinner]

The difference between the wages of skilled labour and those of common labour, is founded upon this principle.

The policy of Europe considers the labour of all mechanicks, artificers, and manufacturers, as skilled labour; and that of all country labourers as common labour. It seems to suppose that of the former to be of a more nice and delicate nature than that of the latter. It is so perhaps in some cases; but in the greater part it is quite otherwise, as I shall endeavour to shew by and by. The laws and customs of Europe, therefore, in order to qualify any person for exercising the one species of labour, impose the necessity of an apprenticeship, though with different degrees of rigour in different places. They leave the other free and open to every body. During the continuance of the apprenticeship, the whole labour of the apprentice belongs to his master. In the mean time he must, in many cases, be maintained by his parents or relations, and in almost all cases must be cloathed by them. Some money too is commonly given to the master for teaching him his trade. They who cannot give money, give time, or become bound for more than the usual number of years; a consideration which, though it is not always advantageous to the master, on account of the usual idleness of apprentices,* is always disadvantageous to the apprentice. In country labour, on the contrary, the labourer, while he is employed about the easier, learns the more difficult parts of his business, and his own labour maintains him through all the different stages of his employment. It is reasonable, therefore, that in Europe the wages of mechanicks, artificers, and manufacturers, should be somewhat higher than those of common labourers. They are so accordingly, and their superior gains make them in most places be considered as a superior rank of people. This superiority, however, is generally very small; the daily or weekly earnings of journeymen in the more common sorts of manufactures, such as those of plain linen and woollen cloth, computed at an average, are, in most places, very little more than the day wages of common labourers. Their employment, indeed, is more steady and uniform, and the superiority of their earnings, taking the whole year together, may be somewhat greater. It seems evidently, however, to be no greater than what is sufficient to compensate the superior expence of their education.

Education in the ingenious arts and in the liberal professions, is still more tedious and expensive. The pecuniary recompence, therefore, of painters and sculptors, of lawyers and physicians, ought to be much more liberal: and it is so accordingly.

The profits of stock seem to be very little affected by the easiness or difficulty of learning the trade in which it is employed. All the different ways in which stock is commonly employed in great towns seem, in reality, to be almost equally easy and equally difficult to learn. One branch either of foreign or domestick trade, cannot well be a much more intricate business than another.

Thirdly, The wages of labour in different occupations vary with the constancy or inconstancy of employment.

Employment is much more constant in some trades than in others. In the greater part of manufactures, a journeyman may be pretty sure of employment almost every day in the year that he is able to work. A mason or bricklayer, on the contrary, can work neither in hard frost nor in foul weather, and his employment at all other times depends upon the occasional calls of his customers. He is liable, in consequence, to be frequently without any. What he earns, therefore, while he is employed, must not only maintain him while he is idle, but make him some compensation for those anxious and desponding moments which the thought of so precarious a situation must sometimes occasion. Where the computed earnings of the greater part of manufacturers, accordingly, are nearly upon a level with the day wages of common labourers, those of masons and bricklayers are generally from one-half more to double those wages. Where common labourers earn four and five shillings a week, masons and bricklayers frequently earn seven and eight; where the former earn six, the latter often earn nine and ten; and where the former earn nine and ten, as in London, the latter commonly earn fifteen and eighteen.* No species of skilled labour, however, seems more easy to learn than that of masons and bricklayers. Chairmen* in London, during the summer season, are said sometimes to be employed as bricklayers. The high wages of those workmen, therefore, are not so much the recompence of their skill, as the compensation for the inconstancy of their employment.

A house carpenter seems to exercise rather a nicer and more ingenious trade than a mason. In most places, however, for it is not universally so, his day-wages are somewhat lower. His employment, though it depends much, does not depend so entirely upon the occasional calls of his customers; and it is not liable to be interrupted by the weather.

When the trades which generally afford constant employment, happen in a particular place not to do so, the wages of the workmen always rise a good deal above their ordinary proportion to those of common labour. In London almost all journeymen artificers are liable to be called upon and dismissed by their masters from day to day, and from week to week, in the same manner as day-labourers in other places. The lowest order of artificers, journeymen taylors, accordingly, earn there half a crown a-day, though eighteen-pence may be reckoned the wages of common labour. In small towns and country-villages, the wages of journeymen taylors frequently scarce equal those of common labour; but in London they are often many weeks without employment, particularly during the summer.*

When the inconstancy of employment is combined with the hardship, disagreeableness and dirtiness of the work, it sometimes raises the wages of the most common labour above those of the most skilful artificers. A collier* working by the piece is supposed, at Newcastle, to earn commonly about double, and in many parts of Scotland about three times the wages of common labour. His high wages arise altogether from the hardship, disagreeableness, and dirtiness of his work. His employment may, upon most occasions, be as constant as he pleases. The coal-heavers in London exercise a trade which in hardship, dirtiness, and disagreeableness, almost equals that of colliers; and from the unavoidable irregularity in the arrivals of coal-ships, the employment of the greater part of them is necessarily very inconstant. If colliers, therefore, commonly earn double and triple the wages of common labour, it ought not to seem unreasonable that coal-heavers should sometimes earn four and five times those wages. In the enquiry made into their condition a few years ago, it was found that at the rate at which they were then paid, they could earn from six to ten shillings a day. Six shillings are about four times the wages of common labour in London, and in every particular trade, the lowest common earnings may always be considered as those of the far greater number. How extravagant soever those earnings may appear, if they were more than sufficient to compensate all the disagreeable circumstances of the business, there would soon be so great a number of competitors as, in a trade which has no exclusive privilege, would quickly reduce them to a lower rate.

The constancy or inconstancy of employment cannot affect the ordinary profits of stock in any particular trade. Whether the stock is or is not constantly employed depends, not upon the trade, but the trader.

Fourthly, The wages of labour vary according to the small or great trust which must be reposed in the workmen.

The wages of goldsmiths and jewellers are every-where superior to those of many other workmen, not only of equal, but of much superior ingenuity; on account of the precious materials with which they are intrusted.

We trust our health to the .physician; our fortune and sometimes our life and reputation to the lawyer and attorney. Such confidence could not safely be reposed in people of a very mean or low condition. Their reward must be such, therefore, as may give them that rank in the society which so important a trust requires. The long time and the great expence which must be laid out in their education, when combined with this circumstance, necessarily enhance still further the price of their labour.

When a person employs only his own stock in trade, there is no trust; and the credit which he may get from other people, depends, not upon the nature of his trade, but upon their opinion of his fortune, probity, and prudence. The different rates of profit, therefore, in the different branches of trade, cannot arise from the different degrees of trust reposed in the traders.

Fifthly, the wages of labour in different employments vary according to the probability or improbability of success in them.

The probability that any particular person shall ever be qualified for the employment to which he is educated, is very different in different occupations. In the greater part of mechanick trades, success is almost certain; but very uncertain in the liberal professions. Put your son apprentice to a shoemaker, there is little doubt of his learning to make a pair of shoes: But send him to study the law, it is at least twenty to one if ever he makes such proficiency as will enable him to live by the business. In a perfectly fair lottery, those who draw the prizes ought to gain all that is lost by those who draw the blanks. In a profession where twenty fail for one that succeeds, that one ought to gain all that should have been gained by the unsuccessful twenty. The counsellor at law* who, perhaps, at near forty years of age, begins to make something by his profession, ought to receive the retribution, not only of his own so tedious and expensive education, but of that of more than twenty others who are never likely to make any thing by it. How extravagant soever the fees of counsellors at law may sometimes appear, their real retribution is never equal to this. Compute in any particular place, what is likely to be annually gained, and what is likely to be annually spent, by all the different workmen in any common trade, such as that of shoemakers or weavers, and you will find that the former sum will generally exceed the latter. But make the same computation with regard to all the counsellors and students of law, in all the different inns of court, and you will find that their annual gains bear but a very small proportion to their annual expence, even though you rate the former as high, and the latter as low, as can well be done. The lottery of the law, therefore, is very far from being a perfectly fair lottery; and that, as well as many other liberal and honourable professions, are, in point of pecuniary gain, evidently under-recompenced.

Those professions keep their level, however, with other occupations, and, notwithstanding these discouragements, all the most generous and liberal spirits are eager to crowd into them. Two different causes contribute to recommend them. First, the desire of the reputation which attends upon superior excellence in any of them; and, secondly, the natural confidence which every man has more or less, not only in his own abilities, but in his own good fortune.

To excel in any profession, in which but few arrive at mediocrity, is the most decisive mark of what is called genius or superior talents. The publick admiration which attends upon such distinguished abilities, makes always a part of their reward; a greater or smaller in proportion as it is higher or lower in degree. It makes a considerable part of that reward in the profession of physick; a still greater perhaps in that of law; in poetry and philosophy it makes almost the whole.

There are some very agreeable and beautiful talents of which the possession commands a certain sort of admiration; but of which the exercise for the sake of gain is considered, whether from reason or prejudice, as a sort of publick prostitution. The pecuniary recompence, therefore, of those who exercise them in this manner, must be sufficient, not only to pay for the time, labour, and expence of acquiring the talents, but for the discredit which attends the employment of them as the means of subsistence. The exorbitant rewards of players, opera-singers, opera-dancers, &c. are founded upon those two principles; the rarity and beauty of the talents, and the discredit of employing them in this manner. It seems absurd at first sight that we should despise their persons, and yet reward their talents with the most profuse liberality. While we do the one, however, we must of necessity do the other. Should the publick opinion or prejudice ever alter with regard to such occupations, their pecuniary recompence would quickly diminish. More people would apply to them, and the competition would quickly reduce the price of their labour. Such talents, though far from being common, are by no means so rare as is imagined. Many people possess them in great perfection, who disdain to make this use of them; and many more are capable of acquiring them, if any thing could be made honourably by them.

The over-weening conceit which the greater part of men have of their own abilities, is an antient evil remarked by the philosophers and moralists of all ages. Their absurd presumption in their own good fortune, has been less taken notice of. It is, however, if possible, still more universal. There is no man living who, when in tolerable health and spirits, has not some share of it. The chance of gain is by every man more or less over-valued, and the chance of loss is by most men under-valued, and by scarce any man, who is in tolerable health and spirits, valued more than it is worth.

That the chance of gain is naturally over-valued, we may learn from the universal success of lotteries. The world neither ever saw, nor ever will see, a perfectly fair lottery; or one in which the whole gain compensated the whole loss; because the undertaker could make nothing by it. In the state lotteries* the tickets are really not worth the price which is paid by the original subscribers, and yet commonly sell in the market for twenty, thirty, and sometimes forty per cent. advance. The vain hope of gaining some of the great prizes is the sole cause of this demand. The soberest people scarce look upon it as a folly to pay a small sum for the chance of gaining ten or twenty thousand pounds; though they know that even that small sum is perhaps twenty or thirty per cent. more than the chance is worth. In a lottery in which no prize exceeded twenty pounds, though in other respects it approached much nearer to a perfectly fair one than the common state lotteries, there would not be the same demand for tickets. In order to have a better chance for some of the great prizes, some people purchase several tickets, and others, small shares in a still greater number. There is not, however, a more certain proposition in mathematicks, than that the more tickets you adventure upon, the more likely you are to be a loser. Adventure upon all the tickets in the lottery, and you lose for certain; and the greater the number of your tickets the nearer you approach to this certainty.

That the chance of loss is frequently under-valued, and scarce ever valued more than it is worth, we may learn from the very moderate profit of insurers.* In order to make insurance, either from fire or sea-risk, a trade at all, the common premium must be sufficient to compensate the common losses, to pay the expence of management, and to afford such a profit as might have been drawn from an equal capital employed in any common trade. The person who pays no more than this, evidently pays no more than the real value of the risk, or the lowest price at which he can reasonably expect to insure it. But though many people have made a little money by insurance, very few have made a great fortune; and from this consideration alone, it seems evident enough, that the ordinary balance of profit and loss is not more advantageous in this, than in other common trades by which so many people make fortunes. Moderate, however, as the premium of insurance commonly is, many people despise the risk too much to care to pay it. Taking the whole kingdom at an average, nineteen houses in twenty, or rather perhaps ninety-nine in a hundred, are not insured from fire. Sea risk is more alarming to the greater part of people, and the proportion of ships insured to those not insured is much greater. Many sail, however, at all seasons, and even in time of war, without any insurance. This may sometimes perhaps be done without any imprudence. When a great company, or even a great merchant, has twenty or thirty ships at sea, they may, as it were, insure one another. The premium saved upon them all, may more than compensate such losses as they are likely to meet with in the common course of chances. The neglect of insurance upon shipping, however, in the same manner as upon houses, is, in most cases, the effect of no such nice calculation, but of mere thoughtless rashness and presumptuous contempt of the risk.

The contempt of risk and the presumptuous hope of success, are in no period of life more active than at the age at which young people chuse their professions. How little the fear of misfortune is then capable of balancing the hope of good luck, appears still more evidently in the readiness of the common people to enlist as soldiers, or to go to sea, than in the eagerness of those of better fashion to enter into what are called the liberal professions.

What a common soldier may lose is obvious enough. Without regarding the danger, however, young volunteers never enlist so readily as at the beginning of a new war; and though they have scarce any chance of preferment, they figure to themselves, in their youthful fancies, a thousand occasions of acquiring honour and distinction which never occur. These romantick hopes make the whole price of their blood. Their pay is less than that of common labourers,* and in actual service their fatigues are much greater.

The lottery of the sea is not altogether so disadvantageous as that of the army. The son of a creditable labourer or artificer may frequently go to sea with his father's consent; but if he enlists as a soldier, it is always without it. Other people see some chance of his making something by the one trade: nobody but himself sees any of his making any thing by the other. The great admiral is less the object of publick admiration than the great general, and the highest success in the sea service promises a less brilliant fortune and reputation than equal success in the land. The same difference runs through all the inferior degrees of preferment in both. By the rules of precedency a captain in the navy ranks with a colonel in the army: but he does not rank with him in the common estimation. As the great prizes in the lottery are less, the smaller ones must be more numerous. Common sailors, therefore, more frequently get some fortune and preferment than common soldiers; and the hope of those prizes is what principally recommends the trade. Though their skill and dexterity are much superior to that of almost any artificers, and though their whole life is one continual scene of hardship and danger, yet for all this dexterity and skill, for all those hardships and dangers, while they remain in the condition of common sailors, they receive scarce any other recompence but the pleasure of exercising the one and of surmounting the other. Their wages are not greater than those of common labourers at the port which regulates the rate of seamens wages. As they are continually going from port to port, the monthly pay of those who sail from all the different ports of Great Britain, is more nearly upon a level than that of any other workmen in those different places; and the rate of the port to and from which the greatest number sail, that is the port of London, regulates that of all the rest. At London the wages of the greater part of the different classes of workmen are about double those of the same classes at Edinburgh. But the sailors who sail from the port of London seldom earn above three or four shillings a month more than those who sail from the port of Leith, and the difference is frequently not so great. In time of peace, and in the merchant service, the London price is from a guinea to about seven-and-twenty shillings the calendar month. A common labourer in London, at the rate of nine or ten shillings a week, may earn in the calendar month from forty to five-and-forty shillings. The sailor, indeed, over and above his pay, is supplied with provisions. Their value, however, may not perhaps always exceed the difference between his pay and that of the common labourer; and though it sometimes should, the excess will not be clear gain to the sailor, because he cannot share it with his wife and family, whom he must maintain out of his wages at home.

The dangers and hair-breadth escapes of a life of adventures, instead of disheartening young people, seem frequently to recommend a trade to them. A tender mother, among the inferior ranks of people, is often afraid to send her son to school at a sea-port town, lest the sight of the ships and the conversation and adventures of the sailors should entice him to go to sea. The distant prospect of hazards, from which we can hope to extricate ourselves by courage and address, is not disagreeable to us, and does not raise the wages of labour in any employment. It is otherwise with those in which courage and address can be of no avail. In trades which are known to be very unwholesome, the wages of labour are always remarkably high. Unwholesomeness is a species of disagreeableness, and its effects upon the wages of labour are to be ranked under that general head.

In all the different employments of stock, the ordinary rate of profit varies more or less with the certainty or uncertainty of the returns. These are in general less uncertain in the inland than in the foreign trade, and in some branches of foreign trade than in others; in the trade to North America, for example, than in that to Jamaica.* The ordinary rate of profit always rises more or less with the risk. It does not, however, seem to rise in proportion to it, or so as to compensate it compleately. Bankruptcies are most frequent in the most hazardous trades. The most hazardous of all trades, that of a smuggler,* though when the adventure succeeds it is likewise the most profitable, is the infallible road to bankruptcy. The presumptuous hope of success seems to act here as upon all other occasions, and to entice so many adventures into those hazardous trades, that their competition reduces the profit below what is sufficient to compensate the risk. To compensate it compleatly, the common returns ought, over and above the ordinary profits of stock, not only to make up for all occasional losses, but to afford a surplus profit to the adventurers of the same nature with the profit of insurers. But if the common returns were sufficient for all this, bankruptcies would not be more frequent in these than in other trades.

Of the five circumstances, therefore, which vary the wages of labour, two only affect the profits of stock; the agreeableness or disagreeableness of the business, and the risk or security with which it is attended. In point of agreeableness or disagreeableness, there is little or no difference in the far greater part of the different employments of stock; but a great deal in those of labour; and the ordinary profit of stock, though it rises with the risk, does not always seem to rise in proportion to it. It should follow from all this, that, in the same society or neighbourhood, the average and ordinary rates of profit in the different employments of stock should be more nearly upon a level than the pecuniary wages of the different sorts of labour.

They are so accordingly. The difference between the earnings of a common labourer and those of a well employed lawyer or physician, is evidently much greater, than that, between the ordinary profits in any two different branches of trade. The apparent difference, besides, in the profits of different trades, is generally a deception arising from our not always distinguishing what ought to be considered as wages, from what ought to be considered as profit.

Apothecaries' profit is become a bye-word, denoting something uncommonly extravagant.* This great apparent profit, however, is frequently no more than the reasonable wages of labour. The skill of an apothecary is a much nicer and more delicate matter than that of any artificer whatever; and the trust which is reposed in him is of much greater importance. He is the physician of the poor in all cases, and of the rich when the distress or danger is not very great. His reward, therefore, ought to be suitable to his skill and his trust, and it arises generally from the price at which he sells his drugs. But the whole drugs which the best employed apothecary, in a large market town, will sell in a year, may not perhaps cost him above thirty or forty pounds. Though he should sell them, therefore, for three or four hundred, or at a thousand per cent. profit, this may frequently be no more than the reasonable wages of his labour charged, in the only way in which he can charge them, upon the price of his drugs. The greater part of the apparent profit is real wages disguised in the garb of profit.

In a small sea-port town, a little grocer will make forty or fifty per cent. upon a stock of a single hundred pounds, while a considerable wholesale merchant in the same place will scarce make eight or ten per cent. upon a stock of ten thousand. The trade of the grocer may be necessary for the conveniency of the inhabitants, and the narrowness of the market may not admit the employment of a larger capital in the business. The man, however, must not only live by his trade, but live by it suitably to the qualifications which it requires. Besides possessing a little capital, he must be able to read, write, and account, and must be a tolerable judge too of, perhaps, fifty or sixty different sorts of goods, their prices, qualities, and the markets where they are to be had cheapest. He must have all the knowledge, in short, that is necessary for a great merchant, which nothing hinders him from becoming but the want of a sufficient capital. Thirty or forty pounds a year cannot be considered as too great a recompence for the labour of a person so accomplished. Deduct this from the seemingly great profits of his capital, and little more will remain, perhaps, than the ordinary profits of stock. The greater part of the apparent profit is, in this case too, real wages.

The difference between the apparent profit of the retail and that of the wholesale trade, is much less in the capital than in small towns and country villages. Where ten thousand pounds can be employed in the grocery trade, the wages of the grocer's labour make but a very trifling addition to the real profits of so great a stock. The apparent profits of the wealthy retailer, therefore, are there more nearly upon a level with those of the wholesale merchant. It is upon this account that goods sold by retail are generally as cheap and frequently much cheaper in the capital than in small towns and country villages. Grocery goods, for example, are generally much cheaper; bread and butcher's meat frequently as cheap. It costs no more to bring grocery goods to the great town than to the country village; but it costs a great deal more to bring corn and cattle, as the greater part of them must be brought from a much greater distance. The prime cost* of grocery goods, therefore, being the same in both places, they are cheapest where the least profit is charged upon them. The prime cost of bread and butcher's-meat is greater in the great town than in the country village; and though the profit is less, therefore, they are not always cheaper there, but often equally cheap. In such articles as bread and butcher's meat, the same cause, which diminishes apparent profit, increases prime cost. The extent of the market, by giving employment to greater stocks, diminishes apparent profit; but by requiring supplies from a greater distance, it increases prime cost. This diminution of the one and increase of the other seem, in most cases, nearly to counter-balance one another; which is probably the reason that, though the prices of corn and cattle are commonly very different in different parts of the kingdom, those of bread and butcher's-meat are generally very nearly the same through the greater part of it.

Though the profits of stock both in the wholesale and retail trade are generally less in the capital than in small towns and country villages, yet great fortunes are frequently acquired from small beginnings in the former, and scarce ever in the latter. In small towns and country villages, on account of the narrowness of the market, trade cannot always be extended as stock extends. In such places, therefore, though the rate of a particular person's profits may be very high, the sum or amount of them can never be very great, nor consequently that of his annual accumulation. In great towns, on the contrary, trade can be extended as stock increases, and the credit of a frugal and thriving man increases much faster than his stock. His trade is extended in proportion to the amount of both, and the sum or amount of his profits is in proportion to the extent of his trade, and his annual accumulation in proportion to the amount of his profits. It seldom happens, however, that great fortunes are made even in great towns by any one regular, established, and well-known branch of business, but in consequence of a long life of industry, frugality, and attention. Sudden fortunes, indeed, are sometimes made in such places by what is called the trade of speculation. The speculative merchant exercises no one regular, established, or well-known branch of business. He is a corn merchant this year, and a wine merchant the next, and a sugar, tobacco, or tea merchant the year after. He enters into every trade when he foresees that it is likely to be more than commonly profitable, and he quits it when he foresees that its profits are likely to return to the level of other trades. His profits and losses, therefore, can bear no regular proportion to those of any one established and well-known branch of business. A bold adventurer may sometimes acquire a considerable fortune by two or three successful speculations; but is just as likely to lose one by two or three unsuccessful ones. This trade can be carried on no where but in great towns. It is only in places of the most extensive commerce and correspondence that the intelligence requisite for it can be had.

The five circumstances above mentioned, though they occasion considerable inequalities in the wages of labour and profits of stock, occasion none in the whole of the advantages and disadvantages, real or imaginary, of the different employments of either. The nature of those circumstances is such, that they make up for a small pecuniary gain in some, and counterbalance a great one in others.

In order, however, that this equality may take place in the whole of their advantages or disadvantages, three things are requisite even where there is the most perfect freedom. First, the employments must be well known and long established in the neighbourhood; secondly, they must be in their ordinary, or what may be called their natural state; and, thirdly, they must be the sole or principal employments of those who occupy them.

First, this equality can take place only in those employments which are well known, and have been long established in the neighbourhood.

Where all other circumstances are equal, wages are generally higher in new than in old trades. When a projector attempts to establish a new manufacture, he must at first entice his workmen from other employments by higher wages than they can either earn in their own trades, or than the nature of his work would otherwise require, and a considerable time must pass away before he can venture to reduce them to the common level. Manufactures for which the demand arises altogether from fashion and fancy, are continually changing, and seldom last long enough to be considered as old established manufactures. Those, on the contrary, for which the demand arises chiefly from use or necessity, are less liable to change, and the same form or fabrick may continue in demand for whole centuries together. The wages of labour, therefore, are likely to be higher in manufactures of the former, than in those of the latter kind. Birmingham deals chiefly in manufactures of the former kind; Sheffield in those of the latter;* and the wages of labour in those two different places, are said to be suitable to this difference in the nature of their manufactures.

The establishment of any new manufacture, of any new branch of commerce, or of any new practice in agriculture, is always a speculation, from which the projector promises himself extraordinary profits. These profits sometimes are very great, and sometimes, more frequently, perhaps, they are quite otherwise; but in general they bear no regular proportion to those of other old trades in the neighbourhood. If the project succeeds, they are commonly at first very high. When the trade or practice becomes thoroughly established and well known, the competition reduces them to the level of other trades.

Secondly, this equality in the whole of the advantages and disadvantages of the different employments of labour and stock, can take place only in the ordinary, or what may be called the natural state of those employments.

The demand for almost every different species of labour, is sometimes greater and sometimes less than usual. In the one case the advantages of the employment rise above, in the other they fall below the common level. The demand for country labour is greater at hay-time and harvest, than during the greater part of the year; and wages rise with the demand. In time of war, when forty or fifty thousand sailors are forced from the merchant service into that of the king, the demand for sailors to merchant ships necessarily rises with their scarcity, and their wages upon such occasions commonly rise from a guinea and seven-and-twenty-shillings, to forty shillings and three pounds a month. In a decaying manufacture, on the contrary, many workmen, rather than quit their old trade, are contented with smaller wages than would otherwise be suitable to the nature of their employment.

The profits of stock vary with the price of the commodities in which it is employed. As the price of any commodity rises above the ordinary or average rate, the profits of at least some part of the stock that is employed in bringing it to market, rise above their proper level, and as it falls they sink below it. All commodities are more or less liable to variations of price, but some are much more so than others. In all commodities which are produced by human industry, the quantity of industry annually employed is necessarily regulated by the annual demand, in such a manner that the average annual produce may, as nearly as possible, be equal to the average annual consumption. In some employments, it has already been observed,* the same quantity of industry will always produce the same, or very nearly the same quantity of commodities. In the linen or woollen manufactures, for example, the same number of hands will annually work up very nearly the same quantity of linen and woollen cloth. The variations in the market price of such commodities, therefore, can arise only from some accidental variation in the demand. A publick mourning raises the price of black cloth. But as the demand for most sorts of plain linen and woollen cloth is pretty uniform, so is likewise the price. But there are other employments in which the same quantity of industry will not always produce the same quantity of commodities. The same quantity of industry, for example, will, in different years, produce very different quantities of corn, wine, hops, sugar, tobacco, &c. The price of such commodities, therefore, varies not only with the variations of demand, but with the much greater and more frequent variations of quantity, and is consequently extremely fluctuating. But the profit of some of the dealers must necessarily fluctuate with the price of the commodities. The operations of the speculative merchant are principally employed about such commodities. He endeavours to buy them up when he foresees that their price is likely to rise, and to sell them when it is likely to fall.

Thirdly, This equality in the whole of the advantages and disadvantages of the different employments of labour and stock; can take place only in such as are the sole or principal employments of those who occupy them.

When a person derives his subsistence from one employment, which does not occupy the greater part of his time; in the intervals of his leisure he is often willing to work at another

FALL TERM TEXTBOOKS RETURNS

5241 CASH 1   0381 0340 006

978019283546 NEW
SMITH/WEALTH OF NA   MDS 1   9.95
02   DISCOUNT 10.0   1.00-
            SUBTOTAL   8.95
   8.25% Sales Tax   .74
              TOTAL   9.69

ACCOUNT NUMBER   XXXXXXXXXXXX0982
   Visa/Mastercard   9.69
Expiration Date   XX/XX
   Authorization   017053

            DISCOUNT TOTAL   1.00-
ALL SALES ARE FINAL

                    11/13/04 5:13 PM

for less wages than would otherwise suit the nature of the employment.

There still subsists in many parts of Scotland a set of people called Cotters or Cottagers,* though they were more frequent some years ago than they are now. They are a sort of out-servants of the landlords and farmers. The usual reward which they receive from their masters is a house, a small garden for pot-herbs, as much grass as will feed a cow, and, perhaps, an acre or two of bad arable land. When their master has occasion for their labour, he gives them, besides, two pecks of oatmeal a week, worth about sixteen-pence sterling. During a great part of the year he has little or no occasion for their labour, and the cultivation of their own little possession is not sufficient to occupy the time which is left at their own disposal. When such occupiers were more numerous than they are at present, they are said to have been willing to give their spare time for a very small recompence to any body, and to have wrought for less wages than other labourers. In antient times they seem to have been common all over Europe. In countries ill cultivated and worse inhabited, the greater part of landlords and farmers could not otherwise provide themselves with the extraordinary number of hands, which country labour requires at certain seasons. The daily or weekly recompence which such labourers occasionally received from their masters, was evidently not the whole price of their labour. Their small tenement made a considerable part of it. This daily or weekly recompence, however, seems to have been considered as the whole of it, by many writers who have collected the prices of labour and provisions in antient times, and who have taken pleasure in representing both as wonderfully low.

The produce of such labour comes frequently cheaper to market than would otherwise be suitable to its nature. Stockings in many parts of Scotland are knit much cheaper than they can any-where be wrought upon the loom. They are the work of servants and labourers, who derive the principal part of their subsistence from some other employment. More than a thousand pair of Shetland stockings are annually imported

into Leith, of which the price is from five-pence to seven-pence
a pair. At Learwick, the small capital of the Shetland islands,
ten-pence a day, I have been assured, is a common price of
common labour. In the same islands they knit worsted stockings
to the value of a guinea a pair and upwards.

The spinning of linen yarn is carried on in Scotland nearly
in the same way as the knitting of stockings, by servants who
are chiefly hired for other purposes. They earn but a very
scanty subsistence, who endeavour to get their whole livelihood
by either of those trades. In most parts of Scotland she is a
good spinner who can earn twenty-pence a week.*

In opulent countries the market is generally so extensive,
that any one trade is sufficient to employ the whole labour and
stock of those who occupy it. Instances of people's living by
one employment, and at the same time deriving some little
advantage from another, occur chiefly in poor countries. The
following instance, however, of something of the same kind is
to be found in the capital of a very rich one. There is no city
in Europe, I believe, in which house-rent is dearer than in
London, and yet I know no capital in which a furnished
apartment can be hired so cheap. Lodging is not only much
cheaper in London than in Paris; it is much cheaper than in
Edinburgh of the same degree of goodness; and what may seem
extraordinary, the dearness of house-rent is the cause of the
cheapness of lodging. The dearness of house-rent in London
arises, not only from those causes which render it dear in all
great capitals, the dearness of labour, the dearness of all the
materials of building, which must generally be brought from a
great distance, and above all the dearness of ground-rent, every
landlord acting the part of a monopolist, and frequently exacting a higher rent for a single acre of bad land in a town, than
can be had for a hundred of the best in the country; but it
arises in part from the peculiar manners and customs of the
people, which oblige every master of a family to hire a whole
house from top to bottom. A dwelling-house in England means
every thing that is contained under the same roof. In France,
Scotland, and many other parts of Europe, it frequently means

no more than a single story.* A tradesman in London is obliged
to hire a whole house in that part of the town where his
customers live. His shop is upon the ground-floor, and he and
his family sleep in the garret; and he endeavours to pay a part
of his house-rent by letting the two middle stories to lodgers.
He expects to maintain his family by his trade, and not by his
lodgers. Whereas, at Paris and Edinburgh, the people who let
lodgings, have commonly no other means of subsistence; and
the price of the lodging must pay, not only the rent of the
house, but the whole expence of the family.

PART II

Inequalities occasioned by the Policy of Europe

Such are the inequalities in the whole of the advantages and
disadvantages of the different employments of labour and stock,
which the defect of any of the three requisites above-mentioned
must occasion, even where there is the most perfect liberty.
But the policy of Europe, by not leaving things at perfect
liberty, occasions other inequalities of much greater importance.

It does this chiefly in the three following ways. First, by
restraining the competition in some employments to a smaller
number than would otherwise be disposed to enter into them;
secondly, by increasing it in others beyond what it naturally
would be; and, thirdly, by obstructing the free circulation of
labour and stock, both from employment to employment and
from place to place.*

First, The policy of Europe occasions a very important
inequality in the whole of the advantages and disadvantages of
the different employments of labour and stock, by restraining
the competition in some employments to a smaller number than
might otherwise be disposed to enter into them.

The exclusive privileges of corporations* are the principal
means it makes use of for this purpose.

The exclusive privilege of an incorporated trade necessarily
restrains the competition, in the town where it is established,

to those who are free of the trade. To have served an apprenticeship in the town, under a master properly qualified, is
commonly the necessary requisite for obtaining this freedom.
The bye-laws of the corporation regulate sometimes the number of apprentices which any master is allowed to have, and
almost always the number of years which each apprentice is
obliged to serve. The intention of both regulations is to restrain
the competition to a much smaller number than might otherwise be disposed to enter into the trade. The limitation of the
number of apprentices restrains it directly. A long term of
apprenticeship restrains it more indirectly, but as effectually,
by increasing the expence of education.

In Sheffield no master cutler can have more than one apprentice at a time, by a bye-law of the corporation. In Norfolk
and Norwich no master weaver can have more than two
apprentices, under pain of forfeiting five pounds a month to
the king. No master hatter can have more than two apprentices
any-where in England, or in the English plantations, under
pain of forfeiting five pounds a month, half to the king, and
half to him who shall sue in any court of record. Both these
regulations, though they have been confirmed by a publick law
of the kingdom, are evidently dictated by the same corporation
spirit which enacted the bye-law of Sheffield. The silk weavers
in London* had scarce been incorporated a year when they
enacted a bye-law, restraining any master from having more
than two apprentices at a time. It required a particular act of
parliament to rescind this bye-law.

Seven years seem antiently to have been, all over Europe,
the usual term established for the duration of apprenticeships
in the greater part of incorporated trades. All such incorporations were antiently called universities; which indeed is the
proper Latin name for any incorporation whatever.* The university of smiths, the university of taylors, &c. are expressions
which we commonly meet with in the old charters of antient
towns. When those particular incorporations which are now
peculiarly called universities were first established, the term of
years which it was necessary to study, in order to obtain the

degree of master of arts, appears evidently to have been copied from the term of apprenticeship in common trades, of which the incorporations were much more antient. As to have wrought seven years under a master properly qualified, was necessary, in order to intitle any person to become a master, and to have himself apprentices in a common trade; so to have studied seven years under a master properly qualified, was necessary to entitle him to become a master, teacher, or doctor (words antiently synonimous) in the liberal arts, and to have scholars or apprentices (words likewise originally synonimous) to study under him.

By the 5th of Elizabeth, commonly called the Statute of Apprenticeship,* it was enacted, that no person should for the future exercise any trade, craft, or mystery at that time exercised in England, unless he had previously served to it an apprenticeship of seven years at least; and what before had been the bye-law of many particular corporations, became in England the general and publick law of all trades carried on in market towns. For though the words of the statute are very general, and seem plainly to include the whole kingdom, by interpretation its operation has been limited to market towns, it having been held that in country villages a person may exercise several different trades, though he has not served a seven years apprenticeship to each, they being necessary for the conveniency of the inhabitants, and the number of people frequently not being sufficient to supply each with a particular sett of hands.

By a strict interpretation of the words too the operation of this statute has been limited to those trades which were established in England before the 5th of Elizabeth, and has never been extended to such as have been introduced since that time. This limitation has given occasion to several distinctions which, considered as rules of police, appear as foolish as can well be imagined. It has been adjudged, for example, that a coach-maker can neither himself make nor employ journeymen to make his coach-wheels, but must buy them of a master wheel-wright; this latter trade having been exercised in England before the 5th of Elizabeth. But a wheel-wright, though he has never served an apprenticeship to a coach-maker, may either himself make or employ journeymen to make coaches; the trade of a coach-maker not being within the statute, because not exercised in England at the time when it was made. The manufactures of Manchester, Birmingham, and Wolverhampton, are many of them, upon this account, not within the statute; not having been exercised in England before the 5th of Elizabeth.

In France, the duration of apprenticeships is different in different towns and in different trades. In Paris, five years is the term required in a great number; but before any person can be qualified to exercise the trade as a master, he must, in many of them, serve five years more as a journeyman. During this latter term he is called the companion of his master, and the term itself is called his companionship.

In Scotland there is no general law which regulates universally the duration of apprenticeships. The term is different in different corporations. Where it is long, a part of it may generally be redeemed by paying a small fine. In most towns too a very small fine is sufficient to purchase the freedom of any corporation. The weavers of linen and hempen cloth, the principal manufactures of the country, as well as all other artificers subservient to them, wheel-makers, reel-makers,* &c. may exercise their trades in any town corporate without paying any fine. In all towns corporate all persons are free to sell butcher's-meat upon any lawful day of the week. Three years is in Scotland a common term of apprenticeship, even in some very nice trades; and in general I know of no country in Europe in which corporation laws are so little oppressive.

The property which every man has in his own labour, as it is the original foundation of all other property, so it is the most sacred and inviolable.* The patrimony of a poor man lies in the strength and dexterity of his hands; and to hinder him from employing this strength and dexterity in what manner he thinks proper without injury to his neighbour, is a plain violation of this most sacred property. It is a manifest encroachment upon the just liberty both of the workman, and of those who might be disposed to employ him. As it hinders the one from working at what he thinks proper, so it hinders the others from employing whom they think proper. To judge whether he is fit to be employed, may surely be trusted to the discretion of the employers whose interest it so much concerns. The affected anxiety of the law-giver lest they should employ an improper person, is evidently as impertinent as it is oppressive.

The institution of long apprenticeships can give no security that insufficient workmanship shall not frequently be exposed to publick sale. When this is done it is generally the effect of fraud, and not of inability; and the longest apprenticeship can give no security against fraud. Quite different regulations are necessary to prevent this abuse. The sterling mark upon plate, and the stamps* upon linen and woollen cloth, give the pur-chaser much greater security than any statute of apprenticeship. He generally looks at these, but never thinks it worth while to enquire whether the workman had served a seven years appren-ticeship.

The institution of long apprenticeships has no tendency to form young people to industry. A journeyman who works by the piece is likely to be industrious, because he derives a benefit from every exertion of his industry. An apprentice is likely to be idle, and almost always is so, because he has no immediate interest to be otherwise. In the inferior employments, the sweets of labour consist altogether in the recompence of labour. They who are soonest in a condition to enjoy the sweets of it, are likely soonest to conceive a relish for it, and to acquire the early habit of industry. A young man naturally conceives an aversion to labour, when for a long time he receives no benefit from it. The boys who are put out apprentices from publick charities* are generally bound for more than the usual number of years, and they generally turn out very idle and worthless.

Apprenticeships were altogether unknown to the antients. The reciprocal duties of master and apprentice make a consider-able article in every modern code. The Roman law is perfectly silent with regard to them. I know no Greek or Latin word (I might venture, I believe, to assert that there is none) which expresses the idea we now annex to the word Apprentice, a servant bound to work at a particular trade for the benefit of a master, during a term of years, upon condition that the master shall teach him that trade.

Long apprenticeships are altogether unnecessary. The arts, which are much superior to common trades, such as those of making clocks and watches,* contain no such mystery as to require a long course of instruction. The first invention of such beautiful machines, indeed, and even that of some of the instruments employed in making them, must, no doubt, have been the work of deep thought and long time, and may justly be considered as among the happiest efforts of human ingenuity. But when both have been fairly invented and are well understood, to explain to any young man, in the compleatest manner, how to apply the instruments and how to construct the machines, cannot well require more than the lessons of a few weeks: perhaps those of a few days might be sufficient. In the common mechanick trades, those of a few days might certainly be sufficient. The dexterity of hand, indeed, even in common trades, cannot be acquired without much practice and experience. But a young man would practise with much more diligence and attention, if from the beginning he wrought as a journeyman, being paid in proportion to the little work which he could execute, and paying in his turn for the materials which he might sometimes spoil through awkwardness and inexperience. His education would generally in this way be more effectual, and always less tedious and expensive. The master, indeed, would be a loser. He would lose all the wages of the apprentice, which he now saves, for seven years together. In the end, perhaps, the apprentice himself would be a loser. In a trade so easily learnt he would have more competitors, and his wages, when he came to be a compleat workman, would be much less than at present. The same increase of competition would reduce the profits of the masters as well as the wages of the workmen. The trades, the crafts, the mysteries, would all be losers. But the publick would be a gainer, the work of all artificers coming in this way much cheaper to market.

It is to prevent this reduction of price, and consequently of wages and profit, by restraining that free competition which would most certainly occasion it, that all corporations, and the greater part of corporation laws, have been established. In order to erect a corporation, no other authority in antient times was requisite in many parts of Europe, but that of the town corporate in which it was established. In England, indeed, a charter from the king was likewise necessary. But this prerogative of the crown seems to have been reserved rather for extorting money from the subject, than for the defence of the common liberty against such oppressive monopolies. Upon paying a fine to the king, the charter seems generally to have been readily granted; and when any particular class of artificers or traders thought proper to act as a corporation without a charter, such adulterine* guilds, as they were called, were not always disfranchised upon that account, but obliged to fine annually to the king for permission to exercise their usurped privileges.[5] The immediate inspection of all corporations, and of the bye-laws which they might think proper to enact for their own government, belonged to the town corporate in which they were established; and whatever discipline was exercised over them, proceeded commonly, not from the king, but from that greater incorporation of which those subordinate ones were only parts or members.

The government of towns corporate was altogether in the hands of traders and artificers; and it was the manifest interest of every particular class of them, to prevent the market from being over-stocked, as they commonly express it, with their own particular species of industry; which is in reality to keep it always under-stocked. Each class was eager to establish regulations proper for this purpose, and, provided it was allowed to do so, was willing to consent that every other class

---

[5] See Madox Firma Burgi, p. 26, &c. ['Anciently, a Gild either Religious or Secular could not legally be set-up without the King's Licence. If any Persons erected a Gild without warrant, that is, without the King's Leave, it was a Trespass, and they were lyable to be punished for it.' Thomas Madox, *Firma Burgi* (London, 1726), 26.] [Campbell and Skinner]

should do the same. In consequence of such regulations, indeed, each class was obliged to buy the goods they had occasion for from every other within the town, somewhat dearer than they otherwise might have done. But in recompence, they were enabled to sell their own just as much dearer; so that so far it was as broad as long, as they say; and in the dealings of the different classes within the town with one another, none of them were losers by these regulations. But in their dealings with the country they were all great gainers; and in these latter dealings consists the whole trade which supports and enriches every town.

Every town draws its whole subsistence, and all the materials of its industry, from the country.* It pays for these chiefly in two ways: first, by sending back to the country a part of those materials wrought up and manufactured; in which case their price is augmented by the wages of the workmen, and the profits of their masters or immediate employers: secondly, by sending to it a part both of the rude and manufactured produce, either of other countries, or of distant parts of the same country, imported into the town; in which case too the original price of those goods is augmented by the wages of the carriers or sailors, and by the profits of the merchants who employ them. In what is gained upon the first of those two branches of commerce, consists the advantage which the town makes by its manufactures; in what is gained upon the second, the advantage of its inland and foreign trade. The wages of the workmen, and the profits of their different employers, make up the whole of what is gained upon both. Whatever regulations, therefore, tend to increase those wages and profits beyond what they otherwise would be, tend to enable the town to purchase, with a smaller quantity of its labour, the produce of a greater quantity of the labour of the country. They give the traders and artificers in the town an advantage over the landlords, farmers, and labourers in the country, and break down that natural equality which would otherwise take place in the commerce which is carried on between them. The whole annual produce of the labour of the society is annually divided between those two different sets of people. By means of those regulations a greater share of it is given to the inhabitants of the town than would otherwise fall to them; and a less to those of the country.

The price which the town really pays for the provisions and materials annually imported into it, is the quantity of manufactures and other goods annually exported from it. The dearer the latter are sold, the cheaper the former are bought. The industry of the town becomes more, and that of the country less advantageous.

That the industry which is carried on in towns is, everywhere in Europe, more advantageous than that which is carried on in the country, without entering into any very nice computations, we may satisfy ourselves by one very simple and obvious observation. In every country of Europe we find, at least, a hundred people who have acquired great fortunes from small beginnings by trade and manufactures, the industry which properly belongs to towns, for one who has done so by that which properly belongs to the country, the raising of rude produce by the improvement and cultivation of land. Industry, therefore, must be better rewarded, the wages of labour and the profits of stock must evidently be greater in the one situation than in the other. But stock and labour naturally seek the most advantageous employment. They naturally, therefore, resort as much as they can to the town, and desert the country.

The inhabitants of a town, being collected into one place, can easily combine together. The most insignificant trades carried on in towns have accordingly, in some place or other, been incorporated; and even where they have never been incorporated, yet the corporation spirit, the jealousy of strangers, the aversion to take apprentices, or to communicate the secret of their trade, generally prevail in them, and often teach them, by voluntary associations and agreements, to prevent that free competition which they cannot prohibit by bye-laws. The trades which employ but a small number of hands, run most easily into such combinations. Half a dozen wool-combers,* perhaps, are necessary to keep a thousand spinners and weavers at work. By combining not to take apprentices they can not only engross the employment, but reduce the whole manufacture into a sort of slavery to themselves, and raise the price of their labour much above what is due to the nature of their work.

The inhabitants of the country, dispersed in distant places, cannot easily combine together. They have not only never been incorporated, but the corporation spirit never has prevailed among them. No apprenticeship has ever been thought necessary to qualify for husbandry, the great trade of the country. After what are called the fine arts, and the liberal professions, however, there is perhaps no trade which requires so great a variety of knowledge and experience. The innumerable volumes which have been written upon it in all languages, may satisfy us, that among the wisest and most learned nations, it has never been regarded as a matter very easily understood. And from all those volumes we shall in vain attempt to collect that knowledge of its various and complicated operations, which is commonly possessed even by the common farmer; how contemptuously soever the very contemptible authors of some of them may sometimes affect to speak of him. There is scarce any common mechanick trade, on the contrary, of which all the operations may not be as compleatly and distinctly explained in a pamphlet of a very few pages, as it is possible for words illustrated by figures to explain them. In the history of the arts, now publishing by the French academy of sciences, several of them are actually explained in this manner.* The direction of operations, besides, which must be varied with every change of the weather, as well as with many other accidents, requires much more judgment and discretion, than that of those which are always the same or very nearly the same.

Not only the art of the farmer, the general direction of the operations of husbandry, but many inferior branches of country labour require much more skill and experience than the greater part of mechanick trades. The man who works upon brass and iron, works with instruments and upon materials of which the temper is always the same, or very nearly the same. But the man who ploughs the ground with a team of horses or oxen, works with instruments of which the health, strength, and temper are very different upon different occasions. The condition of the materials which he works upon too is as variable as that of the instruments which he works with, and both require to be managed with much judgment and discretion. The common ploughman, though generally regarded as the pattern of stupidity and ignorance, is seldom defective in this judgment and discretion.* He is less accustomed, indeed, to social intercourse than the mechanick who lives in a town. His voice and language are more uncouth and more difficult to be understood by those who are not used to them. His understanding, however, being accustomed to consider a greater variety of objects, is generally much superior to that of the other, whose whole attention from morning till night is commonly occupied in performing one or two very simple operations. How much the lower ranks of people in the country are really superior to those of the town, is well known to every man whom either business or curiosity has led to converse much with both. In China and Indostan accordingly both the rank and the wages of country labourers are said to be superior to those of the greater part of artificers and manufacturers. They would probably be so every where, if corporation laws and the corporation spirit did not prevent it.

The superiority which the industry of the towns has every where in Europe over that of the country, is not altogether owing to corporations and corporation laws. It is supported by many other regulations. The high duties upon foreign manufactures and upon all goods imported by alien merchants, all tend to the same purpose. Corporation laws enable the inhabitants of towns to raise their prices, without fearing to be under-sold by the free competition of their own countrymen. Those other regulations secure them equally against that of foreigners. The enhancement of price occasioned by both is every where finally paid by the landlords, farmers, and labourers of the country, who have seldom opposed the establishment of such monopolies. They have commonly neither inclination nor fitness to enter into combinations; and the clamour and sophistry of merchants and manufacturers easily persuade them that the private interest of a part, and of a subordinate part of the society, is the general interest of the whole.

In Great Britain the superiority of the industry of the towns over that of the country, seems to have been greater formerly than in the present times. The wages of country labour approach nearer to those of manufacturing labour, and the profits of stock employed in agriculture to those of trading and manufacturing stock, than they are said to have done in the last century, or in the beginning of the present. This change may be regarded as the necessary, though very late consequence of the extraordinary encouragement given to the industry of the towns. The stock accumulated in them comes in time to be so great, that it can no longer be employed with the antient profit in that species of industry which is peculiar to them. That industry has its limits like every other; and the increase of stock, by increasing the competition, necessarily reduces the profit. The lowering of profit in the town forces out stock to the country, where, by creating a new demand for country labour, it necessarily raises its wages. It then spreads itself, if I may say so, over the face of the land, and by being employed in agriculture is in part restored to the country, at the expence of which, in a great measure, it had originally been accumulated in the town. That every where in Europe the greatest improvements of the country have been owing to such overflowings of the stock originally accumulated in the towns, I shall endeavour to show hereafter;* and at the same time to demonstrate, that though some countries have by this course attained to a considerable degree of opulence, it is in itself necessarily slow, uncertain, liable to be disturbed and interrupted by innumerable accidents, and in every respect contrary to the order of nature and of reason. The interests, prejudices, laws and customs which have given occasion to it, I shall endeavour to explain as fully and distinctly as I can in the third and fourth books of this enquiry.

People of the same trade seldom meet together, even for merriment and diversion, but the conversation ends in a conspiracy against the publick, or in some contrivance to raise prices. It is impossible indeed to prevent such meetings, by any law which either could be executed, or would be consistent with liberty and justice. But though the law cannot hinder people of the same trade from sometimes assembling together, it ought to do nothing to facilitate such assemblies; much less to render them necessary.

A regulation which obliges all those of the same trade in a particular town to enter their names and places of abode in a publick register, facilitates such assemblies. It connects individuals who might never otherwise be known to one another, and gives every man of the trade a direction where to find every other man of it.

A regulation which enables those of the same trade to tax themselves in order to provide for their poor, their sick, their widows and orphans,* by giving them a common interest to manage, renders such assemblies necessary.

An incorporation not only renders them necessary, but makes the act of the majority binding upon the whole. In a free trade an effectual combination cannot be established but by the unanimous consent of every single trader, and it cannot last longer than every single trader continues of the same mind. The majority of a corporation can enact a bye-law with proper penalties, which will limit the competition more effectually and more durably than any voluntary combination whatever.

The pretence that corporations are necessary for the better government of the trade, is without any foundation. The real and effectual discipline which is exercised over a workman, is not that of his corporation, but that of his customers. It is the fear of losing their employment which restrains his frauds and corrects his negligence. An exclusive corporation necessarily weakens the force of this discipline. A particular set of workmen must then be employed, let them behave well or ill. It is upon this account that in many large incorporated towns no tolerable workmen are to be found, even in some of the most necessary trades. If you would have your work tolerably executed, it must be done in the suburbs, where the workmen having no exclusive privilege, have nothing but their character to depend upon, and you must then smuggle it into the town as well as you can.

It is in this manner that the policy of Europe, by restraining the competition in some employments to a smaller number than would otherwise be disposed to enter into them, occasions a very important inequality in the whole of the advantages and disadvantages of the different employments of labour and stock.

Secondly, The policy of Europe, by increasing the competition in some employments beyond what it naturally would be, occasions another inequality of an opposite kind in the whole of the advantages and disadvantages of the different employments of labour and stock.

It has been considered as of so much importance that a proper number of young people should be educated for certain professions, that, sometimes the publick, and sometimes the piety of private founders have established many pensions, scholarships, exhibitions, bursaries, &c. for this purpose, which draw many more people into those trades than could otherwise pretend to follow them. In all christian countries, I believe, the education of the greater part of churchmen is paid for in this manner. Very few of them are educated altogether at their own expence. The long, tedious and expensive education, therefore, of those who are, will not always procure them a suitable reward, the church being crowded with people who, in order to get employment, are willing to accept of a much smaller recompence than what such an education would otherwise have entitled them to; and in this manner the competition of the poor takes away the reward of the rich. It would be indecent, no doubt, to compare either a curate or a chaplain with a journeyman in any common trade. The pay of a curate or chaplain, however, may very properly be considered as of the same nature with the wages of a journeyman. They are, all three, paid for their work according to the contract which they may happen to make with their respective superiors. Till after the middle of the fourteenth century, five merks, containing about as much silver as ten pounds of our present money, was in England the usual pay of a curate or stipendiary parish priest, as we find it regulated by the decrees of several different national councils. At the same period four-pence a day, containing the same quantity of silver as a shilling of our present money, was declared to be the pay of a master mason, and three-pence a day, equal to nine-pence of our present money, that of a journeyman mason.[6] The wages of both these labourers, therefore, supposing them to have been constantly employed, were much superior to those of the curate. The wages of the master mason, supposing him to have been without employment one-third of the year, would have fully equalled them. By the 12th of Queen Anne, c.12,* it is declared, "That whereas for want of sufficient maintenance and encouragement to curates, the cures* have in several places been meanly supplied, the bishop is, therefore, empowered to appoint by writing under his hand and seal a sufficient certain stipend or allowance, not exceeding fifty and not less than twenty pounds a year". Forty pounds a year is reckoned at present very good pay for a curate, and notwithstanding this act of parliament, there are many curacies under twenty pounds a year. There are journeymen shoemakers in London who earn forty pounds a year, and there is scarce an industrious workman of any kind in that metropolis who does not earn more than twenty. This last sum indeed does not exceed what is frequently earned by common labourers in many country parishes. Whenever the law has attempted to regulate the wages of workmen, it has always been rather to lower them than to raise them. But the law has upon many occasions attempted to raise the wages of curates, and for the dignity of the church, to oblige the rectors of parishes to give them more than the wretched maintenance which they themselves might be willing to accept of. And in both cases

---

[6] See the Statute of labourers, 25 Ed.III. [25 Edward III, 2 (1350) in *Statutes of the Realm*, i.311; 25 Edward II, st.I in Ruffhead's edition.] [Campbell and Skinner]

the law seems to have been equally ineffectual, and has never either been able to raise the wages of curates or to sink those of labourers to the degree that was intended; because it has never been able to hinder either the one from being willing to accept of less than the legal allowance, on account of the indigence of their situation and the multitude of their competitors; or the other from receiving more, on account of the contrary competition of those who expected to derive either profit or pleasure from employing them.

The great benefices and other ecclesiastical dignities support the honour of the church, notwithstanding the mean circumstances of some of its inferior members. The respect paid to the profession too makes some compensation even to them for the meanness of their pecuniary recompence. In England, and in all Roman Catholick countries, the lottery of the church is in reality much more advantageous than is necessary. The example of the churches of Scotland, of Geneva,* and of several other protestant churches, may satisfy us that in so creditable a profession, in which education is so easily procured, the hopes of much more moderate benefices will draw a sufficient number of learned, decent, and respectable men into holy orders.

In professions in which there are no benefices, such as law and physick, if an equal proportion of people were educated at the publick expence, the competition would soon be so great, as to sink very much their pecuniary reward. It might then not be worth any man's while to educate his son to either of those professions at his own expence. They would be entirely abandoned to such as had been educated by those publick charities, whose numbers and necessities would oblige them in general to content themselves with a very miserable recompence, to the entire degradation of the now respectable professions of law and physick.

That unprosperous race of men commonly called men of letters, are pretty much in the situation which lawyers and physicians probably would be in upon the foregoing supposition. In every part of Europe the greater part of them have been educated for the church, but have been hindered by different reasons from entering into holy orders.* They have generally, therefore, been educated at the publick expence, and their numbers are every-where so great as commonly to reduce the price of their labour to a very paultry recompence.

Before the invention of the art of printing, the only employment by which a man of letters could make any thing by his talents, was that of a publick or private teacher, or by communicating to other people the curious and useful knowledge which he had acquired himself: And this is still surely a more honourable, a more useful, and in general even a more profitable employment than that other of writing for a bookseller,* to which the art of printing has given occasion. The time and study, the genius, knowledge, and application requisite to qualify an eminent teacher of the sciences, are at least equal to what is necessary for the greatest practitioners in law and physick. But the usual reward of the eminent teacher bears no proportion to that of the lawyer or physician;* because the trade of the one is crowded with indigent people who have been brought up to it at the publick expence; whereas those of the other two are incumbered with very few who have not been educated at their own. The usual recompence, however, of publick and private teachers, small as it may appear, would undoubtedly be less than it is, if the competition of those yet more indigent men of letters who write for bread was not taken out of the market. Before the invention of the art of printing, a scholar and a beggar seem to have been terms very nearly synonimous. The different governors of the universities before that time appear to have often granted licences to their scholars to beg.

In antient times, before any charities of this kind had been established for the education of indigent people to the learned professions, the rewards of eminent teachers appear to have been much more considerable. Isocrates,* in what is called his discourse against the sophists, reproaches the teachers of his own times with inconsistency. "They make the most magnificent promises to their scholars", says he, "and undertake to teach to be wise, to be happy, and to be just, and in return for so important a service they stipulate the paultry reward of four or five minae. They who teach wisdom", continues he, "ought certainly to be wise themselves; but if any man was to sell such a bargain for such a price, he would be convicted of the most evident folly." He certainly does not mean here to exaggerate the reward, and we may be assured that it was not less than he represents it. Four minae were equal to thirteen pounds six shillings and eight pence: five minae to sixteen pounds thirteen shillings and four pence. Something not less than the largest of those two sums, therefore, must at that time have been usually paid to the most eminent teachers at Athens. Isocrates himself demanded ten minae, or thirty-three pounds six shillings and eight pence, from each scholar. When he taught at Athens, he is said to have had an hundred scholars. I understand this to be the number whom he taught at one time, or who attended what we would call one course of lectures, a number which will not appear extraordinary from so great a city to so famous a teacher, who taught too what was at that time the most fashionable of all sciences, rhetorick. He must have made, therefore, by each course of lectures, a thousand minae, or 3,333 *l.* 6*s.* 8*d.* A thousand minae, accordingly, is said by Plutarch in another place, to have been his Didactron,* or usual price of teaching. Many other eminent teachers in those times appear to have acquired great fortunes. Gorgias made a present to the temple of Delphi of his own statue in solid gold. We must not, I presume, suppose that it was as large as the life. His way of living, as well as that of Hippias and Protagoras,* two other eminent teachers of those times, is represented by Plato as splendid even to ostentation. Plato himself is said to have lived with a good deal of magnificence. Aristotle, after having been tutor to Alexander and most munificently rewarded, as it is universally agreed, both by him and his father Phillip, thought it worth while, notwithstanding, to return to Athens, in order to resume the teaching of his school. Teachers of the sciences were probably in those times less common than they came to be in an age or two afterwards, when the competition had probably somewhat re-duced both the price of their labour and the admiration for their persons. The most eminent of them, however, appear always to have enjoyed a degree of consideration much superior to any of the like profession in the present times. The Athen-ians sent Carneades the academick, and Diogenes the stoick,* upon a solemn embassy to Rome; and though their city had then declined from its former grandeur, it was still an inde-pendent and considerable republick. Carneades too was a Baby-lonian by birth, and as there never was a people more jealous of admitting foreigners to publick offices than the Athenians, their consideration for him must have been very great.

This inequality is upon the whole, perhaps, rather advant-ageous than hurtful to the publick. It may somewhat degrade the profession of a publick teacher; but the cheapness of literary education is surely an advantage which greatly over-balances this trifling inconveniency. The publick too might derive still greater benefit from it, if the constitution of those schools and colleges, in which education is carried on,* was more reason-able than it is at present through the greater part of Europe.

Thirdly, The policy of Europe, by obstructing the free circulation of labour and stock both from employment to employment, and from place to place, occasions in some cases a very inconvenient inequality in the whole of the advantages and disadvantages of their different employments.

The statute of apprenticeship obstructs the free circulation of labour from one employment to another, even in the same place. The exclusive privileges of corporations* obstruct it from one place to another, even in the same employment.

It frequently happens that while high wages are given to the workmen in one manufacture, those in another are obliged to content themselves with bare subsistence. The one is in an advancing state, and has, therefore, a continual demand for new hands: The other is in a declining state, and the super-abundance of hands is continually increasing. Those two manu-factures may sometimes be in the same town, and sometimes in the same neighbourhood, without being able to lend the least assistance to one another. The statute of apprenticeship may oppose it in the one case, and both that and an exclusive corporation in the other. In many different manufactures, however, the operations are so much alike, that the workmen could easily change trades with one another, if those absurd laws did not hinder them. The arts of weaving plain linen and plain silk, for example, are almost entirely the same. That of weaving plain woollen is somewhat different; but the difference is so insignificant, that either a linen or a silk weaver might become a tolerable workman in a very few days. If any of those three capital manufactures, therefore, were decaying, the workmen might find a resource in one of the other two which was in a more prosperous condition; and their wages would neither rise too high in the thriving, nor sink too low in the decaying manufacture. The linen manufacture indeed is, in England, by a particular statute, open to every body; but, as it is not much cultivated through the greater part of the country, it can afford no general resource to the workmen of other decaying manufactures, who, wherever the statute of apprenticeship takes place, have no other choice but either to come upon the parish,* or to work as common labourers, for which, by their habits, they are much worse qualified than for any sort of manufacture that bears any resemblance to their own. They generally, therefore, chuse to come upon the parish.

Whatever obstructs the free circulation of labour from one employment to another, obstructs that of stock likewise; the quantity of stock which can be employed in any branch of business depending very much upon that of the labour which can be employed in it. Corporation laws, however, give less obstruction to the free circulation of stock from one place to another than to that of labour. It is every-where much easier for a wealthy merchant to obtain the privilege of trading in a town corporate, than for a poor artificer to obtain that of working in it.

The obstruction which corporation laws give to the free circulation of labour is common, I believe, to every part of Europe. That which is given to it by the poor laws* is, so far as I know, peculiar to England. It consists in the difficulty which a poor man finds in obtaining a settlement, or even in being allowed to exercise his industry in any parish but that to which he belongs. It is the labour of artificers and manufacturers only of which the free circulation is obstructed by corporation laws. The difficulty of obtaining settlements obstructs even that of common labour. It may be worth while to give some account of the rise, progress, and present state of this disorder, the greatest perhaps of any in the police of England.*

When by the destruction of monasteries the poor had been deprived of the charity of those religious houses, after some other ineffectual attempts for their relief, it was enacted by the 43d of Elizabeth, c.2. that every parish should be bound to provide for its own poor; and that overseers of the poor should be annually appointed, who, with the churchwardens, should raise by a parish rate, competent sums for this purpose.

By this statute the necessity of providing for their own poor was indispensably imposed upon every parish. Who were to be considered as the poor of each parish, became, therefore, a question of some importance. This question, after some variation, was at last determined by the 13th and 14th of Charles II. when it was enacted, that forty days undisturbed residence should gain any person a settlement in any parish; but that within that time it should be lawful for two justices of the peace, upon complaint made by the churchwardens or overseers of the poor, to remove any new inhabitant to the parish where he was last legally settled; unless he either rented a tenement of ten pounds a year, or could give such security for the discharge of the parish where he was then living, as those justices should judge sufficient.

Some frauds, it is said, were committed in consequence of this statute; parish officers sometimes bribing their own poor to go clandestinely to another parish, and by keeping themselves concealed for forty days to gain a settlement there, to the discharge of that to which they properly belonged. It was enacted, therefore, by the 1st of James II. that the forty days undisturbed residence of any person necessary to gain a settlement, should be accounted only from the time of his delivering notice in writing, of the place of his abode and the number of his family, to one of the churchwardens or overseers of the parish where he came to dwell.

But parish officers, it seems, were not always more honest with regard to their own, than they had been with regard to other parishes, and sometimes connived at such intrusions, receiving the notice, and taking no proper steps in consequence of it. As every person in a parish, therefore, was supposed to have an interest to prevent as much as possible their being burdened by such intruders, it was further enacted by the 3d of William III. that the forty days residence should be accounted only from the publication of such notice in writing on Sunday in the church, immediately after divine service.

"After all," says Doctor Burn,* "this kind of settlement, by continuing forty days after publication of notice in writing, is very seldom obtained; and the design of the acts is not so much for gaining of settlements, as for the avoiding of them, by persons coming into a parish clandestinely: for the giving of notice is only putting a force upon the parish to remove. But if a person's situation is such, that it is doubtful whether he is actually removeable or not, he shall by giving of notice compel the parish either to allow him a settlement uncontested, by suffering him to continue forty days; or, by removing him, to try the right".

This statute, therefore, rendered it almost impracticable for a poor man to gain a new settlement in the old way, by forty days inhabitancy. But that it might not appear to preclude altogether the common people of one parish from ever establishing themselves with security in another, it appointed four other ways by which a settlement might be gained without any notice delivered or published. The first was, by being taxed to parish rates and paying them; the second, by being elected into an annual parish office and serving in it a year; the third, by serving an apprenticeship in the parish; the fourth, by being hired into service there for a year, and continuing in the same service during the whole of it.

Nobody can gain a settlement by either of the two first ways, but by the publick deed of the whole parish, who are too well aware of the consequences to adopt any new-comer who has nothing but his labour to support him, either by taxing him to parish rates, or by electing him into a parish office.

No married man can well gain any settlement in either of the two last ways. An apprentice is scarce ever married; and it is expressly enacted, that no married servant shall gain any settlement by being hired for a year. The principal effect of introducing settlement by service, has been to put out in a great measure the old fashion of hiring for a year, which before had been so customary in England, that even at this day, if no particular term is agreed upon, the law intends that every servant is hired for a year. But masters are not always willing to give their servants a settlement by hiring them in this manner; and servants are not always willing to be so hired, because as every last settlement discharges all the foregoing, they might thereby lose their original settlement in the places of their nativity, the habitation of their parents and relations.

No independent workman, it is evident, whether labourer or artificer, is likely to gain any new settlement either by apprenticeship or by service. When such a person, therefore, carried his industry to a new parish, he was liable to be removed, how healthy and industrious soever, at the caprice of any churchwarden or overseer, unless he either rented a tenement of ten pounds a year, a thing impossible for one who has nothing but his labour to live by; or could give such security for the discharge of the parish as two justices of the peace should judge sufficient. What security they shall require, indeed, is left altogether to their discretion; but they cannot well require less than thirty pounds, it having been enacted, that the purchase even of a free-hold estate of less than thirty pounds value, shall not gain any person a settlement, as not being sufficient for the discharge of the parish. But this is a security which scarce

any man who lives by labour can give; and much greater
security is frequently demanded.

In order to restore in some measure that free circulation of
labour which those different statutes had almost entirely taken
away, the invention of certificates was fallen upon. By the 8th
and 9th of William III it was enacted, that if any person should
bring a certificate from the parish where he was last legally
settled, subscribed by the churchwardens and overseers of the
poor, and allowed by two justices of the peace, that every other
parish should be obliged to receive him; that he should not be
removeable merely upon account of his being likely to become
chargeable, but only upon his becoming actually chargeable,
and that then the parish which granted the certificate should
be obliged to pay the expence both of his maintenance and of
his removal. And in order to give the most perfect security to
the parish where such certificated man should come to reside,
it was further enacted by the same statute, that he should gain
no settlement there by any means whatever, except either by
renting a tenement of ten pounds a year, or by serving upon
his own account in an annual parish office for one whole year;
and consequently neither by notice, nor by service, nor by
apprenticeship, nor by paying parish rates. By the 12th of
Queen Anne too, stat. I. c. 18. it was further enacted, that
neither the servants nor apprentices of such certificated man
should gain any settlement in the parish where he resided
under such certificate.

How far this invention has restored that free circulation of
labour which the preceding statutes had almost entirely taken
away, we may learn from the following very judicious observation of Doctor Burn. "It is obvious," says he, "that there are
divers good reasons for requiring certificates with persons
coming to settle in any place; namely, that persons residing
under them can gain no settlement, neither by apprenticeship,
nor by service, nor by giving notice, nor by paying parish rates;
that they can settle neither apprentices nor servants; that if
they become chargeable, it is certainly known whither to
remove them, and the parish shall be paid for the removal, and

for their maintenance in the mean time; and that if they fall sick, and cannot be removed, the parish which gave the certificate must maintain them: none of all which can be without a certificate. Which reasons will hold proportionably for parishes not granting certificates in ordinary cases; for it is far more than an equal chance, but that they will have the certificated persons again, and in a worse condition".* The moral of this observation seems to be, that certificates ought always to be required by the parish where any poor man comes to reside, and that they ought very seldom to be granted by that which he proposes to leave. "There is somewhat of hardship in this matter of certificates" says the same very intelligent author in his History of the Poor Laws,* "by putting it in the power of a parish officer, to imprison a man as it were for life; however inconvenient it may be for him to continue at that place where he has had the misfortune to acquire what is called a settlement, or whatever advantage he may propose to himself by living elsewhere".

Though a certificate carries along with it no testimonial of good behaviour, and certifies nothing but that the person belongs to the parish to which he really does belong, it is altogether discretionary in the parish officers either to grant or to refuse it. A mandamus* was once moved for, says Doctor Burn, to compel the church-wardens and overseers to sign a certificate; but the court of King's Bench rejected the motion as a very strange attempt.*

The very unequal price of labour which we frequently find in England in places at no great distance from one another, is probably owing to the obstruction which the law of settlements gives to a poor man who would carry his industry from one parish to another without a certificate. A single man, indeed, who is healthy and industrious, may sometimes reside by sufferance without one; but a man with a wife and family who should attempt to do so, would in most parishes be sure of being removed, and if the single man should afterwards marry, he would generally be removed likewise. The scarcity of hands in one parish, therefore, cannot always be relieved by their super-abundance in another, as it is constantly in Scotland, and, I believe, in all other countries where there is no difficulty of settlement. In such countries, though wages may sometimes rise a little in the neighbourhood of a great town, or wherever else there is an extraordinary demand for labour, and sink gradually as the distance from such places increases, till they fall back to the common rate of the country; yet we never meet with those sudden and unaccountable differences in the wages of neighbouring places which we sometimes find in England, where it is often more difficult for a poor man to pass the artificial boundary of a parish, than an arm of the sea or a ridge of high mountains, natural boundaries which sometimes separate very distinctly different rates of wages in other countries.

To remove a man who has committed no misdemeanour from the parish where he chuses to reside, is an evident violation of natural liberty and justice. The common people of England, however, so jealous of their liberty, but like the common people of most other countries never rightly understanding wherein it consists, have now for more than a century together suffered themselves to be exposed to this oppression without a remedy. Though men of reflection too have sometimes complained of the law of settlements as a publick grievance; yet it has never been the object of any general popular clamour, such as that against general warrants,* an abusive practice undoubtedly, but such a one as was not likely to occasion any general oppression. There is scarce a poor man in England of forty years of age, I will venture to say, who has not in some part of his life felt himself most cruelly oppressed by this ill-contrived law of settlements.

I shall conclude this long chapter with observing, that though antiently it was usual to rate wages, first by general laws extending over the whole kingdom, and afterwards by particular orders of the justices of peace in every particular county, both these practices have now gone entirely into disuse. "By the experience of above four hundred years," says Doctor Burn, "it seems time to lay aside all endeavours to bring under strict regulations, what in its own nature seems incapable of minute limitation: for if all persons in the same kind of work were to receive equal wages, there would be no emulation, and no room left for industry or ingenuity".*

Particular acts of parliament, however, still attempt sometimes to regulate wages in particular trades and in particular places. Thus the 8th of George III. prohibits under heavy penalties all master taylors in London, and five miles round it, from giving, and their workmen from accepting, more than two shillings and seven-pence halfpenny a day, except in the case of a general mourning.* Whenever the legislature attempts to regulate the differences between masters and their workmen, its counsellors are always the masters. When the regulation, therefore, is in favour of the workmen, it is always just and equitable; but it is sometimes otherwise when in favour of the masters. Thus the law which obliges the masters in several different trades to pay their workmen in money and not in goods, is quite just and equitable. It imposes no real hardship upon the masters. It only obliges them to pay that value in money, which they pretended to pay, but did not always really pay, in goods. This law is in favour of the workmen; but the 8th of George III. is in favour of the masters. When masters combine together in order to reduce the wages of their workmen, they commonly enter into a private bond or agreement, not to give more than a certain wage under a certain penalty. Were the workmen to enter into a contrary combination of the same kind, not to accept of a certain wage under a certain penalty, the law would punish them very severely; and if it dealt impartially, it would treat the masters in the same manner. But the 8th of George III. enforces by law that very regulation which masters sometimes attempt to establish by such combinations. The complaint of the workmen, that it puts the ablest and most industrious upon the same footing with an ordinary workman, seems perfectly well founded.

In antient times too it was usual to attempt to regulate the profits of merchants and other dealers, by rating the price both of provisions and other goods. The assize of bread* is, so far as I know, the only remnant of this ancient usage. Where there is an exclusive corporation, it may perhaps be proper to regulate the price of the first necessary of life. But where there is none, the competition will regulate it much better than any assize. The method of fixing the assize of bread established by the 31st of George II. could not be put in practice in Scotland, on account of a defect in the law; its execution depending upon the office of clerk of the market, which does not exist there. This defect was not remedied till the 3d of George III. The want of an assize occasioned no sensible inconveniency, and the establishment of one, in the few places where it has yet taken place, has produced no sensible advantage. In the greater part of the towns of Scotland, however, there is an incorporation of bakers who claim exclusive privileges, though they are not very strictly guarded.

The proportion between the different rates both of wages and profit in the different employments of labour and stock, seems not to be much affected, as has already been observed,* by the riches or poverty, the advancing, stationary, or declining state of the society. Such revolutions in the publick welfare, though they affect the general rates both of wages and profit, must in the end affect them equally in all different employments. The proportion between them, therefore, must remain the same, and cannot well be altered, at least for any considerable time, by any such revolutions.

CHAPTER XI

Of the Rent of Land*

RENT, considered as the price paid for the use of land, is naturally the highest which the tenant can afford to pay in the actual circumstances of the land. In adjusting the terms of the lease, the landlord endeavours to leave him no greater share of the produce than what is sufficient to keep up the stock from which he furnishes the seed, pays the labour, and purchases and maintains the cattle and other instruments of husbandry, together with the ordinary profits of farming stock in the neighbourhood. This is evidently the smallest share with which the tenant can content himself without being a loser, and the landlord seldom means to leave him any more. Whatever part of the produce, or, what is the same thing, whatever part of its price, is over and above this share, he naturally endeavours to reserve to himself as the rent of his land, which is evidently the highest the tenant can afford to pay in the actual circumstances of the land. Sometimes, indeed, the liberality, more frequently the ignorance, of the landlord, makes him accept of somewhat less than this portion; and sometimes too, though more rarely, the ignorance of the tenant makes him undertake to pay somewhat more, or to content himself with somewhat less than the ordinary profits of farming stock in the neighbourhood. This portion, however, may still be considered as the natural rent of land, or the rent for which it is naturally meant that land should for the most part be let.

The rent of land, it may be thought, is frequently no more than a reasonable profit or interest for the stock laid out by the landlord upon its improvement.* This, no doubt, may be partly the case upon some occasions; for it can scarce ever be more than partly the case. The landlord demands a rent even for unimproved land, and the supposed interest or profit upon the expence of improvement is generally an addition to this original rent. Those improvements, besides, are not always made by the stock of the landlord, but sometimes by that of the tenant. When the lease comes to be renewed, however, the landlord commonly demands the same augmentation of rent, as if they had been all made by his own.

He sometimes demands rent for what is altogether incapable of human improvement. Kelp is a species of sea-weed,* which, when burnt, yields an alkaline salt, useful for making glass, soap, and for several other purposes. It grows in several parts of Great Britain, particularly in Scotland, upon such rocks only as lie within the high water mark, which are twice every day covered with the sea, and of which the produce, therefore, was never augmented by human industry. The landlord, however, whose estate is bounded by a kelp shore of this kind, demands a rent for it as much as for his corn fields.

The sea in the neighbourhood of the islands of Shetland is more than commonly abundant in fish, which make a great part of the subsistence of their inhabitants. But in order to profit by the produce of the water, they must have a habitation upon the neighbouring land. The rent of the landlord is in proportion, not to what the farmer can make by the land, but to what he can make both by the land and by the water. It is partly paid in sea-fish,* and one of the very few instances in which rent makes a part of the price of that commodity, is to be found in that country.

The rent of land, therefore, considered as the price paid for the use of the land, is naturally a monopoly price. It is not at all proportioned to what the landlord may have laid out upon the improvement of the land, or to what he can afford to take; but to what the farmer can afford to give.

Such parts only of the produce of land can commonly be brought to market of which the ordinary price is sufficient to replace the stock which must be employed in bringing them thither, together with its ordinary profits. If the ordinary price is more than this, the surplus part of it will naturally go to the rent of the land. If it is not more, though the commodity may be brought to market, it can afford no rent to the landlord.

Whether the price is, or is not more, depends upon the demand.

There are some parts of the produce of land for which the demand must always be such as to afford a greater price than what is sufficient to bring them to market; and there are others for which it either may or may not be such as to afford this greater price. The former must always afford a rent to the landlord. The latter sometimes may, and sometimes may not, according to different circumstances.

Rent, it is to be observed, therefore, enters into the composition of the price of commodities in a different way from wages and profit. High or low wages and profit, are the causes of high or low price; high or low rent is the effect of it. It is because high or low wages and profit must be paid, in order to bring a particular commodity to market, that its price is high or low. But it is because its price is high or low; a great deal more, or very little more, or no more, than what is sufficient to pay those wages and profit, that it affords a high rent, or a low rent, or no rent at all.

The particular consideration, first, of those parts of the produce of land which always afford some rent; secondly, of those which sometimes may and sometimes may not afford rent; and, thirdly, of the variations which, in the different periods of improvement, naturally take place, in the relative value of those two different sorts of rude produce, when compared both with one another and with manufactured commodities, will divide this chapter into three parts.

PART I

Of the Produce of Land which always affords Rent

As men, like all other animals, naturally multiply in proportion to the means of their subsistence,* food is always, more or less, in demand. It can always purchase or command a greater or smaller quantity of labour, and somebody can always be found who is willing to do something, in order to obtain it. The quantity of labour, indeed, which it can purchase, is not always equal to what it could maintain, if managed in the most œconomical manner, on account of the high wages which are sometimes given to labour. But it can always purchase such a quantity of labour as it can maintain, according to the rate at which that sort of labour is commonly maintained in the neighbourhood.

But land, in almost any situation, produces a greater quantity of food than what is sufficient to maintain all the labour necessary for bringing it to market, in the most liberal way in which that labour is ever maintained. The surplus too is always more than sufficient to replace the stock which employed that labour, together with its profits. Something, therefore, always remains for a rent to the landlord.

The most desart moors in Norway and Scotland produce some sort of pasture for cattle, of which the milk and the increase are always more than sufficient, not only to maintain all the labour necessary for tending them, and to pay the ordinary profit to the farmer or owner of the herd or flock; but to afford some small rent to the landlord. The rent increases in proportion to the goodness of the pasture. The same extent of ground not only maintains a greater number of cattle, but as they are brought within a smaller compass, less labour becomes requisite to tend them, and to collect their produce. The landlord gains both ways; by the increase of the produce, and by the diminution of the labour which must be maintained out of it.

The rent of land not only varies with its fertility, whatever be its produce, but with its situation, whatever be its fertility. Land in the neighbourhood of a town, gives a greater rent than land equally fertile in a distant part of the country. Though it may cost no more labour to cultivate the one than the other, it must always cost more to bring the produce of the distant land to market. A greater quantity of labour, therefore, must be maintained out of it; and the surplus, from which are drawn both the profit of the farmer and the rent of the landlord, must be diminished. But in remote parts of the country the rate of profit, as has already been shown,* is generally higher than in the neighbourhood of a large town. A smaller proportion of this diminished surplus, therefore, must belong to the landlord.

Good roads, canals, and navigable rivers,* by diminishing the expence of carriage, put the remote parts of the country more nearly upon a level with those in the neighbourhood of the town. They are upon that account the greatest of all improvements. They encourage the cultivation of the remote, which must always be the most extensive circle of the country. They are advantageous to the town, by breaking down the monopoly of the country in its neighbourhood. They are advantageous even to that part of the country. Though they introduce some rival commodities into the old market, they open many new markets to its produce. Monopoly, besides, is a great enemy to good management, which can never be universally established but in consequence of that free and universal competition which forces every body to have recourse to it for the sake of self-defence. It is not more than fifty years ago that some of the counties in the neighbourhood of London, petitioned the parliament against the extension of the turnpike roads into the remoter counties. Those remoter counties, they pretended, from the cheapness of labour, would be able to sell their grass and corn cheaper in the London market than themselves, and would thereby reduce their rents, and ruin their cultivation. Their rents, however, have risen, and their cultivation has been improved since that time. . . .

PART II

Of the Produce of Land which sometimes does, and sometimes does not, afford Rent

Human food seems to be the only produce of land which always and necessarily affords some rent to the landlord. Other sorts of produce sometimes may and sometimes may not, according to different circumstances.

After food, cloathing and lodging are the two great wants of mankind.*

Land in its original rude state can afford the materials of cloathing and lodging to a much greater number of people than it can feed. In its improved state it can sometimes feed a greater number of people than it can supply with those materials; at least in the way in which they require them, and are willing to pay for them. In the one state, therefore, there is always a super-abundance of those materials, which are frequently, upon that account, of little or no value. In the other there is often a scarcity, which necessarily augments their value. In the one state a great part of them is thrown away as useless, and the price of what is used is considered as equal only to the labour and expence of fitting it for use, and can, therefore, afford no rent to the landlord. In the other they are all made use of, and there is frequently a demand for more than can be had. Somebody is always willing to give more for every part of them than what is sufficient to pay the expence of bringing them to market. Their price, therefore, can always afford some rent to the landlord.

The skins of the larger animals were the original materials of cloathing. Among nations of hunters and shepherds, therefore, whose food consists chiefly in the flesh of those animals, every man, by providing himself with food, provides himself with the materials of more cloathing than he can wear. If there was no foreign commerce, the greater part of them would be thrown away as things of no value. This was probably the case among the hunting nations of North America,* before their country was discovered by the Europeans, with whom they now exchange their surplus peltry,* for blankets, fire-arms, and brandy, which gives it some value. In the present commercial state of the known world, the most barbarous nations, I believe, among whom land property is established, have some foreign commerce of this kind, and find among their wealthier neighbours such a demand for all the materials of cloathing, which their land produces, and which can neither be wrought up nor consumed at home, as raises their price above what it costs to send them to those wealthier neighbours. It affords, therefore, some rent to the landlord. When the greater part of the highland cattle were consumed on their own hills, the exportation of their hides made the most considerable article of the commerce of that country, and what they were exchanged for afforded some addition to the rent of the highland estates. The wool of England, which in old times could neither be consumed nor wrought up at home, found a market in the then wealthier and more industrious country of Flanders, and its price afforded something to the rent of the land which produced it. In countries not better cultivated than England was then, or than the highlands of Scotland are now,* and which had no foreign commerce, the materials of cloathing would evidently be so super-abundant, that a great part of them would be thrown away as useless, and no part could afford any rent to the landlord.

The materials of lodging cannot always be transported to so great a distance as those of cloathing, and do not so readily become an object of foreign commerce. When they are super-abundant in the country which produces them, it frequently happens, even in the present commercial state of the world, that they are of no value to the landlord. A good stone quarry in the neighbourhood of London would afford a considerable rent. In many parts of Scotland and Wales it affords none. Barren timber for building is of great value in a populous and well-cultivated country, and the land which produces it, affords a considerable rent. But in many parts of North America the landlord would be much obliged to any body who would carry away the greater part of his large trees. In some parts of the highlands of Scotland the bark is the only part of the wood which, for want of roads and water-carriage, can be sent to market. The timber is left to rot upon the ground. When the materials of lodging are so super-abundant, the part made use of is worth only the labour and expence of fitting it for that use. It affords no rent to the landlord, who generally grants the use of it to whoever takes the trouble of asking it. The demand of wealthier nations, however, sometimes enables him to get a rent for it. The paving of the streets of London* has enabled the owners of some barren rocks on the coast of

Scotland to draw a rent from what never afforded any before. The woods of Norway and of the coasts of the Baltick,
find a market in many parts of Great Britain which they could
not find at home, and thereby afford some rent to their
proprietors.

Countries are populous, not in proportion to the number of
people whom their produce can cloath and lodge, but in
proportion to that of those whom it can feed. When food is
provided, it is easy to find the necessary cloathing and lodging.
But though these are at hand, it may often be difficult to find
food. In some parts even of the British dominions what is called
A House, may be built by one day's labour of one man. The
simplest species of cloathing, the skins of animals, requires
somewhat more labour to dress and prepare them for use. They
do not, however, require a great deal. Among savage and
barbarous nations, a hundredth or little more than a hundredth
part of the labour of the whole year, will be sufficient to
provide them with such cloathing and lodging as satisfy the
greater part of the people. All the other ninety-nine parts are
frequently no more than enough to provide them with food.

But when by the improvement and cultivation of land the
labour of one family can provide food for two, the labour of
half the society becomes sufficient to provide food for the
whole. The other half, therefore, or at least the greater part of
them, can be employed in providing other things, or in satisfying the other wants and fancies of mankind. Cloathing and
lodging, houshold furniture, and what is called Equipage,* are
the principal objects of the greater part of those wants and
fancies. The rich man consumes no more food than his poor
neighbour. In quality it may be very different, and to select
and prepare it may require more labour and art; but in quantity
it is very nearly the same. But compare the spacious palace
and great wardrobe of the one, with the hovel and the few rags
of the other, and you will be sensible that the difference
between their cloathing, lodging and houshold furniture, is
almost as great in quantity as it is in quality. The desire of
food is limited in every man by the narrow capacity of the

human stomach; but the desire of the conveniencies and ornaments of building, dress, equipage, and houshold furniture,
seems to have no limit or certain boundary. Those, therefore,
who have the command of more food than they themselves can
consume, are always willing to exchange the surplus, or, what
is the same thing, the price of it, for gratifications of this other
kind. What is over and above satisfying the limited desire, is
given for the amusement of those desires which cannot be
satisfied, but seem to be altogether endless.* The poor, in order
to obtain food, exert themselves to gratify those fancies of the
rich, and to obtain it more certainly, they vie with one another
in the cheapness and perfection of their work. The number of
workmen increases with the increasing quantity of food, or with
the growing improvement and cultivation of the lands; and as
the nature of their business admits of the utmost subdivisions
of labour, the quantity of materials which they can work up,
increases in a much greater proportion than their numbers.
Hence arises a demand for every sort of material which human
invention can employ, either usefully or ornamentally, in building, dress, equipage, or houshold furniture; for the fossils and
minerals contained in the bowels of the earth; the precious
metals, and the precious stones.

Food is in this manner, not only the original source of rent,
but every other part of the produce of land which afterwards
affords rent, derives that part of its value from the improvement of the powers of labour in producing food by means of
the improvement and cultivation of land.

Those other parts of the produce of land, however, which
afterwards afford rent, do not afford it always. Even in improved and cultivated countries, the demand for them is not
always such as to afford a greater price than what is sufficient
to pay the labour, and replace, together with its ordinary
profits, the stock which must be employed in bringing them
to market. Whether it is or is not such, depends upon different
circumstances.

Whether a coal-mine, for example, can afford any rent,
depends partly upon its fertility, and partly upon its situation.

A mine of any kind may be said to be either fertile or barren, according as the quantity of mineral which can be brought from it by a certain quantity of labour, is greater or less than what can be brought by an equal quantity from the greater part of other mines of the same kind.

Some coal-mines advantageously situated, cannot be wrought on account of their barrenness. The produce does not pay the expence. They can afford neither profit nor rent.

There are some of which the produce is barely sufficient to pay the labour, and replace, together with its ordinary profits, the stock employed in working them. They afford some profit to the undertaker of the work, but no rent to the landlord. They can be wrought advantageously by nobody but the landlord, who being himself undertaker of the work, gets the ordinary profit of the capital which he employs in it. Many coal-mines in Scotland* are wrought in this manner, and can be wrought in no other. The landlord will allow nobody else to work them without paying some rent, and nobody can afford to pay any. . . .

PART III

Of the Variations in the Proportion between the respective Values of that Sort of Produce which always affords Rent, and of that which sometimes does, and sometimes does not, afford Rent

The increasing abundance of food, in consequence of increasing improvement and cultivation, must necessarily increase the demand for every part of the produce of land which is not food, and which can be applied either to use or to ornament. In the whole progress of improvement, it might therefore be expected, there should be only one variation in the comparative values of those two different sorts of produce. The value of that sort which sometimes does and sometimes does not afford rent, should constantly rise in proportion to that which always affords some rent. As art and industry advance, the materials of cloathing and lodging, the useful fossils and minerals of the earth, the precious metals and the precious stones should gradually come to be more and more in demand, should gradually exchange for a greater and a greater quantity of food, or in other words, should gradually become dearer and dearer. This accordingly has been the case with most of these things upon most occasions, and would have been the case with all of them upon all occasions, if particular accidents had not upon some occasions increased the supply of some of them in a still greater proportion than the demand. . . .

Conclusion Of The Chapter

. . . The whole annual produce of the land and labour of every country, or what comes to the same thing, the whole price of that annual produce, naturally divides itself, it has already been observed,* into three parts; the rent of land, the wages of labour, and the profits of stock; and constitutes a revenue to three different orders of people; to those who live by rent, to those who live by wages, and to those who live by profit. These are the three great, original and constituent orders of every civilized society, from whose revenue that of every other order is ultimately derived.

The interest of the first of those three great orders, it appears from what has been just now said, is strictly and inseparably connected with the general interest of the society. Whatever either promotes or obstructs the one, necessarily promotes or obstructs the other. When the publick deliberates concerning any regulation of commerce or police,* the proprietors of land never can mislead it, with a view to promote the interest of their own particular order; at least, if they have any tolerable knowledge of that interest. They are, indeed, too often defective in this tolerable knowledge. They are the only one of the three orders whose revenue costs them neither labour nor care, but comes to them, as it were, of its own accord, and independent of any plan or project of their own. That indolence, which is the natural effect of the ease and security of their situation, renders them too often, not only ignorant, but incapable of that application of mind* which is necessary in order to foresee and understand the consequences of any publick regulation.

The interest of the second order, that of those who live by wages, is as strictly connected with the interest of the society as that of the first. The wages of the labourer, it has already been shewn,* are never so high as when the demand for labour is continually rising, or when the quantity employed is every year increasing considerably. When this real wealth of the society becomes stationary, his wages are soon reduced to what is barely enough to enable him to bring up a family, or to continue the race of labourers. When the society declines, they fall even below this. The order of proprietors may, perhaps, gain more by the prosperity of the society, than that of labourers: but there is no order that suffers so cruelly from its decline. But though the interest of the labourer is strictly connected with that of the society, he is incapable either of comprehending that interest, or of understanding its connection with his own. His condition leaves him no time to receive the necessary information, and his education and habits are commonly such as to render him unfit to judge even though he was fully informed. In the publick deliberations, therefore, his voice is little heard and less regarded, except upon some particular occasions, when his clamour is animated, set on, and supported by his employers, not for his, but their own particular purposes.

His employers constitute the third order, that of those who live by profit. It is the stock that is employed for the sake of profit, which puts into motion the greater part of the useful labour of every society. The plans and projects of the employers of stock regulate and direct all the most important operations of labour, and profit is the end proposed by all those plans and projects. But the rate of profit does not, like rent and wages, rise with the prosperity, and fall with the declension of the society. On the contrary, it is naturally low in rich, and high in poor countries, and it is always highest in the countries which are going fastest to ruin. The interest of this third order, therefore, has not the same connection with the general interest of the society as that of the other two. Merchants and master manufacturers are, in this order, the two classes of people who commonly employ the largest capitals, and who by their wealth draw to themselves the greatest share of the publick considera-tion. As during their whole lives they are engaged in plans and projects, they have frequently more acuteness of understanding than the greater part of country gentlemen. As their thoughts, however, are commonly exercised rather about the interest of their own particular branch of business, than about that of the society, their judgment, even when given with the greatest candour (which it has not been upon every occasion) is much more to be depended upon with regard to the former of those two objects, than with regard to the latter. Their superiority over the country gentleman is, not so much in their know-ledge of the publick interest, as in their having a better knowledge of their own interest than he has of his. It is by this superior knowledge of their own interest that they have frequently imposed upon his generosity, and persuaded him to give up both his own interest and that of the publick, from a very simple but honest conviction, that their interest, and not his, was the interest of the publick. The interest of the dealers, however, in any particular branch of trade or manufactures, is always in some respects different from, and even opposite to, that of the publick. To widen the market and to narrow the competition, is always the interest of the dealers. To widen the market may frequently be agreeable enough to the interest of the publick; but to narrow the competition must always be against it, and can serve only to enable the dealers, by raising their profits above what they naturally would be, to levy, for their own benefit, an absurd tax upon the rest of their fellow-citizens. The proposal of any new law or regulation of com-merce which comes from this order, ought always to be listened to with great precaution, and ought never to be adopted till after having been long and carefully examined, not only with the most scrupulous, but with the most suspicious attention. It comes from an order of men, whose interest is never exactly the same with that of the publick, who have generally an interest to deceive and even to oppress the publick, and who accordingly have, upon many occasions, both deceived and oppressed it. . . .

BOOK II

Of the Nature, Accumulation, and Employment of Stock

INTRODUCTION

IN that rude state of society in which there is no division of labour, in which exchanges are seldom made, and in which every man provides every thing for himself, it is not necessary that any stock should be accumulated or stored up beforehand in order to carry on the business of the society. Every man endeavours to supply by his own industry his own occasional wants as they occur. When he is hungry, he goes to the forest to hunt; when his coat is worn out, he cloaths himself with the skin of the first large animal he kills: and when his hut begins to go to ruin, he repairs it, as well as he can, with the trees and the turf that are nearest it.

But when the division of labour has once been thoroughly introduced, the produce of a man's own labour can supply but a very small part of his occasional wants. The far greater part of them are supplied by the produce of other mens labour, which he purchases with the produce, or, what is the same thing, with the price of the produce of his own. But this purchase cannot be made till such time as the produce of his own labour has not only been compleated, but sold. A stock of goods of different kinds, therefore, must be stored up somewhere sufficient to maintain him, and to supply him with the materials and tools of his work till such time, at least, as both these events can be brought about. A weaver cannot apply himself entirely to his peculiar business, unless there is beforehand stored up somewhere, either in his own possession or in that of some other person, a stock sufficient to maintain him, and to supply him with the materials and tools of his work, till he has not only compleated, but sold his web. This accumulation must, evidently, be previous to his applying his industry for so long a time to such a peculiar business.

As the accumulation of stock must, in the nature of things, be previous to the division of labour, so labour can be more and more subdivided in proportion only as stock is previously more and more accumulated. The quantity of materials which the same number of people can work up, increases in a great proportion as labour comes to be more and more subdivided; and as the operations of each workman are gradually reduced to a greater degree of simplicity, a variety of new machines come to be invented for facilitating and abridging those operations. As the division of labour advances, therefore, in order to give constant employment to an equal number of workmen, an equal stock of provisions, and a greater stock of materials and tools than what would have been necessary in a ruder state of things, must be accumulated beforehand. But the number of workmen in every branch of business generally increases with the division of labour in that branch, or rather it is the increase of their number which enables them to class and subdivide themselves in this manner.

As the accumulation of stock is previously necessary for carrying on this great improvement in the productive powers of labour, so that accumulation naturally leads to this improvement. The person who employs his stock in maintaining labour, necessarily wishes to employ it in such a manner as to produce as great a quantity of work as possible. He endeavours, therefore, both to make among his workmen the most proper distribution of employment, and to furnish them with the best machines which he can either invent or afford to purchase. His abilities in both these respects are generally in proportion to the extent of his stock, or to the number of people whom it can employ. The quantity of industry, therefore, not only increases in every country with the increase of the stock which employs it, but, in consequence of that increase, the same quantity of industry produces a much greater quantity of work.

Such are in general the effects of the increase of stock upon industry and its productive powers.

In the following book I have endeavoured to explain the nature of stock, the effects of its accumulation into capitals of different kinds, and the effects of the different employments of those capitals. This book is divided into five chapters. In the first chapter, I have endeavoured to show what are the different parts or branches into which the stock, either of an individual, or of a great society, naturally divides itself. In the second, I have endeavoured to explain the nature and operation of money considered as a particular branch of the general stock of the society. The stock which is accumulated into a capital, may either be employed by the person to whom it belongs, or it may be lent to some other person. In the third and fourth chapters, I have endeavoured to examine the manner in which it operates in both these situations. The fifth and last chapter treats of the different effects which the different employments of capital immediately produce upon the quantity both of national industry, and of the annual produce of land and labour.

CHAPTER I

Of the Division of Stock

WHEN the stock which a man possesses is no more than sufficient to maintain him for a few days or a few weeks, he seldom thinks of deriving any revenue from it. He consumes it as sparingly as he can, and endeavours by his labour to acquire something which may supply its place before it be consumed altogether. His revenue is, in this case, derived from his labour only. This is the state of the greater part of the labouring poor in all countries.

But when he possesses stock sufficient to maintain him for months or years, he naturally endeavours to derive a revenue from the greater part of it; reserving only so much for his immediate consumption as may maintain him till this revenue begins to come in. His whole stock, therefore, is distinguished into two parts. That part which, he expects, is to afford him this revenue, is called his capital. The other is that which supplies his immediate consumption; and which consists either, first, in that portion of his whole stock which was originally reserved for this purpose; or, secondly, in his revenue, from whatever source derived, as it gradually comes in; or, thirdly, in such things as had been purchased by either of these in former years, and which are not yet entirely consumed; such as a stock of cloaths, household furniture, and the like. In one, or other, or all of these three articles, consists the stock which men commonly reserve for their own immediate consumption.

There are two different ways in which a capital may be employed so as to yield a revenue or profit to its employer.

First, it may be employed in raising, manufacturing, or purchasing goods, and selling them again with a profit. The capital employed in this manner yields no revenue or profit to its employer, while it either remains in his possession, or continues in the same shape. The goods of the merchant yield him no revenue or profit till he sells them for money, and the money yields him as little till it is again exchanged for goods. His capital is continually going from him in one shape, and returning to him in another, and it is only by means of such circulation, or successive exchanges, that it can yield him any profit. Such capitals, therefore, may very properly be called circulating capitals.

Secondly, it may be employed in the improvement of land, in the purchase of useful machines and instruments of trade,* or in suchlike things as yield a revenue or profit without changing masters, or circulating any further. Such capitals, therefore, may very properly be called fixed capitals.

Different occupations require very different proportions between the fixed and circulating capitals employed in them.

The capital of a merchant, for example, is altogether a circulating capital. He has occasion for no machines or instruments of trade, unless his shop, or warehouse, be considered as such.

Some part of the capital of every master artificer or manufacturer must be fixed in the instruments of his trade. This part, however, is very small in some, and very great in others. A master taylor requires no other instruments of trade but a parcel of needles. Those of the master shoemaker are a little, though but a very little, more expensive. Those of the weaver rise a good deal above those of the shoemaker. The far greater part of the capital of all such master artificers, however, is circulated, either in the wages of their workmen, or in the price of their materials, and repaid with a profit by the price of the work.

In other works a much greater fixed capital is required. In a great iron-work, for example, the furnace for melting the ore, the forge, the slitt-mill,* are instruments of trade which cannot be erected without a very great expence. In coal-works and mines of every kind, the machinery necessary both for drawing out the water and for other purposes, is frequently still more expensive.

That part of the capital of the farmer which is employed in the instruments of agriculture is a fixed; that which is employed in the wages and maintenance of his labouring servants, is a circulating capital. He makes a profit of the one by keeping it in his own possession, and of the other by parting with it. The price or value of his labouring cattle is a fixed capital in the same manner as that of the instruments of husbandry: Their maintenance is a circulating capital in the same manner as that of the labouring servants. The farmer makes his profit by keeping the labouring cattle, and by parting with their maintenance. Both the price and the maintenance of the cattle which are bought in and fattened, not for labour, but for sale, are a circulating capital. The farmer makes his profit by parting with them. A flock of sheep or a herd of cattle that, in a breeding country, is bought in, neither for labour, nor for sale, but in order to make a profit by their wool, by their milk, and by their increase, is a fixed capital. The profit is made by keeping them. Their maintenance is a circulating capital. The profit is made by parting with it; and it comes back with both its own profit, and the profit upon the whole price of the cattle, in the price of the wool, the milk, and the increase. The whole value of the seed too is properly a fixed capital. Though it goes backwards and forwards between the ground and the granary, it never changes masters, and therefore does not properly circulate. The farmer makes his profit, not by its sale, but by its increase.

The general stock of any country or society is the same with that of all its inhabitants or members, and therefore naturally divides itself into the same three portions, each of which has a distinct function or office.

The First, is that portion which is reserved for immediate consumption, and of which the characteristick is, that it affords no revenue or profit. It consists in the stock of food, cloaths, household furniture, &c. which have been purchased by their proper consumers, but which are not yet entirely consumed. The whole stock of mere dwelling-houses too subsisting at any one time in the country, make a part of this first portion. The stock that is laid out in a house, if it is to be the dwelling-house of the proprietor, ceases from that moment to serve in the function of a capital, or to afford any revenue to its owner. A dwelling-house, as such, contributes nothing to the revenue of its inhabitant; and though it is, no doubt, extremely useful to him, it is as his cloaths and household furniture are useful to him, which, however, make a part of his expence, and not of his revenue. If it is to be lett to a tenant for rent, as the house itself can produce nothing, the tenant must always pay the rent out of some other revenue which he derives either from labour, or stock, or land. Though a house, therefore, may yield a revenue to its proprietor, and thereby serve in the function of a capital to him, it cannot yield any to the publick, nor serve in the function of a capital to it, and the revenue of the whole body of the people can never be in the smallest degree increased by it. Cloaths, and household furniture, in the same manner, sometimes yield a revenue, and thereby serve in the function of a capital to particular persons. In countries where masquerades are common, it is a trade to let out masquerade dresses for a night. Upholsterers frequently lett furniture by the month or by the year. Undertakers lett the furniture of funerals by the day and by the week. Many people lett furnished houses, and get a rent, not only for the use of the house, but for that of the furniture. The revenue, however, which is derived from such things, must always be ultimately drawn from some other source of revenue. Of all parts of the stock, either of an individual, or of a society, reserved for immediate consumption, what is laid out in houses is most slowly consumed. A stock of cloaths may last several years: a stock of furniture half a century or a century: but a stock of houses, well built and properly taken care of, may last many centuries. Though the period of their total consumption, however, is more distant, they are still as really a stock reserved for immediate consumption as either cloaths or household furniture.

The Second of the three portions into which the general stock of the society divides itself, is the fixed capital; of which the characteristick is, that it affords a revenue or profit without circulating or changing masters. It consists chiefly of the four following articles:

First, of all useful machines and instruments of trade which facilitate and abridge labour:

Secondly, of all those profitable buildings which are the means of procuring a revenue, not only to their proprietor who letts them for a rent, but to the person who possesses them and pays that rent for them; such as shops, warehouses, workhouses,* farmhouses, with all their necessary buildings; stables, granaries, &c. These are very different from mere dwelling houses. They are a sort of instruments of trade, and may be considered in the same light:

Thirdly, of the improvements of land, of what has been profitably laid out in clearing, draining, enclosing, manuring, and reducing it into the condition most proper for tillage and culture. An improved farm may very justly be regarded in the same light as those useful machines which facilitate and abridge labour, and by means of which, an equal circulating capital can afford a much greater revenue to its employer. An improved farm is equally advantageous and more durable than any of those machines, frequently requiring no other repairs than the most profitable application of the farmer's capital employed in cultivating it:

Fourthly, of the acquired and useful abilities of all the inhabitants or members of the society. The acquisition of such talents, by the maintenance of the acquirer during his education, study, or apprenticeship, always costs a real expence, which is a capital fixed and realized, as it were, in his person. Those talents, as they make a part of his fortune, so do they likewise of that of the society to which he belongs. The improved dexterity of a workman may be considered in the same light as a machine or instrument of trade which facilitates and abridges labour, and which, though it costs a certain expence, repays that expence with a profit.

The third and last of the three portions into which the general stock of the society naturally divides itself, is the circulating capital; of which the characteristick is, that it affords a revenue only by circulating or changing masters. It is composed likewise of four parts:

First, of the money by means of which all the other three are circulated and distributed to their proper consumers:

Secondly, of the stock of provisions which are in the possession of the butcher, the grazier,* the farmer, the corn-merchant, the brewer, &c. and from the sale of which they expect to derive a profit:

Thirdly, of the materials, whether altogether rude, or more or less manufactured, of cloaths, furniture, and building, which are not yet made up into any of those three shapes, but which remain in the hands of the growers, the manufacturers, the mercers* and drapers, the timber-merchants, the carpenters and joiners, the brickmakers, &c.

Fourthly, and lastly, of the work which is made up and compleated, but which is still in the hands of the merchant or manufacturer, and not yet disposed of or distributed to the proper consumers; such as the finished work which we frequently find ready-made in the shops of the smith, the cabinet-maker, the goldsmith, the jeweller, the china-merchant, &c. The circulating capital consists in this manner, of the provisions, materials, and finished work of all kinds that are in the hands of their respective dealers, and of the money that is necessary for circulating and distributing them to those who are finally to use, or to consume them.

Of these four parts three, provisions, materials, and finished work, are, either annually, or in a longer or shorter period, regularly withdrawn from it, and placed either in the fixed capital or in the stock reserved for immediate consumption.

Every fixed capital is both originally derived from, and requires to be continually supported by a circulating capital. All useful machines and instruments of trade are originally derived from a circulating capital, which furnishes the materials of which they are made, and the maintenance of the workmen who make them. They require too a capital of the same kind to keep them in constant repair.

No fixed capital can yield any revenue but by means of a circulating capital. The most useful machines and instruments of trade will produce nothing without the circulating capital which affords the materials they are employed upon, and the maintenance of the workmen who employ them. Land, however improved, will yield no revenue without a circulating capital, which maintains the labourers who cultivate and collect its produce.

To maintain and augment the stock which may be reserved for immediate consumption, is the sole end and purpose both of the fixed and circulating capitals. It is this stock which feeds, cloaths, and lodges the people. Their riches or poverty depends upon the abundant or sparing supplies which those two capitals can afford to the stock reserved for immediate consumption.

So great a part of the circulating capital being continually withdrawn from it, in order to be placed in the other two branches of the general stock of the society; it must in its turn require continual supplies, without which it would soon cease to exist. These supplies are principally drawn from three sources, the produce of land, of mines, and of fisheries. These afford continual supplies of provisions and materials, of which part is afterwards wrought up into finished work, and by which are replaced the provisions, materials, and finished work continually withdrawn from the circulating capital. From mines too is drawn what is necessary for maintaining and augmenting that part of it which consists in money. For though, in the ordinary course of business, this part is not, like the other three, necessarily withdrawn from it, in order to be placed in the other two branches of the general stock of the society, it must, however, like all other things, be wasted and worn out at last, and sometimes too be either lost or sent abroad, and must, therefore, require continual, though, no doubt, much smaller supplies.

Land, mines, and fisheries, require all both a fixed and a circulating capital to cultivate them; and their produce replaces with a profit, not only those capitals, but all the others in the society. Thus the farmer annually replaces to the manufacturer the provisions which he had consumed and the materials which he had wrought up the year before; and the manufacturer replaces to the farmer the finished work which he had wasted and worn out in the same time. This is the real exchange that is annually made between those two orders of people, though it seldom happens that the rude produce of the one and the manufactured produce of the other, are directly bartered for one another; because it seldom happens that the farmer sells his corn and his cattle, his flax and his wool, to the very same person of whom he chuses to purchase the cloaths, furniture, and instruments of trade which he wants. He sells, therefore, his rude produce for money, with which he can purchase, wherever it is to be had, the manufactured produce he has occasion for. Land even replaces, in part, at least, the capitals with which fisheries and mines are cultivated. It is the produce of land which draws the fish from the waters; and it is the produce of the surface of the earth which extracts the minerals from its bowels.*

The produce of land, mines, and fisheries, when their natural fertility is equal, is in proportion to the extent and proper application of the capitals employed about them. When the capitals are equal and equally well applied, it is in proportion to their natural fertility.

In all countries where there is tolerable security,* every man of common understanding will endeavour to employ whatever stock he can command in procuring either present enjoyment or future profit. If it is employed in procuring present enjoyment, it is a stock reserved for immediate consumption. If it is employed in procuring future profit, it must procure this profit either by staying with him, or by going from him. In the one case it is a fixed, in the other it is a circulating capital. A man must be perfectly crazy who, where there is tolerable security, does not employ all the stock which he commands, whether it be his own or borrowed of other people, in some one or other of those three ways.

In those unfortunate countries, indeed, where men are continually afraid of the violence of their superiors, they frequently bury and conceal a great part of their stock, in order to have it always at hand to carry with them to some place of safety, in case of their being threatened with any of those disasters to which they consider themselves as at all times exposed. This is said to be a common practice in Turkey, in Indostan, and, I believe, in most other governments of Asia. It seems to have been a common practice among our ancestors during the violence of the feudal government. Treasure-trove was in those times considered as no contemptible part of the revenue of the greatest sovereigns in Europe. It consisted in such treasure as was found concealed in the earth, and to which no particular person could prove any right. This was regarded in those times as so important an object, that it was always considered as belonging to the sovereign, and neither to the finder nor to the proprietor of the land, unless the right to it had been conveyed to the latter by an express clause in his charter. It was put upon the same footing with gold and silver mines, which, without a special clause in the charter, were never supposed to be comprehended in the general grant of the lands, though mines of lead, copper, tin, and coal were, as things of smaller consequence.

CHAPTER II

Of Money considered as a particular Branch of the general Stock of the Society, or of the Expence of maintaining the National Capital

IT has been shewn in the first Book,* that the price of the greater part of commodities resolves itself into three parts, of which one pays the wages of the labour, another the profits of the stock, and a third the rent of the land which had been employed in producing and bringing them to market: that there are, indeed, some commodities of which the price is made up of two of those parts only, the wages of labour, and the profits of stock: and a very few in which it consists altogether in one, the wages of labour: but that the price of every commodity necessarily resolves itself into some one, or other, or all of these three parts; every part of it which goes neither to rent nor to wages, being necessarily profit to somebody.

Since this is the case, it has been observed, with regard to every particular commodity, taken separately; it must be so with regard to all the commodities which compose the whole annual produce of the land and labour of every country, taken complexly. The whole price or exchangeable value of that annual produce, must resolve itself into the same three parts, and be parcelled out among the different inhabitants of the country, either as the wages of their labour, the profits of their stock, or the rent of their land.

But though the whole value of the annual produce of the land and labour of every country is thus divided among and constitutes a revenue to its different inhabitants, yet as in the rent of a private estate we distinguish between the gross rent and the neat rent, so may we likewise in the revenue of all the inhabitants of a great country.

The gross rent of a private estate comprehends whatever is paid by the farmer; the neat rent, what remains free to the landlord, after deducting the expence of management, of repairs, and all other necessary charges; or what, without hurting his estate, he can afford to place in his stock reserved for immediate consumption, or to spend upon his table, equipage, the ornaments of his house and furniture, his private enjoyments and amusements. His real wealth is in proportion, not to his gross, but to his neat rent.

The gross revenue of all the inhabitants of a great country, comprehends the whole annual produce of their land and labour; the neat revenue, what remains free to them after deducting the expence of maintaining; first, their fixed; and, secondly, their circulating capital; or what, without encroaching upon their capital, they can place in their stock reserved for immediate consumption, or spend upon their subsistence, conveniencies, and amusements. Their real wealth too is in proportion, not to their gross, but to their neat revenue.

The whole expence of maintaining the fixed capital, must evidently be excluded from the neat revenue of the society. Neither the materials necessary for supporting their useful machines and instruments of trade, their profitable buildings, &c. nor the produce of the labour necessary for fashioning those materials into the proper form, can ever make any part of it. The price of that labour may indeed make a part of it; as the workmen so employed may place the whole value of their wages in their stock reserved for immediate consumption. But in other sorts of labour, both the price and the produce go to this stock, the price to that of the workmen, the produce to that of other people, whose subsistence, conveniencies, and amusements, are augmented by the labour of those workmen.

The intention of the fixed capital is to increase the productive powers of labour, or to enable the same number of labourers to perform a much greater quantity of work. In a farm where all the necessary buildings, fences, drains, communications, &c. are in the most perfect good order, the same number of labourers and labouring cattle will raise a much greater produce, than in one of equal extent and equally good ground, but not furnished with equal conveniencies. In manufactures the same number of hands, assisted with the best machinery, will work up a much greater quantity of goods than with more imperfect instruments of trade. The expence which is properly laid out upon a fixed capital of any kind, is always repaid with great profit, and increases the annual produce by a much greater value than that of the support which such improvements require. This support, however, still requires a certain portion of that produce. A certain quantity of materials, and the labour of a certain number of workmen, both of which might have been immediately employed to augment the food, cloathing and lodging, the subsistence and conveniencies of the society, are thus diverted to another employment, highly advantageous indeed, but still different from this one. It is upon this account that all such improvements in mechanicks, as enable the same number of workmen to perform an equal quantity of work, with cheaper and simpler machinery than had been usual before, are always regarded as advantageous to every society. A certain quantity of materials, and the labour of a certain number of workmen, which had before been employed in supporting a more complex and expensive machinery, can afterwards be applied to augment the quantity of work which that or any other machinery is useful only for performing. The undertaker of some great manufactory who employs a thousand a-year in the maintenance of his machinery, if he can reduce this expence to five hundred, will naturally employ the other five hundred in purchasing an additional quantity of materials to be wrought up by an additional number of workmen. The quantity of that work, therefore, which his machinery was useful only for performing, will naturally be augmented, and with it all the advantage and conveniency which the society can derive from that work.

The expence of maintaining the fixed capital in a great country, may very properly be compared to that of repairs in a private estate. The expence of repairs may frequently be necessary for supporting the produce of the estate, and consequently both the gross and the neat rent of the landlord. When by a more proper direction, however, it can be diminished without occasioning any diminution of produce, the gross rent remains at least the same as before, and the neat rent is necessarily augmented.

But though the whole expence of maintaining the fixed capital is thus necessarily excluded from the neat revenue of the society, it is not the same case with that of maintaining the circulating capital. Of the four parts of which this latter capital is composed, money, provisions, materials, and finished work, the three last, it has already been observed, are regularly withdrawn from it, and placed either in the fixed capital of the society, or in their stock reserved for immediate consumption. Whatever portion of those consumable goods is not employed in maintaining the former, goes all to the latter, and makes a part of the neat revenue of the society. The maintenance of those three parts of the circulating capital, therefore, withdraws no portion of the annual produce from the neat revenue of the society, besides what is necessary for maintaining the fixed capital.

The circulating capital of a society is in this respect different from that of an individual. That of an individual is totally excluded from making any part of his neat revenue, which must consist altogether in his profits. But though the circulating capital of every individual makes a part of that of the society to which he belongs, it is not upon that account totally excluded from making a part likewise of their neat revenue. Though the whole goods in a merchant's shop must by no means be placed in his own stock reserved for immediate consumption, they may in that of other people, who, from a revenue derived from other funds, may regularly replace their value to him, together with its profits, without occasioning any diminution either of his capital or of theirs.

Money, therefore, is the only part of the circulating capital of a society, of which the maintenance can occasion any diminution in their neat revenue.

The fixed capital, and that part of the circulating capital which consists in money, so far as they affect the revenue of the society, bear a very great resemblance to one another.

First, as those machines and instruments of trade, &c. require a certain expence, first to erect them, and afterwards to support them, both which expences, though they make a part of the gross, are deductions from the neat revenue of the society; so the stock of money which circulates in any country must require a certain expence, first to collect it, and afterwards to support it, both which expences, though they make a part of the gross, are, in the same manner, deductions from the neat revenue of the society. A certain quantity of very valuable materials, gold and silver, and of very curious labour, instead of augmenting the stock reserved for immediate consumption, the subsistence, conveniences, and amusements of individuals, is employed in supporting that great but expensive instrument of commerce, by means of which every individual in the society has his subsistence, conveniencies, and amusements, regularly distributed to him in their proper proportions.

Secondly, as the machines and instruments of trade, &c. which compose the fixed capital either of an individual or of a society, make no part either of the gross or of the neat revenue of either; so money, by means of which the whole revenue of the society is regularly distributed among all its different members, makes itself no part of that revenue. The great wheel of circulation* is altogether different from the goods which are circulated by means of it. The revenue of the society consists altogether in those goods, and not in the wheel which circulates them. In computing either the gross or the neat revenue of any society, we must always, from their whole annual circulation of money and goods, deduct the whole value of the money, of which not a single farthing can ever make any part of either.

It is the ambiguity of language only which can make this proposition appear either doubtful or paradoxical. When properly explained and understood, it is almost self-evident.

When we talk of any particular sum of money, we sometimes mean nothing but the metal pieces of which it is composed; and sometimes we include in our meaning some obscure reference to the goods which can be had in exchange for it, or to the power of purchasing which the possession of it conveys. Thus when we say, that the circulating money of England has been computed at eighteen millions, we mean only to express the amount of the metal pieces, which some writers have computed, or rather have supposed to circulate in that country. But when we say that a man is worth fifty or a hundred pounds a-year, we mean commonly to express not only the amount of the metal pieces which are annually paid to him, but the value of the goods which he can annually purchase or consume. We mean commonly to ascertain what is or ought to be his way of living, or the quantity and quality of the necessaries and conveniencies of life in which he can with propriety indulge himself.

When, by any particular sum of money, we mean not only to express the amount of the metal pieces of which it is composed, but to include in its signification some obscure reference to the goods which can be had in exchange for them, the wealth or revenue which it in this case denotes, is equal only to one of the two values which are thus intimated somewhat ambiguously by the same word, and to the latter more properly than to the former, to the money's worth more properly than to the money.

Thus if a guinea* be the weekly pension of a particular person, he can in the course of the week purchase with it a certain quantity of subsistence, conveniencies, and amusements. In proportion as this quantity is great or small, so are his real riches, his real weekly revenue. His weekly revenue is certainly not equal both to the guinea, and to what can be purchased with it, but only to one or other of those two equal values; and to the latter more properly than to the former, to the guinea's worth rather than to the guinea.

If the pension of such a person was paid to him, not in gold, but in a weekly bill* for a guinea, his revenue surely would not so properly consist in the piece of paper, as in what he could get for it. A guinea may be considered as a bill for a certain quantity of necessaries and conveniencies upon all the tradesmen in the neighbourhood. The revenue of the person to whom it is paid, does not so properly consist in the piece of gold, as in what he can get for it, or in what he can exchange it for. If it could be exchanged for nothing, it would, like a bill upon a bankrupt, be of no more value than the most useless piece of paper.

Though the weekly, or yearly revenue of all the different inhabitants of any country, in the same manner, may be, and in reality frequently is paid to them in money, their real riches, however, the real weekly or yearly revenue of all of them taken together, must always be great or small in proportion to the quantity of consumable goods which they can all of them purchase with this money. The whole revenue of all of them taken together is evidently not equal to both the money and the consumable goods; but only to one or other of those two values, and to the latter more properly than to the former.

Though we frequently, therefore, express a person's revenue by the metal pieces which are annually paid to him, it is because the amount of those pieces regulates the extent of his power of purchasing, or the value of the goods which he can annually afford to consume. We still consider his revenue as consisting in this power of purchasing or consuming, and not in the pieces which convey it.

But if this is sufficiently evident even with regard to an individual, it is still more so with regard to a society. The amount of the metal pieces which are annually paid to an individual, is often precisely equal to his revenue, and is upon that account the shortest and best expression of its value. But the amount of the metal pieces which circulate in a society, can never be equal to the revenue of all its members. As the same guinea which pays the weekly pension of one man to-day, may pay that of another tomorrow, and that of a third the day thereafter, the amount of the metal pieces which annually circulate in any country, must always be of much less value than the whole money pensions annually paid with them. But the power of purchasing, or the goods which can successively be bought with the whole of those money pensions as they are successively paid, must always be precisely of the same value with those pensions; as must likewise be the revenue of the different persons to whom they are paid. That revenue, therefore, cannot consist in those metal pieces, of which the amount is so much inferior to its value, but in the power of purchasing, in the goods which can successively be bought with them as they circulate from hand to hand.

Money, therefore, the great wheel of circulation, the great instrument of commerce, like all other instruments of trade, though it makes a part and a very valuable part of the capital, makes no part of the revenue of the society to which it belongs; and though the metal pieces of which it is composed, in the course of their annual circulation, distribute to every man the revenue which properly belongs to him, they make themselves no part of that revenue.

Thirdly, and lastly, the machines and instruments of trade, &c. which compose the fixed capital, bear this further resemblance to that part of the circulating capital which consists in money; that as every saving in the expence of erecting and supporting those machines, which does not diminish the productive powers of labour, is an improvement of the neat revenue of the society; so every saving in the expence of collecting and supporting that part of the circulating capital which consists in money, is an improvement of exactly the same kind.

It is sufficiently obvious, and it has partly too been explained already, in what manner every saving in the expence of supporting the fixed capital is an improvement of the neat revenue of the society. The whole capital of the undertaker of every work is necessarily divided between his fixed and his circulating capital. While his whole capital remains the same, the smaller the one part, the greater must necessarily be the other. It is the circulating capital which furnishes the materials and wages of labour, and puts industry into motion. Every saving, therefore, in the expence of maintaining the fixed capital, which does not diminish the productive powers of labour, must increase the fund which puts industry into motion, and consequently the annual produce of land and labour, the real revenue of every society.

The substitution of paper in the room of gold and silver money, replaces a very expensive instrument of commerce with one much less costly, and sometimes equally convenient. Circulation comes to be carried on by a new wheel, which it costs less both to erect and to maintain than the old one. But in what manner this operation is performed, and in what manner it tends to increase either the gross or the neat revenue of the society, is not altogether so obvious, and may therefore require some further explication.

There are several different sorts of paper money,* but the circulating notes of banks and bankers are the species which is best known, and which seems best adapted for this purpose.

When the people of any particular country have such confidence in the fortune, probity, and prudence of a particular banker, as to believe that he is always ready to pay upon demand such of his promissory notes as are likely to be at any time presented to him; those notes come to have the same currency as gold and silver money, from the confidence that such money can at any time be had for them.

A particular banker lends among his customers his own promissory notes, to the extent, we shall suppose, of a hundred thousand pounds. As those notes serve all the purposes of money, his debtors pay him the same interest as if he had lent them so much money. This interest is the source of his gain. Though some of those notes are continually coming back upon him for payment, part of them continue to circulate for months and years together. Though he has generally in circulation, therefore, notes to the extent of a hundred thousand pounds, twenty thousand pounds in gold and silver may, frequently be a sufficient provision for answering occasional demands. By this operation, therefore, twenty thousand pounds in gold and silver perform all the functions which a hundred thousand could otherwise have performed. The same exchanges may be made, the same quantity of consumable goods may be circulated and distributed to their proper consumers, by means of his promissory notes, to the value of a hundred thousand pounds, as by an equal value of gold and silver money. Eighty thousand pounds of gold and silver, therefore, can, in this manner, be spared from the circulation of the country; and if different operations of the same kind should, at the same time, be carried on by many different banks and bankers, the whole circulation may thus be conducted with a fifth part only of the gold and silver which would otherwise have been requisite.

Let us suppose, for example, that the whole circulating money of some particular country amounted, at a particular time, to one million sterling, that sum being then sufficient for circulating the whole annual produce of their land and labour. Let us suppose too, that some time thereafter, different banks and bankers issued promissory notes, payable to the bearer, to the extent of one million, reserving in their different coffers two hundred thousand pounds for answering occasional demands. There would remain, therefore, in circulation, eight hundred thousand pounds in gold and silver, and a million of bank notes, or eighteen hundred thousand pounds of paper and money together. But the annual produce of the land and labour of the country had before required only one million to circulate and distribute it to its proper consumers, and that annual produce cannot be immediately augmented by those operations of banking. One million, therefore, will be sufficient to circulate it after them. The goods to be bought and sold being precisely the same as before, the same quantity of money will be sufficient for buying and selling them. The channel of circulation, if I may be allowed such an expression, will remain precisely the same as before. One million we have supposed sufficient to fill that channel. Whatever, therefore, is poured into it beyond this sum, cannot run in it, but must overflow. One million eight hundred thousand pounds are poured into it. Eight hundred thousand pounds, therefore, must overflow, that sum being over and above what can be employed in the circulation of the country. But though this sum cannot be employed at home, it is too valuable to be allowed to lie idle. It will, therefore, be sent abroad, in order to seek that profitable employment which it cannot find at home. But the paper cannot go abroad;* because at a distance from the banks which issue it, and from the country in which payment of it can be exacted by law, it will not be received in common payments. Gold and silver, therefore, to the amount of eight hundred thousand pounds will be sent abroad, and the channel of home circulation will remain filled with a million of paper, instead of the million of those metals which filled it before.

But though so great a quantity of gold and silver is thus sent abroad, we must not imagine it is sent abroad for nothing, or that its proprietors make a present of it to foreign nations. They will exchange it for foreign goods of some kind or another, in order to supply the consumption either of some other foreign country, or of their own.

If they employ it in purchasing goods in one foreign country in order to supply the consumption of another, or in what is called the carrying trade, whatever profit they make will be an addition to the neat revenue of their own country. It is like a new fund, created for carrying on a new trade; domestick business being now transacted by paper, and the gold and silver being converted into a fund for this new trade.

If they employ it in purchasing foreign goods for home consumption, they may either, first, purchase such goods as are likely to be consumed by idle people who produce nothing, such as foreign wines, foreign silks, &c.; or, secondly, they may purchase an additional stock of materials, tools, and provisions, in order to maintain and employ an additional number of industrious people, who re-produce, with a profit, the value of their annual consumption.

So far as it is employed in the first way, it promotes prodigality, increases expence and consumption without increasing production, or establishing any permanent fund for supporting that expence, and is in every respect hurtful to the society.

So far as it is employed in the second way, it promotes industry; and though it increases the consumption of the society, it provides a permanent fund for supporting that consumption, the people who consume re-producing, with a profit, the whole value of their annual consumption. The gross revenue of the society, the annual produce of their land and labour, is increased by the whole value which the labour of those workmen adds to the materials upon which they are employed; and their neat revenue by what remains of this value, after deducting what is necessary for supporting the tools and instruments of their trade.

That the greater part of the gold and silver which, being forced abroad by those operations of banking, is employed in purchasing foreign goods for home consumption, is and must be employed in purchasing those of this second kind, seems not only probable but almost unavoidable.* Though some particular men may sometimes increase their expence very considerably though their revenue does not increase at all, we may be assured that no class or order of men ever does so; because, though the principles of common prudence do not always govern the conduct of every individual, they always influence that of the majority of every class or order. But the revenue of idle people, considered as a class or order, cannot, in the smallest degree, be increased by those operations of banking. Their expence in general, therefore, cannot be much increased by them, though that of a few individuals among them may, and in reality sometimes is. The demand of idle people, therefore, for foreign goods, being the same, or very nearly the same, as before, a very small part of the money, which being forced abroad by those operations of banking, is employed in purchasing foreign goods for home consumption, is likely to be employed in purchasing those for their use. The greater part of it will naturally be destined for the employment of industry, and not for the maintenance of idleness.

When we compute the quantity of industry which the circulating capital of any society can employ, we must always have regard to those parts of it only, which consist in provisions, materials, and finished work: the other, which consists in money, and which serves only to circulate those three, must always be deducted. In order to put industry into motion, three things are requisite; materials to work upon, tools to work with, and the wages or recompence for the sake of which the work is done. Money is neither a material to work upon, nor a tool to work with; and though the wages of the workman are commonly paid to him in money, his real revenue, like that of all other men, consists, not in the money, but in the money's worth; not in the metal pieces, but in what can be got for them.

The quantity of industry which any capital can employ, must, evidently, be equal to the number of workmen whom it can supply with materials, tools, and a maintenance suitable to the nature of the work. Money may be requisite for purchasing the materials and tools of the work, as well as the maintenance of the workmen. But the quantity of industry which the whole capital can employ, is certainly not equal both to the money which purchases, and to the materials, tools, and maintenance, which are purchased with it; but only to one or other of those two values, and to the latter more properly than to the former.

When paper is substituted in the room of gold and silver money, the quantity of the materials, tools, and maintenance, which the whole circulating capital can supply, may be increased by the whole value of gold and silver which used to be employed in purchasing them. The whole value of the great wheel of circulation and distribution, is added to the goods which are circulated and distributed by means of it. The operation, in some measure, resembles that of the undertaker of some great work, who, in consequence of some improvement in mechanicks, takes down his old machinery and adds the difference between its price and that of the new to his circulating capital, to the fund from which he furnishes materials and wages to his workmen. . . .

It is not by augmenting the capital of the country, but by rendering a greater part of that capital active and productive than would otherwise be so, that the most judicious operations of banking can increase the industry of the country. That part of his capital which a dealer is obliged to keep by him unemployed, and in ready money for answering occasional demands, is so much dead stock, which, so long as it remains in this situation, produces nothing either to him or to his country.

The judicious operations of banking enable him to convert this dead stock into active and productive stock; into materials to work upon, into tools to work with, and into provisions and subsistence to work for; into stock which produces something both to himself and to his country. The gold and silver money which circulates in any country, and by means of which, the produce of its land and labour is annually circulated and distributed to the proper consumers, is, in the same manner as the ready money of the dealer, all dead stock. It is a very valuable part of the capital of the country, which produces nothing to the country. The judicious operations of banking, by substituting paper in the room of a great part of this gold and silver, enables the country to convert a great part of this dead stock into active and productive stock; into stock which produces something to the country. The gold and silver money which circulates in any country may very properly be compared to a highway, which, while it circulates and carries to market all the grass and corn of the country, produces itself not a single pile of either. The judicious operations of banking, by providing, if I may be allowed so violent a metaphor, a sort of waggon-way through the air; enable the country to convert, as it were, a great part of its highways into good pastures and corn fields, and thereby to increase very considerably the annual produce of its land and labour. The commerce and industry of the country, however, it must be acknowledged, though they may be somewhat augmented, cannot be altogether so secure, when they are thus, as it were, suspended upon the Daedalian wings* of paper money, as when they travel about upon the solid ground of gold and silver. Over and above the accidents to which they are exposed from the unskilfulness of the conductors of this paper money, they are liable to several others, from which no prudence or skill of those conductors can guard them.

An unsuccessful war, for example, in which the enemy got possession of the capital, and consequently of that treasure which supported the credit of the paper money, would occasion a much greater confusion in a country where the whole circulation was carried on by paper, than in one where the greater part of it was carried on by gold and silver. The usual instrument of commerce having lost its value, no exchanges could be made but either by barter or upon credit. All taxes having been usually paid in paper money, the prince would not have wherewithal either to pay his troops, or to furnish his magazines; and the state of the country would be much more irretrievable than if the greater part of its circulation had consisted in gold and silver. A prince, anxious to maintain his dominions at all times in the state in which he can most easily defend them, ought, upon this account, to guard, not only against that excessive multiplication of paper money* which ruins the very banks which issue it; but even against that multiplication of it, which enables them to fill the greater part of the circulation of the country with it.

The circulation of every country may be considered as divided into two different branches; the circulation of the dealers with one another, and the circulation between the dealers and the consumers. Though the same pieces of money, whether paper or metal, may be employed sometimes in the one circulation and sometimes in the other, yet as both are constantly going on at the same time, each requires a certain stock of money of one kind or another, to carry it on. The value of the goods circulated between the different dealers, never can exceed the value of those circulated between the dealers and the consumers; whatever is bought by the dealers, being ultimately destined to be sold to the consumers. The circulation between the dealers, as it is carried on by wholesale, requires generally a pretty large sum for every particular transaction. That between the dealers and the consumers, on the contrary, as it is generally carried on by retail, frequently requires but very small ones, a shilling, or even a halfpenny, being often sufficient. But small sums circulate much faster than large ones. A shilling changes masters more frequently than a guinea, and a halfpenny more frequently than a shilling. Though the annual purchases of all the consumers, therefore, are at least equal in value to those of all the dealers, they can generally be transacted with a much smaller quantity of money; the same pieces, by a more rapid circulation, serving as the instrument of many more purchases of the one kind than of the other.

Paper money may be so regulated, as either to confine itself very much to the circulation between the different dealers, or to extend itself likewise to a great part of that between the dealers and the consumers. Where no bank notes are circulated under ten pounds value, as in London,* paper money confines itself very much to the circulation between the dealers. When a ten pound bank note comes into the hands of a consumer, he is generally obliged to change it at the first shop where he has occasion to purchase five shillings worth of goods, so that it often returns into the hands of a dealer, before the consumer has spent the fortieth part of the money. Where bank notes are issued for so small sums as twenty shillings, as in Scotland,* paper money extends itself to a considerable part of the circulation between dealers and consumers. Before the act of parliament,* which put a stop to the circulation of ten and five shilling notes, it filled a still greater part of that circulation. In the currencies of North America, paper was commonly issued for so small a sum as a shilling, and filled almost the whole of that circulation. In some paper currencies of Yorkshire,* it was issued even for so small a sum as a sixpence.

Where the issuing of bank notes for such very small sums is allowed and commonly practised, many mean people* are both enabled and encouraged to become bankers. A person whose promissory note* for five pounds, or even for twenty shillings, would be rejected by every body, will get it to be received without scruple when it is issued for so small a sum as a sixpence. But the frequent bankruptcies to which such beggarly bankers must be liable, may occasion a very considerable inconveniency, and sometimes even a very great calamity to many poor people who had received their notes in payment.

It were better, perhaps, that no bank notes were issued in any part of the kingdom for a smaller sum than five pounds.

Paper money would then, probably, confine itself, in every part of the kingdom, to the circulation between the different dealers, as much as it does at present in London, where no bank notes are issued under ten pounds value; five pounds being, in most parts of the kingdom, a sum which, though it will purchase, perhaps, little more than half the quantity of goods, is as much considered, and is as seldom spent all at once, as ten pounds are amidst the profuse expence of London.

Where paper money, it is to be observed, is pretty much confined to the circulation between dealers and dealers, as at London, there is always plenty of gold and silver. Where it extends itself to a considerable part of the circulation between dealers and consumers, as in Scotland, and still more in North America, it banishes gold and silver almost entirely from the country; almost all the ordinary transactions of its interior commerce being thus carried on by paper. The suppression of ten and five shilling bank notes, somewhat relieved the scarcity of gold and silver in Scotland; and the suppression of twenty shilling notes, would probably relieve it still more. Those metals are said to have become more abundant in America, since the suppression of some of their paper currencies. They are said, likewise, to have been more abundant before the institution of those currencies.

Though paper money should be pretty much confined to the circulation between dealers and dealers, yet banks and bankers might still be able to give nearly the same assistance to the industry and commerce of the country, as they had done when paper money filled almost the whole circulation. The ready money which a dealer is obliged to keep by him, for answering occasional demands, is destined altogether for the circulation between himself and other dealers, of whom he buys goods. He has no occasion to keep any by him for the circulation between himself and the consumers, who are his customers, and who bring ready money to him, instead of taking any from him. Though no paper money, therefore, was allowed to be issued, but for such sums as would confine it pretty much to the circulation between dealers and dealers; yet, partly by discounting real bills of exchange, and partly by lending upon cash accounts,* banks and bankers might still be able to relieve the greater part of those dealers from the necessity of keeping any considerable part of their stock by them, unemployed and in ready money, for answering occasional demands. They might still be able to give the utmost assistance which banks and bankers can, with propriety, give to traders of every kind.

To restrain private people, it may be said, from receiving in payment the promissory notes of a banker, for any sum whether great or small, when they themselves are willing to receive them; or, to restrain a banker from issuing such notes, when all his neighbours are willing to accept of them, is a manifest violation of that natural liberty which it is the proper business of law, not to infringe, but to support. Such regulations may, no doubt, be considered as in some respect a violation of natural liberty. But those exertions of the natural liberty of a few individuals, which might endanger the security of the whole society, are, and ought to be, restrained by the laws of all governments; of the most free, as well as of the most despotical. The obligation of building party walls, in order to prevent the communication of fire, is a violation of natural liberty, exactly of the same kind with the regulations of the banking trade which are here proposed.

A paper money consisting in bank notes, issued by people of undoubted credit, payable upon demand without any condition, and in fact always readily paid as soon as presented, is, in every respect, equal in value to gold and silver money; since gold and silver money can at any time be had for it. Whatever is either bought or sold for such paper, must necessarily be bought or sold as cheap as it could have been for gold and silver.

The increase of paper money, it has been said, by augmenting the quantity, and consequently diminishing the value of the whole currency, necessarily augments the money price of commodities. But as the quantity of gold and silver, which is taken from the currency, is always equal to the quantity of paper which is added to it, paper money does not necessarily increase the quantity of the whole currency. From the beginning of the last century to the present time, provisions never were cheaper in Scotland than in 1759,* though, from the circulation of ten and five shilling bank notes, there was then more paper money in the country than at present. The proportion between the price of provisions in Scotland and that in England, is the same now as before the great multiplication of banking companies in Scotland. Corn is, upon most occasions, fully as cheap in England as in France; though there is a great deal of paper money in England, and scarce any in France.* In 1751 and in 1752, when Mr. Hume published his Political Discourses,* and soon after the great multiplication of paper money in Scotland, there was a very sensible rise in the price of provisions, owing, probably, to the badness of the seasons, and not to the multiplication of paper money.*

It would be otherwise, indeed, with a paper money consisting in promissory notes, of which the immediate payment depended, in any respect, either upon the good will of those who issued them; or upon a condition which the holder of the notes might not always have it in his power to fulfil; or of which the payment was not exigible till after a certain number of years, and which in the mean time bore no interest. Such a paper money would, no doubt, fall more or less below the value of gold and silver, according as the difficulty or uncertainty of obtaining immediate payment was supposed to be greater or less; or according to the greater or less distance of time at which payment was exigible. . . .

If bankers are restrained from issuing any circulating bank notes, or notes payable to the bearer, for less than a certain sum; and if they are subjected to the obligation of an immediate and unconditional payment of such bank notes as soon as presented, their trade may, with safety to the publick, be rendered in all other respects perfectly free. The late multiplication of banking companies in both parts of the united kingdom,* an event by which many people have been much alarmed, instead of diminishing, increases the security of the publick. It obliges all of them to be more circumspect in their conduct, and, by not extending their currency beyond its due proportion to their cash, to guard themselves against those malicious runs, which the rivalship of so many competitors is always ready to bring upon them. It restrains the circulation of each particular company within a narrower circle, and reduces their circulating notes to a smaller number. By dividing the whole circulation into a greater number of parts, the failure of any one company, an accident which, in the course of things, must sometimes happen, becomes of less consequence to the publick. This free competition too obliges all bankers to be more liberal in their dealings with their customers, lest their rivals should carry them away. In general, if any branch of trade, or any division of labour, be advantageous to the publick, the freer and more general the competition, it will always be the more so.

CHAPTER III

Of the Accumulation of Capital, or of productive and unproductive Labour

THERE is one sort of labour which adds to the value of the subject upon which it is bestowed: There is another which has no such effect. The former, as it produces a value, may be called productive; the latter, unproductive[7] labour.* Thus the labour of a manufacturer adds, generally, to the value of the materials which he works upon, that of his own maintenance, and of his master's profit. The labour of a menial servant, on the contrary, adds to the value of nothing. Though the manufacturer has his wages advanced to him by his master, he, in reality, costs him no expence, the value of those wages being generally restored, together with a profit, in the improved value of the subject upon which his labour is bestowed. But the maintenance of a menial servant never is restored. A man grows rich by employing a multitude of manufacturers: He grows poor, by maintaining a multitude of menial servants. The labour of the latter, however, has its value, and deserves its reward as well as that of the former. But the labour of the manufacturer fixes and realizes itself in some particular subject or vendible commodity, which lasts for some time at least after that labour is past. It is, as it were, a certain quantity of labour stocked and stored up to be employed, if necessary, upon some other occasion. That subject, or what is the same thing, the price of that subject, can afterwards, if necessary, put into motion a quantity of labour equal to that which had originally produced it. The labour of the menial servant, on the contrary, does not fix or realize itself in any particular subject or vendible

---

[7] Some French authors of great learning and ingenuity have used those words in a different sense. In the last chapter of the fourth book, I shall endeavour to show that their sense is an improper one.

commodity. His services generally perish in the very instant of their performance, and seldom leave any trace or value behind them, for which an equal quantity of service could afterwards be procured.

The labour of some of the most respectable orders in the society is, like that of menial servants, unproductive of any value, and does not fix or realize itself in any permanent subject, or vendible commodity, which endures after that labour is past, and for which an equal quantity of labour could afterwards be procured. The sovereign, for example, with all the officers both of justice and war who serve under him, the whole army and navy, are unproductive labourers. They are the servants of the publick, and are maintained by a part of the annual produce of the industry of other people. Their service, how honourable, how useful, or how necessary soever, produces nothing for which an equal quantity of service can afterwards be procured. The protection, security, and defence of the commonwealth, the effect of their labour this year, will not purchase its protection, security, and defence, for the year to come. In the same class must be ranked, some both of the gravest and most important, and some of the most frivolous professions: churchmen, lawyers, physicians, men of letters of all kinds; players, buffoons, musicians, opera-singers, opera-dancers, &c. The labour of the meanest of these has a certain value, regulated by the very same principles which regulate that of every other sort of labour; and that of the noblest and most useful, produces nothing which could afterwards purchase or procure an equal quantity of labour. Like the declamation of the actor, the harangue of the orator, or the tune of the musician, the work of all of them perishes in the very instant of its production.*

Both productive and unproductive labourers, and those who do not labour at all, are all equally maintained by the annual produce of the land and labour of the country. This produce, how great soever, can never be infinite, but must have certain limits. According, therefore, as a smaller or greater proportion of it is in any one year employed in maintaining unproductive hands, the more in the one case and the less in the other will remain for the productive, and the next year's produce will be greater or smaller accordingly; the whole annual produce, if we except the spontaneous productions of the earth, being the effect of productive labour.

Though the whole annual produce of the land and labour of every country, is, no doubt, ultimately destined for supplying the consumption of its inhabitants, and for procuring a revenue to them; yet when it first comes either from the ground, or from the hands of the productive labourers, it naturally divides itself into two parts. One of them, and frequently the largest, is, in the first place, destined for replacing a capital, or for renewing the provisions, materials, and finished work, which had been withdrawn from a capital; the other for constituting a revenue either to the owner of this capital, as the profit of his stock; or to some other person, as the rent of his land. Thus, of the produce of land, one part replaces the capital of the farmer; the other pays his profit and the rent of the landlord; and thus constitutes a revenue both to the owner of this capital, as the profits of his stock; and to some other person, as the rent of his land. Of the produce of a great manufactory, in the same manner, one part, and that always the largest, replaces the capital of the undertaker of the work; the other pays his profit, and thus constitutes a revenue to the owner of this capital.

That part of the annual produce of the land and labour of any country which replaces a capital, never is immediately employed to maintain any but productive hands. It pays the wages of productive labour only. That which is immediately destined for constituting a revenue either as profit or as rent, may maintain indifferently either productive or unproductive hands.

Whatever part of his stock a man employs as a capital, he always expects is to be replaced to him with a profit. He employs it, therefore, in maintaining productive hands only; and after having served in the function of a capital to him, it constitutes a revenue to them. Whenever he employs any part of it in maintaining unproductive hands of any kind, that part is, from that moment, withdrawn from his capital, and placed in his stock reserved for immediate consumption.

Unproductive labourers, and those who do not labour at all, are all maintained by revenue; either, first, by that part of the annual produce which is originally destined for constituting a revenue to some particular persons, either as the rent of land or as the profits of stock; or, secondly, by that part which, though originally destined for replacing a capital and for maintaining productive labourers only, yet when it comes into their hands, whatever part of it is over and above their necessary subsistence, may be employed in maintaining indifferently either productive or unproductive hands. Thus, not only the great landlord or the rich merchant, but even the common workman, if his wages are considerable, may maintain a menial servant; or he may sometimes go to a play or a puppet-show, and so contribute his share towards maintaining one set of unproductive labourers; or he may pay some taxes, and thus help to maintain another set, more honourable and useful, indeed, but equally unproductive. No part of the annual produce, however, which had been originally destined to replace a capital, is ever directed towards maintaining unproductive hands, till after it has put into motion its full complement of productive labour, or all that it could put into motion in the way in which it was employed. The workman must have earned his wages by work done, before he can employ any part of them in this manner. That part too is generally but a small one. It is his spare revenue only, of which productive labourers have seldom a great deal. They generally have some, however; and in the payment of taxes the greatness of their number may compensate, in some measure, the smallness of their contribution. The rent of land and the profits of stock are every where, therefore, the principal sources from which unproductive hands derive their subsistence. These are the two sorts of revenue of which the owners have generally most to spare. They might both maintain indifferently either productive or unproductive hands. They seem, however, to have some predilection for the latter. The expence of a great lord feeds generally more idle than industrious people. The rich merchant, though with his capital he maintains industrious people only, yet by his expence, that is, by the employment of his revenue, he feeds commonly the very same sort as the great lord.

The proportion, therefore, between the productive and unproductive hands, depends very much in every country upon the proportion between that part of the annual produce, which, as soon as it comes either from the ground or from the hands of the productive labourers, is destined for replacing a capital, and that which is destined for constituting a revenue, either as rent, or as profit. This proportion is very different in rich from what it is in poor countries.

Thus, at present, in the opulent countries of Europe, a very large, frequently the largest portion of the produce of the land, is destined for replacing the capital of the rich and independent farmer; the other for paying his profits, and the rent of the landlord. But antiently, during the prevalency of the feudal government, a very small portion of the produce was sufficient to replace the capital employed in cultivation. It consisted commonly in a few wretched cattle, maintained altogether by the spontaneous produce of uncultivated land, and which might, therefore, be considered as a part of that spontaneous produce. It generally too belonged to the landlord, and was by him advanced to the occupiers of the land. All the rest of the produce properly belonged to him too, either as rent for his land, or as profit upon this paultry capital. The occupiers of land were generally bondmen, whose persons and effects were equally his property. Those who were not bondmen were tenants at will, and though the rent which they paid was often nominally little more than a quit-rent,* it really amounted to the whole produce of the land. Their lord could at all times command their labour in peace, and their service in war. Though they lived at a distance from his house, they were equally dependant upon him as his retainers who lived in it. But the whole produce of the land undoubtedly belongs to him, who can dispose of the labour and service of all those whom it maintains. In the present state of Europe, the share of the landlord seldom exceeds a third, sometimes not a fourth part of the whole produce of the land.* The rent of land, however, in all the improved parts of the country, has been tripled and quadrupled since those antient times; and this third or fourth part of the annual produce is, it seems, three or four times greater than the whole had been before. In the progress of improvement, rent, though it increases in proportion to the extent, diminishes in proportion to the produce of the land.

In the opulent countries of Europe, great capitals are at present employed in trade and manufactures. In the antient state, the little trade that was stirring, and the few homely and coarse manufactures that were carried on, required but very small capitals. These, however, must have yielded very large profits. The rate of interest was no where less than ten per cent. and their profits must have been sufficient to afford this great interest. At present the rate of interest, in the improved parts of Europe, is no where higher than six per cent. and in some of the most improved it is so low as four, three, and two per cent. Though that part of the revenue of the inhabitants which is derived from the profits of stock is always much greater in rich than in poor countries, it is because the stock is much greater: in proportion to the stock the profits are generally much less.

That part of the annual produce, therefore, which, as soon as it comes either from the ground, or from the hands of the productive labourers, is destined for replacing a capital, is not only much greater in rich than in poor countries, but bears a much greater proportion to that which is immediately destined for constituting a revenue either as rent or as profit. The funds destined for the maintenance of productive labour, are not only much greater in the former than in the latter, but bear a much greater proportion to those which, though they may be employed to maintain either productive or unproductive hands, have generally a predilection for the latter.

The proportion between those different funds necessarily determines in every country the general character of the inhabitants as to industry or idleness. We are more industrious than our forefathers; because in the present times the funds destined for the maintenance of industry, are much greater in proportion to those which are likely to be employed in the maintenance of idleness, than they were two or three centuries ago. Our ancestors were idle for want of a sufficient encouragement to industry. It is better, says the proverb, to play for nothing, than to work for nothing. In mercantile and manufacturing towns, where the inferior ranks of people are chiefly maintained by the employment of capital, they are in general industrious, sober, and thriving; as in many English, and in most Dutch towns. In those towns which are principally supported by the constant or occasional residence of a court, and in which the inferior ranks of people are chiefly maintained by the spending of revenue, they are in general idle, dissolute, and poor; as at Rome, Versailles, Compiegne, and Fontainbleau. If you except Rouen and Bourdeaux, there is little trade or industry in any of the parliament towns of France;* and the inferior ranks of people, being chiefly maintained by the expence of the members of the courts of justice, and of those who come to plead before them, are in general idle and poor. The great trade of Rouen and Bourdeaux seems to be altogether the effect of their situation. Rouen is necessarily the entrepôt* of almost all the goods which are brought either from foreign countries, or from the maritime provinces of France, for the consumption of the great city of Paris. Bourdeaux is in the same manner the entrepôt of the wines which grow upon the banks of the Garonne, and of the rivers which run into it, one of the richest wine countries in the world, and which seems to produce the wine fittest for exportation, or best suited to the taste of foreign nations. Such advantageous situations necessarily attract a great capital by the great employment which they afford it; and the employment of this capital is the cause of the industry of those two cities. In the other parliament towns of France, very little more capital seems to be employed than what is necessary for supplying their own consumption; that is, little more than the smallest capital which can be employed in them. The same thing may be said of Paris, Madrid, and Vienna. Of those three cities, Paris is by far the most industrious; but Paris itself is the principal market of all the manufactures established at Paris, and its own consumption is the principal object of all the trade which it carries on. London, Lisbon, and Copenhagen, are, perhaps, the only three cities in Europe, which are both the constant residence of a court, and can at the same time be considered as trading cities, or as cities which trade not only for their own consumption, but for that of other cities and countries. The situation of all the three is extremely advantageous, and naturally fits them to be the entrepôts of a great part of the goods destined for the consumption of distant places. In a city where a great revenue is spent, to employ with advantage a capital for any other purpose than for supplying the consumption of that city, is probably more difficult than in one in which the inferior ranks of people have no other maintenance but what they derive from the employment of such a capital. The idleness of the greater part of the people who are maintained by the expence of revenue, corrupts, it is probable, the industry of those who ought to be maintained by the employment of capital, and renders it less advantageous to employ a capital there than in other places. There was little trade or industry in Edinburgh before the union.* When the Scotch parliament was no longer to be assembled in it, when it ceased to be the necessary residence of the principal nobility and gentry of Scotland, it became a city of some trade and industry. It still continues, however, to be the residence of the principal courts of justice in Scotland, of the boards of customs and excise, &c. A considerable revenue, therefore, still continues to be spent in it. In trade and industry it is much inferior to Glasgow,* of which the inhabitants are chiefly maintained by the employment of capital. The inhabitants of a large village, it has sometimes been observed, after having made considerable progress in manufactures, have become idle and poor, in consequence of a great lord's having taken up his residence in their neighbourhood.*

The proportion between capital and revenue, therefore, seems every where to regulate the proportion between industry and idleness. Wherever capital predominates, industry prevails: wherever revenue, idleness. Every increase or diminution of capital, therefore, naturally tends to increase or diminish the real quantity of industry, the number of productive hands, and consequently the exchangeable value of the annual produce of the land and labour of the country, the real wealth and revenue of all its inhabitants.

Capitals are increased by parsimony, and diminished by prodigality and misconduct.

Whatever a person saves from his revenue he adds to his capital, and either employs it himself in maintaining an additional number of productive hands, or enables some other person to do so, by lending it to him for an interest, that is, for a share of the profits. As the capital of an individual can be increased only by what he saves from his annual revenue or his annual gains, so the capital of a society, which is the same with that of all the individuals who compose it, can be increased only in the same manner.

Parsimony,* and not industry, is the immediate cause of the increase of capital. Industry, indeed, provides the subject which parsimony accumulates. But whatever industry might acquire, if parsimony did not save and store up, the capital would never be the greater.

Parsimony, by increasing the fund which is destined for the maintenance of productive hands, tends to increase the number of those hands whose labour adds to the value of the subject upon which it is bestowed. It tends therefore to increase the exchangeable value of the annual produce of the land and labour of the country. It puts into motion an additional quantity of industry, which gives an additional value to the annual produce.

What is annually saved is as regularly consumed as what is annually spent, and nearly in the same time too; but it is consumed by a different set of people. That portion of his revenue which a rich man annually spends, is in most cases consumed by idle guests, and menial servants, who leave nothing behind them in return for their consumption. That portion which he annually saves, as for the sake of the profit it is immediately employed as a capital, is consumed in the same manner, and nearly in the same time too, but by a different set of people, by labourers, manufacturers, and artificers, who re-produce with a profit the value of their annual consumption. His revenue, we shall suppose, is paid him in money. Had he spent the whole, the food, cloathing, and lodging which the whole could have purchased, would have been distributed among the former set of people. By saving a part of it, as that part is for the sake of the profit immediately employed as a capital either by himself or by some other person, the food, cloathing, and lodging, which may be purchased with it, are necessarily reserved for the latter. The consumption is the same, but the consumers are different.

By what a frugal man annually saves, he not only affords maintenance to an additional number of productive hands, for that or the ensuing year, but, like the founder of a publick workhouse, he establishes as it were a perpetual fund for the maintenance of an equal number in all times to come. The perpetual allotment and destination of this fund, indeed, is not always guarded by any positive law, by any trust-right or deed of mortmain.* It is always guarded, however, by a very powerful principle, the plain and evident interest of every individual to whom any share of it shall ever belong. No part of it can ever afterwards be employed to maintain any but productive hands, without an evident loss to the person who thus perverts it from its proper destination.

The prodigal perverts it in this manner. By not confining his expence within his income, he encroaches upon his capital. Like him who perverts the revenues of some pious foundation to profane purposes, he pays the wages of idleness with those funds which the frugality of his forefathers had, as it were, consecrated to the maintenance of industry. By diminishing the funds destined for the employment of productive labour, he necessarily diminishes, so far as it depends upon him, the quantity of that labour which adds a value to the subject upon which it is bestowed, and, consequently, the value of the annual produce of the land and labour of the whole country, the real wealth and revenue of its inhabitants. If the prodigality of some was not compensated by the frugality of others, the conduct of every prodigal, by feeding the idle with the bread of the industrious, tends not only to beggar himself, but to impoverish his country.

Though the expence of the prodigal should be altogether in home-made, and no part of it in foreign commodities, its effect upon the productive funds of the society would still be the same. Every year there would still be a certain quantity of food and cloathing, which ought to have maintained productive, employed in maintaining unproductive hands. Every year, therefore, there would still be some diminution in what would otherwise have been the value of the annual produce of the land and labour of the country.

This expence, it may be said indeed, not being in foreign goods, and not occasioning any exportation of gold and silver, the same quantity of money would remain in the country as before. But if the quantity of food and cloathing, which were thus consumed by unproductive, had been distributed among productive hands, they would have reproduced, together with a profit, the full value of their consumption. The same quantity of money would in this case equally have remained in the country, and there would besides have been a reproduction of an equal value of consumable goods. There would have been two values instead of one.

The same quantity of money, besides, cannot long remain in any country, in which the value of the annual produce diminishes. The sole use of money is to circulate consumable goods. By means of it, provisions, materials, and finished work, are bought and sold, and distributed to their proper consumers. The quantity of money, therefore, which can be annually employed in any country must be determined by the value of the consumable goods annually circulated within it. These must consist either in the immediate produce of the land and labour of the country itself, or in something which had been purchased with some part of that produce. Their value, therefore, must diminish as the value of that produce diminishes, and along with it the quantity of money which can be employed in circulating them. But the money which by this annual diminution of produce is annually thrown out of domestick circulation will not be allowed to lie idle. The interest of whoever possesses it, requires that it should be employed. But having no employment at home, it will, in spite of all laws and prohibitions, be sent abroad, and employed in purchasing consumable goods which may be of some use at home. Its annual exportation will in this manner continue for some time to add something to the annual consumption of the country beyond the value of its own annual produce. What in the days of its prosperity had been saved from that annual produce, and employed in purchasing gold and silver, will contribute for some little time to support its consumption in adversity. The exportation of gold and silver is, in this case, not the cause, but the effect of its declension, and may even, for some little time, alleviate the misery of that declension.

The quantity of money, on the contrary, must in every country naturally increase as the value of the annual produce increases. The value of the consumable goods annually circulated within the society being greater, will require a greater quantity of money to circulate them. A part of the increased produce, therefore, will naturally be employed in purchasing, wherever it is to be had, the additional quantity of gold and silver necessary for circulating the rest. The increase of those metals will in this case be the effect, not the cause, of the publick prosperity. Gold and silver are purchased every where in the same manner. The food, cloathing, and lodging, the revenue and maintenance of all those whose labour or stock is employed in bringing them from the mine to the market, is the price paid for them in Peru as well as in England. The country which has this price to pay, will never be long without the quantity of those metals which it has occasion for; and no country will ever long retain a quantity which it has no occasion for.

Whatever, therefore, we may imagine the real wealth and revenue of a country to consist in, whether in the value of the annual produce of its land and labour, as plain reason seems to dictate; or in the quantity of the precious metals which circulate within it, as vulgar prejudices suppose; in either view of the matter, every prodigal appears to be a publick enemy, and every frugal man a publick benefactor.

The effects of misconduct are often the same as those of prodigality. Every injudicious and unsuccessful project in agriculture, mines, fisheries, trade, or manufactures, tends in the same manner to diminish the funds destined for the maintenance of productive labour. In every such project, though the capital is consumed by productive hands only, yet, as by the injudicious manner in which they are employed, they do not reproduce the full value of their consumption, there must always be some diminution in what would otherwise have been the productive funds of the society.

It can seldom happen, indeed, that the circumstances of a great nation can be much affected either by the prodigality or misconduct of individuals; the profusion or imprudence of some being always more than compensated by the frugality and good conduct of others.

With regard to profusion, the principle, which prompts to expence, is the passion for present enjoyment; which, though sometimes violent and very difficult to be restrained, is in general only momentary and occasional. But the principle which prompts to save, is the desire of bettering our condition, a desire which, though generally calm and dispassionate, comes with us from the womb, and never leaves us till we go into the grave. In the whole interval which separates those two moments, there is scarce perhaps a single instant in which any man is so perfectly and completely satisfied with his situation, as to be without any wish of alteration or improvement, of any kind. An augmentation of fortune is the means by which the greater part of men propose and wish to better their condition.* It is the means the most vulgar and the most obvious; and the most likely way of augmenting their fortune, is to save and accumulate some part of what they acquire, either regularly and annually, or upon some extraordinary occasions. Though the principle of expence, therefore, prevails in almost all men upon some occasions, and in some men upon almost all occasions, yet in the greater part of men, taking the whole course of their life at an average, the principle of frugality seems not only to predominate, but to predominate very greatly.

With regard to misconduct, the number of prudent and successful undertakings is every where much greater than that of injudicious and unsuccessful ones. After all our complaints of the frequency of bankruptcies, the unhappy men who fall into this misfortune make but a very small part of the whole number engaged in trade, and all other sorts of business; not much more perhaps than one in a thousand. Bankruptcy is perhaps the greatest and most humiliating calamity which can befal an innocent man. The greater part of men, therefore, are sufficiently careful to avoid it. Some, indeed, do not avoid it; as some do not avoid the gallows.

Great nations are never impoverished by private, though they sometimes are by publick prodigality and misconduct. The whole, or almost the whole publick revenue, is in most countries employed in maintaining unproductive hands. Such are the people who compose a numerous and splendid court, a great ecclesiastical establishment, great fleets and armies, who in time of peace produce nothing, and in time of war acquire nothing which can compensate the expence of maintaining them, even while the war lasts. Such people, as they themselves produce nothing, are all maintained by the produce of other men's labour. When multiplied, therefore, to an unnecessary number, they may in a particular year consume so great a share of this produce, as not to leave a sufficiency for maintaining the productive labourers, who should reproduce it next year. The next year's produce, therefore, will be less than that of the foregoing, and if the same disorder should continue, that of the third year will be still less than that of the second. Those unproductive hands, who should be maintained by a part only of the spare revenue of the people, may consume so great a share of their whole revenue, and thereby oblige so great a number to encroach upon their capitals, upon the funds destined for the maintenance of productive labour, that all the frugality and good conduct of individuals may not be able to compensate the waste and degradation of produce occasioned by this violent and forced encroachment.

This frugality and good conduct, however, is upon most occasions, it appears from experience, sufficient to compensate, not only the private prodigality and misconduct of individuals, but the publick extravagance of government. The uniform, constant, and uninterrupted effort of every man to better his condition, the principle from which publick and national, as well as private opulence is originally derived, is frequently powerful enough to maintain the natural progress of things toward improvement, in spite both of the extravagance of government, and of the greatest errors of administration.* Like the unknown principle of animal life, it frequently restores health and vigour to the constitution, in spite, not only of the disease, but of the absurd prescriptions of the doctor.

The annual produce of the land and labour of any nation can be increased in its value by no other means, but by increasing either the number of its productive labourers, or the productive powers of those labourers who had before been employed. The number of its productive labourers, it is evident, can never be much increased, but in consequence of an increase of capital, or of the funds destined for maintaining them. The productive powers of the same number of labourers cannot be increased, but in consequence either of some addition and improvement to those machines and instruments which facilitate and abridge labour; or of a more proper division and distribution of employment. In either case an additional capital is almost always required. It is by means of an additional capital only that the undertaker of any work can either provide his workmen with better machinery, or make a more proper distribution of employment among them. When the work to be done consists of a number of parts, to keep every man constantly employed in one way, requires a much greater capital than where every man is occasionally employed in every different part of the work. When we compare, therefore, the state of a nation at two different periods, and find, that the annual produce of its land and labour is evidently greater at the latter than at the former, that its lands are better cultivated, its manufactures more numerous and more flourishing, and its trade more extensive, we may be assured that its capital must have increased during the interval between those two periods, and that more must have been added to it by the good conduct of some, than had been taken from it either by the private misconduct of others, or by the publick extravagance of government. But we shall find this to have been the case of almost all nations, in all tolerably quiet and peaceable times, even of those who have not enjoyed the most prudent and parsimonious governments. To form a right judgment of it, indeed, we must compare the state of the country at periods somewhat distant from one another. The progress is frequently so gradual, that, at near periods, the improvement is not only not sensible, but from the declension either of certain branches of industry, or of certain districts of the country, things which sometimes happen though the country in general be in great prosperity, there frequently arises a suspicion, that the riches and industry of the whole are decaying.

The annual produce of the land and labour of England, for example, is certainly much greater than it was, a little more than a century ago, at the restoration of Charles II. Though at present, few people, I believe, doubt of this, yet during this period, five years have seldom passed away in which some book or pamphlet has not been published, written too with such abilities as to gain some authority with the publick, and pretending to demonstrate that the wealth of the nation was fast declining, that the country was depopulated, agriculture neglected, manufactures decaying, and trade undone.* Nor have these publications been all party pamphlets, the wretched offspring of falshood and venality. Many of them have been written by very candid and very intelligent people; who wrote nothing but what they believed, and for no other reason but because they believed it.

The annual produce of the land and labour of England again, was certainly much greater at the restoration, than we can suppose it to have been about an hundred years before, at the accession of Elizabeth. At this period too, we have all reason to believe, the country was much more advanced in improvement, than it had been about a century before, towards the close of the dissensions between the houses of York and Lancaster. Even then it was, probably, in a better condition than it had been at the Norman conquest, and at the Norman conquest, than during the confusion of the Saxon Heptarchy.* Even at this early period, it was certainly a more improved country than at the invasion of Julius Caesar, when its inhabitants were nearly in the same state with the savages in North America.*

In each of those periods, however, there was, not only much private and publick profusion, many expensive and unnecessary wars, great perversion of the annual produce from maintaining productive to maintain unproductive hands; but sometimes, in the confusion of civil discord, such absolute waste and destruction of stock, as might be supposed, not only to retard, as it certainly did, the natural accumulation of riches, but to have left the country, at the end of the period, poorer than at the beginning. Thus, in the happiest and most fortunate period of them all, that which has passed since the restoration, how many disorders and misfortunes have occurred, which, could they have been foreseen, not only the impoverishment, but the total ruin of the country would have been expected from them? The fire and the plague of London, the two Dutch wars, the disorders of the revolution, the war in Ireland, the four expensive French wars of 1688, 1702, 1742, and 1756, together with the two rebellions of 1715 and 1745.* In the course of the four French wars, the nation has contracted more than a hundred and forty-five millions of debt, over and above all the other extraordinary annual expence which they occasioned, so that the whole cannot be computed at less than two hundred

millions. So great a share of the annual produce of the land
and labour of the country, has, since the revolution, been
employed upon different occasions, in maintaining an extraordinary number of unproductive hands. But had not those
wars given this particular direction to so large a capital, the
greater part of it would naturally have been employed in
maintaining productive hands, whose labour would have replaced, with a profit, the whole value of their consumption.
The value of the annual produce of the land and labour of the
country, would have been considerably increased by it every
year, and every year's increase would have augmented still
more that of the following year. More houses would have been
built, more lands would have been improved, and those which
had been improved before would have been better cultivated,
more manufactures would have been established, and those
which had been established before would have been more
extended; and to what height the real wealth and revenue of
the country might, by this time, have been raised, it is not
perhaps very easy even to imagine.

But though the profusion of government must, undoubtedly,
have retarded the natural progress of England towards wealth
and improvement, it has not been able to stop it. The annual
produce of its land and labour is, undoubtedly, much greater
at present than it was either at the restoration or at the
revolution. The capital, therefore, annually employed in cultivating this land, and in maintaining this labour, must likewise
be much greater. In the midst of all the exactions of government, this capital has been silently and gradually accumulated
by the private frugality and good conduct of individuals, by
their universal, continual, and uninterrupted effort to better
their own condition. It is this effort, protected by law and
allowed by liberty to exert itself in the manner that is most
advantageous, which has maintained the progress of England
towards opulence and improvement in almost all former times,
and which, it is to be hoped, will do so in all future times.
England, however, as it has never been blessed with a very
parsimonious government, so parsimony has at no time been

the characteristical virtue of its inhabitants. It is the highest impertinence and presumption, therefore, in kings and ministers, to pretend to watch over the œconomy of private people, and to restrain their expence either by sumptuary laws, or by prohibiting the importation of foreign luxuries.* They are themselves always, and without any exception, the greatest spendthrifts in the society. Let them look well after their own expence, and they may safely trust private people with theirs. If their own extravagance does not ruin the state, that of their subjects never will.

As frugality increases, and prodigality diminishes the publick capital, so the conduct of those, whose expence just equals their revenue, without either accumulating or encroaching, neither increases nor diminishes it. Some modes of expence, however, seem to contribute more to the growth of publick opulence than others.

The revenue of an individual may be spent, either in things which are consumed immediately, and in which one day's expence can neither alleviate nor support that of another; or it may be spent in things more durable, which can therefore be accumulated, and in which every day's expence may, as he chuses, either alleviate or support and heighten the effect of that of the following day. A man of fortune, for example, may either spend his revenue in a profuse and sumptuous table, and in maintaining a great number of menial servants, and a multitude of dogs and horses; or contenting himself with a frugal table and few attendants, he may lay out the greater part of it in adorning his house or his country villa, in useful or ornamental buildings, in useful or ornamental furniture, in collecting books, statues, pictures; or in things more frivolous, jewels, baubles, ingenious trinkets of different kinds; or, what is most trifling of all, in amassing a great wardrobe of fine cloaths, like the favourite and minister of a great prince who died a few years ago.* Were two men of equal fortune to spend their revenue, the one chiefly in the one way, the other in the other, the magnificence of the person whose expence had been chiefly in durable commodities, would be continually increasing, every day's expence contributing something to support and heighten the effect of that of the following day: that of the other, on the contrary, would be no greater at the end of the period than at the beginning. The former too would, at the end of the period, be the richer man of the two. He would have a stock of goods of some kind or other, which, though it might not be worth all that it cost, would always be worth something. No trace or vestige of the expence of the latter would remain, and the effects of ten or twenty years profusion would be as completely annihilated as if they had never existed.

As the one mode of expence is more favourable than the other to the opulence of an individual, so is it likewise to that of a nation. The houses, the furniture, the cloathing of the rich, in a little time, become useful to the inferior and middling ranks of people. They are able to purchase them when their superiors grow weary of them, and the general accommodation of the whole people is thus gradually improved, when this mode of expence becomes universal among men of fortune. In countries which have long been rich, you will frequently find the inferior ranks of people in possession both of houses and furniture perfectly good and entire, but of which neither the one could have been built, nor the other have been made for their use. What was formerly a seat of the family of Seymour, is now an inn upon the Bath road. The marriage-bed of James the First of Great Britain, which his Queen brought with her from Denmark, as a present fit for a sovereign to make to a sovereign, was, a few years ago, the ornament of an alehouse at Dunfermline. In some ancient cities, which either have been long stationary, or have gone somewhat to decay, you will sometimes scarce find a single house which could have been built for its present inhabitants. If you go into those houses too, you will frequently find many excellent, though antiquated pieces of furniture, which are still very fit for use, and which could as little have been made for them. Noble palaces, magnificent villas, great collections of books, statues, pictures, and other curiosities, are frequently both an ornament and an honour, not only to the neighbourhood, but to the whole country to which they belong. Versailles is an ornament and a honour to France, Stowe and Wilton to England.* Italy continues to command some sort of veneration by the number of monuments of this kind which it possesses, though the wealth which produced them has decayed, and though the genius which planned them seems to be extinguished, perhaps from not having the same employment.

The expence too, which is laid out in durable commodities, is favourable, not only to accumulation, but to frugality. If a person should at any time exceed in it, he can easily reform without exposing himself to the censure of the publick. To reduce very much the number of his servants, to reform his table from great profusion to great frugality, to lay down his equipage* after he has once set it up, are changes which cannot escape the observation of his neighbours, and which are supposed to imply some acknowledgment of preceding bad conduct. Few, therefore, of those who have once been so unfortunate as to launch out too far into this sort of expence, have afterwards the courage to reform, till ruin and bankruptcy oblige them. But if a person has, at any time, been at too great an expence in building, in furniture, in books or pictures, no imprudence can be inferred from his changing his conduct. These are things in which further expence is frequently rendered unnecessary by former expence; and when a person stops short, he appears to do so, not because he has exceeded his fortune, but because he has satisfied his fancy.

The expence, besides, that is laid out in durable commodities, gives maintenance, commonly, to a greater number of people, than that which is employed in the most profuse hospitality. Of two or three hundred weight of provisions, which may sometimes be served up at a great festival, onehalf, perhaps, is thrown to the dunghill, and there is always a great deal wasted and abused. But if the expence of this entertainment had been employed in setting to work, masons, carpenters, upholsterers, mechanicks, &c. a quantity of provisions, of equal value, would have been distributed among a still greater number of people, who would have bought them in pennyworths and pound weights, and not have lost or thrown away a single ounce of them. In the one way, besides, this expence maintains productive, in the other unproductive hands. In the one way, therefore, it increases, in the other, it does not increase, the exchangeable value of the annual produce of the land and labour of the country.

I would not, however, by all this be understood to mean, that the one species of expence always betokens a more liberal or generous spirit than the other. When a man of fortune spends his revenue chiefly in hospitality, he shares the greater part of it with his friends and companions; but when he employs it in purchasing such durable commodities, he often spends the whole upon his own person, and gives nothing to any body without an equivalent. The latter species of expence, therefore, especially when directed towards frivolous objects, the little ornaments of dress and furniture, jewels, trinkets, gewgaws,* frequently indicates, not only a trifling, but a base and selfish disposition. All that I mean is, that the one sort of expence, as it always occasions some accumulation of valuable commodities, as it is more favourable to private frugality, and, consequently, to the increase of the publick capital, and as it maintains productive, rather than unproductive hands, conduces more than the other to the growth of publick opulence.

[Chapter IV *Of Stock lent at Interest** has been omitted from this edition.]

CHAPTER V

Of the different Employment of Capitals

THOUGH all capitals are destined for the maintenance of productive labour only, yet the quantity of that labour, which equal capitals are capable of putting into motion, varies extremely according to the diversity of their employment; as does likewise the value which that employment adds to the annual produce of the land and labour of the country.

A capital may be employed in four different ways: either, first, in procuring the rude produce annually required for the use and consumption of the society; or, secondly, in manufacturing and preparing that rude produce for immediate use and consumption; or, thirdly, in transporting either the rude or manufactured produce from the places where they abound to those where they are wanted; or, lastly, in dividing particular portions of either into such small parcels as suit the occasional demands of those who want them. In the first way are employed the capitals of all those who undertake the improvement or cultivation of lands, mines, or fisheries; in the second, those of all master manufacturers; in the third, those of all wholesale merchants; and in the fourth, those of all retailers. It is difficult to conceive that a capital should be employed in any way which may not be classed under some one or other of those four.

Each of those four methods of employing a capital is essentially necessary either to the existence or extension of the other three, or to the general conveniency of the society.

Unless a capital was employed in furnishing rude produce to a certain degree of abundance, neither manufactures nor trade of any kind could exist.

Unless a capital was employed in manufacturing that part of the rude produce which requires a good deal of preparation before it can be fit for use and consumption, it either would never be produced, because there could be no demand for it;

or if it was produced spontaneously, it would be of no value in exchange, and could add nothing to the wealth of the society.

Unless a capital was employed in transporting, either the rude or manufactured produce, from the places where it abounds to those where it is wanted, no more of either could be produced than was necessary for the consumption of the neighbourhood. The capital of the merchant exchanges the surplus produce of one place for that of another, and thus encourages the industry and increases the enjoyments of both.

Unless a capital was employed in breaking and dividing certain portions either of the rude or manufactured produce, into such small parcels as suit the occasional demands of those who want them, every man would be obliged to purchase a greater quantity of the goods he wanted, than his immediate occasions required. If there was no such trade as a butcher, for example, every man would be obliged to purchase a whole ox or a whole sheep at a time. This would generally be inconvenient to the rich, and much more so to the poor. If a poor workman was obliged to purchase a month's or six months provisions at a time, a great part of the stock which he employs as a capital in the instruments of his trade, or in the furniture of his shop, and which yields him a revenue, he would be forced to place in that part of his stock which is reserved for immediate consumption, and which yields him no revenue. Nothing can be more convenient for such a person than to be able to purchase his subsistence from day to day, or even from hour to hour as he wants it. He is thereby enabled to employ almost his whole stock as a capital. He is thus enabled to furnish work to a greater value, and the profit, which he makes by it in this way, much more than compensates the additional price which the profit of the retailer imposes upon the goods. The prejudices of some political writers against shopkeepers and tradesmen, are altogether without foundation.* So far is it from being necessary, either to tax them, or to restrict their numbers, that they can never be multiplied so as to hurt the publick, though they may so as to hurt one another. The quantity of grocery goods, for example, which can be sold in a particular town, is limited by the demand of that town and its neighbourhood. The capital, therefore, which can be employed in the grocery trade cannot exceed what is sufficient to purchase that quantity. If this capital is divided between two different grocers, their competition will tend to make both of them sell cheaper, than if it were in the hands of one only; and if it were divided among twenty, their competition would be just so much the greater, and the chance of their combining together, in order to raise the price, just so much the less. Their competition might perhaps ruin some of themselves; but to take care of this is the business of the parties concerned, and it may safely be trusted to their discretion. It can never hurt either the consumer, or the producer; on the contrary, it must tend to make the retailers both sell cheaper and buy dearer, than if the whole trade was monopolized by one or two persons. Some of them, perhaps, may sometimes decoy a weak customer to buy what he has no occasion for. This evil, however, is of too little importance to deserve the publick attention, nor would it necessarily be prevented by restricting their numbers. It is not the multitude of ale-houses, to give the most suspicious example, that occasions a general disposition to drunkenness among the common people; but that disposition arising from other causes necessarily gives employment to a multitude of ale-houses.*

The persons whose capitals are employed in any of those four ways are themselves productive labourers. Their labour, when properly directed, fixes and realizes itself in the subject or vendible commodity upon which it is bestowed, and generally adds to its price the value at least of their own maintenance and consumption. The profits of the farmer, of the manufacturer, of the merchant, and retailer, are all drawn from the price of the goods which the two first produce, and the two last buy and sell. Equal capitals, however, employed in each of those four different ways, will immediately put into motion very different quantities of productive labour, and augment too in very different porportions the value of the annual produce of the land and labour of the society to which they belong.

The capital of the retailer replaces, together with its profits, that of the merchant of whom he purchases goods, and thereby enables him to continue his business. The retailer himself is the only productive labourer whom it immediately employs. In his profits, consists the whole value which its employment adds to the annual produce of the land and labour of the society.

The capital of the wholesale merchant replaces, together with their profits, the capitals of the farmers and manufacturers of whom he purchases the rude and manufactured produce which he deals in, and thereby enables them to continue their respective trades. It is by this service chiefly that he contributes indirectly to support the productive labour of the society, and to increase the value of its annual produce. His capital employs too the sailors and carriers who transport his goods from one place to another, and it augments the price of those goods by the value, not only of his profits, but of their wages. This is all the productive labour which it immediately puts into motion, and all the value which it immediately adds to the annual produce. Its operation in both these respects is a good deal superior to that of the capital of the retailer.

Part of the capital of the master manufacturer is employed as a fixed capital in the instruments of his trade, and replaces, together with its profits, that of some other artificer of whom he purchases them. Part of his circulating capital is employed in purchasing materials, and replaces, with their profits, the capitals of the farmers and miners of whom he purchases them. But a great part of it is always, either annually, or in a much shorter period, distributed among the different workmen whom he employs. It augments the value of those materials by their wages, and by their masters profits upon the whole stock of wages, materials, and instruments of trade employed in the business. It puts immediately into motion, therefore, a much greater quantity of productive labour, and adds a much greater value to the annual produce of the land and labour of the society, than an equal capital in the hands of any wholesale merchant.

No equal capital puts into motion a greater quantity of productive labour than that of the farmer. Not only his labouring servants, but his labouring cattle, are productive labourers. In agriculture too nature labours along with man; and though her labour costs no expence, its produce has its value, as well as that of the most expensive workmen. The most important operations of agriculture seem intended, not so much to increase, though they do that too, as to direct the fertility of nature towards the production of the plants most profitable to man. A field overgrown with briars and brambles may frequently produce as great a quantity of vegetables as the best cultivated vineyard or corn field. Planting and tillage frequently regulate more than they animate the active fertility of nature; and after all their labour, a great part of the work always remains to be done by her. The labourers and labouring cattle, therefore, employed in agriculture, not only occasion, like the workmen in manufactures, the reproduction of a value equal to their own consumption, or to the capital which employs them, together with its owners profits; but of a much greater value. Over and above the capital of the farmer and all its profits, they regularly occasion the reproduction of the rent of the landlord. This rent may be considered as the produce of those powers of nature, the use of which the landlord lends to the farmer. It is greater or smaller according to the supposed extent of those powers, or in other words, according to the supposed natural or improved fertility of the land. It is the work of nature which remains after deducting or compensating every thing which can be regarded as the work of man. It is seldom less than a fourth, and frequently more than a third of the whole produce.* No equal quantity of productive labour employed in manufactures can ever occasion so great a reproduction. In them nature does nothing; man does all; and the reproduction must always be in proportion to the strength of the agents that occasion it. The capital employed in agriculture, therefore, not only puts into motion a greater quantity of productive labour than any equal capital employed in manufactures, but in proportion too to the quantity of productive labour which it employs, it adds a much greater value to the annual produce of the land and labour of the country, to the real wealth and revenue of its inhabitants. Of all the ways in which a capital can be employed, it is by far the most advantageous to the society.*

The capitals employed in the agriculture and in the retail trade of any society, must always reside within that society. Their employment is confined almost to a precise spot, to the farm, and to the shop of the retailer. They must generally too, though there are some exceptions to this, belong to resident members of the society.

The capital of a wholesale merchant, on the contrary, seems to have no fixed or necessary residence anywhere, but may wander about from place to place, according as it can either buy cheap or sell dear.

The capital of the manufacturer must no doubt reside where the manufacture is carried on; but where this shall be is not always necessarily determined. It may frequently be at a great distance both from the place where the materials grow, and from that where the complete manufacture is consumed. Lyons is very distant both from the places which afford the materials of its manufactures, and from those which consume them. The people of fashion in Sicily are cloathed in silks made in other countries, from the materials which their own produces. Part of the wool of Spain is manufactured in Great Britain, and some part of that cloth is afterwards sent back to Spain.

Whether the merchant whose capital exports the surplus produce of any society be a native or a foreigner, is of very little importance. If he is a foreigner, the number of their productive labourers is necessarily less than if he had been a native by one man only; and the value of their annual produce, by the profits of that one man. The sailors or carriers whom he employs may still belong indifferently either to his country, or to their country, or to some third country, in the same manner as if he had been a native. The capital of a foreigner gives a value to their surplus produce equally with that of a native, by exchanging it for something for which there is a demand at home. It as effectually replaces the capital of the person who produces that surplus, and as effectually enables him to continue his business; the service by which the capital of a wholesale merchant chiefly contributes to support the productive labour, and to augment the value of the annual produce of the society to which he belongs.

It is of more consequence that the capital of the manufacturer should reside within the country. It necessarily puts into motion a greater quantity of productive labour, and adds a greater value to the annual produce of the land and labour of the society. It may, however, be very useful to the country, though it should not reside within it. The capitals of the British manufacturers who work up the flax and hemp annually imported from the coasts of the Baltic,* are surely very useful to the countries which produce them. Those materials are a part of the surplus produce of those countries which, unless it was annually exchanged for something which is in demand there, would be of no value, and would soon cease to be produced. The merchants who export it, replace the capitals of the people who produce it, and thereby encourage them to continue the production; and the British manufacturers replace the capitals of those merchants.

A particular country, in the same manner as a particular person, may frequently not have capital sufficient both to improve and cultivate all its lands, to manufacture and prepare their whole rude produce for immediate use and consumption, and to transport the surplus part either of the rude or manufactured produce to those distant markets where it can be exchanged for something for which there is a demand at home. The inhabitants of many different parts of Great Britain have not capital sufficient to improve and cultivate all their lands. The wool of the southern counties of Scotland is, a great part of it, after a long land carriage through very bad roads, manufactured in Yorkshire, for want of a capital to manufacture it at home. There are many little manufacturing towns in Great Britain, of which the inhabitants have not capital sufficient to transport the produce of their own industry to those distant markets where there is demand and consumption for it. If there are any merchants among them, they are properly only the agents of wealthier merchants who reside in some of the greater commercial cities.

When the capital of any country is not sufficient for all those three purposes, in proportion as a greater share of it is employed in agriculture, the greater will be the quantity of productive labour which it puts into motion within the country; as will likewise be the value which its employment adds to the annual produce of the land and labour of the society. After agriculture, the capital employed in manufactures puts into motion the greatest quantity of productive labour, and adds the greatest value to the annual produce. That which is employed in the trade of exportation, has the least effect of any of the three.

The country, indeed, which has not capital sufficient for all those three purposes, has not arrived at that degree of opulence for which it seems naturally destined. To attempt, however, prematurely and with an insufficient capital, to do all the three, is certainly not the shortest way for a society, no more than it would be for an individual, to acquire a sufficient one. The capital of all the individuals of a nation, has its limits in the same manner as that of a single individual, and is capable of executing only certain purposes. The capital of all the individuals of a nation is increased in the same manner as that of a single individual, by their continually accumulating and adding to it whatever they save out of their revenue. It is likely to increase the fastest, therefore, when it is employed in the way that affords the greatest revenue to all the inhabitants of the country, as they will thus be enabled to make the greatest savings. But the revenue of all the inhabitants of the country is necessarily in proportion to the value of the annual produce of their land and labour.

It has been the principal cause of the rapid progress of our American colonies towards wealth and greatness, that almost their whole capitals have hitherto been employed in agriculture. They have no manufactures, those houshold and coarser manufactures excepted which necessarily accompany the progress of agriculture, and which are the work of the women and children in every private family. The greater part both of the exportation and coasting trade of America, is carried on by the capitals of merchants who reside in Great Britain.* Even the stores and warehouses from which goods are retailed in some provinces, particularly in Virginia and Maryland, belong many of them to merchants who reside in the mother country, and afford one of the few instances of the retail trade of a society being carried on by the capitals of those who are not resident members of it. Were the Americans, either by combination or by any other sort of violence, to stop the importation of European manufactures,* and, by thus giving a monopoly to such of their own countrymen as could manufacture the like goods, divert any considerable part of their capital into this employment, they would retard instead of accelerating the further increase in the value of their annual produce, and would obstruct instead of promoting the progress of their country towards real wealth and greatness. This would be still more the case, were they to attempt, in the same manner, to monopolize to themselves their whole exportation trade.

The course of human prosperity, indeed, seems scarce ever to have been of so long continuance as to enable any great country to acquire capital sufficient for all those three purposes; unless, perhaps, we give credit to the wonderful accounts of the wealth and cultivation of China, of those of antient Egypt, and of the antient state of Indostan. Even those three countries, the wealthiest, according to all accounts, that ever were in the world, are chiefly renowned for their superiority in agriculture and manufactures. They do not appear to have been eminent for foreign trade. The antient Egyptians had a superstitious antipathy to the sea; a superstition nearly of the same kind prevails among the Indians; and the Chinese have never excelled in foreign commerce.* The greater part of the surplus produce of all those three countries seems to have been always exported by foreigners, who gave in exchange for it something else for which they found a demand there, frequently gold and silver.

It is thus that the same capital will in any country put into motion a greater or smaller quantity of productive labour, and add a greater or smaller value to the annual produce of its land and labour, according to the different proportions in which it is employed in agriculture, manufactures, and wholesale trade. The difference too is very great, according to the different sorts of wholesale trade in which any part of it is employed.

All wholesale trade, all buying in order to sell again by wholesale, may be reduced to three different sorts. The home trade, the foreign trade of consumption, and the carrying trade. The home trade is employed in purchasing in one part of the same country, and selling in another, the produce of the industry of that country. It comprehends both the inland and the coasting trade. The foreign trade of consumption is employed in purchasing foreign goods for home consumption. The carrying trade is employed in transacting the commerce of foreign countries, or in carrying the surplus produce of one to another. . . .

The capital . . . employed in the home-trade of any country will generally give encouragement and support to a greater quantity of productive labour in that country, and increase the value of its annual produce more than an equal capital employed in the foreign trade of consumption: and the capital employed in this latter trade has in both these respects a still greater advantage over an equal capital employed in the carrying trade. The riches, and so far as power depends upon riches, the power of every country, must always be in proportion to the value of its annual produce, the fund from which all taxes must ultimately be paid. But the great object of the political œconomy of every country, is to encrease the riches and power of that country. It ought, therefore, to give no preference nor superior encouragement to the foreign trade of consumption above the home-trade, nor to the carrying trade above either of the other two. It ought neither to force nor to allure into either of those two channels, a greater share of the capital of the country than what would naturally flow into them of its own accord.*

Each of those different branches of trade, however, is not only advantageous, but necessary and unavoidable, when the course of things, without any constraint or violence, naturally introduces it.

When the produce of any particular branch of industry exceeds what the demand of the country requires, the surplus must be sent abroad, and exchanged for something for which there is a demand at home. Without such exportation, a part of the productive labour of the country must cease, and the value of its annual produce diminish. The land and labour of Great Britain produce generally more corn, woollens, and hard ware,* than the demand of the home-market requires. The surplus part of them, therefore, must be sent abroad, and exchanged for something for which there is a demand at home. It is only by means of such exportation, that this surplus can acquire a value sufficient to compensate the labour and expence of producing it. The neighbourhood of the sea coast, and the banks of all navigable rivers, are advantageous situations for industry,* only because they facilitate the exportation and exchange of such surplus produce for something else which is more in demand there.

When the foreign goods which are thus purchased with the surplus produce of domestick industry exceed the demand of the home-market, the surplus part of them must be sent abroad again, and exchanged for something more in demand at home. About ninety-six thousand hogsheads* of tobacco are annually purchased in Virginia and Maryland, with a part of the surplus produce of British industry. But the demand of Great Britain does not require, perhaps, more than fourteen thousand. If the remaining eighty-two thousand, therefore, could not be sent abroad and exchanged for something more in demand at home, the importation of them must cease immediately, and with it the productive labour of all those inhabitants of Great Britain, who are at present employed in preparing the goods with which these eighty-two thousand hogsheads are annually purchased. Those goods, which are part of the produce of the land and labour of Great Britain, having no market at home, and being deprived of that which they had abroad, must cease to be produced. The most round-about foreign trade of consumption, therefore, may, upon some occasions, be as necessary for supporting the productive labour of the country, and the value of its annual produce, as the most direct.

When the capital stock of any country is increased to such a degree, that it cannot be all employed in supplying the consumption, and supporting the productive labour of that particular country, the surplus part of it naturally disgorges itself into the carrying trade, and is employed in performing the same offices to other countries. The carrying trade is the natural effect and symptom of great national wealth: but it does not seem to be the natural cause of it. Those statesmen who have been disposed to favour it with particular encouragements, seem to have mistaken the effect and symptom for the cause. Holland, in proportion to the extent of the land and the number of its inhabitants, by far the richest country in Europe,* has, accordingly, the greatest share of the carrying trade of Europe. England, perhaps the second richest country of Europe, is likewise supposed to have a considerable share of it; though what commonly passes for the carrying trade of England, will frequently, perhaps, be found to be no more than a round-about foreign trade of consumption. Such are, in a great measure, the trades which carry the goods of the East and West Indies, and of America, to different European markets. Those goods are generally purchased either immediately with the produce of British industry, or with something else which had been purchased with that produce, and the final returns of those trades are generally used or consumed in Great Britain. The trade which is carried on in British bottoms between the different ports of the Mediterranean, and some trade of the same kind carried on by British merchants between the different ports of India, make, perhaps, the principal branches of what is properly the carrying trade of Great Britain.

The extent of the home-trade and of the capital which can be employed in it, is necessarily limited by the value of the surplus produce of all those distant places within the country which have occasion to exchange their respective productions with one another. That of the foreign trade of consumption, by the value of the surplus produce of the whole country and of what can be purchased with it. That of the carrying trade, by the value of the surplus produce of all the different countries in the world. Its possible extent, therefore, is in a manner infinite in comparison of that of the other two, and is capable of absorbing the greatest capitals.

The consideration of his own private profit, is the sole motive which determines the owner of any capital to employ it either in agriculture, in manufactures, or in some particular branch of the wholesale or retail trade. The different quantities of productive labour which it may put into motion, and the different values which it may add to the annual produce of the land and labour of the society, according as it is employed in one or other of those different ways, never enter into his thoughts. In countries, therefore, where agriculture is the most profitable of all employments, and farming and improving the most direct roads to a splendid fortune, the capitals of individuals will naturally be employed in the manner most advantageous to the whole society. The profits of agriculture, however, seem to have no superiority over those of other employments in any part of Europe. Projectors, indeed, in every corner of it, have within these few years amused the public with most magnificent accounts of the profits to be made by the cultivation and improvement of land.* Without entering into any particular discussion of their calculations, a very simple observation may satisfy us that the result of them must be false. We see every day the most splendid fortunes that have been acquired in the course of a single life by trade and manufactures,* frequently from a very small capital, sometimes from no capital. A single instance of such a fortune acquired by agriculture in the same time, and from such a capital, has not, perhaps, occurred in Europe during the course of the present century. In all the great countries of Europe, however, much good land still remains uncultivated, and the greater part of what is cultivated is far from being improved to the degree of which it is capable. Agriculture, therefore, is almost every where capable of absorbing a much greater capital than has ever yet been employed in it. What circumstances in the policy of Europe have given the trades which are carried on in towns so great an advantage over that which is carried on in the country, that private persons frequently find it more for their advantage to employ their capitals in the most distant carrying trades of Asia and America, than in the improvement and cultivation of the most fertile fields in their own neighbourhood, I shall endeavour to explain at full length in the two following books.

BOOK III

Of the different Progress of Opulence in different Nations

CHAPTER I

Of the natural Progress of Opulence

THE great commerce of every civilized society, is that carried on between the inhabitants of the town and those of the country.* It consists in the exchange of rude for manufactured produce, either immediately, or by the intervention of money, or of some sort of paper which represents money. The country supplies the town with the means of subsistence, and the materials of manufacture. The town repays this supply by sending back a part of the manufactured produce to the inhabitants of the country. The town, in which there neither is nor can be any reproduction of substances, may very properly be said to gain its whole wealth and subsistence from the country. We must not, however, upon this account, imagine that the gain of the town is the loss of the country. The gains of both are mutual and reciprocal, and the division of labour is in this, as in all other cases, advantageous to all the different persons employed in the various occupations into which it is subdivided. The inhabitants of the country purchase of the town a greater quantity of manufactured goods, with the produce of a much smaller quantity of their own labour, than they must have employed had they attempted to prepare them themselves. The town affords a market for the surplus produce of the country, or what is over and above the maintenance of the cultivators, and it is there that the inhabitants of the country exchange it for something else which is in demand

among them. The greater the number and revenue of the
inhabitants of the town, the more extensive is the market which
it affords to those of the country; and the more extensive that
market, it is always the more advantageous to a great number.
The corn which grows within a mile of the town, sells there
for the same price with that which comes from twenty miles
distance. But the price of the latter must generally, not only
pay the expence of raising and bringing it to market, but afford
too the ordinary profits of agriculture to the farmer. The
proprietors and cultivators of the country, therefore, which lies
in the neighbourhood of the town, over and above the ordinary
profits of agriculture, gain, in the price of what they sell, the
whole value of the carriage of the like produce that is brought
from more distant parts, and they save, besides, the whole
value of this carriage in the price of what they buy. Compare
the cultivation of the lands in the neighbourhood of any
considerable town, with that of those which lie at some distance
from it, and you will easily satisfy yourself how much the
country is benefited by the commerce of the town. Among all
the absurd speculations that have been propagated concerning the balance of trade,* it has never been pretended that
either the country loses by its commerce with the town, or the
town by that with the country which maintains it.

As subsistence is, in the nature of things, prior to conveniency and luxury, so the industry which procures the former,
must necessarily be prior to that which ministers to the latter.
The cultivation and improvement of the country, therefore,
which affords subsistence, must, necessarily, be prior to the
increase of the town, which furnishes only the means of
conveniency and luxury. It is the surplus produce of the
country only, or what is over and above the maintenance of
the cultivators, that constitutes the subsistence of the town,
which can therefore increase only with the increase of this
surplus produce. The town, indeed, may not always derive its
whole subsistence from the country in its neighbourhood, or
even from the territory to which it belongs, but from very
distant countries; and this, though it forms no exception from

the general rule, has occasioned considerable variations in the progress of opulence in different ages and nations.

That order of things which necessity imposes in general, though not in every particular country, is, in every particular country, promoted by the natural inclinations of man. If human institutions had never thwarted those natural inclinations, the towns could no-where have increased beyond what the improvement and cultivation of the territory in which they were situated could support; till such time, at least, as the whole of that territory was compleatly cultivated and improved. Upon equal, or nearly equal profits, most men will chuse to employ their capitals rather in the improvement and cultivation of land, than either in manufactures or in foreign trade. The man who employs his capital in land, has it more under his view and command, and his fortune is much less liable to accidents than that of the trader, who is obliged frequently to commit it, not only to the winds and the waves, but to the more uncertain elements of human folly and injustice, by giving great credits in distant countries to men, with whose character and situation he can seldom be thoroughly acquainted. The capital of the landlord, on the contrary, which is fixed in the improvement of his land, seems to be as well secured as the nature of human affairs can admit of. The beauty of the country besides, the pleasures of a country life, the tranquillity of mind which it promises, and wherever the injustice of human laws does not disturb it, the independency which it really affords, have charms that more or less attract every body; and as to cultivate the ground was the original destination of man, so in every stage of his existence he seems to retain a predilection for this primitive employment.*

Without the assistance of some artificers, indeed, the cultivation of land cannot be carried on, but with great inconveniency and continual interruption. Smiths, carpenters, wheel-wrights, and plough-wrights, masons, and bricklayers, tanners, shoe-makers, and taylors, are people, whose service the farmer has frequent occasion for. Such artificers too stand, occasionally, in need of the assistance of one another; and as their residence is not, like that of the farmer, necessarily tied down to a precise spot, they naturally settle in the neighbourhood of one another, and thus form a small town or village. The butcher, the brewer, and the baker, soon join them, together with many other artificers and retailers, necessary or useful for supplying their occasional wants, and who contribute still further to augment the town. The inhabitants of the town and those of the country are mutually the servants of one another. The town is a continual fair or market, to which the inhabitants of the country resort, in order to exchange their rude for manufactured produce. It is this commerce which supplies the inhabitants of the town both with the materials of their work, and the means of their subsistence. The quantity of the finished work which they sell to the inhabitants of the country, necessarily regulates the quantity of the materials and provisions which they buy. Neither their employment nor subsistence, therefore, can augment, but in proportion to the augmentation of the demand from the country for finished work; and this demand can augment only in proportion to the extension of improvement and cultivation. Had human institutions, therefore, never disturbed the natural course of things,* the progressive wealth and increase of the towns would, in every political society, be consequential, and in proportion to the improvement and cultivation of the territory or country.

In our North American colonies, where uncultivated land is still to be had upon easy terms, no manufactures for distant sale have ever yet been established in any of their towns. When an artificer has acquired a little more stock than is necessary for carrying on his own business in supplying the neighbouring country, he does not, in North America, attempt to establish with it a manufacture for more distant sale, but employs it in the purchase and improvement of uncultivated land. From artificer he becomes planter, and neither the large wages nor the easy subsistence which that country affords to artificers, can bribe him rather to work for other people than for himself. He feels that an artificer is the servant of his customers, from whom he derives his subsistence; but that a planter who cultivates his own land, and derives his necessary subsistence from the labour of his own family, is really a master, and independent of all the world.

In countries, on the contrary, where there is either no uncultivated land, or none that can be had upon easy terms, every artificer who has acquired more stock than he can employ in the occasional jobs of the neighbourhood, endeavours to prepare work for more distant sale. The smith erects some sort of iron, the weaver some sort of linen or woollen manufactory. Those different manufactures come, in process of time, to be gradually subdivided, and thereby improved and refined in a great variety of ways, which may easily be conceived, and which it is therefore unnecessary to explain any further.

In seeking for employment to a capital, manufactures are, upon equal or nearly equal profits, naturally preferred to foreign commerce, for the same reason that agriculture is naturally preferred to manufactures. As the capital of the landlord or farmer is more secure than that of the manufacturer, so the capital of the manufacturer, being at all times more within his view and command, is more secure than that of the foreign merchant. In every period, indeed, of every society, the surplus part both of the rude and manufactured produce, or that for which there is no demand at home, must be sent abroad in order to be exchanged for something for which there is some demand at home. But whether the capital, which carries this surplus produce abroad, be a foreign or a domestick one, is of very little importance. If the society has not acquired sufficient capital both to cultivate all its lands, and to manufacture in the compleatest manner the whole of its rude produce, there is even a considerable advantage that that rude produce should be exported by a foreign capital, in order that the whole stock of the society may be employed in more useful purposes. The wealth of antient Egypt, that of China and Indostan, sufficiently demonstrate that a nation may attain a very high degree of opulence, though the greater part of its exportation trade be carried on by foreigners. The progress of our North American and West Indian colonies would have been much less rapid, had no capital but what belonged to themselves been employed in exporting their surplus produce.*

According to the natural course of things, therefore, the greater part of the capital of every growing society is, first, directed to agriculture, afterwards to manufactures, and last of all to foreign commerce. This order of things is so very natural, that in every society that had any territory, it has always, I believe, been in some degree observed. Some of their lands must have been cultivated before any considerable towns could be established, and some sort of coarse industry of the manufacturing kind must have been carried on in those towns, before they could well think of employing themselves in foreign commerce.

But though this natural order of things must have taken place in some degree in every such society, it has, in all the modern states of Europe, been, in many respects, entirely inverted. The foreign commerce of some of their cities has introduced all their finer manufactures, or such as were fit for distant sale; and manufactures and foreign commerce together, have given birth to the principal improvements of agriculture. The manners and customs which the nature of their original government introduced, and which remained after that government was greatly altered, necessarily forced them into this unnatural and retrograde order.

CHAPTER II

*Of the Discouragement of Agriculture in the antient
State of Europe after the Fall of the Roman Empire* *

WHEN the German and Scythian nations over-ran the western
provinces of the Roman empire, the confusions which followed
so great a revolution lasted for several centuries. The rapine
and violence which the barbarians exercised against the antient
inhabitants, interrupted the commerce between the towns and
the country. The towns were deserted, and the country was
left uncultivated, and the western provinces of Europe, which
had enjoyed a considerable degree of opulence under the
Roman empire, sunk into the lowest state of poverty and
barbarism. During the continuance of those confusions, the
chiefs and principal leaders of those nations, acquired or
usurped to themselves the greater part of the lands of those
countries. A great part of them was uncultivated; but no part
of them, whether cultivated or uncultivated, was left without
a proprietor. All of them were engrossed, and the greater part
by a few great proprietors.

This original engrossing of uncultivated lands, though a
great, might have been but a transitory evil. They might soon
have been divided again, and broke into small parcels either
by succession or by alienation. The law of primogeniture
hindered them from being divided by succession: the introduction of entails prevented their being broke into small parcels
by alienation.*

When land, like moveables, is considered as the means only
of subsistence and enjoyment, the natural law of succession
divides it, like them, among all the children of the family; of
all of whom the subsistence and enjoyment may be supposed
equally dear to the father. This natural law of succession
accordingly took place among the Romans, who made no more
distinction between elder and younger, between male and

female, in the inheritance of lands, than we do in the distribution of moveables.* But when land was considered as the means, not of subsistence merely, but of power and protection, it was thought better that it should descend undivided to one. In those disorderly times, every great landlord was a sort of petty prince. His tenants were his subjects. He was their judge, and in some respects their legislator in peace, and their leader in war. He made war according to his own discretion, frequently against his neighbours, and sometimes against his sovereign. The security of a landed estate, therefore, the protection which its owner could afford to those who dwelt on it, depended upon its greatness. To divide it was to ruin it, and to expose every part of it to be oppressed and swallowed up by the incursions of its neighbours.* The law of primogeniture, therefore, came to take place, not immediately, indeed, but in process of time, in the succession of landed estates, for the same reason that it has generally taken place in that of monarchies, though not always at their first institution. That the power, and consequently the security of the monarchy, may not be weakened by division, it must descend entire to one of the children. To which of them so important a preference shall be given, must be determined by some general rule, founded not upon the doubtful distinctions of personal merit, but upon some plain and evident difference which can admit of no dispute. Among the children of the same family, there can be no indisputable difference but that of sex, and that of age. The male sex is universally preferred to the female; and when all other things are equal, the elder everywhere takes place of the younger. Hence the origin of the right of primogeniture, and of what is called lineal succession.

Laws frequently continue in force long after the circumstances, which first gave occasion to them, and which could alone render them reasonable, are no more. In the present state of Europe, the proprietor of a single acre of land is as perfectly secure of his possession as the proprietor of a hundred thousand. The right of primogeniture, however, still continues to be respected, and as of all institutions it is the fittest to support the pride of family distinctions, it is still likely to endure for many centuries. In every other respect, nothing can be more contrary to the real interest of a numerous family, than a right which, in order to enrich one, beggars all the rest of the children.

Entails are the natural consequences of the law of primogeniture. They were introduced to preserve a certain lineal succession, of which the law of primogeniture first gave the idea, and to hinder any part of the original estate from being carried out of the proposed line either by gift, or devise,* or alienation; either by the folly, or by the misfortune of any of its successive owners. They were altogether unknown to the Romans. Neither their substitutions nor fideicommisses* bear any resemblance to entails, though some French lawyers have thought proper to dress the modern institution in the language and garb of those antient ones.

When great landed estates were a sort of principalities, entails might not be unreasonable. Like what are called the fundamental laws of some monarchies, they might frequently hinder the security of thousands from being endangered by the caprice or extravagance of one man. But in the present state of Europe, when small as well as great estates derive their security from the laws of their country, nothing can be more completely absurd. They are founded upon the most absurd of all suppositions, the supposition that every successive generation of men have not an equal right to the earth, and to all that it possesses; but that the property of the present generation should be restrained and regulated according to the fancy of those who died perhaps five hundred years ago. Entails, however, are still respected through the greater part of Europe, in those countries particularly in which noble birth is a necessary qualification for the enjoyment either of civil or military honours. Entails are thought necessary for maintaining this exclusive privilege of the nobility to the great offices and honours of their country; and that order having usurped one unjust advantage over the rest of their fellow-citizens, lest their poverty should render it ridiculous, it is thought reasonable that they should have another. The common law of England, indeed, is said to abhor perpetuities,* and they are accordingly more restricted there than in any other European monarchy; though even England is not altogether without them. In Scotland more than one-fifth, perhaps more than one-third part of the whole lands of the country, are at present supposed to be under strict entail.

Great tracts of uncultivated land were, in this manner, not only engrossed by particular families, but the possibility of their being divided again was as much as possible precluded for ever. It seldom happens, however, that a great proprietor is a great improver.* In the disorderly times which gave birth to those barbarous institutions, the great proprietor was sufficiently employed in defending his own territories, or in extending his jurisdiction and authority over those of his neighbours. He had no leisure to attend to the cultivation and improvement of land. When the establishment of law and order afforded him this leisure, he often wanted the inclination, and almost always the requisite abilities. If the expence of his house and person either equalled or exceeded his revenue, as it did very frequently, he had no stock to employ in this manner. If he was an œconomist,* he generally found it more profitable to employ his annual savings in new purchases, than in the improvement of his old estate. To improve land with profit, like all other commercial projects, requires an exact attention to small savings and small gains, of which a man born to a great fortune, even though naturally frugal, is very seldom capable. The situation of such a person naturally disposes him to attend rather to ornament which pleases his fancy, than to profit for which he has so little occasion. The elegance of his dress, of his equipage, of his house, and houshold furniture, are objects which from his infancy he has been accustomed to have some anxiety about. The turn of mind which this habit naturally forms, follows him when he comes to think of the improvement of land. He embellishes perhaps four or five hundred acres in the neighbourhood of his house, at ten times the expence which the land is worth after all his improvements; and finds that if he was to improve his whole estate in the same manner, and he has little taste for any other, he would be a bankrupt before he had finished the tenth part of it. There still remain in both parts of the united kingdom some great estates which have continued without interruption in the hands of the same family since the times of feudal anarchy. Compare the present condition of those estates with the possessions of the small proprietors in their neighbourhood, and you will require no other argument to convince you how unfavourable such extensive property is to improvement.

If little improvement was to be expected from such great proprietors, still less was to be hoped for from those who occupied the land under them. In the antient state of Europe, the occupiers of land were all tenants at will.* They were all or almost all slaves; but their slavery was of a milder kind than that known among the antient Greeks and Romans, or even in our West Indian colonies. They were supposed to belong more directly to the land than to their master. They could, therefore, be sold with it, but not separately. They could marry, provided it was with the consent of their master; and he could not afterwards dissolve the marriage by selling the man and wife to different persons. If he maimed or murdered any of them, he was liable to some penalty, though generally but to a small one. They were not, however, capable of acquiring property. Whatever they acquired was acquired to their master, and he could take it from them at pleasure. Whatever cultivation and improvement could be carried on by means of such slaves, was properly carried on by their master. It was at his expence. The seed, the cattle, and the instruments of husbandry were all his. It was for his benefit. Such slaves could acquire nothing but their daily maintenance. It was properly the proprietor himself, therefore, that, in this case, occupied his own lands, and cultivated them by his own bondmen. This species of slavery still subsists in Russia, Poland, Hungary, Bohemia, Moravia, and other parts of Germany. It is only in the western and south-western provinces of Europe, that it has gradually been abolished altogether.

But if great improvements are seldom to be expected from great proprietors, they are least of all to be expected when they employ slaves for their workmen. The experience of all ages and nations, I believe, demonstrates that the work done by slaves, though it appears to cost only their maintenance, is in the end the dearest of any.* A person who can acquire no property, can have no other interest but to eat as much, and to labour as little as possible. Whatever work he does beyond what is sufficient to purchase his own maintenance, can be squeezed out of him by violence only, and not by any interest of his own. In antient Italy, how much the cultivation of corn degenerated, how unprofitable it became to the master when it fell under the management of slaves, is remarked by both Pliny and Columella.* In the time of Aristotle it had not been much better in antient Greece. Speaking of the ideal republick described in the laws of Plato, to maintain five thousand idle men (the number of warriors supposed necessary for its defence) together with their women and servants, would require, he says, a territory of boundless extent and fertility, like the plains of Babylon.*

The pride of man makes him love to domineer, and nothing mortifies him so much as to be obliged to condescend to persuade his inferiors. Wherever the law allows it, and the nature of the work can afford it, therefore, he will generally prefer the service of slaves to that of freemen. The planting of sugar and tobacco can afford the expence of slave-cultivation. The raising of corn, it seems, in the present times, cannot. In the English colonies, of which the principal produce is corn, the far greater part of the work is done by freemen. The late resolution of the Quakers in Pennsylvania* to set at liberty all their negro slaves, may satisfy us that their number cannot be very great. Had they made any considerable part of their property, such a resolution could never have been agreed to. In our sugar colonies, on the contrary, the whole work is done by slaves, and in our tobacco colonies a very great part of it. The profits of a sugar-plantation in any of our West Indian colonies are generally much greater than those of any other cultivation that is known either in Europe or America: And the profits of a tobacco plantation, though inferior to those of sugar, are superior to those of corn, as has already been observed. Both can afford the expence of slave-cultivation, but sugar can afford it still better than tobacco. The number of negroes accordingly is much greater, in proportion to that of whites, in our sugar than in our tobacco colonies.*

To the slave cultivators of antient times, gradually succeeded a species of farmers known at present in France by the name of Metayers. They are called in Latin, Coloni Partiarii.* They have been so long in disuse in England that at present I know no English name for them. The proprietor furnished them with the seed, cattle, and instruments of husbandry, the whole stock, in short, necessary for cultivating the farm. The produce was divided equally between the proprietor and the farmer, after setting aside what was judged necessary for keeping up the stock, which was restored to the proprietor when the farmer either quitted, or was turned out of the farm.

Land occupied by such tenants is properly cultivated at the expence of the proprietor, as much as that occupied by slaves. There is, however, one very essential difference between them. Such tenants, being freemen, are capable of acquiring property, and having a certain proportion of the produce of the land, they have a plain interest that the whole produce should be as great as possible, in order that their own proportion may be so. A slave, on the contrary, who can acquire nothing but his maintenance, consults his own ease by making the land produce as little as possible over and above that maintenance. It is probable that it was partly upon account of this advantage, and partly upon account of the encroachments which the sovereign, always jealous of the great lords, gradually encouraged their villains to make upon their authority, and which seem at last to have been such as rendered this species of servitude altogether inconvenient, that tenure in villanage* gradually wore out through the greater part of Europe. The time and manner, however, in which so important a revolution was brought about, is one of the most obscure points in modern history.

The church of Rome claims great merit in it; and it is certain that so early as the twelfth century, Alexander III. published a bull for the general emancipation of slaves.* It seems, however, to have been rather a pious exhortation, than a law to which exact obedience was required from the faithful. Slavery continued to take place almost universally for several centuries afterwards, till it was gradually abolished by the joint operation of the two interests above mentioned, that of the proprietor on the one hand, and that of the sovereign on the other. A villain enfranchised, and at the same time allowed to continue in possession of the land, having no stock of his own, could cultivate it only by means of what the landlord advanced to him, and must, therefore, have been what the French call a Metayer.

It could never, however, be the interest even of this last species of cultivators to lay out, in the further improvement of the land, any part of the little stock which they might save from their own share of the produce, because the lord, who laid out nothing, was to get one-half of whatever it produced. The tithe, which is but a tenth of the produce, is found to be a very great hindrance to improvement. A tax, therefore, which amounted to one half, must have been an effectual bar to it. It might be the interest of a metayer to make the land produce as much as could be brought out of it by means of the stock furnished by the proprietor; but it could never be his interest to mix any part of his own with it. In France, where five parts out of six of the whole kingdom are said to be still occupied by this species of cultivators, the proprietors complain that their metayers take every opportunity of employing the masters cattle rather in carriage than in cultivation; because in the one case they get the whole profits to themselves, in the other they share them with their landlord. This species of tenants still subsists in some parts of Scotland. They are called steel-bow tenants.* Those antient English tenants, who are said by Chief Baron Gilbert and Doctor Blackstone* to have been rather bailiffs of the landlord than farmers properly so called, were probably of the same kind.

To this species of tenancy succeeded, though by very slow degrees, farmers properly so called, who cultivated the land with their own stock, paying a rent certain to the landlord. When such farmers have a lease for a term of years, they may sometimes find it for their interest to lay out part of their capital in the further improvement of the farm; because they may sometimes expect to recover it, with a large profit, before the expiration of the lease. The possession even of such farmers, however, was long extremely precarious, and still is so in many parts of Europe. They could before the expiration of their term be legally outed of their lease, by a new purchaser; in England, even by the fictitious action of a common recovery.* If they were turned out illegally by the violence of their master, the action by which they obtained redress was extremely imperfect. It did not always re-instate them in the possession of the land, but gave them damages which never amounted to the real loss. Even in England, the country perhaps of Europe where the yeomanry has always been most respected, it was not till about the 14th of Henry the VIIth* that the action of ejectment was invented, by which the tenant recovers, not damages only but possession, and in which his claim is not necessarily concluded by the uncertain decision of a single assize. This action has been found so effectual a remedy that, in the modern practice, when the landlord has occasion to sue for the possession of the land, he seldom makes use of the actions which properly belong to him as landlord, the writ of right or the writ of entry, but sues in the name of his tenant, by the writ of ejectment. In England, therefore, the security of the tenant is equal to that of the proprietor. In England besides a lease for life of forty shillings a year value is a freehold, and entitles the lessee to vote for a member of parliament; and as a great part of the yeomanry have freeholds of this kind, the whole order becomes respectable to their landlords on account of the political consideration which this gives them. There is, I believe, nowhere in Europe, except in England, any instance of the tenant building upon the land of which he had no lease, and trusting that the honour of his landlord would take no advantage of so important an improvement. Those laws and customs so favourable to the yeomanry, have perhaps contributed more to the present grandeur of England than all their boasted regulations of commerce taken together.

The law which secures the longest leases against successors of every kind is, so far as I know, peculiar to Great Britain. It was introduced into Scotland so early as 1449, by a law of James the IId.* Its beneficial influence, however, has been much obstructed by entails; the heirs of entail being generally restrained from letting leases for any long term of years, frequently for more than one year. A late act of parliament* has, in this respect, somewhat slackened their fetters, though they are still by much too strait. In Scotland, besides, as no leasehold gives a vote for a member of parliament,* the yeomanry are upon this account less respectable to their landlords than in England.

In other parts of Europe, after it was found convenient to secure tenants both against heirs and purchasers, the term of their security was still limited to a very short period; in France, for example, to nine years from the commencement of the lease. It has in that country, indeed, been lately extended to twenty-seven, a period still too short to encourage the tenant to make the most important improvements. The proprietors of land were antiently the legislators of every part of Europe. The laws relating to land, therefore, were all calculated for what they supposed the interest of the proprietor. It was for his interest, they had imagined, that no lease granted by any of his predecessors should hinder him from enjoying, during a long term of years, the full value of his land. Avarice and injustice are always short-sighted, and they did not foresee how much this regulation must obstruct improvement, and thereby hurt in the long-run the real interest of the landlord.

The farmers too, besides paying the rent, were antiently, it was supposed, bound to perform a great number of services to the landlord, which were seldom either specified in the lease, or regulated by any precise rule, but by the use and wont of the manor or barony. These services, therefore, being almost entirely arbitrary, subjected the tenant to many vexations. In Scotland the abolition of all services, not precisely stipulated in the lease,* has in the course of a few years very much altered for the better the condition of the yeomanry of that country.

The public services to which the yeomanry were bound, were not less arbitrary than the private ones. To make and maintain the high roads, a servitude which still subsists,* I believe, every where, though with different degrees of oppression in different countries, was not the only one. When the king's troops, when his household or his officers of any kind passed through any part of the country, the yeomanry were bound to provide them with horses, carriages, and provisions, at a price regulated by the purveyor. Great Britain is, I believe, the only monarchy in Europe where the oppression of purveyance has been entirely abolished. It still subsists in France and Germany.

The publick taxes to which they were subject were as irregular and oppressive as the services. The antient lords, though extremely unwilling to grant themselves any pecuniary aid to their sovereign, easily allowed him to tallage, as they called it, their tenants, and had not knowledge enough to foresee how much this must in the end affect their own revenue. The taille, as it still subsists in France, may serve as an example of those antient tallages. It is a tax upon the supposed profits of the farmer, which they estimate by the stock that he has upon the farm. It is his interest, therefore, to appear to have as little as possible, and consequently to employ as little as possible in its cultivation, and none in its improvement. Should any stock happen to accumulate in the hands of a French farmer, the taille is almost equal to a prohibition of its ever being employed upon the land. This tax besides is supposed to dishonour whoever is subject to it, and to degrade him below, not only the rank of a gentleman, but that of a burgher, and whoever rents the lands of another becomes subject to it. No gentleman, nor even any burgher who has stock, will submit to this degradation. This tax, therefore, not only hinders the stock which accumulates upon the land from being employed in its improvement, but drives away all other stock from it. The antient tenths and fifteenths,* so usual in England in former times, seem, so far as they affected the land, to have been taxes of the same nature with the taille.

Under all these discouragements, little improvement could be expected from the occupiers of land. That order of people, with all the liberty and security which law can give, must always improve under great disadvantages. The farmer compared with the proprietor, is as a merchant who trades with borrowed money compared with one who trades with his own. The stock of both may improve, but that of the one, with only equal good conduct, must always improve more slowly than that of the other, on account of the large share of the profits which is consumed by the interest of the loan. The lands cultivated by the farmer must, in the same manner, with only equal good conduct, be improved more slowly than those cultivated by the proprietor; on account of the large share of the produce which is consumed in the rent, and which, had the farmer been proprietor, he might have employed in the further improvement of the land. The station of a farmer besides is, from the nature of things, inferior to that of a proprietor. Through the greater part of Europe the yeomanry are regarded as an inferior rank of people, even to the better sort of tradesmen and mechanicks, and in all parts of Europe to the great merchants and master manufacturers. It can seldom happen, therefore, that a man of any considerable stock should quit the superior, in order to place himself in an inferior station. Even in the present state of Europe, therefore, little stock is likely to go from any other profession to the improvement of land in the way of farming. More does perhaps in Great Britain than in any other country, though even there the great stocks which are, in some places, employed in farming, have generally been acquired by farming, the trade, perhaps, in which of all others stock is commonly acquired most slowly. After small proprietors, however, rich and great farmers are, in every country, the principal improvers. There are more such perhaps in England than in any other European monarchy. In the republican governments of Holland and of Berne in Switzerland, the farmers are said to be not inferior to those of England.*

The antient policy of Europe was, over and above all this, unfavourable to the improvement and cultivation of land, whether carried on by the proprietor or by the farmer; first, by the general prohibition of the exportation of corn without a special licence, which seems to have been a very universal regulation; and secondly, by the restraints which were laid upon the inland commerce, not only of corn but of almost every other part of the produce of the farm, by the absurd laws against engrossers, regrators, and forestallers, and by the privileges of fairs and markets.* It has already been observed in what manner the prohibition of the exportation of corn, together with some encouragement given to the importation of foreign corn, obstructed the cultivation of antient Italy, naturally the most fertile country in Europe, and at that time the seat of the greatest empire in the world. To what degree such restraints upon the inland commerce of this commodity, joined to the general prohibition of exportation, must have discouraged the cultivation of countries less fertile, and less favourably circumstanced, it is not perhaps very easy to imagine.

CHAPTER III

Of the Rise and Progress of Cities and Towns, after the Fall of the Roman Empire

THE inhabitants of cities and towns were, after the fall of the Roman empire, not more favoured than those of the country. They consisted, indeed, of a very different order of people from the first inhabitants of the antient republicks of Greece and Italy. These last were composed chiefly of the proprietors of lands, among whom the publick territory was originally divided, and who found it convenient to build their houses in the neighbourhood of one another, and to surround them with a wall, for the sake of common defence. After the fall of the Roman empire, on the contrary, the proprietors of land seem generally to have lived in fortified castles on their own estates, and in the midst of their own tenants and dependants. The towns were chiefly inhabited by tradesmen and mechanicks, who seem in those days to have been of servile, or very nearly of servile condition. The privileges which we find granted by antient charters to the inhabitants of some of the principal towns in Europe, sufficiently shew what they were before those grants. The people to whom it is granted as a privilege, that they might give away their own daughters in marriage without the consent of their lord, that upon their death their own children, and not their lord, should succeed to their goods, and that they might dispose of their own effects by will, must, before those grants, have been either altogether, or very nearly in the same state of villanage with the occupiers of land in the country.

They seem, indeed, to have been a very poor, mean sett of people, who used to travel about with their goods from place to place, and from fair to fair, like the hawkers and pedlars of the present times. In all the different countries of Europe then, in the same manner as in several of the Tartar governments of Asia at present,* taxes used to be levied upon the persons and goods of travellers, when they passed through certain manors, when they went over certain bridges, when they carried about their goods from place to place in a fair, when they erected in it a booth or stall to sell them in. These different taxes were known in England by the names of passage, pontage, lastage, and stallage.* Sometimes the king, sometimes a great lord, who had, it seems, upon some occasions, authority to do this, would grant to particular traders, to such particularly as lived in their own demesnes,* a general exemption from such taxes. Such traders, though in other respects of servile, or very nearly of servile condition, were upon this account called Free-traders. They in return usually paid to their protector a sort of annual poll-tax.* In those days protection was seldom granted without a valuable consideration, and this tax might, perhaps, be considered as compensation for what their patrons might lose by their exemption from other taxes. At first, both those poll-taxes and those exemptions seem to have been altogether personal, and to have affected only particular individuals, during either their lives, or the pleasure of their protectors. In the very imperfect accounts which have been published from Domesday-book, of several of the towns of England, mention is frequently made, sometimes of the tax which particular burghers paid, each of them, either to the king, or to some other great lord, for this sort of protection; and sometimes of the general amount only of all those taxes.[8]

[8] See Brady's historical treatise of Cities and Burroughs, p. 3, &c. [For example: '. . . the Kings of England kept this Burg [Yarmouth] in their own Hands, and received by their Officers the Profits of the Port, until the time of King John, who in the 9th year of his Reign Granted the Burg in Fee-Farm to the Burgesses for ever, at the Rent of Fifty Five Pounds by the Year to be paid by the Provost or Bayliff of Yarmouth, and Granted they should yearly chuse a Bayliff amongst themselves, fit both to serve him, and themselves.' After a number of similar instances from Domesday Brady continued, 'By these instances we find the Burgesses or Tradesmen in great Towns, had in those times their Patrons under whose Protection they Traded, and paid an acknowledgement therefor, or else were in a more Servile Condition, as being in Dominio Regis vel aliorum, altogether under the power of the King, or other Lords, and it seems to me that then they Traded not, as being in any Merchant-Gild, Society and Community, but meerly under the Liberty and Protection given them by

But how servile soever may have been originally the condition of the inhabitants of the towns, it appears evidently, that they arrived at liberty and independency much earlier than the occupiers of land in the country. That part of the king's revenue which arose from such poll-taxes in any particular town, used commonly to be lett in farm, during a term of years for a rent certain, sometimes to the sheriff of the county, and sometimes to other persons. The burghers themselves frequently got credit enough to be admitted to farm the revenues of this sort which arose out of their own town, they becoming jointly and severally answerable for the whole rent.[9] To lett a farm in this manner was quite agreeable to the usual œconomy* of, I believe, the sovereigns of all the different countries of Europe; who used frequently to lett whole manors to all the tenants of those manors, they becoming jointly and severally answerable for the whole rent; but in return being allowed to collect it in their own way, and to pay it into the king's exchequer by the hands of their own bailiff, and being thus altogether freed from the insolence of the king's officers; a circumstance in those days regarded as of the greatest importance.

their Lords and Patrons, who probably might have Power from the King to Licence such a number in this or that Port, or Trading Town . . . ' (R. Brady, *Cities and Boroughs* (London, 1711), 3 and 16.)] [Campbell and Skinner]

[9] See Madox Firma Burgi, p. 18, also History of the Exchequer, chap. 10. Sect. v. p. 223, first edition. ['The yearly profit which the King made of his Cities Towns or Burghs was commonly raised and paid to Him in a sundry manner . . . sometimes the King was pleased to demise or let his Town to the Townsmen thereof at Ferm, that is to say, either in Fee-ferm, or at Ferm for Years.' But Madox does not suggest the development came necessarily from the farming of the poll tax. 'The yearly Ferme of Towns arose out of certain locata or demised things that yielded Issues or profit. Insomuch that when a Town was committed to a Sherif Fermer or *Custos*, such Fermer or *Custos* well knew how to raise the Ferme out of the ordinary issues of the Towns, with an overplus of profit to himself.' (T. Madox, *Firma Burgi* 18 and 251.) 'From the reign of K. William I, down to the succeeding times, the King . . . used to let-out the several Counties of England upon a yearly Ferm or Rent concerted between the Crown and the Fermer, or else to commit them to Custody.' (Madox, *The History and Antiquities of the Exchequer* (London, 1711), 223.) In Letter 115 addressed to Lord Hailes, dated 15 January 1769 Smith also described Madox's work as the *History of the Exchequer* (*Correspondence*, 139).] [Campbell and Skinner]

At first, the farm of the town was probably lett to the burghers, in the same manner as it had been to other farmers, for a term of years only. In process of time, however, it seems to have become the general practice to grant it to them in fee, that is for ever, reserving a rent certain never afterwards to be augmented. The payment having thus become perpetual, the exemptions, in return for which it was made, naturally became perpetual too. Those exemptions, therefore, ceased to be personal, and could not afterwards be considered as belonging to individuals as individuals, but as burghers of a particular burgh, which, upon this account, was called a Free-burgh, for the same reason that they had been called Free-burghers or Free-traders.

Along with this grant, the important privileges above mentioned, that they might give away their own daughters in marriage, that their children should succeed to them, and that they might dispose of their own effects by will, were generally bestowed upon the burghers of the town to whom it was given. Whether such privileges had before been usually granted along with the freedom of trade, to particular burghers, as individuals, I know not. I reckon it not improbable that they were, though I cannot produce any direct evidence of it. But however this may have been, the principal attributes of villanage and slavery being thus taken away from them, they now, at least, became really free in our present sense of the word Freedom.

Nor was this all. They were generally at the same time erected into a commonality or corporation, with the privilege of having magistrates and a town-council of their own, of making bye-laws for their own government, of building walls for their own defence, and of reducing all their inhabitants under a sort of military discipline, by obliging them to watch and ward; that is, as antiently understood, to guard and defend those walls against all attacks and surprises by night as well as by day. In England they were generally exempted from suit to the hundred and county courts;* and all such pleas as should arise among them, the pleas of the crown excepted, were left to the decision of their own magistrates. In other countries much greater and more extensive jurisdictions were frequently granted to them.[10]

It might, probably, be necessary to grant to such towns as were admitted to farm their own revenues, some sort of compulsive jurisdiction to oblige their own citizens to make payment. In those disorderly times it might háve been extremely inconvenient to have left them to seek this sort of justice from any other tribunal. But it must seem extraordinary that the sovereigns of all the different countries of Europe, should have exchanged in this manner for a rent certain, never more to be augmented, that branch of their revenue, which was, perhaps, of all others the most likely to be improved by the natural course of things, without either expence or attention of their own: and that they should, besides, have in this manner voluntarily erected a sort of independent republicks in the heart of their own dominions.*

In order to understand this, it must be remembered, that in those days the sovereign of perhaps no country in Europe, was able to protect, through the whole extent of his dominions, the weaker part of his subjects from the oppression of the great lords. Those whom the law could not protect, and who were not strong enough to defend themselves, were obliged either to have recourse to the protection of some great lord, and in order to obtain it to become either his slaves or vassals; or to enter into a league of mutual defence for the common protection of one another. The inhabitants of cities and burghs, considered as single individuals, had no power to defend themselves: but by entering into a league of mutual defence with their neighbours, they were capable of making no contemptible resistance. The lords despised the burghers, whom they considered not only as of a different order, but as a parcel of emancipated slaves, almost of a different species from them-

[10] See Madox Firma Burgi: See also Pfeffel in the remarkable events under Frederick II. and his successors of the house of Suabia. [The heading 'événe-ments remarquables sous Frédéric II' is used by Pfeffel for several similar chapters. C. F. Pfeffel von Kriegelstein, *Nouvel Abrégé chronologique de l'histoire et du droit publique d'Allemagne* (Paris, 1766), i.284–307.] [Campbell and Skinner]

selves. The wealth of the burghers never failed to provoke their envy and indignation, and they plundered them upon every occasion without mercy or remorse. The burghers naturally hated and feared the lords. The king hated and feared them too; but though perhaps he might despise, he had no reason either to hate or fear the burghers. Mutual interest, therefore, disposed them to support the king, and the king to support them against the lords. They were the enemies of his enemies, and it was his interest to render them as secure and independent of those enemies as he could. By granting them magistrates of their own, the privilege of making bye-laws for their own government, that of building walls for their own defence, and that of reducing all their inhabitants under a sort of military discipline, he gave them all the means of security and independency of the barons which it was in his power to bestow. Without the establishment of some regular government of this kind, without some authority to compel their inhabitants to act according to some certain plan or system, no voluntary league of mutual defence could either have afforded them any permanent security, or have enabled them to give the king any considerable support. By granting them the farm of their town in fee, he took away from those whom he wished to have for his friends, and, if one may say so, for his allies, all ground of jealousy and suspicion that he was ever afterwards to oppress them, either by raising the farm rent of their town, or by granting it to some other farmer.

The princes who lived upon the worst terms with their barons, seem accordingly to have been the most liberal in grants of this kind to their burghs. King John of England,* for example, appears to have been a most munificent benefactor to his towns.[11] Philip the First of France* lost all authority over his barons. Towards the end of his reign, his son Lewis, known afterwards by the name of Lewis the Fat, consulted, according

---

[11] See Madox. ['King John granted some of his Towns in Normandy, to wit, to Falaise, Danfront, and Caen, that they might have a *Communa* during his pleasure.' (T. Madox, *Firma Burgi*, 35.)] [Campbell and Skinner]

to Father Daniel,* with the bishops of the royal demesnes, concerning the most proper means of restraining the violence of the great lords. Their advice consisted of two different proposals. One was to erect a new order of jurisdiction, by establishing magistrates and a town council in every considerable town of his demesnes. The other was to form a new militia, by making the inhabitants of those towns, under the command of their own magistrates, march out upon proper occasions to the assistance of the king. It is from this period, according to the French antiquarians, that we are to date the institution of the magistrates and councils of cities in France.* It was during the unprosperous reigns of the princes of the house of Suabia that the greater part of the free towns of Germany received the first grants of their privileges, and that the famous Hanseatic league* first became formidable.[12]

The militia of the cities seems, in those times, not to have been inferior to that of the country, and as they could be more readily assembled upon any sudden occasion, they frequently had the advantage in their disputes with the neighbouring lords. In countries, such as Italy and Switzerland, in which, on account either of their distance from the principal seat of government, of the natural strength of the country itself, or of some other reason, the sovereign came to lose the whole of his authority, the cities generally became independent republicks, and conquered all the nobility in their neighbourhood; obliging them to pull down their castles in the country, and to live, like other peaceable inhabitants, in the city. This is the short history of the republick of Berne,* as well as of several other cities in Switzerland. If you except Venice, for of that city the history is somewhat different, it is the history of all the considerable Italian republicks, of which so great a number arose and perished, between the end of the twelfth and the beginning of the sixteenth century.

In countries such as France or England, where the authority of the sovereign, though frequently very low, never was de-

[12] See Pfeffel.

stroyed altogether, the cities had no opportunity of becoming entirely independent. They became, however, so considerable that the sovereign could impose no tax upon them, besides the stated farm-rent of the town, without their own consent. They were, therefore, called upon to send deputies to the general assembly of the states of the kingdom, where they might join with the clergy and the barons in granting, upon urgent occasions, some extraordinary aid to the king. Being generally too more favourable to his power, their deputies seem, sometimes, to have been employed by him as a counter-balance in those assemblies to the authority of the great lords. Hence the origin of the representation of burghs in the states general* of all the great monarchies in Europe.

Order and good government, and along with them the liberty and security of individuals, were, in this manner, established in cities at a time when the occupiers of land in the country were exposed to every sort of violence. But men in this defenceless state naturally content themselves with their necessary subsistence; because to acquire more might only tempt the injustice of their oppressors. On the contrary, when they are secure of enjoying the fruits of their industry, they naturally exert it to better their condition, and to acquire not only the necessaries, but the conveniencies and elegancies of life. That industry, therefore, which aims at something more than necessary subsistence, was established in cities long before it was commonly practised by the occupiers of land in the country. If in the hands of a poor cultivator, oppressed with the servitude of villanage, some little stock should accumulate, he would naturally conceal it with great care from his master, to whom it would otherwise have belonged, and take the first opportunity of running away to a town. The law was at that time so indulgent to the inhabitants of towns, and so desirous of diminishing the authority of the lords over those of the country, that if he could conceal himself there from the pursuit of his lord for a year, he was free for ever.* Whatever stock, therefore, accumulated in the hands of the industrious part of the inhabitants of the country, naturally took refuge in cities, as the only sanctuaries in which it could be secure to the person that acquired it.

The inhabitants of a city, it is true, must always ultimately derive their subsistence, and the whole materials and means of their industry from the country. But those of a city, situated near either the sea-coast or the banks of a navigable river, are not necessarily confined to derive them from the country in their neighbourhood. They have a much wider range, and may draw them from the most remote corners of the world, either in exchange for the manufactured produce of their own industry, or by performing the office of carriers between distant countries, and exchanging the produce of one for that of another. A city might in this manner grow up to great wealth and splendor, while not only the country in its neighbourhood, but all those to which it traded, were in poverty and wretchedness. Each of those countries, perhaps, taken singly, could afford it but a small part, either of its subsistence, or of its employment; but all of them taken together could afford it both a great subsistence and a great employment. There were, however, within the narrow circle of the commerce of those times, some countries that were opulent and industrious. Such was the Greek empire as long as it subsisted, and that of the Saracens during the reigns of the Abassides. Such too was Egypt till it was conquered by the Turks, some part of the coast of Barbary, and all those provinces of Spain which were under the government of the Moors.*

The cities of Italy seem to have been the first in Europe which were raised by commerce to any considerable degree of opulence. Italy lay in the center of what was at that time the improved and civilized part of the world. The cruzades* too, though by the great waste of stock and destruction of inhabitants which they occasioned, they must necessarily have retarded the progress of the greater part of Europe, were extremely favourable to that of some Italian cities. The great armies which marched from all parts to the conquest of the Holy Land, gave extraordinary encouragement to the shipping of Venice, Genoa, and Pisa, sometimes in transporting them thither, and always in supplying them with provisions. They were the commis- saries, if one may say so, of those armies; and the most destructive frenzy that ever befel the European nations, was a source of opulence to those republicks.

The inhabitants of trading cities, by importing the improved manufactures and expensive luxuries of richer countries, af- forded some food to the vanity of the great proprietors, who eagerly purchased them with great quantities of the rude produce of their own lands. The commerce of a great part of Europe in those times accordingly, consisted chiefly in the exchange of their own rude, for the manufactured produce of more civilized nations. Thus the wool of England used to be exchanged for the wines of France, and the fine cloths of Flanders, in the same manner as the corn of Poland is at this day exchanged for the wines and brandies of France, and for the silks and velvets of France and Italy.

A taste for the finer and more improved manufactures, was in this manner introduced by foreign commerce into countries where no such works were carried on. But when this taste became so general as to occasion a considerable demand, the merchants, in order to save the expence of carriage, naturally endeavoured to establish some manufactures of the same kind in their own country. Hence the origin of the first manufac- tures for distant sale that seem to have been established in the western provinces of Europe, after the fall of the Roman empire.

No large country, it must be observed, ever did or could subsist without some sort of manufactures being carried on in it; and when it is said of any such country that it has no manufactures, it must always be understood of the finer and more improved, or of such as are fit for distant sale. In every large country, both the cloathing and houshold furniture of the far greater part of the people, are the produce of their own industry. This is even more universally the case in those poor countries which are commonly said to have no manufactures, than in those rich ones that are said to abound in them. In the latter, you will generally find, both in the cloaths and houshold furniture of the lowest rank of people, a much greater proportion of foreign productions than in the former.

Those manufactures which are fit for distant sale, seem to have been introduced into different countries in two different ways.

Sometimes they have been introduced, in the manner above mentioned, by the violent operation, if one may say so, of the stocks of particular merchants and undertakers, who established them in imitation of some foreign manufactures of the same kind. Such manufactures, therefore, are the offspring of foreign commerce, and such seem to have been the antient manufactures of silks, velvets, and brocades, which flourished in Lucca* during the thirteenth century. They were banished from thence by the tyranny of one of Machiavel's heroes, Castruccio Castracani.* In 1310, nine hundred families were driven out of Lucca, of whom thirty-one retired to Venice, and offered to introduce there the silk manufacture.[13] Their offer was accepted; many privileges were conferred upon them, and they began the manufacture with three hundred workmen. Such too seem to have been the manufactures of fine cloths that antiently flourished in Flanders, and which were introduced into England in the beginning of the reign of Elizabeth; and such are the present silk manufactures of Lyons and Spital-fields.* Manufactures introduced in this manner are generally employed upon foreign materials, being imitations of foreign manufactures. When the Venetian manufacture was first established the materials were all brought from Sicily and the Levant. The more antient manufacture of Lucca was likewise carried on with foreign materials. The cultivation of mulberry trees, and the breeding of silk worms, seem not to have been common in the northern parts of Italy before the sixteenth century. Those arts were not introduced into France till the reign of Charles IX. The manufactures of Flanders were carried on chiefly with Spanish and English wool. Spanish wool was

---

[13] See Sandi Istoria Civile de Vinezia, Part 2. vol. 1. page 247, and 256. [V. Sandi, *Principj di Storia Civile della Republica de Venezia* (Venice, 1755), part 2, i.258.] [Campbell and Skinner]

the material, not of the first woollen manufacture of England, but of the first that was fit for distant sale. More than one half the materials of the Lyons manufacture is at this day foreign silk; when it was first established, the whole or very nearly the whole was so. No part of the materials of the Spital-fields manufacture is ever likely to be the produce of England. The seat of such manufactures, as they are generally introduced by the scheme and project of a few individuals, is sometimes established in a maritime city, and sometimes in an inland town, according as their interest, judgment or caprice happen to determine.

At other times manufactures for distant sale grow up naturally, and as it were of their own accord, by the gradual refinement of those houshold and coarser manufactures which must at all times be carried on even in the poorest and rudest countries. Such manufactures are generally employed upon the materials which the country produces, and they seem frequently to have been first refined and improved in such inland countries as were, not indeed at a very great, but at a considerable distance from the sea coast, and sometimes even from all water carriage. An inland country naturally fertile and easily cultivated, produces a great surplus of provisions beyond what is necessary for maintaining the cultivators, and on account of the expence of land carriage, and inconveniency of river navigation, it may frequently be difficult to send this surplus abroad. Abundance, therefore, renders provisions cheap, and encourages a great number of workmen to settle in the neighbourhood, who find that their industry can there procure them more of the necessaries and conveniencies of life than in other places. They work up the materials of manufacture which the land produces, and exchange their finished work, or what is the same thing the price of it, for more materials and provisions. They give a new value to the surplus part of the rude produce, by saving the expence of carrying it to the water side, or to some distant market; and they furnish the cultivators with something in exchange for it that is either useful or agreeable to them, upon easier terms than they could have obtained it before. The cultivators get a better price for their surplus produce, and can purchase cheaper other conveniencies which they have occasion for. They are thus both encouraged and enabled to increase this surplus produce by a further improvement and better cultivation of the land; and as the fertility of the land had given birth to the manufacture, so the progress of the manufacture re-acts upon the land, and increases still further its fertility. The manufacturers first supply the neighbourhood, and afterwards, as their work improves and refines, more distant markets. For though neither the rude produce, nor even the coarse manufacture, could, without the greatest difficulty, support the expence of a considerable land carriage, the refined and improved manufacture easily may. In a small bulk it frequently contains the price of a great quantity of rude produce. A piece of fine cloth, for example, which weighs only eighty pounds, contains in it, the price, not only of eighty pounds weight of wool, but sometimes of several thousand weight of corn, the maintenance of the different working people, and of their immediate employers. The corn, which could with difficulty have been carried abroad in its own shape, is in this manner virtually exported in that of the complete manufacture, and may easily be sent to the remotest corners of the world. In this manner have grown up naturally, and as it were of their own accord, the manufactures of Leeds, Halifax, Sheffield, Birmingham, and Wolverhampton.* Such manufactures are the offspring of agriculture. In the modern history of Europe, their extension and improvement have generally been posterior to those which were the offspring of foreign commerce.* England was noted for the manufacture of fine cloths made of Spanish wool, more than a century before any of those which now flourish in the places above mentioned were fit for foreign sale. The extension and improvement of these last could not take place but in consequence of the extension and improvement of agriculture, the last and greatest effect of foreign commerce, and of the manufactures immediately introduced by it, and which I shall now proceed to explain.

CHAPTER IV

How the Commerce of the Towns contributed to the Improvement of the Country

THE increase and riches of commercial and manufacturing towns, contributed to the improvement and cultivation of the countries to which they belonged, in three different ways.

First, by affording a great and ready market for the rude produce of the country, they gave encouragement to its cultivation and further improvement. This benefit was not even confined to the countries in which they were situated, but extended more or less to all those with which they had any dealings. To all of them they afforded a market for some part either of their rude or manufactured produce, and consequently gave some encouragement to the industry and improvement of all. Their own country, however, on account of its neighbourhood, necessarily derived the greatest benefit from this market. Its rude produce being charged with less carriage, the traders could pay the growers a better price for it, and yet afford it as cheap to the consumers as that of more distant countries.

Secondly, the wealth acquired by the inhabitants of cities was frequently employed in purchasing such lands as were to be sold, of which a great part would frequently be uncultivated. Merchants are commonly ambitious of becoming country gentlemen, and when they do, they are generally the best of all improvers.* A merchant is accustomed to employ his money chiefly in profitable projects; whereas a mere country gentleman is accustomed to employ it chiefly in expence. The one often sees his money go from him and return to him again with a profit: the other, when once he parts with it, very seldom expects to see any more of it. Those different habits naturally affect their temper and disposition in every sort of business. A merchant is commonly a bold; a country gentleman, a timid undertaker. The one is not afraid to lay out at once a large capital upon the improvement of his land, when he has a probable prospect of raising the value of it in proportion to the expence. The other, if he has any capital, which is not always the case, seldom ventures to employ it in this manner. If he improves at all, it is commonly not with a capital, but with what he can save out of his annual revenue. Whoever has had the fortune to live in a mercantile town situated in an unimproved country, must have frequently observed how much more spirited the operations of merchants were in this way, than those of mere country gentlemen. The habits, besides, of order, œconomy and attention, to which mercantile business naturally forms a merchant, render him much fitter to execute, with profit and success, any project of improvement.

Thirdly, and lastly, commerce and manufactures gradually introduced order and good government, and with them, the liberty and security of individuals, among the inhabitants of the country, who had before lived almost in a continual state of war with their neighbours, and of servile dependency upon their superiors. This, though it has been the least observed, is by far the most important of all their effects. Mr. Hume* is the only writer who, so far as I know, has hitherto taken notice of it.

In a country which has neither foreign commerce, nor any of the finer manufactures, a great proprietor, having nothing for which he can exchange the greater part of the produce of his lands which is over and above the maintenance of the cultivators, consumes the whole in rustick hospitality at home. If this surplus produce is sufficient to maintain a hundred or a thousand men, he can make use of it in no other way than by maintaining a hundred or a thousand men. He is at all times, therefore, surrounded with a multitude of retainers and dependants, who having no equivalent to give in return for their maintenance, but being fed entirely by his bounty, must obey him, for the same reason that soldiers must obey the prince who pays them. Therefore the extension of commerce and manufactures in Europe, the hospitality of the rich and the great, from the sovereign down to the smallest baron, exceeded every thing which in the present times we can easily form a notion of. Westminster-hall was the dining-room of William Rufus, and might frequently, perhaps, not be too large for his company. It was reckoned a piece of magnificence in Thomas Becket, that he strowed the floor of his hall with clean hay or rushes in the season, in order that the knights and squires, who could not get seats, might not spoil their fine cloaths when they sat down on the floor to eat their dinner. The great earl of Warwick* is said to have entertained every day at his different manors, thirty thousand people; and though the number here may have been exaggerated, it must, however, have been very great to admit of such exaggeration. A hospitality nearly of the same kind was exercised not many years ago in many different parts of the highlands of Scotland.* It seems to be common in all nations to whom commerce and manufactures are little known. I have seen, says Doctor Pocock,* an Arabian chief dine in the streets of a town where he had come to sell his cattle, and invite all passengers, even common beggars, to sit down with him and partake of his banquet.

The occupiers of land were in every respect as dependent upon the great proprietor as his retainers. Even such of them as were not in a state of villanage, were tenants at will, who paid a rent in no respect equivalent to the subsistence which the land afforded them. A crown, half a crown, a sheep, a lamb, was some years ago in the highlands of Scotland a common rent for lands which maintained a family. In some places it is so at this day,* nor will money at present purchase a greater quantity of commodities there than in other places. In a country where the surplus produce of a large estate must be consumed upon the estate itself, it will frequently be more convenient for the proprietor, that part of it be consumed at a distance from his own house, provided they who consume it are as dependent upon him as either his retainers or his menial servants. He is thereby saved from the embarrassment of either too large a company or too large a family. A tenant at will, who possesses land sufficient to maintain his family for little more than a quit-rent,* is as dependent upon the proprietor as any servant or retainer whatever, and must obey him with as little reserve. Such a proprietor, as he feeds his servants and retainers at his own house, so he feeds his tenants at their houses. The subsistence of both is derived from his bounty, and its continuance depends upon his good pleasure.

Upon the authority which the great proprietors necessarily had in such a state of things over their tenants and retainers, was founded the power of the antient barons. They necessarily became the judges in peace, and the leaders in war, of all who dwelt upon their estates. They could maintain order and execute the law within their respective demesnes, because each of them could there turn the whole force of all the inhabitants against the injustice of any one. No other person had sufficient authority to do this. The king in particular had not. In those antient times he was little more than the greatest proprietor in his dominions, to whom, for the sake of common defence against their common enemies, the other great proprietors paid certain respects. To have enforced payment of a small debt within the lands of a great proprietor, where all the inhabitants were armed and accustomed to stand by one another, would have cost the king, had he attempted it by his own authority, almost the same effort as to extinguish a civil war. He was, therefore, obliged to abandon the administration of justice through the greater part of the country, to those who were capable of administering it; and for the same reason to leave the command of the country militia to those whom that militia would obey.

It is a mistake to imagine that those territorial jurisdictions took their origin from the feudal law. Not only the highest jurisdictions both civil and criminal, but the power of levying troops, of coining money, and even that of making bye-laws for the government of their own people, were all rights possessed allodially* by the great proprietors of land several centuries before even the name of the feudal law was known in Europe. The authority and jurisdiction of the Saxon lords in England, appear to have been as great before the conquest, as that of any of the Norman lords after it. But the feudal law is not supposed to have become the common law of England till after the conquest. That the most extensive authority and jurisdictions were possessed by the great lords in France allodially, long before the feudal law was introduced into that country, is a matter of fact that admits of no doubt. That authority and those jurisdictions all necessarily flowed from the state of property and manners just now described. Without remounting to the remote antiquities of either the French or English monarchies, we may find in much later times many proofs that such effects must always flow from such causes. It is not thirty years ago since Mr. Cameron of Lochiel,* a gentleman of Lochabar in Scotland, without any legal warrant whatever, not being what was then called a lord of regality,* nor even a tenant in chief, but a vassal of the duke of Argyle, and without being so much as a justice of peace, used, notwithstanding, to exercise the highest criminal jurisdiction over his own people. He is said to have done so with great equity, though without any of the formalities of justice; and it is not improbable that the state of that part of the country at that time made it necessary for him to assume this authority in order to maintain the publick peace. That gentleman, whose rent never exceeded five hundred pounds a year, carried, in 1745, eight hundred of his own people into the rebellion with him.

The introduction of the feudal law, so far from extending, may be regarded as an attempt to moderate the authority of the great allodial lords. It established a regular subordination, accompanied with a long train of services and duties, from the king down to the smallest proprietor. During the minority of the proprietor, the rent, together with the management of his lands, fell into the hands of his immediate superior, and, consequently, those of all great proprietors into the hands of the king, who was charged with the maintenance and education of the pupil, and who, from his authority as guardian, was supposed to have a right of disposing of him in marriage, provided it was in a manner not unsuitable to his rank. But though this institution necessarily tended to strengthen the authority of the king, and to weaken that of the great proprietors, it could not do either sufficiently for establishing order and good government among the inhabitants of the country; because it could not alter sufficiently that state of property and manners from which the disorders arose. The authority of government still continued to be, as before, too weak in the head and too strong in the inferior members, and the excessive strength of the inferior members was the cause of the weakness of the head. After the institution of feudal subordination, the king was as incapable of restraining the violence of the great lords as before. They still continued to make war according to their own discretion, almost continually upon one another, and very frequently upon the king; and the open country still continued to be a scene of violence, rapine, and disorder.

But what all the violence of the feudal institutions could never have effected, the silent and insensible operation of foreign commerce and manufactures gradually brought about.* These gradually furnished the great proprietors with something for which they could exchange the whole surplus produce of their lands, and which they could consume themselves without sharing it either with tenants or retainers. All for ourselves, and nothing for other people, seems, in every age of the world, to have been the vile maxim of the masters of mankind. As soon, therefore, as they could find a method of consuming the whole value of their rents themselves, they had no disposition to share them with any other persons. For a pair of diamond buckles perhaps, or for something as frivolous and useless, they exchanged the maintenance, or what is the same thing, the price of the maintenance of a thousand men for a year, and with it the whole weight and authority which it could give them. The buckles, however, were to be all their own, and no other human creature was to have any share of them; whereas in the more antient method of expence they must have shared with at least a thousand people. With the judges that were to determine the preference, this difference was perfectly decisive; and thus, for the gratification of the most childish, the meanest and the most sordid of all vanities, they gradually bartered their whole power and authority.

In a country where there is no foreign commerce, nor any of the finer manufactures, a man of ten thousand a year cannot well employ his revenue in any other way than in maintaining, perhaps, a thousand families, who are all of them necessarily at his command. In the present state of Europe, a man of ten thousand a year can spend his whole revenue, and he generally does so, without directly maintaining twenty people, or being able to command more than ten footmen not worth the commanding. Indirectly, perhaps, he maintains as great or even a greater number of people than he could have done by the antient method of expence. For though the quantity of precious productions for which he exchanges his whole revenue be very small, the number of workmen employed in collecting and preparing it, must necessarily have been very great. Its great price generally arises from the wages of their labour, and the profits of all their immediate employers. By paying that price he indirectly pays all those wages and profits, and thus indirectly contributes to the maintenance of all the workmen and their employers. He generally contributes, however, but a very small proportion to that of each, to very few perhaps a tenth, to many not a hundredth, and to some not a thousandth, nor even a ten thousandth part of their whole annual maintenance. Though he contributes, therefore, to the maintenance of them all, they are all more or less independent of him, because generally they can all be maintained without him.

When the great proprietors of land spend their rents in maintaining their tenants and retainers, each of them maintains entirely all his own tenants and all his own retainers. But when they spend them in maintaining tradesmen and artificers, they may, all of them taken together, perhaps, maintain as great, or, on account of the waste which attends rustick hospitality, a greater number of people than before. Each of them, however, taken singly, contributes often but a very small share to the maintenance of any individual of this greater number. Each tradesman or artificer derives his subsistence from the employment, not of one, but of a hundred or a thousand different customers. Though in some measure obliged to them all, therefore, he is not absolutely dependent upon any one of them.

The personal expence of the great proprietors having in this manner gradually increased, it was impossible that the number of their retainers should not as gradually diminish, till they were at last dismissed altogether. The same cause gradually led them to dismiss the unnecessary part of their tenants. Farms were enlarged, and the occupiers of land, notwithstanding the complaints of depopulation, reduced to the number necessary for cultivating it, according to the imperfect state of cultivation and improvement in those times. By the removal of the unnecessary mouths, and by exacting from the farmer the full value of the farm, a greater surplus, or what is the same thing, the price of a greater surplus, was obtained for the proprietor, which the merchants and manufacturers soon furnished him with a method of spending upon his own person in the same manner as he had done the rest. The same cause continuing to operate, he was desirous to raise his rents above what his lands, in the actual state of their improvement, could afford. His tenants could agree to this upon one condition only, that they should be secured in their possession, for such a term of years as might give them time to recover with profit whatever they should lay out in the further improvement of the land. The expensive vanity of the landlord made him willing to accept of this condition; and hence the origin of long leases.

Even a tenant at will, who pays the full value of the land, is not altogether dependent upon the landlord. The pecuniary advantages which they receive from one another, are mutual and equal, and such a tenant will expose neither his life nor his fortune in the service of the proprietor. But if he has a lease for a long term of years, he is altogether independent; and his landlord must not expect from him even the most trifling service beyond what is either expressly stipulated in the lease, or imposed upon him by the common and known law of the country.

The tenants having in this manner become independent, and the retainers being dismissed, the great proprietors were no longer capable of interrupting the regular execution of justice, or of disturbing the peace of the country. Having sold their birth-right, not like Esau for a mess of pottage* in time of hunger and necessity, but in the wantonness of plenty, for trinkets and baubles, fitter to be the play-things of children than the serious pursuits of men, they became as insignificant as any substantial burgher or tradesman in a city. A regular government was established in the country as well as in the city, nobody having sufficient power to disturb its operations in the one, any more than in the other.

It does not, perhaps, relate to the present subject, but I cannot help remarking it, that very old families, such as have possessed some considerable estate from father to son for many successive generations, are very rare in commercial countries. In countries which have little commerce, on the contrary, such as Wales or the highlands of Scotland, they are very common. The Arabian histories seem to be all full of genealogies, and there is a history written by a Tartar Khan, which has been translated into several European languages, and which contains scarce any thing else; a proof that antient families are very common among those nations.* In countries where a rich man can spend his revenue in no other way than by maintaining as many people as it can maintain, he is not apt to run out, and his benevolence it seems is seldom so violent as to attempt to maintain more than he can afford. But where he can spend the greatest revenue upon his own person, he frequently has no bounds to his expence, because he frequently has no bounds to his vanity, or to his affection for his own person. In commercial countries, therefore, riches, in spite of the most violent regulations of law to prevent their dissipation, very seldom remain long in the same family. Among simple nations, on the contrary, they frequently do without any regulations of law; for among nations of shepherds, such as the Tartars and Arabs, the consumable nature of their property necessarily renders all such regulations impossible.

A revolution of the greatest importance to the publick happiness, was in this manner brought about by two different orders of people, who had not the least intention to serve the publick. To gratify the most childish vanity was the sole motive of the great proprietors. The merchants and artificers, much less ridiculous, acted merely from a view to their own interest, and in pursuit of their own pedlar principle of turning a penny wherever a penny was to be got. Neither of them had either knowledge or foresight of that great revolution which the folly of the one, and the industry of the other, was gradually bringing about.

It is thus that through the greater part of Europe the commerce and manufactures of cities, instead of being the effect, have been the cause and occasion of the improvement and cultivation of the country.

This order, however, being contrary to the natural course of things, is necessarily both slow and uncertain. Compare the slow progress of those European countries of which the wealth depends very much upon their commerce and manufactures, with the rapid advances of our North American colonies, of which the wealth is founded altogether in agriculture. Through the greater part of Europe, the number of inhabitants is not supposed to double in less than five hundred years. In several of our North American colonies, it is found to double in twenty or five-and-twenty years.* In Europe, the law of primogeniture, and perpetuities of different kinds, prevent the division of great estates, and thereby hinder the multiplication of small proprietors. A small proprietor, however, who knows every part of his little territory, who views it with all the affection which property, especially small property, naturally inspires, and who upon that account takes pleasure not only in cultivating but in adorning it, is generally of all improvers the most industrious, the most intelligent, and the most successful.* The same regulations, besides, keep so much land out of the market, that there are always more capitals to buy than there is land to sell, so that what is sold always sells at a monopoly price. The rent never pays the interest of the purchase-money, and is besides burdened with repairs and other occasional charges, to which the interest of money is not liable. To purchase land is every where in Europe a most unprofitable employment of a small capital. For the sake of the superior security, indeed, a man of moderate circumstances, when he retires from business, will sometimes chuse to lay out his little capital in land. A man of profession too, whose revenue is derived from another source, often loves to secure his savings in the same way. But a young man, who, instead of applying to trade or to some profession, should employ a capital of two or three thousand pounds in the purchase and cultivation of a small piece of land, might indeed expect to live very happily, and very independently, but must bid adieu, for ever, to all hope of either great fortune or great illustration,* which by a different employment of his stock he might have had the same chance of acquiring with other people. Such a person too, though he cannot aspire at being a proprietor, will often disdain to be a farmer. The small quantity of land, therefore, which is brought to market, and the high price of what is brought thither, prevents a great number of capitals from being employed in its cultivation and improvement which would otherwise have taken that direction. In North America, on the contrary, fifty or sixty pounds is often found a sufficient stock to begin a plantation with. The purchase and improvement of uncultivated land, is there the most profitable employment of the smallest as well as of the greatest capitals, and the most direct road to all the fortune and illustration which can be acquired in that country. Such land, indeed, is in North America to be had almost for nothing, or at a price much below the value of the natural produce; a thing impossible in Europe, or, indeed, in any country where all lands have long been private property. If landed estates, however, were divided equally among all the children, upon the death of any proprietor who left a numerous family, the estate would generally be sold. So much land would come to market, that it could no longer sell at a monopoly price. The free rent of the land would go nearer to pay the interest of the purchase-money, and a small capital might be employed in purchasing land as profitably as in any other way.

England, on account of the natural fertility of the soil, of the great extent of the sea-coast in proportion to that of the whole country, and of the many navigable rivers which run through it, and afford the conveniency of water carriage to some of the most inland parts of it, is perhaps as well fitted by nature as any large country in Europe, to be the seat of foreign commerce, of manufactures for distant sale, and of all the improvements which these can occasion. From the beginning of the reign of Elizabeth too,* the English legislature has been peculiarly attentive to the interests of commerce and manufactures, and in reality there is no country in Europe, Holland itself not excepted, of which the law is, upon the whole, more favourable to this sort of industry. Commerce and manufactures have accordingly been continually advancing during all this period. The cultivation and improvement of the country has, no doubt, been gradually advancing too: But it seems to have followed slowly, and at a distance, the more rapid progress of commerce and manufactures. The greater part of the country must probably have been cultivated before the reign of Elizabeth; and a very great part of it still remains uncultivated, and the cultivation of the far greater part, much inferior to what it might be. The law of England, however, favours agriculture not only indirectly by the protection of commerce, but by several direct encouragements. Except in times of scarcity, the exportation of corn is not only free, but encouraged by a bounty. In times of moderate plenty, the importation of foreign corn is loaded with duties that amount to a prohibition. The importation of live cattle, except from Ireland, is prohibited at all times, and it is but of late that it was permitted from thence. Those who cultivate the land, therefore, have a monopoly* against their countrymen for the two greatest and most important articles of land produce, bread and butcher's meat. These encouragements, though at bottom, perhaps, as I shall endeavour to show hereafter, altogether illusory, sufficiently demonstrate at least the good intention of the legislature to favour agriculture. But what is of much more importance than all of them, the yeomanry of England are rendered as secure, as independent, and as respectable as law can make them. No country, therefore, in which the right of primogeniture takes place, which pays tithes, and where perpetuities, though contrary to the spirit of the law, are admitted in some cases, can give more encouragement to agriculture than England. Such, however, notwithstanding, is the state of its cultivation. What would it have been, had the law given no direct encouragement to agriculture besides what arises indirectly from the progress of commerce, and had left the yeomanry in the same condition as in most other countries of Europe? It is now more than two hundred years since the beginning of the reign of Elizabeth, a period as long as the course of human prosperity usually endures.*

France seems to have had a considerable share of foreign commerce near a century before England was distinguished as a commercial country. The marine of France was considerable, according to the notions of the times, before the expedition of Charles the VIIIth to Naples.* The cultivation and improvement of France, however, is, upon the whole, inferior to that of England. The law of the country has never given the same direct encouragement to agriculture.

The foreign commerce of Spain and Portugal* to the other parts of Europe, though chiefly carried on in foreign ships, is very considerable. That to their colonies is carried on in their own, and is much greater, on account of the great riches and extent of those colonies. But it has never introduced any considerable manufactures for distant sale into either of those countries, and the greater part of both still remains uncultivated. The foreign commerce of Portugal is of older standing than that of any great country in Europe, except Italy.

Italy is the only great country of Europe which seems to have been cultivated and improved in every part, by means of foreign commerce and manufactures for distant sale. Before the invasion of Charles the VIIIth, Italy, according to Guicciardin,* was cultivated not less in the most mountainous and barren parts of the country, than in the plainest and most fertile. The advantageous situation of the country, and the great number of independent states which at that time subsisted in it, probably contributed not a little to this general cultivation. It is not impossible too, notwithstanding this general expression of one of the most judicious and reserved of modern historians, that Italy was not at that time better cultivated than England is at present.

The capital, however, that is acquired to any country by commerce and manufactures, is all a very precarious and uncertain possession, till some part of it has been secured and realized in the cultivation and improvement of its lands. A merchant, it has been said very properly, is not necessarily the citizen of any particular country. It is in a great measure indifferent to him from what place he carries on his trade; and a very trifling disgust will make him remove his capital, and together with it all the industry which it supports, from one country to another. No part of it can be said to belong to any particular country, till it has been spread as it were over the face of that country, either in buildings, or in the lasting improvement of lands. No vestige now remains of the great wealth, said to have been possessed by the greater part of the Hans towns,* except in the obscure histories of the thirteenth and fourteenth centuries. It is even uncertain where some of them were situated, or to what towns in Europe the Latin names given to some of them belong. But though the misfortunes of Italy in the end of the fifteenth and beginning of the sixteenth centuries greatly diminished the commerce and manufactures of the cities of Lombardy and Tuscany, those countries still continue to be among the most populous and best cultivated in Europe. The civil wars of Flanders, and the Spanish government which succeeded them, chased away the great commerce of Antwerp, Ghent, and Bruges. But Flanders still continues to be one of the richest, best cultivated, and most populous provinces of Europe. The ordinary revolutions of war and government easily dry up the sources of that wealth which arises from commerce only. That which arises from the more solid improvements of agriculture, is much more durable, and cannot be destroyed but by those more violent convulsions occasioned by the depredations of hostile and barbarous nations continued for a century or two together; such as those that happened for some time before and after the fall of the Roman empire in the western provinces of Europe.

BOOK IV

Of Systems of political Œconomy*

INTRODUCTION

POLITICAL œconomy, considered as a branch of the science of a statesman or legislator, proposes two distinct objects; first, to provide a plentiful revenue or subsistence for the people, or more properly to enable them to provide such a revenue or subsistence for themselves; and secondly, to supply the state or commonwealth with a revenue sufficient for the publick services. It proposes to enrich both the people and the sovereign.

The different progress of opulence in different ages and nations, has given occasion to two different systems of political œconomy, with regard to enriching the people. The one may be called the system of commerce, the other that of agriculture. I shall endeavour to explain both as fully and distinctly as I can, and shall begin with the system of commerce. It is the modern system, and is best understood in our own country and in our own times.

CHAPTER I

Of the Principle of the commercial, or mercantile System

THAT wealth consists in money, or in gold and silver, is a popular notion which naturally arises from the double function of money, as the instrument of commerce, and as the measure of value. In consequence of its being the instrument of commerce, when we have money we can more readily obtain whatever else we have occasion for, than by means of any other commodity. The great affair, we always find, is to get money. When that is obtained, there is no difficulty in making any subsequent purchase. In consequence of its being the measure of value, we estimate that of all other commodities by the quantity of money which they will exchange for. We say of a rich man that he is worth a great deal, and of a poor man that he is worth very little money. A frugal man, or a man eager to be rich, is said to love money; and a careless, a generous, or a profuse man, is said to be indifferent about it. To grow rich is to get money; and wealth and money, in short, are, in common language, considered as in every respect synonymous.*

A rich country, in the same manner as a rich man, is supposed to be a country abounding in money; and to heap up gold and silver in any country is supposed to be the readiest way to enrich it. For some time after the discovery of America, the first enquiry of the Spaniards, when they arrived upon any unknown coast, used to be, if there was any gold or silver to be found in the neighbourhood? By the information which they received, they judged whether it was worth while to make a settlement there, or if the country was worth the conquering. Plano Carpino,* a monk sent ambassador from the king of France to one of the sons of the famous Gengis Khan, says that the Tartars used frequently to ask him, if there was plenty of sheep and oxen in the kingdom of France? Their enquiry had the same object with that of the Spaniards. They wanted to know if the country was rich enough to be worth the conquering. Among the Tartars, as among all other nations of shepherds, who are generally ignorant of the use of money, cattle are the instruments of commerce and the measures of value. Wealth, therefore, according to them, consisted in cattle, as according to the Spaniards it consisted in gold and silver. Of the two, the Tartar notion, perhaps, was the nearest to the truth.

Mr. Locke* remarks a distinction between money and other moveable goods. All other moveable goods, he says, are of so consumable a nature that the wealth which consists in them cannot be much depended on, and a nation which abounds in them one year may, without any exportation, but merely by their own waste and extravagance, be in great want of them the next. Money, on the contrary, is a steady friend, which, though it may travel about from hand to hand, yet if it can be kept from going out of the country, is not very liable to be wasted and consumed. Gold and silver, therefore, are, according to him, the most solid and substantial part of the moveable wealth of a nation, and to multiply those metals ought, he thinks, upon that account, to be the great object of its political œconomy.

Others* admit that if a nation could be separated from all the world, it would be of no consequence how much, or how little money circulated in it. The consumable goods which were circulated by means of this money, would only be exchanged for a greater or a smaller number of pieces; but the real wealth or poverty of the country, they allow, would depend altogether upon the abundance or scarcity of those consumable goods. But it is otherwise, they think, with countries which have connections with sovereign nations, and which are obliged to carry on foreign wars, and to maintain fleets and armies in distant countries. This, they say, cannot be done, but by sending abroad money to pay them with; and a nation cannot send much money abroad, unless it has a good deal at home. Every such nation, therefore, must endeavour in time of peace to accumulate gold and silver, that, when occasion requires, it may have wherewithal to carry on foreign wars.

In consequence of these popular notions, all the different nations of Europe have studied, though to little purpose, every possible means of accumulating gold and silver in their respective countries. Spain and Portugal, the proprietors of the principal mines which supply Europe with those metals, have either prohibited their exportation under the severest penalties, or subjected it to a considerable duty. The like prohibition seems antiently to have made a part of the policy of most other European nations. It is even to be found, where we should least of all expect to find it, in some old Scotch acts of parliament, which forbid under heavy penalties the carrying gold or silver *forth of the kingdom.** The like policy antiently took place both in France and England.

When those countries became commercial, the merchants found this prohibition, upon many occasions, extremely inconvenient. They could frequently buy more advantageously with gold and silver than with any other commodity, the foreign goods which they wanted, either to import into their own, or to carry to some other foreign country. They remonstrated, therefore, against this prohibition as hurtful to trade.

They represented, first, that the exportation of gold and silver in order to purchase foreign goods, did not always diminish the quantity of those metals in the kingdom. That, on the contrary, it might frequently increase that quantity; because, if the consumption of foreign goods was not thereby increased in the country, those goods might be re-exported to foreign countries, and being there sold for a large profit, might bring back much more treasure than was originally sent out to purchase them. Mr. Mun* compares this operation of foreign trade to the seed-time and harvest of agriculture. "If we only behold," says he, "the actions of the husbandman in the seed-time, when he casteth away much good corn into the ground, we shall account him rather a madman than a husbandman. But when we consider his labours in the harvest, which is the end of his endeavours, we shall find the worth and plentiful increase of his actions."

They represented, secondly, that this prohibition could not hinder the exportation of gold and silver, which, on account of the smallness of their bulk in proportion to their value, could easily be smuggled abroad. That this exportation could only be prevented by a proper attention to, what they called, the balance of trade.* That when the country exported to a greater value than it imported, a balance became due to it from foreign nations, which was necessarily paid to it in gold and silver, and thereby increased the quantity of those metals in the kingdom. But that when it imported to a greater value than it exported, a contrary balance became due to foreign nations, which was necessarily paid to them in the same manner, and thereby diminished that quantity. That in this case to prohibit the exportation of those metals could not prevent it, but only, by making it more dangerous, render it more expensive. That the exchange was thereby turned more against the country which owed the balance, than it otherwise might have been; the merchant who purchased a bill upon the foreign country being obliged to pay the banker who sold it, not only for the natural risk, trouble and expence of sending the money thither, but for the extraordinary risk arising from the prohibition. But that the more the exchange was against any country, the more the balance of trade became necessarily against it; the money of that country becoming necessarily of so much less value, in comparison with that of the country to which the balance was due. That if the exchange between England and Holland, for example, was five per cent. against England, it would require a hundred and five ounces of silver in England to purchase a bill for a hundred ounces of silver in Holland: that a hundred and five ounces of silver in England, therefore, would be worth only a hundred ounces of silver in Holland, and would purchase only a proportionable quantity of Dutch goods: but that a hundred ounces of silver in Holland, on the contrary, would be worth a hundred and five ounces in England, and would purchase a proportionable quantity of English goods: That the

English goods which were sold to Holland would be sold so much cheaper; and the Dutch goods which were sold to England, so much dearer, by the difference of the exchange; that the one would draw so much less Dutch money to England, and the other so much more English money to Holland as this difference amounted to: and that the balance of trade, therefore, would necessarily be so much more against England, and would require a greater balance of gold and silver to be exported to Holland.

Those arguments were partly solid and partly sophistical. They were solid so far as they asserted that the exportation of gold and silver in trade might frequently be advantageous to the country. They were solid too in asserting that no prohibition could prevent their exportation, when private people found any advantage in exporting them. But they were sophistical in supposing, that either to preserve or to augment the quantity of those metals required more the attention of government, than to preserve or to augment the quantity of any other useful commodities, which the freedom of trade, without any such attention, never fails to supply in the proper quantity. They were sophistical too, perhaps, in asserting that the high price of exchange necessarily increased, what they called, the un-favourable balance of trade, or occasioned the exportation of a greater quantity of gold and silver. That high price, indeed, was extremely disadvantageous to the merchants who had any money to pay in foreign countries. They paid so much dearer for the bills which their bankers granted them upon those countries. But though the risk arising from the prohibition might occasion some extraordinary expence to the bankers, it would not necessarily carry any more money out of the country. This expence would generally be all laid out in the country, in smuggling the money out of it, and could seldom occasion the exportation of a single six-pence beyond the precise sum drawn for. The high price of exchange too would naturally dispose the merchants to endeavour to make their exports nearly balance their imports, in order that they might have this high exchange to pay upon as small a sum as possible. The high price of exchange, besides, must necessarily have operated as a tax, in raising the price of foreign goods, and thereby diminishing their consumption. It would tend, therefore, not to increase, but to diminish, what they called, the unfavourable balance of trade, and consequently the exportation of gold and silver.

Such as they were, however, those arguments convinced the people to whom they were addressed. They were addressed by merchants to parliaments, and to the councils of princes, to nobles and to country gentlemen; by those who were supposed to understand trade, to those who were conscious to themselves that they knew nothing about the matter. That foreign trade enriched the country, experience demonstrated to the nobles and country gentlemen, as well as to the merchants; but how, or in what manner, none of them well knew. The merchants knew perfectly in what manner it enriched themselves. It was their business to know it. But to know in what manner it enriched the country, was no part of their business. This subject never came into their consideration, but when they had occasion to apply to their country for some change in the laws relating to foreign trade. It then became necessary to say something about the beneficial effects of foreign trade, and the manner in which those effects were obstructed by the laws as they then stood. To the judges who were to decide the business, it appeared a most satisfactory account of the matter, when they were told that foreign trade brought money into the country, but that the laws in question hindered it from bringing so much as it otherwise would do. Those arguments therefore produced the wished-for effect. The prohibition of exporting gold and silver was in France and England confined to the coin of those respective countries. The exportation of foreign coin and of bullion was made free. In Holland, and in some other places, this liberty was extended even to the coin of the country. The attention of government was turned away from guarding against the exportation of gold and silver, to watch over the balance of trade, as the only cause which could occasion any augmentation or diminution of those metals. From one fruitless care it was turned away to another care much more intricate, much more embarrassing, and just equally fruitless. The title of Mun's book, England's Treasure in Foreign Trade,* became a fundamental maxim in the political œconomy, not of England only, but of all other commercial countries. The inland or home trade, the most important of all, the trade in which an equal capital affords the greatest revenue, and creates the greatest employment to the people of the country, was considered as subsidiary only to foreign trade. It neither brought money into the country, it was said, nor carried any out of it. The country therefore could never become either richer or poorer by means of it, except so far as its prosperity or decay might indirectly influence the state of foreign trade. . . .

It is not because wealth consists more essentially in money than in goods, that the merchant finds it generally more easy to buy goods with money, than to buy money with goods; but because money is the known and established instrument of commerce, for which every thing is readily given in exchange, but which is not always with equal readiness to be got in exchange for every thing. The greater part of goods besides are more perishable than money,* and he may frequently sustain a much greater loss by keeping them. When his goods are upon hand too, he is more liable to such demands for money as he may not be able to answer, than when he has got their price in his coffers. Over and above all this, his profit arises more directly from selling than from buying, and he is upon all these accounts generally much more anxious to exchange his goods for money, than his money for goods. But though a particular merchant, with abundance of goods in his warehouse, may sometimes be ruined by not being able to sell them in time, a nation or country is not liable to the same accident. The whole capital of a merchant frequently consists in perishable goods destined for purchasing money. But it is but a very small part of the annual produce of the land and labour of a country which can ever be destined for purchasing gold and silver from their neighbours. The far greater part is circulated and consumed among themselves; and even of the surplus which is sent abroad, the greater part is generally destined for the purchase of other foreign goods. Though gold and silver, therefore, could not be had in exchange for the goods destined to purchase them, the nation would not be ruined. It might, indeed, suffer some loss and inconveniency, and be forced upon some of those expedients which are necessary for supplying the place of money. The annual produce of its land and labour, however, would be the same, or very nearly the same, as usual, because the same, or very nearly the same consumable capital would be employed in maintaining it. And though goods do not always draw money so readily as money draws goods, in the long-run they draw it more necessarily than even it draws them. Goods can serve many other purposes besides purchasing money, but money can serve no other purpose besides purchasing goods. Money, therefore, necessarily runs after goods, but goods do not always or necessarily run after money. The man who buys, does not always mean to sell again, but frequently to use or to consume; whereas he who sells, always means to buy again. The one may frequently have done the whole, but the other can never have done more than the one-half of his business. It is not for its own sake that men desire money, but for the sake of what they can purchase with it.*

Consumable commodities, it is said, are soon destroyed; whereas gold and silver are of a more durable nature, and, were it not for this continual exportation, might be accumulated for ages together, to the incredible augmentation of the real wealth of the country. Nothing, therefore, it is pretended, can be more disadvantageous to any country, than the trade which consists in the exchange of such lasting for such perishable commodities. We do not, however, reckon that trade disadvantageous which consists in the exchange of the hardware of England for the wines of France; and yet hardware is a very durable commodity, and was it not for this continual exportation, might too be accumulated for ages together, to the incredible augmentation of the pots and pans of the country.

But it readily occurs that the number of such utensils is in every country necessarily limited by the use which there is for them; that it would be absurd to have more pots and pans than were necessary for cooking the victuals usually consumed there; and that if the quantity of victuals were to increase, the number of pots and pans would readily increase along with it, a part of the increased quantity of victuals being employed in purchasing them, or in maintaining an additional number of workmen whose business it was to make them. It should as readily occur that the quantity of gold and silver is in every country limited by the use which there is for those metals; that their use consists in circulating commodities as coin, and in affording a species of houshold furniture as plate; that the quantity of coin in every country is regulated by the value of the commodities which are to be circulated by it: increase that value, and immediately a part of it will be sent abroad to purchase, wherever it is to be had, the additional quantity of coin requisite for circulating them: that the quantity of plate is regulated by the number and wealth of those private families who chuse to indulge themselves in that sort of magnificence: increase the number and wealth of such families, and a part of this increased wealth will most probably be employed in purchasing, wherever it is to be found, an additional quantity of plate: that to attempt to increase the wealth of any country, either by introducing or by detaining in it an unnecessary quantity of gold and silver, is as absurd as it would be to attempt to increase the good cheer of private families, by obliging them to keep an unnecessary number of kitchen utensils. As the expence of purchasing those unnecessary utensils would diminish instead of increasing either the quantity or goodness of the family provisions; so the expence of purchasing an unnecessary quantity of gold and silver must, in every country, as necessarily diminish the wealth which feeds, cloaths, and lodges, which maintains and employs the people. Gold and silver, whether in the shape of coin or of plate, are utensils, it must be remembered, as much as the furniture of the kitchen. Increase the use for them, increase the consumable commodities which are to be circulated, managed, and prepared by means of them, and you will infallibly increase the quantity; but if you attempt, by extraordinary means, to increase the quantity, you will as infallibly diminish the use and even the quantity too, which in those metals can never be greater than what the use requires. Were they ever to be accumulated beyond this quantity, their transportation is so easy, and the loss which attends their lying idle and unemployed so great, that no law could prevent their being immediately sent out of the country.

It is not always necessary to accumulate gold and silver, in order to enable a country to carry on foreign wars, and to maintain fleets and armies in distant countries. Fleets and armies are maintained, not with gold and silver, but with consumable goods.* The nation which, from the annual produce of its domestick industry, from the annual revenue arising out of its lands, labour, and consumable stock, has wherewithal to purchase those consumable goods in distant countries, can maintain foreign wars there. . . .

I thought it necessary, though at the hazard of being tedious, to examine at full length this popular notion that wealth consists in money, or in gold and silver. Money in common language, as I have already observed, frequently signifies wealth; and this ambiguity of expression has rendered this popular notion so familiar to us, that even they, who are convinced of its absurdity, are very apt to forget their own principles, and in the course of their reasonings to take it for granted as a certain and undeniable truth. Some of the best English writers upon commerce set out with observing, that the wealth of a country consists, not in its gold and silver only, but in its lands, houses, and consumable goods of all different kinds. In the course of their reasonings, however, the lands, houses, and consumable goods seem to slip out of their memory, and the strain of their argument frequently supposes that all wealth consists in gold and silver, and that to multiply those metals is the great object of national industry and commerce.

The two principles being established, however, that wealth consisted in gold and silver, and that those metals could be brought into a country which had no mines only by the balance of trade, or by exporting to a greater value than it imported; it necessarily became the great object of political œconomy to diminish as much as possible the importation of foreign goods for home-consumption, and to increase as much as possible the exportation of the produce of domestick industry. Its two great engines for enriching the country, therefore, were restraints upon importation, and encouragements to exportation.*

The restraints upon importation were of two kinds.

First, Restraints upon the importation of such foreign goods for home-consumption as could be produced at home, from whatever country they were imported.

Secondly, Restraints upon the importation of goods of almost all kinds from those particular countries with which the balance of trade was supposed to be disadvantageous.

Those different restraints consisted sometimes in high duties, and sometimes in absolute prohibitions.

Exportation was encouraged sometimes by drawbacks, sometimes by bounties, sometimes by advantageous treaties of commerce with foreign states, and sometimes by the establishment of colonies in distant countries.

Drawbacks were given upon two different occasions. When the home-manufactures were subject to any duty or excise, either the whole or a part of it was frequently drawn back upon their exportation; and when foreign goods liable to a duty were imported in order to be exported again, either the whole or a part of this duty was sometimes given back upon such exportation.

Bounties were given for the encouragement either of some beginning manufactures, or of such sorts of industry of other kinds as were supposed to deserve particular favour.

By advantageous treaties of commerce, particular privileges were procured in some foreign state for the goods and merchants of the country, beyond what were granted to those of other countries.

By the establishment of colonies in distant countries, not only particular privileges, but a monopoly was frequently procured for the goods and merchants of the country which established them.

The two sorts of restraints upon importation abovementioned, together with these four encouragements to exportation, constitute the six principal means by which the commercial system proposes to increase the quantity of gold and silver in any country by turning the balance of trade in its favour. . . .

CHAPTER II

Of Restraints upon the Importation from foreign Countries of such Goods as can be produced at Home

BY restraining, either by high duties, or by absolute prohibitions, the importation of such goods from foreign countries as can be produced at home, the monopoly of the home-market* is more or less secured to the domestick industry employed in producing them. Thus the prohibition of importing either live cattle or salt provisions from foreign countries secures to the graziers of Great Britain the monopoly of the home-market for butchers-meat. The high duties upon the importation of corn, which in times of moderate plenty amount to a prohibition, give a like advantage to the growers of that commodity. The prohibition of the importation of foreign woollens is equally favourable to the woollen manufacturers. The silk manufacture, though altogether employed upon foreign materials, has lately obtained the same advantage. The linen manufacture has not yet obtained it, but is making great strides towards it. Many other sorts of manufacturers have, in the same manner, obtained in Great Britain, either altogether, or very nearly a monopoly against their countrymen. The variety of goods of which the importation into Great Britain is prohibited, either absolutely, or under certain circumstances, greatly exceeds what can easily be suspected by those who are not well acquainted with the laws of the customs.

That this monopoly of the home-market frequently gives great encouragement to that particular species of industry which enjoys it, and frequently turns towards that employment a greater share of both the labour and stock of the society than would otherwise have gone to it, cannot be doubted. But whether it tends either to increase the general industry of the society, or to give it the most advantageous direction, is not, perhaps, altogether so evident.

The general industry of the society never can exceed what the capital of the society can employ. As the number of workmen that can be kept in employment by any particular person must bear a certain proportion to his capital, so the number of those that can be continually employed by all the members of a great society, must bear a certain proportion to the whole capital of that society, and never can exceed that proportion. No regulation of commerce can increase the quantity of industry in any society beyond what its capital can maintain. It can only divert a part of it into a direction into which it might not otherwise have gone; and it is by no means certain that this artificial direction is likely to be more advantageous to the society than that into which it would have gone of its own accord.*

Every individual is continually exerting himself to find out the most advantageous employment for whatever capital he can command. It is his own advantage, indeed, and not that of the society, which he has in view. But the study of his own advantage naturally, or rather necessarily leads him to prefer that employment which is most advantageous to the society.

First, every individual endeavours to employ his capital as near home as he can, and consequently as much as he can in the support of domestick industry; provided always that he can thereby obtain the ordinary, or not a great deal less than the ordinary profits of stock.

Thus upon equal or nearly equal profits, every wholesale merchant naturally prefers the home-trade to the foreign trade of consumption, and the foreign trade of consumption to the carrying trade. In the home-trade his capital is never so long out of his sight as it frequently is in the foreign trade of consumption. He can know better the character and situation of the persons whom he trusts, and if he should happen to be deceived, he knows better the laws of the country from which he must seek redress. In the carrying trade, the capital of the merchant is, as it were, divided between two foreign countries, and no part of it is ever necessarily brought home, or placed under his own immediate view and command. The capital

which an Amsterdam merchant employs in carrying corn from
Konnigsberg to Lisbon, and fruit and wine from Lisbon to
Konnigsberg, must generally be the one-half of it at Konnigsberg and the other half at Lisbon. No part of it need ever come
to Amsterdam. The natural residence of such a merchant
should either be at Konnigsberg or Lisbon, and it can only be
some very particular circumstances which can make him prefer
the residence of Amsterdam. The uneasiness, however, which
he feels at being separated so far from his capital, generally
determines him to bring part both of the Konnigsberg goods
which he destines for the market of Lisbon, and of the Lisbon
goods which he destines for that of Konnigsberg, to Amsterdam: and though this necessarily subjects him to a double
charge of loading and unloading, as well as to the payment of
some duties and customs, yet for the sake of having some part
of his capital always under his own view and command, he
willingly submits to this extraordinary charge; and it is in this
manner that every country which has any considerable share
of the carrying trade, becomes always the emporium, or general
market, for the goods of all the different countries whose trade
it carries on. The merchant, in order to save a second loading
and unloading, endeavours always to sell in the home-market
as much of the goods of all those different countries as he can,
and thus, so far as he can, to convert his carrying trade into
a foreign trade of consumption. A merchant, in the same
manner, who is engaged in the foreign trade of consumption,
when he collects goods for foreign markets, will always be glad,
upon equal or nearly equal profits, to sell as great a part of
them at home as he can. He saves himself the risk and trouble
of exportation, when, so far as he can, he thus converts his
foreign trade of consumption into a home-trade. Home is in
this manner the center, if I may say so, round which the
capitals of the inhabitants of every country are continually
circulating, and towards which they are always tending, though
by particular causes they may sometimes be driven off and
repelled from it towards more distant employments. But a
capital employed in the home-trade, it has already been

shown,* necessarily puts into motion a greater quantity of domestic industry, and gives revenue and employment to a greater number of the inhabitants of the country, than an equal capital employed in the foreign trade of consumption: and one employed in the foreign trade of consumption has the same advantage over an equal capital employed in the carrying trade. Upon equal, or only nearly equal profits, therefore, every individual naturally inclines to employ his capital in the manner in which it is likely to afford the greatest support to domestick industry, and to give revenue and employment to the greatest number of people of his own country.

Secondly, every individual who employs his capital in the support of domestick industry, necessarily endeavours so to direct that industry, that its produce may be of the greatest possible value.

The produce of industry is what it adds to the subject or materials upon which it is employed. In proportion as the value of this produce is great or small, so will likewise be the profits of the employer. But it is only for the sake of profit that any man employs a capital in the support of industry; and he will always, therefore, endeavour to employ it in the support of that industry of which the produce is likely to be of the greatest value, or to exchange for the greatest quantity either of money or of other goods.

But the annual revenue of every society is always precisely equal to the exchangeable value of the whole annual produce of its industry, or rather is precisely the same thing with that exchangeable value. As every individual, therefore, endeavours as much as he can both to employ his capital in the support of domestick industry, and so to direct that industry that its produce may be of the greatest value; every individual necessarily labours to render the annual revenue of the society as great as he can. He generally, indeed, neither intends to promote the publick interest, nor knows how much he is promoting it. By preferring the support of domestick to that of foreign industry, he intends only his own security; and by directing that industry in such a manner as its produce may be of the greatest value, he intends only his own gain, and he is in this, as in many other cases, led by an invisible hand to promote an end which was no part of his intention.* Nor is it always the worse for the society that it was no part of it. By pursuing his own interest he frequently promotes that of the society more effectually than when he really intends to promote it. I have never known much good done by those who affected to trade for the publick good. It is an affectation, indeed, not very common among merchants, and very few words need be employed in dissuading them from it.

What is the species of domestick industry which his capital can employ, and of which the produce is likely to be of the greatest value, every individual, it is evident, can, in his local situation, judge much better than any statesman or lawgiver can do for him. The stateman, who should attempt to direct private people in what manner they ought to employ their capitals, would not only load himself with a most unnecessary attention, but assume an authority which could safely be trusted, not only to no single person, but to no council or senate whatever, and which would nowhere be so dangerous as in the hands of a man who had folly and presumption enough to fancy himself fit to exercise it.

To give the monopoly of the home-market to the produce of domestick industry, in any particular art or manufacture, is in some measure to direct private people in what manner they ought to employ their capitals, and must, in almost all cases, be either a useless or a hurtful regulation. If the produce of domestick can be brought there as cheap as that of foreign industry, the regulation is evidently useless. If it cannot, it must generally be hurtful. It is the maxim of every prudent master of a family, never to attempt to make at home what it will cost him more to make than to buy. The taylor does not attempt to make his own shoes, but buys them of the shoemaker. The shoemaker does not attempt to make his own cloaths, but employs a taylor. The farmer attempts to make neither the one nor the other, but employs those different artificers. All of them find it for their interest to employ their whole industry in a way in which they have some advantage over their neighbours, and to purchase with a part of its produce, or what is the same thing, with the price of a part of it, whatever else they have occasion for.

What is prudence in the conduct of every private family, can scarce be folly in that of a great kingdom. If a foreign country can supply us with a commodity cheaper than we ourselves can make it, better buy it of them with some part of the produce of our own industry, employed in a way in which we have some advantage. The general industry of the country, being always in proportion to the capital which employs it, will not thereby be diminished, no more than that of the above-mentioned artificers; but only left to find out the way in which it can be employed with the greatest advantage. It is certainly not employed to the greatest advantage, when it is thus directed towards an object which it can buy cheaper than it can make. The value of its annual produce is certainly more or less diminished, when it is thus turned away from producing commodities evidently of more value than the commodity which it is directed to produce. According to the supposition, that commodity could be purchased from foreign countries cheaper than it can be made at home. It could, therefore, have been purchased with a part only of the commodities, or, what is the same thing, with a part only of the price of the commodities, which the industry employed by an equal capital, would have produced at home, had it been left to follow its natural course. The industry of the country, therefore, is thus turned away from a more, to a less advantageous employment, and the exchangeable value of its annual produce, instead of being increased, according to the intention of the lawgiver, must necessarily be diminished by every such regulation.

By means of such regulations, indeed, a particular manufacture may sometimes be acquired sooner than it could have been otherwise, and after a certain time may be made at home as cheap or cheaper than in the foreign country. But through the industry of the society may be thus carried with advantage into a particular channel sooner than it could have been otherwise, it will by no means follow that the sum total, either of its industry, or of its revenue, can ever be augmented by any such regulation. The industry of the society can augment only in proportion as its capital augments, and its capital can augment only in proportion to what can be gradually saved out of its revenue. But the immediate effect of every such regulation is to diminish its revenue, and what diminishes its revenue, is certainly not very likely to augment its capital faster than it would have augmented of its own accord, had both capital and industry been left to find out their natural employments.

Though for want of such regulations the society should never acquire the proposed manufacture, it would not, upon that account, necessarily be the poorer in any one period of its duration. In every period of its duration its whole capital and industry might still have been employed, though upon different objects, in the manner that was most advantageous at the time. In every period its revenue might have been the greatest which its capital could afford, and both capital and revenue might have been augmented with the greatest possible rapidity.

The natural advantages which one country has over another in producing particular commodities are sometimes so great, that it is acknowledged by all the world to be in vain to struggle with them. By means of glasses, hotbeds, and hotwalls, very good grapes can be raised in Scotland, and very good wine too can be made of them at about thirty times the expence for which at least equally good can be brought from foreign countries. Would it be a reasonable law to prohibit the importation of all foreign wines, merely to encourage the making of claret and burgundy in Scotland? But if there would be a manifest absurdity in turning towards any employment, thirty times more of the capital and industry of the country, than would be necessary to purchase from foreign countries an equal quantity of the commodities wanted, there must be an absurdity, though not altogether so glaring, yet exactly of the same kind, in turning towards any such employment a thirtieth, or even a three hundredth part more of either. Whether the advantages which one country has over another, be natural or acquired, is in this respect of no consequence. As long as the one country has those advantages, and the other wants them, it will always be more advantageous for the latter, rather to buy of the former than to make. It is an acquired advantage only, which one artificer has over his neighbour, who exercises another trade; and yet they both find it more advantageous to buy of one another, than to make what does not belong to their particular trades. . . .

The case in which it may sometimes be a matter of deliberation how far it is proper to continue the free importation of certain foreign goods, is, when some foreign nation restrains by high duties or prohibitions the importation of some of our manufactures into their country. Revenge in this case naturally dictates retaliation, and that we should impose the like duties and prohibitions upon the importation of some or all of their manufactures into ours. Nations, accordingly seldom fail to retaliate in this manner. The French have been particularly forward to favour their own manufactures by restraining the importation of such foreign goods as could come into competition with them. In this consisted a great part of the policy of Mr. Colbert,* who, notwithstanding his great abilities, seems in this case to have been imposed upon by the sophistry of merchants and manufacturers, who are always demanding of monopoly against their countrymen. It is at present the opinion of the most intelligent men in France that his operations of this kind have not been beneficial to his country. That minister, by the tarif of 1667, imposed very high duties upon a great number of foreign manufactures. Upon his refusing to moderate them in favour of the Dutch, they in 1671 prohibited the importation of the wines, brandies, and manufactures of France. The war of 1672* seems to have been in part occasioned by this commercial dispute. The peace of Nimeguen put an end to it in 1678, by moderating some of those duties in favour of the Dutch, who in consequence took off their prohibition. It was about the same time that the French and English began mutually to oppress each other's industry, by the like duties and prohibitions, of which the French, however, seem to have set the first example. The spirit of hostility which has subsisted between the two nations ever since,* has hitherto hindered them from being moderated on either side. In 1697 the English prohibited the importation of bonelace, the manufacture of Flanders. The government of that country, at that time under the dominion of Spain, prohibited in return the importation of English woollens. In 1700, the prohibition of importing bone-lace into England, was taken off upon condition that the importation of English woollens into Flanders should be put on the same footing as before.

There may be good policy in retaliations of this kind, when there is a probability that they will procure the repeal of the high duties or prohibitions complained of. The recovery of a great foreign market will generally more than compensate the transitory inconveniency of paying dearer during a short time for some sorts of goods. To judge whether such retaliations are likely to produce such an effect, does not, perhaps, belong so much to the science of a legislator, whose deliberations ought to be governed by general principles which are always the same, as to the skill of that insidious and crafty animal, vulgarly called a statesman or politician,* whose councils are directed by the momentary fluctuations of affairs. When there is no probability that any such repeal can be procured, it seems a bad method of compensating the injury done to certain classes of our people, to do another injury ourselves, not only to those classes, but to almost all the other classes of them. When our neigh-bours prohibit some manufacture of ours, we generally pro-hibit, not only the same, for that alone would seldom affect them considerably, but some other manufacture of theirs. This may no doubt give encouragement to some particular class of workmen among ourselves, and by excluding some of their rivals, may enable them to raise their price in the home-market. Those workmen, however, who suffered by our neighbours prohibition will not be benefited by ours. On the contrary, they and almost all the other classes of our citizens will thereby be obliged to pay dearer than before for certain goods. Every such law, therefore, imposes a real tax upon the whole country, not in favour of that particular class of workmen who were injured by our neighbours prohibition, but of some other class.

The case in which it may sometimes be a matter of deliberation, how far, or in what manner it is proper to restore the free importation of foreign goods, after it has been for some time interrupted, is, when particular manufactures, by means of high duties or prohibitions upon all foreign goods which can come into competition with them, have been so far extended as to employ a great multitude of hands. Humanity may in this case require that the freedom of trade should be restored only by slow gradations, and with a good deal of reserve and circumspection. Were those high duties and prohibitions taken away all at once, cheaper foreign goods of the same kind might be poured so fast into the home market, as to deprive all at once many thousands of our people of their ordinary employment and means of subsistence. The disorder which this would occasion might no doubt be very considerable. It would in all probability, however, be much less than is commonly imagined, for the two following reasons:

First, all those manufactures, of which any part is commonly exported to other European countries without a bounty, could be very little affected by the freest importation of foreign goods. Such manufactures must be sold as cheap abroad as any other foreign goods of the same quality and kind, and consequently must be sold cheaper at home. They would still, therefore, keep possession of the home market, and though a capricious man of fashion might sometimes prefer foreign wares, merely because they were foreign, to cheaper and better goods of the same kind that were made at home, this folly could, from the nature of things, extend to so few, that it could make no sensible impression upon the general employment of the people. But a great part of all the different branches of our woollen manufacture, of our tanned leather, and of our hardware, are annually exported to other European countries without any bounty, and these are the manufactures which employ the greatest number of hands. The silk, perhaps, is the manufacture which would suffer the most by this freedom of trade, and after it the linen, though the latter much less than the former.

Secondly, though a great number of people should, by thus restoring the freedom of trade, be thrown all at once out of their ordinary employment and common method of subsistence, it would by no means follow that they would thereby be deprived either of employment or subsistence. By the reduction of the army and navy at the end of the late war* more than a hundred thousand soldiers and seamen, a number equal to what is employed in the greatest manufactures, were all at once thrown out of their ordinary employment; but, though they no doubt suffered some inconveniency, they were not thereby deprived of all employment and subsistence. The greater part of the seamen, it is probable, gradually betook themselves to the merchant-service as they could find occasion, and in the mean time both they and the soldiers were absorbed in the great mass of the people, and employed in a great variety of occupations. Not only no great convulsion, but no sensible disorder arose from so great a change in the situation of more than a hundred thousand men, all accustomed to the use of arms, and many of them to rapine and plunder. The number of vagrants was scarce anywhere sensibly increased by it, even the wages of labour were not reduced by it in any occupation, so far as I have been able to learn, except in that of seamen in the merchant-service. But if we compare together the habits of a soldier and of any sort of manufacturer, we shall find that those of the latter do not tend so much to disqualify him from being employed in a new trade, as those of the former from being employed in any. The manufacturer has always been accustomed to look for his subsistence from his labour only: the soldier to expect it from his pay. Application and industry have been familiar to the one; idleness and dissipation to the other. But it is surely much easier to change the direction of industry from one sort of labour to another, than to turn idleness and dissipation to any. To the greater part of manufactures besides, it has already been observed,* there are other collateral manufactures of so similar a nature, that a workman can easily transfer his industry from one of them to another. The greater part of such workmen too are occasionally employed in country labour. The stock which employed them in a particular manufacture before, will still remain in the country to employ an equal number of people in some other way. The capital of the country remaining the same, the demand for labour will likewise be the same, or very nearly the same, though it may be exerted in different places and for different occupations. Soldiers and seamen, indeed, when discharged from the king's service, are at liberty to exercise any trade, within any town or place of Great Britain or Ireland.* Let the same natural liberty of exercising what species of industry they please be restored to all his majesty's subjects, in the same manner as to soldiers and seamen; that is, break down the exclusive privileges of corporations, and repeal the statute of apprenticeship, both which are real encroachments upon natural liberty, and add to these the repeal of the law of settlements,* so that a poor workman, when thrown out of employment either in one trade or in one place, may seek for it in another trade or in another place, without the fear either of a prosecution or of a removal, and neither the publick nor the individuals will suffer much more from the occasional disbanding some particular classes of manufacturers, than from that of soldiers. Our manufacturers have no doubt great merit with their country, but they cannot have more than those who defend it with their blood, nor deserve to be treated with more delicacy.

To expect, indeed, that the freedom of trade should ever be entirely restored in Great Britain, is as absurd as to expect that an Oceana or Utopia* should ever be established in it. Not only the prejudices of the publick, but what is much more unconquerable, the private interests of many individuals, irresistibly oppose it. Were the officers of the army to oppose with the same zeal and unanimity any reduction in the number of forces, with which master manufacturers set themselves against every law that is likely to increase the number of their rivals in the home market; were the former to animate their soldiers, in the same manner as the latter enflame their workmen, to attack with violence and outrage the proposers of any such regulation; to attempt to reduce the army would be as dangerous as it has now become to attempt to diminish in any respect the monopoly which our manufacturers have obtained against us. This monopoly has so much increased the number of some particular tribes of them, that, like an overgrown standing army, they have become formidable to the government, and upon many occasions intimidate the legislature.* The member of parliament who supports every proposal for strengthening this monopoly, is sure to acquire not only the reputation of understanding trade, but great popularity and influence with an order of men whose numbers and wealth render them of great importance. If he opposes them, on the contrary, and still more if he has authority enough to be able to thwart them, neither the most acknowledged probity, nor the highest rank, nor the greatest publick services can protect him from the most infamous abuse and detraction, from personal insults, nor sometimes from real danger, arising from the insolent outrage of furious and disappointed monopolists.

The undertaker of a great manufacture who, by the home markets being suddenly laid open to the competition of foreigners, should be obliged to abandon his trade, would no doubt suffer very considerably. That part of his capital which had usually been employed in purchasing materials and in paying his workmen, might, without much difficulty, perhaps, find another employment. But that part of it which was fixed in workhouses, and in the instruments of trade, could scarce be disposed of without considerable loss. The equitable regard, therefore, to his interest requires that changes of this kind should never be introduced suddenly, but slowly, gradually, and after a very long warning. The legislature, were it possible that its deliberations could be always directed, not by the clamorous importunity of partial interests, but by an extensive view of the general good, ought upon this very account, perhaps, to be particularly careful neither to establish any new monopolies of this kind, nor to extend further those which are already established. Every such regulation introduces some degree of real disorder into the constitution of the state, which it will be difficult afterwards to cure without occasioning another disorder.

How far it may be proper to impose taxes upon the importation of foreign goods, in order, not to prevent their importation, but to raise a revenue for government, I shall consider hereafter when I come to treat of taxes.* Taxes imposed with a view to prevent, or even to diminish importation, are evidently as destructive of the revenue of the customs as of the freedom of trade.

CHAPTER III

Of the extraordinary Restraints upon the Importation of Goods of almost all Kinds, from those Countries with which the Balance is supposed to be disadvantageous

PART I

Of the Unreasonableness of those Restraints even upon the Principles of the Commercial System

TO lay extraordinary restraints upon the importation of goods of almost all kinds, from those particular countries with which the balance of trade is supposed to be disadvantageous, is the second expedient by which the commercial system proposes to increase the quantity of gold and silver. Thus in Great Britain Silesia lawns* may be imported for home consumption, upon paying certain duties. But French cambricks* and lawns are prohibited to be imported, except into the port of London, there to be warehoused for exportation. Higher duties are imposed upon the wines of France than upon those of Portugal, or indeed of any other country. By what is called the impost 1692, a duty of five and twenty per cent., of the rate value, was laid upon all French goods;* while the goods of other nations were, the greater part of them, subjected to much lighter duties, seldom exceeding five per cent. The wine, brandy, salt and vinegar of France were indeed excepted; these commodities being subjected to other heavy duties, either by other laws, or by particular clauses of the same law. In 1696, a second duty of twenty-five per cent., the first not having been thought a sufficient discouragement, was imposed upon all French goods, except brandy; together with a new duty of five and twenty pounds upon the ton of French wine, and another of fifteen pounds upon the ton of French vinegar.

French goods have never been omitted in any of those general subsidies, or duties of five per cent., which have been imposed upon all, or the greater part of the goods enumerated in the book of rates. If we count the one third and two third subsidies* as making a compleat subsidy between them, there have been five of these general subsidies; so that before the commencement of the present war seventy-five per cent. may be considered as the lowest duty, to which the greater part of the goods of the growth, produce, or manufacture of France were liable. But upon the greater part of goods, those duties are equivalent to a prohibition. The French in their turn have, I believe, treated our goods and manufactures just as hardly; though I am not so well acquainted with the particular hardships which they have imposed upon them. Those mutual restraints have put an end to almost all fair commerce between the two nations, and smugglers are now the principal importers,* either of British goods into France, or of French goods into Great Britain. The principles which I have been examining in the foregoing chapter took their origin from private interest and the spirit of monopoly; those which I am going to examine in this, from national prejudice and animosity. They are, accordingly, as might well be expected, still more unreasonable. They are so, even upon the principles of the commercial system.*

First, though it were certain that in the case of a free trade between France and England, for example, the balance would be in favour of France, it would by no means follow that such a trade would be disadvantageous to England, or that the general balance of its whole trade would thereby be turned more against it. If the wines of France are better and cheaper than those of Portugal, or its linens than those of Germany, it would be more advantageous for Great Britain to purchase both the wine and the foreign linen which it had occasion for of France, than of Portugal and Germany. Though the value of the annual importations from France would thereby be greatly augmented, the value of the whole annual importations would be diminished, in proportion as the French goods of the same quality were cheaper than those of the other two countries. This would be the case, even upon the supposition that the whole French goods imported were to be consumed in Great Britain.

But, secondly, a great part of them might be re-exported to other countries, where, being sold with profit, they might bring back a return equal in value, perhaps, to the prime cost of the whole French goods imported. What has frequently been said of the East India trade* might possibly be true of the French; that though the greater part of East India goods were bought with gold and silver, the re-exportation of a part of them to other countries, brought back more gold and silver to that which carried on the trade than the prime cost of the whole amounted to. One of the most important branches of the Dutch trade, at present, consists in the carriage of French goods to other European countries. Some part even of the French wine drank in Great Britain is clandestinely imported from Holland and Zealand. If there was either a free trade between France and England, or if French goods could be imported upon paying only the same duties as those of other European nations, to be drawn back upon exportation, England might have some share of a trade which is found so advantageous to Holland.

Thirdly, and lastly, there is no certain criterion by which we can determine on which side what is called the balance between any two countries lies, or which of them exports to the greatest value. National prejudice and animosity, prompted always by the private interest of particular traders, are the principles which generally direct our judgment upon all questions concerning it. . . .

PART II

Of the Unreasonableness of those extraordinary Restraints upon other Principles

. . . It is a losing trade, it is said, which a workman carries on with the alehouse; and the trade which a manufacturing nation would naturally carry on with a wine country, may be considered as a trade of the same nature. I answer, that the trade with the alehouse is not necessarily a losing trade. In its own nature it is just as advantageous as any other, though, perhaps, somewhat more liable to be abused.* The employment of a brewer, and even that of a retailer of fermented liquors, are as necessary divisions of labour as any other. It will generally be more advantageous for a workman to buy of the brewer the quantity he has occasion for, than to brew it himself, and if he is a poor workman, it will generally be more advantageous for him to buy it, by little and little of the retailer, than a large quantity of the brewer. He may no doubt buy too much of either, as he may of any other dealers in his neighbourhood, of the butcher, if he is a glutton, or of the draper, if he affects to be a beau among his companions. It is advantageous to the great body of workmen, notwithstanding, that all these trades should be free, though this freedom may be abused in all of them, and is more likely to be so, perhaps, in some than in others. Though individuals, besides, may sometimes ruin their fortunes by an excessive consumption of fermented liquors, there seems to be no risk that a nation should do so. Though in every country there are many people who spend upon such liquors more than they can afford, there are always many more who spend less. It deserves to be remarked too that, if we consult experience, the cheapness of wine seems to be a cause, not of drunkenness, but of sobriety. The inhabitants of the wine countries are in general the soberest people in Europe; witness the Spaniards, the Italians, and the inhabitants of the southern provinces of France. People are seldom guilty of excess in what is their daily fare. Nobody affects the character of liberality and good fellowship, by being profuse of a liquor which is as cheap as small beer.* On the contrary, in the countries which, either from excessive heat or cold, produce no grapes, and where wine consequently is dear and a rarity, drunkenness is a common vice, as among the northern nations,* and all those who live between the tropics, the negroes, for example, on the coast of Guinea. When a French regiment comes from some of the northern provinces of France, where

wine is somewhat dear, to be quartered in the southern, where
it is very cheap, the soldiers, I have frequently heard it
observed, are at first debauched by the cheapness and novelty
of good wine; but after a few months residence, the greater
part of them become as sober as the rest of the inhabitants.
Were the duties upon foreign wines, and the excises upon malt,
beer, and ale, to be taken away all at once, it might, in the
same manner, occasion in Great Britain a pretty general and
temporary drunkenness among the middling and inferior ranks
of people, which would probably be soon followed by a permanent and almost universal sobriety.* At present drunkenness
is by no means the vice of people of fashion, or of those who
can easily afford the most expensive liquors. A gentleman
drunk with ale, has scarce ever been seen among us. The
restraints upon the wine trade in Great Britain, besides, do not
so much seem calculated to hinder the people from going, if I
may say so, to the alehouse, as from going where they can buy
the best and cheapest liquor. They favour the wine trade of
Portugal, and discourage that of France. The Portuguese, it is
said, indeed, are better customers for our manufactures than
the French, and should therefore be encouraged in preference
to them. As they give us their custom, it is pretended, we
should give them ours. The sneaking arts of underling tradesmen are thus erected into political maxims for the conduct of
a great empire: for it is the most underling tradesmen only
who make it a rule to employ chiefly their own customers. A
great trader purchases his goods always where they are cheapest
and best, without regard to any little interest of this kind.

By such maxims as these, however, nations have been taught
that their interest consisted in beggaring all their neighbours.
Each nation has been made to look with an invidious eye upon
the prosperity of all the nations with which it trades, and to
consider their gain as its own loss. Commerce, which ought
naturally to be, among nations, as among individuals, a bond
of union and friendship,* has become the most fertile source
of discord and animosity. The capricious ambition of kings and
ministers has not, during the present and the preceding cen-

tury, been more fatal to the repose of Europe, than the impertinent jealousy of merchants and manufacturers. The violence and injustice of the rulers of mankind is an ancient evil, for which, I am afraid, the nature of human affairs can scarce admit of a remedy. But the mean rapacity, the monopolizing spirit of merchants and manufacturers, who neither are, nor ought to be the rulers of mankind, though it cannot perhaps be corrected, may very easily be prevented from disturbing the tranquillity of any body but themselves.

That it was the spirit of monopoly which originally both invented and propagated this doctrine, cannot be doubted; and they who first taught it were by no means such fools as they who believed it. In every country it always is and must be the interest of the great body of the people to buy whatever they want of those who sell it cheapest. The proposition is so very manifest, that it seems ridiculous to take any pains to prove it; nor could it ever have been called in question, had not the interested sophistry of merchants and manufacturers confounded the common sense of mankind. Their interest is, in this respect, directly opposite to that of the great body of the people.* As it is the interest of the freemen of a corporation to hinder the rest of the inhabitants from employing any workmen but themselves, so it is the interest of the merchants and manufacturers of every country to secure to themselves the monopoly of the home market. Hence in Great Britain, and in most other European countries, the extraordinary duties upon almost all goods imported by alien merchants. Hence the high duties and prohibitions upon all those foreign manufactures which can come into competition with our own. Hence too the extraordinary restraints upon the importation of almost all sorts of goods from those countries with which the balance of trade is supposed to be disadvantageous; that is, from those against whom national animosity happens to be most violently inflamed.

The wealth of a neighbouring nation, however, though dangerous in war and politicks, is certainly advantageous in trade. In a state of hostility it may enable our enemies to maintain fleets and armies superior to our own; but in a state of peace and commerce it must likewise enable them to exchange with us to a greater value, and to afford a better market, either for the immediate produce of our own industry, or for whatever is purchased with that produce. As a rich man is likely to be a better customer to the industrious people in his neighbourhood, than a poor, so is likewise a rich nation. A rich man, indeed, who is himself a manufacturer, is a very dangerous neighbour to all those who deal in the same way. All the rest of the neighbourhood, however, by far the greatest number, profit by the good market which his expence affords them. They even profit by his under-selling the poorer workmen who deal in the same way with him. The manufacturers of a rich nation, in the same manner, may no doubt be very dangerous rivals to those of their neighbours. This very competition, however, is advantageous to the great body of the people, who profit greatly besides by the good market which the great expence of such a nation affords them in every other way. Private people who want to make a fortune, never think of retiring to the remote and poor provinces of the country, but resort either to the capital or to some of the great commercial towns. They know, that, where little wealth circulates, there is little to be got, but that where a great deal is in motion, some share of it may fall to them. The same maxims which would in this manner direct the common sense of one, or ten, or twenty individuals, should regulate the judgment of one, or ten, or twenty millions, and should make a whole nation regard the riches of its neighbours, as a probable cause and occasion for itself to acquire riches. A nation that would enrich itself by foreign trade is certainly most likely to do so when its neighbours are all rich, industrious, and commercial nations. A great nation surrounded on all sides by wandering savages and poor barbarians might, no doubt, acquire riches by the cultivation of its own lands, and by its own interior commerce, but not by foreign trade. It seems to have been in this manner that the antient Egyptians and the modern Chinese* acquired their great wealth. The antient Egyptians, it is said, neglected foreign commerce, and the modern Chinese, it is known, hold it in the utmost contempt, and scarce deign to afford it the decent protection of the laws. The modern maxims of foreign commerce, by aiming at the impoverishment of all our neighbours, so far as they are capable of producing their intended effect, tend to render that very commerce insignificant and contemptible.

It is in consequence of these maxims that the commerce between France and England has in both countries been subjected to so many discouragements and restraints. If those two countries, however, were to consider their real interest, without either mercantile jealousy or national animosity, the commerce of France might be more advantageous to Great Britain than that of any other country, and for the same reason that of Great Britain to France. France is the nearest neighbour to Great Britain. In the trade between the southern coast of England and the northern and north-western coasts of France, the returns might be expected, in the same manner as in the inland trade, four, five, or six times in the year. The capital, therefore, employed in this trade, could in each of the two countries keep in motion four, five, or six times the quantity of industry, and afford employment and subsistence to four, five, or six times the number of people, which an equal capital could do in the greater part of the other branches of foreign trade. Between the parts of France and Great Britain most remote from one another, the returns might be expected, at least, once in the year, and even this trade would so far be at least equally advantageous as the greater part of the other branches of our foreign European trade. It would be, at least, three times more advantageous, than the boasted trade with our North American colonies, in which the returns were seldom made in less than three years, frequently not in less than four or five years.* France, besides, is supposed to contain twenty-four millions of inhabitants. Our North American colonies were never supposed to contain more than three millions:* And France is a much richer country than North America; though, on account of the more unequal distribution of riches, there is much more poverty and beggary in the one country, than in the other. France, therefore, could afford a market at least eight times more extensive, and, on account of the superior frequency of the returns, four and twenty times more advantageous, than that which our North American colonies ever afforded. The trade of Great Britain would be just as advantageous to France, and, in proportion to the wealth, population and proximity of the respective countries, would have the same superiority over that which France carries on with her own colonies. Such is the very great difference between that trade which the wisdom of both nations has thought proper to discourage, and that which it has favoured the most.

But the very same circumstances which would have rendered an open and free commerce between the two countries so advantageous, to both, have occasioned the principal obstructions to that commerce. Being neighbours, they are necessarily enemies, and the wealth and power of each becomes, upon that account, more formidable to the other; and what would increase the advantage of national friendship, serves only to inflame the violence of national animosity. They are both rich and industrious nations; and the merchants and manufacturers of each, dread the competition of the skill and activity of those of the other. Mercantile jealousy is excited, and both inflames, and is itself inflamed, by the violence of national animosity: And the traders of both countries have announced, with all the passionate confidence of interested falsehood, the certain ruin of each, in consequence of that unfavourable balance of trade, which, they pretend, would be the infallible effect of an unrestrained commerce with the other.

There is no commercial country in Europe of which the approaching ruin has not frequently been foretold by the pretended doctors of this system, from an unfavourable balance of trade. After all the anxiety, however, which they have excited about this, after all the vain attempts of almost all trading nations to turn that balance in their own favour and against their neighbours, it does not appear that any one nation in Europe has been in any respect impoverished by this cause.

Every town and country, on the contrary, in proportion as they have opened their ports to all nations; instead of being ruined by this free trade, as the principles of the commercial system would lead us to expect, have been enriched by it. Though there are in Europe, indeed, a few towns which in some respects deserve the name of free ports, there is no country which does so. Holland, perhaps, approaches the nearest to this character of any, though still very remote from it; and Holland, it is acknowledged, not only derives its whole wealth, but a great part of its necessary subsistence, from foreign trade.

There is another balance, indeed, which has already been explained, very different from the balance of trade, and which, according as it happens to be either favourable or unfavourable, necessarily occasions the prosperity or decay of every nation. This is the balance of the annual produce and consumption. If the exchangeable value of the annual produce, it has already been observed, exceeds that of the annual consumption, the capital of the society must annually increase in proportion to this excess. The society in this case lives within its revenue, and what is annually saved out of its revenue, is naturally added to its capital, and employed so as to increase still further the annual produce. If the exchangeable value of the annual produce, on the contrary, fall short of the annual consumption, the capital of the society must annually decay in proportion to this deficiency. The expence of the society in this case exceeds its revenue, and necessarily encroaches upon its capital. Its capital, therefore, must necessarily decay, and, together with it, the exchangeable value of the annual produce of its industry.

This balance of produce and consumption is entirely different from, what is called, the balance of trade. It might take place in a nation which had no foreign trade, but which was entirely separated from all the world. It may take place in the whole globe of the earth, of which the wealth, population, and improvement may be either gradually increasing or gradually decaying.

The balance of produce and consumption may be constantly in favour of a nation, though what is called the balance of trade be generally against it. A nation may import to a greater value than it exports for half a century, perhaps, together; the gold and silver which comes into it during all this time may be all immediately sent out of it; its circulating coin may gradually decay, different sorts of paper money* being substituted in its place, and even the debts too which it contracts in the principal nations with whom it deals, may be gradually increasing; and yet its real wealth, the exchangeable value of the annual produce of its lands and labour, may, during the same period, have been increasing in a much greater proportion. The state of our North American colonies,* and of the trade which they carried on with Great Britain, before the commencement of the present disturbances,[14] may serve as a proof that this is by no means an impossible supposition.

[14] This paragraph was written in the year 1775. [Britain and North America were at war from 1776.]

[Chapter IV *Of Drawbacks* has been omitted from this edition.]

CHAPTER V

*Of Bounties**

BOUNTIES upon exportation are, in Great Britain, frequently petitioned for, and sometimes granted to the produce of particular branches of domestick industry. By means of them our merchants and manufacturers, it is pretended, will be enabled to sell their goods as cheap, or cheaper than their rivals in the foreign market. A greater quantity, it is said, will thus be exported, and the balance of trade consequently turned more in favour of our own country. We cannot give our workmen a monopoly in the foreign, as we have done in the home market. We cannot force foreigners to buy their goods, as we have done our own countrymen. The next best expedient, it has been thought, therefore, is to pay them for buying. It is in this manner that the mercantile system proposes to enrich the whole country, and to put money into all our pockets by means of the balance of trade.

Bounties, it is allowed, ought to be given to those branches of trade only which cannot be carried on without them. But every branch of trade in which the merchant can sell his goods for a price which replaces to him, with the ordinary profits of stock, the whole capital employed in preparing and sending them to market, can be carried on without a bounty. Every such branch is evidently upon a level with all the other branches of trade which are carried on without bounties, and cannot therefore require one more than they. Those trades only require bounties in which the merchant is obliged to sell his goods for a price which does not replace to him his capital, together with the ordinary profit; or in which he is obliged to sell them for less than it really costs him to send them to market. The bounty is given in order to make up this loss, and to encourage him to continue, or perhaps to begin, a trade of which the expence is supposed to be greater than the returns, of which every operation eats up a part of the capital employed in it, and which is of such a nature, that, if all other trades resembled it, there would soon be no capital left in the country.

The trades, it is to be observed, which are carried on by means of bounties, are the only ones which can be carried on between two nations for any considerable time together, in such a manner as that one of them shall always and regularly lose, or sell its goods for less than it really costs to send them to market. But if the bounty did not repay to the merchant what he would otherwise lose upon the price of his goods, his own interest would soon oblige him to employ his stock in another way, or to find out a trade in which the price of the goods would replace to him, with the ordinary profit, the capital employed in sending them to market. The effect of bounties, like that of all the other expedients of the mercantile system, can only be to force the trade of a country into a channel much less advantageous than that in which it would naturally run of its own accord.

The ingenious and well-informed author of the tracts upon the corn trade* has shown very clearly, that since the bounty upon the exportation of corn was first established, the price of the corn exported, valued moderately enough, has exceeded that of the corn imported, valued very high, by a much greater sum than the amount of the whole bounties which have been paid during that period. This, he imagines, upon the true principles of the mercantile system, is a clear proof that this forced corn trade is beneficial to the nation; the value of the exportation exceeding that of the importation by a much greater sum than the whole extraordinary expence which the publick has been at in order to get it exported. He does not consider that this extraordinary expence, or the bounty, is the smallest part of the expence which the exportation of corn really costs the society. The capital which the farmer employed in raising it must likewise be taken into the account. Unless the price of the corn when sold in the foreign markets replaces, not only the bounty, but this capital, together with the ordinary profits of stock, the society is a loser by the difference, or the national stock is so much diminished. But the very reason for which it has been thought necessary to grant a bounty, is the supposed insufficiency of the price to do this. . . .

I answer, that whatever extension of the foreign market can be occasioned by the bounty, must, in every particular year, be altogether at the expence of the home market; as every bushel of corn which is exported by means of the bounty, and which would not have been exported without the bounty, would have remained in the home market to increase the consumption, and to lower the price of that commodity. The corn bounty, it is to be observed, as well as every other bounty upon exportation, imposes two different taxes upon the people; first, the tax which they are obliged to contribute, in order to pay the bounty; and secondly, the tax which arises from the advanced price of the commodity in the home-market, and which, as the whole body of the people are purchasers of corn, must, in this particular commodity, be paid by the whole body of the people. In this particular commodity, therefore, this second tax, is by much the heaviest of the two. Let us suppose that, taking one year with another, the bounty of five shillings upon the exportation of the quarter of wheat, raises the price of that commodity in the home-market, only sixpence the bushel,* or four shillings the quarter, higher than it otherways would have been in the actual state of the crop. Even upon this very moderate supposition, the great body of the people, over and above contributing the tax which pays the bounty of five shillings upon every quarter of wheat exported, must pay another of four shillings upon every quarter which they themselves consume. But, according to the very well informed author of the tracts upon the corn-trade, the average proportion of the corn exported to that consumed at home, is not more than that of one to thirty-one. For every five shillings, therefore, which they contribute to the payment of the first tax, they must contribute six pounds four shillings to the payment of the second. So very heavy a tax upon the first necessary of life, must either reduce the subsistence of the labouring poor, or it must occasion some augmentation in their pecuniary wages, proportionable to that in the pecuniary price of their subsistence. So far as it operates in the one way, it must reduce the ability of the labouring poor to educate and bring up their children, and must, so far, tend to restrain the population of the country. So far as it operates in the other, it must reduce the ability of the employers of the poor, to employ so great a number as they otherwise might do, and must, so far, tend to restrain the industry of the country. The extraordinary exportation of corn, therefore, occasioned by the bounty, not only, in every particular year, diminishes the home, just as much as it extends the foreign market and consumption, but, by restraining the population and industry of the country, its final tendency is to stunt and restrain the gradual extension of the home-market; and thereby, in the long run, rather to diminish, than to augment, the whole market and consumption of corn.

This enhancement of the money price of corn, however, it has been thought, by rendering that commodity more profitable to the farmer, must necessarily encourage its production.

I answer, that this might be the case if the effect of the bounty was to raise the real price of corn, or to enable the farmer, with an equal quantity of it, to maintain a greater number of labourers in the same manner, whether liberal, moderate, or scanty, that other labourers are commonly maintained in his neighbourhood. But neither the bounty, it is evident, nor any other human institution, can have any such effect. It is not the real, but the nominal price* of corn, which can in any considerable degree be affected by the bounty. And though the tax which that institution imposes upon the whole body of the people, may be very burdensome to those who pay it, it is of very little advantage to those who receive it.

The real effect of the bounty is not so much to raise the real value of corn, as to degrade the real value of silver;* or to make an equal quantity of it exchange for a smaller quantity, not only of corn, but of all other home-made commodities: for the money price of corn regulates that of all other home-made commodities.

It regulates the money price of labour, which must always be such as to enable the labourer to purchase a quantity of corn sufficient to maintain him and his family either in the liberal, moderate, or scanty manner in which the advancing, stationary or declining circumstances of the society oblige his employers to maintain him.

It regulates the money price of all the other parts of the rude produce of land, which, in every period of improvement, must bear a certain proportion to that of corn, though this proportion is different in different periods. It regulates, for example, the money price of grass and hay, of butcher's meat, of horses, and the maintenance of horses, of land carriage consequently, or of the greater part of the inland commerce of the country.

By regulating the money price of all the other parts of the rude produce of land, it regulates that of the materials of almost all manufactures. By regulating the money price of labour, it regulates that of manufacturing art and industry. And by regulating both, it regulates that of the compleat manufacture. The money price of labour, and of every thing that is the produce either of land or labour, must necessarily either rise or fall in proportion to the money price of corn.

Though in consequence of the bounty, therefore, the farmer should be enabled to sell his corn for four shillings the bushel instead of three and sixpence, and to pay his landlord a money rent proportionable to this rise in the money price of his produce; yet if, in consequence of this rise in the price of corn, four shillings will purchase no more home-made goods of any other kind than three and sixpence would have done before, neither the circumstances of the farmer, nor those of the landlord, will be much mended by this change. The farmer will not be able to cultivate much better: the landlord will not be able to live much better. In the purchase of foreign commodities this enhancement in the price of corn may give them some little advantage. In that of home-made commodities it can give them none at all. And almost the whole expence of the farmer, and the far greater part, even of that of the landlord, is in home-made commodities. . . .

There is, perhaps, but one set of men in the whole common-wealth to whom the bounty either was or could be essentially serviceable. These were the corn merchants, the exporters and importers of corn. In years of plenty the bounty necessarily occasioned a greater exportation than would otherwise have taken place; and by hindering the plenty of one year from relieving the scarcity of another, it occasioned in years of scarcity a greater importation than would otherwise have been necessary. It increased the business of the corn merchant in both; and in years of scarcity, it not only enabled him to import a greater quantity, but to sell it for a better price, and consequently with a greater profit than he could otherwise have made, if the plenty of one year had not been more or less hindered from relieving the scarcity of another. It is in this set of men, accordingly, that I have observed the greatest zeal for the continuance or renewal of the bounty.

Our country gentlemen, when they imposed the high duties upon the importation of foreign corn, which in times of moderate plenty amount to a prohibition,* and when they established the bounty, seem to have imitated the conduct of our manufacturers. By the one institution, they secured to themselves the monopoly of the home-market, and by the other they endeavoured to prevent that market from ever being over-stocked with their commodity. By both they endeavoured to raise its real value, in the same manner as our manufacturers had, by the like institutions, raised the real value of many different sorts of manufactured goods. They did not perhaps attend to the great and essential difference which nature has established between corn and almost every other sort of goods. When either by the monopoly of the home-market, or by a bounty upon exportation, you enable our woollen or linen manufacturers to sell their goods for somewhat a better price than they otherwise could get for them, you raise, not only the nominal, but the real price of those goods. You render them equivalent to a greater quantity of labour and subsistence, you encrease not only the nominal, but the real profit, the real wealth and revenue of those manufacturers, and you enable them either to live better themselves, or to employ a greater quantity of labour in those particular manufactures. You really encourage those manufactures, and direct towards them a greater quantity of the industry of the country, than what would probably go to them of its own accord. But when by the like institutions you raise the nominal or money-price of corn, you do not raise its real value. You do not increase the real wealth, the real revenue either of our farmers or country gentlemen. You do not encourage the growth of corn, because you do not enable them to maintain and employ more labourers in raising it. The nature of things has stamped upon corn a real value which cannot be altered by merely altering its money price. No bounty upon exportation, no monopoly of the home market, can raise that value. The freest competition cannot lower it. Through the world in general that value is equal to the quantity of labour which it can maintain, and in every particular place it is equal to the quantity of labour which it can maintain in the way, whether liberal, moderate, or scanty, in which labour is commonly maintained in that place. Woollen or linen cloth are not the regulating commodities by which the real value of all other commodities must be finally measured and determined. Corn is. The real value of every other commodity is finally measured and determined by the proportion which its average money price bears to the average money price of corn. The real value of corn does not vary with those variations in its average money price, which sometimes occur from one century to another. It is the real value of silver which varies with them.

Bounties upon the exportation of any home-made commodity are liable, first, to that general objection which may be made to all the different expedients of the mercantile system; the objection of forcing some part of the industry of the country into a channel less advantageous than that in which it would run of its own accord: and, secondly, to the particular objection of forcing it, not only into a channel that is less advantageous, but into one that is actually disadvantageous; the trade which cannot be carried on but by means of a bounty being necessarily a losing trade. The bounty upon the exportation of corn is liable to this further objection, that it can in no respect promote the raising of that particular commodity of which it was meant to encourage the production. When our country gentlemen, therefore, demanded the establishment of the bounty, though they acted in imitation of our merchants and manufacturers, they did not act with that compleat comprehension of their own interest which commonly directs the conduct of those two other orders of people.* They loaded the publick revenue with a very considerable expence; they imposed a very heavy tax upon the whole body of the people; but they did not, in any sensible degree, increase the real value of their own commodity; and by lowering somewhat the real value of silver, they discouraged, in some degree, the general industry of the country, and, instead of advancing, retarded more or less the improvement of their own lands, which necessarily depends upon the general industry of the country.

To encourage the production of any commodity, a bounty upon production, one should imagine, would have a more direct operation, than one upon exportation. It would, besides, impose only one tax upon the people, that which they must contribute in order to pay the bounty. Instead of raising, it would tend to lower the price of the commodity in the home market; and thereby, instead of imposing a second tax upon the people, it might, at least, in part, repay them for what they had contributed to the first. Bounties upon production, however, have been very rarely granted. The prejudices established by the commercial system have taught us to believe, that national wealth arises more immediately from exportation than from production. It has been more favoured accordingly, as the more immediate means of bringing money into the country. Bounties upon production, it has been said too, have been found by experience more liable to frauds than those upon exportation. How far this is true, I know not. That bounties upon exportation have been abused to many fraudulent purposes, is very well known. But it is not the interest of merchants and manufacturers, the great inventors of all these expedients, that the home market should be overstocked with their goods, an event which a bounty upon production might sometimes occasion. A bounty upon exportation, by enabling them to send abroad the surplus part, and to keep up the price of what remains in the home market, effectually prevents this. Of all the expedients of the mercantile system, accordingly, it is the one of which they are the fondest. I have known the different undertakers of some particular works agree privately among themselves to give a bounty out of their own pockets upon the exportation of a certain proportion of the goods which they dealt in. This expedient succeeded so well, that it more than doubled the price of their goods in the home market, notwithstanding a very considerable increase in the produce. The operation of the bounty upon corn must have been wonderfully different, if it has lowered the money price of that commodity. . . .

Digression concerning the Corn Trade and Corn Laws*

I cannot conclude this chapter concerning bounties, without observing that the praises which have been bestowed upon the law which establishes the bounty upon the exportation of corn, and upon that system of regulations which is connected with it, are altogether unmerited. A particular examination of the nature of the corn trade, and of the principal British laws which relate to it, will sufficiently demonstrate the truth of this assertion. The great importance of this subject must justify the length of the digression.

The trade of the corn merchant is composed of four different branches, which, though they may sometimes be all carried on by the same person, are in their own nature four separate and distinct trades. These are, first, the trade of the inland dealer; secondly, that of the merchant importer for home consumption; thirdly, that of the merchant exporter of home produce for foreign consumption; and, fourthly, that of the merchant carrier, or of the importer of corn in order to export it again.

I. The interest of the inland dealer, and that of the great body of the people, how opposite soever they may at first sight

appear, are, even in years of the greatest scarcity, exactly the
same. It is his interest to raise the price of his corn as high as
the real scarcity of the season requires, and it can never be his
interest to raise it higher. By raising the price he discourages
the consumption, and puts every body more or less, but
particularly the inferior ranks of people, upon thrift and good
management. If, by raising it too high, he discourages the
consumption so much that the supply of the season is likely
to go beyond the consumption of the season, and to last for
some time after the next crop begins to come in, he runs the
hazard, not only of losing a considerable part of his corn by
natural causes, but of being obliged to sell what remains of it
for much less than what he might have had for it several
months before. If by not raising the price high enough he
discourages the consumption so little, that the supply of the
season is likely to fall short of the consumption of the season,
he not only loses a part of the profit which he might otherwise
have made, but he exposes the people to suffer before the end
of the season, instead of the hardships of a dearth, the dreadful
horrors of a famine. It is the interest of the people that their
daily, weekly, and monthly consumption, should be proportioned as exactly as possible to the supply of the season. The
interest of the inland corn dealer is the same. By supplying
them, as nearly as he can judge, in this proportion, he is likely
to sell all his corn for the highest price, and with the greatest
profit; and his knowledge of the state of the crop, and of his
daily, weekly, and monthly sales, enable him to judge, with
more or less accuracy, how far they really are supplied in this
manner. Without intending the interest of the people, he is
necessarily led, by a regard to his own interest, to treat them,
even in years of scarcity, pretty much in the same manner as
the prudent master of a vessel is sometimes obliged to treat
his crew.* When he foresees that provisions are likely to run
short, he puts them upon short allowance. Though from excess
of caution he should sometimes do this without any real
necessity, yet all the inconveniencies which his crew can thereby suffer are inconsiderable in comparison of the danger,

misery, and ruin, to which they might sometimes be exposed by a less provident conduct. Though from excess of avarice, in the same manner, the inland corn merchant should sometimes raise the price of his corn somewhat higher than the scarcity of the season requires, yet all the inconveniencies which the people can suffer from this conduct, which effectually secures them from a famine in the end of the season, are inconsiderable in comparison of what they might have been exposed to by a more liberal way of dealing in the beginning of it. The corn merchant himself is likely to suffer the most by this excess of avarice; not only from the indignation which it generally excites against him, but, though he should escape the effects of this indignation, from the quantity of corn which it necessarily leaves upon his hands in the end of the season, and which, if the next season happens to prove favourable, he must always sell for a much lower price than he might otherwise have had.

Were it possible, indeed, for one great company of merchants to possess themselves of the whole crop of an extensive country, it might, perhaps, be their interest to deal with it as the Dutch are said to do with the spiceries of the Molluccas,* to destroy or throw away a considerable part of it, in order to keep up the price of the rest. But it is scarce possible, even by the violence of law, to establish such an extensive monopoly with regard to corn; and, wherever the law leaves the trade free, it is of all commodities the least liable to be engrossed or monopolized by the force of a few large capitals, which buy up the greater part of it. Not only its value far exceeds what the capitals of a few private men are capable of purchasing, but, supposing they were capable of purchasing it, the manner in which it is produced renders this purchase altogether impracticable. As in every civilized country it is the commodity of which the annual consumption is the greatest, so a greater quantity of industry is annually employed in producing corn than in producing any other commodity. When it first comes from the ground too, it is necessarily divided among a greater number of owners than any other commodity; and these owners can never be collected into one place like a number of independent manufacturers, but are necessarily scattered through all the different corners of the country. These first owners either immediately supply the consumers in their own neighbourhood, or they supply other inland dealers who supply those consumers. The inland dealers in corn, therefore, including both the farmer and the baker, are necessarily more numerous than the dealers in any other commodity, and their dispersed situation renders it altogether impossible for them to enter into any general combination.* If in a year of scarcity therefore, any of them should find that he had a good deal more corn upon hand than, at the current price, he could hope to dispose of before the end of the season, he would never think of keeping up this price to his own loss, and to the sole benefit of his rivals and competitors, but would immediately lower it, in order to get rid of his corn before the new crop began to come in. The same motives, the same interests, which would thus regulate the conduct of any one dealer, would regulate that of every other, and oblige them all in general to sell their corn at the price which, according to the best of their judgment, was most suitable to the scarcity or plenty of the season.

Whoever examines, with attention, the history of the dearths and famines which have afflicted any part of Europe, during either the course of the present or that of the two preceding centuries, of several of which we have pretty exact accounts, will find, I believe, that a dearth never has arisen from any combination among the inland dealers in corn, nor from any other cause but a real scarcity, occasioned sometimes, perhaps, and in some particular places, by the waste of war, but in by far the greatest number of cases, by the fault of the seasons; and that a famine has never arisen from any other cause but the violence of government attempting, by improper means, to remedy the inconveniencies of a dearth.

In an extensive corn country, between all the different parts of which there is a free commerce and communication, the scarcity occasioned by the most unfavourable seasons can never be so great as to produce a famine; and the scantiest crop, if managed with frugality and œconomy, will maintain, through the year, the same number of people that are commonly fed in a more affluent manner by one of moderate plenty. The seasons most unfavourable to the crop are those of excessive drought or excessive rain. But, as corn grows equally upon high and low lands, upon grounds that are disposed to be too wet, and upon those that are disposed to be too dry, either the drought or the rain which is hurtful to one part of the country is favourable to another; and though both in the wet and in the dry season the crop is a good deal less than in one more properly tempered, yet in both what is lost in one part of the country is in some measure compensated by what is gained in the other. In rice countries, where the crop not only requires a very moist soil, but where in a certain period of its growing it must be laid under water, the effects of a drought are much more dismal. Even in such countries, however, the drought is, perhaps, scarce ever so universal as necessarily to occasion a famine, if the government would allow a free trade. The drought in Bengal, a few years ago, might probably have occasioned a very great dearth. Some improper regulations, some injudicious restraints imposed by the servants of the East India Company upon the rice trade, contributed, perhaps, to turn that dearth into a famine.*

When the government, in order to remedy the inconveniencies of a dearth, orders all the dealers to sell their corn at what it supposes a reasonable price, it either hinders them from bringing it to market, which may sometimes produce a famine even in the beginning of the season; or if they bring it thither, it enables the people, and thereby encourages them to consume it so fast, as must necessarily produce a famine before the end of the season. The unlimited, unrestrained freedom of the corn trade,* as it is the only effectual preventative of the miseries of a famine, so it is the best palliative of the inconveniencies of a dearth; for the inconveniencies of a real scarcity cannot be remedied; they can only be palliated. No trade deserves more the full protection of the law, and no trade requires it so much; because no trade is so much exposed to popular odium.

In years of scarcity the inferior ranks of people impute their distress to the avarice of the corn merchant, who becomes the object of their hatred and indignation. Instead of making profit upon such occasions, therefore, he is often in danger of being utterly ruined, and of having his magazines* plundered and destroyed by their violence.* It is in years of scarcity, however, when prices are high, that the corn merchant expects to make his principal profit. He is generally in contract with some farmers to furnish him for a certain number of years with a certain quantity of corn at a certain price. This contract price is settled according to what is supposed to be the moderate and reasonable, that is, the ordinary or average price, which, before the late years of scarcity, was commonly about eight-and-twenty-shillings for the quarter of wheat, and for that of other grain in proportion. In years of scarcity, therefore, the corn merchant buys a great part of his corn for the ordinary price, and sells it for a much higher. That this extraordinary profit, however, is no more than sufficient to put his trade upon a fair level with other trades, and to compensate the many losses which he sustains upon other occasions, both from the perishable nature of the commodity itself, and from the frequent and unforeseen fluctuations of its price, seems evident enough, from this single circumstance, that great fortunes are as seldom made in this as in any other trade. The popular odium, however, which attends it in years of scarcity, the only years in which it can be very profitable, renders people of character and fortune averse to enter into it. It is abandoned to an inferior set of dealers; and millers, bakers, mealmen, and meal factors, together with a number of wretched hucksters,* are almost the only middle people that, in the home market, come between the grower and the consumer.

The ancient policy of Europe, instead of discountenancing this popular odium against a trade so beneficial to the publick, seems, on the contrary, to have authorised and encouraged it.

By the 5th and 6th of Edward VI. cap. 14. it was enacted, That whoever should buy any corn or grain with intent to sell it again, should be reputed an unlawful engrosser,* and should, for the first fault, suffer two months imprisonment, and forfeit the value of the corn; for the second, suffer six months imprisonment, and forfeit double the value; and for the third, be set in the pillory, suffer imprisonment during the king's pleasure, and forfeit all his goods and chattels. The ancient policy of most other parts of Europe was no better than that of England.

Our ancestors seem to have imagined that the people would buy their corn cheaper of the farmer than of the corn merchant, who, they were afraid, would require, over and above the price which he paid to the farmer, an exorbitant profit to himself. They endeavoured, therefore, to annihilate his trade altogether. They even endeavoured to hinder as much as possible any middle man of any kind from coming in between the grower and the consumer; and this was the meaning of the many restraints which they imposed upon the trade of those whom they called kidders* or carriers of corn, a trade which nobody was allowed to exercise without a licence ascertaining his qualifications as a man of probity and fair dealing. The authority of three justices of the peace was, by the statute of Edward VI. necessary, in order to grant this licence. But even this restraint was afterwards thought insufficient, and by a statute of Elizabeth,* the privilege of granting it was confined to the quarter-sessions.

The antient policy of Europe endeavoured in this manner to regulate agriculture, the great trade of the country, by maxims quite different from those which it established with regard to manufactures, the great trade of the towns. By leaving the farmer no other customers but either the consumers or their immediate factors, the kidders and carriers of corn, it endeavoured to force him to exercise the trade, not only of a farmer, but of a corn merchant or corn retailer. On the contrary, it in many cases prohibited the manufacturer from exercising the trade of a shop-keeper, or from selling his own goods by retail. It meant by the one law to promote the general interest of the country, or to render corn cheap, without, perhaps, its being well understood how this was to be done. By the other it meant to promote that of a particular order of men, the shopkeepers, who would be so much undersold by the manufacturer, it was supposed, that their trade would be ruined if he was allowed to retail at all.

The manufacturer, however, though he had been allowed to keep a shop, and to sell his own goods by retail, could not have undersold the common shopkeeper. Whatever part of his capital he might have placed in his shop, he must have withdrawn it from his manufacture. In order to carry on his business on a level with that of other people, as he must have had the profit of a manufacturer on the one part, so he must have had that of a shopkeeper upon the other. Let us suppose, for example, that in the particular town where he lived, ten per cent. was the ordinary profit both of manufacturing and shopkeeping stock; he must in this case have charged upon every piece of his own goods which he sold in his shop, a profit of twenty per cent. When he carried them from his workhouse to his shop, he must have valued them at the price for which he could have sold them to a dealer or shop-keeper, who would have bought them by wholesale. If he valued them lower, he lost a part of the profit of his manufac-turing capital. When again he sold them from his shop, unless he got the same price at which a shopkeeper would have sold them, he lost a part of the profit of his shopkeeping capital. Though he might appear, therefore, to make a double profit upon the same piece of goods, yet as these goods made suc-cessively a part of two distinct capitals, he made but a single profit upon the whole capital employed about them; and if he made less than this profit, he was a loser, or did not employ his whole capital with the same advantage as the greater part of his neighbours.

What the manufacturer was prohibited to do, the farmer was in some measure enjoined to do; to divide his capital between two different employments; to keep one part of it in his granaries and stack yard, for supplying the occasional de-mands of the market; and to employ the other in the cultivation of his land. But as he could not afford to employ the latter for less than the ordinary profits of farming stock, so he could as little afford to employ the former for less than the ordinary profits of mercantile stock. Whether the stock which really carried on the business of the corn merchant belonged to the person who was called a farmer, or to the person who was called a corn merchant, an equal profit was in both cases requisite, in order to indemnify its owner for employing it in this manner; in order to put his business upon a level with other trades, and in order to hinder him from having an interest to change it as soon as possible for some other. The farmer, therefore, who was thus forced to exercise the trade of a corn merchant, could not afford to sell his corn cheaper than any other corn merchant would have been obliged to do in the case of a free competition.

The dealer who can employ his whole stock in one single branch of business, has an advantage of the same kind with the workman who can employ his whole labour in one single operation.* As the latter acquires a dexterity which enables him, with the same two hands, to perform a much greater quantity of work; so the former acquires so easy and ready a method of transacting his business, of buying and disposing of his goods, that with the same capital he can transact a much greater quantity of business. As the one can commonly afford his work a good deal cheaper, so the other can commonly afford his goods somewhat cheaper than if his stock and attention were both employed about a greater variety of objects. The greater part of manufacturers could not afford to retail their own goods so cheap as a vigilant and active shop-keeper, whose sole business it was to buy them by wholesale, and to retail them again. The greater part of farmers could still less afford to retail their own corn, or to supply the inhabitants of a town, at perhaps four or five miles distance from the greater part of them, so cheap as a vigilant and active corn merchant, whose sole business it was to purchase corn by wholesale, to collect it into a great magazine, and to retail it again.

The law which prohibited the manufacturer from exercising the trade of a shopkeeper, endeavoured to force this division in the employment of stock to go on faster than it might otherwise have done. The law which obliged the farmer to exercise the trade of a corn merchant, endeavoured to hinder it from going on so fast. Both laws were evident violations of natural liberty, and therefore unjust; and they were both too as impolitick as they were unjust. It is the interest of every society, that things of this kind should never either be forced or obstructed. The man who employs either his labour or his stock in a greater variety of ways than his situation renders necessary, can never hurt his neighbour by underselling him. He may hurt himself, and he generally does so. Jack of all trades will never be rich, says the proverb. But the law ought always to trust people with the care of their own interest, as in their local situations they must generally be able to judge better of it than the legislator can do.* The law, however, which obliged the farmer to exercise the trade of a corn merchant, was by far the most pernicious of the two.

It obstructed, not only that division in the employment of stock which is so advantageous to every society, but it obstructed likewise the improvement and cultivation of the land. By obliging the farmer to carry on two trades instead of one, it forced him to divide his capital into two parts, of which one only could be employed in cultivation. But if he had been at liberty to sell his whole crop to a corn merchant as fast as he could thresh it out, his whole capital might have returned immediately to the land, and have been employed in buying more cattle, and hiring more servants, in order to improve and cultivate it better. But by being obliged to sell his corn by retail, he was obliged to keep a great part of his capital in his granaries and stack yard through the year, and could not, therefore, cultivate so well as with the same capital he might otherwise have done. This law, therefore, necessarily obstructed the improvement of the land, and, instead of tending to render corn cheaper, must have tended to render it scarcer, and therefore dearer, than it would otherwise have been.

After the business of the farmer, that of the corn merchant is in reality the trade which, if properly protected and encouraged, would contribute the most to the raising of corn. It would support the trade of the farmer in the same manner as the trade of the wholesale dealer supports that of the manufacturer.

The wholesale dealer, by affording a ready market to the manufacturer, by taking his goods off his hand as fast as he can make them, and by sometimes even advancing their price to him before he has made them, enables him to keep his whole capital, and sometimes even more than his whole capital, constantly employed in manufacturing, and consequently to manufacture a much greater quantity of goods than if he was obliged to dispose of them himself to the immediate consumers, or even to the retailers. As the capital of the wholesale merchant too is generally sufficient to replace that of many manufacturers, this intercourse between him and them interests the owner of a large capital to support the owners of a great number of small ones, and to assist them in those losses and misfortunes which might otherwise prove ruinous to them.

An intercourse of the same kind universally established between the farmers and the corn merchants, would be attended with effects equally beneficial to the farmer. They would be enabled to keep their whole capitals, and even more than their whole capitals, constantly employed in cultivation. In case of any of those accidents, to which no trade is more liable than theirs, they would find in their ordinary customer, the wealthy corn merchant, a person who had both an interest to support them, and the ability to do it, and they would not, as at present, be entirely dependent upon the forbearance of their landlord, or the mercy of his steward. Were it possible, as perhaps it is not, to establish this intercourse universally, and all at once, were it possible to turn all at once the whole farming stock of the kingdom to its proper business, the cultivation of land, withdrawing it from every other employment into which any part of it may be at present diverted, and were it possible, in order to support and assist upon occasion the operations of this great stock, to provide all at once another stock almost equally great, it is not perhaps very easy to imagine how great, how extensive, and how sudden would be the improvement which this change of circumstances would alone produce upon the whole face of the country.

The statute of Edward VI., therefore, by prohibiting as much as possible any middle man from coming in between the grower and the consumer, endeavoured to annihilate a trade, of which the free exercise is not only the best palliative of the inconveniencies of a dearth, but the best preventative of that calamity: after the trade of the farmer, no trade contributing so much to the growing of corn as that of the corn merchant.

The rigour of this law was afterwards softened by several subsequent statutes, which successively permitted the engrossing of corn when the price of wheat should not exceed twenty, twenty-four, thirty-two, and forty shillings the quarter. At last, by the 15th of Charles II. c. 7. the engrossing or buying of corn in order to sell it again, as long as the price of wheat did not exceed forty-eight shillings the quarter, and that of other grain in proportion, was declared lawful to all persons not being forestallers, that is, not selling again in the same market within three months.* All the freedom which the trade of the inland corn dealer has ever yet enjoyed, was bestowed upon it by this statute. The statute of the twelfth of the present king, which repeals almost all the other ancient laws against engrossers and forestallers, does not repeal the restrictions of this particular statute, which therefore still continue in force.

This statute, however, authorises in some measure two very absurd popular prejudices.

First, it supposes that when the price of wheat has risen so high as forty-eight shillings the quarter, and that of other grain in proportion, corn is likely to be so engrossed as to hurt the people. But from what has been already said, it seems evident enough that corn can at no price be so engrossed by the inland dealers as to hurt the people: and forty-eight shillings the quarter besides, though it may be considered as a very high price, yet in years of scarcity it is a price which frequently takes place immediately after harvest, when scarce any part of the new crop can be sold off, and when it is impossible even for ignorance to suppose that any part of it can be so engrossed as to hurt the people.

Secondly, it supposes that there is a certain price at which corn is likely to be forestalled, that is, bought up in order to be sold again soon after in the same market, so as to hurt the people. But if a merchant ever buys up corn, either going to a particular market or in a particular market, in order to sell it again soon after in the same market, it must be because he judges that the market cannot be so liberally supplied through the whole season as upon that particular occasion, and that the price, therefore, must soon rise. If he judges wrong in this, and if the price does not rise, he not only loses the whole profit of the stock which he employs in this manner, but a part of the stock itself, by the expence and loss which necessarily attend the storing and keeping of corn. He hurts himself, therefore, much more essentially than he can hurt even the particular people whom he may hinder from supplying themselves upon that particular market day, because they may afterwards supply themselves just as cheap upon any other market day. If he judges right, instead of hurting the great body of the people, he renders them a most important service. By making them feel the inconveniencies of a dearth somewhat earlier than they otherwise might do, he prevents their feeling them afterwards so severely as they certainly would do, if the cheapness of price encouraged them to consume faster than suited the real scarcity of the season. When the scarcity is real, the best thing that can be done for the people is to divide the inconveniencies of it as equally as possible through all the different months, and weeks, and days of the year. The interest of the corn merchant makes him study to do this as exactly as he can; and as no other person can have either the same interest, or the same knowledge, or the same abilities to do it so exactly as he, this most important operation of commerce ought to be trusted entirely to him; or, in other words, the corn trade, so far at least as concerns the supply of the home-market, ought to be left perfectly free.

The popular fear of engrossing and forestalling may be compared to the popular terrors and suspicions of witchcraft. The unfortunate wretches accused of this latter crime were not more innocent of the misfortunes imputed to them, than those who have been accused of the former. The law which put an end to all prosecutions against witchcraft, which put it out of any man's power to gratify his own malice by accusing his neighbour of that imaginary crime, seems effectually to have put an end to those fears and suspicions, by taking away the great cause which encouraged and supported them. The law which should restore entire freedom to the inland trade of corn, would probably prove as effectual to put an end to the popular fears of engrossing and forestalling.

The 15th of Charles II. c. 7. however, with all its imperfections, has perhaps contributed more both to the plentiful supply of the home market, and to the increase of tillage, than any other law in the statute book. It is from this law that the inland corn trade has derived all the liberty and protection which it has ever yet enjoyed; and both the supply of the home market, and the interest of tillage, are much more effectually promoted by the inland, than either by the importation or exportation trade.

The proportion of the average quantity of all sorts of grain imported into Great Britain to that of all sorts of grain consumed, it has been computed by the author of the tracts upon the corn trade, does not exceed that of one to five hundred and seventy. For supplying the home market, therefore, the importance of the inland trade must be to that of the importation trade as five hundred and seventy to one.

The average quantity of all sorts of grain exported from Great Britain does not, according to the same author, exceed the one-and-thirtieth part of the annual produce. For the encouragement of tillage, therefore, by providing a market for the home produce, the importance of the inland trade must be to that of the exportation trade as thirty to one.

I have no great faith in political arithmetick,* and I mean not to warrant the exactness of either of these computations. I

mention them only in order to show of how much less consequence, in the opinion of the most judicious and experienced
persons, the foreign trade of corn is than the home trade. The
great cheapness of corn in the years immediately preceding the
establishment of the bounty, may perhaps, with reason, be
ascribed in some measure to the operation of this statute of
Charles II., which had been enacted about five-and-twenty
years before, and which had therefore full time to produce its
effect. . . .

Were all nations to follow the liberal system of free exportation and free importation, the different states into which a great
continent was divided would so far resemble the different
provinces of a great empire. As among the different provinces
of a great empire the freedom of the inland trade appears, both
from reason and experience, not only the best palliative of a
dearth, but the most effectual preventative of a famine; so
would the freedom of the exportation and importation trade be
among the different states into which a great continent was
divided. The larger the continent, the easier the communication
through all the different parts of it, both by land and by water,
the less would any one particular part of it ever be exposed to
either of these calamities, the scarcity of any one country being
more likely to be relieved by the plenty of some other. But
very few countries have entirely adopted this liberal system.
The freedom of the corn trade is almost every where more or
less restrained, and, in many countries, is confined by such
absurd regulations, as frequently aggravate the unavoidable
misfortune of a dearth, into the dreadful calamity of a famine.
The demand of such countries for corn may frequently become
so great and so urgent, that a small state in their neighbourhood, which happened at the same time to be labouring under
some degree of dearth, could not venture to supply them
without exposing itself to the like dreadful calamity. The very
bad policy of one country may thus render it in some measure
dangerous and imprudent to establish what would otherwise be
the best policy in another. The unlimited freedom of exportation, however, would be much less dangerous in great states,

in which the growth being much greater, the supply could seldom be much affected by any quantity of corn that was likely to be exported. In a Swiss canton, or in some of the little states of Italy, it may, perhaps, sometimes be necessary to restrain the exportation of corn. In such great countries as France or England it scarce ever can. To hinder, besides, the farmer from sending his goods at all times to the best market, is evidently to sacrifice the ordinary laws of justice to an idea of publick utility, to a sort of reasons of state; an act of legislative authority which ought to be exercised only, which can be pardoned only in cases of the most urgent necessity.* The price at which the exportation of corn is prohibited, if it is ever to be prohibited, ought always to be a very high price.

The laws concerning corn may every where be compared to the laws concerning religion. The people feel themselves so much interested in what relates either to their subsistence in this life, or to their happiness in a life to come, that government must yield to their prejudices, and, in order to preserve the publick tranquillity, establish that system which they approve of. It is upon this account, perhaps, that we so seldom find a reasonable system established with regard to either of those two capital objects. . . .

That system of laws, therefore, which is connected with the establishment of the bounty, seems to deserve no part of the praise which has been bestowed upon it. The improvement and prosperity of Great Britain, which has been so often ascribed to those laws, may very easily be accounted for by other causes. That security which the laws in Great Britain give to every man that he shall enjoy the fruits of his own labour, is alone sufficient to make any country flourish, notwithstanding these and twenty other absurd regulations of commerce; and this security was perfected by the revolution, much about the same time that the bounty was established.* The natural effort of every individual to better his own condition,* when suffered to exert itself with freedom and security, is so powerful a principle, that it is alone, and without any assistance, not only capable of carrying on the society to wealth and prosperity, but of surmounting a hundred impertinent obstructions with which the folly of human laws too often incumbers its operations; though the effect of these obstructions is always more or less either to encroach upon its freedom, or to diminish its security. In Great Britain industry is perfectly secure; and though it is far from being perfectly free, it is as free or freer than in any other part of Europe.*

Though the period of the greatest prosperity and improvement of Great Britain, has been posterior to that system of laws which is connected with the bounty, we must not upon that account impute it to those laws. It has been posterior likewise to the national debt. But the national debt has most assuredly not been the cause of it.* . . .

[Chapter VI *Of Treaties of Commerce* has been omitted from this edition.]

CHAPTER VII

Of Colonies

PART FIRST

Of the Motives for establishing new Colonies

THE interest which occasioned the first settlement of the different European colonies in America and the West Indies, was not altogether so plain and distinct as that which directed the establishment of those of ancient Greece and Rome.*

All the different states of ancient Greece possessed, each of them, but a very small territory, and when the people in any one of them multiplied beyond what that territory could easily maintain, a part of them were sent in quest of a new habitation in some remote and distant part of the world; the warlike neighbours who surrounded them on all sides, rendering it difficult for any of them to enlarge very much its territory at home. The colonies of the Dorians resorted chiefly to Italy and Sicily, which in the times preceding the foundation of Rome, were inhabited by barbarous and uncivilized nations: those of the Ionians and Eolians, the two other great tribes of the Greeks, to Asia Minor and the islands of the Egean Sea, of which the inhabitants seem at that time to have been pretty much in the same state as those of Sicily and Italy. The mother city, though she considered the colony as a child, at all times entitled to great favour and assistance, and owing in return much gratitude and respect, yet considered it as an emancipated child, over whom she pretended to claim no direct authority or jurisdiction. The colony settled its own form of government, enacted its own laws, elected its own magistrates, and made peace or war with its neighbours as an independent state, which had no occasion to wait for the approbation or consent of the mother city. Nothing can be more plain and

distinct than the interest which directed every such establishment.

Rome, like most of the other ancient republicks, was originally founded upon an Agrarian law, which divided the publick
territory in a certain proportion among the different citizens
who composed the state. The course of human affairs, by
marriage, by succession, and by alienation,* necessarily de-
ranged this original division, and frequently threw the lands,
which had been allotted for the maintenance of many different
families into the possession of a single person. To remedy this
disorder, for such it was supposed to be, a law was made,
restricting the quantity of land which any citizen could possess
to five hundred jugera, about three hundred and fifty English
acres. This law, however, though we read of its having been
executed upon one or two occasions, was either neglected or
evaded, and the inequality of fortunes went on continually
increasing. The greater part of the citizens had no land, and
without it the manners and customs of those times rendered it
difficult for a freeman to maintain his independency. In the
present times, though a poor man has no land of his own, if
he has a little stock, he may either farm the lands of another,
or he may carry on some little retail trade; and if he has no
stock, he may find employment either as a country labourer,
or as an artificer. But, among the ancient Romans, the lands
of the rich were all cultivated by slaves, who wrought under
an overseer, who was likewise a slave; so that a poor freeman
had little chance of being employed either as a farmer or as a
labourer. All trades and manufactures too, even the retail trade,
were carried on by the slaves of the rich for the benefit of
their masters, whose wealth, authority, and protection made it
difficult for a poor freeman to maintain the competition against
them. The citizens, therefore, who had no land, had scarce any
other means of subsistence but the bounties of the candidates
at the annual elections. The tribunes, when they had a mind
to animate the people against the rich and the great, put them
in mind of the antient division of lands, and represented that law
which restricted this sort of private property as the fundamental

law of the republick.* The people became clamorous to get
land, and the rich and the great, we may believe, were perfectly
determined not to give them any part of theirs. To satisfy them
in some measure, therefore, they frequently proposed to send
out a new colony. But conquering Rome was, even upon such
occasions, under no necessity of turning out her citizens to
seek their fortune, if one may say so, through the wide world,
without knowing where they were to settle. She assigned them
lands generally in the conquered provinces of Italy, where,
being within the dominions of the republick, they could never
form any independent state; but were at best but a sort of
corporation, which, though it had the power of enacting bye-
laws for its own government, was at all times subject to
the correction, jurisdiction, and legislative authority of the
mother city. The sending out a colony of this kind, not only
gave some satisfaction to the people, but often established a
sort of garrison too in a newly conquered province, of which
the obedience might otherwise have been doubtful. A Roman
colony, therefore, whether we consider the nature of the establishment itself, or the motives for making it, was altogether
different from a Greek one. The words accordingly, which in
the original languages denote those different establishments,
have very different meanings. The Latin word (*Colonia*) signifies simply a plantation. The Greek word (αποιχια), on the
contrary, signifies a separation of dwelling, a departure from
home, a going out of the house.* But, though the Roman
colonies were in many respects different from the Greek ones,
the interest which prompted to establish them was equally
plain and distinct. Both institutions derived their origin
either from irresistible necessity, or from clear and evident
utility.

The establishment of the European colonies in America and
the West Indies arose from no necessity: and though the utility
which has resulted from them has been very great, it is not
altogether so clear and evident. It was not understood at their
first establishment, and was not the motive either of that
establishment or of the discoveries which gave occasion to it,

and the nature, extent, and limits of that utility are not, perhaps, well understood at this day. . . .

Finding nothing either in the animals or vegetables of the newly discovered countries, which could justify a very advantageous representation of them, Columbus* turned his view towards their minerals; and in the richness of the productions of this third kingdom, he flattered himself, he had found a full compensation for the insignificancy of those of the other two. The little bits of gold with which the inhabitants ornamented their dress, and which, he was informed, they frequently found in the rivulets and torrents that fell from the mountains, were sufficient to satisfy him that those mountains abounded with the richest gold mines. St. Domingo,* therefore, was represented as a country abounding with gold, and, upon that account (according to the prejudices not only of the present times, but of those times), an inexhaustible source of real wealth to the crown and kingdom of Spain. When Columbus, upon his return from his first voyage, was introduced with a sort of triumphal honours to the sovereigns of Castile and Arragon, the principal productions of the countries which he had discovered were carried in solemn procession before him. The only valuable part of them consisted in some little fillets,* bracelets, and other ornaments of gold, and in some bales of cotton. The rest were mere objects of vulgar wonder and curiosity; some reeds of an extraordinary size, some birds of a very beautiful plumage, and some stuffed skins of the huge alligator and manati;* all of which were preceded by six or seven of the wretched natives, whose singular colour and appearance added greatly to the novelty of the shew.*

In consequence of the representations of Columbus, the council of Castile determined to take possession of countries of which the inhabitants were plainly incapable of defending themselves. The pious purpose of converting them to Christianity sanctified the injustice of the project. But the hope of finding treasures of gold there, was the sole motive which prompted to undertake it; and to give this motive the greater weight, it was proposed by Columbus that the half of all the gold and silver that should be found there should belong to the crown. This proposal was approved of by the council.

As long as the whole or the far greater part of the gold, which the first adventurers imported into Europe, was got by so very easy a method as the plundering of the defenceless natives, it was not perhaps very difficult to pay even this heavy tax. But when the natives were once fairly stript of all that they had, which, in St. Domingo, and in all the other countries discovered by Columbus, was done compleatly in six or eight years, and when in order to find more it had become necessary to dig for it in the mines, there was no longer any possibility of paying this tax. The rigorous exaction of it, accordingly, first occasioned, it is said, the total abandoning of the mines of St. Domingo, which have never been wrought since. It was soon reduced therefore to a third; then to a fifth; afterwards to a tenth; and at last to a twentieth part of the gross produce of the gold mines. The tax upon silver continued for a long time to be a fifth of the gross produce. It was reduced to a tenth only in the course of the present century. But the first adventurers do not appear to have been much interested about silver. Nothing less precious than gold seemed worthy of their attention.

All the other enterprizes of the Spaniards in the new world, subsequent to those of Columbus, seem to have been prompted by the same motive. It was the sacred thirst of gold that carried Oieda, Nicuessa, and Vasco Nugnes de Balboa, to the isthmus of Darien, that carried Cortez to Mexico, and Almagro and Pizzarro to Chili and Peru.* When those adventurers arrived upon any unknown coast, their first enquiry was always if there was any gold to be found there; and according to the information which they received concerning this particular, they determined either to quit the country or to settle in it.

Of all those expensive and uncertain projects, however, which bring bankruptcy upon the greater part of the people who engage in them, there is none perhaps more perfectly ruinous than the search after new silver and gold mines. It is perhaps the most disadvantageous lottery in the world, or the one in which the gain of those who draw the prizes bears the least proportion to the loss of those who draw the blanks: for though the prizes are few and the blanks many, the common price of a ticket is the whole fortune of a very rich man. Projects of mining, instead of replacing the capital employed in them, together with the ordinary profits of stock, commonly absorb both capital and profit. They are the projects, therefore, to which of all others a prudent law-giver, who desired to increase the capital of his nation, would least chuse to give any extraordinary encouragement, or to turn towards them a greater share of that capital than what would go to them of its own accord. Such in reality is the absurd confidence which almost all men have in their own good fortune, that wherever there is the least probability of success, too great a share of it is apt to go to them of its own accord. . . .

The first adventurers of all the other nations of Europe, who attempted to make settlements in America, were animated by the like chimerical views; but they were not equally successful. It was more than a hundred years after the first settlement of the Brazils, before any silver, gold, or diamond mines were discovered there. In the English, French, Dutch, and Danish colonies, none have ever yet been discovered; at least none that are at present supposed to be worth the working. The first English settlers in North America, however, offered a fifth of all the gold and silver which should be found there to the king, as a motive for granting them their patents. In the patents to Sir Walter Raleigh,* to the London and Plymouth companies, to the council of Plymouth, &c. this fifth was accordingly reserved to the crown. To the expectation of finding gold and silver mines, those first settlers too joined that of discovering a north-west passage to the East Indies. They have hitherto been disappointed in both.

PART SECOND

Causes of the Prosperity of new Colonies

The colony of a civilized nation which takes possession, either of a waste country, or of one so thinly inhabited, that the natives easily give place to the new settlers, advances more rapidly to wealth and greatness than any other human society.

The colonists carry out with them a knowledge of agriculture and of other useful arts, superior to what can grow up of its own accord in the course of many centuries among savage and barbarous nations. They carry out with them too the habit of subordination, some notion of the regular government which takes place in their own country, of the system of laws which support it, and of a regular administration of justice; and they naturally establish something of the same kind in the new settlement.* But among savage and barbarous nations, the natural progress of law and government is still slower than the natural progress of arts, after law and government have been so far established, as is necessary for their protection. Every colonist gets more land than he can possibly cultivate. He has no rent, and scarce any taxes to pay. No landlord shares with him in its produce, and the share of the sovereign is commonly but a trifle. He has every motive to render as great as possible a produce, which is thus to be almost entirely his own. But his land is commonly so extensive, that with all his own industry, and with all the industry of other people whom he can get to employ, he can seldom make it produce the tenth part of what it is capable of producing. He is eager, therefore, to collect labourers from all quarters, and to reward them with the most liberal wages. But those liberal wages, joined to the plenty and cheapness of land, soon make those labourers leave him in order to become landlords themselves, and to reward, with equal liberality, other labourers, who soon leave them for the same reason that they left their first master. The liberal reward of labour encourages marriage. The children, during the tender years of infancy, are well fed and properly taken care of, and when they are grown up, the value of their labour greatly over-pays their maintenance. When arrived at maturity, the high price of labour, and the low price of land, enable them to establish themselves in the same manner as their fathers did before them.*

In other countries, rent and profit eat up wages, and the two superior orders of people oppress the inferior one. But in new colonies, the interest of the two superior orders obliges them to treat the inferior one with more generosity and humanity; at least, where that inferior one is not in a state of slavery. Waste lands, of the greatest natural fertility, are to be had for a trifle. The increase of revenue which the proprietor, who is always the undertaker, expects from their improvement, constitutes his profit; which in these circumstances is commonly very great. But this great profit cannot be made without employing the labour of other people in clearing and cultivating the land; and the disproportion between the great extent of the land and the small number of the people, which commonly takes place in new colonies, makes it difficult for him to get this labour. He does not, therefore, dispute about wages, but is willing to employ labour at any price. The high wages of labour encourage population. The cheapness and plenty of good land encourage improvement, and enable the proprietor to pay those high wages. In those wages consists almost the whole price of the land; and though they are high, considered as the wages of labour, they are low, considered as the price of what is so very valuable. What encourages the progress of population and improvement, encourages that of real wealth and greatness.*

The progress of many of the antient Greek colonies towards wealth and greatness, seems accordingly to have been very rapid. In the course of a century or two, several of them appear to have rivalled, and even to have surpassed their mother cities. Syracuse and Agrigentum in Sicily, Tarentum and Locri in Italy, Ephesus and Miletus in Lesser Asia, appear by all accounts to have been at least equal to any of the cities of antient Greece. Though posterior in their establishment, yet all the arts of refinement, philosophy, poetry, and eloquence, seem to have been cultivated as early, and to have been improved as highly in them, as in any part of the mother country. The schools of the two oldest Greek philosophers, those of Thales and Pythagoras,* were established, it is remarkable, not in antient Greece, but the one in an Asiatick, the other in an Italian colony. All those colonies had established themselves in countries inhabited by savage and barbarous nations, who easily gave place to the new settlers. They had plenty of good land, and as they were altogether independent of the mother city, they were at liberty to manage their own affairs in the way that they judged was most suitable to their own interest. . . .

But there are no colonies of which the progress has been more rapid than that of the English in North America.

Plenty of good land, and liberty to manage their own affairs their own way, seem to be the two great causes of the prosperity of all new colonies. . . .

To prohibit a great people, however, from making all that they can of every part of their own produce, or from employing their stock and industry in the way that they judge most advantageous to themselves, is a manifest violation of the most sacred rights of mankind.* Unjust, however, as such prohibitions may be, they have not hitherto been very hurtful to the colonies. Land is still so cheap, and, consequently, labour so dear among them, that they can import from the mother country, almost all the more refined or more advanced manufactures cheaper than they could make them for themselves.* Though they had not, therefore, been prohibited from establishing such manufactures, yet in their present state of improvement, a regard to their own interest would, probably, have prevented them from doing so. In their present state of improvement, those prohibitions, perhaps, without cramping their industry, or restraining it from any employment to which it would have gone of its own accord, are only impertinent badges of slavery imposed upon them, without any sufficient reason, by the groundless jealousy of the merchants and manufacturers of the mother country. In a more advanced state they might be really oppressive and insupportable. . . .

But though the policy of Great Britain with regard to the trade of her colonies has been dictated by the same mercantile spirit* as that of other nations, it has, however, upon the whole, been less illiberal and oppressive than that of any of them.

In every thing, except their foreign trade, the liberty of the English colonists to manage their own affairs their own way is complete. It is in every respect equal to that of their fellow-citizens at home, and is secured in the same manner, by an assembly of the representatives of the people, who claim the sole right of imposing taxes for the support of the colony government.* The authority of this assembly over-awes the executive power, and neither the meanest nor the most obnoxious colonist, as long as he obeys the law, has any thing to fear from the resentment, either of the governor, or of any other civil or military officer in the province. The colony assemblies, though, like the house of commons in England, they are not always a very equal representation of the people, yet they approach more nearly to that character; and as the executive power either has not the means to corrupt them, or, on account of the support which it receives from the mother country, is not under the necessity of doing so, they are perhaps in general more influenced by the inclinations of their constituents. The councils, which, in the colony legislatures, correspond to the House of Lords in Great Britain, are not composed of an hereditary nobility. In some of the colonies, as in three of the governments of New England,* those councils are not appointed by the king, but chosen by the representatives of the people. In none of the English colonies is there any hereditary nobility. In all of them, indeed, as in all other free countries, the descendant of an old colony family is more respected than an upstart of equal merit and fortune: but he is only more respected, and he has no privileges by which he can be troublesome to his neighbours. Before the commencement of the present disturbances, the colony assemblies had not only the legislative, but a part of the executive power. In Connecticut and Rhode Island, they elected the governor. In the other colonies they appointed the revenue officers who collected the taxes imposed by those respective assemblies, to whom those officers were immediately responsible. There is more equality, therefore, among the English colonists than among the inhabitants of the mother country. Their manners are more republican, and their governments, those of three of the provinces of New England in particular, have hitherto been more republican too. . . .

It is in the progress of the North American colonies, however, that the superiority of the English policy chiefly appears. The progress of the sugar colonies of France has been at least equal, perhaps superior, to that of the greater part of those of England; and yet the sugar colonies of England enjoy a free government nearly of the same kind with that which takes place in her colonies of North America. But the sugar colonies of France are not discouraged, like those of England, from refining their own sugar; and, what is of still greater importance, the genius of their government naturally introduces a better management of their negro slaves.*

In all European colonies the culture of the sugar-cane is carried on by negro slaves. The constitution of those who have been born in the temperate climate of Europe could not, it is supposed, support the labour of digging the ground under the burning sun of the West Indies; and the culture of the sugar-cane, as it is managed at present, is all hand labour, though, in the opinion of many, the drill plough might be introduced into it with great advantage. But, as the profit and success of the cultivation which is carried on by means of cattle, depend very much upon the good management of those cattle; so the profit and success of that which is carried on by slaves, must depend equally upon the good management of those slaves; and in the good management of their slaves the French planters, I think it is generally allowed, are superior to the English. The law, so far as it gives some weak protection to the slave against the violence of his master, is likely to be better executed in a colony where the government is in a great measure arbitrary, than in one where it is altogether free. In every country where the unfortunate law of slavery is established, the magistrate, when he protects the slave, intermeddles in some measure in the management of the private property of the master; and, in a free country, where the master is perhaps either a member of the colony assembly, or an elector of such a member, he dare not do this but with the greatest caution and circumspection. The respect which he is obliged to pay to the master, renders it more difficult for him to protect the slave. But in a country where the government is in a great measure arbitrary, where it is usual for the magistrate to intermeddle even in the management of the private property of individuals, and to send them, perhaps, a lettre de cachet* if they do not manage it according to his liking, it is much easier for him to give some protection to the slave; and common humanity naturally disposes him to do so. The protection of the magistrate renders the slave less contemptible in the eyes of his master, who is thereby induced to consider him with more regard, and to treat him with more gentleness. Gentle usage renders the slave not only more faithful, but more intelligent, and therefore, upon a double account, more useful. He approaches more to the condition of a free servant, and may possess some degree of integrity and attachment to his master's interest, virtues which frequently belong to free servants, but which never can belong to a slave, who is treated as slaves commonly are in countries where the master is perfectly free and secure.

That the condition of a slave is better under an arbitrary than under a free government, is, I believe, supported by the history of all ages and nations. In the Roman history, the first time we read of the magistrate interposing to protect the slave from the violence of his master, is under the emperors. When Vedius Pollio, in the presence of Augustus,* ordered one of his slaves, who had committed a slight fault, to be cut into pieces and thrown into his fish pond in order to feed his fishes, the emperor commanded him, with indignation, to emancipate immediately, not only that slave, but all the others that belonged to him. Under the republick no magistrate could have had authority enough to protect the slave, much less to punish the master.

The stock, it is to be observed, which has improved the sugar colonies of France, particularly the great colony of St. Domingo, has been raised almost entirely from the gradual improvement and cultivation of those colonies. It has been almost altogether the produce of the soil and of the industry of the colonists, or, what comes to the same thing, the price of that produce gradually accumulated by good management, and employed in raising a still greater produce. But the stock which has improved and cultivated the sugar colonies of England has, a great part of it, been sent out from England, and has by no means been altogether the produce of the soil and industry of the colonists.* The prosperity of the English sugar colonies has been, in a great measure, owing to the great riches of England, of which a part has overflowed, if one may say so, upon those colonies. But the prosperity of the sugar colonies of France has been entirely owing to the good conduct of the colonists, which must therefore have had some superiority over that of the English; and this superiority has been remarked in nothing so much as in the good management of their slaves.

Such have been the general outlines of the policy of the different European nations with regard to their colonies.

The policy of Europe, therefore, has very little to boast of, either in the original establishment, or, so far as concerns their internal government, in the subsequent prosperity of the colonies of America.

Folly and injustice seem to have been the principles which presided over and directed the first project of establishing those colonies; the folly of hunting after gold and silver mines, and the injustice of coveting the possession of a country whose harmless natives, far from having ever injured the people of Europe, had received the first adventurers with every mark of kindness and hospitality.*

The adventurers, indeed, who formed some of the later establishments, joined, to the chimerical project of finding gold and silver mines, other motives more reasonable and more laudable; but even these motives do very little honour to the policy of Europe.

The English puritans, restrained at home, fled for freedom to America, and established there the four governments of New England. The English catholicks, treated with much greater injustice, established that of Maryland; the Quakers, that of Pensylvania. The Portuguese Jews, persecuted by the inquisition, stript of their fortunes, and banished to Brazil,* introduced, by their example, some sort of order and industry among the transported felons and strumpets, by whom that colony was originally peopled, and taught them the culture of the sugar-cane. Upon all these different occasions it was, not the wisdom and policy, but the disorder and injustice of the European governments, which peopled and cultivated America.*

In effectuating some of the most important of these establishments, the different governments of Europe had as little merit as in projecting them. The conquest of Mexico was the project, not of the council of Spain, but of a governor of Cuba;* and it was effectuated by the spirit of the bold adventurer to whom it was entrusted, in spite of every thing which that governor, who soon repented of having trusted such a person, could do to thwart it. The conquerors of Chili and Peru, and of almost all the other Spanish settlements upon the continent of America, carried out with them no other publick encouragement, but a general permission to make settlements and conquests in the name of the king of Spain. Those adventures were all at the private risk and expence of the adventurers. The government of Spain contributed scarce any thing to any of them. That of England contributed as little towards effectuating the establishment of some of its most important colonies in North America.

When those establishments were effectuated, and had become so considerable as to attract the attention of the mother country, the first regulations which she made with regard to them had always in view to secure to herself the monopoly of their commerce; to confine their market, and to enlarge her own at their expence, and, consequently, rather to damp and discourage, than to quicken and forward the course of their prosperity. In the different ways in which this monopoly has been exercised, consists one of the most essential differences in the policy of the different European nations with regard to their colonies. The best of them all, that of England, is only somewhat less illiberal and oppressive than that of any of the rest.

In what way, therefore, has the policy of Europe contributed either to the first establishment, or to the present grandeur of the colonies of America? In one way, and in one way only, it has contributed a good deal. *Magna virûm Mater!** It bred and formed the men who were capable of atchieving such great actions, and of laying the foundation of so great an empire; and there is no other quarter of the world of which the policy is capable of forming, or has ever actually and in fact formed such men. The colonies owe to the policy of Europe the education and great views of their active and enterprizing founders; and some of the greatest and most important of them, so far as concerns their internal government, owe to it scarce any thing else.

PART THIRD

Of the Advantages which Europe has derived from the Discovery of America, and from that of a Passage to the East Indies by the Cape of Good Hope.

... The monopoly of the colony trade besides, by forcing towards it a much greater proportion of the capital of Great Britain than what would naturally have gone to it, seems to have broken altogether that natural balance which would otherwise have taken place among all the different branches of British industry.* The industry of Great Britain, instead of being accommodated to a great number of small markets, has been principally suited to one great market. Her commerce, instead of running in a great number of small channels, has been taught to run principally in one great channel. But the whole system of her industry and commerce has thereby been rendered less secure; the whole state of her body politick less healthful, than it otherwise would have been. In her present condition, Great Britain resembles one of those unwholesome bodies in which some of the vital parts are overgrown, and which, upon that account, are liable to many dangerous disorders scarce incident to those in which all the parts are more properly proportioned. A small stop in that great blood-vessel, which has been artificially swelled beyond its natural dimensions, and through which an unnatural proportion of the industry and commerce of the country has been forced to circulate, is very likely to bring on the most dangerous disorders upon the whole body politick.* The expectation of a rupture with the colonies, accordingly, has struck the people of Great Britain with more terror than they ever felt for a Spanish armada, or a French invasion. It was this terror, whether well or ill grounded, which rendered the repeal of the stamp act,* among the merchants at least, a popular measure. In the total exclusion from the colony market, was it to last only for a few years, the greater part of our merchants used to fancy that they foresaw an entire stop to their trade; the greater part of our master manufacturers, the entire ruin of their business; and the greater part of our workmen, an end of their employment. A rupture with any of our neighbours upon the continent, though likely too to occasion some stop or interruption in the employments of some of all these different orders of people, is foreseen, however, without any such general emotion. The blood, of which the circulation is stopt in some of the smaller vessels, easily disgorges itself into the greater, without occasioning any dangerous disorder; but, when it is stopt in any of the greater vessels, convulsions, apoplexy, or death, are the immediate and unavoidable consequences. If but one of those overgrown manufactures, which by means either of bounties, or of the monopoly of the home and colony markets, have been artificially raised up to an unnatural height, finds some small stop or interruption in its employment, it frequently occasions a mutiny and disorder alarming to government, and embarrassing even to the deliberations of the legislature. How great, therefore, would be the disorder and confusion, it was thought, which must necessarily be occasioned by a sudden and entire stop in the employment of so great a proportion of our principal manufacturers?

Some moderate and gradual relaxation of the laws which give to Great Britain the exclusive trade to the colonies, till it is rendered in a great measure free, seems to be the only expedient which can, in all future times, deliver her from this danger, which can enable her or even force her to withdraw some part of her capital from this overgrown employment, and to turn it, though with less profit, towards other employments; and which, by gradually diminishing one branch of her industry and gradually increasing all the rest, can by degrees restore all the different branches of it to that natural, healthful, and proper proportion which perfect liberty necessarily establishes, and which perfect liberty can alone preserve. To open the colony trade all at once to all nations, might not only occasion some transitory inconveniency, but a great permanent loss to the greater part of those whose industry or capital is at present engaged in it. The sudden loss of the employment even of the ships which import the eighty-two thousand hogsheads of tobacco, which are over and above the consumption of Great Britain,* might alone be felt very sensibly. Such are the unfortunate effects of all the regulations of the mercantile system! They not only introduce very dangerous disorders into the state of the body politick, but disorders which it is often difficult to remedy, without occasioning, for a time at least, still greater disorders. In what manner, therefore, the colony trade ought gradually to be opened; what are the restraints which ought first, and what are those which ought last to be taken away; or in what manner the natural system of perfect liberty and justice ought gradually to be restored, we must leave to the wisdom of future statesmen and legislators to determine. . . .

If the manufactures of Great Britain, however, have been advanced, as they certainly have, by the colony trade, it has not been by means of the monopoly of that trade, but in spite of the monopoly. The effect of the monopoly has been, not to augment the quantity, but to alter the quality and shape of a part of the manufactures of Great Britain, and to accommodate to a market, from which the returns are slow and distant,* what would otherwise have been accommodated to one from which the returns are frequent and near. Its effect has consequently been to turn a part of the capital of Great Britain from an employment in which it would have maintained a greater quantity of manufacturing industry, to one in which it maintains a much smaller, and thereby to diminish, instead of increasing, the whole quantity of manufacturing industry maintained in Great Britain.

The monopoly of the colony trade, therefore, like all the other mean and malignant expedients of the mercantile system, depresses the industry of all other countries, but chiefly that of the colonies, without in the least increasing, but on the contrary diminishing, that of the country in whose favour it is established.

The monopoly hinders the capital of that country, whatever may at any particular time be the extent of that capital, from maintaining so great a quantity of productive labour as it would otherwise maintain, and from affording so great a revenue to the industrious inhabitants as it would otherwise afford. But as capital can be increased only by savings from revenue,* the monopoly, by hindering it from affording so great a revenue as it would otherwise afford, necessarily hinders it from increasing so fast as it would otherwise increase, and consequently from maintaining a still greater quantity of productive labour, and affording a still greater revenue to the industrious inhabitants of that country. One great original source of revenue, therefore, the wages of labour, the monopoly must necessarily have rendered at all times less abundant than it otherwise would have been.

By raising the rate of mercantile profit, the monopoly discourages the improvement of land.* The profit of improvement depends upon the difference between what the land actually produces, and what, by the application of a certain capital, it can be made to produce. If this difference affords a greater profit than what can be drawn from an equal capital in any mercantile employment, the improvement of land will draw capital from all mercantile employments. If the profit is less, mercantile employments will draw capital from the improvement of land. Whatever therefore raises the rate of mercantile profit, either lessens the superiority or increases the inferiority of the profit of improvement; and in the one case hinders capital from going to improvement, and in the other draws capital from it. But by discouraging improvement, the monopoly necessarily retards the natural increase of another great original source of revenue, the rent of land. By raising the rate of profit too the monopoly necessarily keeps up the market rate of interest higher than it otherwise would be. But the price of land in proportion to the rent which it affords, the number of years purchase which is commonly paid for it, necessarily falls as the rate of interest rises, and rises as the rate of interest falls. The monopoly, therefore, hurts the interest of the landlord two different ways, by retarding the natural increase, first, of his rent, and secondly, of the price which he would get for his land in proportion to the rent which it affords.

The monopoly indeed, raises the rate of mercantile profit, and thereby augments somewhat the gain of our merchants. But as it obstructs the natural increase of capital, it tends rather to diminish than to increase the sum total of the revenue which the inhabitants of the country derive from the profits of stock; a small profit upon a great capital generally affording a greater revenue than a great profit upon a small one. The monopoly raises the rate of profit, but it hinders the sum of profit from rising so high as it otherwise would do.

All the original sources of revenue,* the wages of labour, the rent of land, and the profits of stock, the monopoly renders much less abundant than they otherwise would be. To promote the little interest of one little order of men in one country, it hurts the interest of all other orders of men in that country, and of all men in all other countries.

It is solely by raising the ordinary rate of profit that the monopoly either has proved or could prove advantageous to any one particular order of men. But besides all the bad effects to the country in general, which have already been mentioned as necessarily resulting from a high rate of profit; there is one more fatal, perhaps, than all these put together, but which, if we may judge from experience, is inseparably connected with it. The high rate of profit seems every where to destroy that parsimony which in other circumstances is natural to the character of the merchant.* When profits are high, that sober virtue seems to be superfluous, and expensive luxury to suit better the affluence of his situation. But the owners of the great mercantile capitals are necessarily the leaders and conductors of the whole industry of every nation, and their example has a much greater influence upon the manners of the whole industrious part of it than that of any other order of men. If his employer is attentive and parsimonious, the workman is very likely to be so too; but if the master is dissolute and disorderly, the servant who shapes his work according to the pattern which his master prescribes to him, will shape his life too according to the example which he sets him. Accumulation is thus prevented in the hands of all those who are naturally the most disposed to accumulate; and the funds destined for the maintenance of productive labour receive no augmentation from the revenue of those who ought naturally to augment them the most. The capital of the country, instead of increasing, gradually dwindles away, and the quantity of productive labour maintained in it grows every day less and less. Have the exorbitant profits of the merchants of Cadiz and Lisbon augmented the capital of Spain and Portugal? Have they alleviated the poverty, have they promoted the industry of those two beggarly countries?* Such has been the tone of mercantile expence in those two trading cities, that those exorbitant profits, far from augmenting the general capital of the country, seem scarce to have been sufficient to keep up the capitals upon which they were made. Foreign capitals are every day intruding themselves, if I may say so, more and more into the trade of Cadiz and Lisbon. It is to expel those foreign capitals from a trade which their own grows every day more and more insufficient for carrying on, that the Spaniards and Portugueze endeavour every day to straiten more and more the galling bands of their absurd monopoly. Compare the mercantile manners of Cadiz and Lisbon with those of Amsterdam, and you will be sensible how differently the conduct and character of merchants are affected by the high and by the low profits of stock. The merchants of London, indeed, have not yet generally become such magnificent lords as those of Cadiz and Lisbon; but neither are they in general such attentive and parsimonious burghers as those of Amsterdam. They are supposed, however, many of them, to be a good deal richer than the greater part of the former, and not quite so rich as many of the latter. But the rate of their profit is commonly much lower than that of the former, and a good deal higher than that of the latter. Light come light go, says the proverb; and the ordinary tone of expence seems every where to be regulated, not so much according to the real ability of spending, as to the supposed facility of getting money to spend.

It is thus that the single advantage which the monopoly procures to a single order of men is in many different ways hurtful to the general interest of the country.

To found a great empire for the sole purpose of raising up a people of customers, may at first sight appear a project fit only for a nation of shopkeepers.* It is, however, a project altogether unfit for a nation of shopkeepers; but extremely fit for a nation whose government is influenced by shopkeepers. Such statesmen, and such statesmen only, are capable of fancying that they will find some advantage in employing the blood and treasure of their fellow citizens, to found and to maintain such an empire. Say to a shopkeeper, Buy me a good estate, and I shall always buy my cloaths at your shop, even though I should pay somewhat dearer than what I can have them for at other shops; and you will not find him very forward to embrace your proposal. But should any other person buy you such an estate, the shopkeeper would be much obliged to your benefactor if he would enjoin you to buy all your cloaths at his shop. England purchased for some of her subjects, who found themselves uneasy at home, a great estate in a distant country. The price, indeed, was very small, and instead of thirty years purchase, the ordinary price of land in the present times, it amounted to little more than the expence of the different equipments which made the first discovery, reconnoitred the coast, and took a fictitious possession of the country. The land was good and of great extent, and the cultivators having plenty of good ground to work upon, and being for some time at liberty to sell their produce where they pleased, became in the course of little more than thirty or forty years (between 1620 and 1660) so numerous and thriving a people, that the shopkeepers and other traders of England wished to secure to themselves the monopoly of their custom. Without pretending, therefore, that they had paid any part, either of the original purchase-money, or of the subsequent expence of improvement, they petitioned the parliament that the cultivators of America might for the future be confined to their shop; first, for buying all the goods which they wanted from Europe; and, secondly, for selling all such parts of their own produce as those traders might find it convenient to buy. For they did not find it convenient to buy every part of it. Some parts of it imported into England might have interfered with some of the trades which they themselves carried on at home. Those particular parts of it, therefore, they were willing that the colonists should sell where they could; the farther off the better; and upon that account proposed that their market should be confined to the countries south of Cape Finisterre. A clause in the famous act of navigation* established this truly shopkeeper proposal into a law.

The maintenance of this monopoly has hitherto been the principal, or more properly perhaps the sole end and purpose of the dominion which Great Britain assumes over her colonies. In the exclusive trade, it is supposed, consists the great advantage of provinces, which have never yet afforded either revenue or military force for the support of the civil government, or the defence of the mother country. The monopoly is the principal badge of their dependency, and it is the sole fruit which has hitherto been gathered from that dependency. Whatever expence Great Britain has hitherto laid out in maintaining this dependency, has really been laid out in order to support this monopoly. The expence of the ordinary peace establishment of the colonies amounted, before the commencement of the present disturbances, to the pay of twenty regiments of foot; to the expence of the artillery, stores, and extraordinary provisions with which it was necessary to supply them; and to the expence of a very considerable naval force which was constantly kept up, in order to guard, from the smuggling vessels of other nations, the immense coast of North America, and that of our West Indian islands. The whole expence of this peace establishment was a charge upon the revenue of Great Britain, and was, at the same time, the smallest part of what the dominion of the colonies has cost the mother country. If we would know the amount of the whole, we must add to the annual expence of this peace establishment the interest of the sums which, in consequence of her considering her colonies as provinces subject to her dominion, Great Britain has upon different occasions laid out upon their defence. We must add to it, in particular, the whole expence of the late war, and a great part of that of the war which preceded it.* The late war was altogether a colony quarrel, and the whole expence of it, in whatever part of the world it may have been laid out, whether in Germany or the East Indies, ought justly to be stated to the account of the colonies. It amounted to more than ninety millions sterling, including not only the new debt which was contracted, but the two shillings in the pound additional land tax, and the sums which were every year borrowed from the sinking fund.* The Spanish war which began in 1739, was principally a colony quarrel. Its principal object was to prevent the search of the colony ships which carried on a contraband trade with the Spanish main. This whole expence is, in reality, a bounty which has been given in order to support a monopoly. The pretended purpose of it was to encourage the manufactures, and to increase the commerce of Great Britain. But its real effect has been to raise the rate of mercantile profit, and to enable our merchants to turn into a branch of trade, of which the returns are more slow and distant than those of the greater part of other trades, a greater proportion of their capital than they otherwise would have done; two events which, if a bounty could have prevented, it might perhaps have been very well worth while to give such a bounty.

Under the present system of management, therefore, Great Britain derives nothing but loss from the dominion which she assumes over her colonies.

To propose that Great Britain should voluntarily give up all authority over her colonies, and leave them to elect their own magistrates, to enact their own laws, and to make peace and war as they might think proper, would be to propose such a measure as never was, and never will be adopted, by any nation in the world.* No nation ever voluntarily gave up the dominion of any province, how troublesome soever it might be to govern it, and how small soever the revenue which it afforded might be in proportion to the expence which it occasioned. Such sacrifices, though they might frequently be agreeable to the interest, are always mortifying to the pride of every nation, and what is perhaps of still greater consequence, they are always contrary to the private interest of the governing part of it, who would thereby be deprived of the disposal of many places of trust and profit, of many opportunities of acquiring wealth and distinction, which the possession of the most turbulent, and, to the great body of the people, the most unprofitable province seldom fails to afford. The most visionary enthusiast would scarce be capable of proposing such a measure, with any serious hopes at least of its ever being adopted. If it was adopted, however, Great Britain would not only be immediately freed from the whole annual expence of the peace establishment of the colonies, but might settle with them such a treaty of commerce as would effectually secure to her a free trade, more advantageous to the great body of the people, though less so to the merchants, than the monopoly which she at present enjoys. By thus parting good friends, the natural affection of the colonies to the mother country, which, perhaps, our late dissentions have well nigh extinguished, would quickly revive.* It might dispose them not only to respect, for whole centuries together, that treaty of commerce which they had concluded with us at parting, but to favour us in war as well as in trade, and, instead of turbulent and factious subjects, to become our most faithful, affectionate, and generous allies; and the same sort of parental affection on the one side, and filial respect on the other, might revive between Great Britain and her colonies, which used to subsist between those of ancient Greece and the mother city from which they descended. . . .

Towards the declension of the Roman republick, the allies of Rome, who had borne the principal burden of defending the state and extending the empire, demanded to be admitted to all the privileges of Roman citizens. Upon being refused, the social war broke out. During the course of that war Rome granted those privileges to the greater part of them, one by one, and in proportion as they detached themselves from the general confederacy. The parliament of Great Britain insists upon taxing the colonies; and they refuse to be taxed by a parliament in which they are not represented.* If to each colony, which should detach itself from the general confederacy, Great Britain should allow such a number of representatives as suited the proportion of what it contributed to the publick revenue of the empire, in consequence of its being subjected to the same taxes, and in compensation admitted to the same freedom of trade with its fellow-subjects at home; the number of its representatives to be augmented as the proportion of its contribution might afterwards augment; a new method of acquiring importance, a new and more dazzling object of ambition would be presented to the leading men of each colony. Instead of piddling for the little prizes which are to found in what may be called the paltry raffle of colony faction; they might then hope, from the presumption which men naturally have in their own ability and good fortune, to draw some of the great prizes which sometimes come from the wheel of the great state lottery of British politicks. Unless this or some other method is fallen upon, and there seems to be none more obvious than this, of preserving the importance and of gratifying the ambition of the leading men of America, it is not very probable that they will ever voluntarily submit to us; and we ought to consider that the blood which must be shed in forcing them to do so, is, every drop of it, the blood either of those who are, or of those whom we wish to have for our fellow-citizens. They are very weak who flatter themselves that, in the state to which things have come, our colonies will be easily conquered by force alone. The persons who now govern the resolutions of that they call their continental congress, feel in themselves at this moment a degree of importance which, perhaps, the greatest subjects in Europe scarce feel. From shopkeepers, tradesmen, and attornies, they are become states-men and legislators, and are employed in contriving a new form of government for an extensive empire, which, they flatter themselves, will become, and which, indeed, seems very likely to become, one of the greatest and most formidable that ever was in the world. Five hundred different people, perhaps, who in different ways act immediately under the continental con-gress; and five hundred thousand, perhaps, who act under those five hundred, all feel in the same manner a proportionable rise in their own importance. Almost every individual of the gov-erning party in America, fills, at present in his own fancy, a station superior, not only to what he had ever filled before, but to what he had ever expected to fill; and unless some new object of ambition is presented either to him or to his leaders, if he has the ordinary spirit of a man, he will die in defence of that station. . . .

The discovery of America, and that of a passage to the East Indies by the Cape of Good Hope, are the two greatest and most important events recorded in the history of mankind.* Their consequences have already been very great: but, in the short period of between two and three centuries which has elapsed since these discoveries were made, it is impossible that the whole extent of their consequences can have been seen. What benefits, or what misfortunes to mankind may hereafter result from those great events no human wisdom can foresee. By uniting, in some measure, the most distant parts of the world, by enabling them to relieve one another's wants, to increase one another's enjoyments, and to encourage one another's industry, their general tendency would seem to be beneficial. To the natives, however, both of the East and West Indies, all the commercial benefits which can have resulted from those events have been sunk and lost in the dreadful misfortunes which they have occasioned. These misfortunes, however, seem to have arisen rather from accident than from any thing in the nature of those events themselves. At the particular time when these discoveries were made, the superiority of force happened to be so great on the side of the Europeans, that they were enabled to commit with impunity every sort of injustice in those remote countries. Hereafter, perhaps, the natives of those countries may grow stronger, or those of Europe may grow weaker, and the inhabitants of all the different quarters of the world may arrive at that equality of courage and force which, by inspiring mutual fear, can alone overawe the injustice of independent nations into some sort of respect for the rights of one another. But nothing seems more likely to establish this equality of force than that mutual communication of knowledge and of all sorts of improvements which an extensive commerce from all countries to all countries naturally, or rather necessarily, carries along with it.

In the mean time one of the principal effects of those discoveries has been to raise the mercantile system to a degree of splendor and glory which it could never otherwise have attained to. It is the object of that system to enrich a great nation rather by trade and manufactures than by the improvement and cultivation of land, rather by the industry of the towns than by that of the country.* But, in consequence of those discoveries, the commercial towns of Europe, instead of being the manufacturers and carriers for but a very small part of the world (that part of Europe which is washed by the

Atlantic ocean, and the countries which lie round the Baltick and Mediterranean seas), have now become the manufacturers for the numerous and thriving cultivators of America, and the carriers, and in some respects the manufacturers too, for almost all the different nations of Asia, Africa, and America. Two new worlds have been opened to their industry, each of them much greater and more extensive than the old one, and the market of one of them growing still greater and greater every day. . . .

In the trade to America every nation endeavours to engross as much as possible the whole market of its own colonies, by fairly excluding all other nations from any direct trade to them. During the greater part of the sixteenth century, the Portugueze endeavoured to manage the trade to the East Indies in the same manner, by claiming the sole right of sailing in the Indian seas, on account of the merit of having first found out the road to them. The Dutch still continue to exclude all other European nations from any direct trade to their spice islands. Monopolies of this kind are evidently established against all other European nations, who are thereby not only excluded from a trade to which it might be convenient for them to turn some part of their stock, but are obliged to buy the goods which that trade deals in somewhat dearer, than if they could import them themselves directly from the countries which produce them.

But since the fall of the power of Portugal, no European nation has claimed the exclusive right of sailing in the Indian seas, of which the principal ports are now open to the ships of all European nations. Except in Portugal, however, and within these few years in France, the trade to the East Indies has in every European country been subjected to an exclusive company. Monopolies of this kind are properly established against the very nation which erects them. The greater part of that nation are thereby not only excluded from a trade to which it might be convenient for them to turn some part of their stock, but are obliged to buy the goods which that trade deals in, somewhat dearer than if it was open and free to all their countrymen. Since the establishment of the English East India company, for example, the other inhabitants of England, over and above being excluded from the trade, must have paid in the price of the East India goods which they have consumed, not only for all the extraordinary profits which the company may have made upon those goods in consequence of their monopoly, but for all the extraordinary waste which the fraud and abuse, inseparable from the management of the affairs of so great a company, must necessarily have occasioned.* The absurdity of this second kind of monopoly, therefore, is much more manifest than that of the first.

Both these kinds of monopolies derange more or less the natural distribution of the stock of the society: but they do not always derange it in the same way.

Monopolies of the first kind always attract to the particular trade in which they are established, a greater proportion of the stock of the society than what would go to that trade of its own accord.

Monopolies of the second kind, may sometimes attract stock towards the particular trade in which they are established, and sometimes repel it from that trade according to different circumstances. In poor countries they naturally attract towards that trade more stock than would otherwise go to it. In rich countries they naturally repel from it a good deal of stock which would otherwise go to it. . . .

The English and Dutch companies, though they have established no considerable colonies, . . . have both made considerable conquests in the East Indies. But in the manner in which they both govern their new subjects, the natural genius of an exclusive company has shown itself most distinctly. In the spice islands the Dutch are said to burn all the spiceries which a fertile season produces beyond what they expect to dispose of in Europe with such a profit as they think sufficient. In the islands where they have no settlements, they give a premium to those who collect the young blossoms and green leaves of the clove and nutmeg trees which naturally grow there, but which this savage policy has now, it is said, almost compleatly extirpated. Even in the islands where they have settlements they have very much reduced, it is said, the number of those trees. If the produce even of their own islands was much greater than what suited their market, the natives, they suspect, might find means to convey some part of it to other nations; and the best way, they imagine, to secure their own monopoly, is to take care that no more shall grow than what they themselves carry to market. By different arts of oppression they have reduced the population of several of the Moluccas* nearly to the number which is sufficient to supply with fresh provisions and other necessaries of life their own insignificant garrisons, and such of their ships as occasionally come there for a cargo of spices. Under the government even of the Portugueze, however, those islands are said to have been tolerably well inhabited. The English company have not yet had time to establish in Bengal so perfectly destructive a system. The plan of their government, however, has had exactly the same tendency. It has not been uncommon, I am well assured, for the chief, that is, the first clerk of a factory, to order a peasant to plough up a rich field of poppies, and sow it with rice or some other grain. The pretence was, to prevent a scarcity of provisions; but the real reason, to give the chief an opportunity of selling at a better price a large quantity of opium, which he happened then to have upon hand. Upon other occasions the order has been reversed; and a rich field of rice or other grain has been ploughed up, in order to make room for a plantation of poppies; when the chief foresaw that extraordinary profit was likely to be made by opium.* The servants of the company have upon several occasions attempted to establish in their own favour the monopoly of some of the most important branches, not only of the foreign, but of the inland trade of the country. Had they been allowed to go on, it is impossible that they should not at some time or another have attempted to restrain the production of the particular articles of which they had thus usurped the monopoly, not only to the quantity which they themselves could purchase, but to that which they could expect to sell with such a profit as they might think sufficient. In the course of a century or two, the policy of the English company would in this manner have probably proved as compleatly destructive as that of the Dutch.

Nothing, however, can be more directly contrary to the real interest of those companies, considered as the sovereigns of the countries which they have conquered, than this destructive plan. In almost all countries the revenue of the sovereign is drawn from that of the people. The greater the revenue of the people, therefore, the greater the annual produce of their land and labour, the more they can afford to the sovereign. It is his interest, therefore, to increase as much as possible that annual produce. But if this is the interest of every sovereign, it is peculiarly so of one whose revenue, like that of the sovereign of Bengal, arises chiefly from a land-rent. That rent must necessarily be in proportion to the quantity and value of the produce, and both the one and the other must depend upon the extent of the market. The quantity will always be suited with more or less exactness to the consumption of those who can afford to pay for it, and the price which they will pay will always be in proportion to the eagerness of their competition. It is the interest of such a sovereign, therefore, to open the most extensive market for the produce of his country, to allow the most perfect freedom of commerce, in order to increase as much as possible the number and the competition of buyers; and upon this account to abolish, not only all monopolies, but all restraints upon the transportation of the home produce from one part of the country to another, upon its exportation to foreign countries, or upon the importation of goods of any kind for which it can be exchanged. He is in this manner most likely to increase both the quantity and value of that produce, and consequently of his own share of it, or of his own revenue.

But a company of merchants are, it seems, incapable of considering themselves as sovereigns, even after they have become such. Trade, or buying in order to sell again, they still consider as their principal business, and by a strange absurdity, regard the character of the sovereign as but an appendix to that of the merchant, as something which ought to be made subservient to it, or by means of which they may be enabled to buy cheaper in India, and thereby to sell with a better profit in Europe. They endeavour for this purpose to keep out as much as possible all competitors from the market of the countries which are subject to their government, and consequently to reduce, at least, some part of the surplus produce of those countries to what is barely sufficient for supplying their own demand, or to what they can expect to sell in Europe with such a profit as they may think reasonable. Their mercantile habits draw them in this manner, almost necessarily, though perhaps insensibly, to prefer upon all ordinary occasions the little and transitory profit of the monopolist to the great and permanent revenue of the sovereign, and would gradually lead them to treat the countries subject to their government nearly as the Dutch treat the Moluccas. It is the interest of the East India company, considered as sovereigns, that the European goods which are carried to their Indian dominions, should be sold there as cheap as possible; and that the Indian goods which are brought from thence should bring there as good a price, or should be sold there as dear as possible. But the reverse of this is their interest as merchants. As sovereigns, their interest is exactly the same with that of the country which they govern. As merchants their interest is directly opposite to that interest.

But if the genius of such a government, even as to what concerns its direction in Europe, is in this manner essentially and perhaps incurably faulty, that of its administration in India is still more so.* That administration is necessarily composed of a council of merchants, a profession no doubt extremely respectable, but which in no country in the world carries along with it that sort of authority which naturally over-awes the people, and without force commands their willing obedience. Such a council can command obedience only by the military force with which they are accompanied, and their government is therefore necessarily military and despotical. Their proper business, however, is that of merchants. It is to sell, upon their masters account, the European goods consigned to them, and to buy in return Indian goods for the European market. It is to sell the one as dear and to buy the other as cheap as possible, and consequently to exclude as much as possible all rivals from the particular market where they keep their shop. The genius of the administration, therefore, so far as concerns the trade of the company, is the same as that of the direction. It tends to make government subservient to the interest of monopoly, and consequently to stunt the natural growth of some parts at least of the surplus produce of the country to what is barely sufficient for answering the demand of the company.

All the members of the administration, besides, trade more or less upon their own account, and it is in vain to prohibit them from doing so. Nothing can be more compleatly foolish than to expect that the clerks of a great counting-house at ten thousand miles distance, and consequently almost quite out of sight, should, upon a simple order from their masters, give up at once doing any sort of business upon their own account, abandon for ever all hopes of making a fortune, of which they have the means in their hands, and content themselves with the moderate salaries which those masters allow them, and which, moderate as they are, can seldom be augmented, being commonly as large as the real profits of the company trade can afford. In such circumstances, to prohibit the servants of the company from trading upon their own account, can have scarce any other effect than to enable the superior servants, under pretence of executing their masters order, to oppress such of the inferior ones as have had the misfortune to fall under their displeasure. The servants naturally endeavour to establish the same monopoly in favour of their own private trade as of the publick trade of the company. If they are suffered to act as they could wish, they will establish this monopoly openly and directly, by fairly prohibiting all other people from trading in the articles in which they chuse to deal; and this, perhaps, is the best and least oppressive way of establishing it. But if by an order from Europe they are prohibited from doing this, they will, notwithstanding, endeavour to establish a monopoly of the same kind, secretly and indirectly, in a way that is much more destructive to the country. They will employ the whole authority of government, and pervert the administration of justice, in order to harass and ruin those who interfere with them in any branch of commerce which, by means of agents, either concealed, or at least not publickly avowed, they may chuse to carry on. But the private trade of the servants will naturally extend to a much greater variety of articles than the publick trade of the company. The publick trade of the company extends no further than the trade with Europe, and comprehends a part only of the foreign trade of the country. But the private trade of the servants may extend to all the different branches both of its inland and foreign trade. The monopoly of the company can tend only to stunt the natural growth of that part of the surplus produce which, in the case of a free trade, would be exported to Europe. That of the servants tends to stunt the natural growth of every part of the produce in which they chuse to deal, of what is destined for home consumption, as well as of what is destined for exportation; and consequently to degrade the cultivation of the whole country, and to reduce the number of its inhabitants. It tends to reduce the quantity of every sort of produce, even that of the necessaries of life, whenever the servants of the company chuse to deal in them, to what those servants can both afford to buy and expect to sell with such a profit as pleases them.

From the nature of their situation too the servants must be more disposed to support with rigorous severity their own interest against that of the country which they govern, than their masters can be to support theirs. The country belongs to their masters, who cannot avoid having some regard for the interest of what belongs to them. But it does not belong to the servants. The real interest of their masters, if they were capable of understanding it, is the same with that of the country,[15] and

---

[15] The interest of every proprietor of India Stock, however, is by no means the same with that of the country in the government of which his vote gives him some influence. See Book V. Chap. i. Part 3d.

it is from ignorance chiefly, and the meanness of mercantile prejudice, that they ever oppress it. But the real interest of the servants is by no means the same with that of the country, and the most perfect information would not necessarily put an end to their oppressions. The regulations accordingly which have been sent out from Europe, though they have been frequently weak, have upon most occasions been well-meaning. More intelligence and perhaps less good-meaning has sometimes appeared in those established by the servants in India. It is a very singular government in which every member of the administration wishes to get out of the country, and consequently to have done with the government, as soon as he can, and to whose interest, the day after he has left it and carried his whole fortune with him,* it is perfectly indifferent though the whole country was swallowed up by an earthquake.

I mean not, however, by any thing which I have here said, to throw any odious imputation upon the general character of the servants of the East India company, and much less upon that of any particular persons. It is the system of government, the situation in which they are placed, that I mean to censure; not the character of those who have acted in it. They acted as their situation naturally directed, and they who have clamoured the loudest against them would, probably, not have acted better themselves.* In war and negociation, the councils of Madras and Calcutta* have upon several occasions conducted themselves with a resolution and decisive wisdom which would have done honour to the senate of Rome in the best days of that republick. The members of those councils, however, had been bred to professions very different from war and politicks. But their situation alone, without education, experience, or even example, seems to have formed in them all at once the great qualities which it required, and to have inspired them both with abilities and virtues which they themselves could not well know that they possessed. If upon some occasions, therefore, it has animated them to actions of magnanimity which could not well have been expected from them, we should not wonder

if upon others it has prompted them to exploits of somewhat
a different nature.

Such exclusive companies, therefore, are nuisances in every
respect; always more or less inconvenient to the countries in
which they are established, and destructive to those which have
the misfortune to fall under their government.

CHAPTER VIII

Conclusion of the Mercantile System*

THOUGH the encouragement of exportation, and the discouragement of importation are the two great engines by which the mercantile system proposes to enrich every country, yet with regard to some particular commodities, it seems to follow an opposite plan: to discourage exportation and to encourage importation. Its ultimate object, however, it pretends, is always the same, to enrich the country by an advantageous balance of trade. It discourages the exportation of the materials of manufacture, and of the instruments of trade, in order to give our own workmen an advantage, and to enable them to undersell those of other nations in all foreign markets: and by restraining, in this manner, the exportation of a few commodities, of no great price, it proposes to occasion a much greater and more valuable exportation of others. It encourages the importation of the materials of manufacture, in order that our own people may be enabled to work them up more cheaply, and thereby prevent a greater and more valuable importation of the manufactured commodities. I do not observe, at least in our Statute Book, any encouragement given to the importation of the instruments of trade. When manufactures have advanced to a certain pitch of greatness, the fabrication of the instruments of trade becomes itself the object of a great number of very important manufactures. To give any particular encouragement to the importation of such instruments, would interfere too much with the interest of those manufactures. Such importation, therefore, instead of being encouraged, has frequently been prohibited. . . .

The exportation, however, of the instruments of trade, properly so called, is commonly restrained, not by high duties, but by absolute prohibitions. Thus by the 7th and 8th of William III. chap. 20. sect. 8.* the exportation of frames or engines for knitting gloves or stockings is prohibited under the penalty, not only of the forfeiture of such frames or engines, so exported, or attempted to be exported, but of forty pounds, one half to the king, the other to the person who shall inform or sue for the same. In the same manner by the 14th Geo. III. chap. 71.* the exportation to foreign parts, of any utensils made use of in the cotton, linen, woollen and silk manufactures, is prohibited under the penalty, not only of the forfeiture of such utensils, but of two hundred pounds, to be paid by the person who shall offend in this manner, and likewise of two hundred pounds to be paid by the master of the ship who shall knowingly suffer such utensils to be loaded on board his ship.

When such heavy penalties were imposed upon the exportation of the dead instruments of trade, it could not well be expected that the living instrument, the artificer,* should be allowed to go free. Accordingly, by the 5 Geo. I. chap. 27.* the person who shall be convicted of enticing any artificer of, or in any of the manufactures of Great Britain, to go into any foreign parts in order to practice or teach his trade, is liable for the first offence to be fined in any sum not exceeding one hundred pounds, and to three months imprisonment, and until the fine shall be paid; and for the second offence, to be fined in any sum at the discretion of the court, and to imprisonment for twelve months, and until the fine shall be paid. By the 23 Geo. II. chap. 13.* this penalty is increased for the first offence to five hundred pounds for every artificer so enticed, and to twelve months imprisonment, and until the fine shall be paid; and for the second offence, to one thousand pounds, and to two years imprisonment, and until the fine shall be paid.

By the former of those two statutes, upon proof that any person has been enticing any artificer, or that any artificer has promised or contracted to go into foreign parts for the purposes aforesaid, such artificer may be obliged to give security at the discretion of the court, that he shall not go beyond the seas, and may be committed to prison until he give such security.

If any artificer has gone beyond the seas, and is exercising or teaching his trade in any foreign country, upon warning being given to him by any of his majesty's ministers or consuls abroad, or by one of his majesty's secretaries of state for the time being, if he does not, within six months after such warning, return into this realm, and from thenceforth abide and inhabit continually within the same, he is from thenceforth declared incapable of taking any legacy devised* to him within this kingdom, or of being executor or administrator to any person, or of taking any lands within this kingdom by descent, devise, or purchase. He likewise forfeits to the king, all his lands, goods and chattels, is declared an alien in every respect, and is put out of the king's protection.

It is unnecessary, I imagine, to observe, how contrary such regulations are to the boasted liberty of the subject, of which we affect to be so very jealous; but which, in this case, is so plainly sacrificed to the futile interests of our merchants and manufacturers.

The laudable motive of all these regulations, is to extend our own manufactures, not by their own improvement, but by the depression of those of all our neighbours, and by putting an end, as much as possible, to the troublesome competition of such odious and disagreeable rivals. Our master manufacturers think it reasonable, that they themselves should have the monopoly of the ingenuity of all their countrymen. Though by restraining, in some trades, the number of apprentices which can be employed at one time, and by imposing the necessity of a long apprenticeship in all trades, they endeavour, all of them, to confine the knowledge of their respective employments to as small a number as possible;* they are unwilling, however, that any part of this small number should go abroad to instruct foreigners.

Consumption is the sole end and purpose of all production; and the interest of the producer ought to be attended to, only so far as it may be necessary for promoting that of the consumer. The maxim is so perfectly self-evident, that it would be absurd to attempt to prove it. But in the mercantile system, the interest of the consumer is almost constantly sacrificed to that of the producer; and it seems to consider production, and not consumption, as the ultimate end and object of all industry and commerce.

In the restraints upon the importation of all foreign commodities which can come into competition with those of our own growth, or manufacture, the interest of the home-consumer is evidently sacrificed to that of the producer. It is altogether for the benefit of the latter, that the former is obliged to pay that enhancement of price which this monopoly almost always occasions.

It is altogether for the benefit of the producer that bounties are granted upon the exportation of some of his productions. The home-consumer is obliged to pay, first, the tax which is necessary for paying the bounty, and secondly, the still greater tax which necessarily arises from the enhancement of the price of the commodity in the home market.

By the famous treaty of commerce with Portugal,* the consumer is prevented by high duties from purchasing of a neighbouring country, a commodity which our own climate does not produce, but is obliged to purchase it of a distant country, though it is acknowledged that the commodity of the distant country is of a worse quality than that of the near one. The home-consumer is obliged to submit to this inconveniency, in order that the producer may import into the distant country some of his productions upon more advantageous terms than he would otherwise have been allowed to do. The consumer, too, is obliged to pay, whatever enhancement in the price of those very productions, this forced exportation may occasion in the home-market.

But in the system of laws which has been established for the management of our American and West Indian colonies, the interest of the home-consumer has been sacrificed to that of the producer with a more extravagant profusion than in all our other commercial regulations. A great empire has been established for the sole purpose of raising up a nation of customers who should be obliged to buy from the shops of our different producers, all the goods with which these could supply them. For the sake of that little enhancement of price which this monopoly might afford our producers, the home-consumers have been burdened with the whole expence of maintaining and defending that empire. For this purpose, and for this purpose only, in the two last wars, more than two hundred millions have been spent, and a new debt of more than a hundred and seventy millions has been contracted over and above all that had been expended for the same purpose in former wars.* The interest of this debt alone is not only greater than the whole extraordinary profit, which, it ever could be pretended, was made by the monopoly of the colony trade, but than the whole value of that trade or than the whole value of the goods, which at an average have been annually exported to the colonies.

It cannot be very difficult to determine who have been the contrivers of this whole mercantile system; not the consumers, we may believe, whose interest has been entirely neglected; but the producers whose interest has been so carefully attended to; and among this latter class our merchants and manufacturers have been by far the principal architects. In the mercantile regulations, which have been taken notice of in this chapter, the interest of our manufacturers has been most peculiarly attended to; and the interest, not so much of the consumers, as that of some other sets of producers, has been sacrificed to it.

CHAPTER IX

*Of the agricultural Systems, or of those Systems of
political Œconomy, which represent the Produce of
Land as either the sole or the principal Source of the
Revenue and Wealth of every Country*

THE agriculture systems of political œconomy will not require
so long an explanation as that which I have thought it necessary
to bestow upon the mercantile or commercial system.

That system which represents the produce of land as the sole
source of the revenue and wealth of every country, has, so far
as I know, never been adopted by any nation, and it at present
exists only in the speculations of a few men of great learning
and ingenuity in France.* It would not, surely, be worth while
to examine at great length the errors of a system which never
has done, and probably never will do any harm in any part of
the world. I shall endeavour to explain, however, as distinctly
as I can, the great outlines of this very ingenious system.

Mr. Colbert,* the famous minister of Lewis XIV, was a man
of probity, of great industry and knowledge of detail; of great
experience and acuteness in the examination of publick accounts, and of abilities, in short, every way fitted for introducing method and good order into the collection and expenditure
of the publick revenue. That minister had unfortunately em-
braced all the prejudices of the mercantile system, in its nature
and essence a system of restraint and regulation, and such as
could scarce fail to be agreeable to a laborious and plodding
man of business, who had been accustomed to regulate the
different departments of publick offices, and to establish the
necessary checks and controuls for confining each to its proper
sphere. The industry and commerce of a great country he
endeavoured to regulate upon the same model as the departments of a publick office; and instead of allowing every man

to pursue his own interest his own way, upon the liberal plan of equality, liberty and justice, he bestowed upon certain branches of industry extraordinary privileges, while he laid others under as extraordinary restraints. He was not only disposed, like other European ministers, to encourage more the industry of the towns than that of the country; but, in order to support the industry of the towns, he was willing even to depress and keep down that of the country. In order to render provisions cheap to the inhabitants of the towns, and thereby to encourage manufactures and foreign commerce, he prohibited altogether the exportation of corn, and thus excluded the inhabitants of the country from every foreign market for by far the most important part of the produce of their industry. This prohibition, joined to the restraints imposed by the antient provincial laws of France upon the transportation of corn from one province to another, and to the arbitrary and degrading taxes which are levied upon the cultivators in almost all the provinces, discouraged and kept down the agriculture of that country very much below the state to which it would naturally have risen in so very fertile a soil and so very happy a climate. This state of discouragement and depression was felt more or less in every different part of the country, and many different enquiries were set on foot concerning the causes of it. One of those causes appeared to be the preference given, by the institutions of Mr. Colbert, to the industry of the towns above that of the country.

If the rod be bent too much one way, says the proverb, in order to make it straight you must bend it as much the other. The French philosophers, who have proposed the system which represents agriculture as the sole source of the revenue and wealth of every country, seem to have adopted this proverbial maxim; and as in the plan of Mr. Colbert the industry of the towns was certainly over-valued in comparison with that of the country; so in their system it seems to be as certainly under-valued.

The different orders of people who have ever been supposed to contribute in any respect towards the annual produce of the land and labour of the country, they divide into three classes. The first is the class of the proprietors of land. The second is the class of the cultivators, of farmers and country labourers, whom they honour with the peculiar appellation of the productive class. The third is the class of artificers, manufacturers and merchants, whom they endeavour to degrade by the humiliating appellation of the barren or unproductive class.

The class of proprietors contributes to the annual produce by the expence which they may occasionally lay out upon the improvement of the land, upon the buildings, drains, enclosures and other ameliorations, which they may either make or maintain upon it, and by means of which the cultivators are enabled, with the same capital, to raise a greater produce, and consequently to pay a greater rent. This advanced rent may be considered as the interest or profit due to the proprietor upon the expence or capital which he thus employs in the improvement of his land. Such expences are in this system called ground expences (depenses foncieres).

The cultivators or farmers contribute to the annual produce by what are in this system called the original and annual expences (depenses primitives et depenses annuelles) which they lay out upon the cultivation of the land. The original expences consist in the instruments of husbandry, in the stock of cattle, in the seed, and in the maintenance of the farmer's family, servants and cattle, during at least a great part of the first year of his occupancy, or till he can receive some return from the land. The annual expences consist in the seed, in the wear and tear of the instruments of husbandry, and in the annual maintenance of the farmer's servants and cattle, and of his family too, so far as any part of them can be considered as servants employed in cultivation. That part of the produce of the land which remains to him after paying the rent, ought to be sufficient, first, to replace to him within a reasonable time, at least during the term of his occupancy, the whole of his original expences, together with the ordinary profits of stock; and, secondly, to replace to him annually the whole of his annual expences, together likewise with the ordinary profits of stock. Those two sorts of expences are two capitals which the farmer employs in cultivation; and unless they are regularly restored to him, together with a reasonable profit, he cannot carry on his employment upon a level with other employments; but, from a regard to his own interest, must desert it as soon as possible, and seek some other. That part of the produce of the land which is thus necessary for enabling the farmer to continue his business, ought to be considered as a fund sacred to cultivation, which if the landlord violates, he necessarily reduces the produce of his own land, and in a few years not only disables the farmer from paying this racked rent,* but from paying the reasonable rent which he might otherwise have got for his land. The rent which properly belongs to the landlord, is no more than the neat produce which remains after paying in the compleatest manner all the necessary expences which must be previously laid out in order to raise the gross, or the whole produce. It is because the labour of the cultivators, over and above paying compleatly all those necessary expences, affords a neat produce of this kind, that this class of people are in this system peculiarly distinguished by the honourable appellation of the productive class. Their original and annual expences are for the same reason called, in this system, productive expences, because, over and above replacing their own value, they occasion the annual reproduction of this neat produce.

The ground expences, as they are called, or what the landlord lays out upon the improvement of his land, are in this system too honoured with the appellation of productive expences. Till the whole of those expences, together with the ordinary profits of stock, have been compleatly repaid to him by the advanced rent which he gets from his land, that advanced rent ought to be regarded as sacred and inviolable, both by the church and by the king; ought to be subject neither to tithe nor to taxation. If it is otherwise, by discouraging the improvement of land, the church discourages the future increase of her own tithes, and the king the future increase of his own taxes. As in a well-ordered state of things, therefore, those ground expences, over and above reproducing in the compleatest manner their own value, occasion likewise after a certain time a reproduction of a neat produce, they are in this system considered as productive expences.

The ground expences of the landlord, however, together with the original and the annual expences of the farmer, are the only three sorts of expences which in this system are considered as productive. All other expences and all other orders of people, even those who in the common apprehensions of men are regarded as the most productive, are in this account of things represented as altogether barren and unproductive. . . .

The labour of artificers and manufacturers never adds any thing to the value of the whole annual amount of the rude produce of the land. It adds indeed greatly to the value of some particular parts of it. But the consumption which in the mean time it occasions of other parts, is precisely equal to the value which it adds to those parts; so that the value of the whole amount is not, at any one moment of time, in the least augmented by it. The person who works the lace of a pair of fine ruffles, for example, will sometimes raise the value of perhaps a pennyworth of flax to thirty pounds sterling. But though at first sight he appears thereby to multiply the value of a part of the rude produce about seven thousand and two hundred times, he in reality adds nothing to the value of the whole annual amount of the rude produce. The working of that lace costs him perhaps two years labour. The thirty pounds which he gets for it when it is finished, is no more than the repayment of the subsistence which he advances to himself during the two years that he is employed about it. The value which, by every day's, month's, or year's labour, he adds to the flax, does no more than replace the value of his own consumption during that day, month, or year. At no moment of time, therefore, does he add any thing to the value of the whole annual amount of the rude produce of the land: the portion of that produce which he is continually consuming, being always equal to the value which he is continually producing. The extreme poverty of the greater part of the persons employed in this expensive, though trifling manufacture, may satisfy us that the price of their work does not in ordinary cases exceed the value of their subsistence. It is otherwise with the work of farmers and country labourers. The rent of the landlord is a value, which, in ordinary cases, it is continually producing, over and above replacing, in the most compleat manner, the whole consumption, the whole expence laid out upon the employment and maintenance both of the workmen and of their employer.

Artificers, manufacturers and merchants, can augment the revenue and wealth of their society, by parsimony only; or, as it is expressed in this system, by privation, that is, by depriving themselves of a part of the funds destined for their own subsistence. They annually reproduce nothing but those funds. Unless, therefore, they annually save some part of them, unless they annually deprive themselves of the enjoyment of some part of them, the revenue and wealth of their society can never be in the smallest degree augmented by means of their industry. Farmers and country labourers, on the contrary, may enjoy compleatly the whole funds destined for their own subsistence, and yet augment at the same time the revenue and wealth of their society. Over and above what is destined for their own subsistence, their industry annually affords a neat produce, of which the augmentation necessarily augments the revenue and wealth of their society. Nations, therefore, which, like France or England, consist in a great measure of proprietors and cultivators, can be enriched by industry and enjoyment. Nations, on the contrary, which, like Holland and Hamburgh, are composed chiefly of merchants, artificers and manufacturers, can grow rich only through parsimony and privation. As the interest of nations so differently circumstanced, is very different, so is likewise the common character of the people.* In those of the former kind, liberality, frankness, and good fellowship, naturally make a part of that common character. In the latter, narrowness, meanness, and a selfish disposition, averse to all social pleasure and enjoyment.

The unproductive class, that of merchants, artificers, and manufacturers, is maintained and employed altogether at the expence of the two other classes, of that of proprietors, and of that of cultivators. They furnish it both with the materials of its work and with the fund of its subsistence, with the corn and cattle which it consumes while it is employed about that work. The proprietors and cultivators finally pay both the wages of all the workmen of the unproductive class, and the profits of all their employers. Those workmen and their employers are properly the servants of the proprietors and cultivators. They are only servants who work without doors, as menial servants work within. Both the one and the other, however, are equally maintained at the expence of the same masters. The labour of both is equally unproductive. It adds nothing to the value of the sum total of the rude produce of the land. Instead of increasing the value of that sum total, it is a charge and expence which must be paid out of it.

The unproductive class, however, is not only useful, but greatly useful to the other two classes. By means of the industry of merchants, artificers and manufacturers, the proprietors and cultivators can purchase both the foreign goods and the manufactured produce of their own country which they have occasion for, with the produce of a much smaller quantity of their own labour, than what they would be obliged to employ, if they were to attempt, in an aukward and unskilful manner, either to import the one, or to make the other for their own use. By means of the unproductive class, the cultivators are delivered from many cares which would otherwise distract their attention from the cultivation of land. The superiority of produce, which, in consequence of this undivided attention, they are enabled to raise, is fully sufficient to pay the whole expence which the maintenance and employment of the unproductive class costs either the proprietors, or themselves. The industry of merchants, artificers, and manufacturers, though in its own nature altogether unproductive, yet contributes in this manner indirectly to increase the produce of the land. It increases the productive powers of productive labour, by leaving it at liberty to confine itself to its proper employment, the cultivation of land; and the plough goes frequently the easier and the better by means of the labour of the man whose business is most remote from the plough.

It can never be the interest of the proprietors and cultivators to restrain or to discourage in any respect the industry of merchants, artificers and manufacturers. The greater the liberty which this unproductive class enjoys, the greater will be the competition in all the different trades which compose it, and the cheaper will the other two classes be supplied, both with foreign goods and with the manufactured produce of their own country.

It can never be the interest of the unproductive class to oppress the other two classes. It is the surplus produce of the land, or what remains after deducting the maintenance, first, of the cultivators, and afterwards, of the proprietors, that maintains and employs the unproductive class. The greater this surplus, the greater must likewise be the maintenance and employment of that class. The establishment of perfect justice, of perfect liberty, and of perfect equality, is the very simple secret which most effectually secures the highest degree of prosperity to all the three classes. . . .

Some speculative physicians seem to have imagined that the health of the human body could be preserved only by a certain precise regimen of diet and exercise, of which every, the smallest, violation necessarily occasioned some degree of disease or disorder proportioned to the degree of the violation. Experience, however, would seem to show that the human body frequently preserves, to all appearance at least, the most perfect state of health under a vast variety of different regimens; even under some which are generally believed to be very far from being perfectly wholesome. But the healthful state of the human body, it would seem, contains in itself some unknown principle of preservation, capable either of preventing or of correcting, in many respects, the bad effects even of a very faulty regimen. Mr. Quesnai, who was himself a physician, and a very speculative physician,* seems to have entertained a notion of the same kind concerning the political body, and to have imagined that it would thrive and prosper only under a certain precise regimen, the exact regimen of perfect liberty and perfect justice. He seems not to have considered that in the political body, the natural effort which every man is continually making to better his own condition,* is a principle of preservation capable of preventing and correcting, in many respects, the bad effects of a political œconomy, in some degree, both partial and oppressive. Such a political œconomy, though it no doubt retards more or less, is not always capable of stopping altogether the natural progress of a nation towards wealth and prosperity, and still less of making it go backwards. If a nation could not prosper without the enjoyment of perfect liberty and perfect justice, there is not in the world a nation which could ever have prospered. In the political body, how-ever, the wisdom of nature has fortunately made ample provi-sion for remedying many of the bad effects of the folly and injustice of man; in the same manner as it has done in the natural body, for remedying those of his sloth and intem-perance.

The capital error of this system, however, seems to lie in its representing the class of artificers, manufacturers and mer-chants, as altogether barren and unproductive. The following observations may serve to show the impropriety of this repres-entation.*

First, this class, it is acknowledged, reproduces annually the value of its own annual consumption, and continues, at least, the existence of the stock or capital which maintains and employs it. But upon this account alone the denomination of barren or unproductive should seem to be very improperly applied to it. We should not call a marriage barren or unpro-ductive, though it produced only a son and a daughter, to replace the father and mother, and though it did not increase the number of the human species, but only continued it as it was before. Farmers and country labourers, indeed, over and above the stock which maintains and employs them, reproduce annually a neat produce, a free rent to the landlord. As a marriage which affords three children is certainly more productive than one which affords only two; so the labour of farmers and country labourers is certainly more productive than that of merchants, artificers and manufacturers.* The superior produce of the one class, however, does not render the other barren or unproductive.

Secondly, it seems, upon this account, altogether improper to consider artificers, manufacturers and merchants, in the same light as menial servants. The labour of menial servants does not continue the existence of the fund which maintains and employs them. Their maintenance and employment is altogether at the expence of their masters, and the work which they perform is not of a nature to repay that expence. That work consists in services which perish generally in the very instant of their performance,* and does not fix or realize itself in any vendible commodity which can replace the value of their wages and maintenance. The labour, on the contrary, of artificers, manufacturers and merchants, naturally does fix and realize itself in some such vendible commodity. It is upon this account that, in the chapter in which I treat of productive and unproductive labour,* I have classed artificers, manufacturers and merchants, among the productive labourers, and menial servants among the barren or unproductive. . . .

This system,* however, with all its imperfections is, perhaps, the nearest approximation to the truth that has yet been published upon the subject of political œconomy,* and is upon that account well worth the consideration of every man who wishes to examine with attention the principles of that very important science. Though in representing the labour which is employed upon land as the only productive labour, the notions which it inculcates are perhaps too narrow and confined; yet in representing the wealth of nations as consisting, not in the unconsumable riches of money,* but in the consumable goods annually reproduced by the labour of the society; and in representing perfect liberty* as the only effectual expedient for rendering this annual reproduction the greatest possible, its doctrine seems to be in every respect as just as it is generous and liberal. Its followers are very numerous; and as men are fond of paradoxes, and of appearing to understand what surpasses the comprehension of ordinary people, the paradox which it maintains, concerning the unproductive nature of manufacturing labour, has not perhaps contributed a little to increase the number of its admirers. They have for some years past made a pretty considerable sect, distinguished in the French republick of letters by the name of, The Œconomists.* Their works have certainly been of some service to their country; not only by bringing into general discussion, many subjects which had never been well examined before, but by influencing in some measure the publick administration in favour of agriculture.* It has been in consequence of their representations, accordingly, that the agriculture of France has been delivered from several of the oppressions which it before laboured under. The term during which such a lease can be granted, as will be valid against every future purchaser or proprietor of the land, has been prolonged from nine to twenty-seven years. The antient provincial restraints upon the transportation of corn from one province of the kingdom to another, have been entirely taken away, and the liberty of exporting it to all foreign countries, has been established as the common law of the kingdom in all ordinary cases. This sect, in their works, which are very numerous, and which treat not only of what is properly called Political Œconomy, or of the nature and causes of the wealth of nations, but of every other branch of the system of civil government, all follow implicitly, and without any sensible variation, the doctrine of Mr. Quesnai.* There is upon this account little variety in the greater part of their works. The most distinct and best connected account of this doctrine is to be found in a little book written by Mr. Mercier de la Riviere,* sometime Intendant of Martinico, intitled, The natural and essential Order of Political Societies. The admiration of this whole sect for their master, who was himself a man of the greatest modesty and simplicity, is not inferior to that of any of the antient philosophers for the founders of their respective systems. "There have been, since the world began," says a very diligent and respectable author, the Marquis de Mirabeau,* "three great inventions which have principally given stability to political societies, independent of many other inventions which have enriched and adorned them. The first, is the invention of writing, which alone gives human nature the power of transmitting, without alteration, its laws, its contracts, its annals, and its discoveries. The second, is the invention of money, which binds together all the relations between civilized societies. The third, is the Œconomical Table, the result of the other two, which completes them both by perfecting their object; the great discovery of our age, but of which our posterity will reap the benefit." . . .

The greatest and most important branch of the commerce of every nation, it has already been observed,* is that which is carried on between the inhabitants of the town and those of the country. The inhabitants of the town draw from the country the rude produce which constitutes both the materials of their work and the fund of their subsistence; and they pay for this rude produce by sending back to the country a certain portion of it manufactured and prepared for immediate use. The trade which is carried on between these two different sets of people, consists ultimately in a certain quantity of rude produce exchanged for a certain quantity of manufactured produce. The dearer the latter, therefore, the cheaper the former; and whatever tends in any country to raise the price of manufactured produce, tends to lower that of the rude produce of the land, and thereby to discourage agriculture. The smaller the quantity of manufactured produce which any given quantity of rude produce, or, what comes to the same thing, which the price of any given quantity of rude produce is capable of purchasing, the smaller the exchangeable value of that given quantity of rude produce; the smaller the encouragement which either the landlord has to increase its quantity by improving, or the farmer by cultivating the land. Whatever, besides, tends to diminish in any country the number of artificers and manufacturers, tends to diminish the home market, the most important of all markets for the rude produce of the land, and thereby still further to discourage agriculture.

Those systems, therefore, which preferring agriculture to all other employments, in order to promote it, impose restraints upon manufactures and foreign trade, act contrary to the very end which they propose, and indirectly discourage that very species of industry which they mean to promote. They are so far, perhaps, more inconsistent than even the mercantile system. That system, by encouraging manufactures and foreign trade more than agriculture, turns a certain portion of the capital of the society from supporting a more advantageous, to support a less advantageous species of industry. But still it really and in the end encourages that species of industry which it means to promote. Those agricultural systems, on the contrary, really and in the end discourage their own favourite species of industry.

It is thus that every system which endeavours, either, by extraordinary encouragements, to draw towards a particular species of industry a greater share of the capital of the society than what would naturally go to it; or, by extraordinary restraints, to force from a particular species of industry some share of the capital which would otherwise be employed in it; is in reality subversive of the great purpose which it means to promote. It retards, instead of accelerating, the progress of the society towards real wealth and greatness; and diminishes, instead of increasing, the real value of the annual produce of its land and labour.

All systems either of preference or of restraint, therefore, being thus completely taken away, the obvious and simple system of natural liberty establishes itself of its own accord.* Every man, as long as he does not violate the laws of justice, is left perfectly free to pursue his own interest his own way, and to bring both his industry and capital into competition with those of any other man, or order of men. The sovereign is completely discharged from a duty, in the attempting to perform which he must always be exposed to innumerable delusions, and for the proper performance of which no human wisdom or knowledge could ever be sufficient; the duty of superintending the industry of private people, and of directing it towards the employments most suitable to the interest of the society. According to the system of natural liberty, the sovereign has only three duties to attend to; three duties of great importance, indeed, but plain and intelligible to common understandings: first, the duty of protecting the society from the violence and invasion of other independent societies; secondly, the duty of protecting, as far as possible, every member of the society from the injustice or oppression of every other member of it, or the duty of establishing an exact administration of justice; and, thirdly, the duty of erecting and maintaining certain publick works and certain publick institutions, which it can never be for the interest of any individual, or small number of individuals, to erect and maintain; because the profit could never repay the expence to any individual or small number of individuals, though it may frequently do much more than repay it to a great society.

The proper performance of those several duties of the sovereign necessarily supposes a certain expence; and this expence again necessarily requires a certain revenue to support it. In the following book, therefore, I shall endeavour to explain; first, what are the necessary expences of the sovereign or commonwealth; and which of those expences ought to be defrayed by the general contribution of the whole society; and which of them, by that of some particular part only, or of some particular members of the society: secondly, what are the different methods in which the whole society may be made to contribute towards defraying the expences incumbent on the whole society, and what are the principal advantages and inconveniencies of each of those methods: and, thirdly, what are the reasons and causes which have induced almost all modern governments to mortgage some part of this revenue, or to contract debts, and what have been the effects of those debts upon the real wealth, the annual produce of the land and labour of the society. The following book, therefore, will naturally be divided into three chapters.

BOOK V

Of the Revenue of the Sovereign or Commonwealth*

CHAPTER I

Of the Expences of the Sovereign or Commonwealth

PART FIRST

Of the Expence of Defence

THE first duty of the sovereign, that of protecting the society from the violence and invasion of other independent societies, can be performed only by means of a military force. But the expence both of preparing this military force in time of peace, and of employing it in time of war, is very different in the different states of society, in the different periods of improvement.*

Among nations of hunters, the lowest and rudest state of society, such as we find it among the native tribes of North America,* every man is a warrior as well as a hunter. When he goes to war, either to defend his society, or to revenge the injuries which have been done to it by other societies, he maintains himself by his own labour, in the same manner as when he lives at home. His society, for in this state of things there is properly neither sovereign nor commonwealth, is at no sort of expence, either to prepare him for the field, or to maintain him while he is in it.

Among nations of shepherds,* a more advanced state of society, such as we find it among the Tartars and Arabs, every man is, in the same manner, a warrior. Such nations have commonly no fixed habitation, but live, either in tents, or in a sort of covered waggons which are easily transported from place to place. The whole tribe or nation changes its situation according to the different seasons of the year, as well as according to other accidents. When its herds and flocks have consumed the forage of one part of the country, it removes to another, and from that to a third. In the dry season, it comes down to the banks of the rivers; in the wet season it retires to the upper country. When such a nation goes to war, the warriors will not trust their herds and flocks to the feeble defence of their old men, their women and children; and their old men, their women and children, will not be left behind without defence and without subsistence. The whole nation, besides, being accustomed to a wandering life, even in time of peace, easily takes the field in time of war. Whether it marches as an army, or moves about as a company of herdsmen, the way of life is nearly the same, though the object proposed by it be very different. They all go to war together, therefore, and every one does as well as he can. Among the Tartars, even the women have been frequently known to engage in battle. If they conquer, whatever belongs to the hostile tribe is the recompence of the victory. But if they are vanquished, all is lost, and not only their herds and flocks, but their women and children, become the booty of the conqueror. Even the greater part of those who survive the action are obliged to submit to him for the sake of immediate subsistence. The rest are commonly dissipated and dispersed in the desart.

The ordinary life, the ordinary exercises of a Tartar or Arab, prepare him sufficiently for war. Running, wrestling, cudgel-playing, throwing the javelin, drawing the bow, &c. are the common pastimes of those who live in the open air, and are all of them the images of war. When a Tartar or Arab actually goes to war, he is maintained, by his own herds and flocks which he carries with him, in the same manner as in peace. His chief or sovereign, for those nations have all chiefs or sovereigns, is at no sort of expence in preparing him for the field; and when he is in it, the chance of plunder is the only pay which he either expects or requires.

An army of hunters can seldom exceed two or three hundred men. The precarious subsistence which the chace affords could seldom allow a greater number to keep together for any considerable time. An army of shepherds, on the contrary, may sometimes amount to two or three hundred thousand. As long as nothing stops their progress, as long as they can go on from one district, of which they have consumed the forage, to another which is yet entire; there seems to be scarce any limit to the number who can march on together. A nation of hunters can never be formidable to the civilized nations in their neighbourhood. A nation of shepherds may. Nothing can be more contemptible than an Indian war in North America. Nothing, on the contrary, can be more dreadful than a Tartar invasion has frequently been in Asia. The judgment of Thucydides,* that both Europe and Asia could not resist the Scythians united, has been verified by the experience of all ages. The inhabitants of the extensive, but defenceless plains of Scythia or Tartary, have been frequently united under the dominion of the chief of some conquering horde or clan; and the havock and devastation of Asia have always signalized their union. The inhabitants of the inhospitable desarts of Arabia, the other great nation of shepherds, have never been united but once; under Mahomet and his immediate successors. Their union, which was more the effect of religious enthusiasm than of conquest, was signalized in the same manner. If the hunting nations of America should ever become shepherds, their neighbourhood would be much more dangerous to the European colonies than it is at present.

In a yet more advanced state of society,* among those nations of husbandmen who have little foreign commerce and no other manufactures, but those coarse and houshold ones which almost every private family prepares for its own use; every man, in the same manner, either is a warrior, or easily becomes such. They who live by agriculture generally pass the whole day in the open air, exposed to all the inclemencies of the seasons. The hardiness of their ordinary life prepares them for the fatigues of war, to some of which their necessary occupations bear a great analogy. The necessary occupation of a ditcher prepares him to work in the trenches, and to fortify a camp as well as to enclose a field. The ordinary pastimes of such husbandmen are the same as those of shepherds, and are in the same manner the images of war. But as husbandmen have less leisure than shepherds, they are not so frequently employed in those pastimes. They are soldiers, but soldiers not quite so much masters of their exercise. Such as they are, however, it seldom costs the sovereign or commonwealth any expence to prepare them for the field.

Agriculture, even in its rudest and lowest state, supposes a settlement; some sort of fixed habitation which cannot be abandoned without great loss. When a nation of mere husbandmen, therefore, goes to war, the whole people cannot take the field together. The old men, the women and children, at least, must remain at home to take care of the habitation. All the men of the military age, however, may take the field, and, in small nations of this kind, have frequently done so. In every nation the men of the military age are supposed to amount to about a fourth or a fifth part of the whole body of the people. If the campaign too should begin after seed-time, and end before harvest, both the husbandman and his principal labourers can be spared from the farm without much loss. He trusts that the work which must be done in the mean time can be well enough executed by the old men, the women and the children. He is not unwilling, therefore, to serve without pay during a short campaign, and it frequently costs the sovereign or commonwealth as little to maintain him in the field as to prepare him for it. The citizens of all the different states of antient Greece seem to have served in this manner till after the second Persian war;* and the people of Peloponesus till after the Peloponesian war.* The Peloponesians, Thucydides observes,* generally left the field in the summer, and returned home to reap the harvest. The Roman people under their kings, and during the first ages of the republick, served in the same manner. It was not till the siege of Veii,* that they, who staid at home, began to contribute something towards maintaining those who went to war. In the European monarchies, which were founded upon the ruins of the Roman empire, both before and for some time after the establishment of what is properly called the feudal law,* the great lords, with all their immediate dependents, used to serve the crown at their own expence. In the field, in the same manner as at home, they maintained themselves by their own revenue, and not by any stipend or pay which they received from the king upon that particular occasion.

In a more advanced state of society,* two different causes contribute to render it altogether impossible that they, who take the field, should maintain themselves at their own expence. Those two causes are, the progress of manufactures, and the improvement in the art of war.*

Though a husbandman should be employed in an expedition, provided it begins after seed-time and ends before harvest, the interruption of his business will not always occasion any considerable diminution of his revenue. Without the intervention of his labour, nature does herself the greater part of the work which remains to be done. But the moment that an artificer, a smith, a carpenter, or a weaver, for example, quits his workhouse, the sole source of his revenue is completely dried up. Nature does nothing for him, he does all for himself. When he takes the field, therefore, in defence of the publick, as he has no revenue to maintain himself, he must necessarily be maintained by the publick. But in a country of which a great part of the inhabitants are artificers and manufacturers, a great part of the people who go to war must be drawn from those classes, and must therefore be maintained by the publick as long as they are employed in its service.*

When the art of war too has gradually grown up to be a very intricate and complicated science, when the event of war ceases to be determined, as in the first ages of society, by a single irregular skirmish or battle, but when the contest is generally spun out through several different campaigns, each of which lasts during the greater part of the year; it becomes universally necessary that the publick should maintain those who serve the publick in war, at least while they are employed in that service. Whatever in time of peace might be the ordinary occupation of those who go to war, so very tedious and expensive a service would otherwise be by far too heavy a burden upon them. After the second Persian war, accordingly, the armies of Athens seem to have been generally composed of mercenary troops; consisting, indeed, partly of citizens, but partly too of foreigners; and all of them equally hired and paid at the expence of the state. From the time of the siege of Veii, the armies of Rome received pay for their service during the time which they remained in the field. Under the feudal governments the military service both of the great lords and of their immediate dependents was, after a certain period, universally exchanged for a payment in money, which was employed to maintain those who served in their stead.

The number of those who can go to war, in proportion to the whole number of the people, is necessarily much smaller in a civilized, than in a rude state of society. In a civilized society, as the soldiers are maintained altogether by the labour of those who are not soldiers, the number of the former can never exceed what the latter can maintain, over and above maintaining, in a manner suitable to their respective stations, both themselves and the other officers of government, and law, whom they are obliged to maintain. In the little agrarian states of antient Greece, a fourth or a fifth part of the whole body of the people considered themselves as soldiers, and would sometimes, it is said, take the field. Among the civilized nations of modern Europe, it is commonly computed, that not more than one hundredth part of the inhabitants of any country can be employed as soldiers, without ruin to the country which pays the expence of their service.*

The expence of preparing the army for the field seems not to have become considerable in any nation, till long after that of maintaining it in the field had devolved entirely upon the sovereign or commonwealth. In all the different republicks of antient Greece, to learn his military exercises, was a necessary part of education imposed by the state upon every free citizen.

In every city there seems to have been a publick field, in which, under the protection of the publick magistrate, the young people were taught their different exercises by different masters. In this very simple institution, consisted the whole expence which any Grecian state seems ever to have been at, in preparing its citizens for war. In antient Rome the exercises of the Campus Martius answered the same purpose with those of the Gymnasium* in antient Greece. Under the feudal governments, the many publick ordinances that the citizens of every district should practise archery as well as several other military exercises,* were intended for promoting the same purpose, but do not seem to have promoted it so well. Either from want of interest in the officers entrusted with the execution of those ordinances, or from some other cause, they appear to have been universally neglected; and in the progress of all those governments, military exercises seem to have gone gradually into disuse among the great body of the people.

In the republicks of antient Greece and Rome, during the whole period of their existence, and under the feudal governments for a considerable time after their first establishment, the trade of a soldier was not a separate, distinct trade, which constituted the sole or principal occupation of a particular class of citizens. Every subject of the state, whatever might be the ordinary trade or occupation by which he gained his livelihood, considered himself, upon all ordinary occasions, as fit likewise to exercise the trade of a soldier, and upon many extraordinary occasions as bound to exercise it.

The art of war, however, as it is certainly the noblest of all arts,* so in the progress of improvement it necessarily becomes one of the most complicated among them. The state of the mechanical, as well as of some other arts, with which it is necessarily connected, determines the degree of perfection to which it is capable of being carried at any particular time. But in order to carry it to this degree of perfection, it is necessary that it should become the sole or principal occupation of a particular class of citizens, and the division of labour is as necessary for the improvement of this, as of every other art.

Into other arts the division of labour is naturally introduced by the prudence of individuals, who find that they promote their private interest better by confining themselves to a particular trade, than by exercising a great number. But it is the wisdom of the state only which can render the trade of a soldier a particular trade separate and distinct from all others. A private citizen who, in time of profound peace, and without any particular encouragement from the publick, should spend the greater part of his time in military exercises, might, no doubt, both improve himself very much in them, and amuse himself very well; but he certainly would not promote his own interest. It is the wisdom of the state only which can render it for his interest to give up the greater part of his time to this peculiar occupation: and states have not always had this wisdom, even when their circumstances had become such, that the preservation of their existence required that they should have it.

A shepherd has a great deal of leisure; a husbandman, in the rude state of husbandry, has some; an artificer or manufacturer has none at all. The first may, without any loss, employ a great deal of his time in martial exercises; the second may employ some part of it; but the last cannot employ a single hour in them without some loss, and his attention to his own interest naturally leads him to neglect them altogether. These improvements in husbandry too, which the progress of arts and manufactures necessarily introduces, leave the husbandman as little leisure as the artificer. Military exercises come to be as much neglected by the inhabitants of the country as by those of the town, and the great body of the people becomes altogether unwarlike. That wealth, at the same time, which always follows the improvements of agriculture and manufactures, and which in reality is no more than the accumulated produce of those improvements, provokes the invasion of all their neighbours. An industrious, and upon that account a wealthy nation, is of all nations the most likely to be attacked; and unless the state takes some new measures for the publick defence, the natural habits of the people render them altogether incapable of defending themselves.

In these circumstances, there seem to be but two methods, by which the state can make any tolerable provision for the publick defence.

It may either, first, by means of a very rigorous police, and in spite of the whole bent of the interest, genius and inclinations of the people, enforce the practice of military exercises, and oblige either all the citizens of the military age, or a certain number of them, to join in some measure the trade of a soldier to whatever other trade or profession they may happen to carry on.

Or, secondly, by maintaining and employing a certain number of citizens in the constant practice of military exercises, it may render the trade of a soldier a particular trade, separate and distinct from all others.

If the state has recourse to the first of those two expedients, its military force is said to consist in a militia; if to the second, it is said to consist in a standing army. The practice of military exercises is the sole or principal occupation of the soldiers of a standing army, and the maintenance or pay which the state affords them is the principal and ordinary fund of their subsistence. The practice of military exercises is only the occasional occupation of the soldiers of a militia, and they derive the principal and ordinary fund of their subsistence from some other occupation. In a militia, the character of the labourer, artificer, or tradesman, predominates over that of the soldier: in a standing army, that of the soldier predominates over every other character; and in this distinction seems to consist the essential difference between those two different species of military force.

Militias have been of several different kinds.* In some countries the citizens destined for defending the state, seem to have been exercised only, without being, if I may say so, regimented; that is, without being divided into separate and distinct bodies of troops, each of which performed its exercises under its own proper and permanent officers. In the republicks of antient Greece and Rome, each citizen, as long as he remained at home, seems to have practised his exercises either separately and independently, or with such of his equals as he liked best; and not to have been attached to any particular body of troops till he was actually called upon to take the field. In other countries, the militia has not only been exercised, but regimented. In England, in Switzerland, and, I believe, in every other country of modern Europe, where any imperfect military force of this kind has been established, every militia-man is, even in time of peace, attached to a particular body of troops, which performs its exercises under its own proper and permanent officers.

Before the invention of fire-arms, that army was superior in which the soldiers had, each individually, the greatest skill and dexterity in the use of their arms. Strength and agility of body were of the highest consequence, and commonly determined the fate of battles. But this skill and dexterity in the use of their arms, could be acquired only, in the same manner as fencing is at present, by practising, not in great bodies, but each man separately, in a particular school, under a particular master, or with his own particular equals and companions. Since the invention of fire-arms, strength and agility of body, or even extraordinary dexterity and skill in the use of arms, though they are far from being of no consequence, are, however, of less consequence. The nature of the weapon, though it by no means puts the aukward upon a level with the skilful, puts him more nearly so than he ever was before. All the dexterity and skill, it is supposed, which are necessary for using it, can be well enough acquired by practising in great bodies.

Regularity, order, and prompt obedience to command, are qualities which, in modern armies, are of more importance towards determining the fate of battles, than the dexterity and skill of the soldiers in the use of their arms. But the noise of fire-arms, the smoke, and the invisible death to which every man feels himself every moment exposed, as soon as he comes within cannon-shot, and frequently a long time before the battle can be well said to be engaged, must render it very difficult to maintain any considerable degree of this regularity, order, and prompt obedience, even in the beginning of a modern battle. In an antient battle there was no noise but what arose from the human voice; there was no smoke, there was no invisible cause of wounds or death. Every man, till some mortal weapon actually did approach him, saw clearly that no such weapon was near him. In these circumstances, and among troops who had some confidence in their own skill and dexterity in the use of their arms, it must have been a good deal less difficult to preserve some degree of regularity and order, not only in the beginning, but through the whole progress of an antient battle, and till one of the two armies was fairly defeated. But the habits of regularity, order, and prompt obedience to command, can be acquired only by troops which are exercised in great bodies.

A militia, however, in whatever manner it may be either disciplined or exercised, must always be much inferior to a well disciplined and well exercised standing army.

The soldiers, who are exercised only once a week, or once a month, can never be so expert in the use of their arms, as those who are exercised every day, or every other day; and though this circumstance may not be of so much consequence in modern, as it was in antient times, yet the acknowledged superiority of the Prussian troops,* owing, it is said, very much to their superior expertness in their exercise, may satisfy us that it is, even at this day, of very considerable consequence.

The soldiers, who are bound to obey their officer only once a week or once a month, and who are at all other times at liberty to manage their own affairs their own way, without being in any respect accountable to him, can never be under the same awe in his presence, can never have the same disposition to ready obedience, with those whose whole life and conduct are every day directed by him, and who every day even rise and go to bed, or at least retire to their quarters, according to his orders. In what is called discipline, or in the habit of ready obedience, a militia must always be still more inferior to a standing army, than it may sometimes be in what is called the manual exercise, or in the management and use of its arms. But in modern war the habit of ready and instant obedience is of much greater consequence than a considerable superiority in the management of arms.

Those militias which, like the Tartar or Arab militia, go to war under the same chieftains whom they are accustomed to obey in peace, are by far the best. In respect for their officers, in the habit of ready obedience, they approach nearest to standing armies. The highland militia, when it served under its own chieftains, had some advantage of the same kind. As the highlanders, however, were not wandering, but stationary shepherds, as they had all a fixed habitation, and were not, in peaceable times, accustomed to follow their chieftain from place to place; so in time of war they were less willing to follow him to any considerable distance, or to continue for any long time in the field. When they had acquired any booty they were eager to return home, and his authority was seldom sufficient to detain them.* In point of obedience they were always much inferior to what is reported of the Tartars and Arabs. As the highlanders too, from their stationary life, spend less of their time in the open air, they were always less accustomed to military exercises, and were less expert in the use of their arms than the Tartars and Arabs are said to be.

A militia of any kind, it must be observed, however, which has served for several successive campaigns in the field, becomes in every respect a standing army. The soldiers are every day exercised in the use of their arms, and, being constantly under the command of their officers, are habituated to the same prompt obedience which takes place in standing armies. What they were before they took the field, is of little importance. They necessarily become in every respect a standing army, after they have passed a few campaigns in it. Should the war in America drag out through another campaign, the American militia may become in every respect a match for that standing army, of which the valour appeared, in the last war, at least not inferior to that of the hardiest veterans of France and Spain.*

This distinction being well understood, the history of all ages, it will be found, bears testimony to the irresistible superiority which a well-regulated standing army has over a militia. . . .

Men of republican principles have been jealous of a standing army as dangerous to liberty.* It certainly is so, wherever the interest of the general and that of the principal officers are not necessarily connected with the support of the constitution of the state. The standing army of Caesar destroyed the Roman republick. The standing army of Cromwell* turned the long parliament out of doors. But where the sovereign is himself the general, and the principal nobility and gentry of the country the chief officers of the army; where the military force is placed under the command of those who have the greatest interest in the support of the civil authority, because they have themselves the greatest share of that authority, a standing army can never be dangerous to liberty. On the contrary, it may in some cases be favourable to liberty.* The security which it gives to the sovereign renders unnecessary that troublesome jealousy, which, in some modern republicks, seems to watch over the minutest actions, and to be at all times ready to disturb the peace of every citizen. Where the security of the magistrate, though supported by the principal people of the country, is endangered by every popular discontent; where a small tumult is capable of bringing about in a few hours a great revolution, the whole authority of government must be employed to suppress and punish every murmur and complaint against it. To a sovereign, on the contrary, who feels himself supported, not only by the natural aristocracy of the country, but by a well-regulated standing army, the rudest, the most groundless, and the most licentious remonstrances can give little disturbance. He can safely pardon or neglect them, and his consciousness of his own superiority naturally disposes him to do so. That degree of liberty which approaches to licentiousness can be tolerated only in countries where the sovereign is secured by a well-regulated standing army. It is in such countries only, that the publick safety does not require, that the sovereign should be trusted with any discretionary power, for suppressing even the impertinent wantonness of this licentious liberty.

The first duty of the sovereign, therefore, that of defending the society from the violence and injustice of other independent societies, grows gradually more and more expensive, as the society advances in civilization. The military force of the society, which originally cost the sovereign no expence either in time of peace or in time of war, must, in the progress of improvement, first be maintained by him in time of war, and afterwards even in time of peace.

The great change introduced into the art of war by the invention of fire-arms, has enhanced still further both the expence of exercising and disciplining any particular number of soldiers in time of peace, and that of employing them in time of war. Both their arms and their ammunition are become more expensive. A musquet is a more expensive machine than a javelin or a bow and arrows; a cannon or a mortar, than a balista or a catapulta.* The powder, which is spent in a modern review, is lost irrecoverably, and occasions a very considerable expence. The javelins and arrows which were thrown or shot in an antient one, could easily be picked up again, and were besides of very little value. The cannon and the mortar are, not only much dearer, but much heavier machines than the balista or catapulta, and require a greater expence, not only to prepare them for the field, but to carry them to it. As the superiority of the modern artillery too, over that of the antients, is very great; it has become much more difficult, and consequently much more expensive, to fortify a town so as to resist even for a few weeks the attack of that superior artillery. In modern times many different causes contribute to render the defence of the society more expensive. The unavoidable effects of the natural progress of improvement have, in this respect, been a good deal enhanced by a great revolution in the art of war, to which a mere accident, the invention of gun-powder,* seems to have given occasion.

In modern war the great expence of fire-arms gives an evident advantage to the nation which can best afford that expence; and consequently, to an opulent and civilized, over a poor and barbarous nation. In antient times the opulent and civilized found it difficult to defend themselves against the poor and barbarous nations. In modern times the poor and barbarous find it difficult to defend themselves against the opulent and civilized. The invention of fire-arms, an invention which at first sight appears to be so pernicious, is certainly favourable both to the permanency and to the extension of civilization.*

PART SECOND

Of the Expence of Justice

The second duty of the sovereign, that of protecting, as far as possible, every member of the society from the injustice or oppression of every other member of it, or the duty of establishing an exact administration of justice, requires too very different degrees of expence in the different periods of society.

Among nations of hunters, as there is scarce any property, or at least none that exceeds the value of two or three days labour; so there is seldom any established magistrate or any regular administration of justice. Men who have no property can injure one another only in their persons or reputations. But when one man kills, wounds, beats, or defames another, though he to whom the injury is done suffers, he who does it receives no benefit. It is otherwise with the injuries to property. The benefit of the person who does the injury is often equal to the loss of him who suffers it. Envy, malice, or resentment, are the only passions which can prompt one man to injure another in his person or reputation. But the greater part of men are not very frequently under the influence of those passions; and the very worst men are so only occasionally. As their gratification too, how agreeable soever it may be to certain characters, is not attended with any real or permanent advantage, it is in the greater part of men commonly restrained by prudential considerations. Men may live together in society with some tolerable degree of security, though there is no civil magistrate to protect them from the injustice of those passions. But avarice and ambition in the rich, in the poor the hatred of labour and the love of present ease and enjoyment, are the passions which prompt to invade property, passions much more steady in their operation, and much more universal in their influence. Wherever there is great property, there is great inequality. For one very rich man, there must be at least five hundred poor, and the affluence of the few supposes the indigence of the many. The affluence of the rich excites the indignation of the poor, who are often both driven by want, and prompted by envy, to invade his possessions. It is only under the shelter of the civil magistrate that the owner of that valuable property, which is acquired by the labour of many years, or perhaps of many successive generations, can sleep a single night in security. He is at all times surrounded by unknown enemies, whom, though he never provoked, he can never appease, and from whose injustice he can be protected only by the powerful arm of the civil magistrate continually held up to chastise it. The acquisition of valuable and extensive property, therefore, necessarily requires the establishment of civil government. Where there is no property, or at least none that exceeds the value of two or three days labour, civil government is not so necessary.

Civil government supposes a certain subordination. But as the necessity of civil government gradually grows up with the acquisition of valuable property, so the principal causes which naturally introduce subordination gradually grow up with the growth of that valuable property.*

The causes or circumstances which naturally introduce subordination, or which naturally, and antecedent to any civil institution, give some men some superiority over the greater part of their brethren, seem to be four in number.

The first of those causes or circumstances is the superiority of personal qualifications, of strength, beauty, and agility of body; of wisdom, and virtue, of prudence, justice, fortitude, and moderation of mind. The qualifications of the body, unless supported by those of the mind, can give little authority in any period of society. He is a very strong man who, by mere strength of body, can force two weak ones to obey him. The qualifications of the mind can alone give very great authority.

They are, however, invisible qualities; always disputable, and generally disputed. No society, whether barbarous or civilized, has ever found it convenient to settle the rules of precedency, of rank and subordination, according to those invisible qualities; but according to something that is more plain and palpable.

The second of those causes or circumstances is the superiority of age. An old man, provided his age is not so far advanced as to give suspicion of dotage, is every where more respected than a young man of equal rank, fortune, and abilities. Among nations of hunters, such as the native tribes of North America, age is the sole foundation of rank and precedency. Among them, father is the appellation of a superior; brother, of an equal; and son, of an inferior. In the most opulent and civilized nations, age regulates rank among those who are in every other respect equal, and among whom, therefore, there is nothing else to regulate it. Among brothers and among sisters, the eldest always take place; and in the succession of the paternal estate every thing which cannot be divided, but must go entire to one person, such as a title of honour, is in most cases given to the eldest. Age is a plain and palpable quality which admits of no dispute.

The third of those causes or circumstances is the superiority of fortune. The authority of riches, however, though great in every age of society, is perhaps greatest in the rudest age of society which admits of any considerable inequality of fortune. A Tartar chief, the increase of whose herds and flocks is sufficient to maintain a thousand men, cannot well employ that increase in any other way than in maintaining a thousand men.* The rude state of his society does not afford him any manufactured produce, any trinkets or baubles of any kind, for which he can exchange that part of his rude produce which is over and above his own consumption. The thousand men whom he thus maintains, depending entirely upon him for their subsistence, must both obey his orders in war, and submit to his jurisdiction in peace. He is necessarily both their general and their judge, and his chieftainship is the necessary effect of the superiority of his fortune. In an opulent and civilized society, a man may possess a much greater fortune, and yet not be able to command a dozen of people. Though the produce of his estate may be sufficient to maintain, and may perhaps actually maintain, more than a thousand people, yet as those people pay for every thing which they get from him, as he gives scarce any thing to any body but in exchange for an equivalent, there is scarce any body who considers himself as entirely dependent upon him, and his authority extends only over a few menial servants. The authority of fortune, however, is very great even in an opulent and civilized society. That it is much greater than that, either of age, or of personal qualities, has been the constant complaint of every period of society which admitted of any considerable inequality of fortune. The first period of society, that of hunters, admits of no such inequality. Universal poverty establishes there universal equality, and the superiority, either of age, or of personal qualities, are the feeble, but the sole foundations of authority and subordination. There is therefore little or no authority or subordination in this period of society.* The second period of society, that of shepherds, admits of very great inequalities of fortune, and there is no period in which the superiority of fortune gives so great authority to those who possess it. There is no period accordingly in which authority and subordination are more perfectly established. The authority of an Arabian scherif* is very great; that of a Tartar khan* altogether despotical.

The fourth of those causes or circumstances is the superiority of birth. Superiority of birth supposes an antient superiority of fortune in the family of the person who claims it. All families are equally ancient; and the ancestors of the prince, though they may be better known, cannot well be more numerous than those of the beggar. Antiquity of family means every where the antiquity either of wealth, or of that greatness which is commonly either founded upon wealth, or accompanied with it. Upstart greatness is every where less respected than antient greatness. The hatred of usurpers, the love of the family of an antient monarch, are, in a great measure, founded upon the contempt which men naturally have for the former, and upon their veneration for the latter. As a military officer submits without reluctance to the authority of a superior by whom he has always been commanded, but cannot bear that his inferior should be set over his head; so men easily submit to a family to whom they and their ancestors have always submitted; but are fired with indignation when another family, in whom they had never acknowledged any such superiority, assumes a dominion over them.

The distinction of birth, being subsequent to the inequality of fortune, can have no place in nations of hunters, among whom all men, being equal in fortune, must likewise be very nearly equal in birth. The son of a wise and brave man may, indeed, even among them, be somewhat more respected than a man of equal merit who has the misfortune to be the son of a fool or a coward. The difference, however, will not be very great; and there never was, I believe, a great family in the world whose illustration* was entirely derived from the inheritance of wisdom and virtue.

The distinction of birth not only may, but always does take place among nations of shepherds.* Such nations are always strangers to every sort of luxury, and great wealth can scarce ever be dissipated among them by improvident profusion. There are no nations accordingly who abound more in families revered and honoured on account of their descent from a long race of great and illustrious ancestors; because there are no nations among whom wealth is likely to continue longer in the same families.

Birth and fortune are evidently the two circumstances which principally set one man above another. They are the two great sources of personal distinction, and are therefore the principal causes which naturally establish authority and subordination among men. Among nations of shepherds both those causes operate with their full force. The great shepherd or herdsman, respected on account of his great wealth, and of the great number of those who depend upon him for subsistence, and revered on account of the nobleness of his birth, and of the immemorial antiquity of his illustrious family, has a natural authority over all the inferior shepherds or herdsmen of his horde or clan. He can command the united force of a greater number of people than any of them. His military power is greater than that of any of them. In time of war they are all of them naturally disposed to muster themselves under his banner, rather than under that of any other person, and his birth and fortune thus naturally procure to him some sort of executive power. By commanding too the united force of a greater number of people than any of them, he is best able to compel any one of them who may have injured another to compensate the wrong. He is the person, therefore, to whom all those who are too weak to defend themselves naturally look up for protection. It is to him that they naturally complain of the injuries which they imagine have been done to them, and his interposition in such cases is more easily submitted to, even by the person complained of, than that of any other person would be. His birth and fortune thus naturally procure him some sort of judicial authority.

It is in the age of shepherds, in the second period of society, that the inequality of fortune first begins to take place, and introduces among men a degree of authority and subordination which could not possibly exist before. It thereby introduces some degree of that civil government which is indispensably necessary for its own preservation: and it seems to do this naturally, and even independent of the consideration of that necessity. The consideration of that necessity comes no doubt afterwards to contribute very much to maintain and secure that authority and subordination. The rich, in particular, are necessarily interested to support that order of things, which can alone secure them in the possession of their own advantages. Men of inferior wealth combine to defend those of superior wealth in the possession of their property, in order that men of superior wealth may combine to defend them in the possession of theirs. All the inferior shepherds and herdsmen feel that the security of their own herds and flocks depends upon the security of those of the great shepherd or herdsman; that the maintenance of their lesser authority depends upon that of his greater authority, and that upon their subordination to him depends his power of keeping their inferiors in subordination to them. They constitute a sort of little nobility, who feel themselves interested to defend the property and to support the authority of their own little sovereign, in order that he may be able to defend their property and to support their authority. Civil government, so far as it is instituted for the security of property, is in reality instituted for the defence of the rich against the poor, or of those who have some property against those who have none at all.* . . .

PART THIRD

Of the Expence of publick Works and publick Institutions

The third and last duty of the sovereign or commonwealth is that of erecting and maintaining those publick institutions and those publick works, which, though they may be in the highest degree advantageous to a great society, are, however, of such a nature, that the profit could never repay the expence to any individual or small number of individuals, and which it, therefore, cannot be expected that any individual or small number of individuals should erect or maintain. The performance of this duty requires too very different degrees of expence in the different periods of society.

After the publick institutions and publick works necessary for the defence of the society, and for the administration of justice, both of which have already been mentioned, the other works and institutions of this kind are chiefly those for facilitating the commerce of the society, and those for promoting the instruction of the people. The institutions for instruction are of two kinds; those for the education of the youth, and those for the instruction of people of all ages. The consideration of the manner in which the expence of those different sorts of publick works and institutions may be most properly defrayed, will divide this third part of the present chapter into three different articles.

ARTICLE I

*Of the publick Works and Institutions for facilitating the
Commerce of the Society*

*And, first, of those which are necessary for facilitating
Commerce in general*

That the erection and maintenance of the publick works which
facilitate the commerce of any country, such as good roads,
bridges, navigable canals, harbours, &c.* must require very
different degrees of expence in the different periods of society,
is evident without any proof. The expence of making and
maintaining the publick roads of any country must evidently
increase with the annual produce of the land and labour of that
country, or with the quantity and weight of the goods which it
becomes necessary to fetch and carry upon those roads. The
strength of a bridge must be suited to the number and weight
of the carriages, which are likely to pass over it. The depth and
the supply of water for a navigable canal must be proportioned
to the number and tunnage of the lighters, which are likely to
carry goods upon it; the extent of a harbour to the number of
the shipping which are likely to take shelter in it.

It does not seem necessary that the expence of those publick
works should be defrayed from that publick revenue, as it is
commonly called, of which the collection and application is in
most countries assigned to the executive power. The greater
part of such publick works may easily be so managed, as to
afford a particular revenue sufficient for defraying their own
expence, without bringing any burden upon the general revenue
of the society.

A highway, a bridge, a navigable canal, for example, may in
most cases be both made and maintained by a small toll upon
the carriages which make use of them: a harbour, by a moderate
port-duty upon the tunnage of the shipping which load or
unload in it. The coinage, another institution for facilitating
commerce, in many countries, not only defrays its own expence, but affords a small revenue or seignorage to the sover-

eign. The post-office,* another institution for the same purpose, over and above defraying its own expence, affords in almost all countries a very considerable revenue to the sovereign.

When the carriages which pass over a highway or a bridge, and the lighters which sail upon a navigable canal, pay toll in proportion to their weight or their tunnage, they pay for the maintenance of those publick works exactly in proportion to the wear and tear which they occasion of them. It seems scarce possible to invent a more equitable way of maintaining such works. This tax or toll too, though it is advanced by the carrier, is finally paid by the consumer, to whom it must always be charged in the price of the goods. As the expence of carriage, however, is very much reduced by means of such publick works, the goods, notwithstanding the toll, come cheaper to the consumer than they could otherwise have done; their price not being so much raised by the toll, as it is lowered by the cheapness of the carriage. The person who finally pays this tax, therefore, gains by the application, more than he loses by the payment of it. His payment is exactly in proportion to his gain. It is in reality no more than a part of that gain which he is obliged to give up in order to get the rest. It seems impossible to imagine a more equitable method of raising a tax.

When the toll upon carriages of luxury, upon coaches, post-chaises,* &c. is made somewhat higher in proportion to their weight, than upon carriages of necessary use, such as carts, waggons, &c. the indolence and vanity of the rich is made to contribute in a very easy manner to the relief of the poor, by rendering cheaper the transportation of heavy goods to all the different parts of the country. . . .

Even those publick works which are of such a nature that they cannot afford any revenue for maintaining themselves, but of which the conveniency is nearly confined to some particular place or district, are always better maintained by a local or provincial revenue, under the management of a local and provincial administration, than by the general revenue of the state, of which the executive power must always have the management. Were the streets of London to be lighted and paved at the expence of the treasury, is there any probability that they would be so well lighted and paved as they are at present, or even at so small an expence? The expence, besides, instead of being raised by a local tax upon the inhabitants of each particular street, parish, or district in London, would, in this case, be defrayed out of the general revenue of the state, and would consequently be raised by a tax upon all the inhabitants of the kingdom, of whom the greater part derive no sort of benefit from the lighting and paving of the streets of London.*

The abuses which sometimes creep into the local and provincial administration of a local and provincial revenue, how enormous soever they may appear, are in reality, however, almost always very trifling, in comparison of those which commonly take place in the administration and expenditure of the revenue of a great empire. They are, besides, much more easily corrected. Under the local or provincial administration of the justices of the peace in Great Britain, the six days labour* which the country people are obliged to give to the reparation of the highways, is not always perhaps very judiciously applied, but it is scarce ever exacted with any circumstances of cruelty or oppression. In France, under the administration of the intendants,* the application is not always more judicious, and the exaction is frequently the most cruel and oppressive. Such Corvées,* as they are called, make one of the principal instruments of tyranny by which those officers chastise any parish or communeauté which has had the misfortune to fall under their displeasure.

Of the Publick Works and Institutions which are necessary for facilitating particular Branches of Commerce

The object of the publick works and institutions above mentioned is to facilitate commerce in general. But in order to facilitate some particular branches of it, particular institutions are necessary, which again require a particular and extraordinary expence.

Some particular branches of commerce, which are carried on with barbarous and uncivilized nations, require extraordinary protection. An ordinary store or counting-house could give little security to the goods of the merchants who trade to the western coast of Africa. To defend them from the barbarous natives, it is necessary that the place where they are deposited, should be, in some measure, fortified. The disorders in the government of Indostan have been supposed to render a like precaution necessary even among that mild and gentle people; and it was under pretence of securing their persons and property from violence, that both the English and French East India Companies were allowed to erect the first forts which they possessed in that country. Among other nations, whose vigorous government will suffer no strangers to possess any fortified place within their territory, it may be necessary to maintain some ambassador, minister, or consul, who may both decide, according to their own customs, the differences arising among his own countrymen; and, in their disputes with the natives, may, by means of his publick character, interfere with more authority, and afford them a more powerful protection, than they could expect from any private man. The interests of commerce have frequently made it necessary to maintain ministers in foreign countries, where the purposes, either of war or alliance, would not have required any. The commerce of the Turkey Company first occasioned the establishment of an ordinary ambassador at Constantinople. The first English embassies to Russia* arose altogether from commercial interests. The constant interference which those interests necessarily occasioned between the subjects of the different states of Europe, has probably introduced the custom of keeping, in all neighbouring countries, ambassadors or ministers constantly resident even in the time of peace. This custom, unknown to antient times, seems not to be older than the end of the fifteenth or beginning of the sixteenth century; that is, than the time when commerce first began to extend itself to the greater part of the nations of Europe, and when they first began to attend to its interests.

It seems not unreasonable, that the extraordinary expence, which the protection of any particular branch of commerce may occasion, should be defrayed by a moderate tax upon that particular branch; by a moderate fine, for example, to be paid by the traders when they first enter into it, or, what is more equal, by a particular duty of so much per cent. upon the goods which they either import into, or export out of, the particular countries with which it is carried on. The protection of trade in general, from pirates and freebooters, is said to have given occasion to the first institution of the duties of customs. But, if it was thought reasonable to lay a general tax upon trade, in order to defray the expence of protecting trade in general, it should seem equally reasonable to lay a particular tax upon a particular branch of trade, in order to defray the extraordinary expence of protecting that branch. . . .

With the right of possessing forts and garrisons, in distant and barbarous countries, is necessarily connected the right of making peace and war in those countries. The joint stock companies* which have had the one right, have constantly exercised the other, and have frequently had it expressly conferred upon them. How unjustly, how capriciously, how cruelly they have commonly exercised it, is too well known from recent experience.

When a company of merchants undertake, at their own risk and expence, to establish a new trade with some remote and barbarous nation, it may not be unreasonable to incorporate them into a joint stock company, and to grant them, in case of their success, a monopoly of the trade for a certain number of years. It is the easiest and most natural way in which the state can recompense them for hazarding a dangerous and expensive experiment, of which the publick is afterwards to reap the benefit. A temporary monopoly of this kind may be vindicated upon the same principles upon which a like mono-poly of a new machine is granted to its inventor, and that of a new book to its author.* But upon the expiration of the term, the monopoly ought certainly to determine;* the forts and garrisons, if it was found necessary to establish any, to be taken into the hands of government, their value to be paid to the company, and the trade to be laid open to all the subjects of the state. By a perpetual monopoly, all the other subjects of the state are taxed very absurdly in two different ways; first, by the high price of goods, which, in the case of a free trade, they could buy much cheaper; and, secondly, by their total exclusion from a branch of business, which it might be both convenient and profitable for many of them to carry on. It is for the most worthless of all purposes too that they are taxed in this manner. It is merely to enable the company to support the negligence, profusion, and malversation* of their own servants, whose disorderly conduct seldom allows the dividend of the company to exceed the ordinary rate of profit in trades which are altogether free, and very frequently makes it fall even a good deal short of that rate. Without a monopoly, however, a joint stock company, it would appear from experience, cannot long carry on any branch of foreign trade. To buy in one market, in order to sell, with profit, in another, when there are many competitors in both; to watch over, not only the occasional variations in the demand, but the much greater and more frequent variations in the competition, or in the supply which that demand is likely to get from other people, and to suit with dexterity and judgment both the quantity and quality of each assortment of goods to all these circumstances, is a species of warfare of which the operations are continually changing, and which can scarce ever be conducted successfully, without such an unremitting exertion of vigilance and attention, as cannot long be expected from the directors of a joint stock company. The East India Company, upon the redemption of their funds, and the expiration of their exclusive privilege, have a right, by act of parliament, to continue a corporation with a joint stock, and to trade in their corporate capacity to the East Indies in common with the rest of their fellow-subjects. But in this situation, the superior vigilance and attention of private adventurers would, in all probability, soon make them weary of the trade. . . .

ARTICLE II

*Of the Expence of the Institutions for the Education of
Youth**

The institutions for the education of the youth may, in the
same manner, furnish a revenue sufficient for defraying their
own expence. The fee or honorary which the scholar pays to
the master naturally constitutes a revenue of this kind.

Even where the reward of the master does not arise altogether from this natural revenue, it still is not necessary that
it should be derived from that general revenue of the society,
of which the collection and application is, in most countries,
assigned to the executive power. Through the greater part of
Europe, accordingly, the endowment of schools and colleges
makes either no charge upon that general revenue, or but a
very small one. It every where arises chiefly from some local
or provincial revenue, from the rent of some landed estate, or
from the interest of some sum of money allotted and put under
the management of trustees for this particular purpose, sometimes by the sovereign himself, and sometimes by some private
donor.

Have those publick endowments contributed in general to
promote the end of their institution? Have they contributed to
encourage the diligence, and to improve the abilities of the
teachers? Have they directed the course of education towards
objects more useful, both to the individual and to the publick,
than those to which it would naturally have gone of its own
accord? It should not seem very difficult to give at least a
probable answer to each of those questions.

In every profession, the exertion of the greater part of those
who exercise it, is always in proportion to the necessity they
are under of making that exertion.* This necessity is greatest
with those to whom the emoluments of their profession are the
only source from which they expect their fortune, or even their
ordinary revenue and subsistence. In order to acquire this
fortune, or even to get this subsistence, they must, in the

course of a year, execute a certain quantity of work of a known value; and, where the competition is free, the rivalship of competitors, who are all endeavouring to justle one another out of employment, obliges every man to endeavour to execute his work with a certain degree of exactness. The greatness of the objects which are to be acquired by success in some particular professions may, no doubt, sometimes animate the exertion of a few men of extraordinary spirit and ambition. Great objects, however, are evidently not necessary in order to occasion the greatest exertions. Rivalship and emulation render excellency, even in mean professions, an object of ambition, and frequently occasion the very greatest exertions. Great objects, on the contrary, alone and unsupported by the necessity of application, have seldom been sufficient to occasion any considerable exertion. In England, success in the profession of the law leads to some very great objects of ambition; and yet how few men, born to easy fortunes, have ever in this country been eminent in that profession!

The endowments of schools and colleges have necessarily diminished more or less the necessity of application in the teachers. Their subsistence, so far as it arises from their salaries, is evidently derived from a fund altogether independent of their success and reputation in their particular professions.

In some universities the salary makes but a part, and frequently but a small part of the emoluments of the teacher, of which the greater part arises from the honoraries or fees of his pupils.* The necessity of application, though always more or less diminished, is not in this case entirely taken away. Reputation in his profession is still of some importance to him, and he still has some dependency upon the affection, gratitude, and favourable report of those who have attended upon his instructions; and these favourable sentiments he is likely to gain in no way so well as by deserving them, that is, by the abilities and diligence with which he discharges every part of his duty.

In other universities the teacher is prohibited from receiving any honorary or fee from his pupils, and his salary constitutes the whole of the revenue which he derives from his office. His interest is, in this case, set as directly in opposition to his duty as it is possible to set it. It is the interest of every man to live as much at his ease as he can; and if his emoluments are to be precisely the same, whether he does, or does not perform some very laborious duty, it is certainly his interest, at least as interest is vulgarly understood, either to neglect it altogether, or, if he is subject to some authority which will not suffer him to do this, to perform it in as careless and slovenly a manner as that authority will permit. If he is naturally active and a lover of labour, it is his interest to employ that activity in any way, from which he can derive some advantage, rather than in the performance of his duty, from which he can derive none.

If the authority to which he is subject resides in the body corporate, the college, or university, of which he himself is a member, and in which the greater part of the other members are, like himself, persons who either are, or ought to be teachers; they are likely to make a common cause, to be all very indulgent to one another, and every man to consent that his neighbour may neglect his duty, provided he himself is allowed to neglect his own. In the university of Oxford, the greater part of the publick professors have, for these many years, given up altogether even the pretence of teaching.*

If the authority to which he is subject resides, not so much in the body corporate of which he is a member, as in some other extraneous persons, in the bishop of the diocese for example; in the governor of the province; or, perhaps, in some minister of state; it is not indeed in this case very likely that he will be suffered to neglect his duty altogether. All that such superiors, however, can force him to do, is to attend upon his pupils a certain number of hours, that is, to give a certain number of lectures in the week or in the year. What those lectures shall be, must still depend upon the diligence of the teacher; and that diligence is likely to be proportioned to the motives which he has for exerting it. An extraneous jurisdiction of this kind, besides, is liable to be exercised both ignorantly and capriciously. In its nature it is arbitrary and discretionary, and the persons who exercise it, neither attending upon the lectures of the teacher themselves, nor perhaps understanding the sciences which it is his business to teach, are seldom capable of exercising it with judgment. From the insolence of office too they are frequently indifferent how they exercise it, and are very apt to censure or deprive him of his office wantonly, and without any just cause. The person subject to such jurisdiction is necessarily degraded by it, and, instead of being one of the most respectable, is rendered one of the meanest and most contemptible persons in the society. It is by powerful protection only that he can effectually guard himself against the bad usage to which he is at all times exposed; and this protection he is most likely to gain, not by ability or diligence in his profession, but by obsequiousness to the will of his superiors, and by being ready, at all times, to sacrifice to that will the rights, the interest, and the honour of the body corporate of which he is a member. Whoever has attended for any considerable time to the administration of a French university, must have had occasion to remark the effects which naturally result from an arbitrary and extraneous jurisdiction of this kind.

Whatever forces a certain number of students to any college or university, independent of the merit or reputation of the teachers, tends more or less to diminish the necessity of that merit or reputation.

The privileges of graduates in arts, in law, physick* and divinity, when they can be obtained only by residing a certain number of years in certain universities, necessarily force a certain number of students to such universities, independent of the merit or reputation of the teachers. The privileges of graduates are a sort of statutes of apprenticeship,* which have contributed to the improvement of education, just as the other statutes of apprenticeship have to that of arts and manufactures.

The charitable foundations of scholarships, exhibitions, bursaries, &c. necessarily attach a certain number of students to certain colleges, independent altogether of the merit of those particular colleges. Were the students upon such charitable foundations left free to chuse what college they liked best, such liberty might perhaps contribute to excite some emulation among different colleges. A regulation, on the contrary, which prohibited even the independent members of every particular college from leaving it, and going to any other, without leave first asked and obtained of that which they meant to abandon, would tend very much to extinguish that emulation.

If in each college the tutor or teacher, who was to instruct each student in all arts and sciences, should not be voluntarily chosen by the student, but appointed by the head of the college; and if, in case of neglect, inability, or bad usage, the student should not be allowed to change him for another, without leave first asked and obtained; such a regulation would not only tend very much to extinguish all emulation among the different tutors of the same college, but to diminish very much in all of them the necessity of diligence and of attention to their respective pupils. Such teachers, though very well paid by their students, might be as much disposed to neglect them, as those who are not paid by them at all, or who have no other recompence but their salary.

If the teacher happens to be a man of sense, it must be an unpleasant thing to him to be conscious, while he is lecturing his students, that he is either speaking or reading nonsense, or what is very little better than nonsense. It must too be unpleasant to him to observe that the greater part of his students desert his lectures; or perhaps attend upon them with plain enough marks of neglect, contempt, and derision. If he is obliged, therefore, to give a certain number of lectures, these motives alone, without any other interest, might dispose him to take some pains to give tolerably good ones. Several different expedients, however, may be fallen upon which will effectually blunt the edge of all those incitements to diligence. The teacher, instead of explaining to his pupils himself, the science in which he proposes to instruct them, may read some book upon it; and if this book is written in a foreign and dead language, by interpreting it to them into their own; or, what would give him still less trouble, by making them interpret it to him, and by now and then making an occasional remark upon it, he may flatter himself that he is giving a lecture. The slightest degree of knowledge and application will enable him to do this without exposing himself to contempt or derision, or saying any thing that is really foolish, absurd, or ridiculous. The discipline of the college, at the same time, may enable him to force all his pupils to the most regular attendance upon this sham-lecture,* and to maintain the most decent and respectful behaviour during the whole time of the performance.

The discipline of colleges and universities is in general contrived, not for the benefit of the students, but for the interest, or more properly speaking, for the ease of the masters. Its object is, in all cases, to maintain the authority of the master, and whether he neglects or performs his duty, to oblige the students in all cases to behave to him as if he performed it with the greatest diligence and ability. It seems to presume perfect wisdom and virtue in the one order, and the greatest weakness and folly in the other. Where the masters, however, really perform their duty, there are no examples, I believe, that the greater part of the students ever neglect theirs. No discipline is ever requisite to force attendance upon lectures which are really worth the attending, as is well known wherever any such lectures are given. Force and restraint may, no doubt, be in some degree requisite in order to oblige children, or very young boys, to attend to those parts of education which it is thought necessary for them to acquire during that early period of life; but after twelve or thirteen years of age,* provided the master does his duty, force or restraint can scarce ever be necessary to carry on any part of education. Such is the generosity of the greater part of young men, that, so far from being disposed to neglect or despise the instructions of their master, provided he shows some serious intention of being of use to them, they are generally inclined to pardon a great deal of incorrectness in the performance of his duty, and sometimes even to conceal from the publick a good deal of gross negligence.

Those parts of education, it is to be observed, for the teaching of which there are no publick institutions, are generally the best taught. When a young man goes to a fencing or a dancing school, he does not, indeed, always learn to fence or to dance very well; but he seldom fails of learning to fence or to dance. The good effects of the riding school are not commonly so evident. The expence of a riding school is so great, that in most places it is a publick institution. The three most essential parts of literary education, to read, write, and account, it still continues to be more common to acquire in private than in publick schools;* and it very seldom happens that any body fails of acquiring them to the degree in which it is necessary to acquire them.

In England the publick schools are much less corrupted than the universities. In the schools the youth are taught, or at least may be taught, Greek and Latin, that is, every thing which the masters pretend to teach, or which, it is expected, they should teach. In the universities the youth neither are taught, nor always can find any proper means of being taught, the sciences, which it is the business of those incorporated bodies to teach. The reward of the schoolmaster in most cases depends principally, in some cases almost entirely, upon the fees or honoraries of his scholars. Schools have no exclusive privileges. In order to obtain the honours of graduation, it is not necessary that a person should bring a certificate of his having studied a certain number of years at a publick school. If upon examination he appears to understand what is taught there, no questions are asked about the place where he learnt it.

The parts of education which are commonly taught in universities, it may, perhaps, be said are not very well taught. But had it not been for those institutions they would not have been commonly taught at all, and both the individual and the publick would have suffered a good deal from the want of those important parts of education. . . .

The abilities, both civil and military, of the Greeks and Romans, will readily be allowed to have been, at least, equal to those of any modern nation. Our prejudice is perhaps rather to over rate them. But except in what related to military exercises, the state seems to have been at no pains to form those great abilities: for I cannot be induced to believe that the musical education of the Greeks* could be of much consequence in forming them. Masters, however, had been found, it seems, for instructing the better sort of people among those nations in every art and science in which the circumstances of their society rendered it necessary or convenient for them to be instructed. The demand for such instruction produced, what it always produces, the talent for giving it; and the emulation which an unrestrained competition never fails to excite, appears to have brought that talent to a very high degree of perfection. In the attention which the antient philosophers excited, in the empire which they acquired over the opinions and principles of their auditors, in the faculty which they possessed of giving a certain tone and character to the conduct and conversation of those auditors; they appear to have been much superior to any modern teachers. In modern times, the diligence of publick teachers is more or less corrupted by the circumstances, which render them more or less independent of their success and reputation in their particular professions. Their salaries too put the private teacher,* who would pretend to come into competition with them, in the same state with a merchant who attempts to trade without a bounty,* in competition with those who trade with a considerable one. If he sells his goods at nearly the same price, he cannot have the same profit, and poverty and beggary at least, if not bankruptcy and ruin, will infallibly be his lot. If he attempts to sell them much dearer, he is likely to have so few customers that his circumstances will not be much mended. The privileges of graduation, besides, are in many countries necessary, or at least extremely convenient to most men of learned professions, that is, to the far greater part of those who have occasion for a learned education. But those privileges can be obtained only by attending the lectures of the publick teachers. The most careful attendance upon the ablest instructions of any private teacher, cannot always give any title to demand them. It is from these different causes that the private teacher of any of the sciences which are commonly taught in universities, is in modern times generally considered as in the very lowest order of men of letters. A man of real abilities can scarce find out a more humiliating or a more unprofitable employment to turn them to. The endowments of schools and colleges have, in this manner, not only corrupted the diligence of publick teachers, but have rendered it almost impossible to have any good private ones.

Were there no publick institutions for education, no system, no science would be taught for which there was not some demand; or which the circumstances of the times did not render it, either necessary, or convenient, or at least fashionable to learn. A private teacher could never find his account in teaching, either an exploded and antiquated system of a science acknowledged to be useful, or a science universally believed to be a mere useless and pedantick heap of sophistry and nonsense. Such systems, such sciences, can subsist no where, but in those incorporated societies for education whose prosperity and revenue are in a great measure independent of their reputation, and altogether independent of their industry. Were there no publick institutions for education, a gentleman, after going through, with application and abilities, the most complete course of education, which the circumstances of the times were supposed to afford, could not come into the world completely ignorant of every thing which is the common subject of conversation among gentlemen and men of the world.*

There are no publick institutions for the education of women,* and there is accordingly nothing useless, absurd, or fantastical in the common course of their education. They are taught what their parents or guardians judge it necessary or useful for them to learn; and they are taught nothing else. Every part of their education tends evidently to some useful purpose; either to improve the natural attractions of their person, or to form their mind to reserve, to modesty, to chastity, and to œconomy:* to render them both likely to become the mistresses of a family, and to behave properly when they have become such. In every part of her life a woman feels

some conveniency or advantage from every part of her education. It seldom happens that a man, in any part of his life,
derives any conveniency or advantage from some of the most
laborious and troublesome parts of his education.

Ought the publick, therefore, to give no attention, it may be
asked, to the education of the people? Or if it ought to give
any, what are the different parts of education which it ought
to attend to in the different orders of the people? and in what
manner ought it to attend to them?

In some cases the state of the society necessarily places the
greater part of individuals in such situations as naturally form
in them, without any attention of government, almost all the
abilities and virtues which that state requires, or perhaps can
admit of. In other cases the state of the society does not place
the greater part of individuals in such situations, and some
attention of government is necessary in order to prevent the
almost entire corruption and degeneracy of the great body of
the people.

In the progress of the division of labour, the employment of
the far greater part of those who live by labour, that is, of the
great body of the people, comes to be confined to a few very
simple operations; frequently to one or two. But the understandings of the greater part of men are necessarily formed by
their ordinary employments.* The man whose whole life is
spent in performing a few simple operations, of which the
effects too are, perhaps, always the same, or very nearly the
same, has no occasion to exert his understanding, or to exercise
his invention in finding out expedients for removing difficulties
which never occur. He naturally loses, therefore, the habit of
such exertion, and generally becomes as stupid and ignorant as
it is possible for a human creature to become. The torpor of
his mind renders him, not only incapable of relishing or bearing
a part in any rational conversation, but of conceiving any
generous, noble, or tender sentiment, and consequently of
forming any just judgment concerning many even of the ordinary duties of private life. Of the great and extensive interests
of his country, he is altogether incapable of judging; and unless

very particular pains have been taken to render him otherwise, he is equally incapable of defending his country in war.* The uniformity of his stationary life naturally corrupts the courage of his mind, and makes him regard with abhorrence the irregular, uncertain, and adventurous life of a soldier. It corrupts even the activity of his body, and renders him incapable of exerting his strength with vigour and perseverance, in any other employment than that to which he has been bred. His dexterity at his own particular trade seems, in this manner, to be acquired at the expence of his intellectual, social, and martial virtues. But in every improved and civilized society this is the state into which the labouring poor, that is, the great body of the people, must necessarily fall, unless government takes some pains to prevent it.

It is otherwise in the barbarous societies, as they are commonly called, of hunters, of shepherds, and even of husbandmen in that rude state of husbandry which precedes the improvement of manufactures, and the extension of foreign commerce. In such societies the varied occupations of every man oblige every man to exert his capacity, and to invent expedients for removing difficulties which are continually occurring. Invention is kept alive, and the mind is not suffered to fall into that drowsy stupidity, which, in a civilized society, seems to benumb the understanding of almost all the inferior ranks of people. In those barbarous societies, as they are called, every man, it has already been observed, is a warrior. Every man too is in some measure a statesman, and can form a tolerable judgment concerning the interest of the society, and the conduct of those who govern it. How far their chiefs are good judges in peace, or good leaders in war, is obvious to the observation of almost every single man among them. In such a society indeed, no man can well acquire that improved and refined understanding, which a few men sometimes possess in a more civilized state. Though in a rude society there is a good deal of variety in the occupations of every individual, there is not a great deal in those of the whole society. Every man does, or is capable of doing, almost every thing which any other man does, or is capable of doing. Every man has a considerable degree of knowledge, ingenuity, and invention; but scarce any man has a great degree. The degree, however, which is commonly possessed, is generally sufficient for conducting the whole simple business of the society. In a civilized state, on the contrary, though there is little variety in the occupations of the greater part of individuals, there is an almost infinite variety in those of the whole society. These varied occupations present an almost infinite variety of objects to the contemplation of those few, who, being attached to no particular occupation themselves, have leisure and inclination to examine the occupations of other people. The contemplation of so great a variety of objects necessarily exercises their minds in endless comparisons and combinations, and renders their understandings, in an extraordinary degree, both acute and comprehensive. Unless those few, however, happen to be placed in some very particular situations, their great abilities, though honourable to themselves, may contribute very little to the good government or happiness of their society. Notwithstanding the great abilities of those few, all the nobler parts of the human character may be, in a great measure, obliterated and extinguished in the great body of the people.

The education of the common people requires, perhaps, in a civilized and commercial society, the attention of the publick more than that of people of some rank and fortune. People of some rank and fortune are generally eighteen or nineteen years of age before they enter upon that particular business, profession, or trade, by which they propose to distinguish themselves in the world. They have before that full time to acquire, or at least to fit themselves for afterwards acquiring, every accomplishment which can recommend them to the publick esteem, or render them worthy of it. Their parents or guardians are generally sufficiently anxious that they should be so accomplished, and are, in most cases, willing enough to lay out the expence which is necessary for that purpose. If they are not always properly educated, it is seldom from the want of expence laid out upon their education; but from the improper application of that expence. It is seldom from the want of masters; but from the negligence and incapacity of the masters who are to be had, and from the difficulty, or rather from the impossibility which there is, in the present state of things, of finding any better. The employments too in which people of some rank or fortune spend the greater part of their lives, are not, like those of the common people, simple and uniform. They are almost all of them extremely complicated, and such as exercise the head more than the hands. The understandings of those who are engaged in such employments can seldom grow torpid for want of exercise. The employments of people of some rank and fortune, besides, are seldom such as harass them from morning to night. They generally have a good deal of leisure, during which they may perfect themselves in every branch either of useful or ornamental knowledge of which they may have laid the foundation, or for which they may have acquired some taste in the earlier part of life.

It is otherwise with the common people. They have little time to spare for education. Their parents can scarce afford to maintain them even in infancy. As soon as they are able to work, they must apply to some trade by which they can earn their subsistence.* That trade too is generally so simple and uniform as to give little exercise to the understanding; while, at the same time, their labour is both so constant and so severe, that it leaves them little leisure and less inclination to apply to, or even to think of any thing else.

But though the common people cannot, in any civilized society, be so well instructed as people of some rank and fortune, the most essential parts of education, however, to read, write, and account, can be acquired at so early a period of life, that the greater part even of those who are to be bred to the lowest occupations, have time to acquire them before they can be employed in those occupations. For a very small expence the publick can facilitate, can encourage, and can even impose upon almost the whole body of the people, the necessity of acquiring those most essential parts of education.*

The publick can facilitate this acquisition by establishing in every parish or district a little school, where children may be taught for a reward so moderate, that even a common labourer may afford it; the master being partly, but not wholly paid by the publick; because if he was wholly, or even principally paid by it, he would soon learn to neglect his business. In Scotland the establishment of such parish schools* has taught almost the whole common people to read, and a very great proportion of them to write and account. In England the establishment of charity schools* has had an effect of the same kind, though not so universally, because the establishment is not so universal. If in those little schools the books, by which the children are taught to read, were a little more instructive than they commonly are: and if, instead of a little smattering of Latin; which the children of the common people are sometimes taught there, and which can scarce ever be of any use to them: they were instructed in the elementary parts of geometry and mechanicks,* the literary education of this rank of people would perhaps be as complete as it can be. There is scarce a common trade which does not afford some opportunities of applying to it the principles of geometry and mechanicks, and which would not therefore gradually exercise and improve the common people in those principles, the necessary introduction to the most sublime as well as to the most useful sciences.

The publick can encourage the acquisition of those most essential parts of education by giving small premiums, and little badges of distinction, to the children of the common people who excel in them.

The publick can impose upon almost the whole body of the people the necessity of acquiring those most essential parts of education, by obliging every man to undergo an examination or probation in them before he can obtain the freedom in any corporation, or be allowed to set up any trade either in a village or town corporate.*

It was in this manner, by facilitating the acquisition of their military and gymnastic exercises, by encouraging it, and even by imposing upon the whole body of the people the necessity of learning those exercises, that the Greek and Roman republicks maintained the martial spirit of their respective citizens. They facilitated the acquisition of those exercises by appointing a certain place for learning and practising them, and by granting to certain masters the privilege of teaching in that place. Those masters do not appear to have had either salaries or exclusive privileges of any kind. Their reward consisted altogether in what they got from their scholars; and a citizen who had learnt his exercises in the publick Gymnasia,* had no sort of legal advantage over one who had learnt them privately, provided the latter had learnt them equally well. Those republicks encouraged the acquisition of those exercises, by bestowing little premiums and badges of distinction upon those who excelled in them. To have gained a prize in the Olympic, Isthmian or Nemaean games,* gave illustration,* not only to the person who gained it, but to his whole family and kindred. The obligation which every citizen was under to serve a certain number of years, if called upon, in the armies of the republick, sufficiently imposed the necessity of learning those exercises without which he could not be fit for that service.

That in the progress of improvement the practice of military exercises, unless government takes proper pains to support it, goes gradually to decay, and, together with it, the martial spirit of the great body of the people, the example of modern Europe sufficiently demonstrates. But the security of every society must always depend, more or less, upon the martial spirit of the great body of the people. In the present times, indeed, that martial spirit alone, and unsupported by a well-disciplined standing army, would not, perhaps, be sufficient for the defence and security of any society. But where every citizen had the spirit of a soldier, a smaller standing army would surely be requisite. That spirit, besides, would necessarily diminish very much the dangers to liberty, whether real or imaginary, which are commonly apprehended from a standing army.* As it would very much facilitate the operations of that army against a foreign invader, so it would obstruct them as much if unfortunately they should ever be directed against the constitution of the state.

The antient institutions of Greece and Rome seem to have been much more effectual, for maintaining the martial spirit of the great body of the people, than the establishment of what are called the militias of modern times. They were much more simple. When they were once established, they executed themselves, and it required little or no attention from government to maintain them in the most perfect vigour. Whereas to maintain even in tolerable execution the complex regulations of any modern militia, requires the continual and painful attention of government, without which they are constantly falling into total neglect and disuse.* The influence, besides, of the antient institutions was much more universal. By means of them the whole body of the people was compleatly instructed in the use of arms. Whereas it is but a very small part of them who can ever be so instructed by the regulations of any modern militia; except, perhaps, that of Switzerland. But a coward, a man incapable either of defending or of revenging himself, evidently wants one of the most essential parts of the character of a man. He is as much mutilated and deformed in his mind, as another is in his body, who is either deprived of some of its most essential members, or has lost the use of them. He is evidently the more wretched and miserable of the two; because happiness and misery, which reside altogether in the mind, must necessarily depend more upon the healthful or unhealthful, the mutilated or entire state of the mind, than upon that of the body. Even though the martial spirit of the people were of no use towards the defence of the society, yet to prevent that sort of mental mutilation, deformity and wretchedness, which cowardice necessarily involves in it, from spreading themselves through the great body of the people, would still deserve the most serious attention of government; in the same manner as it would deserve its most serious attention to prevent a leprosy or any other loathsome and offensive disease, though neither mortal nor dangerous, from spreading itself among them; though, perhaps, no other publick good might result from such attention besides the prevention of so great a publick evil.

The same thing may be said of the gross ignorance and stupidity which, in a civilized society, seem so frequently to benumb the understandings of all the inferior ranks of people. A man, without the proper use of the intellectual faculties of a man, is, if possible, more contemptible than even a coward, and seems to be mutilated and deformed in a still more essential part of the character of human nature. Though the state was to derive no advantage from the instruction of the inferior ranks of people, it would still deserve its attention that they should not be altogether uninstructed. The state, however, derives no inconsiderable advantage from their instruction. The more they are instructed, the less liable they are to the delusions of enthusiasm and superstition, which, among ignorant nations, frequently occasion the most dreadful disorders. An instructed and intelligent people besides are always more decent and orderly than an ignorant and stupid one.* They feel themselves, each individually, more respectable, and more likely to obtain the respect of their lawful superiors, and they are therefore more disposed to respect those superiors. They are more disposed to examine, and more capable of seeing through, the interested complaints of faction and sedition, and they are, upon that account, less apt to be misled into any wanton or unnecessary opposition to the measures of government. In free countries, where the safety of government depends very much upon the favourable judgment which the people may form of its conduct, it must surely be of the highest importance that they should not be disposed to judge rashly or capriciously concerning it.

ARTICLE III

Of the Expence of the Institutions for the Instruction of People of all Ages

The institutions for the instruction of people of all ages are chiefly those for religious instruction.* This is a species of instruction of which the object is not so much to render the

people good citizens in this world, as to prepare them for
another and a better world in a life to come. The teachers of
the doctrine which contains this instruction, in the same manner as other teachers, may either depend altogether for their
subsistence upon the voluntary contributions of their hearers;
or they may derive it from some other fund to which the law
of their country may entitle them; such as a landed estate, a
tythe or land tax, an established salary or stipend. Their
exertion, their zeal and industry, are likely to be much greater
in the former situation than in the latter. In this respect the
teachers of new religions have always had a considerable advantage in attacking those antient and established systems of
which the clergy, reposing themselves upon their benefices, had
neglected to keep up the fervour of faith and devotion in the
great body of the people; and having given themselves up to
indolence, were become altogether incapable of making any
vigorous exertion in defence even of their own establishment.
The clergy of an established and well-endowed religion frequently become men of learning and elegance, who possess all
the virtues of gentlemen, or which can recommend them to
the esteem of gentlemen; but they are apt gradually to lose the
qualities, both good and bad, which gave them authority and
influence with the inferior ranks of people, and which had
perhaps been the original causes of the success and establishment of their religion. Such a clergy, when attacked by a
set of popular and bold, though perhaps stupid and ignorant
enthusiasts, feel themselves as perfectly defenceless as the
indolent, effeminate, and full fed nations of the southern parts
of Asia, when they were invaded by the active, hardy, and
hungry Tartars of the North.* Such a clergy, upon such an
emergency, have commonly no other resource than to call upon
the civil magistrate to persecute, destroy, or drive out their
adversaries, as disturbers of the public peace. It was thus that
the Roman catholic clergy called upon the civil magistrate to
persecute the protestants; and the church of England, to persecute the dissenters; and that in general every religious sect,
when it has once enjoyed for a century or two the security of

a legal establishment, has found itself incapable of making any vigorous defence against any new sect which chose to attack its doctrine or discipline. Upon such occasions the advantage in point of learning and good writing may sometimes be on the side of the established church. But the arts of popularity, all the arts of gaining proselytes, are constantly on the side of its adversaries. In England those arts have been long neglected by the well-endowed clergy of the established church, and are at present chiefly cultivated by the dissenters and by the methodists. The independent provisions, however, which in many places have been made for dissenting teachers, by means of voluntary subscriptions, of trust rights,* and other evasions of the law, seem very much to have abated the zeal and activity of those teachers. They have many of them become very learned, ingenious, and respectable men; but they have in general ceased to be very popular preachers. The methodists, without half the learning of the dissenters, are much more in vogue.* . . .

In every civilized society, in every society where the distinction of ranks has once been completely established, there have been always two different schemes or systems of morality current at the same time; of which the one may be called the strict or austere; the other the liberal, or, if you will, the loose system. The former is generally admired and revered by the common people: The latter is commonly more esteemed and adopted by what are called people of fashion. The degree of disapprobation with which we ought to mark the vices of levity, the vices which are apt to arise from great prosperity, and from the excess of gaiety and good humour, seems to constitute the principal distinction between those two opposite schemes or systems. In the liberal or loose system, luxury, wanton and even disorderly mirth, the pursuit of pleasure to some degree of intemperance, the breach of chastity, at least in one of the two sexes, &c. provided they are not accompanied with gross indecency, and do not lead to falsehood or injustice, are generally treated with a good deal of indulgence, and are easily either excused or pardoned altogether. In the austere system, on the contrary, those excesses are regarded with the utmost

abhorrence and detestation. The vices of levity are always
ruinous to the common people, and a single week's thought-
lessness and dissipation is often sufficient to undo a poor
workman for ever, and to drive him through despair upon
committing the most enormous crimes. The wiser and better
sort of the common people, therefore, have always the utmost
abhorrence and detestation of such excesses, which their experience tells them are so immediately fatal to people of their
condition. The disorder and extravagance of several years, on
the contrary, will not always ruin a man of fashion, and people
of that rank are very apt to consider the power of indulging
in some degree of excess as one of the advantages of their
fortune, and the liberty of doing so without censure or reproach, as one of the privileges which belong to their station.
In people of their own station, therefore, they regard such
excesses with but a small degree of disapprobation, and censure
them either very slightly or not at all.

Almost all religious sects have begun among the common
people, from whom they have generally drawn their earliest,
as well as their most numerous proselytes. The austere system
of morality has, accordingly, been adopted by those sects almost
constantly, or with very few exceptions; for there have been
some. It was the system by which they could best recommend
themselves to that order of people to whom they first proposed
their plan of reformation upon what had been before established. Many of them, perhaps the greater part of them, have
even endeavoured to gain credit by refining upon this austere
system, and by carrying it to some degree of folly and extravagance; and this excessive rigour has frequently recommended
them more than any thing else to the respect and veneration
of the common people.

A man of rank and fortune is by his station the distinguished
member of a great society, who attend to every part of his
conduct, and who thereby oblige him to attend to every part
of it himself. His authority and consideration depend very
much upon the respect which this society bears to him. He
dare not do any thing which would disgrace or discredit him

in it, and he is obliged to a very strict observation of that species of morals, whether liberal or austere, which the general consent of this society prescribes to persons of his rank and fortune. A man of low condition, on the contrary, is far from being a distinguished member of any great society. While he remains in a country village his conduct may be attended to, and he may be obliged to attend to it himself. In this situation, and in this situation only, he may have what is called a character to lose. But as soon as he comes into a great city, he is sunk in obscurity and darkness.* His conduct is observed and attended to by nobody, and he is therefore very likely to neglect it himself, and to abandon himself to every sort of low profligacy and vice. He never emerges so effectually from this obscurity, his conduct never excites so much the attention of any respectable society, as by his becoming the member of a small religious sect. He from that moment acquires a degree of consideration which he never had before. All his brother sectaries are, for the credit of the sect, interested to observe his conduct, and if he gives occasion to any scandal, if he deviates very much from those austere morals which they almost always require of one another, to punish him by what is always a very severe punishment, even where no civil effects attend it, expulsion or excommunication from the sect. In little religious sects, accordingly, the morals of the common people have been almost always remarkably regular and orderly; generally much more so than in the established church. The morals of those little sects, indeed, have frequently been rather disagreeably rigorous and unsocial.*

There are two very easy and effectual remedies, however, by whose joint operation the state might, without violence, correct whatever was unsocial or disagreeably rigorous in the morals of all the little sects into which the country was divided.

The first of those remedies is the study of science and philosophy,* which the state might render almost universal among all people of middling or more than middling rank and fortune; not by giving salaries to teachers in order to make them negligent and idle, but by instituting some sort of probation, even in the higher and more difficult sciences, to be undergone by every person before he was permitted to exercise any liberal profession, or before he could be received as a candidate for any honourable office of trust or profit. If the state imposed upon this order of men the necessity of learning, it would have no occasion to give itself any trouble about providing them with proper teachers. They would soon find better teachers for themselves than any whom the state could provide for them. Science is the great antidote to the poison of enthusiasm and superstition; and where all the superior ranks of people were secured from it, the inferior ranks could not be much exposed to it.

The second of those remedies is the frequency and gaiety of publick diversions.* The state, by encouraging, that is by giving entire liberty to all those who for their own interest would attempt, without scandal or indecency, to amuse and divert the people by painting, poetry, musick, dancing; by all sorts of dramatic representations and exhibitions, would easily dissipate, in the greater part of them, that melancholy and gloomy humour which is almost always the nurse of popular superstition and enthusiasm. Publick diversions have always been the objects of dread and hatred, to all the fanatical promoters of those popular frenzies. The gaiety and good humour which those diversions inspire were altogether inconsistent with that temper of mind, which was fittest for their purpose, or which they could best work upon. Dramatick representations besides, frequently exposing their artifices to publick ridicule, and sometimes even to publick execration, were upon that account, more than all other diversions, the objects of their peculiar abhorrence. . . .

PART IV

Of the Expence of supporting the Dignity of the Sovereign

Over and above the expence necessary for enabling the sovereign to perform his several duties, a certain expence is requisite for the support of his dignity. This expence varies both with the different periods of improvement, and with the different forms of government.

In an opulent and improved society, where all the different orders of people are growing every day more expensive in their houses, in their furniture, in their tables, in their dress, and in their equipage;* it cannot well be expected that the sovereign should alone hold out against the fashion. He naturally, therefore, or rather necessarily becomes more expensive in all those different articles too. His dignity even seems to require that he should become so.

As in point of dignity, a monarch is more raised above his subjects than the chief magistrate of any republick is ever supposed to be above his fellow-citizens; so a greater expence is necessary for supporting that higher dignity. We naturally expect more splendor in the court of a king, than in the mansion-house of a doge or burgo-master.

Conclusion of the Chapter

The expence of defending the society, and that of supporting the dignity of the chief magistrate, are both laid out for the general benefit of the whole society. It is reasonable, therefore, that they should be defrayed by the general contribution of the whole society, all the different members contributing, as nearly as possible, in proportion to their respective abilities.

The expence of the administration of justice too, may, no doubt, be considered as laid out for the benefit of the whole society. There is no impropriety, therefore, in its being defrayed by the general contribution of the whole society. The persons, however, who give occasion to this expence are those who, by their injustice in one way or another, make it necessary to seek redress or protection from the courts of justice. The persons again most immediately benefited by this expence, are those whom the courts of justice either restore to their rights, or maintain in their rights. The expence of the administration of justice, therefore, may very properly be defrayed by the particular contribution of one or other, or both of those two different sets of persons, according as different occasions may require, that is, by the fees of court. It cannot be necessary to have recourse to the general contribution of the whole society, except for the conviction of those criminals who have not themselves any estate or fund sufficient for paying those fees.

Those local or provincial expences of which the benefit is local or provincial (what is laid out, for example, upon the police* of a particular town or district) ought to be defrayed by a local or provincial revenue, and ought to be no burden upon the general revenue of the society. It is unjust that the whole society should contribute towards an expence of which the benefit is confined to a part of the society.

The expence of maintaining good roads and communications is, no doubt, beneficial to the whole society, and may, therefore, without any injustice, be defrayed by the general contribution of the whole society. This expence, however, is most immediately and directly beneficial to those who travel or carry goods from one place to another, and to those who consume such goods. The turnpike tolls in England, and the duties called peages in other countries, lay it altogether upon those two different sets of people, and thereby discharge the general revenue of the society from a very considerable burden.

The expence of the institutions for education and religious instruction, is likewise, no doubt, beneficial to the whole society, and may, therefore, without injustice, be defrayed by the general contribution of the whole society. This expence, however, might perhaps with equal propriety, and even with some advantage, be defrayed altogether by those who receive the immediate benefit of such education and instruction, or by the voluntary contribution of those who think they have occasion for either the one or the other.

When the institutions or publick works which are beneficial to the whole society, either cannot be maintained altogether, or are not maintained altogether by the contribution of such particular members of the society as are most immediately benefited by them, the deficiency must in most cases be made up by the general contribution of the whole society. The general revenue of the society, over and above defraying the expence of defending the society, and of supporting the dignity of the chief magistrate, must make up for the deficiency of many particular branches of revenue. The sources of this general or publick revenue, I shall endeavour to explain in the following chapter.

CHAPTER II

*Of the Sources of the general or publick Revenue of
the Society*

THE revenue which must defray, not only the expence of
defending the society and of supporting the dignity of the chief
magistrate, but all the other necessary expences of government,
for which the constitution of the state has not provided any
particular revenue, may be drawn, either, first, from some fund
which peculiarly belongs to the sovereign or commonwealth,
and which is independent of the revenue of the people; or,
secondly, from the revenue of the people.

PART I

*Of the Funds or Sources of Revenue which may peculiarly
belong to the Sovereign or Commonwealth*

The funds or sources of revenue which may peculiarly belong
to the sovereign or commonwealth must consist, either in stock,
or in land.

The sovereign, like any other owner of stock, may derive a
revenue from it, either by employing it himself, or by lending it. His revenue is in the one case profit, in the other
interest.

The revenue of a Tartar or Arabian chief consists in profit.
It arises principally from the milk and increase of his own herds
and flocks, of which he himself superintends the management,
and is the principal shepherd or herdsman of his own horde
or tribe. It is, however, in this earliest and rudest state of civil
government only that profit has ever made the principal part
of the publick revenue of a monarchical state.

Small republicks have sometimes derived a considerable
revenue from the profit of mercantile projects. The republick
of Hamburgh is said to do so from the profits of a publick

wine cellar and apothecary's shop.[16] The state cannot be very great of which the sovereign has leisure to carry on the trade of a wine merchant or apothecary. The profit of a publick bank has been a source of revenue to more considerable states. It has been so not only to Hamburgh, but to Venice and Amsterdam. A revenue of this kind has even by some people been thought not below the attention of so great an empire as that of Great Britain. Reckoning the ordinary dividend of the bank of England at five and a half per cent. and its capital at ten millions seven hundred and eighty thousand pounds, the neat annual profit, after paying the expence of management, must amount, it is said, to five hundred and ninety-two thousand nine hundred pounds. Government, it is pretended, could borrow this capital at three per cent. interest, and by taking the management of the bank into its own hands, might make a clear profit of two hundred and sixty-nine thousand five hundred pounds a year. The orderly, vigilant, and parsimonious administration of such aristocracies as those of Venice and Amsterdam, is extremely proper, it appears from experience, for the management of a mercantile project of this kind. But whether such a government as that of England; which, whatever may be its virtues, has never been famous for good

---

[16] See Memoires concernant les Droits & Impositions en Europe: tome i. page 73. This work was compiled by the order of the court for the use of a commission employed for some years past in considering the proper means for reforming the finances of France. The account of the French taxes, which takes up three volumes in quarto, may be regarded as perfectly authentic. That of those of other European nations was compiled from such informations as the French ministers at the different courts could procure. It is much shorter, and probably not quite so exact as that of the French taxes.

[*Mémoires concernant les impositions et droits en Europe* (Paris, 1768–9), by J. L. Moreau de Beaumont. Smith mentions this book in Letter 196 addressed to Sir John Sinclair, dated 24 November 1778. In this letter Smith stated that he had had frequent occasion to study a book which had never been properly published, and that he had obtained it 'by the particular favour of Mr. Turgot'. At the same time Smith expressed himself as being unwilling to send the book out of Edinburgh, since 'if any accident should happen to my book, the loss is perfectly irreparable'. Smith believed that there were as few as three copies in Britain at the time (*Correspondence*, 235–6).] [Campbell and Skinner]

œconomy; which, in time of peace, has generally conducted itself with the slothful and negligent profusion that is perhaps natural to monarchies; and in time of war has constantly acted with all the thoughtless extravagance that democracies are apt to fall into; could be safely trusted with the management of such a project must at least be a good deal more doubtful.*

The post-office is properly a mercantile project.* The government advances the expence of establishing the different offices, and of buying or hiring the necessary horses or carriages, and is repaid with a large profit by the duties upon what is carried. It is perhaps the only mercantile project which has been successfully managed by, I believe, every sort of government. The capital to be advanced is not very considerable. There is no mystery in the business. The returns are not only certain, but immediate.

Princes, however, have frequently engaged in many other mercantile projects, and have been willing, like private persons, to mend their fortunes by becoming adventurers in the common branches of trade. They have scarce ever succeeded. The profusion with which the affairs of princes are always managed, renders it almost impossible that they should. The agents of a prince regard the wealth of their master as inexhaustible; are careless at what price they buy; are careless at what price they sell; are careless at what expence they transport his goods from one place to another. Those agents frequently live with the profusion of princes, and sometimes too, in spite of that profusion, and by a proper method of making up their accounts, acquire the fortunes of princes. It was thus, as we are told by Machiavel,* that the agents of Lorenzo of Medicis, not a prince of mean abilities, carried on his trade. The republick of Florence was several times obliged to pay the debt into which their extravagance had involved him. He found it convenient, accordingly, to give up the business of merchant, the business to which his family had originally owed their fortune, and in the latter part of his life to employ both what remained of that fortune, and the revenue of the state of which he had the disposal, in projects and expences more suitable to his station.

No two characters seem more inconsistent than those of trader and sovereign. If the trading spirit of the English East India company renders them very bad sovereigns; the spirit of sovereignty seems to have rendered them equally bad traders. While they were traders only, they managed their trade successfully, and were able to pay from their profits a moderate dividend to the proprietors of their stock. Since they became sovereigns, with a revenue which, it is said, was originally more than three millions sterling, they have been obliged to beg the extraordinary assistance of government in order to avoid immediate bankruptcy. In their former situation, their servants in India considered themselves as the clerks of merchants: In their present situation, those servants consider themselves as the ministers of sovereigns.*

A state may sometimes derive some part of its publick revenue from the interest of money, as well as from the profits of stock. If it has amassed a treasure, it may lend a part of that treasure, either to foreign states, or to its own subjects. . . .

The unstable and perishable nature of stock and credit, however, render them unfit to be trusted to, as the principal funds of that sure, steady and permanent revenue, which can alone give security and dignity to government. The government of no great nation, that was advanced beyond the shepherd state, seems ever to have derived the greater part of its publick revenue from such sources.

Land is a fund of a more stable and permanent nature; and the rent of publick lands, accordingly, has been the principal source of the publick revenue of many a great nation that was much advanced beyond the shepherd state.* From the produce or rent of the publick lands, the ancient republicks of Greece and Italy derived, for a long time, the greater part of that revenue which defrayed the necessary expences of the commonwealth. The rent of the crown lands constituted for a long time the greater part of the revenue of the ancient sovereigns of Europe.

War and the preparation for war, are the two circumstances which in modern times occasion the greater part of the necessary expence of all great states. But in the ancient republicks of Greece and Italy every citizen was a soldier, who both served and prepared himself for service at his own expence. Neither of those two circumstances, therefore, could occasion any very considerable expence to the state. The rent of a very moderate landed estate might be fully sufficient for defraying all the other necessary expences of government.

In the ancient monarchies of Europe, the manners and customs of the times sufficiently prepared the great body of the people for war; and when they took the field, they were, by the condition of their feudal tenures,* to be maintained, either at their own expence, or at that of their immediate lords, without bringing any new charge upon the sovereign. The other expences of government were, the greater part of them, very moderate. The administration of justice, it has been shown,* instead of being a cause of expence, was a source of revenue. The labour of the country people, for three days before and for three days after harvest, was thought a fund sufficient for making and maintaining all the bridges, highways, and other publick works which the commerce of the country was supposed to require. In those days the principal expence of the sovereign seems to have consisted in the maintenance of his own family and houshold. The officers of his houshold, accordingly, were then the great officers of state. The lord treasurer received his rents. The lord steward and lord chamberlain looked after the expence of his family. The care of his stables was committed to the lord constable and the lord marshal. His houses were all built in the form of castles, and seem to have been the principal fortresses which he possessed. The keepers of those houses or castles might be considered as a sort of military governors. They seem to have been the only military officers whom it was necessary to maintain in time of peace. In these circumstances the rent of a great landed estate might, upon ordinary occasions, very well defray all the necessary expences of government. . . .

Though there is not at present, in Europe, any civilized state of any kind which derives the greater part of its publick revenue from the rent of lands which are the property of the state; yet, in all the great monarchies of Europe, there are still many large tracts of land which belong to the crown. They are generally forest; and sometimes forest where, after travelling several miles, you will scarce find a single tree; a mere waste and loss of country in respect both of produce and population. In every great monarchy of Europe the sale of the crown lands would produce a very large sum of money, which, if applied to the payment of the publick debts, would deliver from mortgage a much greater revenue than any which those lands have ever afforded to the crown. In countries where lands, improved and cultivated very highly, and yielding at the time of sale as great a rent as can easily be got from them, commonly sell at thirty years purchase; the unimproved, uncultivated, and low-rented crown lands might well be expected to sell at forty, fifty, or sixty years purchase. The crown might immediately enjoy the revenue which this great price would redeem from mortgage. In the course of a few years it would probably enjoy another revenue. When the crown lands had become private property, they would, in the course of a few years, become well-improved and well-cultivated.* The increase of their produce would increase the population of the country, by augmenting the revenue and consumption of the people. But the revenue which the crown derives from the duties of customs and excise, would necessarily increase with the revenue and consumption of the people.

The revenue which, in any civilized monarchy, the crown derives from the crown lands, though it appears to cost nothing to individuals, in reality costs more to the society than perhaps any other equal revenue which the crown enjoys. It would, in all cases, be for the interest of the society to replace this revenue to the crown by some other equal revenue, and to divide the lands among the people, which could not well be done better, perhaps, than by exposing them to publick sale.

Lands, for the purposes of pleasure and magnificence, parks, gardens, publick walks, &c. possessions which are every where considered as causes of expence, not as sources of revenue, seem to be the only lands which, in a great and civilized monarchy, ought to belong to the crown.

Public stock and publick lands, therefore, the two sources of revenue which may peculiarly belong to the sovereign or commonwealth, being both improper and insufficient funds for defraying the necessary expence of any great and civilized state; it remains that this expence must, the greater part of it, be defrayed by taxes of one kind or another; the people contributing a part of their own private revenue in order to make up a publick revenue to the sovereign or commonwealth.

PART II

Of Taxes

The private revenue of individuals, it has been shewn in the first book of this inquiry, arises ultimately from three different sources; Rent, Profit, and Wages.* Every tax must finally be paid from some one or other of those three different sorts of revenue, or from all of them indifferently. . . .

Before I enter upon the examination of particular taxes, it is necessary to premise the four following maxims with regard to taxes in general.

I. The subjects of every state ought to contribute towards the support of the government, as nearly as possible, in proportion to their respective abilities; that is, in proportion to the revenue which they respectively enjoy under the protection of the state. The expence of government to the individuals of a great nation, is like the expence of management to the joint tenants of a great estate, who are all obliged to contribute in proportion to their respective interests in the estate. In the observation or neglect of this maxim consists, what is called the equality or inequality of taxation. Every tax, it must be observed once for all, which falls finally upon one only of the three sorts of revenue above-mentioned, is necessarily unequal,* in so far as it does not affect the other two. In the following examination of different taxes I shall seldom take much further notice of this sort of inequality, but shall, in most cases, confine my observations to that inequality which is occasioned by a particular tax falling unequally even upon that particular sort of private revenue which is affected by it.

II. The tax which each individual is bound to pay ought to be certain, and not arbitrary. The time of payment, the manner of payment, the quantity to be paid, ought all to be clear and plain to the contributor, and to every other person. Where it is otherwise, every person subject to the tax is put more or less in the power of the tax-gatherer, who can either aggravate the tax upon any obnoxious contributor, or extort, by the terror of such aggravation, some present or perquisite to himself. The uncertainty of taxation encourages the insolence and favours the corruption of an order of men who are naturally unpopular, even where they are neither insolent nor corrupt. The certainty of what each individual ought to pay is, in taxation, a matter of so great importance, that a very considerable degree of inequality, it appears, I believe, from the experience of all nations, is not near so great an evil as a very small degree of uncertainty.

III. Every tax ought to be levied at the time, or in the manner in which it is most likely to be convenient for the contributor to pay it. A tax upon the rent of land or of houses, payable at the same term at which such rents are usually paid, is levied at the time when it is most likely to be convenient for the contributor to pay; or, when he is most likely to have where-withal to pay. Taxes upon such consumable goods as are articles of luxury, are all finally paid by the consumer, and generally in a manner that is very convenient for him. He pays them by little and little, as he has occasion to buy the goods. As he is at liberty too, either to buy, or not to buy as he pleases, it must be his own fault if he ever suffers any considerable inconveniency from such taxes.

IV. Every tax ought to be so contrived as both to take out and to keep out of the pockets of the people as little as possible, over and above what it brings into the publick treasury of the state. A tax may either take out or keep out of the pockets of the people a great deal more than it brings into the publick treasury, in the four following ways. First, the levying of it may require a great number of officers, whose salaries may eat up the greater part of the produce of the tax, and whose perquisites may impose another additional tax upon the people. Secondly, it may obstruct the industry of the people, and discourage them from applying to certain branches of business which might give maintenance and employment to great multitudes. While it obliges the people to pay, it may thus diminish, or perhaps destroy some of the funds, which might enable them more easily to do so. Thirdly, by the forfeitures and other penalties which those unfortunate individuals incur who attempt unsuccessfully to evade the tax, it may frequently ruin them, and thereby put an end to the benefit which the community might have received from the employment of their capitals. An injudicious tax offers a great temptation to smuggling.* But the penalties of smuggling must rise in proportion to the temptation. The law, contrary to all the ordinary principles of justice, first creates the temptation, and then punishes those who yield to it; and it commonly enhances the punishment too in proportion to the very circumstance which ought certainly to alleviate it, the temptation to commit the crime.[17] Fourthly, by subjecting the people to the frequent visits, and the odious examination of the tax-gatherers, it may

[17] See Sketches of the History of Man, page 474. & seq. [By Henry Home, Lord Kames (Edinburgh, 1774). Kames provided in this place the following six rules regarding taxation.

(1) 'That wher-ever there is an opportunity of smuggling, taxes ought to be moderate.'
(2) 'That taxes expensive in the levying ought to be avoided.'
(3) 'To avoid arbitrary taxes.'
(4) 'To remedy the "inequality of riches" as much as possible, by relieving the poor and burdening the rich.'
(5) 'That every tax which tends to impoverish the nation ought to be rejected with indignation.'
(6) 'To avoid taxes that require oath of party.'

expose them to much unnecessary trouble, vexation, and oppression; and though vexation is not, strictly speaking, expence, it is certainly equivalent to the expence at which every man would be willing to redeem himself from it. It is in some one or other of these four different ways that taxes are frequently so much more burdensome to the people than they are beneficial to the sovereign. . . .

While citing Kames's authority, in fact Smith's discussion of taxation as contained in LJ (B) [*Lectures on Jurisprudence* (1766)] illustrates many of the canons above mentioned; for example, equality 310, ed. Cannan 240; economy 311–12, ed. Cannan 240–1; and convenience 314–15, ed. Cannan 242–3. He also emphasized the importance of levying taxes in such a way as to avoid infringing the liberty of the subject at 313(241). In LJ (A) [Lectures on Jurisprudence (1762–3)] vi.34 Smith refers to the 'insolence and oppression' of the officers who collect taxes as being 'still more insupportable' than the tax itself. Francis Hutcheson would also appear to have anticipated at least the canons of conveniency, economy, and equity: 'As to taxes for defraying the publick expences, these are most convenient which are laid on matters of luxury and splendour, rather than the necessaries of life; on foreign products and manufactures, rather than domestick; and such as can be easily raised without many expensive offices for collecting them. But above all, a just proportion to the wealth of people should be observed in whatever is raised from them, otherways than by duties upon foreign products and manufactures, for such duties are often necessary to encourage industry at home, tho' there were no publick expences.' (*A System of Moral Philosophy* (London, 1755), ii.340–1.) Sir James Steuart also grasped the importance of convenience, economy, certainty, and equity in discussing the canons of taxation. See for example, *Principles of Political Œconomy* (London, 1767), V.iv–v.] [Campbell and Skinner]

CHAPTER III

Of publick Debts

IN that rude state of society which precedes the extension of commerce and the improvement of manufactures, when those expensive luxuries which commerce and manufactures can alone introduce, are altogether unknown, the person who possesses a large revenue, I have endeavoured to show in the third book of this enquiry,* can spend or enjoy that revenue in no other way than by maintaining nearly as many people as it can maintain. A large revenue may at all times be said to consist in the command of a large quantity of the necessaries of life. In that rude state of things it is commonly paid in a large quantity of those necessaries, in the materials of plain food and coarse cloathing, in corn and cattle, in wool and raw hides. When neither commerce nor manufactures furnish any thing for which the owner can exchange the greater part of those materials which are over and above his own consumption, he can do nothing with the surplus but feed and cloathe nearly as many people as it will feed and cloathe. A hospitality in which there is no luxury, and a liberality in which there is no ostentation, occasion, in this situation of things, the principal expences of the rich and the great. But these, I have likewise endeavoured to shew in the same book,* are expences by which people are not very apt to ruin themselves. There is not, perhaps, any selfish pleasure so frivolous, of which the pursuit has not sometimes ruined even sensible men. A passion for cock-fighting has ruined many. But the instances, I believe, are not very numerous of people who have been ruined by a hospitality or liberality of this kind; though the hospitality of luxury and the liberality of ostentation have ruined many. Among our feudal ancestors, the long time during which estates used to continue in the same family, sufficiently demonstrates the general disposition of people to live within their income.*

Though the rustick hospitality, constantly exercised by the great land-holders, may not, to us in the present times, seem consistent with that order, which we are apt to consider as inseparably connected with good œconomy, yet we must certainly allow them to have been at least so far frugal as not commonly to have spent their whole income. A part of their wool and raw hides they had generally an opportunity of selling for money. Some part of this money, perhaps, they spent in purchasing the few objects of vanity and luxury, with which the circumstances of the times could furnish them; but some part of it they seem commonly to have hoarded. They could not well indeed do any thing else but hoard whatever money they saved. To trade was disgraceful to a gentleman,* and to lend money at interest, which at that time was considered as usury and prohibited by law,* would have been still more so. In those times of violence and disorder, besides, it was convenient to have a hoard of money at hand, that in case they should be driven from their own home, they might have something of known value to carry with them to some place of safety. The same violence, which made it convenient to hoard, made it equally convenient to conceal the hoard. The frequency of treasure-trove, or of treasure found of which no owner was known, sufficiently demonstrates the frequency in those times both of hoarding and of concealing the hoard. Treasure-trove was then considered as an important branch of the revenue of the sovereign. All the treasure-trove of the kingdom would scarce perhaps in the present times make an important branch of the revenue of a private gentleman of a good estate.

The same disposition to save and to hoard prevailed in the sovereign, as well as in the subjects. Among nations to whom commerce and manufactures are little known, the sovereign, it has already been observed in the fourth book,* is in a situation which naturally disposes him to the parsimony requisite for accumulation. In that situation the expence even of a sovereign cannot be directed by that vanity which delights in the gaudy finery of a court. The ignorance of the times affords but few of the trinkets in which that finery consists. Standing armies are not then necessary, so that the expence even of a sovereign, like that of any other great lord, can be employed in scarce any thing but bounty to his tenants, and hospitality to his retainers. But bounty and hospitality very seldom lead to extravagance; though vanity almost always does. All the antient sovereigns of Europe accordingly, it has already been observed, had treasures. Every Tartar chief in the present times is said to have one.

In a commercial country abounding with every sort of expensive luxury, the sovereign, in the same manner as almost all the great proprietors in his dominions, naturally spends a great part of his revenue in purchasing those luxuries. His own and the neighbouring countries supply him abundantly with all the costly trinkets which compose the splendid, but insignificant pageantry of a court. For the sake of an inferior pageantry of the same kind, his nobles dismiss their retainers, make their tenants independent, and become gradually themselves as insignificant as the greater part of the wealthy burghers in his dominions.* The same frivolous passions, which influence their conduct, influence his. How can it be supposed that he should be the only rich man in his dominions who is insensible to pleasures of this kind? If he does not, what he is very likely to do, spend upon those pleasures so great a part of his revenue as to debilitate very much the defensive power of the state, it cannot well be expected that he should not spend upon them all that part of it which is over and above what is necessary for supporting that defensive power. His ordinary expence becomes equal to his ordinary revenue, and it is well if it does not frequently exceed it. The amassing of treasure can no longer be expected, and when extraordinary exigencies require extraordinary expences, he must necessarily call upon his subjects for an extraordinary aid. The present and the late king of Prussia are the only great princes of Europe who, since the death of Henry IV. of France in 1610, are supposed to have amassed any considerable treasure.* The parsimony which leads to accumulation has become almost as rare in republican as in monarchical governments. The Italian republicks, the United Provinces of the Netherlands, are all in debt. The canton of Berne* is the single republick in Europe which has amassed any considerable treasure. The other Swiss republicks have not. The taste for some sort of pageantry, for splendid buildings, at least, and other publick ornaments, frequently prevails as much in the apparently sober senate-house of a little republick, as in the dissipated court of the greatest king.

The want of parsimony in time of peace, imposes the necessity of contracting debt in time of war. When war comes, there is no money in the treasury but what is necessary for carrying on the ordinary expence of the peace establishment. In war an establishment of three or four times that expence becomes necessary for the defence of the state, and consequently a revenue three or four times greater than the peace revenue. Supposing that the sovereign should have, what he scarce ever has, the immediate means of augmenting his revenue in proportion to the augmentation of his expence, yet still the produce of the taxes, from which this increase of revenue must be drawn, will not begin to come into the treasury till perhaps ten or twelve months after they are imposed. But the moment in which war begins, or rather the moment in which it appears likely to begin, the army must be augmented, the fleet must be fitted out, the garrisoned towns must be put into a posture of defence; that army, that fleet, those garrisoned towns must be furnished with arms, ammunition and provisions. An immediate and great expence must be incurred in that moment of immediate danger, which will not wait for the gradual and slow returns of the new taxes. In this exigency government can have no other resource but in borrowing.

The same commercial state of society which, by the operation of moral causes, brings government in this manner into the necessity of borrowing, produces in the subjects both an ability and an inclination to lend. If it commonly brings along with it the necessity of borrowing, it likewise brings along with it the facility of doing so.*

A country abounding with merchants and manufacturers, necessarily abounds with a set of people through whose hands not only their own capitals, but the capitals of all those who either lend them money, or trust them with goods, pass as frequently, or more frequently, than the revenue of a private man, who, without trade or business, lives upon his income, passes through his hands. The revenue of such a man can regularly pass through his hands only once in a year. But the whole amount of the capital and credit of a merchant, who deals in a trade of which the returns are very quick, may sometimes pass through his hands two, three, or four times in a year. A country abounding with merchants and manufacturers, therefore, necessarily abounds with a set of people who have it at all times in their power to advance, if they chuse to do so, a very large sum of money to government. Hence the ability in the subjects of a commercial state to lend.

Commerce and manufactures can seldom flourish long in any state which does not enjoy a regular administration of justice, in which the people do not feel themselves secure in the possession of their property, in which the faith of contracts is not supported by law, and in which the authority of the state is not supposed to be regularly employed in enforcing the payment of debts from all those who are able to pay. Commerce and manufactures, in short, can seldom flourish in any state in which there is not a certain degree of confidence in the justice of government. The same confidence which disposes great merchants and manufacturers, upon ordinary occasions, to trust their property to the protection of a particular government; disposes them, upon extraordinary occasions, to trust that government with the use of their property. By lending money to government, they do not even for a moment diminish their ability to carry on their trade and manufactures. On the contrary, they commonly augment it. The necessities of the state render government upon most occasions willing to borrow upon terms extremely advantageous to the lender. The security which it grants to the original creditor, is made transferable to any other creditor, and, from the universal confidence in the justice of the state, generally sells in the market for more than was originally paid for it. The merchant or monied man makes money by lending money to government, and instead of diminishing, increases his trading capital. He generally considers it as a favour, therefore, when the administration admits him to share in the first subscription for a new loan. Hence the inclination or willingness in the subjects of a commercial state to lend.

The government of such a state is very apt to repose itself upon this ability and willingness of its subjects to lend it their money on extraordinary occasions. It foresees the facility of borrowing, and therefore dispenses itself from the duty of saving.

In a rude state of society there are no great mercantile or manufacturing capitals. The individuals who hoard whatever money they can save, and who conceal their hoard, do so from a distrust of the justice of government, from a fear that if it was known that they had a hoard, and where that hoard was to be found, they would quickly be plundered. In such a state of things few people would be able, and nobody would be willing, to lend their money to government on extraordinary exigencies. The sovereign feels that he must provide for such exigencies by saving, because he foresees the absolute impossibility of borrowing. This foresight increases still further his natural disposition to save.

The progress of the enormous debts* which at present oppress, and will in the long-run probably ruin, all the great nations of Europe, has been pretty uniform. Nations, like private men, have generally begun to borrow upon what may be called personal credit, without assigning or mortgaging any particular fund for the payment of the debt; and when this resource has failed them, they have gone on to borrow upon assignments or mortgages of particular funds. . . .

It is not contrary to justice that both Ireland and America should contribute towards the discharge of the publick debt of Great Britain. That debt has been contracted in support of the government established by the Revolution,* a government to which the protestants of Ireland* owe, not only the whole authority which they at present enjoy in their own country, but every security which they possess for their liberty, their property, and their religion; a government to which several of the colonies of America owe their present charters, and consequently their present constitution, and to which all the colonies of America owe the liberty, security, and property which they have ever since enjoyed. That publick debt has been contracted in the defence, not of Great Britain alone, but of all the different provinces of the empire; the immense debt contracted in the late war in particular, and a great part of that contracted in the war before, were both properly contracted in defence of America.*

By a union with Great Britain,* Ireland would gain, besides the freedom of trade, other advantages much more important, and which would much more than compensate any increase of taxes that might accompany that union. By the union with England,* the middling and inferior ranks of people in Scotland gained a compleat deliverance from the power of an aristocracy which had always before oppressed them. By an union with Great Britain the greater part of the people of all ranks in Ireland would gain an equally compleat deliverance from a much more oppressive aristocracy; an aristocracy not founded, like that of Scotland, in the natural and respectable distinctions of birth and fortune; but in the most odious of all distinctions, those of religious and political prejudices;* distinctions which, more than any other, animate both the insolence of the oppressors and the hatred and indignation of the oppressed, and which commonly render the inhabitants of the same country more hostile to one another than those of different countries ever are. Without a union with Great Britain, the inhabitants of Ireland are not likely for many ages to consider themselves as one people.

No oppressive aristocracy has ever prevailed in the colonies. Even they, however, would, in point of happiness and tranquillity, gain considerably by a union with Great Britain.* It would, at least, deliver them from those rancorous and virulent factions which are inseperable from small democracies, and which have so frequently divided the affections of their people, and disturbed the tranquillity of their governments, in their form so nearly democratical. In the case of a total separation from Great Britain, which, unless prevented by a union of this kind, seems very likely to take place, those factions would be ten times more virulent than ever. Before the commencement of the present disturbances, the coercive power of the mother-country had always been able to restrain those factions from breaking out into any thing worse than gross brutality and insult. If that coercive power was entirely taken away, they would probably soon break out into open violence and blood-shed. In all great countries which are united under one uniform government, the spirit of party commonly prevails less in the remote provinces than in the centre of the empire. The distance of those provinces from the capital, from the principal seat of the great scramble of faction and ambition, makes them enter less into the views of any of the contending parties, and renders them more indifferent and impartial spectators of the conduct of all. The spirit of party prevails less in Scotland than in England. In the case of a union it would probably prevail less in Ireland than in Scotland, and the colonies would probably soon enjoy a degree of concord and unanimity at present unknown in any part of the British empire. Both Ireland and the colonies, indeed, would be subjected to heavier taxes than any which they at present pay. In consequence, however, of a diligent and faithful application of the publick revenue towards the discharge of the national debt, the greater part of those taxes might not be of long continuance, and the publick revenue of Great Britain might soon be reduced to what was necessary for maintaining a moderate peace establishment.

The territorial acquisitions of the East India Company,* the undoubted right of the crown, that is, of the state and people of Great Britain, might be rendered another source of revenue more abundant, perhaps, than all those already mentioned. Those countries are represented as more fertile, more extens-ive; and in proportion to their extent, much richer and more populous than Great Britain. In order to draw a great revenue from them, it would not probably be necessary, to introduce any new system of taxation into countries which are already sufficiently and more than sufficiently taxed. It might, perhaps, be more proper to lighten, than to aggravate, the burden of those unfortunate countries, and to endeavour to draw a revenue from them, not by imposing new taxes, but by preventing the embezzlement and misapplication of the greater part of those which they already pay.

If it should be found impracticable for Great Britain to draw any considerable augmentation of revenue from any of the resources above mentioned; the only resource which can remain to her is a diminution of her expence. In the mode of collecting, and in that of expending the publick revenue; though in both there may be still room for improvement; Great Britain seems to be at least as œconomical as any of her neighbours. The military establishment which she maintains for her own defence in time of peace, is more moderate than that of any European state which can pretend to rival her either in wealth or in power.* None of those articles, therefore, seem to admit of any considerable reduction of expence. The expence of the peace establishment of the colonies was, before the commencement of the present disturbances, very considerable, and is an expence which may, and if no revenue can be drawn from them, ought certainly to be saved altogether. This constant expence in time of peace, though very great, is insignificant in comparison with what the defence of the colonies has cost us in time of war. The last war, which was undertaken altogether on account of the colonies, cost Great Britain, it has already been observed, upwards of ninety millions. The Spanish war of 1739 was principally undertaken on their account; in which, and in the French war that was the consequence of it, Great Britain spent upwards of forty millions, a great part of which ought justly to be charged to the colonies. In those two wars the colonies cost Great Britain much more than double the sum which the national debt amounted to before the commencement of the first of them.* Had it not been for those wars that debt might, and probably would by this time, have been compleatly paid; and had it not been for the colonies, the former of those wars might not, and the latter certainly would not have been undertaken. It was because the colonies were supposed to be provinces of the British empire, that this expence was laid out upon them. But countries which contribute neither revenue nor military force towards the support of the empire, cannot be considered as provinces. They may perhaps be considered as appendages, as a sort of splendid and showy equipage of the empire. But if the empire can no longer support the expence of keeping up this equipage, it ought certainly to lay it down; and if it cannot raise its revenue in proportion to its expence, it ought, at least, to accommodate its expence to its revenue. If the colonies, notwithstanding their refusal to submit to British taxes, are still to be considered as provinces of the British empire, their defence in some future war may cost Great Britain as great an expence as it ever has done in any former war. The rulers of Great Britain have, for more than a century past, amused the people with the imagination that they possessed a great empire on the west side of the Atlantic. This empire, however, has hitherto existed in imagination only. It has hitherto been, not an empire, but the project of an empire; not a gold mine, but the project of a gold mine; a project which has cost, which continues to cost, and which, if pursued in the same way as it has been hitherto, is likely to cost immense expence, without being likely to bring any profit; for the effects of the monopoly of the colony trade, it has been shewn;* are, to the great body of the people, mere loss instead of profit. It is surely now time that our rulers should either realize this golden dream, in which they have been indulging themselves, perhaps, as well as the people; or, that they should awake from it themselves, and endeavour to awaken the people. If the project cannot be compleated, it ought to be given up. If any of the provinces of the British empire cannot be made to contribute towards the support of the whole empire, it is surely time that Great Britain should free herself from the expence of defending those provinces in time of war, and of supporting any part of their civil or military establishments in time of peace, and endeavour to accommodate her future views and designs to the real mediocrity of her circumstances.

EXPLANATORY NOTES AND COMMENTARY

I have attempted the usual task of an editor, to supply information about people, institutions, customs, and events not necessarily familiar to the modern reader, as well as to give complete references to the range of works (economic, philosophical, literary, historical, and so on) alluded to in Smith's text. In preparing these notes I have benefited greatly from the investigations of earlier annotators of the *Wealth of Nations*: from Edwin Cannan's edition (1904) and from R. H. Campbell and A. S. Skinner's Glasgow edition (1976). Specific debts to their work are recorded below, in square brackets after the relevant note. Beyond this, the range of my notes and commentary, not always strictly relevant to the task of economic elucidation, requires some justification. It is the purpose of this edition to contextualize the *Wealth of Nations* in a wider field of relations and to demonstrate a richer application than its conventional modern presentation as a textbook of economic principles. Consequently, notes draw upon a range of contemporary social, historical, and literary documents.

The following abbreviations for *An Inquiry into the Nature and Causes of the Wealth of Nations* are used: *WN* refers by book, chapter, and (in parentheses) by page to passages in this World's Classics edition; 'Glasgow Edition' refers by page to the two-volume Glasgow edition edited by Campbell and Skinner (1976). References, by short title and page, to other of Smith's works are in each case to the appropriate volumes of the Glasgow edition, though where possible I have also, following the usual practice of Smith's editors, given the original divisions, together with the paragraph numbers added in the margin of the Glasgow edition, in order that any edition may be consulted.

8   *savage nations of hunters and fishers*: significant to the 'scientific' explanation of human progress which dominated French and Scottish debate, in particular, in the second half of the eighteenth century was the stadial theory of economic and social organization. The theory posited four (sometimes three) stages through which societies will in the course of development

progress in fixed order—the hunting, shepherd, farming, and commercial economies. To each of these stages it was recognized that certain social, legal, and political organizations, as well as psychological traits, will correspond. Versions of the theory were propounded in France by Anne-Robert-Jacques Turgot; in Scotland by, among others, Lord Kames, Adam Ferguson, and Adam Smith. Smith's clearest statement of the theory, which underlies several of his historical arguments in *WN*, occurs in *Lectures on Jurisprudence* (1762–3), i. 27–32 (pp. 14–16). (See Ronald L. Meek, *Social Science and the Ignoble Savage* (Cambridge: Cambridge University Press, 1976), 116–30, for an extended analysis of Smith's economic contribution in terms of the four-stages theory.)

10 *political œconomy*: the modern term 'economics' did not exist in Smith's time to describe the collectivity of writings on money, trade, wealth, manufacture, and the like. Throughout the eighteenth century the unattributed term 'œconomy' (subsequently 'economy', from the Greek *oikonomia*) retained as its primary significance 'the management of a house' or 'domestic regulation', as in: 'When we entered, we found an old woman boiling goats-flesh in a kettle . . . she was willing enough to display her whole system of economy' (Samuel Johnson, *A Journey to the Western Islands of Scotland* (1775), ed. J. D. Fleeman (Oxford: Clarendon Press, 1985), 24). 'Political œconomy', cited in the *OED* from 1767, though it can be found in English in the late seventeenth century, is an extension from the domestic context, referring to arguments concerning the laws and management of a national economy, or the formulation of the economy as an aspect of the state. (See Keith Tribe, *Land, Labour, and Economic Discourse* (London: Routledge and Kegan Paul, 1978), 80–109, for a discussion of the formation of a discursive space called 'political œconomy'.)

11 *the division of labour*: Smith was not the first social or economic thinker to identify the division of labour as the key to productivity in the modern commercial society. Anticipations can be found in the writings of the economic pamphleteers of the 1690s. See, for example, Sir William Petty: 'Those who have command of the Sea Trade, may Work at easier Freight with more profit, than others at greater; for as Cloth must be cheaper made, when one Cards, another Spins, another Weaves,

another Draws, another Dresses, another Presses and Packs; than when all the Operations above-mentioned, were clumsily performed by the same hand; so those who command the Trade of Shipping, can build long slight Ships for carrying Masts, Fir-Timber, Boards, Balks, etc.' (*Political Arithmetick* (London, 1690), in *The Economic Writings of Sir William Petty*, ed. C. H. Hull, 2 vols. (Cambridge: Cambridge University Press, 1899), i. 260). John Locke and Bernard Mandeville both put forward early versions of a division-of-labour theory. (See Locke, *Two Treatises of Government* (1690), ed. Peter Laslett (Cambridge: Cambridge University Press, 1960), 315–16; and Mandeville, *The Fable of the Bees* (1723), ed. F. B. Kaye, 2 vols. (Oxford: Clarendon Press, 1924), ii. 284). For an early literary assimilation of the theory, see my Introduction, p. xxiii.

12 *the trade of the pin-maker*: pin-making, Smith's well-known economic model, was socially exemplary, too. As one of the proto-industries of the eighteenth century, it was among the earliest to manifest some of the wider problems of industrialization. Gloucester was famous for pin-making, having by 1802 nine pin factories employing 1,500 workers, many of them children, out of a town-population of 7,600. The industry was directly associated with the launch of the Sunday-School Movement in Gloucester in 1780. (See Josiah Harris, *Robert Raikes, the Man and His Work*, ed. J. Henry Harris (Bristol and London, 1899), 58–9.)

eighteen distinct operations: even before Smith's famous usage, the example of the pin provided a persuasive account of the sophisticated and efficient division of labour. The smallest and commonest of all manufactured items, it yet required a particularly high number of operations before it reached the market. Denis Diderot's essay on the pin describes eighteen different stages in its manufacture (*Encyclopédie ou Dictionnaire Raisonné des Sciences, des Arts, et des Métiers* (Paris, 1755), v. 804–7: 'Épingle'). According to one contemporary commentator on pin-making, 'by the Number of different Hands employed, this Work is quickly dispatched, otherwise it could scarce afford a living Profit' (R. Campbell, *The London Tradesman: Being a Compendious View of All the Trades, Professions, Arts, both Liberal and Mechanic, now practised in the Cities of London and Westminster* (London, 1747), 256).

15   *making of a nail*: of the metal trades in the eighteenth century,
      the manufacture of nails (generally unlike pins) was an outwork
      industry, with iron rods being supplied to workers to forge and
      hammer into nails in their own domestic workshops and with
      little further subdivision of labour. Smith's firsthand account
      could have been gained among the villages around his own
      home town of Kirkcaldy in east Scotland, where the manufac-
      ture of nails was a local industry. William Hutton, travelling in
      1741, noted the employment of women alongside men in the
      domestic nail trade in the Black Country. (*A History of Birming-
      ham to the End of the Year 1780* (Birmingham, 1781), quoted
      in Maxine Berg, *The Age of Manufactures: Industry, Innovation,
      and Work in Britain 1700–1820* (London: Fontana, 1985), 312.)

16   *a metal button*: Birmingham's great prosperity from the late
      eighteenth century was built on the manufacture of such modest
      consumer items as buttons and buckles. Buttons were the
      foundation of the Birmingham-based fortune of William Boul-
      ton, who partnered James Watt in the manufacture of steam
      engines. The individual operations involved in button-making
      in the Birmingham toy trade were described in 1766: 'instead
      of employing the same hand to finish a button or any other
      thing, they subdivide it into as many different hands as possible,
      finding beyond doubt that the human faculties by being con-
      fined to a repetition of the same thing become more expeditious
      and more to be depended on than when obliged or suffered to
      pass from one to another. Thus a button passes through fifty
      hands, and each hand perhaps passes a thousand in a day;
      likewise, by this means, the work becomes so simple that, five
      times in six, children of six or eight years old do it as well as
      men, and earn from tenpence to eight shillings a week' (Lord
      Fitzmaurice, *Life of William Earl of Shelburne*, 2nd edn., 2 vols.
      (London: Macmillan, 1912), i. 276–7).

      A country weaver: Smith's example of the 'sauntering weaver',
      as representative of the wastefulness of undivided labour,
      gained some notoriety. His own pupil and early biographer,
      Dugald Stewart, took issue with Smith, defending the country
      weaver, not on the grounds of economic profitability, but of
      individual and social well-being, maintaining that his 'occasional
      labour in the fields' was preferable to 'those habits of intem-
      perate dissipation in which all workmen who have no variety

of pursuit are prone to indulge' (Dugald Stewart, *Lectures on Political Economy*, in *Collected Works*, ed. Sir William Hamilton, 11 vols. (Edinburgh, 1854–60), viii. 176). Mary Wollstonecraft countered that '[t]he time which, a celebrated writer says, is sauntered away, in going from one part of an employment to another, is the very time that preserves the man from degenerating into a brute' (*An Historical and Moral View of the Origin and Progress of the French Revolution* (London, 1794), i. 519). John Stuart Mill returned to the 'sauntering weaver' to argue vigorously that the division of labour as outlined by Smith might in fact be a bar to efficiency and mental agility in the work-place: 'The habit of passing rapidly from one occupation to another may be acquired, like other habits, by early cultivation; and when it is acquired, there is none of the sauntering which Adam Smith speaks of . . . but the workman comes to each part of his occupation with a freshness and a spirit which he does not retain if he persists in any one part' (*Principles of Political Economy* (1848), ed. W. J. Ashley (London: Longman, Green, and Co., 1923), 127–8). Interestingly, Smith himself makes some of the same criticisms of repetitive labour in *WN*, v. i (p. 429).

application of proper machinery: the three parts of Smith's argument in favour of the division of labour all come together here. Commentators throughout the eighteenth century were fascinated by the possibilities inherent in mechanical inventions. For Defoe in 1697, the period since 1680 was characterized by mechanical inventions: 'But about the Year 1680 began the Art and Mystery of Projecting to creep into the World. Prince *Rupert*, Uncle to King *Charles* the Second, gave great Encouragement to that part of it that respects Engines, and Mechanical Motions . . .' (*An Essay on Projects* (London, 1697), p. 25). By the 1760s and 1770s, there are explicit connections made between the introduction of new machinery into particular trades, the rise of specialized manufactures, gains in productivity, and the expansion of markets. (See A. Anderson, *Historical and Chronological Deduction of the Origin of Commerce from the Earliest Accounts to the Present Times*, 2 vols. (London, 1764), and W. Kenrick, *An Address to the Artists and Manufacturers of Great Britain* (London, 1774).) At the same time, criticisms can be heard of the possible moral and social complications

consequent upon mechanization—among them, the reorganiza-
tion of labour, the promotion of new industries, and the rise
of vice in manufacturing towns. (See [Josiah Tucker] *A Brief
Essay on the Advantages and Disadvantages which respectively
attend France and Great Britain, with regard to Trade* (1750), and
M. Postlethwayt, *Britain's Commercial Interests* (1757).) According to the poet William Blake, '[a] Machine is not a Man nor a
Work of Art, it is destructive of Humanity & of Art: the word
Machination' ('Public Address' (?1811), in *William Blake's Writings*, ed. G. E. Bentley, Jr., 2 vols. (Oxford: Clarendon Press,
1978), ii. 1,037). It is in the context of this complex structure
of opinion that Smith builds his division-of-labour theory.

17 *fire-engines*: steam engines. See Elizabeth Montagu to Matthew
Boulton, 1 Oct. 1778: 'I shall owe to you the richest and the
most beautiful part of my Furniture, and by a Fire Engine of
your improved construction shall in time save money equivalent
to the expence of these articles of elegant luxury' (cited in Neil
McKendrick, 'The Commercialization of Fashion', in McKendrick, John Brewer, and J. H. Plumb, *The Birth of a Consumer
Society: The Commercialization of the Eighteenth Century* (London: Hutchinson, 1983), 70). James Watt, who devised the
separate condenser for the steam engine, worked from 1756
until 1773 at Glasgow University and overlapped there for
a time with Smith. According to Skinner, Smith's story of
the boy and the steam engine is mythical. See T. K. Derry and
T. I. Williams, *A Short History of Technology* (Oxford: Clarendon Press, 1960), 316–19.

18 *woollen coat . . . this homely production*: Mandeville had used the
manufacture of 'the most ordinary *Yorkshire* Cloth' to illustrate
the complex network of labour which supports even the simplest commodity in the consumer society. (See *The Fable of the
Bees*, ed. Kaye, i. 169–70.) In the manufacture of woollen cloth,
the scribbler teases the wool, the fuller beats the cloth to cleanse
and thicken the fibres, and the dresser finishes the fabric.

19 *the glass window*: Smith ends this important first chapter by
imaginatively reassembling his argument as the mundane details
of the life of the 'meanest' workman. The effect is to celebrate
the democratization of consumption as promoted by the division
of labour. The commodities he cites are conspicuously humble.
In his Highland tour of 1773, Dr Johnson noted that the Scottish

'are more frugal of their glass than the English'; and his observations on Scottish windows provide him with an adjusted perspective on society and a corrected vision of social progress—as the small advances of the many—which is very similar to Smith's. Johnson comments: 'But it must be remembered, that life consists not of a series of illustrious actions, or elegant enjoyments; the greater part of our time passes in compliance with necessities, in the performance of daily duties, in the removal of small inconveniencies, in the procurement of petty pleasures ... The true state of every nation is the state of common life. The manners of a people are not to be found in the schools of learning, or the palaces of greatness ... they whose aggregate constitutes the people, are found in the streets, and the villages, in the shops and farms; and from them collectively considered, must the measure of general prosperity be taken. As they approach to delicacy a nation is refined, as their conveniencies are multiplied, a nation, at least a commercial nation, must be denominated wealthy' (*Journey*, ed. Fleeman, 16–17).

20 *ten thousand naked savages*: cf. Locke: 'There cannot be a clearer demonstration of any thing, than several Nations of the *Americans* [American Indians] are of this, who are rich in Land, and poor in all the Comforts of Life ... And a King of a large and fruitful Territory there feeds, lodges, and is clad worse than a day Labourer in *England*' (*Two Treatises of Government*, ed. Laslett, 314–15).

22 *their benevolence only*: 'To expect, that others should serve us for nothing, is unreasonable; therefore all Commerce, that Men can have together, must be a continual bartering of one thing for another. The Seller, who transfers the Property of a Thing, has his own Interest as much at Heart as the Buyer, who purchases that Property; and, if you want or like a thing, the Owner of it, whatever Stock of Provision he may have of the same, or how greatly soever you may stand in need of it, will never part with it, but for a Consideration, which he likes better, than he does the thing you want' (Mandeville, *The Fable of the Bees*, ed. Kaye, ii. 349).

23 *a brazier*: a worker in brass.

effect of the division of labour: 'When we consider how nearly equal all men are in their bodily force, and even in their mental powers and faculties, till cultivated by education, we must necessarily allow, that nothing but their own consent could at first associate them together, and subject them to any authority' (David Hume, 'Of the Original Contract', in *Essays Moral, Political, and Literary* (London: Oxford University Press, 1963), 454).

26 *the market*: by the late seventeenth century the emphasis of the word has changed from a reference to the point of sales to the more elusive concept of consumption controlled by supply and demand, though the two meanings continue to be invoked often at the same time, with the more physical sense of a market-place nostalgically contesting the abstract ground of the later usage. At *WN* III. ii (p. 245), for example, we discover Smith attempting to release trade from the market as *place*, where the market-place appears to resist the notion of 'natural' pricing.

27 *Leith*: two miles east of Edinburgh Old Town, Leith has been the city's seaport since medieval times and was still a separate town in the eighteenth century.

land and water-carriage: Chapter Three as a whole reads like a justificatory celebration of the 'canal mania' which gripped Britain in the late decades of the eighteenth century. In the course of the century engineering works extended navigable rivers, and canals, sanctioned by Acts of Parliament, were financed by incorporated companies issuing shares, bought mainly by interested local parties. By 1772 canals linked the Severn and Mersey; by 1777, the Trent and Mersey; and by 1790 Liverpool, Hull, Birmingham, Bristol, and London were all linked. Over the same period turnpike acts (allowing for the collecting of tolls) ensured that roads also improved. But in Scotland, where a Forth–Clyde canal to link the North Sea and the Atlantic was begun in 1768, neither road nor water communications proceeded at the same speed as in England. Smith perhaps exaggerates the slowness of road-carriage—his estimated travel-times between Edinburgh and London are truer of 1700 than even of 1750. By then the journey could be completed in 150 hours; and in nearer sixty hours by 1790. Turnpikes did not, of course, make haulage cheap; canals, however, did, which is the pertinent point for Smith's argument. Carriage by sea could still be both expensive and hazardous.

28   *London and Calcutta*: at the mouth of the Ganges in North East
      India, Calcutta was the export point for the great English East
      India Company (trading since 1600). It was the late seven-
      teenth-century craze for the cheap and colourful fabrics—calico,
      chintz, and muslin—imported from India which has been seen
      by modern economic historians as fuelling the pamphlet war of
      the 1690s, from which eventually emerged arguments, like
      Smith's, legitimizing a theory of growth based on domestic
      consumption. In 'Considerations on the East-India Trade' (1701),
      for example, Henry Martyn argued that the cheaper consumer
      goods provided by the East India trade would offer incentives
      for higher productivity at home and lead to 'the invention of
      Arts, and Mills, and Engines, to save the labour of Hands in
      other Manufactures' (in J. R. McCulloch (ed.), *A Selection of
      Early English Tracts on Commerce* (1856; repr. Cambridge: Cam-
      bridge University Press, 1952), 590). (See Joyce Appleby, 'Ideo-
      logy and Theory: The Tension between Political and Economic
      Liberalism in Seventeenth-Century England', *American Histor-
      ical Review*, 81 (1976), 499–515.)

29   *the Phenicians and Carthaginians*: the ancient inhabitants of
      Phœnicia, on the coast of present-day Syria, the Phœnicians
      also established the city of Carthage in North Africa.

31   *Of the Origin and Use of Money*: behind Smith's historical
      account in Chapter Four of the origins of money as an exchange
      facility and a measure of value lie the speculations of earlier
      philosophers and commentators—especially Samuel von Pufen-
      dorf, the German author of *De jure naturae et gentium* (Of the
      Law of Nature and Nations) (1672), with its origins in Aristotle;
      and John Locke's account of money in various pamphlets
      (*Considerations of the Lowering of Interest and Raising the Value
      of Money* (1691); *Further Considerations Concerning Raising the
      Value of Money* (1695)), and in his *Two Treatises of Government*
      (ed. Laslett, 317–20). See, too, John Law, *Money and Trade
      Considered* (1705), and Joseph Harris, *An Essay upon Money and
      Coins* (1757). See also *WN*, II ii.

32   *armour of Diomede . . . an hundred oxen*: Homer, *Iliad*, vi. 234–6,
      where Diomedes and Glaucus exchange armour. Since Diomedes'
      suit is plain bronze and Glaucus' is made of gold, the transaction
      gave rise to a proverb used to describe an unequal bargain—
      'gold for bronze'.

32   *Salt . . . dressed leather . . . or the ale-house*: the use of salt in Abyssinia is mentioned by Montesquieu, *De l'esprit des lois* (1748), XXII. i. note. Richard Cantillon pointed out that 'Tobacco, Sugar, and Cocoa' had been used as money in the American colonies (*Essai sur la nature du commerce* (1755), 145; ed. Henry Higgs (London: Macmillan, 1931), 111) [Campbell and Skinner].

33   *Pliny*: Pliny the Elder (*c*.AD 23–79). Servius Tullius ruled in Rome 579–34 BC.

     assaying: the trial of metals by fire to determine the quantity of metal in an ore or alloy, or the fineness of a coin.

34   *aulnagers and stampmasters*: aulnagers were officials employed to examine and attest the quality of woollen goods according to prescribed standards. Goods were then issued with a seal or stamp. Aulnage is the official measurement (by the ell—a variable length in different countries) of cloth. Statutes of 1711 and 1726 provided for the stamping and measurement of cloth.

     Nothing is more useful than water: the contrasting values in use and exchange of water and diamonds is an example used by earlier writers. See von Pufendorf, *De jure naturae et gentium* (1672), v. i. 6, and Law, *Money and Trade Considered* (Edinburgh, 1705), 4.

36   *Labour . . . the real measure . . . of all commodities*: Smith's exposition in the following paragraphs contributes to a larger discussion of labour and its relation to value throughout the eighteenth century. Cf. Locke, *Two Treatises of Government*: 'how much *labour makes the far greatest part of the value* of things, we enjoy in this World' (ed. Laslett, 315); Mandeville, *The Fable of the Bees*: '[I]t is . . . the Labour of the Poor, and not the high and low value that is set on Gold or Silver, which all the Comforts of Life must arise from' (ed. Kaye, i. 301); and Hume, 'Of Commerce': 'Every thing in the world is purchased by labour; and our passions are the only causes of labour' (*Essays Moral, Political, and Literary*, 267).

37   *Wealth, as Mr. Hobbes says, is power*: Thomas Hobbes, *Leviathan* (1651), I. x., distinguishes riches as among the 'instrumentall' (as opposed to the 'Originall' or 'Naturall') forms of power: 'Also Riches joyned with liberality, is Power; because it procureth friends, and servants' (ed. K. R. Minogue (London: Dent, 1973), 43).

39　*abundant mines of America*: Spain early laid claim to the gold and silver mines of South America. As developing techniques allowed their full exploitation (at Potosi, Peru, discovered in 1545, and at Zacatecas, Mexico, discovered in 1548), there seemed to be a limitless flow of wealth. The influx of silver into Spain rose in the last two decades of the sixteenth century to four times what it had been in the 1550s and 1560s. Anglo-Spanish wars from the sixteenth to the eighteenth centuries were partly activated by the struggle to possess this fabulous wealth.

　　fathom: the length of the outstretched arms—by convention, six feet.

40　*perpetual rent . . . particular sum of money*: during his Highland tour of 1773, Johnson refers several times to a local scarcity of money and to the long persistence of certain traditional payments in kind. Like Smith, he is careful to distinguish between money and wealth. On the island of Ulva, he notes the existence of a payment which, 'like others, was, for want of money, made anciently in the produce of the land. *Macquarry* was used to demand a sheep, for which he now takes a crown, by that inattention to the uncertain proportion between the value and the denomination of money, which has brought much disorder into *Europe*. A sheep has always the same power of supplying human wants, but a crown will bring at one time more, at another less' (*Journey*, ed. Fleeman, 119).

42　*corn rent . . . all these fluctuations*: a corn rent is one paid in corn or one determined each year by the price of corn. Writing of the islanders of Col, Johnson observes: 'The rents have, till within seven years, been paid in kind, but the tenants finding that cattle and corn varied in their price, desired for the future to give their landlord money; which, not having yet arrived at the philosophy of commerce, they consider as being every year of the same value' (*Journey*, ed. Fleeman, 106). Throughout the eighteenth century agriculture was the greatest single component in the national economy and Britain's largest industry, in terms of capital investment and labour force. For much of the century production outstripped home demand, forcing prices down. Much grain was exported. But as the home demand for grain was inelastic it did not fall off after bad harvests, when prices rose sharply. After the poor harvests of

1767 the importing of corn, paid for in gold, caused shock-waves through the whole economy. Smith here appears sanguine concerning the short-term fluctuations in the price of corn and their effect on the consumer, the poorer of whom, being heavily dependent on bread, would inevitably foot the bill if prices were unpegged. He returns to the more complex issues surrounding grain prices at *WN*, IV. v (pp. 313 ff.).

45 *superior skill . . . in the wages of labour*: at *WN*, I. x (p. 103), Smith presents an interesting argument in which he justifies, in terms of moral compensation, the high remuneration of those employed in the arts, whose talents we admire but disapprove of when publicly 'prostituted' for gain.

46 *manufactures . . . manufactory*: in 1776 the usage of such terms is wide. Both might refer to the small factory or domestic workshop where labour is employed or to the actual process of making articles or material by physical labour, with or without mechanical power. See, too, Hume's use of 'manufactory' to mean the growing of corn. Writing of England in the early fourteenth century, he comments: 'the raising of corn was a species of manufactory, which few in that age could practise with advantage' (*The History of England from the Invasion of Julius Caesar to the Accession of Henry VII*, 2 vols. (London, 1762), ii. 152).

47 *land . . . private property*: land enclosure had been going on for centuries, either by private agreement among the powerful or by Act of Parliament. It was an effective means of controlling mineral rights as well as of boosting the profits from agriculture. Between 1760 and the end of the century enclosure brought from two to three million acres of common and waste ground in England into cultivation. But at the same time it redefined property in the land in such a way as to jeopardize the open-field strips of the small independent cultivators and the land-use of those cottagers and wage-labourers at the bottom of society. According to Arthur Young, the most celebrated British agriculturalist of the late eighteenth century and himself an enthusiastic supporter of enclosure: 'By nineteen out of twenty Enclosure Bills the poor are injured and most grossly . . . The poor in these parishes may say with truth, "Parliament may be tender of property; all I know is, I had a cow, and an Act of Parliament has taken it from me" ' (quoted in Roy

Porter, *English Social History in the Eighteenth Century* (Harmondsworth: Penguin, 1982), 229). In Scotland the process of enclosure was slower, though accelerated in the later eighteenth century by landlord improvers.

49 *hereafter*: at *WN*, I. xi (p. 146).

50 *Scotch Pebbles*: a kind of agate.

51 *immediately or mediately*: directly and with no intervention; or indirectly, through an intermediate operation.

confounded . . . at least in common language: Smith illustrates this confusion in categories of return at *WN*, I. viii. and x. (pp. 64–5 and 109), in the examples of the independent workman and the apothecary.

harrowers: those employed in breaking up the soil after ploughing.

52 *journeyman*: one who has served an apprenticeship to a trade and is qualified to work at it for days' wages—that is, neither an apprentice nor a master. The term frequently covered both sexes.

53 *natural and market Price*: the distinction between natural and market price is both crucial and perplexing in Smith's advocacy of a system in which markets are allowed to work freely without outside interference. It is at the root of his disagreement, implicit throughout this chapter, with the older Mercantilist position, which favoured the intervention of the state in economic activity. The free-market economy, Smith's paradigm, is advanced here and throughout as somehow 'naturally' producing that balance of supply and demand on which its operations depend; yet at the same time the natural economic forces at work in the market never actually equate market with natural prices. For a discussion of Smith's use of the term 'natural', see my Introduction.

hereafter: at *WN*, I. viii and ix.

advancing, stationary, or declining condition: in 1776 Scotland was as yet a poor country and England was rich. But in terms of growth rates Scotland was, like England, an advancing society. Smith's favourite example of a stationary economy is that of China (*WN*, I. ix (p. 91 and n.)); at *WN*, I. xi, he states that among the European countries perhaps only Portugal and Spain 'have gone backwards' since the discovery of America.

54   *A very poor man . . . effectual demand*: cf. Mandeville: 'If one, who is forced to walk on Foot envies a great Man for keeping a Coach and Six, it will never be with that Violence, or give him that Disturbance which it may to a Man, who keeps a Coach himself, but can only afford to drive with four Horses' (*The Fable of the Bees*, ed. Kaye, i. 136). But as recently as 1766 the bookseller John Newbery published *A History of Little Goody Two Shoes* whose title-page addressed those:

'Who from a State of Rags and Care, | And having Shoes but half a Pair; | Their Fortune and their Fame would fix, | And gallop in a Coach and Six.' | Newbery, who had launched himself by marrying his employer's widow, sold children's books which offered enticing images of upward mobility to the growing class of those with money to spend on leisure and improvement.

55   *famine*: for accounts of famine in Scotland in the late seventeenth century, see Michael Flinn (ed.), *Scottish Population History from the Seventeenth Century to the 1930s* (Cambridge: Cambridge University Press, 1977), 164–86. For improved food distribution after the bad harvest of 1740/1, see T. C. Smout, 'Famine and Famine-Relief in Scotland', in L. M. Cullen and T. C. Smout (eds.), *Comparative Aspects of Scottish and Irish Economic and Social History 1600–1900* (Edinburgh: John Donald, 1976), 25–6. By the 1773 British Corn Law (13 Geo. III, c. 43), a bounty and import system shut off exports and allowed imports whenever the domestic price of grain rose above 48 shillings (£2) per bushel. The whole issue of Corn-Law legislation is discussed in detail at *WN*, IV. v (pp. 313 ff.). The debates over bread prices and the grain trade in the 1760s and 1770s are economically formative and divide thinkers into those who, like Smith, believe food is a 'natural' commodity, and as such should be left to find its own price, and those who see it as a 'political' commodity, its price to be regulated by government intervention, at least in situations of need.

58   *A publick mourning . . . black cloth*: Smith uses the example again at *WN*, I. x, where he also states that legislation setting the daily wages of a tailor could be waived only 'in the case of a general mourning' (p. 143). According to M. Dorothy George: 'During periods of court-mourning [journeymen tailors] were to work at night as well as all day for double wages' (*London*

Life in the Eighteenth Century (1925; Harmondsworth: Penguin, 1966), 205).

58   *regulations of police*: the public regulation or control of price, like the national police of the grain trade in France, which operated virtually uninterrupted from 1769 until 1789. In this case, however, regulation served to stabilize prices below their 'natural price'.

60   *A monopoly*: at *WN*, IV. ii, Smith exclaims against 'the wretched spirit of monopoly', and although elsewhere he admitted its short-term usefulness (*WN*, V. i (p. 418)), he saw it as in general 'a great enemy to good management' (*WN*, I. xi (p. 149)). Here, as in the earlier parts of his argument in favour of 'natural price', he takes another swipe at Mercantilism. As long as monopolies operate, they will hamper a free market whose equilibrium is the result of the continuous creation of new needs and desires to be satisfied by the increasing division of labour. A good example to support Smith's argument is that of the brass and copper industries. Throughout the eighteenth century they were organized in large monopolistic firms whose restrictive practices hindered the expansion of the trade and sought to keep prices high. (See Berg, *The Age of Manufactures*, 291–2.)

exclusive privileges . . . statutes of apprenticeship: Smith expands on employment and apprenticeship restrictions and the advantages which would accrue from their relaxation at *WN*, I. x (pp. 117 ff.). See my note at p. 117 below on the structure of apprenticeships in the eighteenth century.

62   *hereafter*: at *WN*, I. x.

65   *combinations*: from the 1720s statutes were passed restricting workers' combinations (trades unions). Combinations were outlawed among tailors in 1721 and 1767, in the woollen trade in 1726, among hatters in 1777. By the time of the general (anti-) Combinations Acts of 1799 and 1800 there were on the statute book more than forty Acts prohibiting combinations to raise wages. For an extreme view of the 'combinations of masters' at home and abroad (as, for example, in the East India Company), see William Cowper, *The Task* (1785):

> 'Hence merchants, unimpeachable of sin
> Against the charities of domestic life,

> Incorporated, seem at once to lose
> Their nature; and, disclaiming all regard
> For mercy and the common rights of man,
> Build factories with blood, conducting trade
> At the sword's point, and dyeing the white robe
> Of innocent commercial justice red.'

(iv. 676–83)

66   *combination of the workmen*: in many trades ancient usage pro-
      tected the rates for the job. Workers in towns (not yet a large
      percentage of the work-force) were sometimes better placed to
      combine against encroachments, but those in dispersed domestic
      industries, or the victims of monopolistic practices or of rigid
      polarizations between masters and workers, were open to great
      abuse. Domestic nail-makers were notoriously exploited by the
      ironmongers who held them in debt and controlled their wages.
      Spinners, often housewives in the countryside, had no organiza-
      tion for resistance when their wage rates fell, as they very often
      did. In London, journeymen tailors and stay-makers were the
      most powerful combinations in the later eighteenth century.
      Elsewhere, local strikes against wage lowering and mechanization
      could be intimidating and violent affairs. John Kay's home was at-
      tacked in 1753 by workers protesting against his 'flying shuttle'; in
      1765 in London Spitalfields silk-weavers besieged the Duke
      of Bedford's Bloomsbury Square house during their campaign for
      protective tariffs against imported French silks; and in 1779
      hosiers in Nottinghamshire smashed hundreds of Arkwright's
      stocking frames after failing to secure a minimum wage. (See
      E. J. E. Hobsbawm, 'The Machine Breakers', in his *Labouring
      Men: Studies in the History of Labour* (London: Weidenfeld and
      Nicolson, 1964), and John Rule, *The Experience of Labour in
      Eighteenth-Century Industry* (London: Croom Helm, 1981).)

67   *Mr. Cantillon*: Richard Cantillon (1680–1734), an Irish inter-
      national banker who wrote *Essai sur la nature du commerce en
      général* (Essay on the Nature of Trade in General), which was
      not published until 1755 but had circulated from about 1730.
      This work was one of the first synoptic analyses of the economic
      process. Smith draws on it in several places in *WN* (see note
      to p. 32 above). The reference here is to Cantillon's calcula-
      tion of subsistence wages for a labourer and his family (*Essai*,
      ed. Higgs, 33 ff.).

68   *annuitant*: one who receives a yearly income from investments.

69   *London price*: for much of the eighteenth century regional contrasts in wages were extreme, with those in the south and London the highest. Day rates for labour in London in 1775 were between 1*s*. 6*d*., earned by common labourers, and 2*s*. 6*d*., earned by craftsmen. Elizabeth Gilboy argues that wage *rates* increased rapidly between 1760 and 1780, especially in industrializing areas like Lancashire, where demand for labour was strongest—see her *Wages in Eighteenth-Century England* (Cambridge, Mass.: Harvard University Press, 1934). Though by no means consistent on the subject of labourers' wages, Daniel Defoe argued in *The Complete English Tradesman* (1726) in favour of high wages as essential to a high-productivity economy: 'in a word, the working manufacturing people of England eat the fat, and drink the sweet, live better, and fare better, than the working poor of any other nation in Europe . . . As the people get greater wages, so they, I mean the same poorer part of the people, clothe better, and furnish better, and this increases the consumption of the very manufactures they make; then that consumption increases the quantity made, and this creates what we call inland trade, by which innumerable families are employed, and the increase of the people maintained, and by which increase of trade and people the present growing prosperity of this nation is produced' (1839; Gloucester: Alan Sutton Publishing, 1987), 221). Obviously wages and prices must be considered together to get a sense of a standard of living, and even then important non-monetary factors escape the net. However, a picture emerges of rising money wages above rising prices until the third quarter of the century, when the gentle rise in prices (especially food) became much steeper and real wages fell among London workers by as much as 25 per cent. (See Paul Langford, *A Polite and Commercial People: England 1727–1783* (Oxford: Oxford University Press, 1989), 447–59.)

    British colonies in North America: the Thirteen Colonies expanded rapidly from a population of 340,000 in 1700 to 1,200,000 by 1760.

70   *labour of each child*: Smith mentions the profitability of children in the American colonies at *WN*, IV. vii (p. 345).

    China . . . travellers in the present times: Marco Polo visited China in 1275. According to Campbell and Skinner, Smith's contemporary authority for China was probably J. B. Du Halde, *Description géographique, historique, chronologique, politique, et physique de l'Empire de la Chine et de la Tartarie Chinoise* (Paris, 1735). For the significance of the example of China to the Scottish economists, see note to p. 91 below.

72 *English settlements in the East Indies*: originally chartered in 1600 as a trading company, the East India Company was by the mid-eighteenth century granted joint sovereignty (with the Crown) of India. Smith returns to the oppressive economic government of the East India Company and to the contrasting liberality of the policy of the British government towards its American colonies at *WN*, IV. vii. On the corrupt government of the East India Company, see below p. 325 and note and pp. 366 ff. and notes

73 *the wages of labour*: Smith's argument over the next several paragraphs is a characteristically conflated blend of the apparently descriptive and the actually prescriptive. The generalization that the wages of labourers are 'in the present times' more than sufficient for subsistence (at the heart of Smith's advocacy of a high-wage/high-productivity economy) is based only on the irregular evidence that such wages are often higher in the summer than the winter (when need is greater), and that there has been little rise in the money price of labour despite rises in food prices. According to Campbell and Skinner, 'Smith may overestimate the wage rates slightly' (Glasgow Edition, 92, n. 25). Moreover, Smith persistently assumes the male identity of his typical worker. But as Dorothy George concludes from the case of three women found dead from starvation in 1763 in an empty house in Stonecutter Street, London: 'It is significant that all the victims should have been women; there can be little doubt that the hardships of the age bore with especial weight upon them. Social conditions tended to produce a high proportion of widows, deserted wives, and unmarried mothers, while women's occupations were over-stocked, ill-paid, and irregular' (*London Life in the Eighteenth Century*, 174). By suppressing throughout the female contribution to the flourishing commercial society, Smith not only categorizes paid labour as a male preserve but severely distorts the inequalities which existed in wage rates between the sexes, across trades, and in different areas of the country. The picture of the waged labourer is a

more complex composition of comfort and distress; and as Dorothy George notes, strikes in the period often related directly to the rising cost of living. She quotes one contemporary account of the situation: 'If the butchers would be content with a reasonable profit, the journeymen and labourers might be content with less wages; but when they pay so dear for all the necessaries of life, it cannot be so well expected' (ibid. 361, n. 21, from a report in the *London Chronicle* for 12 Dec. 1761).

74 *hereafter*: at *WN*, I. x (pp. 110–11).

75 *Oatmeal*: 'Their native bread is made of oats, or barley. Of oatmeal they spread very thin cakes, coarse and hard, to which unaccustomed palates are not easily reconciled' (Johnson, *Journey*, ed. Fleeman, 44).

76 *publick fiars*: in Scotland these were the average seasonal prices of grain fixed annually by law at the Fiars Court in each district, mainly to determine the payment of rents and ministers' stipends when these were based on the value of crops.

Glasgow, Carron, Ayrshire, &c.: in the later eighteenth century Glasgow was at the centre of an expanding linen industry; in 1759 an ironworks was set up on the River Carron near Falkirk; and agricultural improvers created jobs in Ayrshire.

eight pence a day: 'The common pay of a private man in the infantry was eight pence a-day, a lieutenant two shillings, an ensign eighteen pence' (David Hume, *History of England*, 8 vols. (London, 1778), vi. 178) [Campbell and Skinner].

Lord Chief Justice Hales . . . by begging or stealing: 'a Poor Man and his Wife though able to work, may have four Children, two of them possibly able to work, two not able: The Father and Mother are not able to maintain themselves and their Family in Meat, Drink, Cloathing and House-rent under ten Shillings *per* Week, and so much they might probably get if imployed; This amounts to £26 *per Annum* . . . without a supply Equivalent to this they must live by Begging or Stealing, or Starve' (Matthew Hale, *Discourse touching Provision for the Poor* (London, 1683), 16–17) [Campbell and Skinner].

77 *Mr. Gregory King . . . Doctor Davenant*: Gregory King, 'Natural and Political Observations and Conclusions upon the State and Condition of England 1696'. King is seen by modern historians

as giving one of the most precise pictures, using sample surveys and 'scientific' evidence, of the economic and social structure of England just before the industrial expansion. Charles D'Avenant, *Essay upon the Probable Methods of Making a People Gainers in the Balance of Trade* (1698), in *Political and Commercial Works*, 5 vols. (London, 1771), ii., confirmed the extent of lower-class poverty revealed by King's calculations—that over half the population of late seventeenth-century England were not able to live by their income.

78   *Soap, salt, candles . . . taxes . . . laid upon them*: as governments throughout the century sought greater revenue, the tax-burden swung from land tax (paid by landowners) to indirect taxation on consumer goods (paid by everyone). Per-capita taxation virtually doubled between 1715 and 1803. A large part of these levies were on even the most basic items of consumption—soap, tea, coffee, sugar, bricks, glass, coal, and so on. Contrary to Smith, it could seem that the poor were subsidizing the rich. But see Smith: 'I dislike all taxes that may affect the necessary expenses of the poor' (*Correspondence*, 327). William Blake, poet and social critic, raged against the omnipresent fetters of taxation: 'Lawful Bread, Bought with Lawful Money & a Lawful Heaven seen thro a Lawful Telescope by means of Lawful Window Light. The Holy Ghost & whatever cannot be Taxed is Unlawful & Witchcraft' (Marginalia to Thornton's New Translation of the *Lord's Prayer* (1827), in *William Blake's Writings*, ed. Bentley, ii. 1,515).

luxury extends itself . . . lowest ranks of the people: the attack on lower-class luxury was a commonplace of later-eighteenth-century moral economists. Smith is here specifically addressing those who believed that the labouring classes were by nature idle and improvident—men like the Dissenting minister Richard Price, who lamented in 1773: 'The lower ranks of the people are altered in every respect for the worse, while tea, wheaten bread, and other delicacies are necessaries which were formerly unknown to them' (quoted in Porter, *English Society in the Eighteenth Century*, 236). According to this view, what needed to be ascertained was the precise level at which labour could be recompensed as bare subsistence. Smith's thesis, that in a low-wage economy consumption and therefore productivity suffers (though not so outrageous to moralists as Mandeville's argument of 1723 vigorously representing the economic advantages of gin-drinking among the poor), relies on an intellectual recognition of the economic benefits of democratized consumption and, here at least, on a suspension of the moral argument.

79 *Luxury . . . powers of generation*: the restriction of female sexuality to motherhood is dedicated to economic expansionism in a remarkable range of eighteenth-century texts, by women as well as by men. Writing in 1726 in *Some Considerations upon Street-Walkers with a Proposal for lessening the present Number of them*, Defoe observed: 'The great Use of Women in a Community, is to supply it with Members that may be serviceable, and keep up a Succession' (in *Women in the Eighteenth Century: Constructions of Femininity*, ed. Vivien Jones (London: Routledge, 1990), 69). The word 'luxury', which in eighteenth-century usage can encompass a range of moral and political evils, usually denotes in *WN* no more than a particular kind of economic expenditure, even in a phrase like 'wanton luxury' (I. vii (p. 55)). But in this passage two forms of expansion are in competition. While luxury (and here women are conventionally appealed to as the chief consumers) stimulates the economy and employs productively an expanding work-force, it might also under certain conditions affect the national stock detrimentally. Where population growth is synonymous not just with national power but with further commercial progress, failure to procreate is a source of individual guilt and of socio-economic failure. In other writers, the association of female luxury and infertility is treated in overt terms of moral condemnation. See, for example, the complicated denunciation in Mary Wollstonecraft, *A Vindication of the Rights of Woman* (1792), where it is argued: 'Luxury has introduced a refinement in eating, that destroys the constitution . . . The depravity of the appetite which brings the sexes together, has had a still more fatal effect. Nature must ever be the standard of taste, the gauge of appetite—yet how grossly is nature insulted by the voluptuary . . . Women becoming . . . weaker, in mind and body, than they ought to be, were one of the grand ends of their being taken into the account, that of bearing and nursing children, have not sufficient strength to discharge the first duty of a mother . . . The weak enervated women . . . are unfit to be mothers, though they may

conceive . . .' (ed. Miriam Kramnick (Harmondsworth: Penguin, 1975), 247–9).

79 *foundling hospitals . . . mortality . . . the common people*: the London Foundling Hospital, England's first institutional orphanage, was founded by the philanthropist Thomas Coram, who obtained a charter in 1739. Maintained by charitable subscriptions, it aimed at stopping the exposure, desertion, and murder of unwanted children, and was opened in 1741. For a survey of the London Bills of Mortality recording the baptisms and deaths of children under 5 years of age and of children in parish care, see George, *London Life in the Eighteenth Century*, 399 and 401–5. For the twenty years from 1750 to 1769, the burials of children under 5 were, according to the Bills, 63 per cent of all children christened, though it should be remembered that London Bills of Mortality were not representative of other parts of the country.

80 *no species can ever multiply beyond it*: according to James Steuart's reading of the relationship between population and the food supply, 'the generative faculty resembles a spring loaded with a weight, which always exerts itself in proportion to the diminution of resistance' (*Principles of Political Oeconomy*, i. 20, ed. Skinner, 2 vols. (Edinburgh: Oliver and Boyd, 1966) i. 32) [Campbell and Skinner].

multiplication of labourers: cf. Arthur Young, 'the increase of employment will be found to raise men like mushrooms' (quoted in Porter, *English Society in the Eighteenth Century*, 224). From the 1740s the population of England rose in something more than the 'slow and gradual' fashion described by Smith—from 5.722 million in 1751, to 6.448 million in 1771, and 8.664 million in 1801.

81 *work done by freemen . . . cheaper . . . than that performed by slaves*: Smith expands on the economic disadvantages of slavery at *WN*, III. ii (pp. 238–40) and IV. vii (pp. 348–50). See note to p. 238 below.

liberal reward of labour: cf. Hume, 'Of Commerce', where he states that 'the great advantage of England above any nation at present in the world, or that appears in the records of any story' consists in the extended division of wealth down to the labouring classes: 'It will not, I hope, be considered as a superfluous digression, if I here observe, that as the multitude of mechanical arts is advantageous, so is the great number of persons to whose share the productions of these arts fall ... Every person, if possible, ought to enjoy the fruits of his labour, in a full possession of all the necessaries, and many of the conveniences of life. No one can doubt but such an equality is most suitable to human nature, and diminishes much less from the *happiness* of the rich, than it adds to that of the poor ... Add to this, that where the riches are in few hands, these must enjoy all the power, and will readily conspire to lay the whole burden on the poor, and oppress them still further, to the discouragement of all industry' (*Essays Moral, Political, and Literary*, 271–2). Debated throughout the eighteenth century were the competing economic and moral advantages of the doctrines of beneficial luxury and lower-class poverty.

82   *Ramuzzini ... concerning such diseases*: Bernardino Ramazzini, *De morbis artificum diatriba*, translated into English as *A Treatise of the Diseases of Tradesmen* (London, 1705). Ramazzini's was the standard eighteenth-century work on industrial disease and was, according to its English introduction, translated into all the European languages. Expanding on Smith's reference to the reduced health of the London carpenter, Dorothy George notes: 'In a pair of sawyers, one man was always the top-sawyer; he had the harder work, but escaped the blinding shower of sawdust that affected the eyes of the under-sawyer.' She gives other examples of the physical strain, cruel hours, and dangers of labour in the eighteenth century (*London Life in the Eighteenth Century*, 202–7).

84   *temptations of bad company ... ruin the morals of the other*: Josiah Tucker, Churchman and progressive conservative economist, spent his life in the manufacturing centres of the West country— in Bristol and Gloucester. He saw as the 'capital' disadvantage of the expansion of trade in Great Britain the 'want of subordination in the lower class of people', especially in those gathered in manufacturing towns. He proposed a system of courts or 'guardians of the morals of the manufacturing poor' for controlling vice. (See [Tucker] *A Brief Essay on the Advantages and Disadvantages which respectively attend France and Great Britain, with regard to Trade* (2nd edn., London, 1750), 36 ff.)

85   *Mr. Messance . . . Rouen*: Messance, *Recherches sur la population des généralites d'Auvergne, de Lyon, de Rouen, et de quelques provinces et villes du royaume, avec des réflexions sur la valeur du bled taut en France qu'en Angleterre, depuis 1674, jusqu'en 1764* (Paris, 1766) [Campbell and Skinner]. *Tailles* are taxes.

growing manufactures: Scottish linen manufacture rapidly expanded during the eighteenth century around Dundee in the east and Glasgow in the west. The flourishing woollen trade in the West Riding of Yorkshire (around Halifax) had impressed Daniel Defoe early in the century. See *A Tour Through the Whole Island of Great Britain* (1724–6), ed. Pat Rogers (Harmondsworth: Penguin, 1971), 491–3.

1740, a year of great scarcity: the year 1740/1 saw a serious failure of the Scottish harvest and threatened famine, though none occurred owing to the improved organization of emergency relief. (See note to p. 55 above.)

American stamp act: the Stamp Act of March 1765 levied taxes in the American colonies on, among other things, legal transactions, newspapers, and imported goods, threatening British manufacturers with the loss of an important export market: much Scottish linen was exported to the colonies in the eighteenth century. The money raised was to be used towards the cost of defending the colonies. American resistance made it impossible to enforce the Act, which was repealed early in 1766, but not before a Declaratory Act was passed maintaining Parliament's full sovereignty over the colonies.

91   *hereafter*: at *WN*, II. iii.

China seems to have been long stationary: China's neglect of foreign commerce was a favourite topic among eighteenth-century thinkers. Both Hume and Smith were puzzled by the example of a country which did not fit their theories of economic evolutionism: possessed of great wealth and early advanced in arts, sciences, and manufacture, it yet remained non-progressive. For Hume, 'China is represented as one of the most flourishing empires in the world, though it has very little commerce beyond its own territories' ('Of Commerce', *Essays Moral, Political, and Literary*, 271). Textiles, lacquer work, and wallpaper were imported from China from the seventeenth century and were later copied by European designers and craftsmen, but such exportation was undertaken not by the Chinese but by resident communities of foreign merchants. See *WN*, III. i (p. 231). (See also Hugh Honour, *Chinoiserie: The Vision of Cathay* (London: John Murray, 1961).)

92 *mandarines*: 'a generic name for all grades of Chinese officials, of which there were nine, each distinguished by a particular kind of button' (*OED*). During the eighteenth century there emerged alongside the view of China as a stagnant society a vision of the Chinese as a cruel and untrustworthy race. In the previous chapter (*WN*, I. viii), Smith refers to the practice in China of exposing unwanted children and the fact that some make a living by collecting such children for drowning (p. 71). Here he emphasizes the corruption of the mandarins and the oppression of the poor. See the contemporary hostile account of China by the author of Commander George Anson's *A Voyage Round the World* (1748).

93 *province of Holland*: according to Hume, '[t]he only commercial state that ought to dread the improvements and industry of their neighbours, is such a one as the Dutch, who, enjoying no extent of land, nor possessing any number of native commodities, flourish only by their being the brokers, and factors, and carriers of others . . . But though this consequence may naturally be dreaded . . . [t]he advantage of superior stocks and correspond-ence is so great, that it is not easily overcome' ('Of the Jealousy of Trade', *Essays Moral, Political, and Literary*, 337). A pure trading nation, Holland lost its commercial lead to Britain in the course of the eighteenth century, owing to the raw materials and industries and the colonial trade which proved the basis for the latter's sustained economic improvement.

94 *compound interest*: interest calculated not only on the original capital invested, but also on the interest earned in previous periods. This contrasts with *simple interest*, in which interest is calculated on the original capital only, for all years.

96 *a journeyman taylor*: later in this chapter Smith describes jour-neymen tailors as '[t]he lowest order of artificers' (p. 100).

97 *who follow as a trade . . . as a pastime*: at I. xi. Smith considers the case of those who earn a living as gardeners: 'The circum-stances of gardeners, generally mean, and always moderate, may satisfy us that their great ingenuity is not commonly

over-recompensed. Their delightful art is practised by so many
rich people for amusement, that little advantage is to be made
by those who practise it for profit; because the persons who
should naturally be their best customers, supply themselves
with all their most precious productions' (Glasgow Edition,
169). In Book Three of *The Task* (1785), entitled 'The Garden',
William Cowper attests both to the popularity of gardening as
a hobby in the late eighteenth century (for example, his celebrated description of cucumber growing at iii. 446 ff.), and to
the importance of luxury crops to the labouring economy:

> 'Grudge not, ye rich, (since luxury must have
> His dainties, and the world's more num'rous half
> Lives by contriving delicates for you)
> Grudge not the cost. Ye little know the cares,
> The vigilance, the labour, and the skill,
> That day and night are exercis'd, and hang
> Upon the ticklish balance of suspense,
> That ye may garnish your profuse regales
> With summer fruits brought forth by wintry suns.'
>
> (iii. 544–52)

97   *A poacher . . . in Great Britain*: hunting became increasingly a
pastime of the privileged in the course of the eighteenth
century. From 1671 no one with less than an estate of £100 a
year was permitted to kill game, not even on their own land.
From the mid-eighteenth century game preserves were set up
and poachers severely dealt with. Under an Act of 1770,
nocturnal poaching attached a sentence of six months' imprisonment. A further Act of 1803 prescribed death for poachers
resisting arrest with arms. (See Douglas Hay, 'Poaching and
the Game Laws on Cannock Chase', in D. Day *et al.*, *Albion's
Fatal Tree: Crime and Society in Eighteenth-Century England*
(London: Allen Lane, 1975).) In late eighteenth-century writings, poaching is synonymous with lower-class disaffection and
sloth, as in Hannah More's Cheap Repository Tract, *Black Giles
the Poacher* (Nov. 1796); and yet it remained true that for many
low-income country workers poaching provided a necessary
supplement.

98   *usual idleness of apprentices*: a distinction was drawn between the
apprentice who paid with his labour and who would be a

journeyman when out of his time and the apprentice who came for education and with the support of a good fee. The latter would expect to set up for himself at the end of his training. The idleness of the apprentice was a byword throughout the century. In Hogarth's series of engravings entitled *Industry and Idleness* (1747), apprenticeship represents initiation into the values of a commercial society. The progress of the two apprentices, one industrious and one idle, is reflected in a rigorous system of contrasts through twelve plates, ending with the industrious apprentice married to his master's daughter and made Lord Mayor of London, and the idle apprentice executed at Tyburn. See, too, Hannah More's Cheap Repository Tract, *The Cheapside Apprentice* (June 1796). The tract purports to be written from the condemned cell by the profligate apprentice as a warning to other young men. Separated by fifty years of steady commercialization, both Hogarth and More saw art as at the service of utility and morality, and both espoused the belief that in industry lay the advancement of self and society and the wealth of nations.

99   *the latter commonly earn fifteen and eighteen*: for wages of labourers and craftsmen in the later eighteenth century, see note to p. 69 above.

100   *Chairmen*: those employed in carrying people by sedan-chair, often Irish and Scottish immigrant workers, and generally regarded as the lowest of the unskilled. See Pierre-Jean Grosley, *A Tour to London; or, New Observations on England, and Its Inhabitants*, 2 vols. (London, 1772), where chairmen are described as part of a group, including porters, sailors, and street-workers, who form 'as insolent a rabble as can be met with in countries without law or police' (i. 84).

during the summer: as usual, Smith exaggerates the long-term benefits of the relatively high seasonal wage of the worker with no incentive or habit of saving. Dorothy George (quoting R. Campbell, *The London Tradesman* (1747), 17) writes of midcentury: 'The dead season was a serious thing when the world of fashion deserted London for four or five months at least, and the middle-class demand was comparatively undeveloped. The tailors for instance, in 1747, were said to be "as numerous as locusts, out of business three or four months of the year, and generally as poor as rats" ' (*London Life in the Eighteenth Century*, 263).

100   *A collier*: The 'hardship, disagreeableness and dirtiness', noted
by Smith as the collier's lot, are echoed by literary observers.
Describing the coal-miners of the North of Scotland whom he
encountered on his tour, Defoe wrote: 'what with the dejected
countenances of the men, occasioned by their poverty and hard
labour, and what with the colour or discolouring, which comes
from the coal, both to their clothes and complexions, [they] are
indeed, frightful fellows at first sight' (*A Tour Through the
Whole Island of Great Britain*, 639). In Scotland until the end
of the eighteenth century (1799), colliers, like salt-workers,
existed in a state of slavery and were sold as part of the
machinery of the mines in which they worked. In one of the
first poems to refer to industrialization, Richard Jago's *Edge-
Hill, or, the Rural Prospect Delineated and Moralized* (1767), the
hazard to health of mining is expounded:

> 'Mean while the subterraneous City spreads
> Its covert Streets, and ecchoes with the Noise
> Of swarthy Slaves, and Instruments of Toil.
> They, such the Force of Custom's pow'rful Laws!
> Pursue their sooty Labours, destitute
> Of the Sun's cheering Light, and genial Warmth.
> And oft a chilling Damp, or unctuous Mist,
> Loos'd from the crumbly Caverns, issues forth,
> Stopping the Springs of Life.'

> (iii. 434–42)

102   *The counsellor at law*: before the more diffused professionalization of career structures which characterized Victorian Britain,
entry into the higher reaches of the law and medicine was
jealously guarded by closed oligarchies in the form of the
College of Physicians and the Inns of Court. In the eighteenth
century most practitioners were excluded from the privileges of
these exclusive bodies, and while they remained on the lower
rungs of their professional ladders their esteem was not high.

104   *state lotteries*: these had flourished since 1694 and were viewed
as a legitimate method of raising money for ventures in the
public interest. But from the 1770s their use was more widespread and more open to abuse. Several private lotteries were
authorized by Parliament at this time, and the state lottery helped
fund institutions like the British Museum and projects like Westminster Bridge. There were also illegal private lotteries, called

Little Goes, which were grossly fraudulent. (On lotteries, see Langford, *A Polite and Commercial People*, 572–4.)

105   *moderate profit of insurers*: the Phoenix (1680) and the Sun Fire (1708) pioneered fire insurance in London, while the Royal Exchange Assurance and Lloyd's specialized in marine insurance. Life assurance can be dated to later in the century; friendly societies for the relief of workers and their families are to be found in the seventeenth century but multiplied towards the end of the eighteenth.

106   *Their pay . . . less than that of common labourers*: for soldiers' pay, see note to p. 76 above.

108   *trade to North America . . . to Jamaica*: at *WN*, III. ii (pp. 238–9), Smith comments that the profits from the West Indian sugar plantations 'are generally much greater than those of any other cultivation that is known either in Europe or America'. In 1798 Prime Minister Pitt estimated incomes from the West Indies at four million pounds, as compared with one million from the rest of the world. However, this very profitability rendered the possession of the sugar islands insecure in the mid-century wars between France and Britain.

    The most hazardous of all trades . . . a smuggler: basic commodities as well as luxuries were heavily taxed in eighteenth-century Britain. The smuggler, committed by profession to free trade in imports, is an interesting figure in Smith's industrious society. See note to p. 303 below.

109   *Apothecaries' profit . . . uncommonly extravagant*: apothecaries remained important throughout the eighteenth century as general medical practitioners, especially among the less wealthy. Like craftsmen, they trained on the job by apprenticeships. Of the trade of the apothecary R. Campbell writes: 'There is no Branch of Business, in which a Man requires less Money to set him up, than this very profitable Trade: Ten or twenty Pounds, judiciously applied, will buy Gallipots and Counters, and as many Drugs to fill them as might poison the whole Island. His Profits are unconceivable; Five Hundred *per Cent*. is the least he receives' (*The London Tradesman* (1747), 64).

110   *prime cost*: this includes *variable cost* (which varies directly with the rate of output—for example, labour costs and raw-material

costs) plus *fixed cost* (which does not vary in the short term with output—for example, administrative costs).

112 *Birmingham ... the former kind; Sheffield ... the latter*: Birmingham's prosperity, dating from the later eighteenth century, was built on the manufacture of buttons, buckles, and 'toys' (a label including then much of what we would now term jewellery and fashion items); Sheffield's was founded on the older-established profits of cutlery. Evidence for the high wages in the Birmingham toy industry is provided in Berg, *The Age of Manufactures*, 308.

114 *it has already been observed*: at *WN*, I. vii (pp. 56–7).

115 *Cotters or Cottagers*: on the island of Col in 1773, Johnson noted there was 'a particular mode of undertenure', with 'tenants below the rank of Tacksmen, that have yet smaller tenants under them; for in every place, where money is not the general equivalent, there must be some whose labour is immediately paid by daily food' (*Journey*, ed. Fleeman, 107; and see 73). Smith sees the Scottish cotter, the lowest kind of subtenant, part servant and part independent day-labourer, as the relic of an older way of life, before land improvement drove out its precarious economy. Ten years later Robert Burns's poetic portrayal of family-based subsistence in 'The Cotter's Saturday Night' (1786) is compromised by sentimentality, while George Crabbe's contrastive portraits of the lives of country labourers in his poem *The Village* (1783) paints in harsher colours the hardship of an equivalent English community. In all four studies, the sense is powerful of a pre-commercial economy now finally disappearing.

116 *she is a good spinner ... twenty-pence a week*: at IV. viii. Smith notes: 'but our spinners are poor people, women commonly, scattered about in all different parts of the country, without support or protection' (Glasgow Edition, 644). Spinning (on the distaff) long remained a female and home-based occupation, even after the introduction of technology in the form of spinning-wheels and spinning jennies. The extremely low pay attached to the work, not only in Scotland but throughout Britain, reflected the assumption that women could attend to it alongside or in the intervals from other labours. As late as 1823 Hugh Miller observes of women's role in the harsh economy of the Scottish Highlands: 'Here as in all semi-barbarous countries,

is the woman seen to be regarded rather the drudge than the companion to the man. The husband turns up the land and sows it—the wife conveys the manure to it in a creel, tends the corn, reaps it, hoes the potatoes, digs them up, carries the whole home on her back, when bearing the creel she is also engaged with spinning with the distaff . . .' (cited in Berg, *The Age of Manufactures*, 143). The economy of the cotters depends on self-exploitation within the family. As Smith notes, its spinning and knitting of stockings, more cheaply by hand than with machines, is built on the assumption that such labour, however arduous, is only supplementary. If it were undertaken in workshops, the cost would be higher; as it is, costs are kept low by association with the land and with the family, both of which serve to categorize labour as unspecialized and cheap. Smith's estimate of twenty pence a week as the wage of a good woman spinner is to be compared with his earlier estimate of eight pence a day as 'the most usual wages of common labour' in the Scottish Lowlands (p. 76).

In . . . Scotland . . . a single story: in Edinburgh, for example, before the establishment of the New Town (for which building was only beginning in the 1770s), it was common even for the wealthiest and the best-connected families to occupy a single storey of a large tenement or land, as the houses were called. Defoe was not impressed by the living conditions in Edinburgh in the 1720s, describing the 'thronged buildings, from seven to ten or twelve story high', and complaining that 'in no city in the world so many people live in so little room as at Edinburgh' (*A Tour Through the Whole Island of Great Britain*, 577).

117 *free circulation . . . from place to place*: At *WN*, IV. viii (p. 375), Smith refers to Statutes of 1718 and 1749 penalizing persons 'convicted of enticing any artificer of, or in any of the manufactures of Great Britain, to go into any foreign parts in order to practice or teach his trade'. By 'foreign parts' Smith means other areas of Britain. He comments on this restriction of movement: 'When such heavy penalties were imposed upon the exportation of the dead instruments of trade, it could not well be expected that the living instrument, the artificer, should be allowed to go free.'

exclusive privileges of corporations: long-established trades, like tailoring and wheel-making (Smith's example), were covered by the Elizabethan Statute of Artificers of 1563; that is, they restricted entry, upheld apprenticeships, and by-laws made established rates of pay and terms of work enforceable by magistrates. Such rules gave qualified journeymen a property in their trade and a strong position for collective bargaining. However, in rapidly expanding industries and in unincorporated or newer towns like Birmingham (uncontrolled by craft organizations or guilds), apprenticeship took on a more flexible shape or lapsed altogether, as cheap labour replaced formal training. According to Berg, '[o]f 108 buttonmakers in Birmingham in 1767 only 18 took indentured apprentices or had themselves served as apprentices' (*The Age of Manufactures*, 306; and see Rule, *The Experience of Labour in Eighteenth-Century Industry*). Traditionally, apprenticeships were open to women as well as men in a wide range of trades from weaving to blacksmith's work. Apprenticeship records suggest no fixed conception of appropriate female labour. But in the course of the later eighteenth century rapid expansion undermined the powers of corporations to control labour conditions, and it was to the advantage of employers to take on women and children as cheaper and often unskilled labour. Long term, the consequence was to deny women the security of decent wages and skilled employment and to erode their rights (always fragile) to apprenticeships. In the interest of the freedom of trade, Smith calls (at *WN*, IV. ii) for the abolition of the statute of apprenticeship and exclusive privileges, arguing that these are 'real encroachments upon natural liberty' (p. 299). In retrospect at least, it would seem that the absence of labour protection which such liberty entails worked to widen the gap between workers (now often mere labourers) and employers, who had most to gain from the freedom, and between male and female labour. In 1798 Priscilla Wakefield published *Reflections on the Present Condition of the Female Sex; with suggestions for its improvement*, in which she directly criticized Smith's free-enterprise economy as itself an encroachment on the liberty of women, who are denied access to dignified and well-paid work, pushed out into poverty and enforced prostitution by male workers within the new economic order. Part of her argument is for the return of exclusive privileges in the interests of a more generally productive economy of women as well as men. She would, for example, have male workers excluded from certain markets and functions—like midwifery and shop-work, where the goods for sale target female purchasers.

118   *silk weavers in London*: the by-law was enacted in 1670. George comments of the Spitalfields silk-weavers in the later eighteenth century: 'The excessive number of apprentices taken by the journeymen weavers of Spitalfields had long been complained of. The Spitalfields Act in 1773 which provided for the fixing of wages by Quarter Sessions, forbade weavers to take more than two apprentices, to prevent, as Hanway said, "the scene of misery which they had brought upon themselves". Apprenticeship, however, was by no means rigidly enforced among the London weavers, and in any case their wives and children often wove, whether apprenticed or not. The restriction nevertheless was beneficial' (*London Life in the Eighteenth Century*, 234).

universities . . . any incorporation whatever: 'Latin *universitas* the whole . . . (in later juridical language) society, guild, corporation (whence the medieval academic use *universitas magistrorum et scholarium* [guild of teachers and scholars])' (*OED*). In a letter to William Cullen, 20 Sept. 1774, Smith observed that the monopolistic tendencies of degrees, like apprenticeship statutes in trades, 'have banished almost all useful and solid education from the greater part of Universities' (*Correspondence*, 177).

119   *Statute of Apprenticeship*: see note to p. 117 above.

120   *reel-makers*: those who make reels, cylinders, or spools on which thread is wound.

property . . . in his own labour . . . the most sacred and inviolable: cf. Locke, *Two Treatises of Government*: 'Though the Earth, and all inferior Creatures be common to all Men, yet every Man has a *Property* in his own *Person*. This no Body has any Right to but himself. The *Labour* of his Body, and the *Work* of his Hands, we may say, are properly his' (ed. Laslett, 305–6).

121   *sterling mark . . . stamps*: the hallmark or authorized stamp which guarantees standard quality of plate. For stamps on linen and wool, see note to p. 34 above.

apprentices from publick charities: the apprenticeship of needy or orphaned children by the parish or a charitable institution was a form of poor relief and the most general way of giving a disadvantaged child a start in life. It differed legally from ordinary apprenticeship in the longer term of servitude and the compulsory binding by the overseers with the consent of two justices. Acts of 1767 and 1768 limited the binding of parish boys beyond the age of 21 and stipulated that a minimum fee should be given with them. Poor boys and girls were usually bound to the least skilled and to badly paid trades, often as little more than drudges. Charles Dickens's *Oliver Twist* (1837–8), subtitled *The Parish Boy's Progress*, details the histories of two such apprentices in Oliver himself and Noah Claypole.

122 *making clocks and watches*: watch- and clock-making developed markedly in England from the late seventeenth century, along with the making of other precision and scientific instruments: navigation instruments and microscopes. On his birthday in 1764 George III was given a silver repeating watch which struck the hours and was less than half-an-inch in diameter. Campbell and Skinner note that Smith is rather more generous to the skills of watchmakers in *Lectures on Jurisprudence* (1766), 225 (p. 495).

123 *adulterine*: 'Illegal, unlicensed . . . Adulterine castles, guilds. 1640' (*OED*).

124 *Every town . . . from the country*: see *WN*, III. i (pp. 227–9), for an expansion of this argument.

125 *wool-combers*: those who comb out or card the wool, disentangling the fibres in preparation for spinning. John Dyer, in *The Fleece* (1757), his celebratory epic on the British wool industry, describes this process as part of an extravagant eulogium of the industrious poor in a mid-century workhouse:

> 'With equal scale
> Some deal abroad the well-assorted fleece;
> These card the short, those comb the longer flake;
> Others the harsh and clotted lock receive,
> Yet sever and refine with patient toil,
> And bring to proper use.'

(iii. 275–80)

126 *In the history of the arts . . . explained in this manner*: Smith's reference is to *Descriptions des arts et métiers faites ou approuvées par Messieurs de l'Académie Royale des Sciences* (1761–88).

127 *The common ploughman . . . seldom defective in this judgment and discretion*: several commentators have noted how at this point in his analysis of the conditions for the wealth of nations Smith

disconcertingly abandons his narrow and pragmatic argument in favour of industrial specialization leading to high productivity, to replace it with its antithesis—a portrait of the undivided and consequently varied labour of the ploughman. The shift appears to be from an economic to an imaginative, even poetic, engagement with the nature of production, whereby a superior intelligence and alertness, the consequences of a labour both independent and challenging, make part of the returns of the country worker. As the poetic vision at the heart of Smith's functional commercial economy, the life of the ploughman represents a paradox. Behind Smith's praise of the rural life lies a traditional opposition of town and country values, reaching back to Cicero and Horace, and especially to Virgil, and a classical ideal of virtuous work upon which the unvirtuous spirit of acquisitive commercialism depends. Virgil's *Georgics*, in particular, offers a model for a didactic poetics of rural life and agronomic improvement which in the eighteenth century influenced James Thomson's *The Seasons* (1726–30) and Cowper's *The Task* (1785) as well as *WN*. Kenneth Maclean suggests that Smith's agrarianism anticipates Wordsworth's turn-of-the-century celebration of the greater dignity of rural life. (*Agrarian Age: A Background for Wordsworth*, Yale Studies in English, 115 (New Haven, Conn.: Yale University Press, 1950), 87–103.) A more recent critic adds the qualification that Wordsworth was perhaps less 'poetic' than Smith, and 'capable of a realism which, at this moment in [his] argument, Smith wishes to ignore' (Richard Feingold, *Nature and Society: Later Eighteenth-Century Uses of the Pastoral and Georgic* (Hassocks: Harvester, 1978), 79). According to Feingold's argument, the Smithian Wordsworth is the creator of the sheep-farmer Michael in *Lyrical Ballads* (1800), while his un-Smithian 'realism' dictates the portrait of the country labourer in *The Excursion* (1814):

> 'Turn we then
> To Britons born and bred within the pale
> Of civil polity, and early trained
> To earn, by wholesome labour in the field,
> The bread they eat. A sample should I give
> Of what this stock hath long produced to enrich
> The tender age of life, ye would exclaim,
> "Is this the whistling plough-boy whose shrill notes

Impart new gladness to the morning air!"
Forgive me if I venture to suspect
That many, sweet to hear of in soft verse,
Are of no finer frame. Stiff are his joints;

.   .   .   .

And mark his brow!
Under whose shaggy canopy are set
Two eyes—not dim, but of a healthy stare—
Wide, sluggish, blank, and ignorant, and strange—
Proclaiming boldly that they never drew
A look or motion of intelligence . . .'

(viii. 391–412)

128   *hereafter*: at *WN*, III. iv, entitled 'How the Commerce of the Towns contributed to the Improvement of the Country'.

129   *A regulation . . . to provide for . . . widows and orphans*: Smith has in mind the friendly societies (also known as 'box clubs'), which offered a rudimentary social insurance against sickness, death, and so on, and also served as cover for trades-union activities. An Act of 1793 provided that the rules of friendly societies should be enrolled at quarter sessions.

131   *By the 12th of Queen Anne, c.12*: an Act of 1713.

     cures: 'The spiritual charges of parishioners; the office or function of a curate' (*OED*). In the same paragraph, *curacies* again refers to 'the office of a curate'.

132   *churches of Scotland, of Geneva*: the Presbyterian system of government of the Church of Scotland was established in 1690. As in the case of the Swiss Calvinist Church, its livings would be less prosperous than those of the wealthier and longer-established Church of England and, in parts of mainland Europe, the Roman Catholic Church. In addition, with superintendence invested in courts or councils and not individual bishops, it possibly offered a less attractive career-structure for the ambitious cleric.

133   *entering into holy orders*: in 1740 Smith finished his studies at Glasgow University and went with a Snell Exhibition to Balliol College, Oxford. The purpose of the Snell Foundation was originally to provide a supply of ministers for the Episcopal Church of Scotland, but this was nullified in 1690 by the Presbyterian settlement of the Church. An Oxford attempt to

force entry on Exhibition holders into orders in the Church of England failed in 1744. Smith himself left Oxford in 1746 without seeking ordination. (See R. H. Campbell and A. S. Skinner, *Adam Smith* (Beckenham: Croom Helm, 1985), 23.)

133 *writing for a bookseller*: Smith here appears to stand back from the industry of book-making, which as part of the trade in culture was rapidly expanding in the course of the eighteenth century. Booksellers, operating from shop premises, were the publishers of the day. In 1725 Defoe wrote: 'writing is become a very considerable part of the English commerce. The booksellers are the master manufacturers or employers. The several writers, authors, copyers, subwriters, and all other operators with pen and ink are the workmen employed by the said master manufacturers' (cited in Porter, *English Society in the Eighteenth Century*, 259). While for many this meant poorly paid hackwork, there were also large amounts to be made. Dr Johnson received £1,575 for his *Dictionary* (1755) and Smith £500 for *WN*, when, according to his biographers, his 'income from teaching probably did not exceed £170 per annum' (Campbell and Skinner, *Adam Smith*, 40).

the usual reward . . . no proportion to that of the lawyer or physician: writing on 20 Sept. 1774 to William Cullen, now Professor of the Practice of Medicine at Edinburgh, Smith notes of the large fees commanded by doctors: 'Had the Universities of Oxford and Cambridge been able to maintain themselves in the exclusive privilege of graduating all the doctors who could practise in England, the price of feeling a pulse might by this time have risen from two and three guineas, the price which it has now happily arrived at, to double or triple that sum' (*Correspondence*, 178).

Isocrates: (436–338 BC) an Athenian orator and rhetorician who opened a school of rhetoric in 393. The school soon became famous and pupils flocked to it from all parts of the Greek world. The quotation from *Against the Sophists* was employed in an earlier eighteenth-century treatise on money, Charles Arbuthnot's, *Tables of Ancient Coins, Weights, and Measures* (London, 1727), 198.

134 *Plutarch . . . his Didactron*: (AD 46–126) a philosopher and historian who studied in Athens and travelled to Alexandria and

Rome. His teaching fee is mentioned in Arbuthnot, *Tables of Ancient Coins, Weights, and Measures*, 198.

134   *Gorgias . . . Delphi . . . Hippias . . . Protagoras*: Gorgias (485–380 BC) was a philosopher and rhetorician and the teacher of Isocrates. Plato writes of him in the *Gorgias*. Delphi, in the centre of mainland Greece, was the most important religious centre in its empire. According to Pliny, the statue of himself which Gorgias sent to Delphi was 'the first solid gold statue of a human being', and its richness witnessed to the great profits 'to be made by teaching the art of oratory' (*Natural History*, XXXIII. xxiv., trans. H. Rackham (Loeb edn., 1952), ix. 64–5). Hippias, a sophist and virtual contemporary of Socrates (469–339 BC), is known mainly through his caricatured portrait in two dialogues of Plato, *Hippias major* and *Hippias minor*. His claim was to know everything. Protagoras (485–411 BC) was a rhetorician from Thrace, Northern Greece. At the beginning of the *Protagoras*, Plato describes the intense excitement caused by the arrival of this celebrated teacher in Athens.

135   *Carneades . . . Diogenes the stoick*: influential in the dissemination of Greek learning in the West, Carneades, Diogenes, and Critolaus were three Athenian professors sent as envoys to Rome in 155 BC. They gave public lectures while waiting for the Senate's decision on their plea, and these excited a demand for more Greek knowledge.

    the constitution . . . in which education is carried on: at *WN*, v.i (pp. 420 ff.), Smith considers at some length the subject of education and its benefits to the state.

    exclusive privileges of corporations: in towns with heavy investment in craft corporations there were wide-ranging regulations covering residence, the admission of freemen, and the licensing of trades. In towns without corporation control, labour restrictions were fewer and new enterprise could develop more freely. See note to p. 117 above.

136   *to come upon the parish*: to apply for financial relief from the parish. See the following note.

    the poor laws: Elizabethan legislation of 1601 (modifying an Act of 1598) established the system of every parish in England raising money by a Poor Rate for the relief of indigence. The system lasted until 1834. The Act of Settlement of the Poor of

1662 empowered a parish to send back to the parish of which she or he was a native anyone liable to be a charge on the rates. Every native was deemed to possess a 'settlement' in one parish only—usually by birth, marriage (of a woman to a husband), or being apprenticed there. Anyone requiring relief owing to sickness, incapacity for work, and the like, had the right to relief only in that one parish. In law (though for an unskilled worker not usually in practice), a person needed a certificate before leaving the parish of his or her settlement to obtain work elsewhere. Viewed in its best light, the Act of Settlement served to identify responsibility for the needy (and in this sense it recognized that the needy exist and that responsibility rests somewhere) and to discourage vagrancy. But by the same token it was a licence to deal ruthlessly with the travelling poor and those without a settlement. Unmarried pregnant women were treated cruelly, and the Act's restrictive conditions encouraged ever-meaner interpretation since no parish actually courted responsibility for its poor. In the following report the parish of Cowley, near Oxford, is attempting to refuse the burden of a widow of sixteen years residence and her children, all of whom were born in the parish: 'On Tuesday last began the General Quarter Sessions for this county, at which a remarkable case came before the bench, upon an appeal to an order for removing Elizabeth the widow of Edward Haynes, and her six children from the parish of Cowley in this county, to the place of her settlement when a single woman; upon a presumption that the children were illegitimate, and her marriage illegal' (from *Jackson's Oxford Journal*, 13 Jan. 1770; in Bridget Hill (ed.), *Eighteenth-Century Women: An Anthology* (London: Allen and Unwin, 1984), 176). Smith's objections to the Act are not strictly humanitarian, since his concern is not with the needy or helpless but with the restrictions imposed on a free circulation of labour. Scottish poor relief was established on broadly similar lines to those of the English law, though parish settlement appears to have been a less contentious matter.

137   *the police of England*: the public regulation or administration of England. Campbell and Skinner note of Smith's discussion of the Act of Settlement: 'Even more than in his discussion of the Statute of Apprenticeship Smith concentrates on the statutory basis of the law of settlement and not on its operation.

Interference with the mobility of labour was probably much less in practice than he believed' (Glasgow Edition, 152, n. 50). See D. Marshall, 'The Old Poor Law, 1662–1795', *Economic History Review*, 8 (1937), 1.

138 *Doctor Burn*: Richard Burn, *The Justice of the Peace and Parish Officer* (13th edn., London, 1776), iii. 413 [Campbell and Skinner].

140 *Doctor Burn ... in a worse condition*: Burn, *Justice of the Peace* (8th edn., London, 1764), ii. 274 [Campbell and Skinner].

141 *History of the Poor Laws*: Richard Burn, *History of the Poor Laws* (London, 1764), 235–6 [Campbell and Skinner].

mandamus: 'a juridical writ issued in the king's name from the Court of King's Bench (now, from the Crown side of the King's Bench Division of the High Court of Justice) and directed to an inferior court, a corporation, an officer, etc., commanding some specific thing to be done' (*OED*).

a very strange attempt: Burn, *Justice of the Peace*, (1776), iii. 310 [Campbell and Skinner].

142 *general warrants*: warrants for the apprehension of the persons suspected of an offence, no individual being named or particularly described. Such warrants were obviously intimidatory, able to be issued with little hard proof to uphold them.

Doctor Burn ... for industry or ingenuity: Burn, *History of the Poor Laws*, 130 [Campbell and Skinner].

143 *except in the case of a general mourning*: the Act was of 1768. See note to p. 58 above.

assize of bread: the statutory regulation of the price and weight of bread by the ruling price of grain. See Hannah More's Cheap Repository Tract, *The Cottage Cook; or, Mrs Jones's Cheap Dishes* (Jan. 1797), where a baker is successfully prosecuted for selling bread under regulation weight. The Assize of Bread remained effective throughout the eighteenth century in many market towns. Smith's case for dismantling the assize is based on the claim that it has acted to keep the price of loaves above their 'natural' competitive price.

144 *already been observed*: at *WN*, I. vii (p. 62).

145 *Of the Rent of Land*: this final and longest chapter of Book One has here been reduced to a few pages. I have omitted the lengthy 'Digression concerning the Variations in the Value of

Silver during the Course of the Four last Centuries' and have retained only the outlines of Smith's three explanations of the origins of rent—the monopoly of landlords, the natural productivity of the soil, and the differential income accruing to land of greater marginal fertility—as well as his concluding and famous discussion of the interests of the 'three great, original and constituent orders' which make up society.

145   *upon its improvement*: the second half of the eighteenth century was the great age of landlord improvers, draining and reclaiming waste land, experimenting with new crops, and systematizing stock-breeding. Smith recommends that landlords should improve their ground at WN v. ii on account of their greater capital and ability to take risks (Glasgow Edition, 832). But at *WN*, III. ii (pp. 236–7) and iv (pp. 259–60), he distinguishes between those born to a landed estate and the city-bred merchants who buy into land, arguing that it is the latter who often make the better improvers.

146   *Kelp is a species of sea-weed*: from the late eighteenth century the Highland kelp industry was extremely lucrative to tenants and landlords. But its doom was sealed in 1815 with the removal of the high excise duty on imported sodium sulphate for alkali production. (See L. Rymer, 'The Scottish Kelp Industry', *Scottish Geographical Review*, 90 (1974), 142–52, and Bruce Lenman, *Integration, Enlightenment, and Industrialization: Scotland 1746–1832* (London: Edward Arnold, 1981), 123.) While visiting the Island of Skye in 1773, Johnson observed in almost Smithian terms the landlords' readiness to exploit the natural resource of the kelp industry: 'They have lately found a manufacture considerably lucrative. Their rocks abound with kelp, a sea-plant, of which the ashes are melted into glass. They burn kelp in great quantities, and then send it away in ships, which come regularly to purchase them. This new source of riches has raised the rents of many maritime farms; but the tenants pay, like all other tenants, the additional rent with great unwillingness; because they consider the profits of the kelp as the mere product of personal labour, to which the landlord contributes nothing. However, as any man may be said to give, what he gives the power of gaining, he has certainly as much right to profit from the price of kelp as of any thing else found or raised upon his ground' (*Journey*, ed. Fleeman, 66–7).

146   *rent . . . partly paid in sea-fish*: see Bruce Lenman: 'Shetland had its own class of merchant-lairds who had risen on the ruin of the class of immigrant Scottish lairds who had asserted control over Shetland in the late sixteenth and early seventeenth centuries. Keeping their tenants deliberately at the margin of survival on what were known as fishing tenures, Shetland lairds forced them by threat of eviction and by debt-bondage to concentrate on fishing for fish which had to be handed over to the laird who cured and exported them. Division of farms to secure more hands for the boats ensured that agriculture was incapable of sustaining the population for more than part of the year' (*Integration, Enlightenment, and Industrialization*, 10–11). This mode of fishing tenure is described in Walter Scott's novel of eighteenth-century Shetland life, *The Pirate* (1822), ch. 22.

147   *As men . . . naturally multiply . . . in proportion to the means of their subsistence*: see the note to p. 80 above.

148   *already been shown*: at *WN*, I. ix (Glasgow Edition, 106–7).

149   *Good roads, canals, and navigable rivers*: for improvement in transport and communications in the course of the eighteenth century, see the note to pp. 27–8 above.

    After food . . . the two great wants of mankind: the great thinkers of the Scottish Enlightenment—David Hume, Adam Ferguson, Adam Smith, Lord Kames, William Robertson, and John Millar—sought to redefine the concerns of the historian. They subordinated traditional enquiries into the struggles of princes and the rise and fall of great dynasties to a more general materialist examination of what motivates human behaviour. In a sense they inverted history, fashioning it from the ground up, as the assemblage of universal, anonymous, and often unattractive human needs and appetites in different times and places— food, clothing, shelter, and sexual desire—and not, as was (and is) more usual, from the top down as the specific interventions of the great and the glamorous. See, for example, Smith's comment quoted in my Introduction (p. xxvii).

150   *hunting nations of North America*: for the Scottish Enlightenment historians, as for their French counterparts, the native Indians of the North American continent before the contamination of the European invaders represented all mankind as they must have been in the earliest stage of existence. According to

William Robertson, 'the discovery of the New World enlarged the sphere of contemplation, and presented nations to our view, in stages of their progress, much less advanced than those wherein they have been observed in our continent. In America, man appears under the rudest form in which we can conceive him to subsist . . . That state of primaeval simplicity, which was known in our continent only by the fanciful description of poets, really existed in the other' (*The History of America*, 2 vols. (London, 1777), i. 282–3). Cf. Locke's famous statement almost a century earlier: 'Thus in the beginning all the World was *America*' (*Two Treatises*, ed. Laslett, 319).

150   *peltry*: undressed fur skins; a collective form for *pelts*.

151   *than the highlands of Scotland are now*: it became something of a commonplace to compare the Scottish Highlands, still remote, largely feudal, and considered savage in the mid-eighteenth century, to the state of England in the Middle Ages—or to something much more terrifying. According to Johnson in 1773, for example: 'To the southern inhabitants of Scotland, the state of the mountains and the islands is equally unknown with that of *Borneo* or *Sumatra*' (*Journey*, ed. Fleeman, 72). For Walter Scott, writing in 1814, changes in the Highlands over the previous sixty years, '[t]he gradual influx of wealth, and extension of commerce, have since united to render the present people of Scotland a class of beings as different from their grandfathers, as the existing English are from those of Queen Elizabeth's time' (*Waverley; or, 'Tis Sixty Years Since*, ed. Claire Lamont (Oxford: Oxford University Press, 1981), 340).

paving of the streets of London: the succession of Paving Acts, beginning in 1762, led to great improvements in London's streets and to business for North-East Scotland. Aberdeen was sending granite to London in the late eighteenth century, by which time 'the London market for sets and paving stones alone was providing employment for 600 Aberdeen quarriers' (Bruce Lenman, *An Economic History of Modern Scotland 1660–1976* (London: Batsford, 1977), 108).

152   *Equipage*: a capacious word, including furniture, articles for personal ornament and use, and (as probably meant here) a carriage with or without horses and the attendant servants. As the list implies, 'equipage' relates to the public display of one's

person and wealth. A carriage, like the modern car, was the paramount status symbol.

153   *those desires which ... seem to be altogether endless*: Smith is expressing here the basic tenets (grounded in behavioural psychology) of an expansionist philosophy of commerce formulated as early as the 1690s. It is an amoral argument, which assumes human appetite as the motor of historical change. See, for example, [Dudley North], *Discourse Upon Trade* (London, 1691): 'The main spur to Trade, or rather to Industry and Ingenuity, is the exorbitant Appetites of Men, which they will take pains to gratifie, and so be disposed to work, when nothing else will incline them to it; for did Men content themselves with bare Necessaries, we should have a poor World' (p. 14). N.B. [Nicholas Barbon], in *A Discourse of Trade* (London, 1690), voices similar sentiments: 'Those Expences that most Promote Trade, are in Cloaths and Lodging: In Adorning the Body and the House, There are a Thousand Traders Imploy'd in Cloathing and Decking the Body, and Building, and Furnishing of Houses, for one that is Imploy'd in providing Food ... Man being Naturally Ambitious, the Living Together, occasion Emulation, which is seen by Out-Vying one another in Apparel, Equipage, and Furniture of the House; whereas, if a Man lived Solitary alone, his chiefest Expence, would be Food' (pp. 64–9).

154   *Many coal-mines in Scotland*: landowners may have worked their own coal-mines because only they had the capital resources to do so. T. C. Smout, 'Scottish Landowners and Economic Growth, 1650–1850', *Scottish Journal of Political Economy*, 11 (1964), 220–1 [Campbell and Skinner].

155   *it has already been observed*: at *WN*, I. vi (p. 50).

regulation of commerce or police: a regulation affecting commerce or civil administration, as at pp. 58 and 137 above.

not only ignorant, but incapable of that application of mind: in the next paragraph Smith argues that the waged-labourer, too, is 'incapable' of extended thought. If, in the case of the landlord, inactivity is associated with 'ease and security' of situation, or the absence of labour, in the case of the workman, as is pointed out at *WN*, v. i (p. 429–30), the same ignorance is the result of the division of labour. As elsewhere, Smith interprets the human mind in accordance with Locke's *tabula rasa* theory, its liveliness corresponding to the range of sensations it receives. Smith's model of the energetic man is the merchant, the entrepreneur, or the master-manufacturer. But driven by narrow self-interest, he is a man whose public integrity and acumen are severely compromised. See Smith, *Correspondence*, 286, and the concluding section of this chapter. See, too, my Introduction, pp. xxvii–xxviii.

156   *it has already been shewn*: at *WN*, I. viii (pp. 68–9).

163   *instruments of trade*: Smith uses the phrase 'instruments of trade' with a wide variety of applications. At *WN*, IV. viii (p. 375), he distinguishes between the 'dead instruments', which are machinery, and the 'living instrument', who is the workman himself. Later in this chapter (p. 166), he includes the training and talents in which consists the 'living instrument', the worker, in the nation's fixed capital: 'The improved dexterity of a workman may be considered in the same light as a machine or instrument of trade which facilitates and abridges labour, and which, though it costs a certain expence, repays that expence with a profit.' Compare the argument of another Scottish Enlightenment thinker, Adam Ferguson, in *An Essay on the History of Civil Society* (1767), where 'Manufactures, accordingly, prosper most, where the mind is least consulted, and where the workshop may, without any great effort of imagination, be considered as an engine, the parts of which are men' (ed. Duncan Forbes (Edinburgh: Edinburgh University Press, 1966), 183). The image of society itself as a machine and of each member as a part in its productive engine, though not unique to the Scottish School of social and economic philosophy, was soon associated exclusively with them in the minds of its opponents. According to the radical social critic William Hazlitt, '[t]his is their *idea of a perfect commonwealth*: where each member performs his part in the machine, taking care of himself, and no more concerned about his neighbours, than the iron and wood-work, the pegs and nails in a spinning-jenny. Good screw! good wedge! good ten-penny nail!' ('The New School of Reform', *The Plain Speaker* (1826), in *The Complete Works of William Hazlitt*, ed. P. P. Howe, 21 vols. (London and Toronto: Dent, 1930–4), xii. 182).

163   *the slitt-mill*: 'a mill or machine by which iron bars or plates are slit into nail-rods' (*OED*).

166   *workhouses*: at this date the term covered buildings where work was regularly carried on, like workshops or factories, and was not specific to those houses which proliferated throughout the eighteenth century in towns and rural parishes to provide work in return for food and shelter for the unemployed poor of a parish.

167   *the grazier*: one who pastures cattle and rears them for the market.

      the mercers: dealers in textiles, especially the more costly ones, like silks.

169   *the produce of land . . . minerals from its bowels*: land remained throughout the eighteenth century the prime source of Britain's economic wealth, supplying almost all the country's food (apart from spices and luxuries) and the bulk of its raw industrial materials. Even Dr Johnson, an enthusiastic urbanite, wrote in 1756 expounding the, to him, obvious truth that 'trade and manufactures, however profitable, must yield to the cultivation of lands in usefulness and dignity' ('Further Thoughts on Agriculture', in the *Universal Visitor*, Mar. 1756, in Johnson, *Political Writings*, ed. Donald J. Greene, Yale Edition of the Works of Samuel Johnson (New Haven, Conn. and London: Yale University Press, 1958–), x (1977), 122).

      where there is tolerable security: Smith notes later the important link between personal and political security and economic growth, maintaining: 'Commerce and manufactures can seldom flourish long in any state which does not enjoy a regular administration of justice, in which the people do not feel themselves secure in the possession of their property' (*WN*, v. iii (p. 459)). The link was commonplace. It is assumed behind Alexander Pope's pastoral poem *Windsor Forest* (1713), a panegyric to settled Stuart monarchy and the imperial benefits of trade and commerce after the advantageous (to Britain) settlement of the Treaty of Utrecht.

171   *in the first Book*: at *WN*, I. vi.

175   *The great wheel of circulation*: Smith uses the image of a wheel of circulation a few paragraphs later. The recourse to metaphor

is significant. Like Hume, Smith was convinced of the unimportance of money as such for the wealth of nations. Both argued that there is no virtue in its accumulation as a commodity, but that the real riches of a country lie in its raw materials, its people, and their skills, all of which money merely measures as value. In Hume's words: 'Money is not, properly speaking, one of the subjects of commerce; but only the instrument which men have agreed upon to facilitate the exchange of one commodity for another.' Rejecting the wheel, he chooses another image governed by motion to communicate the essentially substitutive properties which characterize money: '[Money] is none of the wheels of trade: it is the oil which renders the motion of the wheels more smooth and easy' ('Of Money', *Essays Moral, Political, and Literary*, 289). Money's wheel is, of course, fortune's wheel, too, whose mobility is a sign of the uncertainty and risk which attend the complexity of exchanges (substitutions) upon which commerce depends. Interestingly, in the next paragraph Smith adverts to 'the ambiguity of language' which clouds the relation between money and real value. As his argument develops through this chapter he is at some pains to distinguish use from reality. Yet as contemporary thinkers sought to explain, the disambiguation is impossible since the problem was itself the shared ground of economic and linguistic representation. Anne-Robert-Jacques Turgot, whom Smith knew in Paris in the 1760s, was both economist and etymologist, and made a systematic comparison of words and money as social symbols of exchange. (See, for example, his unfinished essay translated as 'Value and Money' (*c.*1769) in *Precursors of Adam Smith*, ed. Ronald L. Meek (London: Dent, 1973), 79–100.) Jean-Jacques Rousseau extended the comparison, arguing that coins, like words, are simply signs; both are languages—words measuring things or the idea of things, and coins measuring value. As the paper-money economy grew during the eighteenth century, the generalized symbolic functions of words and money (now doubly substitutive, since paper money is a representation of a representation) converge even further. Note-issue and the workings of a paper-money economy fascinated not only Smith but Hume and James Steuart among contemporary economic thinkers in Scotland. (For the general theory of linguistic and economic forms, see Michel Foucault, *The Order of Things: An*

Archaeology of the Human Sciences (London: Tavistock Publications, 1970), 174 ff., and Marc Shell, *The Economy of Literature* (Baltimore, Md.: Johns Hopkins, 1978.)

176   *a guinea*: an English gold coin, first struck in 1663 from gold brought from Guinea (in Africa). From 1717 it was current as legal tender at the rate of twenty-one shillings (£1.05).

bill: this could be in the form of a banknote, a promissory note, or even a bill of exchange. Promissory notes were signed documents containing written promises to pay a stated sum to a particular person. Bills of exchange were usually for larger sums than a guinea and were developed in inland trade by merchants who wished to resell goods before making payment for them. In principle similar to a post-dated cheque, a bill of exchange, endorsed on the back by everyone through whose hands it passed, could and did circulate as currency at every level of society. Bills passed from clients to shopkeepers, from retailers to wholesalers, and from manufacturers to their raw suppliers. See the next note.

179   *several different sorts of paper money*: during the course of the eighteenth century, a paper-money economy developed in Britain. Not only bills of exchange and bills of accommodation (for the purpose of raising money on credit), but promissory notes, banknotes, and other forms of credit-worthy paper became vital to an economy desperately short of circulating coin. Credit enabled business to expand by trading on expectations, while interest-rates remained low because capital was plentiful. The Bank of England was founded in 1694, the Bank of Scotland in 1695, and the Royal Bank of Scotland in 1727. In the second half of the century country banks issuing their own notes emerged. There developed other kinds of local credit networks linking producers, distributors, and consumers in often precarious webs of credit. The grave shortage of low-denomination coin could mean that workers were paid infrequently with high-denomination coins, or that employers might resort to trade tokens or deposit payments with local traders to whom the workers must then apply for goods in lieu of wages—a system often tinged with extortion. In Scotland, where coin was chronically scarce, credit was created by a free use of all kinds of written promises to pay. On his visit to Skye with Dr Johnson in 1773, James Boswell found rents were commonly

paid in drovers' bills, obtained from Edinburgh merchants (*Journal of a Tour to the Hebrides* (1785), ed. R. W. Chapman (Oxford: Oxford University Press, 1924; repr. 1970), 330). For much of the eighteenth century Britain remained a collection of regional economies, linked by a system of credit which could ripple through the local network, often via the London banks and the bill-broking facilities of the powerful merchant houses. (See P. G. M. Dickson, *The Financial Revolution in England* (London: Macmillan, 1967); B. L. Anderson, 'Money and the Structure of Credit in the Eighteenth Century', *Business History*, 12 (1970), 85–101; and John Brewer, 'Commercialization and Politics', in McKendrick, Brewer, and Plumb, *The Birth of a Consumer Society*, 203 ff.)

180   *But the paper cannot go abroad*: the discussion of money in this chapter centres on two not necessarily contradictory arguments. One is that coined gold and silver, as merely representative of the value which inheres in those commodities it can command, is itself replaced with no loss by another more convenient medium of exchange. According to this view, the value of coin exists properly in its claim to exchange. The second argument is that, once released in this way from the constraints of *intrinsic* value, coined money can be channelled into those areas of the economy (overseas trade) where the guarantee of *extrinsic* value (which paper claims as money) does not stretch.

182   *not only probable but almost unavoidable*: Smith's argument here builds on those pamphlets of the 1690s (by Dudley North, Nicholas Barbon, and others; see note to p. 153 above) which challenged the balance-of-trade theory, the bedrock of the still-influential Mercantilist explanation of economic prosperity. The Mercantilist ideal (to which Dr Johnson was much attracted) assumed high import tariffs and caution over the export of bullion as part of a philosophy which identified national wealth with a fund of precious metals and the strict regulation of foreign trade, and which advocated state intervention where necessary with a view to obtaining export surpluses. Smith's view is that the bulk of imports serves to increase the industry and productivity of the home market because growth lies in a system of goods and services consumed and renewed. The argument that consumption is the key to national prosperity exposes as unwarranted the Mercantilist fear of chronic imbal-

ance and loss, and rests on the belief that while the individual may be a spendthrift, the greater number, the 'class' or 'order', motivated by the natural impulse for gain, will be both consumers *and* investors. (For a full account of Mercantilist views on the balance of trade, see Jacob Viner, *Studies in the Theory of International Trade* (London: Allen and Unwin, 1937.))

184   *Daedalian wings*: after the legendary Cretan inventor Daedalus, who found a way of flying by means of wings made of birds' feathers. His son Icarus met his death by falling into the sea, after the wax holding his wings had melted when he flew too near the sun.

185   *excessive multiplication of paper money*: between 1745 and 1772 Scotland developed a complex multiple system of public and private banks. In 1746 the British Linen Company was founded, the only chartered bank in the United Kingdom specializing in industrial development—in this case, short-term finance to the Scottish linen industry. In Glasgow, the Ship Bank and Arms Bank, founded in 1750, and later the Thistle Bank, sustained by the magnates of the tobacco trade, constituted an important source of credit for several industries. Over this period the Scottish banking-system saw a fifteen-fold increase in note-issue, clearly revealing the implication of paper money in economic growth. But in 1762 and again in 1772, when the Ayr Bank collapsed, excessive note-issue helped bring on a severe balance-of-payments crisis. Hume, who had grave reservations about the use of paper money and the development of banks, wrote during the financial crises of 1772 from Edinburgh to Smith, then in Kirkcaldy and at work on *WN*: 'We are here in a very melancholy Situation: Continual Bankruptcies, universal Loss of Credit, and endless Suspicions. There are but two standing Houses [private banks] in this Place . . . The Case is little better in London . . . and even the Bank of England is not entirely free from Suspicion. Those of Newcastle, Norwich and Bristol are said to be stopp'd: The Thistle Bank has been reported to be in the same Condition: The Carron Company is reeling, which is one of the greatest Calamities of the whole; as they gave Employment to near 10,000 People. Do these Events any-wise affect your Theory? Or will it occasion the Revisal of any Chapters?' (*Correspondence*, 162). Smith's view, which he outlines in this chapter, is that paper money used

prudently energizes the economy, overcoming the initial lack of capital stock.

186   *as in London*: initially notes were in multiples of £5. Clapham (citing A. Anderson, *Origin of Commerce* (London, 1764), iii. 308), comments: 'Subsequently notes for less than £20 became so rare that when the Bank began a regular issue of £15 and £10 notes, in 1759, contemporaries referred to them as though they were a novelty' (J. H. Clapham, *The Bank of England: A History*, 2 vols. (Cambridge: Cambridge University Press, 1944), i. 146) [Campbell and Skinner].

as in Scotland: the British Linen Company, for example, originally specialized in credit to manufacturers, but it soon began issuing low-denomination notes (for £5, £1, and ten shillings). Unlike normal banknotes, these were receipts for goods but soon became acceptable currency throughout Scotland.

the act of parliament: of 1765 (for Scotland) and 1775 and 1777 (for England), prohibiting the issue of notes smaller than £1 and requiring all notes to be payable on demand.

paper currencies of Yorkshire: where employers were paying wages in notes for very small sums and passing various frauds off against their illiterate workers—for example, offering notes payable only at a future date.

mean people: people in poor or humble circumstances.

promissory note: see note to p. 176 above.

188   *by discounting . . . cash accounts*: not only the customary means by which traders paid for materials or commodities, bills of exchange were themselves traded, merchants and others providing a discount market as well as the banks. Cash accounts allowed customers to draw out sums by way of loans. In both of these ways banking could buttress economic expansion— creating credit and mobilizing the (otherwise inert) savings of the nation.

189   *provisions . . . in 1759*: the fiars price of an imperial quarter of oats at Haddington in 1759 was 9s. 11¼d. The price was lower in twelve of the earlier years of the century, and in only one (1760 at 9s. 10d.) in the later years [Campbell and Skinner].

189   *scarce any in France*: according to Fernand Braudel, France
       suffered for much of the eighteenth century from a 'traumatic
       fear of paper-money and banking' (*The Wheels of Commerce*
       (London: Fontana, 1985), 136), the consequence of the failure
       of John Law's paper-currency strategy. Law, the Scottish author
       of *Money and Trade considered, with a Proposal for Supplying the
       Nation with Money* (1705), induced the Regent Orleans to
       establish the Bank of France in 1716, and in 1717 a West India
       Company, to exploit the Mississippi area. In 1720 he was
       Comptroller General of France. His schemes led to confusion
       and bankruptcy.

       Mr. Hume . . . Political Discourses: David Hume, historian, philo-
       sopher, and friend of Smith. His *Political Discourses* (1752)
       contain a systematic treatment of economics. (See, for example,
       the essays 'Of Commerce', 'Of Money', and 'Of the Balance of
       Trade'.) Pertinent here is Hume's suggestion that the financial
       mechanism might be distorted by the growth of domestic
       banking and paper money. Hume accepted a relation between
       the quantity of money in an economy and the price-level, arguing
       that the short-run effect of an injection of paper-credit is to sink
       the value of money and raise the price of labour and com-
       modities. For a contextualization of Hume's argument, see Istvan
       Hont, 'The "Rich Country–Poor Country" Debate in Scottish
       Classical Political Economy', in Hont and Michael Ignatieff
       (eds.), *Wealth and Virtue* (Cambridge: Cambridge University
       Press, 1983), 271–315.

       not to the multiplication of paper money: for the multiplication
       of paper money in Scotland at this period, see note to p. 185
       above. The year 1771, which saw large-scale banking collapse
       in Britain, also saw serious food riots brought on by poor
       harvests and soaring prices.

       in both parts of the united kingdom: the second half of the
       eighteenth century saw the rise of local country banks. It has been
       estimated that from twelve in 1750, the number had risen to 290
       by 1797 (Porter, *English Society in the Eighteenth Century*, 205).

191   *unproductive labour*: at *WN*, IV. ix (p. 381), Smith describes the
       term 'unproductive' as a 'humiliating appellation', and proceeds
       to expose the interdependency of productive and unproductive
       labour. He attaches the epithet rather differently here. Both

productive and unproductive labour have value, but the value of productive labour is added to the goods it manufactures, so as to be used later, while the value of unproductive labour, 'how honourable, how useful, or how necessary soever' (p. 192), is fixed in no permanent (that is, vendible) commodity and is consumed at once. Only productive labour replenishes circulating capital.

192 *perishes in the very instant of its production*: describing the labour of physicians and lawyers, Hume notes that they 'beget no industry; and it is even at the expense of others they acquire their riches' ('Of Interest', *Essays Moral, Political, and Literary*, 310). Though unproductive labour is marginal to the progressive activity of the economy, Smith makes it clear that its service-oriented model is not without value. Rather, the value, like the 'pleasure and delight' of a concert, is immediately and totally consumed and is capable of sustaining no further production. (See Smith's 'Of the Nature of that Imitation which takes place in what are called the Imitative Arts', *Essays on Philosophical Subjects*, 187–207.)

195 *quit-rent*: a rent, usually of small amount, paid by a tenant to a landlord in lieu of services which might otherwise be required.

196 *seldom exceeds a third . . . of the whole produce of the land*: Smith cites the same figure at *WN*, II. v (p. 217).

197 *the parliament towns of France*: in 1776 there were thirteen towns in France with 'parlements'; that is, with provincial assemblies housing supreme courts of justice.

entrepôt: a commercial centre to which goods are brought for distribution; also, a river- or seaport with facilities for transshipment or storage prior to re-export and without the necessity of customs control. The port of Rotterdam is an entrepôt.

198 *before the union*: the Act of Union of 1707, when the Kingdoms of England and Scotland alike ceased to exist and were incorporated in a United Kingdom of Great Britain, with the loss of a separate Scottish Parliament in Edinburgh. Union opened free trade between Scotland and England, providing ready markets for each country's manufactures.

much inferior to Glasgow: already by the mid-eighteenth century Glasgow was a prosperous mercantile centre, its wealth and industry the result of the western Atlantic trades in the cotton, coffee, sugar, and rum of the British West Indies, in the importation and re-export of the tobacco of the southern colonies of British North America, and in the export of Scottish textiles. For Jedediah Cleishbotham, the fictitious persona who introduces Walter Scott's latest series of novels in 1816, Smith's distinction still holds true. Edinburgh is 'our metropolis of law' and Glasgow 'our metropolis and mart of gain' ('Introduction', *Tales of My Landlord*).

198   *in consequence of a great lord's . . . in their neighbourhood*: cf. *Lectures on Jurisprudence* (1766), 204, where Smith observes: 'Nothing tends so much to corrupt mankind as dependency, while independency still encreases the honesty of the people' (p. 486).

199   *Parsimony*: in arguing that parsimony is a mode of expenditure, Smith distinguishes between the greater quantity of productive labour which savings set in motion and the limited productive power of revenue. Both contribute to the maintenance of a consumer economy, but paradoxically, it is parsimony or frugality which fuels consumption in the long term while prodigality, it is suggested, will exhaust it. In arguing thus, Smith importantly adjusts Mandeville's earlier infamous thesis that private vice is the necessary foundation of the public virtues of the successful capitalist economy. Cf. 'Frugality is like Honesty, a mean starving Virtue . . . Prodigality has a thousand Inventions to keep People from sitting still, that Frugality would never think of . . .' (Mandeville, *The Fable of the Bees*, ed. Kaye, i. 104–5. Thomas Malthus, in *Principles of Political Economy* (1820), later criticized Smith's position, arguing that a rise in savings necessarily diminishes consumption at the same time as it increases the output of consumer goods through increased investment, the result being *under*-consumption.

200   *trust-right or deed of mortmain*: in law, trust-right is the confidence reposed in a person in whom the legal ownership of property is invested to hold or use for the benefit of another; property held 'in mortmain' is held without possibility of transfer. Smith appears to suggest that invested capital may not be legally restricted to this use but that it will remain in everyone's interest to employ it thus and secure it against transfer to some other use.

203   *wish to better their condition*: the economic justification of frugality which Smith has been at pains to expound has its
foundation, he argues, in human nature—the desire to better
our condition. Cf. *The Theory of Moral Sentiments*, I. iii. 2. 1:
'The rich man glories in his riches, because he feels that
they naturally draw upon him the attention of the world . . .'
(pp. 50–1). Characteristic of Scottish Enlightenment thinking,
to which Smith contributes, is the naturalization of a modern
economic theory the original and guarantor of which is psychological; hence the appeals throughout this argument to the
relationship between economic activity and the desire for social status and approval. At Part Six of *The Theory of Moral
Sentiments*, added to the sixth edition of 1790, Smith comments:
'Though it is in order to supply the necessities and conveniencies of the body, that the advantages of external fortune
are originally recommended to us, yet we cannot live long in
the world without perceiving that the respect of our equals,
our credit and rank in the society we live in, depend very much
upon the degree in which we possess, or are supposed to
possess, those advantages. The desire of becoming the proper
objects of this respect, of deserving and obtaining this credit
and rank among our equals, is, perhaps, the strongest of all
our desires, and our anxiety to obtain the advantages of fortune
is accordingly much more excited and irritated by this
desire, than by that of supplying all the necessities and conveniencies of the body, which are always very easily supplied'
(VI. i. 3 (pp. 212–13)). Furthermore, as the passage continues,
it becomes clear that 'prudence' rather than conspicuous consumption promotes this coveted social approbation. Cf. Hume:
'Commerce increases industry, by conveying it readily from one
member of the state to another, and allowing none of it to
perish or become useless. It increases frugality, by giving
occupation to men, and employing them in the arts of gain,
which soon engage their affection, and remove all relish for
pleasure and expense' ('Of Interest', *Essays Moral, Political, and
Literary*, 309).

205   *the extravagance of government . . . administration*: the extravagance
of government is a recurring complaint in *WN*, as is government's
dependence on the frugality of the private individual. See later
in this chapter (at pp. 208–9) and *WN*, V. ii. (pp. 446–7).

206   *and trade undone*: see, for example, *Britannia Languens, or A
      Discourse of Trade: Shewing the Grounds and Reasons of the
      Increase and Decay of Land-Rents, National Wealth and Strength*
      (1680). Recent estimates of Britain's economic development
      during the eighteenth century give an impression of slow but
      steady and widespread growth, with rates of growth in total
      production in the late eighteenth century running well ahead
      of those for the rest of the century. Total production grew by
      1.7 times between 1700 and 1780, and production per capita by
      1.2 times. (See P. Deane and W. A. Cole, *British Economic
      Growth 1688–1959* (Cambridge: Cambridge University Press,
      2nd edn., 1967, and N. F. R. Crafts, 'British Economic Growth,
      1700–1831: A Review of the Evidence', *Economic History Re-
      view*, 36 (1983), 177–99.)

207   *Saxon Heptarchy*: by tradition, the heptarchy were the seven
      kingdoms of the Anglo-Saxons.

      invasion of Julius Caesar . . . the savages in North America: Julius
      Caesar invaded Britain in 55 BC. For the Scottish Enlightenment
      historians, the Indian tribes of North America represented
      society in its most primitive state. See note to p. 150 above.

      fire and the plague of London . . . rebellions of 1715 and 1745:
      Smith's historical survey of the hundred years since Charles
      II's restoration in 1660 proceeds in terms of those misfortunes
      which have disrupted the smooth progress of economic activity.
      The plague refers to the outbreak of bubonic plague in 1665
      and the fire is the Great Fire of London of 1666, in which over
      13,000 houses, eighty-nine churches, and old St Paul's Cathe-
      dral were destroyed. Two Anglo-Dutch Wars, the result of
      Britain's commercial and colonial aggression, were fought dur-
      ing Charles II's reign, between 1665–7 and 1672–4. The revol-
      ution is that of 1688–9 (the Glorious Revolution) when James
      II fled from England and the crowns of England and Scotland
      were offered to his Protestant daughter Mary and son-in-law
      William of Orange. Anglo-Irish hostilities, the consequence of
      James II's attempt to use Ireland as a means to regaining power
      in Britain, followed in 1690. Britain and France were at war
      for much of this hundred-year period, ranged as enemies in
      the War of the League of Augsburg (1689–97), the War of the
      Spanish Succession (1702–13), and the War of the Austrian

Succession (1740–8). From the Seven Years War with France (1756–63) England emerged victorious, but with a National Debt risen from 70 millions to 130 millions. By the rebellions of 1715 and 1745 Smith refers to recent events in Scottish history, when supporters of the Roman Catholic line of the exiled Stuart King James II rose on behalf of his son James, known as the Pretender (claimant) and later on behalf of his grandson, Charles Edward, the Young Pretender. This second rebellion was followed by harsh government reprisals in Scotland and a consolidation of Westminster-centred power. It was in the immediate aftermath of these events that the Scottish Enlightenment thinkers attempted to lay the intellectual foundations for a northern cultural and economic revival.

209   *by sumptuary laws . . . foreign luxuries*: sumptuary laws control expenditure, especially by restraining excess in food, fashion items, and luxury consumption. It was an article of Mercantilist policy (for Mercantilism, see note to p. 182 above) that government intervention was important in regulating, by means of tariff and other laws, the flow of foreign luxuries, a potential drain on the nation's moral and gold reserves. The arguments were easily (and falsely, as Smith implies) allied to patriotism, where 'foreign luxuries' can be equated with the exotic and even the degenerate, while domestic manufactures are assumed to imply simplicity and restraint in consumption. See John Dennis, dramatist and literary critic, in his *An Essay upon Publick Spirit; being a Satyr in Prose upon the Manners and Luxury of the Times, the Chief Source of Our Present Parties and Divisions* (London, 1711), p. vi: 'A Tax upon our Superfluities and our Luxuries, will by rendering us frugal, and consequently industrious, have a Tendency to the augmenting the National Stock of Trade.' See, too, Mandeville, 'The Grumbling Hive', where: 'The haughty *Chloe*, to live Great, | Had made her Husband rob the State: | But now she sells her Furniture, | Which th'*Indies* had been ransack'd for' (*The Fable of the Bees*, ed. Kaye, i. 33–4).

who died a few years ago: one might compare with Smith's account, Alexander Pope's satiric portrait ('Epistle to Bathurst' (1732), ll. 299–314) of the fate of the prodigal as exemplified in the death of George Villiers, second Duke of Buckingham, who, after a life of lavish extravagance, died in 1687 in extreme poverty in a remote Yorkshire inn.

211   *Versailles . . . Stowe and Wilton to England*: among the powerful cultural and economic statements of the later seventeenth and eighteenth centuries were the palaces and private houses of the great. The extravagant formality of the palace and gardens of Versailles, adorned for Louis XIV, became a model for magnificence. At Stowe in Buckinghamshire, Viscount Cobham laid out splendid grounds with temples of Ancient and Modern Virtue and of British Worthies. Wilton House in Wiltshire, a seat of the Earl of Pembroke, was partly redesigned about 1633 under the influence of Inigo Jones. Both Stowe and Wilton represent significant statements about the importance of land-ownership and patriarchal ideals in defining the conditions for national eminence in the eighteenth century—statements which Smith here appears to endorse.

equipage: see note to p. 152 above.

212   *gewgaws*: baubles, showy items without value.

Of Stock lent at Interest: Chapter Four, 'Of Stock lent at Interest', is omitted. Its argument merely confirms and further illustrates that presented in *WN*, II. i–iii. Smith explains in Chapter Four that lending stock (capital) is no different from lending money. As the opening sentences of the chapter state: 'The stock which is lent at interest is always considered as a capital by the lender. He expects that in due time it is to be restored to him, and that in the mean time the borrower is to pay him a certain annual rent for the use of it.' (See Glasgow Edition, 350.)

214   *prejudices . . . against shopkeepers . . . without foundation*: Smith alludes here to the doctrine of the Physiocrats that mercantile stock is 'sterile' and that agriculture is the only source of wealth because it alone produces a surplus, other manufactures merely reproducing what they consume. The Physiocrats, a group of eighteenth-century French economists led by François Quesnay, the king's physician, flourished in France between 1760 and 1770. Quesnay's model of the economic process is usually known as the *Tableau Œconomique* (1758, unpublished). Smith respected Quesnay, whom he knew in Paris in the 1760s, and his thinking on free trade and minimal state intervention

influenced Smith's own, but he found the rigidity of the
Physiocratic doctrines disagreeable. See *WN*, IV. ix for a fuller
discussion of the Physiocratic system. See, too, R. L. Meek,
The Economics of Physiocracy (London: Allen and Unwin, 1962),
and Elizabeth Fox-Genovese, *The Origins of Physiocracy: Economic Revolution and Social Order in Eighteenth-Century France*
(Ithaca, NY: Cornell University Press, 1976).

215   *a multitude of ale-houses*: the tide of complaints against lower-
class drunkenness rose from the middle of the eighteenth
century. In the view of many economic thinkers, the lower ranks
of society were idle and vicious by nature. Their in-built
disposition to debauchery was seen to be exacerbated by the
new working conditions in factories and towns. See, for
example, the combined moral and economic arguments put
forward by Josiah Tucker in *An Impartial Use of Low Priced
Spirituous Liquors . . .* (1751). Tucker proposed a strict control
on the licensing of alehouses, advocating 'Courts . . . with the
Title of Guardians of the *Morals of the manufacturing Poor*',
who might levy fines on, among others, 'all Persons who keep
Cock-Pits, Skittle-Allies . . . or bring Liquors, Cakes, Fruit, or
any like Temptations, to draw People together' ([Tucker], *A
Brief Essay on the Advantages and Disadvantages which respectively attend France and Great Britain, with regard to Trade*,
53–6). By the end of the century alehouses were regarded with
suspicion by the establishment as promoting the drunken assembly of lower-class dissidence. See William Cowper, *The
Task*, where we discover in the alehouse: 'Smith, cobbler,
joiner, he that plies the shears, | And he that kneads the dough;
all loud alike, | All learned, and all drunk!' (iv. 466–78). At v.
ii (Glasgow Edition, 853), Smith discusses taxes on alehouses.

217   *seldom less than a fourth . . . of the whole produce*: see *WN*, II. iii
(p. 196 above) for a similar breakdown.

218   *by far the most advantageous to the society*: cf. *Lectures on
Jurisprudence* (1766): 'Agriculture is of all other arts the most
beneficient to society' (289; p. 522). While rejecting the economic basis of the Physiocratic position—that the labour of the
farmer uniquely produces more than he requires for subsistence—Smith nevertheless endorses at several points the superiority of agricultural productivity. This is not a matter of the
size of profits (where other manufactures regularly surpass

agriculture); rather, it relates to a deeply rooted and exemplary notion of virtuous productivity, and a belief that the proper use of land underlies the progressive march of culture. At times Smith only just steers clear of the unabashed moralized economics of Dr Johnson, who writes that 'Agriculture ... and agriculture alone, can support us without the help of others in certain plenty and genuine dignity ... while our ground is covered with corn and cattle, we can want nothing' ('Further Thoughts on Agriculture' (1756), in *Political Writings*, ed. Greene, x. 124).

219 *from the coasts of the Baltic*: there were strong Scottish trading connections with various Baltic ports and long-settled Scottish merchant colonies in Danzig (modern Gdansk, Poland) and Königsberg (modern Kaliningrad, Lithuania).

221 *by the capitals of merchants who reside in Great Britain*: the big Glasgow tobacco firms operated a store system in the inland areas of Virginia and Maryland around Chesapeake Bay. At these stores local tobacco planters could exchange their crop, usually for a combination of goods and cash. During the 1760s and 1770s expansion in these American colonies was decisively affected by the competitive offers of credit from the Glasgow merchants. According to Bruce Lenman, 'John Glassford, a leading Glasgow "tobacco lord", estimated that in the early 1760s he and his fellows were owed some £500,000 by planters. In 1778 the estimated planter debt to Glasgow was £1,306,000' (*Integration, Enlightenment, and Industrialization*, 43–4). See, too, v. iii (Glasgow Edition, 941–2), where Smith notes the use of tobacco as currency by the British colonies. At *WN*, IV. vii, he observes of the British West Indies: 'The prosperity of the English sugar colonies has been, in a great measure, owing to the great riches of England, of which a part has overflowed, if one may say so, upon those colonies' (p. 350).

Were the Americans ... to stop ... European manufactures: the Anglo-American crisis came to a head in 1776, the year *WN* was published, with the Declaration of Independence and the outbreak of war. At *WN*, IV. vii (pp. 352–4), Smith speculates on the dangers lying in wait for Britain with so much capital tied up in an exclusive American trade. Writing in 1783 at the end of the war and after the loss of the American colonies, he tells his correspondent William Eden, 'I have little anxiety about what becomes of the American commerce. By an equality of treatment to all nations, we might soon open a commerce with the neighbouring nations of Europe infinitely more advantageous than that of so distant a country as America. This is an immense subject . . . I shall only say at present that every extraordinary either encouragement or discouragement that is given to the trade of any country more than to that of another, may, I think, be demonstrated to be in every case a complete piece of dupery, by which the interest of the State and the nation is constantly sacrificed to that of some particular class of traders' (*Correspondence*, 271–2).

221   *The antient Egyptians . . . in foreign commerce*: Montesquieu also refers to the fact that the Egyptians, 'by their religion and their manners were averse to all communication with strangers'. He added that '[t]heir country was the Japan of those times; it possessed everything within itself' (*De l'esprit des lois* (1748), XXI. vi. 13) [Campbell and Skinner]. See note to p. 91 above on China's neglect of foreign commerce.

223   *than what would naturally flow into them of its own accord*: in *Lectures on Jurisprudence* (1766), Smith refers to a 'natural balance of industry' and to the 'natural connection of all trades'. He makes the point that regulation breaks the 'balance of industry' (233–4; p. 498).

  hard ware: metal goods of the kind that Birmingham was already producing in large quantities, such as household utensils, tools, and weapons.

  advantageous situations for industry: see note to pp. 27–8 above.

  hogsheads: a measure of capacity. In the case of tobacco (US), it represents 750 to 1,200 lb. Much of the prosperity of the west coast of Scotland in the eighteenth century derived from the powerful trade in importing and re-exporting tobacco which centred on Glasgow. In the 1760s and 1770s tobacco accounted for almost 50 per cent in value of all Scottish imports from beyond Britain, most of it imported through Greenock and Port Glasgow.

224   *Holland . . . by far the richest country in Europe*: see note to p. 93 above. At IV. vii, Smith observes that '[t]he mercantile capital of Holland is so great that it is, as it were, continually overflowing' (Glasgow Edition, 632).

225   *by the cultivation and improvement of land*: Smith probably has
in mind works like Arthur Young's *A Six Months Tour through
the North of England* (1770), where emphasis rests less on the
moral worth of labour on the land than on the farm as a
business capable of realizing great profits. The similarities with
Physiocratic doctrines, where agriculture provides an origin for
the system of circulation, are marked. For the change in
agricultural treatises around 1750 to accommodate the idea of
the farm as a unit of production, see Keith Tribe, *Land, Labour,
and Economic Discourse* (London: Routledge and Kegan Paul,
1978), 66–79.

by trade and manufactures: at *WN*, I. x (p. 125), Smith has
already remarked on the greater profitability of trade and
manufactures over agriculture. But it was also true, as Smith
elsewhere observes, that: 'Merchants are commonly ambitious
of becoming country gentlemen' (*WN*, III. iv (p. 259)). This
was a commonplace as early as the seventeenth century. On his
tour of England in 1724–6 Defoe commented on the gentrified
aspirations of merchants as the key to the building and buying
up of estates which already threatened to crowd the home counties. In some cases, as he observes of Sir William Scawen, the
merchant family's rise in just one generation had been meteoric.
In Surrey, the Downs near the village of Carshalton are
'crowded with fine houses of the citizens of London; some of
which are built with such a profusion of expense, that they look
rather like seats of the nobility, than the country houses of
citizens and merchants; particularly those of Sir William Scawen,
lately deceased; who besides an immense estate in money has
left, as I was told, one article of nine thousand pounds a year to
his heir; and was himself since the Fire of London, only Mr
Scawen, a Hamborough merchant, dealing by commission, and
not in any view of such an increase of wealth, or any thing like
it' (*A Tour Through the Whole Island of Great Britain*, 167–8).
See, too, Lawrence Stone and Jeanne C. Fawtier Stone, *An Open
Elite? England 1540–1880* (Oxford: Oxford University Press,
1984).

227   *The great commerce ... and those of the country*: Smith makes
this point at various stages in the course of the argument of
WN. See, for example, I. x (p. 124); II. i (pp. 168–9); and IV.
ix (Glasgow Edition, 677) and (p. 390).

228   *absurd speculations . . . concerning the balance of trade*: the attack is upon the Mercantilist position, which maintained the importance of the relationship between a nation's wealth and its balance of foreign trade, and in particular warned against the export of precious metals in payment of foreign goods. At *WN*, IV. i (pp. 278–9), Smith challenges the arguments of the Mercantilist Thomas Mun as outlined in *England's Treasure by Forraign Trade* (1664). Later, at IV. iii, Smith states that 'Nothing, however, can be more absurd than this whole doctrine of the balance of trade' (Glasgow Edition, 488).

229   *retain a predilection for this primitive employment*: at *WN*, II. iv, Smith had observed that '[t]he superior security of land' compensates for its lesser profitability as an investment (Glasgow Edition, 358). For Smith, as for other eighteenth-century writers in the Georgic tradition, agricultural work remains the model of virtuous labour. See note to p. 127 above.

230   *human institutions . . . the natural course of things*: this is Smith's second reference in this chapter to a conflict between human institutions and natural progress. One of the major concerns of the Scottish Enlightenment thinkers, and particularly of Hume and Smith, was the relationship between the institutions of an organized society and its economic development. The concern centres on the competing definitions of society as a community of private interests or of public regulation. It is at one level the relation between those legislative and administrative institutions which constitute and protect human society and that individual 'natural' liberty from government which is the motor of economic development. What is at issue here is the distribution of labour and investment between manufactures and agriculture, town and country. This, in a broadly historical context, is the concern of Book Three. But at the same time that Smith argues that the natural progression of states is from agriculture to manufactures to commerce, he also observes that the characteristic advancement of European states has come about by inverting this natural order under the stimulus of urban demand. Against state intervention to regulate trade and re-route investment capital into agriculture, Smith still argues that optimum distribution, left to itself, will be established naturally. Productivity in one sector (manufacturing) will induce the surplus necessary for exchange in the other (agriculture). In

other words, leave the 'unnatural' alone and it will discover its own 'natural' balance. Redistribution should not be forced.

231 *The wealth of antient Egypt . . . their surplus produce*: Smith has already outlined the advantages to North America and China of an export trade carried on by foreign merchants. See notes to pp. 91 and 221 above.

233 *Of the Discouragement of Agriculture . . . Roman Empire*: this and the next chapter draw heavily on Smith's earlier work as recorded in his *Lectures on Jurisprudence*, where he gives historical elaboration to the rise, progress, and decline of Greece and Rome, and the breakdown of feudal order in the course of the emergence of the 'commercial' stage. In *Lectures on Jurisprudence* (1762–3, iv (pp. 200–69); 1766, 5–99 (pp. 398–437)), the material is presented as a continuing survey ranging from the foundation of Greek civilization to the English Revolution Settlement of 1689. For *WN* the argument is differently divided, with much of the evidence from classical Greek and Roman society absorbed into v. i, and the historical survey beginning here in iii with the fall of Rome. Such a wide sweep of the past characterized the stylized history-writing of other Scottish Enlightenment thinkers, especially Hume, Adam Ferguson, and John Millar. Like them, Smith does not mean to imply that history (as mere antiquity) has any prescriptive force, but that, as a record of how differing modes of subsistence connect at various stages with the development of social institutions, it is both materially instructive and capable of generating laws for understanding social change. The argument here begins with the sack of Rome by Alaric the Visigoth in AD 410 and the end of the Roman Empire in the West, dated to 476.

law of primogeniture . . . entails . . . by alienation: the law of primogeniture fixes right of succession on the first born. Specifically, it is the feudal rule of inheritance by which the whole of the real estate of an intestate passes to the eldest son. An entail settles an estate on a number of persons in predetermined succession so that it cannot be dealt with or redistributed by any one possessor as absolute owner. Alienation is the act of transferring ownership to another and would, where it exists, be a breach of entail. In 1764 the Faculty of Advocates, representing the law in Scotland, inaugurated a national campaign to reform the Scottish law of entail in favour of the smaller landowner-improver who might wish to free the land-market and raise loans. This was directly against the interests of the great dynastic families, for many of whom land signified power and family privilege held in opposition to the pressures for commercial exchange which the abolition of entail would inaugurate. For details of the Scottish campaign, see N. T. Phillipson, 'Lawyers, Landowners, and the Civic Leadership of Post-Union Scotland', *Juridical Review*, NS 21 (1976), 97–120.

233 *natural law of succession . . . in the distribution of moveables*: in *Lectures on Jurisprudence* (1762–3), Smith observes that in Roman law 'the children all shared equally in the estate of the father or master of the family' (i. 94 (p. 40)).

234 *by the incursions of its neighbours*: Lord Stair justified primo-geniture as the means for 'the preservation of the memory and dignity of families, which by frequent divisions of the inherit-ance would become despicable or forgotten' (*Institutions of the Law of Scotland* (1681), III. iv. 22) [Campbell and Skinner]. Lord Stair (1619–95), Lord President of the Court of Session (the Scottish judicature), was an important contributor to the making of Scottish law into a systematic code.

235 *devise*: a testamentary disposition of real property or the clause in a will conveying this.

Neither their substitutions nor fideicommisses: in law, a substitution describes the designation of a person or series of persons to succeed as heir or heirs on the failure of a person or persons previously named. In Roman law, a *fidei-commissum* (noun from past participle of *fidei-committere*: to entrust (a thing) to a person's good faith) was a bequest which a person made by begging an heir or legatee to transfer something to a third person.

236 *perpetuities*: of an estate; the quality, in law, whereby owner-ship is either inalienable (unable to be transferred), or untrans-ferable for a period beyond certain limits fixed by the general law.

seldom . . . a great improver: in a letter of 4 Apr. 1759 Smith wrote to Lord Shelburne: 'We have in Scotland some noblemen whose estates extend from the east to the west sea, who call themselves improvers, and are called so by their countrymen, when they cultivate two or three hundred acres round their own family seat while they allow all the rest of their country to lie waste, almost uninhabited and entirely unimproved, not worthy a shilling the hundred acres, without thinking themselves answerable to God, their country and their Posterity for so shameful as well as so foolish a neglect' (*Correspondence*, 32). According to L. Timperley, around 1770 the 'great landlords' controlled just over 50 per cent of total agrarian wealth, though with huge regional variation ('The Pattern of Landholding in Eighteenth-Century Scotland', in M. L. Parry and T. R. Slater (eds.), *The Making of the Scottish Countryside* (London: Croom Helm, 1980), 137–54).

236 *an œconomist*: a thrifty and effective manager of resources. See note to p. 10 above.

237 *tenants at will*: those who hold at the will or pleasure of the lessor. As the paragraph develops Smith draws a distinction between serfdom, as it once operated in Western Europe and still (in the eighteenth century) operated in Eastern Europe, and slavery proper.

238 *work done by slaves ... the dearest of any*: for similar arguments see *WN*, I. viii (p. 81) and IV. ix, where it is stated that 'Slaves, however, are very seldom inventive; and all the most important improvements, either in machinery, or in the arrangement and distribution of work which facilitate and abridge labour, have been the discoveries of freemen ... The work of the former must, upon that account, generally have been dearer than that of the latter' (Glasgow Edition, 684). Smith argues that, since the self-interest of master and worker is best served by independent labour, then independent labour is likely to be the most productive. On a strictly economic basis, considered separately from any humanitarian debates which would surround the denunciation of slavery later in the eighteenth century, Smith's reasoning, ingenious though it appears, was not new. Josiah Tucker, Churchman and economist, with strong connections in the 'slave port' of Bristol, argued ten years earlier in 1766 against all forms of slavery as 'repugnant to the Interests of Society'. He continues: 'Nay it is known, *experimentally* known, to be incompatible with an extensive Progress, much less with any great Perfection in Manufactures, and the Mechanic Arts ... the Principle holds true in general, that Freedom is a Spur, and Slavery a Discouragement

to Genius, to Industry, and to the Exertion of all the active Powers in human Nature' (*A Sermon Preached in the Parish-Church of Christ-Church, London, on Wednesday May the 7th, 1766* (London, 1766), 19). Cf. John Millar, Smith's pupil at Glasgow University in the 1750s: 'there is ground to believe that the institution of slavery is the chief circumstance that has prevented those contrivances to shorten and facilitate the more laborious employments of the people, which take place in other countries where freedom has been introduced' (*The Origin of the Distinction of Ranks* (1771; 3rd edn., rev., London, 1781), 357).

238   *Pliny and Columella*: Pliny the Elder (AD 23–79), in his *Natural History*, XVIII. iv, trans. H. Rackham (1950), v. 203: 'And we forsooth are surprised that we do not get the same profits from the labour of slave-gangs as used to be obtained from that of generals.' Columella (first century BC), in his treatise on farming, *De re rustica*, i (Preface), 11–12, trans. H. B. Ash (Loeb edn., 1941), i. 9–11.

like the plains of Babylon: Aristotle, *Politics*, 1265a, trans. William Ellis (London: Dent, 1912), 38–9 [Campbell and Skinner]. As references to the conduct of the classical republics suggest, the argument over slavery is not just part of the economic analysis of *WN*, it also contributes to its revaluation of the conditions for political liberty. According to the older civic humanist ideal still evident in the early eighteenth century, such liberty belongs to a restricted male élite. In the revised commercial model, prosperity depends upon the progressive division of social duties (and with them social liberties) down to the lowest members of the state. (For the civic humanist idea of virtue and its reinterpretation in the course of the eighteenth century, see in particular J. G. A. Pocock, 'Cambridge Paradigms and Scotch Philosophers: a study of the relations between the civic humanist and the civil jurisprudential interpretation of eighteenth-century social thought', in Hont and Ignatieff, (eds.), *Wealth and Virtue* 235–52.)

Quakers in Pennsylvania: by a decision of 1758 the Philadelphia Yearly Meeting of Quakers altered its policy on slavery. Henceforth, members buying or selling black slaves were to be excluded from business meetings and from making financial contributions to the Society. In 1760 New England Quakers made the importation of slaves an offence. (See David Brion

Davis, *The Problem of Slavery in Western Culture* (Ithaca, NY: Cornell University Press, 1966), 330.) There was in the 1760s and 1770s an active correspondence between the Pennsylvania Quakers and Dissenters in London which amounted to an anti-slavery campaign. The Pennsylvania Quaker Anthony Benezet published his *Caution and Warning to Great Britain* in 1767. John Millar writes of the modern practice of slavery that: 'The Quakers of Pennsylvania, are the first body of men in those countries, who have discovered any scruples upon that account, and who seem to have thought that the abolition of this practice is a duty they owe to religion and humanity' (*The Origin of the Distinction of Ranks* (1781), 334). As Smith appears to suggest, though, in his qualification of the Quaker decision, the advantages to free-market economics of doing away with slavery as an institution are somewhat compromised by the fact that slaves themselves can measure that capacity to acquire property which defines the successful industry of the free man.

239   *number of negroes . . . in our tobacco colonies*: black slaves were the life-blood of the West Indies sugar economy. Under the agreement between Britain and Spain (the *asiento*), British slave-traders transported a million-and-a-half Africans to work in the plantations in the course of the eighteenth century. According to Millar, '[t]he negro-slaves in the West-Indies are commonly said to exceed the free people nearly as three to one; and it has been supposed that the disproportion between them is daily increasing' (*The Origin of the Distinction of Ranks*, 346). In mid-century the riches that sugar represented and the conflict between Britain and France, the most successful Mercantilist powers, was acted out in constant quarrels over 'ownership' of disputed sugar islands. Significantly, and as a way of linking wealth with lax and careless management, Smith associates the highly expensive slave labour with the growers of the most lucrative crops.

Metayers . . . Coloni Partiarii: *métayers* held land by paying a proportion (usually half) of the produce as rent to the owner, who in turn provided stock and seed. *Métayage* was a widely operating system of land-tenure in France, still a predominantly feudal state in the eighteenth century. It served to distinguish its agricultural activity into the capital investment of the great and the mass dependent labour of the peasant cultivator. *Coloni*

Partiarii—literally, 'cultivators who pay rent with a part of the produce'.

239   *tenure in villanage*: the tenure by which a feudal villein (a serf or bondservant) held land in return for service rendered to the lord.

240   *Alexander III . . . emancipation of slaves*: in *Lectures on Jurisprudence* (1766), Smith gives credit for this to a later twelfth-century pope, Innocent III, but notes the need to distinguish between the political interests of the Church and Christian feeling over the issue of slavery: 'Another cause of the abolition of slavery was the influence of the clergy, but by no means the spirit of Christianity, for our planters are all Christians' (141–2 (p. 454)).

steel-bow tenants: 'steelbow' was a form of tenure in Scotland in which the landlord equipped the tenant with implements and seed. It is described in John Walker, *An Economical History of the Hebrides and Highlands of Scotland*, 2 vols. (Edinburgh, 1808), i. 58–9.

Chief Baron Gilbert and Doctor Blackstone: Sir Geoffrey Gilbert, *A Treatise of Tenures* (3rd edn., London, 1757), 34, and Sir William Blackstone, *Commentaries on the Laws of England*, 4 vols. (Oxford, 1765–9), ii. 141–2 [Campbell and Skinner].

241   *fictitious action of a common recovery*: this was the process, based on a legal fiction, by which an entailed estate was commonly transferred from one party to another.

14th of Henry the VIIth: that is, at the close of the fifteenth century. At v. i, Smith observes: 'When the tenant sued his lord for having unjustly outed him of his lease, the damages which he recovered were by no means equivalent to the possession of the land. Such causes, therefore, for some time, went all to the court of chancery, to the no small loss of the courts of law. It was to draw back such causes to themselves that the courts of law are said to have invented the artificial and fictitious writ of ejectment, the most effectual remedy for an unjust outer or dispossession of land' (Glasgow Edition, 721).

242   *by a law of James the IId*: *Acts of the Parliament of Scotland*, ii. 35 (1449) [Campbell and Skinner].

242   *A late act of parliament*: 10 Geo. III, c. 51 (1770). 'The longer leases were granted on condition that the tenant effected improvements' [Campbell and Skinner].

In Scotland . . . for a member of parliament: 'Though only freeholders could vote in Scotland, a landowner could use his estate for electoral purposes by means of trust dispositions. Scottish politics were notoriously corrupt in the eighteenth century, perhaps no more so than in the general election of 1768. C. E. Adam (ed.), *View of the Political State of Scotland in 1788* (Edinburgh, 1887)' [Campbell and Skinner].

243   *In Scotland . . . not precisely stipulated in the lease*: the Abolition of Heritable Jurisdictions (Scotland) Act of 1747 (20 Geo. II, c. 43), part of government reprisals after the Jacobite uprisings of 1745–6, effectively abolished the hereditary rights of landowners over their tenants and so broke the remaining feudal powers of the Highland chiefs.

a servitude which still subsists: 'Most of the provisions for the maintenance of roads in Scotland, including "statute labour" were reiterated by 5 Geo. I, c. 30 (1718). Statute labour was commuted for a money payment and the turnpike acts enabled additional funds to be obtained through tolls. The first Scottish turnpike act was for the county of Edinburgh in 1713, but improvements were significant only in the last quarter of the eighteenth century' [Campbell and Skinner].

244   *antient tenths and fifteenths*: taxes of one-tenth and one-fifteenth, imposed on personal property in the Middle Ages.

245   *not inferior to those of England*: see Walter Harte, *Essays on Husbandry* (London, 1764), 79, where, after discussing the agriculture of Holland and Berne, he argues: 'That republics are better calculated than monarchies, for the advancement of agriculture.' His reasons may seem strained to the modern reader: 'for most republics (from natural reasons, rather than any strange concurrence of circumstances) are generally situated in a neglected barren soil: And there it is that art and industry make the most shining improvements in husbandry. Add to this, that the common-wealth we are now speaking of, and others of Switzerland in a lesser proportion, are living proofs, that there is, in such sorts of government, something analogous to the advancement of agriculture. The inhabitants are free from

ambition (at least for a considerable time after the first establishment of their community;) Liberty gives them scope to exercise their industry, and equality excites emulation... Besides, small shares of property are better distinguished, secured, and bounded: And, at the same time, more capable of admitting a correct and accurate husbandry.' For Harte, as for other English agrarians, farming was an expression of that liberty and patriotic independence which they believed had characterized republican Rome. In the opening of his work he cites various Roman authors to prove that farming is the worthiest of human activities. We have already had references from Smith to Columella and Pliny (see note to p. 238 above).

245 *laws against engrossers . . . privileges of . . . markets*: the terms 'engrosser', 'regrater', and 'forestaller' all apply to those who buy up commodities in bulk and with a view to enhancing the price and selling them on. Since Tudor times marketing regulations for grain required producers to sell in small quantities directly to the consumer at market. By the eighteenth century this system was rapidly disappearing. An Act of 1773, Thomas Pownall's Corn Law (13 Geo. III, c. 43) repealed Elizabethan legislation against forestalling and regrating. While Smith regarded laws against the speculative purchasing of grain by middlemen as an invasion of the rights of property and an unwarranted interference in the natural workings of the market, others continued to argue (and especially in times of scarcity and high prices) in terms of an older moral economics of distribution which centred on the notion of the individual customer dealing face-to-face with the producer in a regulated market. Smith returns to the vexed issue of grain policing at *WN*, IV. v.

246 *In . . . Europe then . . . Tartar governments of Asia at present*: as a means of illustrating their theory of historical progress, the Scottish Enlightenment thinkers turned habitually to contemporary cross-cultural analogy. The nomadic Tartars of Central Asia provided a favourite exemplum, as at *WN*, III. iv (p. 267 below). Still living in the second, or shepherd, age (see note to p. 80 above), and therefore corresponding to the society of pre-Conquest England, they yet inhabited the world alongside the commercial Scots of the eighteenth century. According to Adam Ferguson's summary of the comparative method, the

modern European historian might discover, 'as in a mirror', in the 'present condition' of the Tartars (sometimes it is the Arab 'clans' or North American tribes) 'the features of our own progenitors'. Ferguson explains: 'If, in advanced years, we would form a just notion of our progress from the cradle, we must have recourse to the nursery, and from the example of those who are still in the period of life we mean to describe, take our representation of past manners, that cannot, in any other way, be recalled' (*An Essay on the History of Civil Society*, ed. Forbes, 81). See, too, Edmund Burke in a letter of 1777 to the Scottish historian William Robertson: 'But now the Great Map of Mankind is unroll'd at once; and there is no state or Gradation of barbarism, and no mode of refinement which we have not at the same instant under our View. The very different Civility of Europe and of China; The barbarism of Persia and Abyssinia. The erratick manners of Tartary, and of arabia. The Savage State of North America, and of New Zealand' (*The Correspondence of Edmund Burke*, 10 vols. (Cambridge: Cambridge University Press, 1958–78), iii, ed. George H. Guttridge (1961), 351.

247   *passage . . . stallage*: at v. ii. Smith refers to Saxon 'Duties of Passage', 'which seem to have been originally established for the same purpose as our turnpike tolls, or the tolls upon our canals and navigable rivers, for the maintenance of the road or of the navigation' (Glasgow Edition, 894). According to one modern historian of the twelfth century, '[t]oll was the great restraint on the development of medieval trade. It was levied on sales and on purchases, in markets and in fairs, on highways and on bridges; nor could the merchant diverge from the straight way in order to avoid it . . . To be quit of toll was therefore the most highly valued franchise which a town could acquire' (A. L. Poole, *Domesday Book to Magna Carta: 1087–1216* (2nd edn., Oxford: Clarendon Press, 1955), 75). For a recent account of medieval tolls, see J. L. Bolton, *The Medieval English Economy 1150–1500* (London: Dent, 1980), 130–1.

demesnes: estates or lands.

Free-traders . . . a sort of annual poll-tax: at v. ii. Smith observes: 'During the barbarous times of feudal anarchy, merchants, like all the other inhabitants of burghs, were considered as little better than emancipated bondmen, whose persons were despised, and whose gains were envied' (Glasgow Edition, 878–9). A poll-tax is a tax of so much a head—that is, on each person alike.

248   *œconomy*: management. See note to p. 236 above.

249   *the hundred . . . courts*: in England a hundred court was a sub-division of the county court, having civil and criminal jurisdiction within a territorial hundred (a division of a county, originally supposed to contain a hundred families).

250   *in the heart of their own dominions*: Hume also noted that: 'The government of cities . . . even under absolute monarchies, is commonly republican' (*History of England* (1778), vi. 295) [Campbell and Skinner].

251   *King John of England*: John ruled as King of England from 1199 to 1216.

       Philip the First of France: Philip I died in 1108, and his son Louis (here Lewis) VI succeeded him in that year.

252   *Father Daniel*: G. Daniel, *Histoire de France* (Amsterdam, 1720), was a work which Smith ordered for Glasgow University Library [Campbell and Skinner].

       institution of the magistrates . . . in France: Hume argued that 'the erecting of these communities was an invention of Lewis the Gross [Louis VI], in order to free the people from slavery under the lords, and to give them protection, by means of certain privileges and a separate jurisdiction' (*History of England* (1778), ii. 118) [Campbell and Skinner].

       Hanseatic league: a powerful political and commercial confederation of mercantile communities in North Germany and elsewhere, trading in the Baltic and North Seas, with the purpose of acquiring monopolies and other privileges. Beginning in the thirteenth century, the League reached its highest point of influence in the middle of the fourteenth century when over a hundred towns belonged to it (including Bremen, Hamburg, Cologne, Riga, and Danzig), not counting depots of Hanseatic members in other towns, such as London, Bruges, and Bergen. The League declined with the emergence of the monarchies and principalities of the modern era, and especially with the competition of the Dutch and English in the Baltic and North Sea trade.

252   *republick of Berne*: see *Lectures on Jurisprudence* (1762–3), v. 46–50 (pp. 288–90), where Smith describes the establishment of European commercial republics.

253   *the states general*: the legislative assembly representing (in France before the Revolution of 1789 and in the Netherlands from the fifteenth century until 1796) the three estates—namely the clergy, the nobles, and the burghers of the whole realm.

       he was free for ever: outlining the ways in which a villein might gain freedom, Poole observes: 'He might also escape to a town where, if he remained unreclaimed for a year and a day, he became free ... It may be assumed that the nascent towns welcomed recruitment from the country, for the admission of escaped rustics is often specially recorded among the privileges of a chartered borough' (*Domesday Book to Magna Carta*, 47).

254   *that of the Saracens ... the Moors*: in his 'History of Astronomy', iv. 22, Smith refers to the development of science and the translation of classical works on astronomy into Arabic as a result of the 'munificence of the Abassides, the second race of the Califfs'. At iv. 23, he remarks that the 'victorious arms of the Saracens carried into Spain the learning, as well as the gallantry, of the East; and along with it ... the Arabian translations of Ptolemy and Aristotle' (in *Essays on Philosophical Subjects*, 68 and 69) [Campbell and Skinner].

       The cruzades: there were three crusades to recover the Holy Land between the eleventh and thirteenth centuries. On the relationship between the crusades and the expansion of trade routes, Poole notes: 'English mariners, a mixture of pilgrim, pirate, and honest trader, participated in the early crusading enterprises to a greater extent than has usually been recognized ... In the later years of the twelfth century there was a small colony of London business men resident at Genoa' (*Domesday Book to Magna Carta*, 94 and 95).

256   *Lucca*: north of Pisa, in north-west Italy.

       one of Machiavel's heroes, Castruccio Castracani: Niccolò Machiavelli (1469–1527), Florentine statesman and political writer, author of *The Prince* (1513), a famous treatise on statecraft. His principal work is *The History of Florence* (1520–5). Castruccio Castracani (1281–1328), who by political ruthlessness and military genius became Lord of Lucca and half of Tuscany, is the subject of Machiavelli's *Life of Castruccio Castracani of Lucca* (1520).

256   *of Lyons and Spital-fields*: Lyons in central southern France and Spitalfields, London, were both centres of the silk industry. A colony of French Huguenot silk-weavers settled in Spitalfields in the London East End in the late seventeenth century, fleeing France and religious persecution after the Revocation of the Edict of Nantes in 1685. With them they brought new methods of workmanship and new styles in weaving.

258   *manufactures of Leeds . . . and Wolverhampton*: the rising prosperity of Halifax and Leeds during the eighteenth century was based on wool and the newer worsted manufacture. Meteoric though this success appeared to be, it had its roots in an industry reaching back to the fifteenth century. Birmingham and Wolverhampton were centres of the hardware trades, Birmingham being famous for, among other things, its fashion items in metal and household utensils; Sheffield was known for cutlery. All gained importance in the later eighteenth century. Like the Yorkshire textile industry, many of the metal trades (especially around Sheffield) kept some capital invested in agriculture; but the divorce between land and trade became greater over the course of the seventeenth and eighteenth centuries. (See Berg, *The Age of Manufactures*, 275.)

offspring of foreign commerce: cf. Hume's argument in 'Of Commerce': 'If we consult history, we shall find, that in most nations foreign trade has preceded any refinement in home manufactures, and given birth to domestic luxury' (*Essays Moral, Political, and Literary*, 270).

259   *Merchants . . . the best of all improvers*: see note to p. 225 above; and T. M. Devine, 'Glasgow Colonial Merchants and Land, 1770–1815', in J. T. Ward and R. G. Wilson (eds.), *Land and Industry: the Landed Estate and the Industrial Revolution* (Newton Abbot: David and Charles, 1971), 205–44. At *WN*, v. ii, Smith suggests the sale of Crown lands to improvers, arguing: 'When the crown lands had become private property, they would, in the course of a few years, become well-improved and well-cultivated' (p. 450).

260   *Mr. Hume*: in 'Of Refinement in the Arts', Hume argues: 'If we consider the matter in a proper light, we shall find, that a

progress in the arts is rather favourable to liberty, and has a natural tendency to preserve, if not produce a free government' (*Essays Moral, Political, and Literary*, 283). In 1776 these were not the novel sentiments that Smith appears to suggest, but rather lay at the basis of the Scottish thinkers' materialist views of commercial progress and political liberty as outlined by Ferguson, Lord Kames, and others. See, for example, the argument outlined in John Millar, *Origin of the Distinction of Ranks* (1781), chap. 5: 'The changes produced in the government of a people, by their progress in Arts, and in polished Manners' (pp. 269–96).

261   *William Rufus . . . Thomas Becket . . . earl of Warwick*: Smith's examples set his argument to the late eleventh and twelfth centuries. William Rufus (William II), son of the Conqueror, was king from 1087 to 1100, and Becket was murdered in 1170. Hume cites the same example of Becket's magnificence in his *History of England* (1778), i. 384, where he also refers to the Earl of Warwick's 30,000 guests (iii. 182). Writing of 'the first and more uncultivated ages of any state', Hume notes in his essay 'Of Money', that at such times 'rustic hospitality' consumes 'the greater part' of the incomes of the powerful (*Essays Moral, Political, and Literary*, 298–9).

the highlands of Scotland: on his travels in 1773 Dr Johnson commented on the splendour of Highland hospitality as comparable to that of the Middle Ages. On Skye it seemed to him that: 'The fictions of the *Gothick* romances were not so remote from credibility as they are now thought. In the full prevalence of the feudal institution, when violence desolated the world, and every baron lived in a fortress, forests and castles were regularly succeeded by each other, and the adventurer might very suddenly pass from the gloom of woods, or the ruggedness of moors, to seats of plenty, gaiety, and magnificence. Whatever is imaged in the wildest tale, if giants, dragons, and enchantment be excepted, would be felt by him, who, wandering in the mountains without a guide, or upon the sea without a pilot, should be carried amidst his terror and uncertainty, to the hospitality and elegance of *Raasay* or *Dunvegan*' (*Journey*, ed. Fleeman, 63).

Doctor Pocock: 'an Arab Prince will often dine in the street, before his door, and call to all that pass, even beggars, in the usual expression, Bismillah, that is, In the name of God; who come and sit down, and when they have done, give their Hamdellilah, that is, God be praised. For the Arabs are great levellers, put everybody on a footing with them; and it is by such generosity and hospitality that they maintain their interest; but the middling people among them, and the Coptis, live but poorly' (Richard Pococke, *A Description of the East and some other Countries* (London, 1743), i. 183) [Cannan].

261   *it is so at this day*: see note to p. 40 above.

      quit-rent: see note to p. 195 above.

262   *allodially*: an allodium is an estate held in absolute ownership; its opposite is an estate held in feud (feudally), that is, under a superior. Smith argues that during the Middle Ages the feudal system, based on the relation of lord and vassal, replaced the independent allodial system of land tenure which pertained in England before the Conquest. Cf. Hume, who states that the Saxons 'found no occasion for the feudal institutions', and that William I 'introduced into England the feudal law, which he found established in France and Normandy' (*History of England* (1778), i. 225 and 253).

263   *Mr. Cameron of Lochiel*: Donald Cameron of Lochiel, one of Prince Charles Edward Stuart's most influential supporters in the 1745/6 uprising. Smith's romantic picture of him as an uncommercialized Gaelic patriarch, stuck in the 'shepherd stage', needs some adjusting. Lochiel was, in fact, an enterprising businessman when it came to the management of his local estates and of trade ventures in North America and the West Indies. (See Bruce Lenman, *The Jacobite Risings in Britain 1589–1746* (London: Eyre Methuen, 1980), 245–6.) On the legitimacy of Lochiel's powers of jurisdiction, Campbell and Skinner, in their note, correct Smith, pointing out that 'Lochiel's situation was not necessarily so devoid of legal authority as Smith implies. Lochiel, and others, could possess baronial rights, derived from their subject superior, in Lochiel's case from Argyll. No written charter need exist, so long as the rights were customarily recognized' (Glasgow Edition, 417).

      lord of regality: one in possession of a territorial jurisdiction which constituted his land a little kingdom in which his courts might try all cases except treason. Regality came to an end in

1747 by the Abolition of Heritable Jurisdictions (Scotland) Act, doing away with the hereditary rights of landowners over their tenants as part of the campaign to break clan power after the 1745/6 uprising.

264 *silent and insensible operation . . . brought about*: in referring to the transition from the feudal state, Kames remarks that 'after the Arts of Peace began to be cultivated, Manufactures and Trade to revive in *Europe*, and Riches to encrease, this institution behoved to turn extreme burdensome. It first tottered, and then fell by its own Weight, as wanting a solid Foundation' (*Essays upon several Subjects Concerning British Antiquities* (Edinburgh, 1747), 155) [Campbell and Skinner].

267 *not like Esau for a mess of pottage*: 'Esau selleth his birthright for a mess of potage' is the heading to Genesis 25 in the Geneva Bible.

antient families . . . common among those nations: in *The Theory of Moral Sentiments*, Smith notes: 'In pastoral countries, and in all countries where the authority of law is not alone sufficient to give perfect security to every member of the state, all the different branches of the same family commonly chuse to live in the neighbourhood of one another . . . The same extensive regard to kindred is said to take place among the Tartars, the Arabs, the Turkomans, and, I believe, among all other nations who are nearly in the same state of society in which the Scots Highlanders were about the beginning of the present century. In commercial countries, where the authority of law is always perfectly sufficient to protect the meanest man in the state, the descendants of the same family, having no such motive for keeping together, naturally separate and disperse, as interest or inclination may direct' (VI. ii. 1. 12–13 (pp. 222–3)). In his *Historical View of the English Government*, 4 vols. (London, 1803), Smith's pupil John Millar remarks how an advanced commercial society unfixes property, family, and the traditional distinctions and identities of rich and poor: 'Property is thus commonly subjected to a constant rotation, which prevents it from conferring upon the owner the habitual respect and consideration, derived from a long continued intercourse between the poor and the rich' (iv. 131).

268 *in twenty or five-and-twenty years*: the same argument and figures are offered at *WN*, I. viii (p. 69).

268   *A small proprietor . . . the most successful*: see notes to pp. 233 and 236 above.

269   *illustration*: distinction, illustriousness.

270   *From the beginning of the reign of Elizabeth too*: Elizabeth came to the throne in 1558.

     Except in times of scarcity . . . a monopoly: the bounty for the exportation of corn was established by I Wm. & Mar., c. 12 (1688). By an Act of 1773, exports were shut off and imports allowed only when the domestic price rose above 48 shillings per bushel. The purpose was to reconcile high prices for producers with a stable price and an adequate supply for the domestic consumer (see note to p. 55 above). The importation of foreign corn was regulated by 22 Car. II, c. 13 (1670). 18 and 19 Car. II, c. 2 (1666) prohibited the importation of live cattle. The importation of cattle from Ireland was allowed by 32 Geo. II, c. 11 (1758) and continued by further Acts in 1765 and 1772. Smith comments on these regulations at IV. ii, where he argues that 'the freest importation of the rude produce of the soil could have no [detrimental] effect upon the agriculture of the country' (Glasgow Edition, 459).

271   *a period as long as . . . prosperity usually endures*: cf. Hume to Lord Kames, 4 Mar. 1758: 'Great empires, great cities, great commerce, all of them receive a check, not from accidental events, but necessary principles' (*The Letters of David Hume*, ed. J. Y. T. Grieg, 2 vols. (Oxford: Clarendon Press, 1932), i. 272) [Campbell and Skinner].

     the expedition of Charles the VIIIth to Naples: in 1494–5. Hume uses the same example in 'Of Refinement in the Arts', to show the problem which arises when the wealth accrued from a nation's industry does not keep pace with the expensive drains of its military ambitions: 'When Charles VIII of France invaded Italy, he carried with him about 20,000 men . . . this armament so exhausted the nation . . .' (*Essays Moral, Political, and Literary*, 280).

     foreign commerce of Spain and Portugal: at I. xi, Smith stated that 'Spain and Portugal . . . are, after Poland, perhaps, the two most beggarly countries in Europe' (Glasgow Edition, 256).

     according to Guicciardin: Francesco Guicciardini (1483–1540), a historian. Most of his works were published posthumously. The reference here is to *Della Istoria d'Italia* (1561; Venice, 1738), i. 2. In *Lectures on Rhetoric and Belles Lettres*, ii. 69–70 (p. 114), Smith describes Guicciardini and Machiavelli as 'the two most famous modern Italian historians' [Campbell and Skinner].

272 *the Hans towns*: see note to p. 252 above.

275 *Of Systems of political Œconomy*: for the term 'political œconomy', see the note to p. 10 above. As the introductory outline to *WN*, IV suggests, Smith lumps together all previous writings on the management of a national economy as representative of two opposed schools of thought—the commercial and the agricultural. Most of *WN*, IV is concerned to expose the flaws in the commercial or Mercantilist system, under which, Smith asserts, the British and other European economies are severely hampered. Only the last chapter gives an outline of and qualified praise to the agricultural or Physiocratic model. On Mercantilism and Physiocracy, see notes to pp. 182 and 214 above and notes throughout *WN*, IV below. Clearly, the inference to be drawn from Smith's rough division is that *WN* offers a new set of principles for the organization of political economy. This, however, like the intellectual honesty of Smith's procedure and the fairness of his representation of the Mercantilist and Physiocratic positions, has been questioned. See Keith Tribe, *Land, Labour, and Economic Discourse*, 107–9.

276 *in every respect synonymous*: the alleged confusion between wealth and money forms a central element in the critique of Mercantilism developed by Hume and Smith. See *WN*, II. ii and notes to pp. 175 and 182 above.

Plano Carpino: there may be a confusion between Plano Carpini, sent as a legate to Pope Innocent IV in 1246, and Guillaume de Rubruquis, sent as ambassador by Louis IX in 1253. Both are mentioned in N. Bergeron's *Voyages faits principalement en Asie dans les xii., xiv., et xv. siècles* (La Haye, 1735) [Cannan].

277 *Mr. Locke*: in *Lectures on Jurisprudence* (1762–3), vi. 135 (p. 381), Locke appears as a Mercantilist, who has lent that system 'somewhat more of a philosophicall air and the appearance of probability by some amendments'. The distinction which Smith allows to Locke is perhaps that money is considered less as the means of free bargaining than as the instrument of the state for the organization and securing of a national

economy. In *Two Treatises of Government*, money is 'some lasting thing that Men might keep without spoiling, and that by mutual consent Men would take in exchange for the truly useful, but perishable Supports of Life' (ed. Laslett, 318–19).

277 *Others*: for example, Hume, who argues that: 'If we consider any one kingdom by itself, it is evident, that the greater or less plenty of money is of no consequence' ('Of Money', *Essays Moral, Political, and Literary*, 289).

278 *carrying gold or silver forth of the kingdom*: Act anent the having of the money furth of the Realme (1487). *Acts of the Parliament of Scotland*, ii. 183 [Campbell and Skinner].

Mr. Mun: Sir Thomas Mun (1571–1641), an English Mercantilist and director of the East India Company. Smith quotes here, slightly inaccurately, from Mun's *England's Treasure by Forraign Trade* (1664; repr. in J. R. McCulloch, *A Select Collection of Early English Tracts on Commerce*), 141. Mun attacked the idea that exports of bullion should be totally prohibited and other restrictions put on trade, arguing that such restrictions invited retaliation in foreign markets and raised domestic prices. Although he thought it unnecessary to achieve an export surplus with each trading partner, he did emphasize, however, its importance in the balance of trade to the country as a whole.

279 *the balance of trade*: for the importance of a favourable balance of trade in Mercantilist descriptions of the economy, see notes to pp. 182 and 228 above. Smith examines the doctrine of the balance of trade in *Lectures on Jurisprudence* (1762–3), vi. 137–70 (pp. 381–94), where he cites among its advocates Mun, Jonathan Swift, Locke, and Mandeville.

282 *England's Treasure in Foreign Trade*: Mun's title is *England's Treasure by Forraign Trade; or, the Ballance of our Forraign Trade is the Rule of our Treasure*.

more perishable than money: Sir William Petty (1623–87) made important contributions to monetary theory, arguing in *Political Arithmetick* (1690) for a hierarchy of productivity in terms of the perishability of goods. Food is the most perishable, followed in ascending order by clothes, furniture, houses, working of mines and fisheries, and eventually the most productive employment (in terms of durability) is that which brings '*Gold and Silver* into the Country: Because those things are not only not perishable, but are esteemed for Wealth at all times, and every where: Whereas other Commodities which are perishable, or whose value depends upon the Fashion; or which are contingently scarce and plentiful, are wealth, but *pro hic & nunc*, as shall be elsewhere said' (*The Economic Writings of Sir William Petty*, ed. Hull, i. 269). According to Tribe, who examines Petty's argument, it is a serious misrepresentation of the Mercantilist position to argue from its preoccupation with gold accumulation. As he sees it, money or bullion serves the Mercantilists as a means to stimulate circulation and not as an end in itself: the more durable a commodity, the greater its exchangeability, where circulation (not accumulation) enhances the power of the state. (See *Land, Labour, and Economic Discourse*, 87–9.)

283   *what they can purchase with it*: see note to p. 175 above. At IV. vi, Smith states: 'But money is a commodity with regard to which every man is a merchant. Nobody buys it but in order to sell it again; and with regard to it there is in ordinary cases no last purchaser or consumer' (Glasgow Edition, 554).

285   *with consumable goods*: in economic writings in general the close connections between trade and war are emphasized, where the extent of a nation's trade depends upon its ability to dominate certain routes and ports. Cf. Hume, 'Of Refinement in the Arts', where, among the advantages of an extended commerce and productivity, 'the increase and consumption of . . . commodities' become 'a kind of *storehouse* of labour, which, in the exigencies of state, may be turned to the public service.' He continues, in direct opposition to the frugality enjoined, in the interests of patriotism and national defence, by certain Mercantilist pamphleteers: 'In a nation, where there is no demand for such superfluities, men sink into indolence, lose all enjoyment of life, and are useless to the public, which cannot maintain or support its fleets and armies from the industry of such slothful members' (*Essays Moral, Political, and Literary*, 279).

286   *restraints . . . exportation*: Smith expands upon these twin doctrines of Mercantilism throughout *WN*, IV. See, especially, IV. viii, where the picture is complicated by certain policies which appear to run counter to the general system.

288   *monopoly of the home-market*: Smith discusses the prohibitions on importing live cattle and corn at *WN*, III. iv (see note to p. 270 above). The importation of foreign woollens was prohibited under an ancient Act of 4 Edw. IV c. 1 (1464). Wool, Britain's chief home as well as export industry in the early period, provided 70 per cent of domestic exports in 1700 and 50 per cent in 1770. (See Berg, *The Age of Manufactures*, 124–5.) The restraints on the importation of silks functioned rather differently. Unlike wool, silk was an expensive luxury commodity whose industry faced fierce foreign competition and was totally dependent on the importation of its raw materials, supplies of which were sometimes interrupted. It was a heavily protected trade in the face of French competition and smuggling. There was a complete ban on foreign silk fabrics between 1765 and 1826, but this did not bring prosperity to the weavers. According to George: 'The trade was subject to periods of over-expansion and subsequent depression, to sudden changes of fashion, to disastrous interruptions from court mourning; it was also seasonal, and the small master was often unable to withstand even seasonal fluctuations' (*London Life in the Eighteenth Century*, 180). See note to p. 60 above for Smith's general opposition to monopolies.

289   *of its own accord*: for Smith's ideal of a 'natural balance of industry', see note to p. 223 above.

290   *it has already been shown*: at II. v (Glasgow Edition, 369).

292   *no part of his intention*: the notion of unintended social outcomes was common to several of the thinkers of the Scottish Enlightenment, who stress that men and women may advance social interest without knowing it and that they can, in seeking the gratification of individual selfishness, fail to appreciate the connection between that gratification and the achievement of general welfare. According to Adam Ferguson, '[e]very step and every movement of the multitude, even in what are termed enlightened ages, are made with equal blindness to the future, and nations stumble upon establishments, which are indeed the result of human action, but not the execution of any human design' (*Essay on the History of Civil Society*, ed. Forbes, 122). In his *Theory of Moral Sentiments*, IV. i. 10, Smith had already argued that an 'invisible hand' distributes, with some approach to equality, the 'necessaries of life' and the basic means to happiness, despite the unequal distribution of wealth in com-

mercial society (pp. 184–5). Now he argues that the self-interested individual unintentionally maximizes the wealth of society for all its members. This is not a reiteration of Mandeville's notorious position that public benefits arise from private vices. Smith's contention is both less colourful and, in fact, less starkly moralized than Mandeville's. For he maintains that, among the private interests motivating the selfish conduct of the rich, 'frugality' will predominate over 'expense', and a code of propriety will control the pursuit of self-improvement (see an earlier stage of this same argument at *WN*, II. iii (pp. 203–4)). Mandeville's commercial vision requires the controlling regulation of a statesman at the helm, while the Smithian principle of propriety assumes a society of independent manufacturers and merchants, whose conduct is self-policing in the context of free-market relations. Only when the sectional interests of some manufacturers, creating monopolies and narrowing competition, threaten the 'natural liberty' of the market will its internal propriety be endangered.

295 *Mr. Colbert*: Jean-Baptiste Colbert (1619–83), one of the chief ministers of Louis XIV of France, concerned mainly with financial and economic policy. See note to p. 379 below.

The war of 1672: the Franco-Dutch War of 1672–9, which was fortified by Colbert's wish to loosen the hold of the Dutch entrepreneurs on the French economy and to capture their world trade. Colbert had erected a prohibitive tariff against the Dutch in 1667 and imposed high sugar duties in 1670–1.

296 *spirit of hostility . . . ever since*: at *WN*, II. iii, Smith refers to Britain's 'four expensive French wars of 1688, 1702, 1742, and 1756' (see note to p. 207 above). Throughout the eighteenth century the English and French struggled for control of the seas and the trading riches of North America, the West Indies, West Africa, and India.

insidious and crafty animal . . . politician: cf. *Lectures on Jurisprudence* (1766), 327: 'They whom we call politicians are not the most remarkable men in the world for probity and punctuality' (p. 539).

298 *end of the late war*: the Seven Years War with France ended in 1763.

it has already been observed: at *WN*, I. x (p. 136).

299   *Soldiers . . . any trade . . . or Ireland*: the privilege was given after particular wars by 12 Car. II, c. 16 (1660); 12 Anne, c. 14 (1712); 3 Geo. III, c. 8 (1762); etc. [Cannan].

exclusive privileges of corporations . . . law of settlements: all regulations restricting the admission to trades and the free movement of a labour force. Viewed as 'encroachments upon natural liberty', they put in question the value of intervention as a method of protecting rights to work. Smith discusses these regulations at *WN*, I. x (see notes to pp. 117 and 136 above).

an Oceana or Utopia: Utopia was an imaginary island, depicted by Sir Thomas More in his *Utopia* (1516) as enjoying a perfect social, legal, and political system. James Harrington's *Commonwealth of Oceana* (1656) was described by Hume, in his essay 'Idea of a Perfect Commonwealth', as 'the only valuable model of a commonwealth, that has yet been offered to the public' (*Essays Moral, Political, and Literary*, 501).

300   *intimidate the legislature*: the advantageous effect of Britain's political and legal infrastructure on commerce in the eighteenth century is noted by modern historians. As Porter explains: 'The state wasn't a clog to trade, as it was elsewhere, though grumbling commercial lobbies were perennially up in arms. There was no profits tax, no capital gains tax. Successive ministries' economic policies switched tariffs to protect home manufactures and cheapen exports' (*English Society in the Eighteenth Century*, 203). Smith notes with suspicion (at *WN*, I. xi (p. 157)) the narrow concerns and self-serving policies of the merchant and master-manufacturer. In opposing the establishment of Chambers of Commerce, Smith argued, in a letter of 1785, '[i]n a Country where Clamour always intimidates and faction often oppresses the Government, the regulations of Commerce are commonly dictated by those who are most interested to deceive and impose upon the Public' (*Correspondence*, 286).

301   *when I come to treat of taxes*: at *WN*, v. ii.

302   *Silesia lawns*: fine linen or cotton fabrics manufactured in Silesia, a province in the east of Germany.

cambricks: a kind of fine white linen originally manufactured at Cambrai in French Flanders.

302   *the impost 1692 . . . upon all French goods*: 4 Wm & Mar., c. 5 (1692). An impost is a custom duty levied on merchandise.

303   *one third and two third subsidies*: exacted by Acts of 1703 and 1704.

smugglers . . . the principal importers: at *WN*, I. x (p. 108), Smith commented on the 'trade' of the smuggler as 'the most hazardous of all trades'. Committed by profession to free trade in imports, the smuggler is an interesting figure in the Smithian economy and the development of commercial capitalism, while his goods form a significant proportion of everyday domestic requirements. Writing to William Eden on 3 Jan. 1780, Smith called for the repeal of prohibitions, arguing that 'our Merchants ought not to complain if we refuse to tax ourselves any longer in order to support a few feeble and languishing branches of their commerce'. Smith was appointed a Commissioner of Customs for Scotland in January 1778, and he observes to Eden that on taking up office he examined the list of prohibited goods and found 'to my great astonishment, that I had scarce a stock, a cravat, a pair of ruffles, or a pocket handkerchief which was not prohibited to be worn or used in Great Britain. I wished to set an example and burnt them all. I will not advise you to examine either your own or Mrs. Edens apparel or household furniture, least you be brought into a scrape of the same kind.' He concludes: 'The sole effect of a prohibition is to hinder the revenue from profiting by the importation' (*Correspondence*, 245–6).

even upon the principles of the commercial system: characteristic of the Mercantilist position was the protected economy, which signalled a strong state and was bound up with ideas of national esteem and economic patriotism. Like Smith, Hume argued in his essays 'Of the Jealousy of Trade' and 'Of the Balance of Trade' that international rivalry promotes domestic industry and that an extended and untrammelled foreign trade actually augments the nation's riches and therefore its power: 'The emulation among rival nations serves rather to keep industry alive in all of them: and any people is happier who possess a variety of manufactures, than if they enjoyed one single great manufacture, in which they are all employed. Their situation is less precarious; and they will feel less sensibly those revolutions and uncertainties, to which every particular branch of commerce will always be exposed' ('Of the Jealousy of Trade', *Essays Moral, Political, and Literary*, 337).

304 *of the East India trade*: A. Anderson commented: 'Objections, and answers to the East India trade ... 1. Its exhausting our Treasure. Answered, We may, by this Trade, draw as much Silver from other Countries as we send to India' (*Historical and Chronological Deduction of the Origin of Commerce* (London, 1764), ii. 452) [Campbell and Skinner].

305 *more liable to be abused*: see note to p. 215 above.

small beer: weak beer.

among the northern nations: cf. Hume, 'Of National Characters': 'The only observation with regard to the difference of men in different climates, on which we can rest any weight, is the vulgar one, that people, in the northern regions, have a greater inclination to strong liquors, and those in the southern to love and women' (*Essays Moral, Political, and Literary*, 218). The distinction was something of a commonplace.

306 *almost universal sobriety*: in *Lectures on Jurisprudence* (1762–3), vi. 86 (363), Smith objected to the view that to increase the price of some liquors would reduce public drunkenness. At v. ii, in the course of a discussion of 'Taxes upon Consumable Commodities', he argues, in the context of 'the morals of the common people', for a distinction between spirits and 'the wholesome and invigorating liquors of beer and ale' (Glasgow Edition, 891).

Commerce ... a bond of union and friendship: for the Scottish Enlightenment thinkers, the early meaning of commerce as the buying and selling of merchandise is often, as here, contained within the context of its later abstracted meaning of interchange or communication (of ideas, emotions, and so on), as in John Millar's assertion that '[t]he acquisition of property ... has also a considerable effect upon the commerce of the sexes' (*Origin of the Distinction of Ranks* (1781), 71). In the socio-economic environment of eighteenth-century Europe, the commercial system mediates all actions and modes of behaviour and negotiates between individuals and the larger formation which comprises them. Cf. Smith's statement near the beginning of *WN*, I. iv: 'Every man thus lives by exchanging, or becomes in some measure a merchant' (p. 31).

307 *great body of the people*: at *WN*, I. xi (p. 157), Smith made the same point. See, too, his concern over the influence of sectional trading interests on government policy as expressed in his correspondence with William Eden at the close of the American War (quoted at note to p. 221 above).

308 *antient Egyptians ... modern Chinese*: two of Smith's favourite examples of powerful nations negligent of foreign trade. See notes to pp. 91 and 221 above.

309 *not in less than four or five years*: partly owing to the greater distances for transportation, but also to the roundabout trade involved in sending tobacco to England prior to its re-export to the Continent.

never ... more than three millions: the Thirteen Colonies had expanded to a population of 1,200,000 by 1760. In 1780 the population of England and Wales was 'more than seven million, and growing at an unprecedentedly fast rate' (Paul Langford, *A Polite and Commercial People: England 1727–1783* (Oxford: Clarendon Press, 1989), 636).

312 *different sorts of paper money*: see note to p. 179 above.

our North American colonies: at *WN*, I. viii (pp. 69–70) and II. v (pp. 220–1), Smith analyses the rapid progress towards wealth of the American colonies and distinguishes between their happy commercial prospects and the present relatively unadvanced state of the American economy.

313 *Of Bounties*: bounties are financial encouragements by the state to merchants or manufacturers to stimulate particular branches of industry. On corn bounties, see notes to pp. 55, 245, and 270. Long extracts have been retained from what may seem an unduly digressive chapter on bounties and, in particular, on encouragements to and regulation of the grain market. This section is, in fact, highly important, not least because, in the Western context, corn (wheat) was and is of all commodities the original and the essential. As Smith here observes: 'Woollen or linen cloth are not the regulating commodities by which the real value of all other commodities must be finally measured and determined. Corn is' (p. 319). Consequently, corn focuses the debate at the centre of free-market economics. As the food of survival, corn is both a natural and a political commodity.

Corn and the grain store represent the site of impassioned confrontation between competing views of society, where the rights to property of the corn merchant challenge, in times of dearth or famine, the rights to survival of the poor: who has prior claim to the most basic human food; and in what sense can it be privately owned? Corn highlights the difficulty of reconciling 'naturally' and 'with justice' (favourite Smithian terms) that inequality of property of the entrepreneurial class and the adequate subsistence of the poor wage-labourer—the linked interests upon which Smith's free commercial model depends. Government control of the market in grain was the central element of Mercantilist economic regulation; and for much of the eighteenth century corn bounties formed part of an attempt to increase British agricultural profitability in the face of over-production. That is, regulation was part of a high-prices and low-wages economy working against the interests of the labouring poor. The effects of controls periodically gave rise through the century to pamphlets on the corn trade, and in many cases restrictions provoked local food riots. But to question such regulation seemed at the time, and still does seem to many commentators, Smith's most radical theoretical claim, for it appears to challenge the very right to survival of the poor. See the opposed modern readings of E. P. Thompson, 'The Moral Economy of the English Crowd in the Eighteenth Century', *Past and Present*, 50 (1971), 76–136, and Gertrude Himmelfarb, *The Idea of Poverty: England in the Early Industrial Age* (1984), especially 50–73. See, too, Thompson's late response in 'The Moral Economy Reviewed', in *Customs in Common* (London: Merlin Press, 1991). In fact, by an Act of 1773 (Thomas Pownall's Corn Law), laws against the speculative purchasing of grain by middlemen had already been decisively repealed though bounties remained. Pownall's bill was the most important piece of corn legislation between the introduction of the bounty in 1688 and the later statutes of 1791–1846. What it represented was a compromise, between regulation and liberalization, in the context of which Smith's endorsement of free trade in grain needs to be seen. Among other things, the Act encouraged warehousing of corn at points of import and export and the manipulation of supplies by merchants. On the other hand, in opposing export bounties which distort price for the benefit of the producer, Smith has also been seen as championing the rights of the consumer. (See Istvan Hont and Michael Ignatieff, 'Needs and Justice in the *Wealth of Nations*: an introductory essay', in Hont and Ignatieff (eds.), *Wealth and Virtue*, 15.)

314   *tracts upon the corn trade*: Charles Smith, *Three Tracts on the Corn-Trade and Corn Laws* (2nd edn., London, 1766; original pamphlets in 1758 and 1759), concerned to abolish the old model of market regulation. It is interesting to note, given the proliferation of pamphlets on the corn trade in the 1760s and 1770s, that Smith mentions specifically only the three tracts by Charles Smith which support so closely his own argument. There is no explicit mention of the French debates over the liberalization of the grain trade which were contemporary with Smith's residence in France in the mid 1760s and, one would imagine, would have influenced his own thinking. Like his quarrel with Mercantilism in general, the overwhelming logic of Smith's argument in this chapter succeeds largely by reducing opposition to a nameless and simplified practice.

315   *bushel*: a dry measure of eight gallons.

316   *not the real . . . the nominal price*: Smith distinguishes between real and nominal price at *WN*, I. v.

      the real value of silver: at I. xi, Smith notes that 'Corn . . . is . . . a more accurate measure of value than any other commodity or sett of commodities . . . therefore, we can judge better of the real value of silver, by comparing it with corn, than by comparing it with any other commodity, or sett of commodities' (Glasgow Edition, 206).

318   *amount to a prohibition*: see note to p. 270 above.

320   *those two other orders of people*: at *WN*, I. xi, Smith observes that 'Merchants and master manufacturers . . . have frequently more acuteness of understanding than the greater part of country gentlemen' (p. 157).

321   *Digression concerning the Corn Trade and Corn Laws*: the crucial section of Smith's argument for a free trade in grain, the digression has been seen as influential on subsequent thinking during the bad harvests, shortages, and high prices of the 1790s, though not directly formative of government policy at this time. See, for example, Edmund Burke, *Thoughts and Details on Scarcity*, written in November 1795, where, in response to

contemporary events, the case is put against government interference with wages, prices, and agricultural merchandizing. The
sufficiency of E. P. Thompson's emotionally powerful argument
(in 'The Moral Economy of the English Crowd'), that what
Smith proposes to abolish in the digression is the moral economy and traditional regulatory system to which the poor appeal,
has been questioned by other writers from an economic and
political perspective and in terms of a more complicating pattern of lower-class agitation, establishment accommodation, and
a shift in the social role of economic activity itself. See Elizabeth Fox-Genovese, 'The Many Faces of Moral Economy: A
Contribution to a Debate', *Past and Present*, 58 (1973), 161–8;
Dale Edward Williams, 'Morals, Markets, and the English
Crowd in 1766', *Past and Present*, 104 (1984), 56–73; and Ian
R. Christie, *Stress and Stability in Late Eighteenth-Century
Britain: Reflections on the British Avoidance of Revolution* (Ox-
ford: Clarendon Press, 1984), 150–5.

322 *obliged to treat his crew*: the image of the prudent shipmaster is
typical in its persuasive power of the subtly moralized rhetoric
of Smith's morally disburdened system of unintended consequences, in terms of which a natural economic order comes into
being. The point that the self-interest of the dealer to maintain
high prices works to ration corn and so preserve it for need is
not, however, as self-evidently beneficial as Smith means it to
appear. For rationing by price may remove supplies from areas
of need to those of greater affluence. Besides, demand for corn
is highly inelastic.

323 *the Molluccas*: the Spice Islands of Dutch Indonesia.

324 *any general combination*: Smith makes the point at *WN*, I. x,
concerning country workers, that 'dispersed in distant places,
[they] cannot easily combine together' (p. 126).

325 *drought in Bengal . . . into a famine*: in 1600 the East India
Company had been formed, at first in the shape of a few small
trading centres, depending for their existence on the tolerance
of local rulers. But as business increased in the eighteenth
century so the commercial and political power of the Company
grew. This was consolidated by the British victory under Robert
Clive over the French in India in 1751. Clive's subsequent defeat
of the local Indian princes at Plassey in 1757 established him as

Governor of Bengal, and Britain as the dominant European power on the subcontinent. By 1772 corruption among Company officials was rife; added to this a terrible famine had killed a third of the local population. In that year the British government intervened in the Company's affairs and Warren Hastings was sent out as Governor-General to reform its legal and financial systems. Smith refers to the local decay practised against the Indian economy by the monopolistic methods and corruption of the Company at *WN*, I. viii (p. 72) and IV. vii (p. 366 below).

325   *unlimited . . . freedom of the corn trade*: cf. J. Arbuthnot ('A Farmer'), 'Let corn flow like water, and it will find its level' (*An Inquiry into the Connection between the Present Price of Provisions and the Size of Farms* (London, 1773), 88), quoted in Thompson, 'The Moral Economy of the English Crowd', 89.

326   *magazines*: storehouses.

by their violence: food riots were a fairly common phenomenon in eighteenth-century Britain whenever fears of shortages or unexpected rises in prices occurred. Such riots were worst in the mid-1760s, the early 1770s, the mid-1790s, and 1799/1800. There is a large body of writings on food riots in eighteenth-century Britain and France, the experiences of both countries forming the larger context to Smith's argument. In particular, recent historians have emphasized the subsistence riot as a women's political activity, the market-place being a female space which represents the moral economic implications of women's functions as family providers (see Cynthia A. Bouton, 'Gendered Behaviour in Subsistence Riots: The French Flour War of 1775', *Journal of Social History*, 23 (1990), 735–54). Ian Christie points out that '[t]he investigation of these riots by historians seems to suggest that they scored a relatively high degree of success' (*Stress and Stability*, 153). Both Bouton and Christie include useful reference lists of recent writings on food riots.

hucksters: a term of reproach for corn retailers (*OED*).

unlawful engrosser: see note to p. 245 above.

327   *kidders*: forestallers, hucksters (origin obscure).

a statute of Elizabeth: 5 Eliz. I, c. 12 (1562), by transferring the power of licensing to quarter sessions, confirmed the impression of stringency in the provision for concessions [Campbell and Skinner].

329   *in one single operation*: this is, of course, the basis of Smith's exposition of the division of labour in the opening chapters of *WN*.

330   *than the legislator can do*: cf. similar sentiments expressed at *WN*, I. x (pp. 120–1) and IV. ii (p. 292). Such a view of individual liberty lies at the heart of Smith's philosophy.

332   *by the 15th of Charles II . . . within three months*: by the Act of 1663: 'It shall be lawfull for all and every person and persons (not forestalling nor selling the same in the same Market within three Months after the buying thereof) to buy in open Market, and to lay up and keep in his and their Granaries or Houses' [Campbell and Skinner]. And see notes to pp. 55 and 270.

334   *political arithmetick*: statistics of trade, revenue, expenditure, population of a state, and so on. See the title of Sir William Petty's *Another Essay in Political Arithmetick, Concerning the Growth of the City of London* (1683). For Smith's reservations on quantitative methods, see *Correspondence*, 288.

336   *only in cases of the most urgent necessity*: Smith's advocacy of freedom in internal trade is uncompromising. Hume, who was also in favour of liberalization, nevertheless believed that the right to private property in grain should be waived 'even in less urgent necessities' than actual starvation; and he allowed for more situations than Smith in which magistrates might open up private granaries and distribute corn to the poor at fixed prices. (See *An Enquiry Concerning the Principles of Morals* (1751), ed. L. A. Selby-Bigge (3rd edn., rev. P. H. Nidditch; Oxford: Clarendon Press, 1975), 186–7).

  by the revolution . . . the bounty was established: the 'Glorious Revolution' of 1688, by which William of Orange and Mary, daughter of James II, were declared joint sovereigns and in return the new monarchs accepted a Bill of Rights, establishing the supremacy of Parliament over the monarchy and shifting the centre of political power. The bounty for the export of corn was established by I Wm. & Mar., c. 12 (1688). Smith is clearly at pains to link the new constitutional security of the individual with the conditions for economic growth at the close of the seventeenth century.

336   *to better his own condition*: see note to p. 203 above. But see,
too, Hume, 'Of Commerce', for an adjustment of this optimistic
view. Hume argues: 'The poverty of the common people is a
natural, if not an infallible effect of absolute monarchy; though
I doubt whether it be always true on the other hand, that their
riches are an infallible result of liberty . . . Where the labourers
and artisans are accustomed to work for low wages, and to retain
but a small part of the fruits of their labour, it is difficult for
them, even in a free government, to better their condition, or
conspire among themselves to heighten their wages' (*Essays
Moral, Political, and Literary*, 272).

337   *freer than in any other part of Europe*: of England in 1729
Montesquieu wrote: 'This nation is passionately fond of liberty
. . . every individual is independent.' And he made the connection: 'England has progressed the farthest of all peoples of the
world in three important things: in piety, in commerce, and in
freedom' (quoted in Porter, *English Society in the Eighteenth
Century*, 271).

national debt . . . not been the cause of it: eighteenth-century rule
was very costly. The National Debt, standing at £14.2 millions
in 1700, had rocketed to £130 millions in 1763 and to £456
millions in 1800. Its basis was the nexus of interests linking the
post-Revolution dynasty, the financial and commercial worlds, and
the tax-paying public. Making war, maintaining empire, and
regulating trade found mutual support in the machinery of the
Debt, but many commentators, like Smith and Hume (in 'Of
Public Credit'), were more conscious of the disadvantages of a
debt that could never actually be repaid. Smith discusses the
National Debt and its relation to economic growth at *WN*, v. iii.

338   *those of ancient Greece and Rome*: it is equally characteristic of
the Scottish Enlightenment thinkers to hope to generate by
analogy laws for understanding the development of societies in
history and to insist, as here, on the impossibility of sustaining
inquiry in such terms. What is of interest is the interplay of
similarities and differences across societies and historical ages.
What becomes clear in the course of this chapter is that, as far
as Smith can see, there is no economic case for colonies and
therefore for empire; that the monopolies which empire establishes, of whatever kind, impoverish the homeland.

339   *by alienation*: see note to p. 233 above.

The tribunes . . . fundamental law of the republick: Smith refers here to the tribunes of the people, officials appointed to protect the interests and rights of the plebeians from the Roman aristocracy. In *Lectures on Rhetoric and Belles Lettres*, he notes of the tribunes: 'The method of these men, who from their attachment to the Populace were called Populares, was to propose Laws for the equall division of Lands and the distributing of Corn at the Publick charge, or else by Largesses and bounties bestowed out of their own private fortune. Of this sort were Clodius, Marius, and others' (ii. 157; p. 156) [Campbell and Skinner].

340   *The Latin word . . . a going out of the house*: Latin *Colonia*, from *colo* (verb), 'I cultivate' and *colonus* (noun), 'a cultivator, farmer'. Greek ἀποικια, from ἀπο (prep.), 'away' and ἡοἰκια (noun), 'house, home'.

341   *Columbus*: Christopher Columbus (*c*.1451–1506), an Italian navigator and adventurer; credited with the discovery of America in 1492. His early voyages were supported by the Spanish monarchs Ferdinand II and Isabella, whose marriage had united the kingdoms of Aragon and Castile. In all, Columbus made four voyages to North and South America, though he died convinced that it had been Asiatic lands which he had explored.

St. Domingo: Hispaniola (Haiti), where Columbus made an early landing.

fillets: ornamental headbands.

manati: or manatee, a freshwater cetacean inhabiting the rivers and estuaries of the tropical Atlantic shore.

added greatly to the novelty of the shew: in 1710 four Iroquois chiefs were brought to England and given an audience with Queen Anne. In 1762 three Cherokee chiefs were paraded in London. There developed a rich English and European literature on the American Indian in the course of the eighteenth century. An Indian princess sold into slavery by her ungrateful English lover (a calculating young merchant) is the heroine of the sentimental tale of Inkle and Yarico, popularized by Steele in the *Spectator*, No. 11 (1711), and recast in many later versions. Prévost's novel *Cleveland* (1732–9) gives an idealized representation of South American Indians; the hero of Voltaire's satirical romance *L'Ingenu* (The Child of Nature) (1767) has been brought up among the Huron (Iroquois) Indians; and, in the context of French Revolutionary debate, the hero of Robert Bage's novel *Hermsprong; or, Man as He Is Not* (1796), also educated among American Indians, brings to British society the idealism and virtues of the natural man and the critical fervour of the born radical. William Wordsworth's *Lyrical Ballads* (1798) contain a poem entitled 'The Complaint of the Forsaken Indian Woman'. The standard early eighteenth-century history, and drawn upon by Smith, was that of the French Jesuit Joseph-François Lafitau, who lived among the Iroquois: *Mœurs des sauvages ameriquains, comparées aux mœurs des premiers temps* (1724). The authoritative late eighteenth-century view is offered by Smith's Scottish contemporary William Robertson, in his *History of America* (1777).

342   *Oieda . . . to Chili and Peru*: Alonzo de Oieda accompanied Columbus on his second voyage. When in 1509 Ferdinand II of Spain established two governments on the American continent, 'one extending from Cape de Vela to the gulf of Darien, and the other from that to Cape Gracias a Dios', Oieda took charge of the former and Diego de Nicuessa the latter (Robertson, *History of America*, i. 192). Vasco Nuñes de Bilboa settled a Spanish colony at Santa Maria on the gulf of Darien and in 1513 marched across the isthmus of Darien (modern Panama), discovering the Pacific Ocean. According to Robertson, 'the intrepidity of Balboa was such as distinguished him among his countrymen, at a period when every adventurer was conspicuous for daring courage' (*History of America*, i. 202). Hernán Cortés (*c.*1485–1547), the conqueror and for a time Governor and Captain-General (for Spain) of Mexico. Diego de Almagro and Francisco Pizarro (*c.*1475–1541), ruthless conquerors of Peru and destroyers of the Inca kingdom. Almagro grew dissatisfied with his share of the Inca spoils and rebelled against Pizarro, but was defeated and killed in 1538. Pizarro was later killed by Almagro's followers.

343   *Sir Walter Raleigh*: (*c.*1554–1618), a favourite of Queen Elizabeth I of England and an early advocate of American colonization. In 1595 he sailed in search of El Dorado, the fabulous city of untold wealth and, though he failed to find it, he

explored three or four hundred miles of the Orinoco valley, Venezuela. With the Earl of Essex in 1597 he made an unsuccessful voyage to destroy the new Spanish Armada and capture the silver fleet, and in 1616 he led an expedition, also unsuccessful, to Guiana in search of gold.

344   *The colonists carry out with them ... in the new settlement*: in his *History of America*, William Robertson employs the evolutionary method favoured by the Scottish sociological historians in order to explain the barbarism and backwardness of the indigenous inhabitants of America before the arrival of the Europeans: 'A naked savage, cowering near the fire in his miserable cabin, or stretched under a few branches which afford him a temporary shelter, has as little inclination as capacity for useless speculation. His thoughts extend not beyond what relates to animal life; and when they are not directed towards some of its concerns, his mind is totally inactive' (*History of America*, i. 312). But Robertson also wishes his 'civilized' readers to be sensitive to the confining perspectives of our own social condition, according to which cultural myopia '[i]t is extremely difficult to procure satisfying and authentic information concerning nations while they remain uncivilized ... For, in every stage of society, the faculties, the sentiments, and desires of men are so accommodated to their own state, that they become standards of excellence to themselves, they affix the idea of perfection and happiness to those attainments which resemble their own, and wherever the objects and enjoyments to which they have been accustomed are wanting, confidently pronounce a people barbarous and miserable' (i. 284). For the effect of the study of the North American Indians upon the Scottish socio-historical theorists, see Meek, *Social Science and the Ignoble Savage*, 37–67.

345   *as their fathers did before them*: Smith has commented at *WN*, I. viii (p. 70) on the high value attached to children in the American colonies; at *WN*, III. i (pp. 230–1), he notes the greater advantage to be had there from land cultivation as opposed to manufacture.

encourages that of real wealth and greatness: the obsession with population of eighteenth-century social commentators is worth considering, where population growth is synonymous with national power and further commercial progress. The idea underlies Robertson's explanation of the low sex-drive of the

impoverished American Indian, whose energies are absorbed in
obtaining subsistence and defending himself from enemies. But
'in those countries of America, where, from the fertility of the
soil, the mildness of the climate, or some farther advances . . .
in improvement, the means of subsistence are more abundant,
and the hardships of savage life are less severely felt, the animal
passion of the sexes becomes more ardent' (*History of America*,
i. 296). In his essay 'Of the Populousness of Ancient Nations',
Hume considered the conditions most favourable to population
and pointed to the connection between the political liberty,
small size, and social equality of ancient republics. Though he
then went on to expose the flaws in the government of ancient
republics, these three conditions relate interestingly to views
expressed by Smith on the rapid progress of the American
colonies, where, it seems, there is an opportunity to correct the
faults of the ancient world.

346   *Thales and Pythagoras*: Thales (*c.*636–546 BC) was born at
Miletus, one of the principal Ionian towns on the coast of Asia
Minor. He is credited by Aristotle with being the founder of
Greek philosophy. Pythagoras, a native of Samos, and active
around 530 BC, was part philosopher and part priest. He settled
at Crotona in Southern Italy.

the most sacred rights of mankind: cf. *WN*, I. x (p. 120 and note).
Locke argues that private property is inviolable. It comes into
being when people mix their labour with the stock originally
given by God to all to have in common: 'Though the Water
running in the Fountain be every ones, yet who can doubt, but
that in the Pitcher is his only who drew it out?' (*Two Treatises
of Government*, ed. Laslett, 307). By the Seven Years War
(1756–63), Britain asserted her dominance over France in the
North Atlantic and effectively affirmed the identity of the
American colonies as a vast loyal market for British manufactures, a source of valuable raw materials, and a new source of
revenue for the Treasury. Elaborate trade- and manufacturing
restrictions worked to confine the industry and diversification
of the colonies and to control by monopolies their exports and
imports through exclusive trading agreements with Britain. In
the decade between the end of the war and the Declaration of
Independence (and incidentally, the publication of *WN*) in
1776, attempts to raise revenue in the American colonies and

to defend the principle of unlimited Parliamentary sovereignty, by the Sugar Tax of 1764 and the Stamp Duty of 1765 (see note to p. 85 above) brought the situation to crisis-point. The colonists insisted on the rights of their own assemblies to exclusive control over internal policies and the raising of revenue. The cry of 'No Taxation without Representation' gained strength as a rallying call. The Whig politician Edmund Burke defended the Americans in his *Speech on Conciliation with the Colonies* (1775), where he argued that even if the British Parliament had the legal right to tax the colonists, to exercise such a right would run counter to the established habit of self-government which characterized America. Thomas Jefferson's Declaration of Independence of 1776 affirmed an important shift of emphasis: where the previous debate appeared to be over the traditional British rights of the colonists against Parliament, now it is asserted that 'all men are created equal', and that what is at stake are 'natural' rights. In Smith's argument throughout this chapter commercial, political, and natural considerations interestingly displace one another.

346 *make them for themselves*: at *WN*, II. v (pp. 220–1), Smith noted that the progress of the American colonies is attributable to a concentration on agriculture. Their domestic manufactures are not yet capable of competing with European imports, and to attempt such competition, he argues there, would retard their growth. This, however, is not an endorsement of Britain's repressive trade regulations.

347 *the same mercantile spirit*: according to Mercantilist theories, colonies were to be seen as valuable sources of raw materials, as a means of adding to the mother country's stock of bullion, as markets for surplus home products, and as dumping-grounds for excess population. The exclusive benefits of trade with colonies ensured a healthy and controlled circulation of wealth and a strong nation. See Montesquieu, *De l'esprit des lois*, XXI. xxi. 10–11: 'The colonies they [European nations] have formed are under a kind of dependence, of which there are but very few instances in all the colonies of the ancients; whether we consider them as holding of the state itself, or of some trading company established in the state. The design of these colonies is, to trade on more advantageous conditions than could otherwise be done with the neighbouring people, with whom all advantages are

reciprocal. It has been established that the metropolis, or mother
country, alone shall trade in the colonies, and that from very good
reason; because the design of the settlement was the extension of
commerce, not the foundation of a city or of a new empire.'

347   *for the support of the colony government*: for contemporary attacks
on this independent right to levy taxes and the consequent
constitutional confrontation, see note to p. 346 above.

three of the governments of New England: among the most vocal
of these was the Massachusetts Assembly, who sent a circular
letter to the other colonies in February 1768 calling for joint
resistance to taxation of any kind without representation, a
position which entailed independence, since sending MPs to
London was not in their minds. Of the four early administra-
tions—Massachusetts, Rhode Island, Connecticut, and New
Hampshire—only New Hampshire was a royal colony.

348   *progress of the sugar colonies . . . their negro slaves*: at *WN*, III. ii
(pp. 238–9), Smith notes of the use of slaves in the sugar colonies
that the enormous profits enjoyed by planters justify what is
otherwise an expensive form of labour. In the late eighteenth
century the exports of the French West Indian island of Saint-
Domingue were one-third more than those of all the British West
Indies combined. As a result the French planter was able to
undersell the British in the European sugar market. But Smith's
argument that such superiority was the consequence of capital
raised almost entirely from the local industry of the French
planters has been challenged by recent historians. Eric Williams
argues that the French planter 'was even more heavily in debt
than his British rival', and that the profitability of Saint-Domingue rested on the 'fertility of its soil, before it was exhausted
by over-cropping' (*From Columbus to Castro: The History of the
Caribbean 1492–1969* (London: André Deutsch, 1970), 239–40).

349   *a lettre de cachet*: originally a letter under the private seal of
the French king containing orders of exile or imprisonment.

Vedius Pollio . . . Augustus: the case is reported by Seneca in
De ira (see Seneca, *Moral Essays*, trans. J. W. Basore, 3
vols. (Loeb edn., 1928–35), i. 348–9). While the Roman republican constitution was believed by eighteenth-century political thinkers to enshrine the principles of liberty, it was agreed
that Augustus was responsible for its destruction. The tyranny

under the emperor Augustus was widely regarded as the model for those absolute monarchies still ruling in parts of Europe and Asia (see Howard D. Weinbrot, *Augustus Caesar in 'Augustan' England: The Decline of a Classical Norm* (Princeton, NJ: Princeton University Press, 1978)). Smith's argument that slaves fare better under despotic governments (like that of France) assumes the non-interference of democratic government in the management of private property: in a free country, where the rights of property are protected and owners have access to government, there is little chance of protecting slaves against injustice or of transforming their conditions. But according to Williams, such views (held by others as well as Smith) were 'fantastic': 'the slave mortality in Saint-Domingue was frightful' (*From Columbus to Castro*, 245).

350 *of the soil and industry of the colonists*: the same point is made concerning the dependency of the American colonies on British capital at *WN*, II. v (pp. 220–1).

every mark of kindness and hospitality: a note of regret for the destruction of a world of innocence is heard in many eighteenth-century accounts of the Americas, including those written by travellers there. The sea-captain George Shelvocke wrote in 1721 (in the journal which gave Coleridge his albatross) that the native Indians of California 'are endowed with all the humanity imaginable, and they make some nations (who would give these poor people the epithet of savages or barbarians) blush to think that they deserve that appellation more than they ... In a word they seem to pass their lives in the purest simplicity of the earliest ages of the world, before discord and contention were heard amongst men' (George Shelvocke, *A Voyage round the World* (1726), ed. W. G. Perrin (London: Cassell and Co., 1928), 224).

351 *The English puritans ... banished to Brazil*: Massachusetts, Rhode Island, Connecticut, and New Hampshire were the four early governments of New England, founded by Puritans leaving England from the 1620s in search of religious freedom. Maryland, named after Queen Henrietta Maria, wife of Charles I, was settled in the 1630s by Catholic gentlemen, their families and followers. In 1681 Charles II granted the territory west of the River Delaware to William Penn, in payment of a debt due by the government to Penn's grandfather. Penn colonized his

grant at once with members of his own faith, the Society of Friends or Quakers, and in 1682 founded the city of Philadelphia. Authorized by papal bull in 1478, in the reigns of Ferdinand and Isabella, Columbus's patrons, the Spanish Inquisition was designed to inquire into the orthodoxy of Jews converted to Christianity. Spanish Jews were expelled from the whole kingdom in 1492. The Inquisition soon became a powerful general instrument of royal absolutism; its jurisdiction extended throughout the Spanish empire and by the late sixteenth century included Portugal. It was not abolished until 1834.

351　*disorder and injustice . . . cultivated America*: cf. Hume: 'Peopled gradually from England by the necessitous and indigent, who, at home, increased neither wealth or populousness, the colonies, which were planted along that tract [from St Augustine to Cape Breton], have promoted the navigation, encouraged the industry, and even multiplied the inhabitants of their mother-country. The spirit of independency, which was reviving in England, here shone forth in its full lustre, and received new accessions of force from the aspiring character of those, who, being discontented with the established church and monarchy, had fought for freedom amid those savage deserts' (*History of England* (1778), vi. 186) [Campbell and Skinner].

　　a governor of Cuba: Cortés fought in the expedition under Diego Velázquez which conquered Cuba (1511–13), and was later sent by Velázquez to explore and trade with the mainland of Central America.

352　*Magna virûm Mater!*: 'Great Mother of men!' (Virgil, *Georgics*, ii. 173–4). The imaginative excitement which the idea of America arouses in Smith and Hume might be compared to Burke's eulogistic acknowledgement of the heroic adventures of the New England whalers: 'Whilst we follow them among the tumbling mountains of ice, and behold them penetrating into the deepest frozen recesses of Hudson's Bay and Davis's Straits, whilst we are looking for them beneath the arctic circle, we hear that they have pierced into the opposite region of polar cold, that they are at the antipodes, and engaged under the frozen serpent of the South. Falkland Island, which seemed too remote and romantic an object for the grasp of national ambition, is but a stage and a resting-place in the progress of their victorious industry' ('Speech on Conciliation with the Colonies', in

Edmund Burke on Government, Politics, and Society, ed. B. W. Hill (Brighton: Harvester, 1975), 169). As in Smith's tribute, the energy of Burke's vision derives from a sense of America as a land of commercial heroism.

352 *all the different branches of British industry*: see note to p. 223 for Smith's views on 'a natural balance of industry'.

353 *the whole body politick*: the sustained development of Smith's graphic medical analogy is worth attending to. The link between the circulation of the blood, the body itself as a circulatory system, and wealth as a circulatory system is consciously exploited in many economic writings from the seventeenth century onwards. François Quesnay, the leader of the Physiocrats, was a surgeon by profession who had written on human physiology and saw in the free circulation of the blood the principle of natural liberty which he was to establish as the law for economic society. His famous *Tableau Œconomique* is the first presentation of a circular-flow equilibrium in the history of economic thought. Smith exploits his analogy here. For Smith's further thoughts on the loss to Britain of the American markets, see his letter to William Eden, 15 Dec. 1783 (*Correspondence*, 271–2), and his 'Thoughts on the State of the Contest with America' (1778) (ibid. 377–85).

repeal of the stamp act: in 1766. see note to p. 85 above.

354 *consumption of Great Britain*: see note to p. 223 above, for the importance to south-west Scotland of the trade in tobacco re-exportation.

355 *returns are slow and distant*: at *WN*, IV iii (p. 309), Smith argues the advantages of trade agreements between France and Britain over those between Britain and the American Colonies, 'in which the returns were seldom made in less than three years, frequently not in less than four or five years'.

only by savings from revenue: as Smith argues at *WN*, II. iii (p. 199).

improvement of land: at *WN*, III. iv (p. 259), it was recognized, however, that land benefits enormously by the subsequent investment of mercantile profits.

356 *All the original sources of revenue*: these are outlined at *WN*, I. vi (p. 50).

357 *natural to the character of the merchant*: for Smith's settled opposition to monopolies, see note to p. 60 above. In criticizing a system which promotes the high profits of the few as damaging even to the interests of the few, Smith's argument follows characteristic lines. State regulation, he asserts, actually hampers that self-regulation in terms of which individuals promote their own good and at the same time (though unintentionally) the good of others. For Smith's explanation of the economic profitability of parsimony, see note to p. 199 above.

those two beggarly countries: see note to p. 271 above.

358 *a nation of shopkeepers*: a phrase often attributed to Napoleon, it was used long before by Adam Smith. It also formed part of a speech said to have been delivered at Philadelphia by Samuel Adams ('A nation of shopkeepers are very seldom so disinterested . . .') in August 1776, five months after the publication of *WN*. According to Patrick Colquhoun, the turn-of-the-century statistician and London magistrate, the prosperity of the English economy was based on a diversified commercial middle class and a widespread system of small investors—that is, a nation of shopkeepers: 'It is not . . . an excess of property to the few, but the extension of it among the mass of the community, which appears most likely to prove beneficial with respect to national wealth and national happiness. Perhaps no other country in the world possesses greater advantages in this respect than Great Britain, and hence that spirit of enterprise and that profitable employment of diffused capitals which has created so many resources for productive labour beyond any other country in Europe' (quoted in Porter, *English Society in the Eighteenth Century*, 97).

359 *famous act of navigation*: by 12 Car. II, c. 18 (1660), so-called non-enumerated commodities could be exported from the American and West Indian colonies directly to other countries. However, they had to be carried in British or plantation vessels owned and largely manned by British subjects. By the Act of 1660, sugar, tobacco, and cotton-wool were among the enumerated goods whose trade was confined to Britain. Navigation Acts throughout the century reclassified enumerated and non-enumerated goods and enforced a monopoly of carrying and entrepôt trade with Britain's major colonial producers.

360   *the late war . . . war which preceded it*: by the 'late war', Smith refers to the Seven Years War (1756–63), a Europe-based and a colonial and naval war. The war preceding it was the Anglo-Spanish naval war of 1739 and the War of the Austrian Succession (1740–8), between Britain on one side and France and Spain on the other. In their colonial aspect the two wars continued the long Anglo-French struggle for control of the seas and of North America, the West Indies, West Africa, and India. By the Treaty of Paris (1763), France ceded Canada to Britain as well as the Middle West of America as far as the Mississippi, and Spain ceded Florida to Britain, representing the effective if temporary hegemony of North America.

     the sinking fund: a fund introduced in 1717 and formed by periodically setting aside revenue to accumulate at interest for the purpose of reducing the principal of the National Debt. At IV. i (Glasgow Edition, 441–2), Smith states that the last war with France cost over £90 millions and added some £75 millions to the National Debt. It is in this context that he suggests, at *WN*, v. iii (pp. 460–1), that the colonies should contribute to the costs incurred in their defence. It was this proposal, adopted by government in 1764/5, which initiated colonial resistance and insistence that their own assemblies should control the raising of revenue.

361   *by any nation in the world*: see *WN*, v. iii, the concluding paragraph of the whole work, where final emphasis is placed on the illusory nature of empire.

362   *would quickly revive*: cf. Smith's 'Thoughts on America': 'tho' Canada, Nova Scotia, and the Floridas were all given up to our rebellious colonies, or were all conquered by them, yet the similarity of language and manners would in most cases dispose the Americans to prefer our alliance to that of any other nation. Their antient affection for the people of this country might revive, if they were once assured that we meant to claim no dominion over them . . . By a federal union with America we should certainly incur much less expense, and might, at the same time, gain as real advantages, as any we have hitherto derived from all the nominal dominion we have ever exercised over them' (*Correspondence*, 383).

     not represented: see note to p. 347.

363   *in the history of mankind*: Bartolomeu Dias (*c.* 1450–1500) was
the Portuguese discoverer of the sea-route to India via the Cape
of Good Hope. Cf.: 'The discovery of the new world, and the
passage to the East Indies by the Cape of Good Hope, is one
of the most important events in the history of the human
species' (G. T. F. Raynal, *Histoire philosophique et politique des
établissemens et du commerce des européens dans les deux Indes*
(Amsterdam, 1775), trans. J. Justamond (Edinburgh, 1777), i. 1)
[Campbell and Skinner]. The book was in Smith's library.

364   *than by that of the country*: according to Smith's schematized
argument in *WN*, IV, this is the basic distinction between
Mercantilist and Physiocratic policy.

366   *must necessarily have occasioned*: the rapacity and abuses of the
British East India Company are often referred to by Smith, as,
for example, in the local decay practised against the Indian
economy: *WN*, I. viii (p. 72). From 1765, when Robert Clive
formally accepted the *diwanni* (land revenues) of Bengal on behalf
of the Company, it was committed to direct political control rather
than to mere commercial activity. The consequence was a transformation of the British perception of India from exotic market
to imperial possession. Clive himself embodied most explicitly the
linkage between political power and personal fortune. In the 1760s
and 1770s furious speculation in East India stock and the government's growing interest in the Company's financial activities
turned attention to the corrupt character of East India politics
(see note to p. 325). At one point, when the Company's affairs
fell into confusion in 1772, it was suggested that Smith might
become a member of a commission to study its dealings (see
Correspondence, 164, n. 5).

367   *Moluccas*: the Spice Islands of Dutch Indonesia.

to be made by opium: At *WN*, IV. v (p. 325), Smith refers to the
abuse of rice production in Bengal as possibly contributing to the
famine of 1772.

369   *is still more so*: constitutional reforms were put in motion by
the Regulating Act of 1773 aimed at giving the East India
Company more stability in London and firmer control in India.
Warren Hastings was sent out as Governor-General of Bengal,
a Supreme Court of Justice was set up, and Bombay and Madras
were placed under the supervision of Bengal. Smith's view is

that such administrative reforms are doomed to failure because they cannot create by legislation long-term concern for the welfare of India on the part of commercial investors and Company officials.

372 *carried his whole fortune with him*: returned East India Company officials, loaded with fortunes and known as 'nabobs', were regarded in Britain as well as in India as dangerously rootless and corrupt. Oliver Goldsmith, in his poem *The Traveller, or A Prospect of Society* (1764), complains of 'The wealth of climes, where savage nations roam, | Pillaged from slaves to purchase slaves at home' (ll. 387–8). William Pitt, now Earl of Chatham and himself influential in forming British foreign policy in India, wrote in 1770 that '[t]he riches of Asia have been poured in upon us, and have brought with them not only Asiatic luxury, but, I fear, Asiatic principles of government. Without connections, without any natural interest in the soil, the importers of foreign gold have forced their way into parliament, by such a torrent of private corruption, as no private hereditary fortune could resist' (*Correspondence of William Pitt, Earl of Chatham*, ed. W. S. Taylor and J. H. Pringle, 4 vols. (London, 1838–40), iii. 405).

not have acted better themselves: Smith later (v. i) observes of the East India merchant-governors: 'No other sovereigns ever were, or, from the nature of things, ever could be, so perfectly indifferent about the happiness or misery of their subjects, the improvement or waste of their dominions, the glory or disgrace of their administration; as, from irresistible moral causes, the greater part of the proprietors of such a mercantile company are, and necessarily must be' (Glasgow Edition, 752). That the East India Company's investment was not the basis for the long-term prosperity and security of the country was ensured by a system which continued to set the self-interests of its officials and investors against the local interests. It is human nature, argues Smith throughout *WN*, to be directed by self-interest and to act as our circumstances dictate.

councils of Madras and Calcutta: the most important early English settlements in India were in Madras, Calcutta, and Bombay, and they were originally independent of one another. By the reforms of 1773 the Governor-General, assisted by a council of four assessors, took up residence in Calcutta, overseeing the other settlements from there.

374   *Conclusion of the Mercantile System: WN*, IV. viii has been reduced here to a very few pages summarizing the main points of Smith's anti-Mercantilist argument. Omitted are specific instances of the prohibitions and bounties which controlled Britain's export-import trade in the eighteenth century: for example, the ban on the importation of foreign woollen cloths and on the exportation of live sheep and wool, controls which, Smith argues, form 'a monopoly against the consumers' (Glasgow Edition, 647).

   William III. chap. 20. sect.8: an Act of 1695.

375   *14th Geo. III. chap. 71*: an Act of 1774. This and the Act of William III (above) were designed to safeguard Britain's textile industries on which so much eighteenth-century prosperity depended.

   the living instrument, the artificer: for the idea of society as a productive machine and each worker a vital part of its engine, see note to p. 163 above.

   5 Geo. I. chap. 27: an Act of 1718.

   23 Geo. II. chap. 13: an Act of 1749.

376   *devised*: bequeathed.

   to as small a number as possible: at *WN*, I. x, Smith argued against the regulations inhibiting the free circulation of labour. See note to p. 117 above.

377   *treaty of commerce with Portugal*: of 1703, by which Britain exported woollen manufactures to Portugal and imported Portuguese wines. Smith details its provisions at IV. vi (here omitted).

378   *in former wars*: for the state of the National Debt after the two recent colonial wars, see notes to pp. 337 and 360 above.

379   *a few men of great learning . . . in France*: for the doctrines of the Physiocrats and Smith's association with them, see note to p. 214 above. The term 'Physiocracy', meaning the rule of nature, was coined in 1767 by Pierre-Samuel du Pont de Nemours. The Physiocrats believed in the existence of a natural order based on the land and regarded the state's role as simply that of preserving property and upholding this natural order. They held that agriculture was the only source of wealth and therefore that this sector should be taxed by a single tax. In

this, and in their advocacy for free trade, their views were directly opposed to those of the Mercantilists. (See Elizabeth Fox-Genovese, *The Origins of Physiocracy*.)

379 *Mr. Colbert*: Jean-Baptiste Colbert, one of Louis XIV's chief ministers, leader of the Council of Finances (1661), Superintendent of Royal Buildings, Arts, and Manufactures (1664), Controller-General of Finances (1665), and Secretary of State for the Navy (1668). Using the new Council of Commerce, established in 1664, he applied a rigorous Mercantilist policy. He encouraged the export of home manufactures and discouraged the import of foreign goods. He discouraged the export of raw materials used in industry and encouraged their import. He forbade craftsmen to emigrate and persuaded foreign skilled workmen—Dutch weavers, German miners, Italian silk- and glass-workers—to settle in France by offering special privileges. His investment in towns kept food prices low, and limitations on the market worked against agriculture. He encouraged the colonization of Canada (New France). Colbert has been seen as responsible for providing the resources which enabled Louis XIV to establish absolutism in France.

382 *racked rent*: rent raised above a fair and reasonable amount.

384 *common character of the people*: in the sociological investigations of the French and Scottish Enlightenment thinkers, the dominant mode of subsistence in a given society was significantly influential on its wider development. Not only will laws and institutions reflect epiphenomenally a society's modes of production at any given time, but human personality will be generated by the same economic means. This assumption underlies the sociological analyses of John Millar, Smith's pupil at Glasgow University. See, for example, his *Origin of the Distinction of Ranks* (1771).

386 *Mr. Quesnai . . . a very speculative physician*: on the link between medical and economic theories, see note to p. 353 above.

387 *to better his own condition*: a belief in the supremacy of natural, individual effort is a frequent argumentative strategy of Smith's (see, for example, p. 203 and note). Such effort surmounts the obstacles of state regulation and confining doctrine and, devolving on to the individual the responsibility for constructing a destiny which is at the same time socially and economically

determined, it appears to absolve the political economist from
the necessity for a fully articulated alternative economic procedure.

387 *impropriety of this representation*: at *WN*, II. iii, Smith argued for
a distinction between what he called there 'productive and unproductive labour', and in a note (to p. 191) he observed that
'[s]ome French authors of great learning and ingenuity have used
those words in a different sense'. He promises: 'In the last chapter
of the fourth book, I shall endeavour to show that their sense is
an improper one.' It would seem, however, from his summary
here that Smith's criticism of the Physiocratic position is based
on a misunderstanding or at least a relocation of their usage of
the terms 'productive' and 'unproductive'. In Physiocratic doctrine, productivity has to do with the system of wealth circulation
and not, as in Smith's reconstruction of their position, the forms
of labour. (See Keith Tribe, *Land, Labour, and Economic Discourse*,
108.)

388 *more productive than that of . . . manufacturers*: see p. 218 above
and note.

in the very instant of their performance: see p. 192 above and
note.

productive . . . labour: at *WN*, II. iii.

This system: of the Physiocrats. According to his biographer and
pupil Dugald Stewart, Smith thought so well of the Physiocrat
leader Quesnay that he intended to dedicate *WN* to him and
was only prevented from doing so by Quesnay's death (Stewart,
'Account of the Life and Writings of Adam Smith, LL.D.', in
Essays on Philosophical Subjects, 304).

political œconomy: see note to p. 10 above.

unconsumable riches of money: according to Keith Tribe, Smith's
assessments of Mercantilism and Physiocracy, which form the
subject of *WN*, IV, both seriously misrepresent these doctrines
and distort all previous writings on the economy of the state by
arbitrarily fixing them in one of two schools. In particular, in
characterizing Mercantilism as a preoccupation with the amassing
of money and the restrictive trade practices which would ensure
this, Smith, according to Tribe, 'simply initiates a popular mis-
conception that has remained to this day' (*Land, Labour, and
Economic Discourse*, 108).

388   *perfect liberty*: the principles of liberty underpinning Physiocratic doctrine were to operate within certain restrictions.
Though the Physiocrats have been seen as providing the economic theory for the French Revolution, their agrarian vision
was centred in the gentleman farmer, not the democratic community of an independent and thriving peasantry. See S. T.
Coleridge's criticism of the popular espousal of Physiocratic
notions in *The Statesman's Manual* (1816): 'It seems a paradox
only to the unthinking, and it is a fact that none, but the unread
in history, will deny, that in periods of popular tumult and
innovation the more abstract a notion is, the more readily has
it been found to combine, the closer has appeared its affinity,
with the feelings of a people and with all their immediate
impulses to action. At the commencement of the French revolution, in the remotest villages every tongue was employed in
echoing and enforcing the almost geometrical abstractions of
the physiocratic politicians and economists. The public roads
were crowded with armed enthusiasts disputing on the inalienable sovereignty of the people, the imprescriptible laws of
the pure reason, and the universal constitution, which, as rising
out of the nature and rights of man as man, all nations
alike were under the obligation of adopting' (*The Collected
Works of Samuel Taylor Coleridge*, 16 vols. (London: Routledge
& Kegan Paul, 1971–), vol. vi, *Lay Sermons*, ed. R. J. White
(1972), 15–16).

389   *The Œconomists*: or the *Secte* were the names by which the
Physiocrats were most commonly known among their contemporaries.

in favour of agriculture: in place of a multiple tax system, the
Physiocrats advocated a single and smaller land tax and the free
movement of agricultural products from province to province
and from country to city. In this way they hoped to remove
the limitations on the market which had worked against agricultural productivity since the time of Colbert. At v. ii, Smith
notes the Physiocratic views on land tax: 'A tax upon the rent of
land which varies with every variation of the rent, or which rises
and falls according to the improvement or neglect of cultivation,
is recommended by that sect of men of letters in France, who
call themselves the œconomists, as the most equitable of all taxes'
(Glasgow Edition, 830).

389   *the doctrine of Mr. Quesnai*: see notes to pp. 214 and 379 above.
Anne-Robert-Jacques Turgot was a follower of Quesnay. He
wrote *Reflections on the Formation and Distribution of Riches*
(1769), and, as minister under Louis XVI, decreed the free
circulation of grain inside France (Sept. 1774), only to have his
experiments in liberalization ruined by the bad harvest of 1774
and the food riots of 1775. Turgot's failure in implementing
Physiocratic policy in the mid-1770s has been seen as discre-
diting the school's claims for a new socio-economic order.
Pierre-Samuel du Pont de Nemours, editor of Quesnay's *Physio-
cratie* (1768), wrote *Origin and Progress of a New Science* [that
is, of political economy] (1767). Two Physiocrat journals appeared in the 1760s, both edited for a time by du Pont: *Journal
de l'agriculture* (1765–6) and *Ephémérides du citoyen* (1768–72),
which advocated an agrarian equivalent of the citizen virtues
constructed in the essays of the English bourgeois periodical
the *Spectator*. Other literary spin-offs included plays, like *Les
Moissonneurs*, translated as *The Reapers: or the Englishman out
of Paris* (1770). (For the literary dissemination of Physiocratic
views, see Kenneth Maclean, *Agrarian Age: A Background for
Wordsworth*, 65–86.) The fashionable appeal of an aristocratic
agrarianism is exemplified by Marie Antoinette playing at shep-
herdesses. In Paris in 1766 Smith mixed with members of the
Physiocratic School at the height of its powers. His library
contained a rich selection of their works.

Mr. Mercier de la Riviere: a member of the Parlement of Paris
and sometime intendant of Martinique. His book is *L'Ordre
naturel et essentiel des sociétés politiques* (1767).

390   *Marquis de Mirabeau*: in his *Philosophie rurale ou économie
générale et politique de l'agriculture, pour servir de suite à l'ami
des hommes*, 3 vols. (Amsterdam, 1763), i. 44 (cited in Maclean,
Agrarian Age, 66). Mirabeau was Quesnay's early collaborator
and propagator of Physiocracy.

it has already been observed: see the opening sentence of *WN*,
III. i (p. 227).

391   *of its own accord*: similar sentiments are expressed at various points
in the argument of *WN*, IV with reference to merchant investors
and the deregulation of colonial trade (see, for example, pp. 292
and 354). Earlier at *WN*, I. x (pp. 120–1), the liberty of the

common workman to employ his labour as he sees fit is defended against apprenticeship regulations. The 'system of natural liberty' extends, it appears, to all areas of the economy from the humblest to the most powerful member.

393 *Of the Revenue of the Sovereign or Commonwealth*: where the argument of *WN*, IV has been directed towards justifying a society of 'natural liberty', *WN*, V seeks to establish the economic role of government and the limits to its powers in such a society: what expenditures properly devolve on the statesman in a free commercial society? what are the legitimate means of raising revenue to support such expenditures? Smith's views on the state organization of services, detailed in *WN*, V. i, are highly topical in the late twentieth century in the emphasis placed on considerations of efficiency, the role of markets, and the possibilities of some services being self-financing. Consequently large sections of Chapter I are presented here. But *WN*, V. ii and iii, which discuss the justice and forms of taxation and the guaranteeing of public debts, have been reduced to a few pages.

in the different periods of improvement: the discussions of *WN*, V. i are set within the context of the influential 'four-stages' theory of social organization, according to which civil and administrative institutions alter as the material basis of society—the way in which people interact with the environment to gain subsistence—changes. The idea of a stadial explanation of social development—usually in terms of the hunting, shepherd, farming, and commercial economies—was widely accepted by Enlightenment thinkers and is more fully explained by Smith in *Lectures on Jurisprudence* (1762–3), i. 27–32 (pp. 14–16) (see note to p. 8 above). Highly speculative, the four-stages theory yet provided, by the law of analogy, what amounted to empirical evidence for the remotest European past in the shape of the varying states of the societies which the modern commercial European encountered. Together with the historical survey presented at *WN*, III. ii and iii, the discussion here offers the fullest treatment in *WN* of the economic roots of social structures.

native tribes of North America: representing mankind in his earliest state (see note to p. 150 above). At *WN*, II. iii (p. 207), Smith observes that 'at the invasion of Julius Caesar' the native British 'were nearly in the same state with the savages in North America'.

393   *nations of shepherds*: see note to p. 246 above.

395   *Thucydides*: the Athenian historian (*c*.462–395 BC). The reference is to his *History of the Peloponnesian War*: 'not only are the nations of Europe unable to compete, but even in Asia, nation against nation, there is none which can make a stand against the Scythians if they all act in concert' (ii. 97, trans. C. F. Smith, 4 vols. (Loeb edn., 1919–23), i. 446–7) [Campbell and Skinner]. The Scottish historical method was given respectable pedigree by reference to the comparative method of Thucydides, often called the father of scientific history. See Ferguson, *An Essay on the History of Civil Society*, ed. Forbes, 80.

   yet more advanced state of society: the agricultural stage, accompanied by the acquisition and settled cultivation of land, the next stage after the nomadic shepherd stage.

396   *the second Persian war*: in 480 BC. During this war battles were fought at Artemisium, Thermopylae, and Salamis, and Athens was sacked by the Persians.

   the Peloponesian war: the Peloponnese is the penninsula forming the southern Greek mainland. The First Peloponnesian War was from *c*.460–446 BC, between Athens and the Spartan alliance. The Second or Great Peloponnesian War was 431–404 BC.

   Thucydides observes: 'For before this summer the enemy's invasions, being of short duration, did not prevent the Athenians from making full use of the land during the rest of the year; but at this time, the occupation being continuous . . . the Athenians were suffering great damage' (*History of the Peloponnesian War*, vii. 27, trans. C. F. Smith, iv. 48–9) [Campbell and Skinner].

   the siege of Veii: the great Etruscan city and rival to Rome in its early days, Veii was besieged and eventually captured in 405–396 BC. Livy records the public payment of Roman soldiers: 'the senate . . . granted the people the most seasonable boon which has ever been bestowed on them by the chiefs of the state, when they decreed, without waiting for any suggestion by the plebs or their tribunes, that the soldiers should be paid from the public treasury, whereas till then every man had served at his own costs' (iv. 59, trans. B. O. Foster, 13 vols. (Loeb edn., 1922), ii. 450–1) [Campbell and Skinner].

397   *the feudal law*: *WN*, III. iv (pp. 262–3), Smith distinguishes allodial from feudal. See the note to p. 262 for the transition from allodial to feudal possession in England during the course of the Middle Ages.

more advanced state of society: referring to the commercial stage.

progress of manufactures . . . art of war: in *Lectures on Jurisprudence* (1762–3), iv. 85 (p. 232), Smith cites the same causes as contributing to the general military decline of advanced society. In 'Of Refinement in the Arts', Hume argues that the higher productivity of a commercial society provides a fund on which the statesman may draw in time of war to employ men in military service. In particular, he notes that improvements in agriculture and manufacture find their equivalents in the military sector: troops raised in a commercial society may be less ferocious than those drawn from barbarous societies, but they are more skilful and better disciplined. Consequently, a rich commercial society is likely to be a greater military power than its less-advanced rivals. He observes: 'Nor need we fear, that men, by losing their ferocity, will lose their martial spirit, or become less daunted and vigorous in defence of their country or their liberty. The arts have no such effect in enervating either the mind or body. On the contrary, industry, their inseparable attendant, adds new force to both' (*Essays Moral, Political, and Literary*, 279–81).

maintained by the publick . . . in its service: at *WN*, II. iii (p. 192), Smith numbers among the 'unproductive labourers' of society '{t]he sovereign . . . with all the officers both of justice and war who serve under him, the whole army and navy . . . They are the servants of the publick, and are maintained by a part of the annual produce of the industry of other people. Their service, how honourable, how useful, or how necessary soever, produces nothing for which an equal quantity of service can afterwards be procured.'

398   *without ruin to the country which pays . . . their service*: Smith employs some of the same calculations and figures in *Lectures on Jurisprudence* (1762–3), iv. 78–81 (pp. 229–31).

399   *the Campus Martius . . . the Gymnasium*: the Plain of Mars, named after the Roman god of war, was an open space outside

the city walls where the youths of Rome performed military exercises and games. The Greek gymnasium was a complex of grounds and buildings dedicated to the same purpose.

399   *other military exercises*: the Wappenshaws in Scotland were one such feudal institution. They were periodical days of muster, when men within a specific area had to turn out for the purpose of review, to check that each was armed in accordance with his rank and ready to take the field if required. In *Old Mortality* (1816), ch. 2, Walter Scott describes the revival of such musters at the end of the seventeenth century.

    the noblest of all arts: cf. 'A Prince, therefore, should have no other object or thought, nor acquire skill in anything, except war, its organization, and its discipline. The art of war is all that is expected of a ruler' (Niccolo Machiavelli, *The Prince*, trans. George Bull (Harmondsworth: Penguin, rev. edn, 1975), 87).

401   *Militias have been of several different kinds*: the revival of the English militia in 1757 brought large numbers of men into temporary military service and gave to the, often far-flung, wars in which Britain was engaged in the second half of the eighteenth century an immediate and domestic sense of theatre. Langford observes of the two great militia camps established in the late 1770s in Kent and Essex: 'They became the objects of intense interest to Londoners. A primitive coach service was organized, and various forms of commercial exploitation took place, including side-shows, prostitution, and gaming. The militia themselves operated in a rather unreal atmosphere, training in the midst of civilian society for a war which might never come close, but which, if it did, would become one of deadly seriousness' (*A Polite and Commercial People*, 628). Agitation for a militia in Scotland in the 1750s and 1760s was all the keener for the knowledge that government considered Scottish loyalty in question after the events of the 1745/6 Jacobite rebellion. The Poker Club was founded in Edinburgh in 1762 to campaign for a Scottish militia. Adam Ferguson and William Robertson were prominent members, as was Smith. An Act for raising a Scottish militia was not passed until 1797, in expectation of a French invasion.

403   *Prussian troops*: during the eighteenth century England's peacetime standing army was small compared to others in Europe:

in war in 1794 its strength was 45,000 compared to the might of Prussia's 190,000. Frederick II (the Great), King of Prussia from 1740 to 1786, had inherited a militarized state and a huge army from his father. This army ranked third or fourth strongest in Europe, while Prussia itself was only the tenth-largest country in size and thirteenth in population.

404 *seldom sufficient to detain them*: in *Lectures on Jurisprudence* (1766), 331–2 (pp. 540–1), Smith links the decline of the martial spirit to economic advancement and cites as evidence the temporary military success of the uncommercialized Scottish Highlanders on their journey south in 1745/6. The Highlanders and the tribes of Central Asia are elsewhere considered as occupying the same social state. See note to p. 267 above.

veterans of France and Spain: every British war of the mid-eighteenth century was sooner or later a war against France and Spain. The British army which faced France and Spain in the Seven Years War (1756–63), in the colonies, and less significantly in Europe, was better trained and more experienced than that which had turned out against the same enemies in the 1740s, when, it was objected by one contemporary that '[t]he far greater part of our *British* soldiers labour'd under the disadvantage, of having never yet had an opportunity to see an enemy in the field' (quoted in Langford, *A Polite and Commercial People*, 621).

405 *as dangerous to liberty*: Smith's advocacy of a standing army over a militia needs to be seen in the context of an earlier Scottish debate, often republican, over the link between state policy and civic liberty, and in particular those qualities necessary to form the virtuous and the free citizen. This debate was made significant and eventually redundant in the context of Union with England, whereby in 1707 the independent Scottish Parliament was sacrificed. The influential tradition in political philosophy which derived virtue from the martial virtue (*virtus*, Latin: 'strength') of the independent soldier-citizen of the Graeco-Roman city republics was bound up with the identity of the citizen as a man actively engaged in the executive assemblies of the community and prepared in the citizen army for the defence of his liberty. To anti-Unonists and republicans like Andrew Fletcher (1653–1716), standing armies assured monarchs of arbitrary power while militias stood for the right of

each subject to defend his liberty (see his *Discourse of Government with relation to Militias* (1698)). Later, in his 'Idea of a Perfect Commonwealth' (*Political Discourses* (1752)), Hume argued that the perfect commonwealth's defence should be entrusted to a universal militia of 20,000 men called out annually in rotation for training. Such a system, Hume felt, would provide the people with the surest guarantee of their liberty. (For the Scottish militia debate, see John Robertson, 'The Scottish Enlightenment at the Limits of the Civic Tradition', in Hont and Ignatieff, (eds.) *Wealth and Virtue*, 137–78.) Smith (pp. 399–400) argues his preference for a standing army largely on economic rather than moral or political grounds—that modern warfare with its expert weapons is necessarily expensive and that it will therefore be conducted more efficiently and economically by a specialized force. But later in the same chapter (at pp. 433–6) he adjusts his preference on social and moral grounds, arguing this time in terms of the welfare of the people.

405   *standing army of Caesar . . . of Cromwell*: disobeying the Senate ruling that he should disband his army, Julius Caesar, the conqueror of Gaul, crossed the Rubicon, the river separating his province from Italy, and marched towards Rome. He achieved the victory in the ensuing civil war which ended the Republic, and was Dictator of Rome from 48–44 BC. Oliver Cromwell (1599–1658), the Puritan general in the English Civil War, created in his New Model Army of the 1640s a power-base which made him the strongest man in England. On 20 April 1653 he brought musketeers into the House and dispersed what was left of the Long Parliament. Thereafter he remained sole ruler by virtue of his position as Commander-in-Chief of the Army.

favourable to liberty: this is a characteristically Smithian piece of arguing in its suggestion that, where civil authority is supported by military might, even the public display of 'licentious liberty' can confidently be tolerated.

406   *mortar . . . catapulta*: a mortar was a short piece of artillery for throwing shells or bombs; the ballista and catapulta were early military engines for hurling stones and other heavy missiles.

406   *the invention of gun-powder*: cf. Francis Bacon: 'It is well to observe the force and virtue and consequence of discoveries, and these are to be seen nowhere more conspicuously than in those three which were unknown to the ancients, and of which the origin, though recent, is obscure and inglorious; namely, printing, gunpowder, and the magnet [Mariner's Needle]. For these three have changed the whole face and state of things throughout the world' (*Novum Organum* (1620), I. 129).

407   *extension of civilization*: in explaining the fall of Rome to the German tribes, Smith observes (v. i): 'It was brought about by the irresistible superiority which the militia of a barbarous, has over that of a civilized nation; which the militia of a nation of shepherds, has over that of a nation of husbandmen, artificers, and manufacturers' (Glasgow Edition, 704). It is only improvements in technology, themselves the consequences of a progressive society, which can come to compensate for the loss of martial vigour which necessarily attends such progress. Langford notes the concern, expressed in several quarters in the late eighteenth century, that advances in military technology were making war increasingly terrible (*A Polite and Commercial People*, 623).

408   *the principal causes ... of that valuable property*: in *Lectures on Jurisprudence* (1762–3), iv. 21, Smith notes that it is in the second stage of society, 'the age of shepherds', that 'government first commences'. And he continues: 'Property makes it absolutely necessary' (p. 208). Cf. Locke, *Two Treatises of Government*: 'whereas Government has no other end but the preservation of Property' (ed. Laslett, 347). In *Origin of the Distinction of Ranks* (1781), John Millar offers one of the fullest explanations of the progress of civilization and of property as the key to the changing relations of society in its various stages. In particular, this work contains one of the most comprehensive contemporary examinations of sexuality as a function of property in history. Millar observes: 'The acquisition of property among shepherds has also a considerable effect upon the commerce of the sexes' (p. 71). In particular, Millar's third chapter, 'The Authority of a Chief over the Members of a Tribe or Village', offers a close comparison with Smith's argument in the next few pages on the four sources of authority.

409 *in maintaining a thousand men*: Smith has considered at *WN*, III. iv (pp. 260–6), and in much the same terms, the variations in the authority of riches in a rude and civilized society.

410 *in this period of society*: cf. Millar, *Origin of the Distinction of Ranks*: 'In the most rude and barbarous ages, little or no property can be acquired by particular persons; and, consequently, there are no differences of rank to interrupt the free intercourse of the sexes. The pride of family as well as the insolence of wealth, is unknown; and there are no distinctions among individuals, but those which arise from their age and experience, from their strength, courage, and other personal qualities' (pp. 18–19).

Arabian scherif: or *shereef*, a descendant of Mohammed through his daughter Fatima. Hence used as the title of certain Arab princes (*OED*).

Tartar khan: a lord or prince; specifically, the title given to the supreme rulers over the Turkish, Tartar, and Mongol tribes during the Middle Ages (*OED*).

411 *illustration*: distinction, illustriousness (as at *WN*, III. iv (p. 269)).

among nations of shepherds: cf. *Lectures on Jurisprudence* (1766), 28 (p. 407): 'In no age is antiquity of family more respected than in this.' See, too, note to p. 267 above.

413 *who have none at all*: Hume argues the point rather differently, commenting that '[n]o one can doubt, that the convention for the distinction of property, and for the stability of possession, is of all circumstances the most necessary to the establishment of human society'. And it is only 'by establishing the rule for the stability of possession' that society renders compatible with its own security those very qualities on which the accumulation of property depends, namely the 'avidity' 'of acquiring goods and possessions for ourselves and our nearest friends', a passion which left unchecked is 'insatiable, perpetual, universal, and directly destructive of society' (*Treatise of Human Nature*, ed. Nidditch, 491–2). What both Smith and Hume take for granted as necessarily emerging in the course of history—institutions which endorse an inequality of property—were attacked by Jean-Jacques Rousseau as injurious to the many, as pandering to the worst elements in human nature, and as a 'fraudulent' social contract: 'Such was, or must have been, the origin of

society and of laws, which put new fetters on the weak and gave new powers to the rich, which irretrievably destroyed natural liberty, established for all time the law of property and inequality, transformed adroit usurpation into irrevocable right, and for the benefit of a few ambitious men subjected the human race thenceforth to labour, servitude and misery' (*Discourse on the Origins and Foundations of Inequality among Men* (1755), trans. Maurice Cranston (Harmondsworth: Penguin, 1984), 122). For Smith and Hume, the emergence of social institutions is in some sense natural; but for Rousseau it is a distortion and a deception played by the rich few upon the many. The two sides of the argument can be seen to inform the challenges to and protection of property rights in the era of the French Revolution.

414 *good roads ... harbours, &c.*: for the importance of good communications and transport facilities to the commercial economy of eighteenth-century Britain, see *WN*, I. iii and I. xi (p. 149) and note to pp. 27–8 above.

415 *The post-office*: from early in the eighteenth century London had its own local penny post, a service which changes in the regulations permitted other cities to emulate only after 1765. Generally speaking, the eighteenth-century postal service was expensive, badly administered, and politically corrupt. Postmasters were given a monopoly of 'posting' travellers in 1660, and they excluded competition.

post-chaises: travelling carriages, either hired privately from stage to stage of a journey, or drawn by horses so hired (*OED*). Unlike a stage-coach, which went along particular routes between major towns at specified times, the post-chaise travelled at the hirer's pleasure, and so it was the most expensive, if also the most rapid and convenient, mode of travel. Parson Woodforde paid the huge sum of £4. 8s. in 1774 for a post-chaise to travel the hundred miles from Oxford to Castle Cary in Somerset, a distance which he covered in a day (see *The Diary of a Country Parson*, ed. John Beresford, 5 vols. (Oxford: Oxford University Press, 1924–31), i. 131).

416 *lighting and paving ... of London*: local Acts for the lighting of London streets became effective from 1736 and operated in terms of a rating system on inhabitants. The first Westminster

Paving Act of 1762 was one of a series of mid-century Improvement Acts establishing, according to Dorothy George, 'a new code of street behaviour'. Acts relating to sewage and the removal of rubbish followed (*London Life in the Eighteenth Century*, 108–9). See note to p. 151.

416   *the six days labour*: known as 'statute labour', this was a definite amount of labour on works of public utility required by statute to be performed by the residents in the district concerned. Money could be paid to commute the service. See note to p. 243.

intendants: in France, officers in charge of departments of public business.

Corvées: forced labour. Suppression of the *corvées* and their replacement by a tiered system of district and provincial representative bodies was an item of Physiocratic policy.

417   *the Turkish Company . . . English embassies to Russia*: from the end of the sixteenth century various joint-stock companies, formed to open up trade in Russia, the Levant, Turkey, and the East Indies, provided diplomatic and managerial services in markets where independent enterprises would have met with little success.

418   *joint stock companies*: business enterprises in which the capital is divided into small units permitting a number of investors to contribute varying amounts to the total, profits being divided between stockholders in proportion to the number of shares they each own. Such companies developed from the late sixteenth century in response to ventures like overseas trading which required high capital investment. Their business was regulated by the Statutory Company Act of 1720.

temporary monopoly . . . of a new book to its author: cf. *Lectures on Jurisprudence* (1762–3), ii. 31–2 (p. 83): 'Some indeed contend that the book is an intire new production of the authors and therefore ought in justice to belong to him and his heirs for ever, and that no one should be allowed to print or sell it but those to whom he has given leave, by the very laws of naturall reason. But it is evident that printing is no more than a speedy way of writing. Now suppose that a man had wrote a book and had lent it to another who took a copy of it, and that he afterwards sold this copy to a third; would there be here any reason to think the writer was injured. I can see none, and the same must hold equally with regard to printing. The only benefit one would have by writing a book, from the natural laws of reason, would be that he would have the first of the market and may be thereby a considerable gainer.' The Copyright Act of 1709 limited copyright in books already published to twenty-one years and in future books to a maximum of twenty-eight years. This act had been recently enforced by a ruling of 1774. If copyright had no limit, the holder (usually the bookseller at this time) could of course use it to keep the price of books as high as the market could stand and so restrain the competition of cheap editions.

418   *determine*: expire.

419   *malversation*: corrupt administration.

420   *Of the Expence . . . for the Education of Youth*: the views which Smith expresses here on university education are supported by a long letter of 20 Sept. 1774 to William Cullen, Professor of the Practice of Medicine at Edinburgh University (see *Correspondence*, 173–9). So closely do the letter and this section of *WN* correspond, that it is likely they were written at the same time (according to Campbell and Skinner, *Adam Smith*, 157). As Smith sees it, university education should be subject to the same system of natural liberty which he advocates for other areas of a commercial society—namely, free competition and market forces. In particular, he suggests that the monopolistic practices of the universities should be curbed in favour of the private enterprise of independent teachers. What is advocated, in effect, is a customer-driven educational model at university level. Smith writes to Cullen: 'I have thought a great deal upon this subject, and have inquired very carefully into the constitution and history of several of the principal Universities of Europe' (*Correspondence*, 174). It is not difficult to discern in these pages an apparent precedent for certain British government policies on higher education as developed in the 1980s. Yet the analogy is historically disturbing and inexact: Smith does not envisage a situation where government holds the purse-strings while at the same time demanding that universities devise educational policies on market principles; further, Smith's argument needs to be seen in the context of a more general attack on the moribund and intellectually marginalized

methods of England's two universities, and not as an anti-intellectual attack *per se*. Far from it; this was an age of high intellectual and scientific achievement and of good-quality free-market instruction—from prestigious Dissenting academies (set up to cater for those excluded by religious qualifications from England's Anglican grammar schools and universities) to public lectures and commercial schools.

420   *in proportion to the necessity . . . that exertion*: cf. Mandeville, *The Fable of the Bees*, Part II: 'you never saw Men so entirely devote themselves to their Calling, and pursue Business with that Eagerness, Dispatch and Perseverance in any Office or Preferment, in which the yearly Income is certain and unalterable, as they often do in those Professions, where the Reward continually accompanies the Labour, and the Fee immediately, either precedes the Service they do to others, as it is with the Lawyers, or follows it, as it is with the Physicians' (ed. Kaye, ii. 355) [Campbell and Skinner].

421   *fees of his pupils*: Smith regarded the Scottish universities, despite 'all their faults', as 'without exception the best seminaries of learning that are to be found any where in Europe'; and he attributed this in some part to the dependency of teachers in the Scottish system on the fees paid directly by their pupils. In Oxford, on the contrary, where Smith had spent six unhappy years as a Snell Exhibitioner, the endowments of the colleges secured large incomes irrespective of industry or excellence. Such financial certainty has the effect, he argues, of absolving the teachers from all effort in their profession (see *Correspondence*, 173–5). Again, cf. Mandeville, *The Fable of the Bees*: 'Professors should, besides their Stipends allowed 'em by the Publick, have Gratifications from every Student they teach, that Self-Interest as well as Emulation and the Love of Glory might spur them on to Labour and Assiduity . . . Universities should be publick Marts for all manner of Literature, as your Annual Fairs . . . are for different Wares and Merchandizes' (ed. Kaye, i. 293–4).

422   *given up . . . even the pretence of teaching*: as the sites of much of the major intellectual activity of the mid-eighteenth century, the Scottish universities became noted for the academic rigour and progressive nature of their teaching at a time when their counterparts in England were labelled backward-looking or

stagnant. While Oxford in the 1740s (Smith was a student there from 1740 to 1746) was the scene of dissipation and political intrigue (much of it Jacobite), the universities of Scotland, with Glasgow and Edinburgh in the van, were forging new syllabuses on high liberal principles, with specialist professors and greater standards of efficiency. Edward Gibbon, a student at Magdalen College, Oxford, in the 1750s, later expressed his disappointment at the education offered him there and criticized the university in consciously Smithian terms: 'From the toil of reading or thinking or writing they had absolved their conscience, and the first shoots of learning and ingenuity withered on the ground without yielding any fruit to the owners or the public . . . The silence of the Oxford professors, which deprives the youth of public instruction, is imperfectly supplied by the tutors, as they are styled, of the several colleges. Instead of confining themselves to a single science . . . they teach or promise to teach either history or mathematics, or ancient literature or moral philosophy; and as it is possible that they may be defective in all, it is highly probable that of some they will be ignorant. They are paid indeed by private contributions; but their appointment depends on the head of the house: their diligence is voluntary, and will consequently be languid, while the pupils themselves and their parents are not indulged in the liberty of choice or change' (*Memoirs of My Life*, ed. Betty Radice (Harmondsworth: Penguin, 1984), 80–1).

423 *physick*: medicine.

a sort of statutes of apprenticeship: for Smith's views on the monopolistic effects of apprenticeship regulations, their failure to ensure skilled work, and their early provision of a model for university degree structures, see *WN*, I. x (pp. 118–21). In his letter to Cullen, Smith observes that the same monopolistic tendencies of university degree regulations 'have banished almost all useful and solid education from the greater part of Universities' (*Correspondence*, 177). Gibbon, too, derives the 'use of academical degrees' from 'the mechanic corporations in which an apprentice, after serving his time, obtains a testimonial of his skill, and a licence to practise his trade and mystery' (*Memoirs of My Life*, 77).

425 *this sham-lecture*: in contrast, John Millar reports on the vigour and erudition of Smith's own lecturing technique as Professor

of Moral Philosophy at Glasgow University: 'There was no situation in which the abilities of Mr Smith appeared to greater advantage than as a Professor. In delivering his lectures, he trusted almost entirely to extemporary elocution. His manner, though not graceful, was plain and unaffected; and, as he seemed to be always interested in the subject, he never failed to interest his hearers . . . By the fulness and variety of his illustrations, the subject gradually swelled in his hands, and acquired a dimension which, without a tedious repetition of the same views, was calculated to seize the attention of his audience, and to afford them pleasure, as well as instruction . . . His reputation as a Professor was accordingly raised very high, and a multitude of students from a great distance resorted to the University, merely upon his account' (in Stewart, 'Account of the Life and Writings of Adam Smith', in *Essays on Philosophical Subjects*, 275–6).

425 *twelve or thirteen years of age*: Smith himself went to Glasgow University in 1737, at the age of 14, which was not at all unusual at that time.

426 *publick schools*: schools endowed for the benefit of the public and carried on under some kind of public management, like the grammar schools, some of which dated from Tudor times.

427 *musical education of the Greeks*: Smith has earlier in this chapter noted that '[i]n the republicks of antient Greece, every free citizen was instructed, under the direction of the publick magistrate, in gymnastic exercises and in musick . . . By . . . musick, it was proposed, at least by the philosophers and historians who have given us an account of those institutions, to humanize the mind, to soften the temper, and to dispose it for performing all the social and moral duties both of publick and private life' (Glasgow Edition, 774).

the private teacher: writing to Cullen on 20 Sept. 1774, concerning what he sees as specific abuses in Scottish medical schools, Smith argued for the advantages of free competition between established institutions and private teachers. Only by abolishing the current monopoly on qualifications held by the universities, he believed, could standards of academic efficiency be guaranteed within those institutions. Smith points to the great eighteenth-century surgeons, anatomists, and physicians, like William Hewson, William Hunter, and William Fordyce, all at that time working outside the university structure, practising medicine and publicly lecturing in London (*Correspondence*, 174). Other contemporary pioneering scientists like Joseph Priestley and Henry Cavendish also worked outside the university system.

427 *without a bounty*: that is, without guaranteed financial subsidy whether he succeeds or fails in his profession. At *WN*, IV. v, Smith attacks bounties in trade as mercantile privileges which distort price for the benefit of the producer (see note to p. 313 above). Here the institutions of higher education enter the market by analogy with two of the greatest instruments of commercial progress, as Smith sees it—the deregularization of skilled labour and of inland and overseas trade.

428 *among gentlemen and men of the world*: Hume, who unlike Smith spent his whole career outside the university system, deals more humorously with what he sees as the obscure deliberations of the learned in their colleges. In 'Of Essay Writing', he presents himself as the effective channel between men of learning and men of the world. As a professional essayist, he employs the language of commercial transaction to describe his own role as literary merchant, who in trading converts to his own as well as society's advantage those profits of learning which would otherwise remain 'unintelligible' (*Essays Moral, Political, and Literary*, 568–70).

no publick institutions for the education of women: this is a curious argument, characterized by that perverse logic which we find in other areas of Smith's analysis (see, for example, his argument concerning the bad economics of slavery at *WN*, IV. vii). Women were, throughout the eighteenth century, educated within the home and exclusively for the performance of domestic duties; very few benefited from organized schooling, and though some received irregular scholarly education from male relatives, all higher institutions of learning were, of course, closed to them. To view this as cause for social congratulation requires us to consider only the efficiency of the provision (or lack of it), and not its justice; nor, having criticized what he sees as the failure of the higher reaches of education, does Smith consider this as an argument for reassessing educational and career opportunities and women's rights to them, as several women commentators (some in response to Smith) were soon to do, notably Mary Wollstonecraft, in *A Vindication of the Rights of Woman* (1792), and Priscilla Wakefield, in *Reflections on the Present Condition of the Female Sex; with suggestions for its improvement* (1798). (See note to p. 117 above.)

428   *œconomy*: household management; cf. p. 236 and note to p. 10 above.

429   *necessarily formed by their ordinary employments*: at *WN*, I x, Smith contrasted the varied labour of the ploughman with the narrowly specialized work of the mechanic and argued that the latter may be highly productive, but that, lacking the stimulation of variety, it left the town labourer the intellectual inferior of his country counterpart, whose 'understanding . . . being accustomed to consider a greater variety of objects, is generally much superior to that of the other, whose whole attention from morning till night is commonly occupied in performing one or two very simple operations' (p. 127). Cf. *Lectures on Jurisprudence* (1766), 328 (p. 539): 'There are some inconveniences, however, arising from a commercial spirit. The first we shall mention is that it confines the views of men. Where the division of labour is brought to perfection, every man has only a simple operation to perform. To this his whole attention is confined, and few ideas pass in his mind but what have an immediate connection with it. When the mind is employed about a variety of objects it is some how expanded and enlarged, and on this account a country artist is generally acknowledged to have a range of thoughts much above a city one.' Such a view of the mechanic was a commonplace in Scottish philosophical writing at this time. See, for example, Adam Ferguson: 'Many mechanical arts, indeed require no capacity; they succeed best under a total suppression of sentiment and reason; and ignorance is the mother of industry as well as of superstition' (*History of Civil Society*, ed. Forbes, 182). See note to p. 163 above.

430   *incapable of defending his country in war*: one persuasive argument for the reintroduction of a militia at this time was that, in providing some compensation for the necessary division of labour in a progressive society, it represented an opportunity for commercial (mechanical) man to rediscover his 'virtue' (strength) in the refurbished ideal of the undivided personality

of the warrior-producer. John Millar contrasts the stupidity and lassitude of the workman in a commercial society with the vigour of his counterpart in a less advanced nation, observing that in a 'rude nation', '[n]o man relies upon the exertions of his neighbour; but each employs, for the relief of his wants, or in defence of what belongs to him, either the strength of his body or the ingenuity of his mind, all the talents which he has been able to acquire, all the faculties with which nature has endowed him . . . Unlike the mechanics of a commercial nation . . . the inhabitants of a rude country have separately preserved, and kept in action, all the original powers of man' (*An Historical View of the English Government*, 4 vols. (London, 1803), iv. 150–1).

432   *by which they can earn their subsistence*: in *Lectures on Jurisprudence* (1766), 329–30, Smith points out that in eighteenth-century Scotland there is little demand for the labour of the very young, owing to the less advanced state of the economy, and consequently more time is given to their education; but this is not the case in the commercial districts of England: 'A boy of 6 or 7 years of age at Birmingham can gain his 3 pence or sixpence a day, and parents find it to be their interest to set them soon to work' (p. 540). The Birmingham toy trades, the result of new technology, made extensive use of children's labour. For the developing importance of child labour to the English family income, see Neil McKendrick, 'Home Demand and Economic Growth: A New View of the Role of Women and Children in the Industrial Revolution', in McKendrick (ed.), *Historical Perspectives: Studies in English Thought and Society, in honour of J. H. Plumb* (London: Europa Publications, 1974), 152–210.

to read, write, and account . . . essential parts of education: Smith here advocates a state policy for universal elementary education; and it is important to note that, while he writes of *encouraging* the poor to send their children to school, he supports the notion of *compulsory* education. At the time, such a view was highly progressive and better explained in terms of Smith's Scottish, as opposed to a British, experience of education. Soame Jenyns still spoke for many when in 1757 he asserted, directly contrary to Smith's view of only twenty years later, that ignorance was 'the appointed lot of all born to poverty and the drudgeries of life . . . the only opiate capable of infusing that sensibility, which can enable them to endure the miseries of the one and the fatigues of the other . . . a cordial, administered by the gracious hand of providence, of which they ought never to be deprived by an ill-judged and improper education' (quoted in Richard D. Altick, *The English Common Reader: A Social History of the Mass Reading Public 1800–1900* (Chicago, Ill.: University of Chicago Press, 1957), 31–2). Smith's concern for the basic ingredients of an elementary-school curriculum is in keeping with the practical emphases on useful learning of late eighteenth-century educationalists and social reformers. However, it is worth pointing out that the early church schools for the children of the poor commonly distinguished between the skills of reading and writing; and while the reading of suitable (usually religious) works was generally encouraged, writing was judged not only unnecessary for most to learn but even likely to endanger social stability, except as it was allied to a particular trade (see Altick, *The English Common Reader*).

433   *In Scotland . . . parish schools*: an act of Privy Council of 1616 laid down that there should be a school in every parish in Scotland. Thanks to the strict Calvinist emphasis on Bible reading, education was available to all social levels in the Scottish Lowlands, as well as a compulsory elementary-school system, long before this was the case further south. Consequently, in the second half of the eighteenth century profound illiteracy was virtually unknown in Scotland, at a time when the actual number of illiterates was rising in the new urban centres of England. In the case of the lowest social groups, no real rise in literacy in England can be registered until about 1800, when it reached only 35 to 40 per cent (Michael Sanderson, 'Literacy and Social Mobility in the Industrial Revolution in England', *Past and Present*, 56 (1972), 75–104).

charity schools: the Society for Promoting Christian Knowledge (SPCK), founded in 1699, set down guide-lines for charity schools which proliferated throughout the eighteenth century. In them boys and girls were taught together according to a narrow curriculum, principally reading and Scripture, the aim being to instill sound habits of morality in the children of the poor. Pupils were given economic rewards, too, in the form of apprenticeships in trade or entrance into domestic service. Supported by voluntary parish subscriptions, charity schools also witnessed to the philanthropic virtues of the more prosperous members of the local community, and served to bind poor and prosperous together in a well-subordinated and harmonious society. Writing in the *Spectator* No. 294 (6 Feb. 1712), Steele called them 'the greatest Instances of publick Spirit the Age has produced'. See, too, M. G. Jones, *The Charity School Movement: A Study of Eighteenth-Century Puritanism in Action* (Cambridge: Cambridge University Press, 1938). In his 'Essay on Charity, and Charity-Schools', added to *The Fable of the Bees* in 1723, Mandeville records his opposition to charity schools, arguing in Mercantilist terms that such institutions are at odds with the economic necessity for a large labouring poor who will only labour while they remain in ignorance (cf. Soame Jenyns in note to p. 432 above). For a directly opposed defence of charity schools, argued in terms of the economic need for liberal opportunity among the poor coupled with submission to civil authority, see Tucker, *A Sermon preached in the Parish-Church of Christ-Church, London, on Wednesday May the 7th, 1766: being the time of the yearly meeting of the children educated in the charity-schools, in and about the cities of London and Westminster* (London, 1766), where it is stated that such schools form 'a Nursery towards the Introduction of Labour, as well as a Seminary for Christian Piety and good Morals' (p. 15).

433   *geometry and mechanicks*: Smith's emphasis is on the practical and long-term advantages of an education which imparts a rudimentary scientific knowledge to the labouring classes. The same educational philosophy can be traced to the Scottish Enlightenment-inspired reading agenda, an austerely utilitarian diet of science and technology for the masses, issued in 1827 by the Society for the Diffusion of Useful Knowledge. Thomas Love Peacock satirized the enterprise in *Crochet Castle* (1831) as the 'Steam Intellect Society'.

in a village or town corporate: Smith's advocacy of a system of compulsory education appears here to supplement or even substitute for certain elements in the regulations governing apprenticeships. In his letter of 20 Sept. 1774 to William Cullen, he criticized the monopolistic tendencies of university degrees and apprenticeship statutes in trades, the effect of which has been to strip such training of its real educational value (*Correspondence*, 177).

434   *Gymnasia*: see note to p. 399 above.

Olympic . . . or Nemaean games: Olympia, where a sanctuary sacred to Zeus became the site of the celebrated Olympic games; Isthmia, near Corinth, site of a temple to Poseidon and a venue for games; and Nemea, where in legend Heracles slew the lion. Here there was a temple to Zeus Nemeus surrounded by a sacred grove in which games were celebrated.

illustration: see note to p. 411.

dangers to liberty . . . from a standing army: see note to p. 405.

435   *total neglect and disuse*: for the lack of a Scottish militia and the recent reintroduction of an English militia, see note to p. 401 above.

436   *more decent . . . than an ignorant and stupid one*: the argument that education is an effective method of policing society and dissolving anti-social behaviour gained ground during the political upheavals of the 1790s. As Maria and Richard Edgeworth, prominent educationalists, observed in their influential *Practical Education*: 'It is the business of education to prevent crimes, and to prevent all those habitual propensities which necessarily lead to their commission' (1798; 2nd edn, 3 vols., London, 1801), i. 354.

for religious instruction: Addison wrote in the *Spectator* No. 112 (9 July 1711): 'It is certain the Country-People would soon degenerate into a kind of Savages and Barbarians, were there not such frequent Returns of a stated Time, in which the whole Village meet together with their best Faces, and in their cleanliest Habits, to converse with one another upon indifferent Subjects, hear their Duties explained to them, and join together in Adoration of the supreme Being.' The Anglican Church, the Church of the Establishment and the nation's largest and wealthiest institution at this time, held a monopoly grip on Oxford and Cambridge Universities, where almost all dons were in holy orders. Rectors and vicars were presented with Church livings by ecclesiastical and lay patrons, and were ensured of an income regardless of the duties they performed. At the end of the seventeenth century the Church of England founded the Society for Promoting Christian Knowledge, which sought the attention of ordinary people through tracts. Towards the close of the eighteenth century Evangelical Anglicans, like Hannah More, established Sunday Schools for adults as well as children, and gave a new boost to the industry in uplifting pamphlet literature. Baptists, Congregationalists, Presbyterians, and other more extreme Dissenting groups were a feature of town life and provided much of the religious sustenance of urban tradesmen and artisans, while from the later part of the century Methodism did much to encourage reading among the labouring classes and to pioneer the popularizing of 'good' literature. See Altick, *The English Common Reader*, 35–8, and T. Laqueur, *Religion and Respectability: Sunday Schools and Working-Class Culture* (New Haven, Conn.: Yale University Press, 1976).

437   *effeminate . . . nations . . . of Asia . . . Tartars of the North*: in *Lectures on Jurisprudence* (1762–3), iii. 41, Smith remarks that the 'Tartars, a savage nation, have overrun all Asia severall times, and Persia above 12 times' (p. 157). Asiatic 'effeminacy', the consequence of excessive advancement and luxury, was a byword in the eighteenth century.

438   *trust rights*: see note to p. 200 above.

   methodists . . . much more in vogue: established in Oxford in 1729 by the brothers John and Charles Wesley, Wesleyanism or Methodism presented the century's strongest challenge to the established Church of England. From its beginnings it was identified with the religious life of the middle and lower classes, and was a popular movement without the rational inquiry and intellectual self-consciousness which characterized many Dissenter sects. On eighteenth-century Methodism, see Langford, *A Polite and Commercial People*, 243–57.

440   *sunk in obscurity and darkness*: although the great expansion of industrial centres was still some way in the future, there was already in the mid-eighteenth century a considerable consensus of opinion among Scottish thinkers that, in Hume's words, large cities are 'destructive to society' and 'beget vice and disorder of all kinds' ('Of the Populousness of Ancient Nations', *Essays Moral, Political, and Literary*, 400). See Adam Ferguson, *Institutes of Moral Philosophy* (1769; 3rd edn., Edinburgh, 1785),

262, and Henry Home, Lord Kames, *Sketches of the History of Man*, 4 vols. (Dublin, 1774), iii. 68–79: 'A Great City considered in Physical, Moral, and Political Views'. Such observations, with their attendant assumptions of identity-loss and of the labourer's need for replacement communities, have been compared to Marx's criticisms of the phenomenon of general estrangement in the industrial-capitalist city and its disintegrating effects on the labourer's personality. Marx himself was given to quoting from this section of *WN*. For an exploration of the affinities and limits of the Smith–Marx analysis, see Ronald L. Meek, *Smith, Marx, and After: Ten Essays in the Development of Economic Thought* (London: Chapman and Hall, 1977), 3–17.

440   *disagreeably rigorous and unsocial:* an apt illustration of Smith's point might be provided by the fictional congregation of Lantern Yard from which George Eliot's Silas Marner is expelled in the 1780s. A victim of the industrializing town with its harsh institutions, Marner is gradually and painfully returned into the village community. The town sect, extreme in its Dissent, is described by Eliot's editor, Q. D. Leavis, as 'ascetic, self-righteous, and emotionally repressive', even though such sects generally 'had the very great value of obliging . . . members to take responsibility, and supply initiative, and cooperate, in the financing and running of a religious organization of their own choice' (*Silas Marner* (1861), ed. Q. D. Leavis (Harmondsworth: Penguin, 1967), 250–1). Self-governing Dissenting conventicles of extreme kinds sprang up throughout the eighteenth century—Antinomian, Millennialist, Moravian, Sandemanian, and so on—all with an emphasis on personal conversion and the literal interpretation of the Bible.

the study of science and philosophy: in the last thirty years of the eighteenth century provincial scientific societies sprang up, like the Lunar Society of Birmingham and the Manchester Literary and Philosophical Society. Local institutions dedicated to rational knowledge and scientific and technological improvements, they represented the enterprise culture of the master-manufacturers and tradesmen of the new industrial centres. What Smith appears to be proposing here is something closer to a compulsory, though privately funded, training and professional entrance qualification for the middle classes in the classical disciplines of natural and moral philosophy (his own specialism) and logic.

441 *publick diversions*: for Smith's belief in toleration as necessary to life in community, and for his concern over the social damage done by extreme religious sects, see *Theory of Moral Sentiments*, III. 6. 12: 'False notions of religion are almost the only causes which can occasion any very gross perversion of our natural sentiments . . . and that principle which gives the greatest authority to the rules of duty, is alone capable of distorting our ideas of them in any considerable degree' (p. 176). In advocating privately funded programmes of entertainment and instruction, Smith addresses the problem of the new urban labourer, deracinated and the equal prey of religious fanaticism and profligacy. Like other educationalists and social reformers of the period, his concern is to offset the potential evil effects of labour-specialization by a programme encouraging individual responsibility and judgement and mutual toleration. This has much to do with the underpinning of existing social structures and the safeguarding of commercial society. For the growth of circulating libraries, theatres, circuses, exhibitions of various kinds, and other structured entertainments in the course of the eighteenth century, see J. H. Plumb, 'The Commercialization of Leisure in Eighteenth-Century England', in McKendrick, Brewer, and Plumb, *The Birth of a Consumer Society*, 265–85.

442 *equipage*: see note to p. 152 above.

443 *police*: civil administration; public order in general.

447 *a good deal more doubtful*: the extravagance of government is a recurring theme in *WN*. See note to p. 205 above.

post-office . . . a mercantile project: see note to p. 415 above.

Machiavel: 'In his commercial affairs he [Lorenzo de Medici] was very unfortunate, from the improper conduct of his agents, who in all their proceedings assumed the deportment of princes rather than of private persons; so that in many places, much of his property was wasted, and he had to be relieved by his country with large sums of money. To avoid similar inconveniences, he withdrew from mercantile pursuits, and invested his property in land and houses, as being less liable to vicissitude' (N. Machiavelli, *History of Florence*, VIII, trans. (London, 1851), 400–1) [Campbell and Skinner].

448 *ministers of sovereigns*: see *WN*, IV. vii (pp. 366–73 and notes), on the maladministrations of the East India Company.

the shepherd state: that is, the second stage of society. See note to p. 8 above.

449 *feudal tenures*: described at *WN*, III. iv.

it has been shown: at v. i (Glasgow Edition, 715–16).

450 *well-improved and well-cultivated*: for Smith's belief that merchants make 'the best of all improvers' of land, see *WN*, III. iv (p. 259).

451 *Rent, Profit, and Wages*: at *WN*, I. vi (p. 50) Smith notes: 'Wages, profit, and rent, are the three original sources of all revenue as well as of all exchangeable value. All other revenue is ultimately derived from some one or other of these.'

Every tax . . . is necessarily unequal: Smith proposes a redistribution of taxation. At this time liquid capital, like profits, escaped direct taxation and in the course of the century the tax burden shifted from land tax (paid by landowners) to indirect taxation on consumables. Consumer taxes hit all levels of society but obviously annexed much of the labourer's pay-packet. See note to p. 78 above on indirect taxation and on Smith's opposition to the taxation of the poor.

453 *temptation to smuggling*: see note to p. 303 above.

455 *in the third book of this enquiry*: at *WN*, III. iv.

in the same book: at *WN*, III. iv (p. 267).

to live within their income: see note to p. 267 above on the unfixing of income and rotation of property in commercial societies.

456 *disgraceful to a gentleman*: in *Lectures on Jurisprudence* (1766), 300, Smith observes: 'In a rude society nothing is honourable but war. In the Odyssey, Ulysses is sometimes asked, by way of affront, whether he be a pirate or a merchant. At that time a merchant was reckoned odious and despicable' (p. 527).

prohibited by law: Christians were forbidden by the Church to engage in usury, that is, to lend money for interest, in England in the Middle Ages; and those Jews who followed this profession found their goods forfeited to the Crown on their death.

456   *in the fourth book*: the points which follow in this paragraph recapitulate the argument at *WN*, IV. i.

457   *in his dominions*: the same point is made at *WN*, III. iv (pp. 266–7).

any considerable treasure: Henry IV of France's huge treasure, built up after the French Wars of Religion (which ended in 1598), was dissipated during the minority of his son Louis XIII. Frederick William I, King of Prussia (1713–1740), raised his annual revenue from 3,655,000 thaler in 1713 to 7,000,000 in 1740, and by his financial prowess turned Prussia from a client state into a great power. His son, Frederick II, raised the revenue to 19,000,000 thaler, and the State treasure from 8,000,000 to 51,000,000 thaler.

458   *canton of Berne*: see Hume, 'Of the Balance of Trade', where he writes that Berne has £300,000 lent at interest and 'about six times as much in their treasury' (*Essays Moral, Political, and Literary*, 330).

the facility of doing so: such an observation is part of Smith's larger argument to show that the evolution of a free-market economy is identical with the realization of a social ethics of 'natural liberty', and that, unchecked by government regulation, need and supply will 'naturally' work together for the advancement and benefit of society at all levels.

460   *the enormous debts*: on the British National Debt at this time, see note to p. 337 above.

by the Revolution: the so-called Glorious Revolution of 1688, when Catholic James II of Great Britain and Ireland was overthrown and replaced by William and Mary. The National Debt, created in 1693, was part of the financial revolution underpinning the authority of the new regime and providing the preconditions for the commercial revolution of the eighteenth century.

the protestants of Ireland: James II attempted to use Ireland as a step to regaining power in Britain. He landed in Ireland with French troops and, with Irish Catholic support, laid siege to the northern Protestants in Londonderry. His Irish-French army was defeated by William at the Battle of the Boyne in 1690. By late 1692 the Irish Parliament was dominated by Protestants. William used the Anglo-Irish landed nobility and gentry to keep the country subservient to English rule.

461   *in defence of America*: see *WN*, IV. vii and notes to p. 360 above.

   a union with Great Britain: French-inspired rebellions and reprisals in Ireland in the 1790s convinced the British Prime Minister Pitt that union was necessary and that the Parliament in Dublin should be incorporated into that in London. An Act of Union became law on 1 Jan. 1801, and the nation became known as the United Kingdom of Great Britain and Ireland.

   the union with England: in 1707, giving the Scots participation in the English economy. See note to p. 198 above.

   of religious and political prejudices: Pitt attempted unsuccessfully to pressurize the Irish Parliament into granting Catholics voting rights in 1793, as part of an attempt to curb the enthusiasm for French politics and the violence of a Catholic peasantry deeply resentful of the Protestant privileges of an Anglo-Irish ruling class.

   by a union with Great Britain: at IV. vii, Smith argues that union with the American colonies could not harm the British constitution: 'That constitution, on the contrary, would be completed by it, and seems to be imperfect without it' (Glasgow Edition, 624–5). He does not consider this as a likely outcome, however.

462   *acquisitions of the East India Company*: see note to p. 325 above.

463   *rival her . . . in power*: see note to p. 403 above.

   before the commencement of the first of them: see notes to p. 360.

464   *it has been shewn*: at *WN*, IV. vii (pp. 352–73).

INDEX

The index has been compiled from Smith's original index, first appended to the third edition of 1784, and from the additions to it by Edwin Cannan in his edition of 1904. New entries have been added where they appear relevant to the purposes of this World's Classics edition. The index covers only the selected text and Smith's notes.

Bhagavad Gita

The Bible Authorized King James Version
  With Apocrypha

Dhammapada

Dharmasūtras

The Koran

The Pañcatantra

**The Sauptikaparvan (from the
  Mahabharata)**

**The Tale of Sinuhe and Other Ancient
  Egyptian Poems**

Upaniṣads

ANSELM OF CANTERBURY   **The Major Works**

THOMAS AQUINAS   **Selected Philosophical Writings**

AUGUSTINE   **The Confessions**
On Christian Teaching

BEDE   **The Ecclesiastical History**

HEMACANDRA   **The Lives of the Jain Elders**

KĀLIDĀSA   **The Recognition of Śakuntalā**

MANJHAN   **Madhumalati**

ŚĀNTIDEVA   **The Bodhicaryàvatàra**

	Classical Literary Criticism
	The First Philosophers: The Presocrats and the Sophists
	Greek Lyric Poetry
ARISTOTLE	The Nicomachean Ethics
BOETHIUS	The Consolation of Philosophy
CAESAR	The Civil War The Gallic War
CATULLUS	The Poems of Catullus
EURIPIDES	Bacchae and Other Plays Medea and Other Plays
HERODOTUS	The Histories
HOMER	The Iliad The Odyssey
HORACE	The Complete Odes and Epodes
JUVENAL	The Satires
MARCUS AURELIUS	The Meditations
OVID	The Love Poems Metamorphoses
PETRONIUS	The Satyricon
PLATO	Defence of Socrates, Euthyphro, and Crito Republic
PLAUTUS	Four Comedies
SOPHOCLES	Antigone, Oedipus the King, and Electra
SUETONIUS	Lives of the Caesars
TACITUS	Histories
VIRGIL	The Aeneid The Eclogues and Georgics